T0206826

COMMODORE
THE AMIGA YEARS

Brian Bagnall
Variant Press

Variant Press
3404 Parkin Avenue
Winnipeg, Manitoba
R3R 2G1

Edited by Nick Lines

Designed by Hayden Sundmark

Manufactured in Canada

Library and Archives Canada Cataloguing in Publication

Bagnall, Brian, 1972-, author
      Commodore : the Amiga years / Brian Bagnall.

Includes bibliographical references and index.
ISBN 978-0-9940310-2-0 (hardcover)

      1. Amiga (Computer)--History. 2. Multimedia systems--
History. I. Title.

QA76.8.A177B34 2017   006.7   C2017-905493-7

Acknowledgments

Prior to this book, all my previous books have been largely solitary efforts, written in secret and launched to the public when they had achieved a high enough level of completeness. This is the first book for me that has come together through a much bigger group effort and there are many people to thank. Foremost, a huge thanks goes to the Kickstarter backers for sticking with this project for the two years it took to complete. Without their initial support, this project never would have lifted off the ground. And not only that, having a crowd behind the project elevated the book in so many ways, from direct help from backers to just raising my own personal standards. Good enough was no longer good enough and with the help of the backers, this history has turned out better than it ever could have been.

I owe a debt of gratitude to Anthony and Nicola Caulfield, Rick Thornquist, and Sam Dyer whose efforts and expert advice helped me to conceive of and execute a successful Kickstarter campaign.

Thanks to Christian Bartsch of *The Software Preservation Society* and Christian Euler for making available legacy materials, paperwork, and documents. Because of their dedicated work, this history has a much more complete and accurate timeline.

Thanks to the former Commodore employees who shared their stories. The young engineers who are now in their 50s and 60s are still excited to talk about these days and remain as fascinated by Commodore as we are. Even those in senior management are excited to talk about Commodore. They are: Ron Nicholson, Bob Welland, Joe Decuir, Hedley Davis, Jeff Porter, Glenn Keller, David Pleasance, Guy Wright, Eric Cotton, Jeff Bruette, David Baraff, Greg Berlin, Bryce Nesbitt, Bill Hart, Don Reisinger, Gerard Bucas, Joe Augenbraun, Eric Lavitsky, Don Gilbreath, Carl Sassenrath, Larry Kaplan, RJ Mical, Dale Luck, Dave Haynie, Robert Russell, Bil Herd, and Thomas Rattigan. If there was enough time, I would have interviewed everyone.

Special thanks to those photographers from the 1980s who allow us a glimpse into the lives they led through those amazing years: Bill Koester, Bob Welland, Chris Collins (modern photos), Dale Luck, David Pleasance, Eric Cotton, Gerard Bucas, Dave Haynie, Jeff Bruette, John Schilling, RJ Mical, Steve Tibbett, Terry Ryan, and Sandy Fisher.

Thanks to the incredibly creative Commodore and Amiga community for keeping the scene thriving so many decades later. Who would have thought there would be so much exciting hardware and software released every week of every year? These machines keep working, improving, and holding their allure for hundreds of thousands of people.

Thanks to Michael Battilana and Cloanto Corporation for helping to keep the spirit of Commodore alive with C64 Forever and Amiga Forever, and for assisting me with the production of this book.

And those who put in so many hours picking through the text with tweezers, pulling out little bugs here and there. I'm talking about the people who reviewed early drafts of this manuscript multiple times and pored over every page: Ceri Stagg, Jared Brookes (the "Comma King"), Matthew Kurth, Dave Farquar, Rick Thornquist, and many others. Having someone spot one of the many errors that crept into the manuscript has never filled me with so much joy and happiness.

And finally, my editor and frequent confidante, Nick Lines. His suggestions helped shape the structure of this book and raise it to a higher level. It is because of his diligent, detail minded changes that this story flows.

Table of Contents

Introduction

What you are about to read is a chronicle of an important company whose computers helped change the world. The Greek historian Polybius believed that historians should only write about events based on interviews with the actual participants, otherwise the historian is bound to get it wrong with inaccurate, revisionist stories based on modern perceptions. That's why I have reached out to the main players who were influential to Commodore. I felt it was important to hear those histories from the source as much as possible (with the information verified of course) and so I have included their quotes as generously as possible throughout the text. This also allows you, the reader, to get to know the thoughts and personalities of these players, giving the story a more personal touch. They are able to capture what is was like being there better than any author ever could.

Factual integrity of the contents of this book was also at the forefront of my mind through this entire process. You will notice even the blemishes of Commodore are included in this book. It is my hope that, if you are a fan of Commodore, this enhances rather than diminishes your love for the company and its products.

The timeline was perhaps the hardest part of this history to reconstruct. You will find dates liberally sprinkled throughout each chapter, but more importantly, the order the events happened is maintained as best I could. Chapters are often segregated into individual topics, such as an Amiga chapter followed by a chapter about the C128. This is because Commodore frequently worked on different products simultaneously and some projects overlapped with each other. Therefore the timeline may jump back at times; a necessary step to avoid attempting to describe multiple projects together in one confusing chapter. I hope you will forgive this small alteration of the timeline.

This book cover the years from 1982, when Amiga came together, right up until almost mid 1987, when a series of events rocked the company and resulted in the departure of many top engineers and executives. A final book will cover the Commodore saga through the golden years of the Amiga to the company's conclusion in 1994. As you will soon notice, this book is the dark middle chapter in the trilogy. Commodore starts with a serious problem that only deepens throughout the book and ends with a cataclysm. I hope you enjoy it.

Brian Bagnall
August 6, 2017

New Management 1984

Prologue: Friday 13th

By 1984, Commodore the computer company had achieved remarkable success while its competition—Atari, Tandy, Texas Instruments and even Apple— were floundering. On January 13, 1984, Commodore's board of directors, led by financier Irving Gould, decided to fire the man who had made that success happen: Jack Tramiel, founder and president.[1]

When Commodore lost Tramiel, it lost the passionate, ruthless engine that drove the company forward. "Jack was the whole personality of the company. There was nobody else," says Commodore engineer Robert Russell. Even though Tramiel treated many of his employees harshly, they were ready to follow him.

Commodore was searching for the next great product to compete against what it saw as the biggest threat at the time, the IBM PC. Unknown to them, a third foe would rise who was capable of obliterating Commodore, gutting the company from within. Commodore needed strong leadership to carry the company's momentum forward.

Marshall Smith

The timing of Jack Tramiel's resignation was a surprise to everyone, including Irving Gould, and he needed an acting CEO very quickly. Gould wanted stable management and turned to friend and former industrial CEO, Marshall Smith. A week later, Smith was voted in.

---

1   This story is told in *Commodore: A Company on the Edge*, published by Variant Press.

According to Gould, Smith "enjoys an excellent reputation as an executive in the area of manufacturing, finance and marketing and is known for his leadership skills in motivating and developing the people who work for him."[2]

"There's a lot of insanity at Commodore," says engineer David Baraff. "I mean they got rid of Jack and they brought in a guy who had no experience in retail or high-tech at all. You couldn't have found a poorer match."

According to Robert Russell, "Once you saw somebody like Marshall Smith, you were like, 'You've got to be kidding me.'"

Smith was previously president of Indian Head Incorporated, a Charlotte, North Carolina company specializing in brakes for the trucking industry. In 1974 the company was acquired by a Netherlands company, Thyssen-Bornemisza N.V., in order to establish a North American presence. Indian Head was renamed Thyssen-Bornemisza Incorporated and Smith became its CEO.

Gould wanted to expand Commodore. He did not want the lean, perennially understaffed company of the past, and did not want to personally approve every expenditure over $1000—unlike Tramiel. "Commodore at that time was ballooning with all these guys being brought down from Northern Telecom [Nortel] up in Canada, like Martin Schabelski," says Russell. "They were big-company guys building empires."

Many of Commodore's top managers had come from Bell Northern Research (a research arm of Northern Telecom), including VP of Technology, Adam Chowaniec and his boss Lloyd Taylor, who was responsible for finding new technology and acquisitions for Commodore. "At that time, a vice president from the research division by the name of Lloyd Taylor had gone down to Commodore to work with Jack Tramiel," explains Baraff. "Lloyd was a technology guy with a semiconductor background and Commodore needed inexpensive computer chips to be cost effective."

Former marketing head Kit Spencer believes the new hires were a key mistake. "Commodore just brought in people from the traditional computer business who weren't in the microcomputer business and they didn't really understand the business they were coming into," he says.

Engineer Yash Terakura was perturbed by the changes he saw happening in Commodore. " They wanted to be IBM," he says. "They got too big and it became very bureaucratic."

---

2 *New York Times.* January 18, 1984. "Business People."

Software developer Neil Harris found the new Commodore less driven than under Tramiel. "After he left, at one point I said to my boss, 'I don't really have that much to work on right now.' And he said, ' Just keep your head down and look busy and that will be fine.' In all the years of working for this company, I never had to look busy."

The Unix Business Computer

Commodore was still basking in the success of the C64 and VIC-20 in 1984. However, the company did not remain complacent and was about to release a followup computer that was intended to be even cheaper than the C64. Called the Plus/4, it frustratingly ended up as a more expensive computer than the C64 with worse technical specs.

Commodore also had the aging PET line of business computers, which had been a bonafide hit in the European business community for a few years. With the IBM PC beginning to take away business market share, Commodore's VP of product development, Lloyd "Red" Taylor, began looking for a worthy successor.

His search for a business machine led him to consider releasing a Unix-based computer. Unix was a well regarded operating system that was popular in universities and research, not to mention among programmers and developers. It had yet to gain a foothold in the business world, however, but it was still early days. Perhaps it had a shot at competing against MS-DOS.

Commodore began developing a UNIX machine to replace the PET computers sometime in 1983.[3] Frank Hughes, the engineer in charge of Commodore's cash register products, became the project leader of the machine with engineer Shiraz Shivji designing the motherboard.

According to Robert Russell, much of the design came together in discussions with Shivji. "Shiraz and I were doing lunch all the time, working on what we wanted to do for the next generation computer," reveals Russell.

The logical chip choice for many computer makers was the 16-bit Motorola 68000, which would end up being famously used in the Amiga and Macintosh. However, at Commodore, this was unthinkable due to an ongoing lawsuit with the chipmaker. "We were still butting heads with Motorola, so Motorola wasn't really an option," says Russell.

---

3   The origins of this project are covered in *Commodore: A Company on the Edge* (2010), Variant Press.

Instead, the PET successor (later called the C900) would use a 16-bit Z8000 chip from semiconductor maker ZiLOG. Commodore, under Jack Tramiel, began talks with ZiLOG to acquire the entire company.

Engineers dubbed it the Z-machine because of the Z8000 chip. Bil Herd loved to tease the Unix group by calling them Z-people. The engineers soon raised the naming stakes to absurd heights and began calling the pens they used Z-pens and the food they ate Z-meals. "They were kind of treated as second rate citizens unfortunately," says Herd.

According to Russell, the deal to acquire ZiLOG fell through. "I remember being in meetings with the top management of ZiLOG while the Commodore guys were negotiating," he recalls. "I think it must have been an issue about price."

According to *Byte* magazine, Commodore acquired a license to manufacture the Z8000 instead. "We were trying to leverage MOS Technology chips," says Russell. "The goal was to do vertical integration. They let me keep the project because they basically negotiated parts at cost for us to continue on with the technology."

The engineers even attempted to create an entertainment system out of the Z-Machine. "At one time we were going to do a gaming version of the Z8000 with the memory mapping chip and everything," recalls Russell. "Once we put it together as a prototype and we were running BASIC on it, it was kind of like, 'This isn't a gaming machine! It's not interesting because there's no way to make it compatible. What the hell is this but just a super fast thing that looks like a Commodore 64.'"

As Commodore expanded during this time, engineers like Russell and Shivji found it difficult to do their jobs. "The engineers that I hired were guys like me who thought, 'This is bullshit.' Guys like Shiraz that were like, 'We're here to do things, we're not here to go fight in meetings and sit across the desk from Martin Schabelski and Joe Krasucki, and argue to try to get things done the right way.'"

Shivji designed the system using a Z8000 chip running at 10 MHz. The system contained a reasonable 256 kilobytes of memory, expandable up to 2 megabytes, and two 1.2 megabyte floppy drives. Shivji completed his prototype motherboard for the Unix system and was able to bring up the system in time for a showing at the upcoming Hanover Fair.

Testing the Waters

In January 1983, Compaq pioneered a new industry by releasing an IBM PC clone. The move was legal because the IBM PC used widely available parts with no custom semiconductor chips. The BIOS code (Basic Input/ Output System) was the only copyrighted part of the IBM PC, so Compaq had its programmers legally reverse-engineer the code.

By early 1984, the IBM PC was seen as an open standard for business computers. With Commodore's PET computers now obsolete, and the Unix machine at least a year away, Commodore Europe needed something to sell its business customers quickly. Commodore's VP of product development, Lloyd Taylor, decided to join the enemy and test the waters with IBM PC clones.

Rather than attempting to design a PC from scratch, Taylor found a Canadian competitor to Compaq that produced a luggable clone called the Hyperion. "We went and bought the design for a luggable PC compatible from Canada called the Bytec-Hyperion," recalls Nicholas Lefevre, Commodore's legal counsel. "We went and cut a deal and got all that technology to hedge our bets if we wanted to be in the PC compatible space."[4]

Lloyd Taylor concluded that Commodore could have an advantage over other clone makers, such as Compaq, if it could manufacture its own Intel 8088 chips. The list price of the 8088 was originally $124.80 when first released and in-house production could result in significant savings. Taylor went to Intel and successfully negotiated a license to become a second source for the Intel 8088, a first for any company before or since. When news of the deal leaked, an industry analyst from the Gartner Group predicted, "Commodore could conceivably become the major supplier of low-cost PC-compatibles, while other companies may be forced to merge or go out of business."[5]

The other factor in Commodore's favor was that IBM was struggling to gain a foothold in Europe. According to *PC Magazine*, "Unlike Commodore, IBM has had difficulties in marketing its PC overseas."[6] IBM had flubbed the release, without special German characters and with poor documentation, making it unsuitable for business use. This left IBM with sluggish sales and in 1984 it was forced to drop prices by 20% in order to reduce inventory.

---

4   *Antic: The Atari 8-bit Podcast.* "ANTIC Interview 46 - Nicholas Lefevre, Attorney for Commodore & Atari"

5   *PC Magazine.* May 1, 1984. p. 52. "Commodore Adds Hyperion, Chips"

6   *PC Magazine.* June 12, 1984. p. 58. "Commodore Launches PC-Compatible Abroad"

Given that Commodore held a vastly superior position to IBM in the European market, it was clear that the time to strike was now, rather than waiting for the upcoming C900 Unix system.

First, Commodore needed to secure one important part of the PC clone. "Of course we needed for the Bytec machine an MS-DOS license if we're going to be able to sell a PC compatible," explains Lefevre.

Unfortunately, the prior year, Jack Tramiel had launched a $24 million antitrust lawsuit against Microsoft. This happened because at the 1983 Summer CES Sig Hartmann, Commodore's VP of software, had announced Commodore would sell *Multiplan* for $99 even before Microsoft had signed the deal. Bill Gates had immediately responded the next day that he would not allow any vendor to sell Multiplan for $99 and cancelled the deal.

Gates was soon reminded that, according to the Sherman Antitrust Act, a manufacturer is not allowed to set prices for its vendors. Jack Tramiel responded by levelling the aforementioned antitrust lawsuit against Microsoft—perhaps not the best way to continue a working partnership.

Back to early 1984, Nicholas Lefevre attempted to acquire an MS-DOS license from Microsoft. He says, "In the meantime of course Steve Ballmer, who is responsible for the OEM deal, is telling me, 'The MS-DOS deal for the Bytec? Someday we'll talk about it.'"

Lefevre approached Bill Gates again at the February 21 Softcon in New Orleans. "I got Bill and he said, 'Okay let's talk. You should talk with my friend Jon Shirley.' He was the new president of Microsoft," says Lefevre.

Lefevre tracked down Microsoft's president and they went into a smoke-filled room. "I met with Jon Shirley and started working out a deal," says Lefevre. "And the idea I say is, 'We'll drop the Multiplan lawsuit if you give us MS-DOS for the Bytec.'"

The two continued working out the details when there was a knock at the door. It was at that moment Lefevre learned of the loathing Microsoft felt towards Commodore. "I open the door and there's Bill Gates," recalls Lefevre. "He asks, 'What's going on here?' Jon says, 'We're trying to work out something on getting rid of the lawsuit in exchange for MS-DOS.' And Bill goes into one of his fits of anger and curses Jack and everything with the Tramiels. 'I will never deal with them. We're not even going to talk about MS-DOS until you dismiss the lawsuit and then we'll talk about terms for that.'"

Commodore dismissed the lawsuit and, as a result, secured MS-DOS for its clones. But it was clear the company would not be able to win the support of one of the most powerful software makers in the industry. One that, in 1983 at least, had been willing to make software for the world's most popular computer.

In March 1984, Lloyd Taylor and Nicholas Lefevre negotiated the license from the makers of the Hyperion luggable, Bytec-Comterm, to rebrand the computer and sell it as a Commodore product.[7] The same month, Bytec-Comterm shipped Commodore dozens of Hyperion kits for assembly and the latter began studying them for cost reductions.

Commodore debuted the Hyperion on April 4 at the massive Hanover Fair in Germany.[8] And, perhaps sending a mixed message, Commodore privately debuted the C900 behind closed doors to select people. The system was obviously in the early alpha stage and lacked a working Unix operating system, although Commodore mentioned it planned to use a version of Unix called Coherent.

At the same show, IBM attended with a massive booth manned by 500 employees. The industry giant was sending a clear message that it would do whatever it took to enter the European business market. The race was on.

Tramel Technology Limited

Earlier in the year, as the drama at Commodore played out that resulted in Jack Tramiel being dismissed from Commodore, its chief rival Atari was keeping close watch. As emails exchanged among Atari employees attest to, the view of Tramiel was not flattering. When an Atari engineer named Dave Sovey was informed of the surprise resignation, he replied, "I wonder what industry he is going to ruin next?"

The two Atari employees had no idea Tramiel would soon be their boss. After his dismissal from Commodore, Tramiel and his wife began a yearlong trip around the world, a lifelong dream for both of them. However, the trip was cut short in April 1984 when Tramiel received a phone call from Steve Ross, the CEO of Warner Communications. Ross had tracked down Tramiel through his youngest son, Gary.[9]

By 1984, Atari was hemorrhaging money and the parent company Warner wanted to be rid of it. But Ross had a reason for calling Tramiel above all other people: Atari had competed head to head against Tramiel while

---

7   *InfoWorld*. March 26, 1984. p. 14. "Commodore pact sparks talk of IBM PC-compatible micro"

8   *InfoWorld*. April 30, 1984. p. 9. "Germany's Fair of Fairs"

9   *Atari Inc: Business is Fun.* (2012) p. 744. Syzygy Press.

he ran Commodore, and knew what an aggressive leader he was. Though Ross wanted to sell off Atari, he also wanted Warner to receive shares in the newly spun-off company. Ross believed if anyone could rescue Atari, and raise the stock price, it was Jack Tramiel.

Tramiel, along with his son Sam, returned to California and met with Ross and executives of Warner Communications. When talks of an acquisition became serious, Tramiel opened up an office at 455 South Mathilda Avenue in Sunnyvale, five minutes from Atari. He called his new venture Tramel Technology Limited (TTL, which coincidentally is also an acronym for Transistor-Transistor Logic). According to Leonard Tramiel, "Our name Tramiel was constantly being mispronounced as *Tra-meal* and my dad hoped that the other spelling would get people to say *Tra-mell*. It didn't work."

After their initial meeting, Tramiel and his sons negotiated throughout the next few months with Warner Communications in New York for the ownership of Atari. The Tramiels had to convince Warner that a deal with them was in its best interest. For starters, Tramel Technology offered to take over all debts and obligations, something that would give Warner Communications a big sigh of relief. Warner would also retain shares in Atari, which it could sell or hold depending on how the company fared after Tramiel took over.

Finally, Tramiel had to convince Warner that he would be the guy to turn Atari around, making Warner's shares in Atari potentially valuable.

The same month, Tramiel began scouring Silicon Valley, searching for development firms with technology to create a C64 killer. On the advice of Commodore executive Lloyd ' Red' Taylor, he eventually made his way to a small start-up with a computer they called the Amiga.

Earthquakes

A Silicon Valley upstart known as Amiga had successfully created a multimedia home computer whose chip technology surpassed that of the competition. But the company's future was on shaky ground, both figuratively and literally. On April 24, 1984 at 1:15 pm, the Morgan Hill earthquake hit California. "That was so remarkable for me because it was my first earthquake ever in my life," recalls Amigas employee RJ Mical. "You could tell the difference between someone from California and someone not from California because all of my coworkers, who knew better, dove under their desks, dove into the doorways, and got themselves into protective positions."

Mical was from Chicago, where earthquakes were unknown. As he recalls, "I'm standing in the middle of the room, riding up and down on the floor with my arms out to the side saying, 'Whee,' like some kid on a surfboard. All my coworkers are shouting, 'Get under the desk you idiot!'"

Rather than find cover for protection, Mical left the building for a better view. "I went running outside past all the plate glass windows and everything," he says. "I was so colossally stupid, but I didn't know. I ran out into the parking lot and it was just the most amazing thing I've ever seen in my life. To see the cars all heaving up and down with their burglar alarms going off one by one; to see these rows of stately palm trees crisscrossing each other as the waves went over them; God, it was just so gorgeous. And then I threw up."

Amiga was soon subject to another earth moving event: a visit from Jack Tramiel. The former Commodore president sat down with Amiga CEO Dave Morse to work out a possible deal. "We mostly met with [his son] Sam and on occasion Jack," says Mical. "I only had hands-folded discussions with them across the table about various things. I also met his son Leonard on a few occasions."

Unknown to the Tramiels, Amiga already had a licensing agreement in the works with Atari, the company TTL soon hoped to acquire. If they had known, they would not have bothered trying to work out a largely redundant licensing agreement, which they would end up getting for free once the Atari deal was signed at the end of June.

After Tramiel was ousted from Commodore, his three sons remained there in high-level positions. "They left a couple of Jack's sons as vice presidents. Of course, Jack was setting up to go into competition with Commodore," remarks Commodore employee David Baraff. "They left Jack's two sons as vice presidents in charge of their divisions, which to me was insane. Leaving his sons in such a high level. I mean how stupid can you be? They stayed with the company for a couple of months and then they joined their father."

Jack Tramiel and his sons were primarily interested in acquiring the chipset for a computer of their own. "They were hard, hard businessmen," says Mical. "They came to understand our situation. The deeper in they got with us and the closer they got to making a deal and understanding our finances and what we had to offer, the more they were able to come to realize how desperate we were."

Initially, the two groups discussed an offer of three dollars per share, with Morse explaining the reasons for the valuation. At first, the Tramiels counter-offered with $2.00. Morse attempted to meet the Tramiels in the middle by lowering his offer to $2.75, but instead he was told, "In that case, our offer is now $1.50."

"Instead of negotiating in a way to get us to say yes, they started negotiating to see how far they could push us to still say yes as the deal got worse and worse," says Mical.

After many meetings, the offer fell to under a dollar per share. "Instead of the deal that they were offering us increasing over time, it decreased. It was pathetic and ridiculous," says Mical.

The aggressive moves by Tramiel threatened to alienate the Amiga team. With the latest offer at 98 cents per share, the talks soon disintegrated. The experience of dealing with the Tramiels left a bitter taste with Dave Morse and the rest of his team.

"I think he's a ruthless business person and he's out to screw anybody if he can make a buck," says Dale Luck. "But he did what he had to do to make money."

For now, Jack Tramiel forgot about Amiga and moved onto different technology, though the company would reenter his target hairs in just a few months. Tramiel also began ramping up his new company. To do this, he required experienced managers and skilled engineers. And he knew exactly where to get some of the best in the industry.

Exodus

Even though Commodore's engineers were working on the Z8000 UNIX machine, the engineers often talked about and planned what they would do for a personal computer to replace the C64. "Those were done during Commodore lunch hours at a cheap fish restaurant," explains Bob Russell. "My engineers were working on the Z8000, mostly hardware guys, and then with Shiraz, we'd all go out and have lunch together."

Shivji favored the National Semiconductor NS32032 processor. "We were choosing our chipset and talking about how we were going to design it and build it," says Russell. "We were sketching it on a napkin."

On May 17, the same day TTL was incorporated, several core east coast engineers departed for California to join Jack Tramiel. "Shiraz Shivji left," recalls Russell. "A bunch of my hardware engineers left, including my best friend at that point in time." Shivji took three of his engineering staff: Arthur Morgan, John Hoenig, and Douglass Renn. "It was mostly my engineering group that left as far as hardware engineers."

C64 Kernel developer John Feagans also departed. "I was working on networking and system applications until I left for Tramel Technology," he recalls. Feagans was developing his GUI ideas that started with *Magic Desk*, in something he called Magic Desk II. The graphical user interface was now without a programmer. It would be impossible for someone else to carry on Feagans' work.[10]

To Russell, it was obvious why his friends and coworkers wanted to leave with the engineer-friendly Tramiel. "It was an opportunity to finally go break out and do something new," explains Russell. "Most of these guys were the type of individuals that Jack's personality appealed to. If you were aggressive and wanted to make something happen and create the next generation Commodore 64, obviously you could do that with Jack a lot easier than you could do it at Commodore."

Curiously, Russell chose to stay with Commodore. "I turned them down and said, 'I have learned all I want to learn from Jack. As much as I like you guys, I want to do something different.'"

In the middle of May, top managers began resigning from Commodore. Sam Tramiel was the first. Next was Tony Tokai, Vice President of Commodore Japan. Jack Tramiel's friend Elie Kenan, who distributed Commodore computers in France under Procep, suddenly dropped Commodore products. Something was happening behind the scenes and Irving Gould believed that "something" was Jack Tramiel.

Others soon followed. "In May, in one week, 35 of us left," recalls Tomczyk. Ira Velinsky, the production designer at Commodore Japan who was working on the Unix case, also resigned.

Lloyd 'Red' Taylor also departed. "When Commodore got rid of Jack Tramiel, you couldn't have shot yourself in both hands and feet any worse than they did," says David Baraff. "When they got rid of Jack, they got rid of the vice presidents that were competent and who knew how to run the business. And Lloyd was one of them."

Resignations included Bernie Witter, vice president of finance, Sam Chin, manager of finance in East Asia, Joe Spiteri, and David Carlone, both of manufacturing, and Gregg Pratt, vice president of operations.

Marketing manager Kit Spencer watched as the talent walked out the door. "When Jack left he took a few key people from Commodore, which diluted the experienced management," he says. " You needed the technical

---

10 Feagans obsession with graphical operating systems did not end with Magic Desk. He went on to port a graphical operating system called GEM for Atari.

geniuses, like the Chucks[11], and you needed somebody with the commercial drive and tunnel vision of a Jack to make him focus on that happening. That's the combination we had at Commodore at one time but it was gone soon after I moved to the Bahamas."

Michael Tomczyk, product manager of the VIC-20, thinks Marshall Smith should have tried harder to retain his employees. "To the best of my knowledge, not one of us was approached by Irving or any one of those grey haired presidents and asked to stay," he says. "They basically let the whole corporate culture and the whole corporate memory die in one week, which was corporate suicide."

Yash Terakura, a Japanese immigrant to the US who helped engineer Commodore's products, did not join the other engineers with Jack Tramiel due to his differences with management. "I was just doing whatever I wanted to, but I wasn't getting much support within the engineering groups because they were headed by Lloyd Taylor and Shiraz Shivji," he says. "Shiraz was kind of a weird guy. Those guys were not exactly the kind of engineers I liked or respected."

Tramiel loyalists like Terakura found themselves in a difficult position. "When Jack quit the company, they didn't like me over there because they thought I was the shadow of Jack Tramiel," says Terakura. "After that, I stayed a little bit, but I just lost interest in Commodore."

Terakura began research into 3D display technology using LCD switching glasses. "I was into some of the 3D displays. It was not an immediately feasible product or anything. That was a totally independent job I was doing and I had nothing to do with any group."

Commodore showed no interest in his work, so Terakura worked with a Portland, Oregon company named Tectronics to develop the technology. "At that time, I was kind of freelancing in the company," he laughs. "What I was doing was not anything the company told me to do." Terakura left Commodore shortly after.

Michael Tomczyk, an inner family member, began writing a book on his experiences with Commodore called *The Home Computer Wars*. He was not asked to join Tramel Technology, Limited. "I think the Tramiel family didn't like Mike's book very much," says Neil Harris. "At the end of the day, they liked operating their business in a very close manner. I think the idea of having Mike, who was an insider, come out for his own personal benefit

---

11 Chuck Peddle was the previous head of engineering at Commodore, responsible for the 6502 chip and more, as detailed in *Commodore: A Company on the Edge* (Variant Press).

and tell the stories was something that they didn't like. And I don't think Mike understood that was what was going on."

Irving Gould was alarmed by the resignations; not by the actual loss of talent, but on the image it projected to shareholders. To counteract this, he issued a vague press statement that indicated new CEO Marshall Smith was just cleaning house. It was nothing of the sort: they were joining Jack Tramiel to fight Commodore.

Worse still for Commodore, Tramiel began planning a C64 killer. He gave the task to his ex-Commodore engineers, headed by Shiraz Shivji. The war was on.

CHAPTER 2

Proto Laptop 1984

Commodore was beginning to branch into different types of computer systems, from Unix workstations to IBM PC clones. While Lloyd "Red" Taylor, Commodore's VP of product development, was still with the company, he spotted an opportunity for portable computers. With the company flush with cash, it seemed now was the time to attempt to enter that market too.

Commodore Optoelectronics

In the 1970's, Commodore's main source of revenue came from calculators and digital watches, manufactured completely in house thanks to Jack Tramiel's obsession with vertical integration. Unlike the rest of Commodore, the LCD operation was not located in Pennsylvania. "There was a group down in Texas which had been Commodore Optoelectronics," explains Dave Haynie.

According to Bil Herd, Commodore was unique among computer companies in this regard. "The thing that Commodore had that nobody else had was glass," says Herd. "There were no American makers of LCD glass."

Through the early eighties, Commodore Optoelectronics was headed by engineer Rodney Blose. By 1984, Commodore still had LCD manufacturing capacity, although it was not getting much use. "The watch business was sort of not going anywhere at the time when I was there," says Commodore executive Gerard Bucas.

At the time, Commodore was not making use of this unique facility because there was no demand for LCD parts as Commodore's calculators and watches were in decline. There was a clear opportunity to sell the loss-making cost centre off as Commodore relocated en masse to Pennsylvania. But they didn't. "Someone decided to move the LCD factory from Dallas to

Pennsylvania and the whole goal of that was to make an LCD computer," says Jeff Porter.

Commodore was finishing off a "luggable" computer based on the Commodore 64 which would eventually be released as the SX-64 Executive. "The SX-64 was a Commodore Japan Limited creation," recalls engineer Hedley Davis. The Tokyo office designed the luggable and contracted Mitsumi to create the special components. "I don't know where they got the design, but that product did ship in some kind of volume."

To take that concept even further, Lloyd Taylor was planning a new product for Commodore that required LCD. He wanted a truly portable computer to redefine the marketplace. "A lot of the guys that were doing the LCD displays for calculators and watches were relocated to Pennsylvania, and they set up shop to build black and white liquid crystal displays for laptop computers," says Commodore engineer Jeff Porter.

When Commodore moved into the massive West Chester facility in 1983, Optoelectronics also moved in. "I got involved with them when they were moving into West Chester, and I introduced them to the facility," recalls Bob Russell. "They originally moved in and they had an LCD production line in the front corner of the West Chester building."

While reconfiguring the Optoelectronics division for new products, the division kept its sword sharp by making internal products for Commodore. "They were doing these specialty LCDs with great big clocks," recalls Russell. "They had ones that were the size of a piece of paper, eight and a half by eleven or so, with big independent LCD sections in it to light up different things. They gave them out as advertising and gifts, handing them out internally."

The LCD plant was also looking for opportunities in the marketplace. "They were mostly internal for Commodore and a couple of pilot projects," says Porter. "One was LCD dimmable rear view mirrors for the auto industry. You actually see those today a little bit but I don't know if that actually panned out for them."

The main reason for Commodore holding onto Optoelectronics was because of its interest in an emerging technology called active-matrix liquid-crystal display. The man who introduced Commodore to the technology was David Baraff. "I came to Commodore from a company called Northern Telecom, which was a Canadian telecommunications company," he explains. "The organization within Northern Telecom I was in was called Bell Northern Research (BNR) and they were in effect the Bell Laboratories of Canada."

Much like its sister Bell Laboratories in the US, BNR was on the leading edge of new experimental technologies. "While I was at BNR, I led a research team which developed the first large area liquid crystal display," he says. "Today liquid crystal displays are common in televisions and computer monitors and telephones, but when we started our project, you could only make a display that was one letter high."

This made the technology practical for advanced calculators but it was not yet good enough for computers. The technology needed an advancement. "We were interested in figuring out how we could get to a full screen," says Baraff. "Obviously I and the other team members were very excited to have a development like that, so we went to the BNR management and said, 'Hey this is the greatest thing since sliced bread. Once you guys get into the display business you can sell a gazillion of these things to the computer industry and eventually, when we develop color, you can sell them to the television industry.'"

BNR felt the development costs and marketing challenges would make the project too risky, something Baraff agrees with today in retrospect. "Management said to us, 'Fellas, we're a telephone company. We're not a computer company and we're not a television company. That will be too far afield.' In other words, they were not interested."

Baraff had a passion for the project and decided to shop the idea around to computer companies that might be more interested. He contacted his former co-worker, Lloyd Taylor, who now worked for Commodore. "I called him because he was unaware of what was going on with Northern, whether or not they wanted the technology," says Baraff. "I said, 'Look we have this flat screen technology. You could use it in portable computers.'"

Unknown to Baraff at the time, the company was close to releasing the SX-64 Executive. "In those days a portable computer was carried around in a big suitcase and had a small cathode ray tube," explains Baraff. "So he said, 'Yeah, why don't you come on down.'"

Baraff presented Commodore with the specs for a proposed LCD screen. After the talks, Taylor was excited about the prospect of a truly lightweight, portable computer that could run on its own batteries, rather than having to be plugged in, as the SX-64 required. In January 1984, he commissioned Commodore engineer Michael North to produce a detailed specification of an LCD portable computer. North was part of an R&D group within Commodore. "He was in the 'sandbox' group of which Bob Russell and Benny Pruden were members," recalls Bil Herd.

While that was going on, Lloyd Taylor offered Baraff the job of head of the Optoelectronics division, and soon Baraff moved from Canada to Pennsylvania. "I went down to Commodore in 1984 and I assembled a team of engineers to start building displays for Commodore and, if they want, to develop a portable computer or a laptop computer."

Baraff's official title at Commodore was manager of liquid crystal display development. He was happy to learn he would not have to develop the manufacturing capability from scratch. "When I got to Commodore there was already a liquid crystal group that was making these smaller displays that were single line displays for other products," he says. "So I did not have to develop a whole manufacturing operation. All I had to do was bring in the technology."

Commodore set up the LCD production group near the massive warehouse. "It would have been on the west side of the warehouse," says Baraff. "When I first got there, my desk was up in the engineering department. But then as we got the facility built, then we moved my office downstairs so I could be closer to the work."

When Baraff arrived, Commodore Optoelectronics was still in the midst of its move from Texas. Commodore gave Baraff everything he needed and then some. "When I got there, they were sort of developing it. It was composed of two large clean rooms, approximately equal in size. The clean rooms each were about thirty feet by twenty feet wide. That was in the clean area for manufacturing. Then there was a non-clean packaging area that was roughly equivalent in size to those two clean rooms combined."

Commodore Optoelectronics also had office space for management, finance and research, including secretaries. "There were about eight offices and each of the offices would have been about fifteen foot square," recalls Baraff.

It was up to Baraff to supercharge the existing facility so it could produce active-matrix displays. "I set up a team and then, although they had liquid crystal manufacturing, there was a lot of high-tech manufacturing equipment that we had to purchase and set up."

Even though it was a small facility, there were two divisions within the LCD operation. "There were two groups, one was the R&D group, that I was the head of, so I reported to the vice president of research and development," says Baraff. "Then there was the manufacturing group, it reported to the vice president of manufacturing."

Once Baraff finished outfitting his department, he quickly produced an active matrix display similar to the prototypes he had developed while at BNR. Within months, Commodore had prototype displays ready.

Compared to other LCD displays at the time, Commodore's new LCD screen was remarkable. It contained 80-columns by 16-rows of text or 1200 characters (compared to 1000 for the Commodore 64). In total, the screen displayed 480 by 128 pixels.

LCD technology was still primitive in 1984 and manufacturing the display was difficult. "They would show me these big panels with so many defects," recalls Russell.

However, the successful production runs produced stunning quality for 1984. "We were doing traditional LCD displays and he was working on active matrix LCD displays which were pretty fricking awesome," says Jeff Porter. "The blacks were super black, the whites were super white on those screens. The contrast was really amazing."

Given the bright future that LCD screens and flat panels in particular had, in computers, televisions, and mobile phones, and Commodore's position as the only North American producer of the technology, it looked like something big could come out of the Commodore Optoelectronics group.

The LCD Portable

By the end of January, Michael North completed his 17 page specification for the LCD portable, which would act as the blueprint for the computer. It is clear the specs are inspired by the Tandy/Radio Shack TRS-80 Model 100 portable computer. "At the time, the rage in laptops was the Radio Shack TRS-80 model 100," says Jeff Porter. "It ran off AA batteries and had a keyboard, and a whopping 8 line 40 character LCD screen to it. So we looked at that and said there's probably a market for something like that."

The Model 100 was especially popular with journalists, who could type up a story and send it off immediately to the publisher with the built-in 300 baud modem. It even contained MS BASIC and was notable as the last product Bill Gates personally coded before he moved into management exclusively.

Commodore's LCD portable shared many features with the Model 100, such as 32 KB RAM, a built in 300-baud modem, MS BASIC, and built in applications. Where it deviated significantly was in the size of the ROM. The Model 100 contained a 32 KB ROM, but Commodore's computer would include 128 KB, courtesy of MOS Technology.

The computer would use a more energy efficient variant of the 6502 processor done in CMOS, running at 1 MHz according to the spec. Long-term plans would be for MOS Technology to manufacture the chips, but for now the engineers would use a Rockwell 65C102 CPU clocked at 2 MHz.

Although the target release computer would come with 32 KB, according to the specs, the unit could contain as little as 16 KB or as much as 1 megabyte. With all the ROM and system software available, the spec called for a Memory Management Unit (MMU).

Commodore intended to dethrone Tandy's LCD laptop computers. "It was like the Tandy-100 only on steroids," recalls Haynie. "It had a bigger display, the software was actually pretty good, there was tons of ROM in there, and it had a lot of [RAM] memory inside. It didn't run anybody else's software, but it was pretty cool."

Lloyd Taylor handed the project over to Joe Krasucki, a two year veteran at Commodore by 1984 and Director of the Consumer Products Division. He, in turn, gave the project to his leading engineer who was just finishing off Commodore's last major release. "I was fresh off the Plus/4, I knew what our chips could do, and I knew we could design our own memory management units, so I did the design for an LCD computer," says Bil Herd.

Much of Herd's initial work on the LCD portable took place while he finished off the Plus/4 in the first half of 1984. "I had approximately 5 months of LCD project lead time and it heavily overlapped with the end of the 264/364 project where we were also doing things like RAM expansion," he says. "There is also a complete MMU spec that I wrote somewhere done in typical VAX EDT editor format with a graph paper drawing that accompanied it."

One key component of the LCD Portable was the internal modem. At the time, Commodore licensed out its modem technology, but now it would gain the ability to handle the technology itself.

Jeff Porter

In March, Commodore would acquire an engineer who would not only develop modem technology, but would also play a key role in determining Commodore's system designs for the next decade, rising through the ranks to lead the engineering department.

Jeff Porter was born and raised in a small town outside of Milwaukee, Wisconsin. After graduating high school in 1975, he studied electrical engineering at Purdue University. While there, he worked two years as a co-op student at Kodak in the apparatus division.

After receiving his B.Sc., Porter went on to earn a Masters in EE from University of Illinois at Urbana-Champaign. In the summer of 1979, Bell Labs hired him into the Home Communications Laboratory, working on consumer products, including modems.

Then in March 1984 a headhunter recruited him for Commodore. "They were originally looking for engineers to do integrated circuit (IC) design," he recalls. "So they brought me in under that premise."

On March 29, the same day a major NFL team controversially packed up and moved states, Porter made his way to Commodore. "I drove to Pennsylvania the same date that the Baltimore Colts were driving to Indianapolis", he recalls.

Porter was slated to work for Commodore Semiconductor Group designing IC's and microchips, even though he was more interested in consumer product design. "I said, 'That's interesting, but who's doing all the circuit boards and all the stuff that the IC's go into?'" he laughs. "They said, 'That's in a different department.' I said, 'Well that might be really nice to work on.' So begrudgingly the manager of that group took me over to the manager of the other group. I sat down for about 10 minutes and we hit it off really well."

The man Porter hit it off with was Joe Krasucki. "He had been around during most of heyday of the C64," says Porter. "He worked for a guy named Adam Chowaniec, a sweetheart of a Canadian."

"He said, 'We've got a couple of things you could be working on. We've got this project for a laptop computer, another project for Unix workstations, and then of course our traditional Commodore 64 stuff. What are you interested in?' I said, 'Laptops would be awesome.'"

The young engineer, who was accustomed to dressing up for work at Bell Labs, began working alongside Bil Herd. "Jeff was the only one of us who knew how to tie a tie, so he was destined to be management," says Herd. "You could find him in his tie at ten o'clock at night."

Despite the cultural differences between Porter and his coworkers, he was well regarded for his engineering abilities and well liked. As a former Bell Labs employee, telecommunications was his specialty. "He knew about modems, a 300 baud modem in particular," says Hedley Davis. "This project had to have a modem in it and I think that's how he got into it."

Commodore Modems

Although Jeff Porter was slated to work on the LCD Portable, his mission soon spread to designing modems in general. "I was the Bell Labs guy, so when I first showed up, they said, 'It's nice that you want to work on that but we need somebody to figure out this modem crap.'"

Commodore wanted faster modems for the 8-bit computers, principally the C64. Porter was disappointed his contribution would be limited to modems. As he says, he "got suckered into redesigning modems at first."

The only modem Commodore sold at the time for the C64, the 1650, was designed by an outside company called Anchor Automation. Dennis Hayes, a pioneering designer of modems for home computers, developed the firmware code. A deal made by former director of marketing Michael Tomczyk meant Commodore had to pay royalties to both parties. "They were basically OEMing that from some guy and he was raking them over the coals," says Porter. "I said, 'I think I can help you with that. I know a few things about building a modem from my Bell Labs days.'"

Now Commodore had snagged its own Dennis Hayes. For his first task, Porter worked on a simple modem, focusing on cost reduction to make it more profitable for Commodore. "There was a 300 baud modem that was dirt cheap," says Porter. The modem was branded the 1660 and would retail for around $30, an astonishing price at the time.

One notable improvement Porter made was the switch from pulse dialing in the 1650 modem to tone dialing. Pulse dialing was a standard way of dialing a phone number that dated back to the late 1800's. It relied on dialing a rotary phone with your finger. The 1650 modem was able to recreate these pulses, but Commodore wanted to support tone dialing, which dialed numbers faster and would not be affected if telephone companies phased out pulse dialing.

Most modems included a simple sound synthesis chip to produce the dialing tones. Porter, however, was focused on cost reducing the 1660. Instead, he decided to use the C64's SID chip to produce the tones. To do this, he included an audio input jack. Users could then attach an included cable-splitter from the audio out on the back of the C64 to the audio in on the 1660 modem. All Porter's modem did was relay the sounds through the modem to the phone line.

Because of the versatility of the SID chip, it was able to generate a range of sounds, including the restricted tones used by AT&T. This made the 1660 modem popular with hackers who used the C64 as a blue box; a device to make long distance calls free of charge. Reportedly hackers could even transmit a tone to make quarters eject from public phones.

In late May 1984, Lloyd Taylor resigned from Commodore to join Jack Tramiel. Commodore promoted former Bell Northern Research employee

Adam Chowaniec to replace him. "This started at the end of Lloyd Taylor's reign and the start of Adam's," says Bill Herd. "Adam Chowaniec was a French-Canadian and he had worked for Lloyd Taylor who was a vice president under Jack."

Porter would go on to complete his 1660 modem design by November 1984, at which time he sent his 1660 prototype to San Jose, California for FCC testing. He fully expected testing and production to be ready in three months, although as it turned out, he would be sorely disappointed.

His next assignment, given to him by his immediate manager Joe Krasuki, was to design a faster 1200-baud modem for the C64. "There was a 1200 baud Hayes compatible modem that was nice and that was pretty unique," says Porter.

By this time, Dennis Hayes, the original designer of the 1650 modem, had established the Hayes standard for modem communications. Porter decided to make his 1200-baud modem compatible with this standard.

Due to his work on modems, and the requirement for an internal modem in the LCD portable, Porter joined the LCD portable team. "We hired Jeff (Joe [Krasuki] and I made the decision) to bring him into the LCD team which I was lead on, due to Jeff's telco and modem experience," says Herd, who was impressed with Porter's thorough knowledge of the telephone system, and specifically the phone lines that transmitted noise, known as FCC part number 68. "My memory is he knew FCC Part 68 subpart J cold, as an example, and we also wanted him to start immediately on a next higher speed modem in parallel."

The LCD portable project began gaining steam within Commodore. However, other changes were afoot within this tumultuous period and would soon turn the project on its head.

Unix Machine 1984

After the departure of many of Commodore's key engineers to join Jack Tramiel, the Unix Z-machine project fell into trouble. Adam Chowaniec, newly positioned as Commodore's VP of technology, attempted to pick up the pieces and try again.

Gerard Bucas

At Commodore, job titles became more important after Jack Tramiel left. "They asked me if I wanted to be director of business machines, which is what the Z8000 was," recalls Bob Russell. Unfortunately, the recent exodus left Commodore devoid of knowledgeable executives. He told Chowaniec, "I don't want to step up to director because I have no mentors here. I have nobody to show me how it's done."

Instead, Russell stepped into the role of director of engineering. "I became management there just because they said, 'You've been around here the longest and you can show the other guys the ropes.' I was already hiring people even though I wasn't a manager, so what the hell. Okay, I'll be a manager."

Unable to find someone within the company to lead the business division, Commodore began looking outside the company. The Unix machine was about to get a big supporter.

Gerard Bucas was born in Holland in 1946 and moved to South Africa at the age of seven. He grew up there and received degrees in economics, business administration and computer science by 1979. Olivetti, an Italian typewriter and computer company, hired him in the same year. He worked out of the head office in Italy in the strategic planning group where he focused on network architectures. "I did that about two years but didn't really want to stay in Italy longer term," he says.

When Olivetti presented an opportunity to move to the United States, he took it. "I went to their so-called advanced technology center, which was based in Cupertino, California," he recalls. "Interestingly enough, it was where they were developing their first PC. In fact, the first PC Olivetti did was actually CP/M, but then after the IBM PC came out, they switched to MS-DOS."

Despite the industry focus on MS-DOS, Bucas developed a deep appreciation of Unix. "I was responsible for what they called advanced software technology, which was a lot of different things like compilers and tools," he recalls. "I got heavily involved in Unix and the whole PC transition [from mainframes/minicomputers]."

In 1984, a job opened up at Commodore that fit Bucas like a glove. "In those days, Commodore was also very interested and active in business computers as opposed to home computers," explains Bucas. "They were developing their own PC's. So this guy said to me, 'Listen, why don't you go? It's your perfect company. Even though it's more than a billion dollar company, they really have no organization and you would fit in well there.' So I said, 'Well, I don't want to move to the east coast, so forget it.'"

Fortunately Commodore did not relent. "The head hunter kept on hassling me. I said, 'Well, I'll go for an interview.'" Bucas was won over by Adam Chowaniec. "I got the job there as director of business system development, which meant I was responsible for all the PC development; a new PC line and Unix workstation they were working on."

Bucas soon noticed the man in charge of Commodore at the time, Marshall Smith, was an unusual choice to run a computer company. "Marshall Smith was so non-technical and almost a non-entity in some sense," he says. "He basically didn't really know the industry and he didn't know the business."

Bucas was right, Marshal Smith was a strange fit for the computer industry. "My first impression of Commodore in front of the building there was Marshall Smith walking out to the Commodore limousine which had been idling and waiting for him with the license plate CBM 1," recalls Commodore consultant Eric Lavitsky. "These were the kind of old school executive types who had no problem exploiting company resources to their own benefit."

Managers within Commodore enjoyed great power due to Smith's lack of understanding and resulting non-interference, which for anyone who worked in the Tramiel organisation must have been a culture shock. "Engineering, including myself, we had a major influence on the whole company," explains Bucas. "Internally, some of us referred to Commodore as a billion-dollar garage shop. They basically had no depth in their organization, which was good for people like myself. I could do just about anything. I could literally decide product strategy, where to spend money, et cetera."

Chowaniec had eyed Bucas for a specific role at Commodore. "I was director of business systems development, which meant that I was responsible for all development that was not related to home computers," explains Bucas. This meant he had no input into the VIC-20 and C64 line of computers, which was managed by his counterpart in the home computer division, Joe Krasuki.

VAX Machines - March 1984

In his new position, Gerard Bucas began to acquire the best equipment available at the time for his engineers. "I'm a big believer in you've got to have the best tools available," he says.

Prior to Bucas, the main systems used by Commodore were IBM mainframes and a single VAX-11/750. "At that time all of the billing and accounting side of the company were run on IBM System/38's, an old IBM system," says Commodore employee Don Gilbreath.

Bucas purchased several Apollo DN660 systems and terminals, primarily to run Mentor CAD software. "We had many workstations for PCB design as well as for chip layout design," he says. "And graphical work stations which, in those days, were really expensive."

Bucas also purchased several Digital Equipment VAX mainframes for the engineering department. "That was our main development machine," he says. "From a development point of view, we used VAX for storing all our projects, all our work, and for email."

Commodore would, over the course of the next year, acquire multiple VAX systems for the various departments, all networked together into a cluster of Vaxen (plural for VAX). The VAX servers would improve communications between employees via intercompany email. Several terminals connected to the VAX cluster were scattered around the engineering department. Engineers would login to a terminal, check their mail, run programs, and log off when done. This new technology changed how engineers communicated from in person meetings to predominantly electronic. "We were certainly an early adopter of email and VAX of course had its own operating system," says Bucas.

In March 1984, the new VAX systems went online. "It's interesting to see how Commodore went from having a lot of money to having no money," says Bob Welland. "They bought a VAX-11/785 when they were very flush with cash, right when I got there. I remember seeing the purchase order, which was just written out by hand, for a machine that cost upwards of two million dollars. And I'm like, 'Wow, you can just spend money like that?' Little did I know the answer later would be no."

The VAX-11/785 was the latest in a line of DEC mainframe systems that ran Ultrix, a flavor of the Unix operating system. This daily usage of Unix gave the engineers an appreciation of the operating system and helped motivate them in the creation of the C900.

Upper management felt it would be important for the engineers to have access to the sales and marketing data on the IBM System/38 mainframe. "All of engineering product bill of materials, all of the stuff you find on the technical side were on Digital VAX machines," says Commodore engineer Don Gilbreath, who was tasked to implement a solution. "One of my first roles was they wanted to fuse those two computer systems together, from the administrative side, to be able to drill right back down to the bill of materials. There was pressure from the top to make that happen. So that was my first skunk project to get that happening."

First he physically linked the systems. "We had to build the protocol converter to actually electrically connect IBM's to Vaxen," he says. "We used a VIC-20 as a custom port. The job wasn't a big problem."

To save money, Commodore elected to use old PET computers as terminals, rather than purchase dozens of expensive DEC VT100 terminals. "They wanted to use their own equipment as the terminals, literally PETs and beyond," says Gilbreath. "It was an interesting project because what I ended up doing was we wrote software for the PET line to make it look like the VT100 from a software point of view. We made a pretty smart terminal software package for the PET and in some cases actually ended up building added circuitry to get high speed serial ports and stuff that it didn't have natively."

Although management wanted the bridge built between engineering and marketing & sales, there was resistance. "The big problem was the politics," says Gilbreath. "No one wanted to give up their own data. The M&S department that ran the IBM didn't want it. They were talking about viruses but they didn't like the idea of losing power to engineering and engineering didn't give a crap about having access to the sales flow."

Unix Project Design and Goals

Bucas' first task as director of business systems was to oversee the completion of the Unix project. "The PET was already basically dead at that point. By the time I got there, the main focus was on a Unix workstation," says Bucas. "They wanted to do a real versatile yet low-cost Unix workstation, which was pretty interesting and pretty visionary at that stage."

He and Bob Russell reviewed the goals of the proposed Unix machine. The vision Russell had for the computer was similar to Sun workstations, except five times less expensive. "We were looking at going after the workstation market," says C900 engineer Bob Welland. "There were plenty of machines in the really high end. The Apollo/Domain existed at the time and the Sun-2 had been announced. It was kind of an interesting market. And we were going to shoot for less than $2,000. So it was much less than what the Sun and Apollos were selling for."

Bucus was enthusiastic about the Unix system, owing to his previous experience at Olivetti's advanced technology group. "I had quite a strong Unix background from my Olivetti days," he says. "Probably six months before I left, Olivetti and AT&T hooked up on a number of levels. Bell Labs was of course where Unix and Berkeley Unix and lot of that came from. I was responsible for advanced technology, so I was very involved with that whole transition between the proprietary operating system that Olivetti had to Unix. It was pretty exciting."

With a Commodore-Motorola lawsuit over the 6500 line of microprocessors still ongoing, the plan remained to use the 16-bit chip from ZiLOG. "The Z8000 was comparable in performance to the 68000," says Welland. "You needed a memory management unit to run Unix. It had, if I'm remembering correctly, a segmenting memory management unit very similar to what the Intel 8086 had. And it was quite a bit faster as well."

ZiLOG itself was on somewhat shaky financial ground at the time. "Today you wouldn't go anywhere near a ZiLOG processor out of fear that the company would go out of business," says Welland. "But ZiLOG was still a presence because they had a lot of success with the Z80. And they were promising another chip called the Z80000 that was supposed to be a much higher performance 32-bit chip. So we were looking at what the arc of what you might consider workstation processors would be."

When it came to 16-bit processors, more companies opted to use the Motorola 68000 over the Z8000. "I wouldn't have chosen the Z8000," admits Welland. "I never really liked it but that decision had been made."

One unique feature of the Z-machine was the ability to act like a shared mainframe computer. "They were going to have terminals to hook into the Unix machine," says Dave Haynie. "They were developing a multiple port card for the thing so you could use it more like the VAX rather than like the workstations."

Coherent Unix OS

In the early 1980s, Commodore's engineers were starting to realize the operating system was as important as the hardware. Unix in particular was highly respected by engineers and academics as the most enduring and complete operating system at the time. It was important for Commodore to get the Unix part of the system right, but Commodore was known more for its hardware than software. IBM had famously licensed the MS-DOS operating system for its PC in 1981. Now Bob Russell began looking outside Commodore for a Unix operating system the company could use—at the same time that the PC clone team was negotiating for MS-DOS.

Unix originated in Bell Labs, AT&T's research division. Computer pioneers Dennis Ritchie and Ken Thompson developed the operating system in 1969 and released it to the outside world in 1973 for the PDP-11. The OS had many impressive features. It was written in the C-language, which meant the code was portable to other hardware. It was multitasking, meaning it could run several computer programs at the same time. It was multi-user, meaning users could login to their specific ID to access computer resources. And finally, it was time-sharing, allowing multiple people to access the same system via terminals.

By the late 1970s, other companies soon recognized the importance of the operating system and began developing their own versions. "There were many flavors of Unix then," explains Commodore engineer Bob Welland. "There was Berkeley Unix, which is what Sun was based on. We were using version 7 Unix which is what AT&T produced." Even Microsoft sold a version of Unix called Xenix.[1]

By the 1980's, local area networks were becoming more popular and Sun Microsystems was the first to take full advantage. "Bill Joy was the guy who had done Berkeley Unix. He was the person who added the networking lay-

---

1   When IBM came to Microsoft for an operating system, Bill Gates offered Xenix and
    tried to get IBM to change the hardware design to use the 68000 processor instead of
    the Intel 8088.

er to Unix, which was a very important advance," says Welland. "He went off and was one of the co-founders of Sun with Andreas Bechtolsheim who is the hardware designer. And then they brought in Scott McNealy who ran Sun for a long time."

With all the different Unix flavors, and Commodore about to have their own, it was becoming a complicated scene. "Everyone wanted their own version of Unix. and that was something that fragmented Unix in a lot of ways," says Welland. "If you were DEC, you owned V7M and so once you've got someone using your VAX machine, they were locked into your operating system."

Businesses were torn between the commercial appeal of offering a popular OS and the financial benefits of trying to lock users into a proprietary OS. "Every one of those hardware makers were thinking, 'If we just adopt a common Unix then what is our value add?' I think that was a valid fear on their part as Intel would prove later," says Welland. "So every one of those companies HP, Apollo, Sun, DEC, anyone who produced Unix had their own version. In general, the software would have to be recompiled but maybe the compilers had subtle differences. I mean it was a mess really."

In order to legally distribute a version of Unix, it had to be a clean room implementation, meaning the programmers could not look at the source code of AT&T Unix while developing their own version. "In those days it was kind of a free for all. In fact AT&T sued Berkeley about basically taking Unix and hacking on it."

Russell found a small software company in Chicago named Mark Williams Company. "Bob Russell was the person who made that choice," says Welland. The company had a Unix operating system called Coherent that dated back to 1980.

Mark Williams Company originally hired a group of programmers from Canada to develop the operating system for the PDP-11. "Bob Schwartz, the founder of Mark Williams, found this bunch of guys at the University of Waterloo who were Unix experts," explains Welland. "He got them all to move to Chicago. It was just an amazing team of people. I learned an astonishing amount from them."

Although the core team was from Canada, Schwartz hired others, among them Bob Welland. It was his job to implement Unix utilities for Coherent.

History records that the IBM PC had a choice of two operating systems: CP/M by Digital Research and MS-DOS by Microsoft. However, there was a third operating system, based on Unix, that almost made the cut. "IBM gave them an early prototype and in fact they were briefly in the running for who was going to provide IBM with their operating system," says Welland.

The main problem in porting Coherent to the IBM PC was that Unix required a Memory Management Unit (MMU) to run properly, something the IBM PC lacked. "It's very difficult to get Unix to run on a processor that doesn't have a memory manager," explains Welland. "Multitasking was a bit much for a machine with a relatively small amount of memory and a floppy drive."

However, a programmer named Johann George succeeded in the task. "They got it running. It was kind of amazing but it took a lot of jumping through hoops," explains Welland.

In many ways, it seems like Unix should have been the operating system picked up by IBM. However, what seems clear on paper can be thwarted by the details. In this case, the price was too high compared to what Microsoft offered, and the OS was really too powerful for the first IBM PC, making it slow and clunky. "In the end, as everyone knows, Microsoft was to get that contract and a large place in the history books," says Welland.

Mark Williams Company continued selling Coherent for the IBM-PC and other microcomputers for $495. But in the aftermath of the lost opportunity with IBM, the engineers deserted the company. "It must have been around 1982 that they had a big falling out with Bob," says Welland. "They all left because they couldn't come up with an adequate equity agreement." Welland himself was among those who scattered to the wind.

Unix continued to advance after they departed but Coherent became somewhat frozen in time. "It was a version 7 Unix clone. Essentially what you had was an operating system developed by a whole bunch of people in a really wild, maniacal couple of years and then they all left," says Welland. "You can't replace those people, they were just too good. And so that made it guaranteed to be obsolete."

By 1984, when Commodore became interested in a Unix clone, the Coherent OS was missing an important feature. "Coherent suffers from one fatal flaw which was that it didn't have a networking layer," says Welland, referring to the lack of a TCP/IP stack. "That's what Berkeley Unix had done and those happened kind of simultaneously to the development of Coherent."

Board Redesign

With the Z-machine project in between teams, Bob Russell decided to re-evaluate the current motherboard designed by Shiraz Shivji. "The first motherboard wasn't very well-designed," says Welland.

Russell decided the problem was due to inexperience with the Z8000 chip itself. Commodore had no engineers with Z8000 experience, so he decided to bring in a consultant named George Robbins to redesign the board. "We ended up bringing in a Z8000 expert and he redesigned the motherboard," says Bob Welland. "He made a huge contribution. Basically he came in with a new motherboard design."

Unofficially called the Z-machine, Commodore chose a new name for the Unix machine. "Commodore marketing had decided that their computer was going to be the Commodore 900," says Dave Haynie.

C900 Design Team Assembled

The loss of key engineers to Atari momentarily paused development of the Z-machine. Only Bob Russell remained to pick up the pieces. As the new motherboard was in development, Russell and Bucas began hiring a new team to continue the work. "There were three different teams on the C900 before they got that to work right," recalls Haynie. "The last of those were George Robbins and Bob Welland."

George Robbins would design the system board, making him the owner of the C900 project, who would drive the other engineers forward. Bob Welland would design the video circuit-board in the C900.

There was top-to-bottom cohesion of the team, due to a mutual love of Unix. "Gerard Bucas, the head of engineering at the time, had a really soft spot in his heart for the C900," says Welland.

George R. Robbins, whom engineers nicknamed 'Grr', was a contractor for Commodore at the time. "He owned the motherboard and all of the ancillary details," explains Welland. "He was an extremely good detail person and he kind of savored that."

Born in 1954, Robbins was a self-taught engineer, a process that took longer than a formal education, and as a result he was in his thirties by the time he entered his profession at Commodore. "He was a little bit older than most of us at the time," says Haynie. "He lived a bohemian lifestyle."

Robbins looked something like a cowboy, with long greying hair that went well past his shoulders and a handlebar moustache. Prior to Commodore, he had spent a lot of time at sea. "He had worked on an oil tanker for a long time," says Bob Welland. "He was responsible for tracking the spare parts. I guess they have a lot of spare parts on an oil tanker. So he had all these stories."

Although he lacked a formal education, his colleagues rated him highly. "You find these guys and they're just so much better than you are. They didn't go to school, they've got big brains, they just pick it up and go," laughs engineer Hedley Davis. "I never was one of those guys. I had to go to school. I didn't have the discipline or the drive or something."

At the same time as Robbins and Welland were starting at Commodore, the VAX server appeared. Robbins fell in love with the machine. "George was very involved with the VAX that we had," says Welland. "He took to the VAX and spent a lot of time making sure that it did what it should do."

Herd was impressed with the ingenuity of the Z-people and their ability to thrive in the Commodore environment. At the massive new West Chester building, space was abundant and there were many rooms available. One night, the Z-people stole the furniture out of the Commodore lobby and made their own lounge so they could relax and smoke. The unauthorized lounge would obviously not last long once managers found out about it, so the Z-people disguised it as a VAX mainframe repair depot. According to Herd, "I was so amused by this that I stopped teasing them for a week."

Engineers often made jests about the distinctive odor that followed Robbins, in good fun since most engineers suffered the same problem from time to time, depending on their work schedule. "The difference between George and me was George didn't do the things for hygiene that I did," says Herd. "We all knew it."

For years, Commodore engineers requested on-site showers due to the odd hours they worked, however management refused. "That was the one thing we could never get," says Haynie, who still sounds frustrated. "Bil had made a deal that if we finished on time we would get showers. We were petitioning for years."

Herd remembers the negotiations. "I was always telling people, 'You need showers. Look, I'm here all the time. You want work out of me? Put a fricking shower in. I'm using a brown tub I fill out of the coffee machine.'"

When Robbins needed sleep at Commodore, he nested. "George was different," explains Herd. "George would sleep in bubble wrap. We called it nesting. You could look under a table and see a whole bunch of bubble wrap and maybe a foot sticking out of it. Then he would walk around with these little red circles on his face after he woke up."

Robbins lived on cafeteria food at Commodore and resorted to vending machines when the cafeteria closed. "He was drop kicking the vending machine," says Herd. "He probably had no change and needed to eat or something."

Robbins' ability to live at Commodore for long periods of time made him one of Commodore's most effective engineers. "I would argue that he was probably the best one, largely because he just worked at it more than anybody else. He never left the building, just always worked," says Hedley Davis.

Working alongside Robbins was 23 year old Robert Welland. Welland was also one of the original Coherent Unix programmers, which made him a valuable hire for the C900 project.

Welland attended Northwestern University for two years starting in 1978, taking Physics and computer science classes, however he dropped out of university before receiving a degree and began working at *itty bitty machine company* located in nearby in Evanston, Illinois. Much like Robbins, his knowledge in computers was largely self-taught. "I started out in high school doing hardware and that was my first passion. And then I switched to software just because that's where the jobs were."

After departing The Mark Williams Company, he worked for a company called Scientific Information Retrieval porting a database to different Unix computers. "I had spent a little time at Sun porting a database to their SUN-1," recalls Welland. As his Fortran code compiled on the system, he routinely popped open the SUN-1 case and studied the graphics board. "I kind of reverse engineered their graphics processor because I was bored."

The SUN-1 graphics board used 7400 series Transistor-Transistor Logic (TTL) chips, those 14-pin chips that looked like little robot bugs. "In those days that board was all TTL so if you knew all your TTL numbers, then you could figure out what the board did just by looking at the chips and looking at their relative location to each other."

Welland began recreating the board logic on paper but his forays into hardware ended when Sun formally asked him to stop looking at its hardware while his code compiled. However, the experience left Welland with a deep interest in computer graphics. In particular, he found the bit blitter to be of interest. "[Andreas] Bechtolsheim had done the first hardware blit, so it's kind of an interesting machine in that regard," he says. "It was a single word blitter which is a funny thing. It's hard to describe how it worked but it's kind of interesting."

In 1984, Welland received a call from his old boss. "The guy who owned Mark Williams, Bob Schwartz, was in contact with Commodore because the C900 was running Coherent, which was Mark Williams' cleanroom clone of Unix," explains Welland. "So Bob introduced me to Bob Russell and so I interviewed with Bob Russell. I went and just visited and it was very cool."

Because of his recent fascination with the SUN-1 graphics board, Welland was eager to do something similar. "I always wanted to do chip design and I was very familiar with hardware and suddenly there's this building full of chip designers," he says. "That was kind of fascinating."

Welland also accepted his offer from Commodore due to a personal relationship. "It was attractive for an odd reason: it was pretty close to Washington D.C. where my then girlfriend had moved."

Russell hired him to work on the video portion of the C900, though in the back of his mind he must have appreciated the Coherent background Welland possessed. "They brought me in to do the video part," he says. "So while I was doing the chip, we worked on the video, just a discrete version of the display."

Welland was extremely focused on computer design and software development, rather than using applications. "At that time I just cared about hardware design and hardware architecture. I could not care less about the software," he says. "I didn't have a computer at home. I was using a Sun-2 for certain things. I brought in a bunch of software for automated VLSI tools. Berkeley had done a tool set for auto-routing and auto-placement and a bunch of stuff that Commodore wasn't doing at the time."

Welland was one of the few engineers at Commodore comfortable in both hardware and software development. "I'm self-taught, so I can jump back and forth," he says in his deep, billowy voice. "I really, really wanted to learn chip design so that was a motivation."

Rounding out the C900 development was a new hire at Commodore, Greg Berlin. Although he would not work on the main C900, he was responsible for engineering the backup tape unit for the C900. "There was a high speed tape drive before the hard drives came out and all kinds of other stuff we were working on," says Berlin.

C900 Video Card

The original C900 computer, designed by Bob Russell and Shiraz Shivji, used a color video chip called the 8563. Two LSI engineers, husband and wife team Kim and Anne Eckert, had begun designing the 8563 chip in early 1983 and it was first produced in early 1984. Although the 8563 would be used in the new C900 design, Bob Welland wanted to add higher resolutions.

Welland was inspired by the monochrome, high resolution Unix machines produced by Sun Microsystems and Xerox. "From studying the Xerox Alto I knew what I wanted to do but I had never done a chip before so there were a lot of things I needed to learn," he says. "The C900 was targeted at the Unix workstation market. It took me little time to suggest what I wanted to make: a high resolution graphics card with a 2D bit-blitter in hardware."

His chip, called the 8724 Video Controller, would have specs comparable to the high end Unix systems of the time. "We were going for resolution as opposed to color. It was 1024 by 800, black and white," says Welland. "The Sun-2 would have been about the same."

To overlay GUI Windows on the screen quickly, Welland would design a bit blitter. "The novel idea behind the C900 video chip was to incorporate a 2D blitter," says Welland. "The idea of bit blit was still quite novel and so I might claim that I brought that idea into Commodore—that was the payoff of my obsession with the Xerox Alto. So far as I know, at the time, this was one of the first attempts to build a 2D blitter in hardware."

Welland was aided by another engineer. "I worked with a wonderful guy called Ferenc Vadovszki, a guy from New Jersey but he was I think of Hungarian gypsy background," says Welland. "Very interesting, a really lovely guy."

It was Welland's first experience with chip design and Vadovszki was even less experienced than Welland. "He was a more junior chip designer in a way that turned out to not be a great thing because I was a junior chip architect," says Welland. "Combine the two of us together and we flailed a lot and struggled a lot because we were both new to that."

Welland relied on several experienced chip designers to guide him along. "The chip designers there were very generous with helping me understand that stuff," says Welland. "I worked pretty closely with Victor Andrade and Kim Eckert. The head of the chip division was Martin Schabelski. He was a nice guy and he let people talk to me. He had to manage what all they did and I'm kind of a knowledge seeking engine so I'll go waste tons of people's time trying to figure stuff out. But they were very nice about trying to bring me up to speed."

Slowly, a little at a time, Welland completed one part after another of his video chip. "I did the easiest part first, which was to build the refresh engine for putting the pixels on the screen," explains Welland. "For this you essentially start with a pixel rate clock and divide it into lines that have a pixel region and a dead region that allows the CRT to direct the electron-beam back to the start of the next line. Using TTL-think, I implemented all of this with counters."

Welland was just following what he knew, designing the circuitry as he had seen it implemented in the SUN-1 card he studied earlier, using Transistor-Transistor Logic (TTL). He soon realized how wasteful this was. "A card like the SUN-1 graphics card would be built this way," he explains. "But when I did a design review of this with the chip designers they balked, asking me if I understood what a counter was. I didn't understand what they were getting at and they pointed out that counters are adders and adders are large (in that era). Why aren't you multiplexing a single adder was the question."

Welland was used to designing digital electronics and found the transition to chip design required a different mindset. "I was used to doing TTL design and chip design is very, very different because you have all the wires you want," he says. "It took quite a bit of a learning curve to realize that you don't just design something like it's TTL and then put it on a chip. You actually think quite differently. And it probably took me about six months to internalize that difference."

Welland soon picked up the differences and started thinking like a chip designer designing with Very Large Scale Integration (VLSI). "This is when it first dawned on me how different and cool VLSI design was," he says. "TTL is limited by the packages you have and so structures that are easy in VLSI, like register files with accumulators, are very difficult and impractical in TTL. In this sense, VLSI can be a much more direct expression of the design intent. I came up to speed pretty quickly, with a lot of help from the VLSI design team."

Despite his inexperience, Welland made rapid progress with the blitter. "He designed a graphics chip for the C900 that had its own blitter, which was a bit more sophisticated in some ways than the Amiga blitter," says Dave Haynie. Getting the chip to work was a whole other endeavor.

Welland felt elated to be designing chips at Commodore, one of the only computer companies with its own semiconductor design groups. "It is hard to convey how amazing Commodore was at that time," says Welland. "Coming from a hardware background where everything was made of TTL except the microprocessors, to find oneself working on the stuff that went into the chips was quite exhilarating."

C900 X-Window GUI

With windowed GUI operating systems coming into fashion, the team wanted one for the C900. At the time there were few options for Unix-based windows. "Everyone was looking at the Mac as the standard-bearer of overlapping windows and also the Sun machines. X-Window didn't exist then," says Welland, referring to the standard windowing GUI for Unix. The first windowing system for Unix was called X version 1, released in May 1984. However, the definitive X11 windows GUI would not come along until September 15, 1987.

At Sun Microsystems, computer pioneer James Gosling was developing a GUI called NeWS. He used a scripting language called PostScript, which was designed for producing vector graphics. "Gosling's design was heavily weighted around PostScript kind of things," says Welland.

Commodore made an early, aborted attempt at a windows interface. "The software team on the C900 needed to write a windows system for the C900 and that's actually a very difficult job," says Welland. "They were struggling a lot with it.

The first attempt was comparatively simple compared to the efforts by Sun, Xerox and Bell Labs. "It had a much more primitive API I would say," says Welland. "Though it had overlapping windows, it was just very traditional in that way. It was structured kind of like X-Window from a software perspective where there is a device driver in the kernel that kind of passed rendering instructions to the windows subsystem so that an app could connect through a kernel driver to change the screen. And that's the kind of thing that, if you're not very familiar with the inner workings of a kernel, you're going to really struggle to get that stuff going. The earlier team had that struggle."

An outside contractor and friend of Welland was able to restart the GUI project and break the stalemate. "I brought in a good friend of mine Rico Tudor, who I had worked with at Mark Williams," recalls Welland. "He's a very good kernel coder and very creative guy. He came from Reed College and had a wonderful software design style that I learned a great deal from. His habit was to compose the smallest piece of code that would do the thing he wanted and then he would optimize for speed. Often this approach seemed insane but it always seemed to work for him and it clarified the core issues."

After helping bring Coherent to the C900 computer, Tudor took on the failed windows GUI, using his minimization-optimization strategy. "He later demonstrated this approach in his implementation of the window system for the C900," says Welland.

The C900 received a professional, compact case design. "All the plastic design, all the case work, and all the molds that had to be cut were being done out of Japan," says Russell. "There was nothing out of the United States."

The lead mechanical engineer was a 30-year old designer of many of the PET computer cases, who delivered the C900 case before departing Commodore for Atari. "We had a US designer Ira Velinsky there but Ira was spending more time dealing with Japan talking Japanese than he was doing much here in the United States," says Russell. "Of course, Ira then went on to Atari too and did case work for them."

Chasing IBM

After the April 1984 Hanover Fair, Commodore had planned to sell rebadged Hyperion computers to the PC market in Europe. But several factors led them to cancel this idea. First, the German customers did not want the strange portable form factor of the Hyperion. They wanted a full-sized IBM PC clone. Second, the Hyperion was not very compatible with existing IBM PC software. And third, MOS Technology was having problems manufacturing the Intel 8088. Commodore ended up deciding against marketing the system, and did not take advantage of the Intel and Hyperion licenses purchased earlier in 1984.

But Commodore was not out of the PC clone business. The general manager of Commodore Germany's Braunschweig factory, Winfried Hoffmann, spotted an opportunity. Compaq was still establishing the PC clone market in North America, leaving the market in Europe open. He determined, independently of Commodore US, to enter the market himself. "He built the factory in Braunschweig without asking Jack or Irving or anybody," says former Commodore engineer Chuck Peddle.

Hoffmann directed his engineers to build a new desktop PC compatible, called the PC-10. The German engineers studied the original IBM PC and the Hyperion, copying circuitry in both for use in the new design.

Although Harald Speyer was the GM of Commodore Germany, he would only be responsible for the overall sales and marketing of the computer in his region. Dave Haynie believes Commodore Germany was forced to deliver IBM PC clones, otherwise it would lose its longtime customers.

Officially, Gerard Bucas was in charge of the development of business computers. When word of the German PC clones came to the halls of

Commodore in Pennsylvania, the project fell under Gerard Bucas' provision. "When I started there, that was really my responsibility: PC's and the Unix workstation, the C900," says Bucas. "That was really all I did for the first one year I was there. When I came to Commodore, they didn't have PC's yet."

Commodore would have no problem obtaining any of the off-the shelf parts that made up the IBM PC, except for the BIOS chip (Basic Input/Output System), responsible for booting up the system. Rather than attempting to develop its own clean-room BIOS, Bucas decided to license the BIOS from Phoenix Technologies of Boston, Massachusetts. The company used the Chinese Wall method of cloning the IBM PC BIOS. Furthermore, the Phoenix BIOS was famed for its high compatibility with the IBM PC. To assuage fears, Phoenix took out $2 million dollar insurance policy against possible copyright-infringement claims by IBM. If IBM attempted to go after Commodore, lawyers from Phoenix would protect them.

Bucas was amazed at how cheap Commodore could acquire keyboards compared to his former employer. "In those days, Olivetti was paying maybe $40 for a keyboard. Commodore, on the other hand, for a C64 keyboard, was probably paying $6. Of course, the C64 sold in much higher volume than Olivetti PCs. By definition, that was one of the reasons why the pricing was different."

The systems were eventually manufactured in Braunschweig for the European market. "The first couple of PC designs were done in Germany and all the PCs were manufactured in Germany and not in West Chester," explains Bucas.

In late 1984, Speyer released the Commodore PC-10. The machine captured a large portion of the European PC market, largely due to competitive pricing over IBM PC computers. "He really did this brilliant job of marketing," says Peddle.

The fact that Commodore was producing PC compatible machines seemed like a major concession in the computer wars by Commodore. Michael Tomczyk disagreed with the new strategy. "After Jack left, the grey haired men that were running the company, none of whom had a computer background, all thought that Commodore should become IBM," he says. "We even started selling IBM PCs in Europe."

The move allowed Commodore to take profits away from IBM, and they became more successful than American clone makers. "We became the largest distributor of IBM PC [clones] in Europe," says Tomczyk.

As Commodore moved closer to becoming yet another maker of unimaginative PC clones, across the country a new company was taking shape. This upstart would shake up Commodore to the core and change the trajectory of personal computers for the rest of the decade.

CHAPTER 4

Hi-Toro
1984

After Jack Tramiel left Commodore, the company was in search of a new hit product. The computers offered by rivals Apple and IBM used very little color and had poor sound. In fact, Commodore's own C64 was the peak of audio-visual capability for home computers.

At the upcoming CES, a new product would catch the attention of Commodore and change its fortunes forever. The computer that would eventually make a quantum leap ahead of the rest had its origins years earlier, when a group of engineers and businessmen haphazardly fell together and decided to design a new video game system.

Larry Kaplan

The first inkling of a revolutionary new computer called the Amiga came from a game developer. Larry Kaplan had developed half a dozen games for Atari before co-founding *Activision* with David Crane, Alan Miller, and Bob Whitehead.

At Activision, he designed *Kaboom!*, a bestselling game for the Atari 2600. However, Kaplan seemed perpetually dissatisfied no matter where he worked. "I was at Activision in early 1982 and bored with doing 2600 games and eager to work on new game hardware," he explains.

During the Consumer Electronics Show (CES) that year, Kaplan saw an early preview of a gaming console from a small and little known Japanese company. "I had seen the Nintendo NES at the CES in June '82 and thought we could do better."[1]

---

1   First-hand interview by digitpress.com retrieved August 20, 2015.

Over lunch one day, Kaplan met with another former Atari employee named Doug Neubauer, a codesigner of the Atari Pokey chip but perhaps most famous for creating the Atari game *Star Raiders*. At the time, Neubauer was creating movie-based games for 20th Century Fox, such as *Mega Force* and *M*A*S*H*. He too wanted to work with better hardware. "I wasn't happy at Activision when Doug and I had lunch," recalls Kaplan. "He wanted to do something together and we both agreed a new game machine was it."

After some discussion, they decided there was one crucial person they needed to contact. "We contacted Jay Miner, who was doing chip design at Zymos," recalls Kaplan.

Jay Miner

The man who would design Commodore's next generation hardware did not work for Commodore. In fact, he was working for its rival, Atari, when he first conceived of the new computer.

Jay Glenn Miner was born May 31, 1932 in Prescott, Arizona. A few years after his birth, Miner's family moved to Southern California. After graduating high school, he signed up for the United States Coast Guard, which took him to Groton, Connecticut for military training. While there, he met Caroline Poplawski and married her in 1952. Like Tramiel, Miner served in the military during the Korean War.

He received his first taste of electronics at Groton in the Coast Guard's Electronics Technician School. After completing the six-month course, he joined the North Atlantic Weather Patrol where he hopped from island to island by boat and helicopter, servicing radar stations and radio installations. With few distractions, he immersed his young mind in electronics.

After serving three years in the barren North Atlantic, Miner enrolled at the University of California, Berkeley in electrical engineering and computer science. By 1958, he completed his electrical engineering degree, with a major in the design of generators and servomotors.

He performed contract work for several years until he landed permanent employment at General Micro Electronics in 1964. At GME, Miner pioneered some of the earliest digital voltmeters and helped design the first MOS (Metal Oxide Semiconductor) calculator chip.

In 1973, Miner left GME to co-found chipmaker Synertek, which eventually became a second source for MOS Technology's 6502 chip. Atari relied on Synertek to fabricate its custom chips for the Atari 2600, and eventually the former poached Miner to design the Atari 2600 video chipset at Cyan Engineering (Atari's research lab in Grass Valley). He went on to design the impressive Atari 400 and 800 systems, admired by users for their graphics capabilities.

Miner was an interesting sight at Cyan Engineering. People who saw him in the halls often had to take a second look because a tiny black shadow seemed to follow his every move. The shadow was actually a little black Cockapoo named Mitchy. "Mitchy had a long history of being involved in the computer industry because Mitchy used to go to Atari with Jay and helped him design the systems there," says fellow engineer RJ Mical.

The dog became a fixture at Atari. Miner had a brass nameplate on his door that read, 'J.G. Miner', and just below it was a smaller nameplate, 'Mitchy'. The canine even had her own tiny photo-ID badge clipped to her collar as she happily trotted through the halls. While Miner worked on his groundbreaking systems, Mitchy sat on a couch watching with puzzlement as her master slaved over diagrams and schematics.

By 1979, he was brainstorming the possibilities offered by a new 16-bit Motorola 68000 microprocessor, which was not yet commercially available.

He and a co-worker named Joe Decuir pitched an idea to Atari for a new computer based on the 68000. "They talked to Atari management about building a more powerful machine and Atari management nixed it," says Decuir's friend, Ron Nicholson. "They wanted to keep on milking the [Atari] 800. So even though they had beat the innovator's dilemma by jumping from the VCS to the 800, they couldn't do it twice in a row."

Miner also felt aggrieved when Atari failed to live up to an agreement despite the commercial success of both products. "They decided not to pay the bonus they promised me and the engineers. So I quit, as did nearly all of the engineers and programmers," says Miner.[2]

Zymos

After leaving Atari, Miner joined a semiconductor start-up named Zymos. A medical device company named Intermedics had purchased Zymos because it wanted a steady supply of ROM chips for its devices. Soon, Miner began designing ROM chips for pacemakers.

Bill Hart, an early investor in Amiga, recalls, "Intermedics had bought this semiconductor company to do ROMs for their pacemakers because there was a very tough market for components back then. They wanted

---

2 *Amiga User International.* June 1988. "The AUI Interview" p. 20.

to make sure that they didn't have to interrupt manufacturing because of shortages."

Intermedics itself was a rising powerhouse. It had launched the first lithium battery pacemaker in 1976, extending the life of the device from 2 to 6 years. "Intermedics made state-of-the-art implantable pacemakers and defibrillators," recalls Nicholson. "Before that time, pacemakers were these big boxes you had to strap on with wires going through holes in your body, and it was a huge disaster at best. Or they were such high powered devices you'd need regular surgery to open them up to replace the battery." Annual sales rapidly grew from $2.2 million in its first year to $155 million by 1981, becoming the second largest manufacturer of pacemakers.

Intermedics soon expanded into dental implants and other products. Amid a flurry of acquisitions with its newfound wealth, the publicly traded Intermedics acquired Zymos. "The funders of Intermedics funded Zymos to make CMOS low power custom chips," explains Nicholson. "To gain the reputation that they could actually succeed and accomplish that, they had to have big names to raise the capital, and Jay Miner was the big name to found Zymos."

Intermedics wanted what is called a captive chip source; one that they had full control over. Miner worked at Zymos happily designing pacemaker chips for Intermedics under his boss, W. Bert Braddock. However, the pacemaker market dealt with modest volumes and Braddock soon found his manufacturing facility sat idle most of the time. "They found that the scale that they had to establish to start a semiconductor company was more than they needed," explains Hart. "So they needed to find outlets for the capacity."

The Proposal

Around this time, Kaplan and Neubauer took Jay Miner to lunch to convince him to design a new video chip. It was an easy conversation. Miner saw a real opportunity, what with the market doing so well for Activision and Atari. He was in.

But the group still needed financing. Miner went to his boss over at Zymos for help. "Jay talked to the president of his company, Bert Braddock, who was interested," explains Kaplan.

Braddock knew just where to get the funding. Billionaire O. Wayne Rollins, the 79th richest person in the United States at the time, had made his fortune in the pest control business, principally through Orkin. He was also the owner of Intermedics and Zymos.

Given the video game boom, the heart of the proposal was creating a console for video games to compete with Atari. "Our business plan was strictly about doing a new game console, with Jay and Doug doing the chip design with Zymos," says Kaplan.

Larry Kaplan would co-design the system and oversee game development, while Jay Miner and Doug Neubauer would design the chips and motherboard. Zymos, in turn, would fabricate the chips and cartridges.

With the proposal in hand, the group approached the most promising millionaire they knew. "Bert talked to his financier, O.W. Rollins of Rollins, Inc.", recalls Larry Kaplan.

When Rollins saw the proposal, he knew that the success of the startup would also help his other investment, the struggling Zymos. "They were looking at where the most ROM chips were going and the answer was in the cartridge business," says Hart. "That was the biggest user of those chips. Activision and Atari were dominating the cartridge businesses at the time."

Rollins insisted on professional management with retail consumer experience. "Rollins found the CEO, David Morse, a vice-president at Tonka Toys in Minnesota," says Kaplan.

Dave Morse, Founder of Amiga

In early 1982, a 39 year old VP of marketing named Dave Morse was dreaming of something bigger, while growing frustrated at his current position in a toy company. At the time, the leading toy companies in North America included names like Hasbro, Kenner, Mattel, Coleco, Fisher Price, and Tonka. Morse had worked at the last since 1970 and had seen the direction consumer products, including toys, were headed.

The source of Morse's frustration was Tonka's unwillingness to enter the market for electronic toys. Tonka was known primarily for a line of steel trucks. "The most famous one is the Mighty Dump, that big yellow dump truck that was the real symbol of Tonka," recalls Don Reisinger, who worked for Morse at Tonka. The Mighty Dump Truck had been a perennial favorite since the 1950's across North America, found in sandboxes, scratched and rusted after years of play by toddlers.

While Tonka had a large variety of vehicles in its toy line, it never strayed too far out of what had always worked. In 1982, Tonka was making a transition from metal toys to plastic. "We redesigned the whole thing from the bottom up, which was risky because it's your biggest item. But in order to maintain the price point, we redesigned it," recalls Reisinger.

Unfortunately for Morse, it was a bad time to suggest an even more radical change. "Dave was pushing Tonka very, very hard to get involved in electronics and toys," says Reisinger. "Not necessarily games but making the vehicles more than just the steel trucks with four wheels on them. And he had a lot of resistance there from everybody from the top right on down."

Morse knew well that hit toys like *Simon* and *Speak & Spell* pointed to the future of the toy industry. However, he held a genuine interest in electronics beyond wanting to join a trend. Earlier in life he had earned a degree in electrical engineering from Tufts University near Boston. He then enrolled at Tuck School of Business, one of six Ivy League business schools in the United States, graduating with an MBA. From there he moved to Minnesota to work for Pillsbury and then Tonka, where he had remained all this time.

As vice-president of marketing, Morse attended CES every year, making sales and watching the trends. One of Tonka's rivals, Coleco, had debuted the ColecoVision video game console at the 1982 summer CES. The system featured the hit game *Donkey Kong*, developed by Nintendo of Japan. Morse decided to follow the trail and visited the Nintendo booth, where the company was demonstrating its *Game & Watch* product.

With several successful coin-operated arcade games under its belt, Nintendo planned to launch a new home console. Representatives began demonstrating early versions of the system behind closed doors in 1982 with a planned launch date of July 1983. However, Nintendo did not have a North American presence, nor did it have the resources needed to form an organization to market, advertise, launch, and distribute the product across the retail space. Instead, it planned to partner with an established toy company for retail distribution.

When Morse met with Nintendo, both parties sensed an opportunity. "Dave told me that he had had discussions with Nintendo about having Tonka represent them in the US market to handle distribution and sales," recalls Bill Hart, a classmate of Morse's at Tuck School of Business. "Tonka was probably one of the strongest brands in the Toys "R" Us portfolio. Nintendo, which was new to the US market, was looking for some real clout in the retail channel and they felt, probably rightly so, that Tonka could give that to them."

When Morse introduced the deal to the board of directors at Tonka, the idea went nowhere. "They turned it down," recalls Hart. "I do know that frustrated Dave."

By 1982, Morse and his wife of 17 years, Lorraine, had two sons. As far as businessmen go, he was a bit of a nerd; more of a Bill Gates than a Steve Ballmer. But there were a few signs of his success, including a large home on a lake in Minneapolis and a Porsche that he delighted in driving.

Hart visited Morse in the summer of 1982 while raising an investment fund. The two discussed opportunities and it seemed to Hart that Morse was getting ready to strike out on his own. "My guess is that Dave had already begun to feel the entrepreneurial bug because when I visited him in Minnesota, he was really interested in everything we were talking about. I think he had in his mind that someday he'd like to take a shot at building a company of his own."

Unknown to Hart, Morse was already actively laying down plans to make his exit from Tonka. Earlier in the year he had hired corporate headhunters to find him a marketing position in Silicon Valley. "Dave had a fair number of recruiters up there that were looking to place him somewhere," recalls Reisinger.

When O. Wayne Rollins saw that the head of marketing for a large US corporation was free and that he held degrees in business and electrical engineering, he thought he would be the perfect person to expand Zymos' ROM sales into the cartridge market. "They wanted him to go start a cartridge company," recalls Hart. Not just to produce cartridge ROMs but to design, program and release games for the Atari 2600 market.

The idea of founding his own video game company appealed to Morse, however, he wanted to make sure he was not setting himself up for failure. "Dave had decided to leave Tonka so he came here, but he told them that he would not agree to do anything until they funded a study that he would do on the market so that he could come back with a more informed business plan," explains Hart.

As part of his research, Bert Braddock introduced Morse to Jay Miner. "When Dave started to study, the guy introduced him to Jay as a resource," says Hart.

That introduction would foster one of the most radical changes in personal computing, though at the time it seemed like business as usual.

The Pixel System

After a few weeks of talking with Jay Miner, Dave Morse became more interested in the video game console. "He went out there and concluded that it didn't make any sense to take on Atari and the other players in that game," says Bill Hart. "He said that technology is going to change and we're behind the curve. We should not do that." Instead, Morse joined Larry Kaplan and Doug Neubauer.

With Morse onboard, Kaplan abruptly quit Activision in June 1982, one week before a planned company trip to Hawaii. "Over the summer we all wrote a business plan."

The business plan was spearheaded by Dave Morse in order to figure out a timetable and how much investment was required. The team developed a 14 page plan that included an analysis of the video game market, the home computer market, a development program, manufacturing, marketing and sales, key personnel, legal and financial requirements.

A name for the company was bandied about until everyone was satisfied. "I wanted to name the company Pixel," recalls Kaplan. The game console they were developing would likewise be called the Pixel System.

The partners proposed three consoles with slightly different specs, each codenamed after Kaplan's wife and two sons. All three Pixel Systems used a 6502 processor running at 4 MHz. "Dave" had 2 KB, cost $53 to manufacture and retailed for $180. "Benj" had 16 KB, cost $107 and retailed for $350. "Sue" had 64 KB of static RAM, cost $229 and retailed for $750. At this point the business plan favored the creation of the Dave prototype.

The business plan noted that the company would be built around three key figures: Larry Kaplan, Dave Morse, and Doug Neubauer. There is only one mention of Jay Miner as the person who "will design the chips for the new game".

The timetable for a production-ready system was two years. Chip design would begin in July 1982, with chip layout complete in October 1983, along with the game console's motherboard. The prototype would debut at CES in January 1984, along with five games. Sales would begin by July 1984. Sales projections included 74,000 consoles and 290,000 cartridges for 1984.

The company required initial capital of $3.6 million. Ownership was broken down as 40% for the employees, 5% for Zymos, and 55% for the investor, which at that time was listed as Hi-Tec Ventures. "Hi-Tec Ventures was Rollins' venture fund for investing," explains Larry Kaplan.

That spring, the partners were wondering where to locate the new company. Surprisingly, the expensive housing market in California was weighing heavily on everyone. "Dave came out a couple times and I went to Minnesota to see him a couple times," recalls Kaplan. "It was late spring and my wife and I looked at houses in Minnesota because we could afford the house on the lake previously owned by the president of General Mills for what our house in Los Altos was worth."

When Braddock and Rollins heard of the search for housing, Intermedics stepped forward on behalf of Morse. "The company loaned money for Dave to move out and buy a house here," says Kaplan. "He maybe moved in August."

The company name Pixel was short lived when due diligence showed another company with a similar name. "There was already a Pixcel and they said it was too close," says Kaplan.

To O. Wayne Rollins, the deal must have looked unbeatable. Not only did he have top people in the video game industry but his chip company Zymos would now have the opportunity to produce custom chips for a game console. It was win-win.

Rollins' Hi-Tec Ventures had previously started a number of "shelf companies", so named because the lawyers set up companies under dummy names, perform the legal paperwork in anticipation of forming new companies and then place the empty company on the shelf. In this case, one of those shelf companies was called Hi-Toro. "Hi-Toro may have been a shelf company and grabbing the name and corporate structure made it easier to get the company started," says Don Reisinger.

The origin of the name was derived from Hi-Tec. "I vaguely remember that Hi Toro came from the name HI-Tec Ventures," says Larry Kaplan. "Hi-Toro was just a placeholder until we could come up with a new one."

Rollins injected the funds into the startup through Intermedics. "In October, Rollins gave Hi-Toro the money to start," recalls Kaplan. If Rollins truly understood the time and expense of designing a console, plus the manufacturing and marketing costs, and the low probability of success, he probably would have balked. However, he knew bug spray, not silicon. To him, owning a video game company for $6 million sounded good.

For Larry Kaplan, the dream of a new console company did not last long. "Dave asked me to ask Nolan Bushnell to be on the board of Hi-Toro," says Kaplan. Unfortunately, the ever persuasive Bushnell turned the tables on Kaplan. "Nolan convinced me he could do a better job of building and selling a new game system, so I jumped ship to work with Nolan." Kaplan was now gone from the fledgling company, never to return.[3]

---

3   Unbeknownst to Kaplan, Bushnell had a non-compete clause with Atari that prohibited him from starting a video game company. Instead, Kaplan joined Atari as VP of consumer software. He would lose that job six months later when the video game market crashed.

Joe

Jay Miner was now 50 years old and looked like a cross between an Amish farmer and Kenny Rogers. He sported a heavy beard on the underside of his jaw and liked to wear pastel blue suits with big collars or loud Hawaiian shirts. With his large frame, Miner was hard to miss.

In his free time with his wife of 30 years, Caroline, he cultivated bonsai trees and enjoyed square dancing, camping, and backpacking. He even found time to build model airplanes.

With Kaplan out of the picture, Miner scrapped the plan for the proposed 8-bit 6502 based computer. Instead, he would attempt to steer things his way and create the 16-bit machine he first envisioned at Atari back in 1979. "Jay had his own axe to grind because he and Bert Braddock were pushing this company ahead trying to do what Jay described as a personal supercomputer," recalls Bill Hart. "So when he got to meet Dave, he managed to convince Dave that that was the real opportunity."

He would need to hire an engineer to back-fill Kaplan's position in order to proceed with the chipset design. Miner turned to an old friend from his Atari days. "Jay Miner calls me up in the fall of 1982 and says, 'Hey let's do another system,'" recalls Joe Decuir.

Like Miner before him, Decuir received a degree in electrical engineering and computer science from Berkeley. However, Decuir was a generation younger than Miner and graduated in 1974. In 1975, a then 24 year old Decuir was an early hire of Atari in the Cyan Engineering research lab. There he helped debug an early prototype of the Atari 2600 before moving on to Los Gatos to apprentice under Jay Miner.

He also worked on two launch titles for the Atari 2600. He programed the core graphics engine of one of his favorite arcade games, *Tank*, which eventually became *Combat* (included with every 2600 system). After that he programmed *Video Olympics* entirely on his own, a mix of games reminiscent of *Pong*.

In the summer of 1977, Decuir returned to Grass Valley with Miner to work on the Atari 400 and 800 computers. It was here they developed the three core chips inside the Atari computers.

After Miner departed Atari for Zymos, Decuir stayed on and finished several projects before leaving to form a startup named Standard Technologies. He and his partners had an idea for an answering machine/automated secretary designed for the IBM PC. "I had two business partners and we were trying to get venture capital," says Decuir.

And then the 32 year old received the aforementioned call from Jay Miner. "I went off with him on a boating trip up the Sacramento Delta and we spent a lot of time fleshing out what we wanted to do," he recalls. Decuir always kept an engineering notebook with doodles and specs of his ideas. Just prior to Miner leaving Atari, the two had discussed the next version of an Atari computer with a 16-bit 68000 or Z8000 chip. Although it was a simplified block drawing, it would become the basis for their next computer.

But the high-level vision for the system came from Morse. "Dave Morse said he wanted us to be able to render cartoons in real time," says Decuir. "Can we sell a game console, in the $200 to $300 retail price point that can render cartoons in real time? Instead of Disney deciding what the story is, your kid, who is playing another kid, determines what the story is."

Hi-Toro contracted Decuir in October of 1982, when his own startup needed money. "In order to keep my company together, I went off and worked as a consultant for Hi-Toro and took the money and split it three ways with my business partners." As such, Decuir was not an official employee of Hi-Toro.

The two system architects began working on the system concept. It was to be a game machine, yet with ports for a floppy drive and a keyboard. This was to be a platform so powerful that programmers could develop games on it directly.

Hi-Toro now had the three ingredients needed for a start-up: a wizard to develop the technology, a business visionary to lead the company, and a money man. Through the rest of 1982, Dave Morse developed the business side while Miner developed the technology. Both men would make radical changes to the original business plan.

But first, the company needed somewhere to work. Morse leased office space at the Koll Oakmead Park, located in Santa Clara at 3350 Scott Boulevard. Built in 1977 by The Koll Company, the industrial site contained 66 separate buildings scattered around a giant parking lot; almost like a condominium complex for small businesses. Each building was approximately 4500 square feet, housing everything from new electronics startups to regional offices for larger companies like Monsanto.

Ron

Doug Neubauer was a key member of Hi-Toro but when Larry Kaplan dropped out of the picture, Neubauer followed suit. Jay Miner now had to find a replacement. His search led him to a 29 year old chip designer at Apple named Ron Nicholson.

Nicholson, like Decuir, was another graduate of Berkeley. "I graduated from Berkeley in '78 with a degree in engineering mathematics and engineering science," he says.

He also attended the Homebrew Computer Club, where he first saw the Apple II. "I did not think that Apple was by far the leading best-in-class machine. I thought they were just one of the better companies that had a lot better press in the Valley."

Despite his indifference to its products, Nicholson soon joined Apple in 1980 and designed the Super Serial Card for the Apple II, which would become a perennial seller for the company. Next he joined the Macintosh group in 1981 where he oversaw the design of a disk controller chip called the Integrated Woz Machine.

Nicholson's next project was to oversee the development of a clock chip for the Macintosh to keep track of the system time. "There were clock chips available back then, but between Burrell [Smith] and Steve [Jobs], they decided they were too big and too inelegant," recalls Nicholson. "And of course by Steve's artistry, nothing big and inelegant can go on the Macintosh motherboard."

Apple wanted two sources to produce the clock chips. Nicholson approached several chip companies, including Zymos, to offer them bids on the chip contract. "I was given Jay's phone number by Steve Jobs and he specifically called out Jay as one of the best chip designers that he knew because they had overlapped when Steve was at Atari," recalls Nicholson.

Nicholson travelled down to Zymos in 1982 and found a pre-Hi-Toro Miner working alongside a technician on a large breadboard emulator of the chip he was designing for a pacemaker. "At the time I met Jay to work on the clock chip, he was just finishing up a brand new programmable pacemaker chip for Intermedics," he recalls.

Both Synertek and Zymos ended up winning the bid for the clock chip, and as a side effect, Nicholson ended up becoming friends with Miner. "Jay is a very gregarious type and so we ended up going out to lunch and being social together," he says. "It turned out that we both were involved in square dancing. Jay was a Challenge dancer and I was learning how to teach beginner square dancing. We were both Berkeley grads. We were both members of the IEEE. There were things in common we could talk about."

Nicholson became disappointed in two aspects of the Macintosh project: the lack of color and the rising cost. "Jeff Raskin originally envisioned the Macintosh as an extremely inexpensive computer he wanted to sell for under a thousand bucks," he recalls. "At this time in the Macintosh project, the cost was going well over a thousand bucks. We are going, 'Well there goes our shot of building a computer for everybody.'" On top of that, Nicholson was denied a training program in VLSI to design a new chip called a bit blitter.

In a bit of fortuitous timing, another opportunity came his way. "Within days, Jay Miner calls and tells me, 'I got this guy who wants to start a company doing an inexpensive color game machine.'"

Nicholson went down to Hi-Toro at 3350 Scott Boulevard in Santa Clara, 15 minutes from Apple. "At that time they had sales, marketing, finance, and some support staff but actually no engineering over there. Jay, even though his ID badge was number two, was not working over there."

Nicholson was at first skeptical. "Apple had an IPO [two years earlier, in 1980] and they were rolling in IPO cash and publicity back then," he says. "You wouldn't want to compete with the Macintosh."

Morse's vision of a gaming console interested Nicholson the most. "He wanted to animate cartoons and have that as the selling point of games. And then he wanted hardware that could have the horsepower to run those games, which was beyond the level of what the Atari, the Commodore 64, or the Apple II could do back then," says Nicholson. "He wanted to produce a platform for doing video games that could be sold in toy stores."

The sales pitch worked and Nicholson was on board. "I said here is a project that is different, that is interesting to me, and wouldn't at all compete with what we are doing on the Mac team," he recalls. Little did Nicholson realize the product would eventually compete head-on with the Mac.

Nicholson started in late 1982 and was surprised to be one of three technical people at the company. "I was employee number 11 and they had 10 other people there, none of them technical," he recalls. "They were all on the other side of the building opposite engineering trying to figure out how to market their products."

Name Change

With 1982 coming to a close, the end-of-year paperwork for taxes and incorporation would have to be filed. They needed a more permanent name to file the paperwork. "Hi-Toro was very short lived," says Reisinger. "It was gone by the end of 1982."

Everyone wanted a name that would come before Apple and Atari in the telephone directory, so they took out a dictionary, turned to Apple, and started browsing backwards. "We spent about half a day in a room with a white board and came up with 200 to 300 names and started the narrowing down process from there," recalls Reisinger.

Everyone agreed that the name should sound friendly. Amigo, as it turns out, is one of the few Spanish words in the English dictionary. More importantly, it exuded friendliness, since Amigo means friend in Spanish. However, it was not quite sexy enough, so someone suggested Amiga, the feminine form of Amigo. "By the end of the day, it was the Amiga," says Reisinger.

Miner was not fond of the name. "I didn't like it much. I thought using a Spanish name wasn't such a good move," he said.[4]

He retaliated by coming up with counter names, though Morse hoped he would give up and get on with his engineering duties. "He spent days coming up with alternatives to it," recalls Nicholson.

With time, Miner accepted that it was the best name they were likely to come up with and Morse incorporated the company under the new name. The ball was rolling and soon it would be bouncing.

---

4 *Amiga User International.* June 1988. "The AUI Interview" p. 20.

Amiga
1982-1983

In the latter half of 1982, Amiga Corporation came together under Dave Morse's leadership. A plan evolved and he was able to secure financing and find office space for the endeavor. Jay Miner had found two promising young engineers to help him design the chips for a proposed new video game system. Now it was time to create a detailed blueprint for how the video and sound chips would interact with the central processor.

Chip Designers

In late December 1982, the trio of Jay Miner, Joe Decuir and Ron Nicholson assembled at 3350 Scott Boulevard, building seven to begin the design of the Amiga chipset.

CEO Dave Morse assigned the engineers a portion of the building. He used the natural split floor plan to separate Engineering and Marketing: "The ten people involved in sales and marketing were on the south side of the building," recalls Nicholson. The engineers set up on the north side.

The engineers had to walk past the bright, airy offices at the south-facing front of the office to get to their labs, which were dark and windowless. Separating the two areas were the washrooms, a small kitchen and a few storage closets. The engineers in the back weren't missing out on much, though, since the front doors opened onto the busy Central Expressway. Other buildings on the site had skylights but not building seven. With few windows along the back, it was kept dark and cool.

Within the engineering section were three rooms: two conference-room-sized offices on either side and a large open area in the middle. "The middle was going to be the lab," explains Nicholson. "On one side of the lab was where we were going to put the software group."

Jay Miner was the undisputed leader of the architectural design. "He definitely would be the one who knew best," explains Nicholson. "Sometimes we'd fight with him but we'd let him resolve the final decision on everything because obviously he'd founded several semiconductor companies before Joe and I had even gotten out of college."

The team first had to settle on a microprocessor. "We wanted to build the best animation we could get and we started with a 16-bit processor," says Joe Decuir. There were three contenders, Motorola's 68000, Zilog's Z8000, and Intel's 8086 processor.

However, Motorola stood out for price. "We were being quoted $12 apiece in large quantity," says Decuir. "That was better than the Zilog people for the Z8000 were offering. And it was much better than Intel was asking for the 8086 family."

Motorola unveiled the chip in 1980, but samples were not publicly available until 1982, just in time for Miner and his engineers to begin work on their new system.

For now, the three engineers resided in one of the two large offices along the side. "We had three desks in it. One was Jay's, one was myself, and one Joe used," says Nicholson. "We actually had old-fashioned desks in there."

Almost as old-fashioned were the design tools they would use for the first few months of development. "The building came with one wall as an entire whiteboard," recalls Nicholson. "We pushed the desks to the side of the room."

With a set of dry markers, the engineers could now begin their collaboration. "We'd take turns scribbling stuff on the whiteboard and erasing it when someone said no, that's not good enough," recalls Nicholson. "That whiteboard just evolved over the first six to twelve weeks."

The engineers came from different schools of thought when it came to computer design. Miner and Decuir came from Atari while Nicholson came from Apple. But there was one goal. "Jay secretly had always wanted to design a personal computer that was almost as powerful as a minicomputer," recalls Nicholson.

Miner hoped the diversity of the team would produce a well rounded design, provided they could weather the conflicting opinions that would inevitably occur. "Of course, because I'd come from a completely different school of design with BTI computer systems and the Apple group than Jay had with mostly the Atari stuff, we had greatly divergent philosophies on how to do certain things," recalls Nicholson. "The Amiga, in one way, ended up being the merger of some technologies that came from technological ideas floating around at both Apple and at Atari."

Rounding out the team and making sure things never got too serious was Mitchy. "There were four beings always in our discussion. It was Jay, Joe, myself, and Mitchy, sometimes napping but sometimes carefully observing the proceedings," says Nicholson. "Occasionally we had to figure out which way to go, left or right. We'd toss it up and say Mitchy, what do you think? One bark for yes, two barks for no."

Sharing the Load

All three engineers (and Mitchy) agreed that, in order to deliver the desired performance, the system would need to have dedicated hardware to offload tasks from the main processor.

These subsystems would need to move data around autonomously, with the CPU setting up a job and letting the subsystems get on with it, interrupting when they finish. The approach is called Direct Memory Access, or DMA.

The DMA engine itself sped up a lot of different parts of the system. "That's a buzzword for an autonomous engine that can transfer data from RAM to various components on the chip," explains Ron Nicholson. "So Direct Memory Access is a separate high-speed processor engine that could transfer stuff between things without the software having to get involved and take up processor time."

The DMA in the computer would also be used to transfer graphics and sound data. "DMA is generally used to transfer data from the disk controller to memory or a serial port's memory," explains Nicholson. "We generalized the DMA so it actually transferred stuff from memory to the blitter, or from the blitter back to memory."

Graphics

With animation at the center of Dave Morse's vision of the video game system, the engineers spent most of their time on the graphics. It didn't hurt that both Jay Miner and Joe Decuir were pioneers in creating computer graphics on the Atari VCS.[1] "Joe Decuir pretty much invented the technology while actually working at Cyan's labs with Jay Miner at Atari," explains Nicholson. "The technology of the time was CRT TVs, these big

1 As described in the book *Racing the Beam* (2009), MIT Press.

huge glass bottles that drew the display on-screen by scanning the beam horizontally across and down the display."

The designers' task was to send a picture from the computer to a television or monitor line by line, via a cable, to make up a single frame. On the Atari 2600, it was up to the game programmer to draw each dot on the screen at the right time and get all the game logic handled for each frame before it was time for the next frame to be displayed. "The Atari 2600 sort of figured out where the dot was being drawn on the display as it was getting scanned horizontally, and that's what they put the timing on. That's called racing the beam," says Nicholson.

On their next computer, the aforementioned Atari 400 and 800, Miner and Decuir refined the design into an integrated chipset to handle the low-level work of displaying graphics. This freed up programmers to concentrate on designing games and made the games faster too. Now they would refine those ideas even further with the Amiga chipset. "One of the things we did on the Amiga was put in a lot of video timing that could follow the beam autonomously, so the processor and the programmer wouldn't have to race the beam with the software," says Nicholson.

For now, the chip designers only worried about the NTSC standard, the mode supported by North American televisions. Later in the design process, they would create an alternate chip to support the European PAL standard.

Miner and his engineers had a major choice to make on the basic design of the graphics system: character based or bitmap based.

Character based systems use blocks (of characters) to make up an image rather than individual pixels. Because of this, they use less memory but do not provide the graphical finesse that would be needed for rendering animated cartoons, which was the aim of the system.

In a bitmap display, each pixel is defined individually, which can use a lot of memory—especially when using colors. A single bit can describe a monochrome pixel, 2 bits can define 4 colors and so on. For a low resolution NTSC screen of 320x200 pixels, each bitmap would take just under 8KB, however memory wasn't the only design factor: moving information around between memory and the graphical system required higher bandwidth.

Miner had seen memory dropping in price, so he chose a bitmap solution, and compromised on a maximum of 5 bits per pixel, allowing 32 colors, and leaving time for other things to happen. Colors were chosen from a palette of 4096 (16 red values, 16 blue values, 16 green values). Combining the corresponding bits in the multiple bitmaps told the system which color to make a pixel.

However, this limitation meant the chipset would not be able to display more colors in the future as memory prices decreased. " A lot of things in the chip architecture weren't that expandable," says Nicholson

The engineers also wanted to improve the resolution of the graphics so that animations would look less blocky and more like cartoons. They settled on four different graphics modes, which could display 320 x 200 and 320 x 400 using 32 colors or 640 x 200 and 640 x 400 using 16 colors.

Nicholson also introduced a seemingly small idea that would later end up giving the Amiga a unique market. "I didn't like the fact that with an Apple II and an Atari, you couldn't hook them up to a VCR," explains Nicholson. "I threw out the idea, 'Let's make it so we can record on a VCR.'"

VCR's were already becoming commonplace in the home, having been introduced in the late 1970's. However, anyone who tried to record video directly from their computer and played it back saw a flickering mess on screen.

The reason was because computers and video game consoles used progressive scan (non-interlaced) video. "When you race the beam, you can do it interlaced or non-interlaced," explains Nicholson. "And non-interlaced is likely to flicker less and refreshes the same dot more often, so game consoles did it. Unfortunately, you couldn't record it on a VCR or mix it with other professional video."

The solution to recording to a VCR was simple. VCR's recorded and played back video in an interlaced format, meaning only every second line of each frame was recorded and displayed. By allowing interlaced video output and the proper timing, a VCR could record the image directly from the computer. "On the Amiga, we made sure to put in interlaced timing on our NTSC PAL synchronization racing the beam, so that it could be recorded," says Nicholson.

In order to get accurate NTSC timing to match the VCR, Decuir and Nicholson went out and did the homework. "I bought a couple textbooks on video timing just make sure we could get it exactly right," says Nicholson, referring to the *Raster Graphics Handbook* (Conrac Corp., 1981). "[It was] one of the first detailed books on how to do video timing."

Blitter

The team also had to figure out how they would produce the cartoon characters required by Dave Morse's vision. At the time, computers used sprites to create fast moving, animated characters on top of backgrounds. "In a sprite engine you have essentially multiple layers," explains Nicholson, referring to the sprite layer and the bitmap layer. "A sprite is essentially a layer that the hardware puts on top of another layer."

In the C64, released just a few months prior in late 1982, the hardware sprites were a key to its success. The VIC-II chip inside the C64 allowed 8 sprites with three different colors, plus transparent pixels, at a resolution of 12 x 21. With some additional programming, it could produce dozens of sprites on screen at the same time.

The three engineers would up the ante, slightly. The chip would allow 8 sprites 16 pixels wide and any height. And they could be composed of three colors plus a transparent color.

If the sprite engine they planned to design sounds uninspired, it is for good reason. The team wanted something more than a bunch of small, flip-frames animating on screen. They wanted fluid animation with shadows and transparencies. Huge shapes or small shapes that could be duplicated many times all over the screen. Shapes that could easily deform into other shapes.

The inspiration came from an impressive military flight simulator Miner and Nicholson had previously visited. The Singer Company was a manufacturer of sewing machines that had diversified into areas of high-technology, including flight simulators. The Link flight simulator was state of the art for the early 1980s. A friend of Miner's at Singer named Al Pound shared the technology with them. "Both Jay and I had seen the flight simulators at Singer-Link," recalls Nicholson. "They showed me around and I had seen their graphics engine."

Each simulator was worth millions of dollars and sold to private airlines, NASA, and the military. Because the company produced the simulators in small volumes, they didn't bother miniaturizing the circuitry into silicon chips. Instead, there were large racks of PCBs and cooling systems to keep the heat under control. During tours, the proud employees pointed visitors to the huge electronics system. "They tried to show off how impressive it was by showing me this big thing," says Nicholson. "That was their graphics engine and it was the size of a UPS delivery truck! It was this monstrous thing."

The experience inspired the engineers to think bigger by thinking smaller. Nicholson wanted to produce those same graphics that the Singer-Link produced in its UPS truck-sized system. And he wanted to put it on a chip.

And instead of costing millions of dollars, he wanted it to sell it as part of a $300 video game system in Toys "R" Us.

In computer graphics, an image, such as a picture of a boat, is a series of bits that make up the image. This is called a bitmap. The special feature of the Singer-Link graphics hardware that interested Miner and Nicholson most was its ability to take one bitmap, such as a background image, and combine it with another bitmap, such as a foreground image like a tree.

This technique had been pioneered, like so many other things, at Xerox PARC when they were inventing the GUI windowing system. The programmers needed to overlay the mouse cursor, as well as overlapping windows, onto an existing bitmapped background.

Since the image is really just computer data stored in memory, in order to combine two bitmaps together, the processor must move all the data of one bitmap into the data of the other bitmap—preferably quickly. This is called a bit block image transfer. The Xerox programmers named the function BitBLT in their code, which they pronounced "bit blit". "Bit blit is actually drawing the image that you want to see in computer memory and cutting a hole out of the background scene and pasting the ball in the appropriate outlined shape," explains Nicholson. "What you see in computer memory is what you see on the screen."

Bit blitting had been done in software before, both at Xerox and at Apple with the Lisa, but tied up the CPU when doing so. The engineers at Singer-Link took the next step, creating it with their truck-sized hardware. When done in hardware, the device was called a blitter and once set on a task could carry on without using CPU resources.

Ron Nicholson had become familiar with bit blitting while at Apple. "I had written blit logic as a learning experience on an Apple II," he recalls. "I started writing this thing that would be a mouse driven ball game on an Apple II." Using a discarded Lisa mouse connected to the Apple II, he began programming. The project never got very far.

Once at Amiga, Nicholson resurrected his demo to help convince Dave Morse that it was possible. "He knew he wanted to do something animating cartoons," recalls Nicholson. "I had whipped together a slightly better demo to show Jay Miner and Dave Morse why we should base the chip engines mostly on blitting rather than yet more and more sprites and overlays."

Once convinced, the team added the blitter, argued over the functionality, and worked on the specifics by diagramming it on the whiteboard in block diagram. "We had already got the blitter done before the end of January," recalls Nicholson. The finished block diagram for the blitter would resemble closely the one that eventually appeared in a patent for the Amiga chipset.

At the time, no other personal computer or gaming system included a blitter. This meant the Amiga computer, when it was released, would command a definitive advantage over anything else on the market. It was also remarkably advanced, allowing up to three image patterns for input to create one output. And it was flexible, allowing not only AND calculations, but OR, NOR, XOR, and other logical functions. It even included something called a barrel shifter which allowed simple horizontal scrolling.

Audio

As part of the goal to bring animated cartoons to a game system, Morse's plan called for a system centered around playing digitally recorded voices and music. This, of course, did not exist in 1982 for any home computer (ignoring the barely understandable hacked attempts). The state of the art at the time was the C64 with its SID chip but it was merely a sound generator, synthetically creating a variety of noises for video games.

According to Nicholson, "The design of the audio actually came from Joe Decuir and myself." Decuir had previous experience with sound while working on the Atari 800 system, which contained the famous Pokey audio chip. Pokey, in turn, had advanced the state of the art from the Atari VCS. "There was a lot more in common between the Atari VCS and the Atari computers," says Decuir. "But there's a huge jump from either of those to the Amiga."

There was a big difference with their new architecture. A synthesizer chip, like the SID, created its own sound waves by generating the sounds from a few numbers to define a tone. With the new design, the chip would play audio directly from memory, without needing the CPU to copy data around.

The data in memory was digital. A series of numbers increasing and decreasing in value could recreate a sound wave. But how to transform the digital sound wave to analog? At the heart of the sound chip would be a Digital-to-Analog Converter, or DAC. "There really wasn't that much synthesis in there, it was just a straight digital analog converter," says Dale Luck, a future employee of Amiga. Once the digital data is converted to an analog signal, the signal is sent to speakers, headphones, or an amplifier where it vibrates the speakers to create the sound waves that travel to our ears.

One big improvement in the sound was that the new chip would be able to produce stereo sound. The chip would have 4 audio channels, each with independent volume control. By dedicating two voices per speaker, stereo was achieved. This sounded noticeably different than monophonic sound produced by the SID chip.

The team also needed a serial bus to allow external devices to connect to the computer. RS232 was the standard protocol for sending data along a serial bus. It had to be fast enough to handle data input and output for devices that might come along in the next five years or so, including printers, modems, mice, keyboards, and other devices.

Nicholson made sure the bus would be fast enough to handle one specific multimedia protocol. When he designed the serial adapter for the Apple II, he was inundated with complaints that it could not achieve speeds of 31.25 kilobits per second. This meant it was not fast enough for MIDI, a protocol for using musical devices with a computer. "I had customer complaints that it didn't do MIDI," he laments. "So I made sure to include a powerful enough serial engine in the Amiga, as well as the disk controller with the raw encoding capability, as well as the keyboard controller." Whether the engineers would eventually include MIDI connector ports was a separate issue.

One curious addition at this stage was a disk controller. After all, why would a video game machine require a disk controller? "A disk controller and all that stuff obviously means that we're designing a personal computer. But no," says Nicholson, maintaining it was still a game machine. "I come from the Woz school of disk controller design. Woz designed a disk controller and the disk controller board has eight chips on it but actually two of the chips are amplifiers, three of the chips are to handle software, the actual disk controller hardware engine was three chips. It's really tiny. And of course it used the Apple II software to do the bulk of the work of decoding."

Miner would not allow features on the chipset that took up large amounts of real estate unless they were truly going to be used. But optional functions could be added, provided the footprint was minimal. "I knew you could put a disk controller on that using almost no gates because there's three chips worth of logic. Once you put it on an ASIC (Application-Specific Integrated Circuit) it is almost irrelevant in terms of the amount of chip area it takes. So that's why we could throw a disk controller on the Amiga chipset without making it a big thing that we had to plan ahead for. Jay definitely wanted to put in the disk controller too but I made sure it fit and didn't slow down the effort."

Using this combination of chips, the Amiga could produce true DMA audio. "In the [8 bit] Atari computer we had DMA audio but it was fairly simple," says Decuir. It was also rarely used, owing to the lack of RAM in the Atari computers to store audio samples. A sample a few seconds long, for example, could eat up so much data that there was little RAM left for the actual game code and graphics data.

The new Amiga system, however, would have more memory. "In the Amiga, we had DMA audio and you could take this piece of memory, sample it at some pre-programmed rate, you could assign where it came from memory in some programmatic fashion, and you could set how long the sample is before you loop back," explains Decuir.

Using this combination, the sampled sound could be modified to produce unusual effects. A recorded voice of an adult, for example, could be played back quicker and at a higher pitch, making a true cartoon-sounding voice. Programmers could also create a musical instrument, such as a piano sound, by looping only the middle portion of a piano sample. This would allow musicians to create and play symphonic music, something that would revolutionize music in games.

Game Machines

Although a $300 game console was the goal, the engineers designed the chipset for a variety of machines. After all, at Atari, Pokey was used in a number of arcade machines as well as the 400 and 800 home computers. Engineers design for the most general case possible that allows flexibility with design. "We knew it could scale," says Joe Decuir.

As the chip design was progressing, the engineers began formalizing several options for the systems they could design around their chipset. "I actually have a set of notes in my notebook from the 4th of February 1983 with our suggested configurations," says Decuir. They envisioned four different machine configurations.

With the C64 an obvious market success by early 1983, the engineers set their target appropriately. "The smallest 1.0 game machine was a 68000 that addressed 128K," says Decuir. "This machine could do things that the Commodore 64 couldn't do, in terms of how fast it can animate and move things around. That was our bottom end machine."

Whether or not it would come with a keyboard or disk drive was up in the air. "We were thinking that a cartridge could be made for the Amiga game machine where you would plug it in and that would add the disk port, the mass storage port, the keyboard port and stuff like that," explains

Nicholson. "It would look a lot like an NES, a console with two joystick controllers."

The second machine, which they labelled 1.5, was aimed at the market for computer networks and terminals. "We were thinking about a 1.5 machine as a smart graphics terminal," explains Decuir. "We would add extra communications to it actually and a built-in modem." As a terminal, it would target the businesses world of shared computing, which was still a popular method of development in 1983 and would later play an important role for the Amiga operating system developers.

Of particular interest is the third machine, which became the favored design. "The 2.0 machine was going to be a simple complete computer but didn't have slots, that would have 128 kilobytes and sockets for another 128 kilobytes."

In light of the recent success of the IBM PC, the engineers created a final concept of a computer for serious computing. "The 3.0 machine was going to have something with slots and mechanicals for a second disk, and maybe a hard drive," says Decuir. This machine would be the culmination of a personal supercomputer that Jay Miner was keen to build.

This supercomputer was for game developers. "We knew that if we built those things, we would sell them to the Activisions of the world to build games on," says Decuir. "What we realized when we built the Atari game machine was that we were building tools for artists to create new experiences for people. When we built the Amiga machine as a game player, we had the same thoughts. We said, 'Ok, we don't know exactly how smart those guys are but let's put a lot of stuff in their hands and let these people run with it.'"

Splitting the Chipset

By February 11, after almost three months of design work, the engineers had defined all the functions that would go into their chipset, all while little Mitchy patiently watched every move. Each part of the chipset was essentially an engine that would perform a function on some data, autonomously. Now they needed to figure out how much real estate each engine would occupy in silicon.

The whiteboard diagrams included the connections between each of the "engines" and the timing of those interactions. The entire system took up more space on the whiteboards than they originally anticipated. "When we ran out of space I actually had to talk Dave Morse into buying us some more whiteboards," recalls Nicholson. "We had one or two more whiteboards."

By March 17, 1983, they knew how large each engine would be. Based on their previous experience designing the Atari computers, the engineers predicted they could fit all the functions into three chips. Now it was time to decide which chips would contain which functions. They would decide based on how many pins each engine used (each chip would have 48 pins) and they would also try to group the functions of each chip into a similar theme. For example, the audio functions on a dedicated audio chip. This would theoretically allow other devices, such as a music synthesizer, to use just the audio chip.

In keeping with the female theme of Amiga Corporation, the engineers used female names for their main chips. The chip containing ports and audio became Portia. "Portia for ports," explains Nicholson. The disk controller also ended up in Portia by default. "We moved stuff around and Portia had enough pins for the disk controller and stuff like that, so that's why that ended up in Portia."

Using the two first letters of Display Adapter, the engineers correspondingly named the graphics chip Daphne. "There was a second device called the data unit, which was collecting and driving the video. That became Daphne," says Decuir. Daphne would contain all the circuitry for displaying bitmap graphics and sprites. Due to having some remaining free pins, it also accepted input from the mouse or analog joystick ports.

The final chip, Agnus, was a contraction of Address Generator. Any chip that needed to access RAM would have to go through Agnus. "There is one device that was originally called the address unit, which became Agnus," says Decuir.

Agnus also contained the blitter and a third engine called the copper, which stands for co-processor. The copper would run in synchronization with the video beam of a monitor, executing commands with precision timing when the beam was at a certain point on the screen. And finally, a few pins were saved for synchronizing the display to an external timing source, such as video from a video camera or VCR.

Curiously, Agnus did not use the traditional spelling of the female name Agnes. According to Jim Williams, a fellow engineer who knew Miner, the reason it deviates from the traditional spelling is because Jay Miner favored the Latin expression agnus dei, meaning "lamb of God".

The fourth major chip in the Amiga would of course be the 68000 processor. Each of these chips was, in effect, a microprocessor. Many call the Amiga a multiprocessor system, since each chip handles its own load of processing tasks in a specific domain. Unlike other computers, the 68000 processor was free much of the time, making it one of the fastest machines of the period. The 7.16 MHz processor speed did little to describe the actual speed compared to other computers.

The three chips in the system mirrored those in the Atari home computers, which also contained three chips with analogous features. "We had similar thoughts in our heads when we partitioned the chipset," says Decuir. "Agnus corresponds to Antic in the Atari computer, GTIA or CTIA corresponds to Daphne in Amiga, and the Pokey chip in the Atari computer corresponds roughly to the Portia chip in the Amiga."

The Amiga computer they were building was largely an evolution on the Atari computers, although it would be a stretch to say there was any theft of Atari intellectual property.

In 1983, Joe Decuir started feeling nervous that, perhaps, someday, a lawyer could make it look like some of the technology originated at Atari. "During the time I was doing design work on what became Amiga, several times I remember asking Dave Morse if I could get indemnified in case there was any legal activity," he recalls. "And I never really did get a good answer." Morse, for his part, didn't need the extra cost of buying the insurance. Plus it was a distraction he frankly didn't want to take on. For now the issue lay dormant, but it would rear up in the following years.

Timing

By March 29, the chipset was divided and it was now up to Joe Decuir to figure out the memory access timings between the various engines in each chip. The chipset was like an assembly line, except instead of something like pies, this assembly line moved data. If the timing is off, an assembly line will grind to a halt and create a huge mess. In this case, the chips would effectively crash the computer.

Apple has had a reputation of stealing ideas from other companies and claiming them as their own, but in this case Amiga stole an idea from Apple to increase performance. "How did we get the performance of the Amiga up there? That's an idea I stole from Woz," says Nicholson.

Up until that time it was common for the processor and the graphics chip to take turns accessing memory. Nicholson introduced the idea of the graphics chip and CPU accessing memory at the same time. "In the Atari, the memory could either do video or handle software; one or the other, not both. Woz designed the Apple II with a double speed memory so that on alternating cycles, called time-division multiplexing, a unified memory system could handle both the video and the 6502 CPU at the same time. Both of them can go full speed."

While Decuir worked on the timing, Nicholson began designing the video game system itself which would lead to a motherboard design. He was also in charge of software for now. Jay Miner would work with Decuir on timing while also concentrating on the massive task of designing the details of the Agnus chip. In the ensuing months, a lot would change with Amiga's finely laid business and engineering plans.

Crash 1983

The original business plan for the 8-bit Pixel system projected zero revenue from sales in 1983 and a loss of $1.4 million. Dave Morse wanted to change those figures and produce a profit for 1983. All he needed were some products to market while Jay Miner developed the video game console.

Business Plan 2.0

With the video game boom at an all time high, and with the partnership with Zymos already established, plus one of Atari's top video game designers—Doug Neubauer—on the team, it was not much of a stretch to consider releasing games for other consoles. This would also support Bert Braddock's initial goal of increasing production for Zymos and was sure to please investor O. Wayne Rollins, who would appreciate the vertical integration of his companies.

The business plan also described a system with better controllers. The new controllers would use a much different technology from the unreliable blister switches found in Atari 2600 joysticks. "There was this conductive rubber technology that was a great switching technology for game controllers," explains Don Reisinger.

Instead of mechanical switches, it used carbon pads that directly contacted the circuit traces on a circuit board. "He looked at this and he said wow, this is a great switching technology for video games," says Reisinger. Not only was it good, but it was also inexpensive to produce.

The company would design slight variations on each joystick and release them for a number of computers and consoles. "At that time, Atari and all the software companies are flying high. ColecoVision was coming. The Mattel Intellivision system was there. We had the TRS-80 system that was there," says Reisinger. "The beauty of it is, other than changing the shell on the device, this technology that he had was adaptable to all of them."

Morse also wanted to develop an expansion for the Atari 2600—of which there were 10 million in homes by the end of 1982—that would allow users to load games into memory from a cassette tape. This was a little more ambitious than joysticks and game cartridges and would require more development time to perfect.

The overall plan to release products ahead of the game console allowed Hi-Toro to establish a distribution channel into retail stores. Morse hoped to leverage his contacts from Tonka. "The guys we are going to sell it to are guys we knew because in those days a lot of the big video game retailers were toy retailers," he recalls. "Those were the guys we had talked to and dealt with at Tonka."

At the time, the plan seemed low risk, dealt in high volumes, and with the huge market for video games it would bring in revenue to sustain development costs. Morse already secured $3.6 million in development funds from O. Wayne Rollins. Now he would need to convince him that an additional $2.4 million for controller and games development would pay off. Given the climate in 1982, it was an easy sell.

With Jay Miner responsible for hiring six engineers and Rollins responsible for hiring a VP of Finance and a Controller, it was left to Morse to hire three marketing managers. And he knew just where to look.

Morse knew who the standout marketing people were at Tonka back in Minnesota. "After he had left Tonka, I'd shared with him that I was tired of some of the decisions being made," recalls Don Reisinger. "He gave me a few little hints along the way that there might be a time when he would call me."

Reisinger had just got back from a trip to New York while working with an ad agency on behalf of Tonka when he got the call. As it turned out, Reisinger was headed to California within the week. "The following Sunday I was going to L.A. to finish up some negotiating with Honda on some licensing work and he called and said, 'Why don't you come to California next Sunday?' This was on a Wednesday."

Morse had a particular talent for persuading those around him. His secret was to assume the other party already agreed with him and proceed from there. "I didn't have to interview for the job," recalls Reisinger. "He said, 'We're going to put your mind at ease. I'm going to have you go out with a real estate person here to see that you're going to be able to afford a house when you move here.' And so I spent probably as much time looking at neighborhoods around Silicon Valley as I did actually talking with Dave."

Morse assured him he would be able to learn more about the business before plunging in and Reisinger accepted the role of Amiga's new director of marketing, but not until negotiating a little more pay. After convincing his wife (a task made easier due to an ice storm back in Minneapolis) the family made the move to California. "I joined Dave in November of 1982," he recalls.

Once set up as director of marketing, Reisinger met the other members of the marketing and sales team. First was Gary McCoy, another hire from Tonka, as VP of sales, Caryn Havis as advertising manager (a recent graduate of San Francisco State University in Business/Corporate Communications) and of course Morse himself overseeing it all.

Morse already had working prototypes of the joystick controller for his new team to market. "That was pretty much done by the time I got there," says Reisinger.

The Power System

While the engineers toiled away on Amiga's chipset, Dave Morse focused on growing the business. "Dave was smart," says investor Bill Hart "He was a guy who understood how to manage technical geniuses and that was key to Dave's success. These guys loved working for Dave."

Morse possessed the charisma and trust that made his employees happy to follow his lead. "He was able to bring out of people things that I think most of them didn't even know they had inside of them," says Don Reisinger. "You wanted to perform because he had both invested in you and trusted in you to pick it up and run with it. And so we all did!"

Morse contracted outside engineering teams to develop video game products. According to Miner, the Amiga products were partly to deflect unwanted curiosity away from their video game system and allow the internal engineers to focus on the Amiga completely. "We hired lots of other people to design peripherals which kept the notorious Silicon Valley spies away from the office. All they could see were joysticks and they weren't too much of a threat."[1]

But the number one priority was to start offering video game products to toy stores in order to raise money. "He was trying to finance the company

1 *Amiga User International.* June 1988. "The AUI Interview" p. 20.

by selling accessories in the existing game market rather than having to get more investment," says Joe Decuir.

Selling video game products would also produce several positive side effects for Amiga. "He had the whole distribution marketing plan in place when I first got there," recalls Ron Nicholson. "He had really thought out the whole thing from getting our brand recognized, establishing our marketing channel, building up some product recognition, integrating the products together—the joystick sort of went with an eventual game machine. He had a very comprehensive plan very early in the game."

According to Reisinger, the products worked together to give gamers a more powerful system. "We decided to use the Power System for all of those dedicated video game items," he says. As long as the products were well received, it would benefit the Amiga name.

The other benefit was that once a whole system of products was introduced, retailers were more likely to buy more from Amiga. "Dave was very much into marketing channels and the more integrated set of solutions you can throw at a big toy store, the more likely it is they'll take the whole bundle," observes Ron Nicholson.

Pro-Stick

Morse's earliest product was the aforementioned joystick. He knew it had to stand out from other joysticks on store shelves. Unlike most joysticks, the carbon contacts were extremely quiet. It offered two buttons, one on either side, that allowed it to work just as well in the left or right hands. But totally unique was the size, easily fitting in the palm of the hand, almost as though he had miniaturized an Atari joystick. After an exhaustive search for names, the marketing team settled on "Pro-Stick".

The Amiga video game console would likely use the same joysticks Dave Morse was getting ready to market at Amiga. "We decided we might as well be compatible with the controllers we were already putting in the channel as well as the whole ecosystem," says Nicholson.

Amiga would produce joysticks for the leading game systems of the day. These included packages of one or two joysticks for the Atari line in striking red and black. The primary obstacle of marketing the joystick to the Atari crowd was the two joysticks already included with the console. Luckily the Atari joysticks used cheap "blister" switches that failed over time, which would make it easier to convince young video gamers to upgrade.

Most home computers and even some video game consoles shared the same joystick connector in the early eighties. This meant the Atari Pro-

Stick would also work in any system with the same 9 pin D-connector, and in principle the basic design did not need to be altered. Despite this, Morse planned to release special versions of the controller for the Commodore VIC-20 and C64 computers in beige and brown.

Morse also created special versions of the Pro-Stick for the hit Coleco Vision and also the Mattel Intellivision. Both of these systems included numeric keypads making them slightly more complicated than the base joystick.

However, as it turned out, the Pro-Stick name was a little too generic. A joystick maker named Newport Machine Design had released an Atari 2600 version of a stand-up arcade joystick called the Newport Prostick. Another company named BP Electronics, Inc. had previously released a joystick for the Atari computers called the Pro-Stick. As a result, Caryn Havis felt the name would be confusing and instead changed the name to the Power-Stick.

Power Module

Dave Morse also intended to market a unique accessory for the Atari 2600 called the Power Module. This was a special cartridge that allowed users to load games from cassette tapes. "That was actually the core for the Power System," says Reisinger. "It was a way to be able to make software that would run on an Atari system without having a ROM cartridge and bypassing the licensing fees."

Gaming press at the time described it as, "An alternative to ROM cartridges for the Atari VCS. Plugged into the game machine, it provides 6K RAM and a microprocessor to receive and use game programs loaded from a cassette recorder. Pre-programmed tapes for the module are much cheaper than ROM cartridges, and the extra RAM enhances graphics and play."[2]

The idea of loading a game from tape into the Atari was not new. The prior year, a company named Starpath released the Supercharger which allowed the same for $69.95. However, Morse would ensure his product stood out in two important ways.

First, the Power Module would include red and blue 3D glasses, which would make some games appear in 3D. Second, players could connect Atari VCS units together with a phone line to play competitively or in co-operation. Although the Power Module did not include a modem, players could connect it to a modem.

---

2 *Digital Antic*. May 1983.

Tape games for the Power Module would sell for $9.95, a lower price than standard Atari cartridges. "A company like us would have had to make the software," says Reisinger. "The software would have been written and then delivered to the consumer in the form of an audiotape, only it would have been a computer tape. And then that software would have been loaded into the Power Module and from there would have been operated on the Atari VCS. And it worked!"

Morse wanted 12 cassette games for the Power Module. Unfortunately Doug Neubauer had left Amiga by now, but he put Morse in touch with a company called Videosoft to create the games. Videosoft was started by engineer Jerry Lawson, a pioneer in the field who headed development of the Fairchild Channel F, an early but mostly forgotten game console. Unfortunately, the Fairchild lost out mainly because the games for the system were bland compared to those offered by Atari.

Videosoft was initially contracted to produce four Atari games for the Power Module, programmed by both Lawson and his employees Mike Glass, Dan McElroy, and Frank Ellis.

Lawson himself programmed a submarine game called *Depth Charge*. The main draw of Depth Charge was that it would use the Power Module to allow two players to compete. Although it was similar in play to the classic *Sea Wolf* arcade game, the multiplayer aspect would hopefully produce a tense situation of hunter and hunted.

The planned 3D games would be a first for the Atari 2600. Lawson created the 3D effect by rapidly flickering images on the screen between red and blue. For example, to make an object appear closer to the player, the two images (red and blue) would be drawn farther apart.

The first game utilizing 3D glasses was called *3-D Ghost Attack*. The programmer incorporated the 3D effect into the gameplay, requiring the cursor to be on the same plane as the ghosts, which were at different depths.

The contractors initially developed the games on Atari computer systems. "The Atari 800 was the first software version we had," says Reisinger. Amiga also planned to release the software on the Atari home computers and the latest hit in video game consoles, the ColecoVision.

In order to make the Amiga name recognizable, every game cartridge, box, advertisement, and manual had the same yellow colored logo in the corner. The logo read, "The Power System. Amiga."

By early 1983 Morse had his products. "Two and a half months after we get there, we were so far along we actually had finished product we're using for the demos," says Reisinger. "We're not using prototypes. We've got relatively finished packaging." The team was now ready to unveil the product line.

American International Toy Fair

Coming from the toy industry, Dave Morse decided to focus his marketing efforts on toy stores. And the principle way to gain access to toy store shelves was the American International Toy Fair, held every February in New York City. The former Tonka employees knew this was where they could make important connections in the retail industry.

Prior to the show, advertising manager Caryn Havis created the sales materials and organized a small display booth. It would be up to the marketing team to find buyers and convince them to carry Amiga's products. With the Power System still in development, Havis could only launch the joystick, although she allowed sneak peeks of the other upcoming products.

At the toy fair there would be plenty of handshakes required, but not by Dave Morse, who preferred to remain low-key. Amiga's VP of sales, Gary McCoy, had the most daunting task of landing clients. Morse would take a secondary support role and answer to McCoy at the show. As Reisinger says, "Dave was in a meeting and he told our VP of sales, 'Look, I'm not much in the sales side. I can schmooze your customers if you need it but selling is your job. You tell me how you want to do it. You want to do it yourself, that's fine. You want to bring reps in, that's fine. I'm not going to stand in your way but it's going to be your responsibility.'"

Trusting the people he hired created a very motivated staff. "It was such that it really drove you to do a good job," says Reisinger. "And Dave was the kind of guy that you wanted to do a good job for."

With a list of retailers in hand, the team met with the leading players at Kay Bee Toys, Toys "R" Us, and general retailers such as Kmart and Sears. "From a sales standpoint, we were basically preaching to the choir because we were the guys they talked to all the time from Tonka," says Reisinger. "In practise, they were more than happy to introduce us to the buyer who's handling video games."

The company attracting the most attention at the show was Coleco, who entered the show with dual hits of Cabbage Patch dolls and a competitor to Amiga's console, the ColecoVision. Now they were attempting to launch the Coleco Adam, a $525 computer, plus an add-on expansion for the console that made it into a full computer.

The Amiga marketing team held a dim view of Coleco at the time due to the dubious preview of the prototype earlier in the year. "We were at a

Winter CES in 1983 and Coleco had launched the Adam with all of this fanfare and hoopla and PR and advertising plans and everything else," recalls Reisinger. "Let's just say a couple of our more ingenious engineers figured out what it was that was actually demonstrating the capabilities of the Adam. They found that tucked under the table were a bunch of Apple II's."

While at Tonka, Reisinger had seen Coleco launch products that were not even close to production. Now they were at it again. "That is emblematic of the kind of company that Coleco was at that time," he says. "Get us the orders and if we get enough orders then we'll figure out how to make the product. You can kind of do it in the toy business but you sure as hell can't do it in the electronics business."

Unlike Coleco, Morse made sure his products were ready for production once they began taking orders. "We went in the opposite direction of Coleco," says Reisinger. "We went in with the real stuff and said, 'Hey guys, you're used to dealing with us. Just because its electronics, we're not changing the way we do business.'"

The Atari 2600 Power-Stick would go on sale at $13.99 each or $19.99 for a pair. As it turned out, the Power-Stick was a huge success with retailers. "About two and a half months after we started we had our first show and the response to the product was absolutely astounding," recalls Reisinger. "Immediate orders. I mean guys were saying, 'Yeah, we're going to take this right now.'"

Joyboard

After completing production models of the Power-Stick, Dave Morse began developing a very unique game controller he planned to unveil at the upcoming Summer CES in June. Consisting of a black platform with a surface area about two feet square, the player stood or kneeled on the platform and leaned in a direction to move. In a moment of inspiration, the team decided to call it the Joyboard.

Internally, the electronics resembled those used in the Power-Stick. "It used that same conductive rubber switching technology so that when you moved on that joyboard, the character moved on screen," explains Don Reisinger.

There was even a joystick port on the Joyboard that the gamer could plug a regular joystick into in order to press the fire button. This allowed players to control regular Atari games using the Joyboard, although in practice it was often impractical because shifting body weight was slower than moving a joystick.

Miner again turned to Videosoft to produce some Joyboard games. "We needed software in order to make the thing make sense at all," says Reisinger. "Any of those accessories, whether they're short term or long term, are totally dependent on how much software support there is. We had three or four games designed for it."

The first game Videosoft began developing was called *Mogul Maniac*, a 3D downhill skiing game. Though the graphics were good for an Atari 2600 game, the gameplay itself was rather shallow. Mogul Maniac would be included in the box with the Joyboard.

A second game, *Off Your Rocker*, was based on the Simon memory game by Milton-Bradley. The third game was called *Surf's Up*. It featured excellent graphics albeit with simplistic surfing game-play. A fourth game called *S.A.C. Alert* was a jet fighter combat game.

In order to get more games for the Power Module, Morse began looking to another contractor called Design Labs with an unreleased arcade game called *Genesis*. Although the arcade game was never produced, Datasoft managed to acquire the home computer rights to the game and ported it to Apple II, Atari 400/800, C64, and IBM PC computers. Morse acquired the rights for the Atari 2600 and contracted Videosoft to program the game in 3D.

Videosoft began work on a third 3D game called *3D Havoc*, essentially an Asteroids clone in which the player shoots asteroids in a 3D asteroid field.

Advertising

In order to reassure retailers that the products wouldn't sit on store shelves unsold, Dave Morse promised them an advertising campaign. Caryn Havis developed the theme of the campaign promoting better scores in video games. This is reflected in the original Pro-Stick name, which implied the stick was for "professional" video game players.

Amiga sought out a prominent Olympic skier named Suzy Chaffee to promote the Joyboard, who was a perfect fit for Mogul Maniac. "That was part of our PR primarily on the Joyboard," says Reisinger. "I worked with Suzy relatively close on that."

Chaffee had never won a medal at the 1968 Winter Olympics but she had made an impact with her silver skin-tight racing suit. Later she became a Ford Model, pioneered freestyle skiing, and became spokesperson for ChapStick lip balm. "You might remember her as Suzy Chapstick and she loved the Joyboard too," says Amiga developer RJ Mical.

Chaffee appeared in print advertising and promotional materials for the Joyboard but she also came in person to events. "We launched the skiing game at Studio 54 in New York," says Reisinger. "Suzy was the demo model on the Joyboard."

The spokesperson did a good job of reaching into people's homes. "She appeared on morning news programs and at toy fairs playing a skiing game to demonstrate the Amiga Joyboard," recalls Mical. "She wore ski clothing, carried poles, and had some fun pretending to ski on the joyboard. We had some fun watching her do this."[3]

Amiga's Power-Stick ads reflect the pride the marketing people had in the technology inside the joysticks, even going so far as to show the metal traces on the printed circuit boards.

By the middle of 1983 it was time to start shipping the first run of joysticks for the upcoming Christmas season. "That was phase one," sums up Reisinger. "It was really an opportunity to bring some cash in relatively quickly with a fairly small investment." If all went well, they could rely on two or three years worth of sales until the game system was ready to launch.

The controllers became a favorite among Atari owners. "The reviews on the product were phenomenal by everybody that reviewed video games back in those days because it was an application of a technology that was so different than what was being used on all of the other stuff in the market," recalls Reisinger. "The performance was there and it did things that the other stuff didn't do."

By the middle of 1983, it looked like Morse's master plan was performing better than he expected. The positive reviews garnered by the Power-Sticks established a quality reputation for the Amiga brand. They were flying off the shelves and more products were on the way.

The Great Video Game Crash

Amiga's short-term revenue stream to fund development of the video game system was now in place. It seemed like an unbeatable plan, especially with the Atari-led video game boom that Jay Miner and Joe Decuir had helped create. "1982 was a banner year," recalls Decuir. "I have an IEEE article

---

3   *Info Magazine.* January 1987. p. 45.

that's dated March of '83 and it's talking about how we've built a four billion dollar business in the video game market."

However, soon Morse's revenue stream began to evaporate. "He didn't anticipate that the whole game market was going to fall apart, which is why they ran out of money in '83," says Decuir.

It was a confusing time for those in the industry. Retailers had been hungry for anything video game related the year before. Too hungry, in fact, to the point where weak products were being thrown onto shelves with a less than stellar reception by video gamers. "They changed from management who knew what consumers wanted in games and how games were built to management that just understood marketing paper towels, toilet tissue and how do you do the accounting so that it made a profit," explains Ron Nicholson. "Once they brought those types in, basically they produced really bad games that essentially destroyed the industry for many years."

As a result of the video game glut, Amiga's games among them, many products sat on shelves unsold. Normally retailers would request refunds but with small video game companies going out of business, retailers were forced to absorb the loss. Once retailers began losing money on video games they wanted nothing more to do with them.

This was most apparent at the June 1983 CES, where Amiga introduced the Joyboard at a suggested retail price of $37.99. However, orders were slow. "The game console sales plummeted and the arcades started to falter," recalls RJ Mical.

The setback made everyone in Amiga marketing sick to their stomachs. All the research and development they had spent time and money on was now worthless, as was the planned two to three year product lifetime. "I thought they had started out with some good product ideas but just at the time when they were getting this stuff out into channels was the great event that caused Atari to bulldoze *E.T.* cartridges by the millions into a desert landfill," says Nicholson.

Amiga had no choice but to launch the Joyboard into the lackluster Christmas market. They had spent too much already to develop and manufacture the Joyboards and now they tried to recoup what they could. "That product did not do well in the market and a fair amount of it was that, by the time it hit, the bottom had pretty much dropped out," says Reisinger.

Morse also abandoned The Power Module, the device that would allow gamers to load Atari 2600 games from tape. It was almost a blessing in disguise, as they could have lost more had it gone to production. "By the time we got it to the point where both the hardware and software were ready, there just wasn't any need for it anymore," says Reisinger. "There was no market for it."

The R&D to include tape loading, RAM, and telecommunications had used up valuable Amiga resources. And now it looked like all of Amiga could be in trouble.

Chip Boards
1983

Dave Morse's plan to support development of his wonder system by selling peripherals and software was derailed by the video game crash, leaving Amiga Corp. with steep financial constraints. It couldn't have happened at a worse time. With the chip architecture done, it was time to begin hiring more engineers to complete the detailed logic design of the chips. Jay Miner had contacts with some of the best chip engineers in Silicon Valley, but with the recent financial woes of the fledgling startup, he would have to hire junior engineers where possible to save money. If all went well, Amiga would soon have functioning prototypes of the chips and could begin coding the system software.

Joe Leaves Amiga

By 1983, Jay Miner and Dave Morse started to have an idea of the resources they would require to complete the Amiga chipset. Miner would need to hire at least eight more engineers and purchase or rent expensive development systems. He would also need to find contractors for short term tasks, such as producing prototypes of the chips.

Morse's division had racked up the majority of the costs so far: salaries for his marketing people, flights and expenses for trade shows, placing ads in magazines, contracting packaging designs, and tooling for his accessories. On the game development front, the contractors he hired were proving expensive. All this, and Amiga had barely released any Atari products, other than the Power-Stick and Joyboard.

Morse and Miner presented their projected budgets to Amiga's VP of finance, who was then able to forecast the burn rate of their remaining capital. The results were not good. They weren't out of money yet and they had some revenue coming in from the Atari products, but the bank account would soon become stressed.

Morse and Miner made a difficult but necessary decision, the first of many. "We had basically drawn out all the timing diagram and system diagrams and chip schematics by the time they ran out of money for me," says Joe Decuir. "I was a consultant to Amiga. Amiga paid me $80,000 over a period from fall 1982 through spring 1983. Yes, I was expensive. In contrast, Ron was a regular employee."

In mid-April, Decuir returned to Standard Technologies where his company would one day design third-party devices for Amiga's upcoming system. "I took that money and split it three ways with my STC business partners," he says.

As a fulltime employee, Ron Nicholson felt his job was safer but he noted something worrying. "Joe Decuir stopped coming around. I found out much later that they stopped offering to pay him."

Growing Amiga

Back in the Amiga engineering department, the engineers were ready to begin designing the chips themselves. It was like they had created a basic map of a city, with roads interconnecting everything and traffic lights timed so that the cars didn't go into gridlock. Now they would begin designing those buildings and neighborhoods in detail.

Jay Miner planned to have teams of two people working on each chip, requiring six engineers total. Agnus was the hardest chip to design, so Miner would take the lead on that one himself. He needed someone with video experience to lead Daphne. And for Portia, someone who could design both analog and digital circuits.

The other three engineers would simulate and test the different parts of the chip as they were being designed. It would be futile to design the entire chip, with thousands of gates, all at once and expect it to work. The lead engineer would need to design the smaller parts one at a time and then pass those designs off to an assistant to simulate the design in software to confirm each part worked before placing it into the chip.

With Decuir out of the picture and Nicholson occupied by systems design and software, Miner would need to hire two more engineers. For now, he would rely heavily on Nicholson's contacts at his former employer, BTI Systems. "This company had tons of really, really bright software and hardware people," says Nicholson.

Chu and Shieu

Miner knew just where to find two technicians to design, simulate, and test the chip circuits. "Jay knew a couple of chip designers from his previous N companies and so he brought in Mark Shieu and Edwin Chu," recalls Ron Nicholson. "He brought them in to do essentially the circuit level design."

Mark Shieu had previously helped develop the Pokey chip at Atari, working under Miner. Now he would fulfill a similar role on Portia, simulating the chip using circuit simulation software called SPICE. By simulating the circuit, the engineers could verify the circuit operation at the transistor level before committing to manufacturing the larger chips.

Shieu and Chu would not have to wait for the engineers to design the entire logic in the entire chip first. Instead, as different circuits in the chips were completed, the pair could begin testing them.

The length of the project would be shortened by starting work before the completed chips were in. "We design from both ends at once," says Nicholson. "We had the big block diagrams but then, to figure out if we could get the performance and size we need, we needed them to look at the process and figure out how big the transistors would be and whether we could fit them all in and whether it would go fast enough."

Once the chip circuits were verified, the engineers could even begin the layout of the chips, adding each circuit one at a time as they were completed.

Glenn Keller

The engineer who would end up designing the detailed logic in Portia seemed like an unlikely candidate to design a disk controller and audio engine, considering he had no prior experience with either and didn't even use computers. Glenn Jay Keller was born in Oklahoma in 1952, but he was destined to travel. "We lived in 17 different places," he laughs.

The reason for his frequent moves had to do with his father's work on a missile system meant to intercept Russian nuclear bombers before they could drop their payload on America. "My dad worked for Western Electric," he says. "He designed the guidance systems for the Nike missiles. It was like an earlier version of the Patriot, designed for bombers instead of missiles. They would put missiles around the city so if the Russian bombers came in they could fight against them."

Project Nike developed a family of four different Nike missiles between 1945 and 1967, when the project became obsolete. However, prior to that, due to his expertise with missile guidance systems, Keller's father joined the

NASA space program. "We lived in Titusville, Florida when all the Moon shots happened. That was pretty cool. We saw all of them take off from our backyard."

Keller followed in his father's engineering footsteps but was more drawn to the frontiers of the ocean than space. In 1971, MIT accepted his application and he embarked on a masters in ocean engineering, graduating in 1976. As an oceanic engineer, Keller hoped to design everything from submersible craft to exotic instruments used in ocean exploration. "I'm the guy that builds all those weird things that the oceanographers use, and ships, and stuff," he says.

When the oil crisis hit in 1973, Western powers began looking for alternative sources of energy. One of those potential sources was the power of ocean waves. The project caught Keller's eye while he was attending MIT, and in 1977 he moved to Scotland to work for Stephen Salter, the inventor of "Salter's duck", a bobbing device that converted wave energy into electrical power.

The British government created the UK Wave Energy program and in turn, the University of Edinburgh received funds for the program. This resulted in them hiring Keller to work for the university.

The experience allowed Keller to develop skills in areas of analog electronics (with the study of waves playing an important role), digital electronics, and working with large water tanks to experiment with waves. "That resulted in some actual power generated from ocean waves," he says. "It was a lot of fun."

In March 1982, with oil prices returning to normal, the UK government shut down the Wave Energy program and Keller returned to the United States ready to continue his career in oceanographic engineering. He soon landed in California, where much of the development of submersibles was occurring. "I was up in the North Bay looking for oceanography jobs and ocean engineering jobs," he recalls. "I talked to some submarine companies and people who had built instruments and stuff like that."

Unfortunately, none of the companies he approached were hiring. He then extended his search out to the East Bay. "Somebody who was doing something that sounded vaguely oceanic was a guy named Joe Decuir," recalls Keller.

Standard Technologies, as Keller found out, had nothing to do with oceanography. It was Joe Decuir's background in bioengineering that sounded 'vaguely oceanic' to Keller. "Joe Decuir was a grad student in bioengineering and had a company he had started in the East Bay," explains Nicholson, referring to Standard Technologies. "Glenn Keller's resume originally went to Joe Decuir and Joe at that time wasn't hiring oceanographers."

Amiga was likewise uninterested in oceanographic engineers but it was looking to hire a chip designer for Portia. Noting Keller's experience with analog and digital electronics, Decuir passed his resume to Amiga. "He said, 'Well, here's the resume of someone who looks really sharp' and gave it to me," says Nicholson.

Eventually Decuir called the 30 year old engineer back and told him, "'Well, I don't have anything, but go talk to my friend in Sunnyvale."

Soon, Keller was boarding a train for what would become a life changing experience. When he exited the train he was greeted by Jay Miner, wearing one of his trademark Hawaiian T-shirts. "I go to Sunnyvale, I show up at the train station, and there is this guy in a Lincoln Continental with a little dog sticking out," laughs Keller.

During the ride to the Amiga offices, Keller had a chance to talk casually with Miner. The two found a connection over their first and middle names. "It probably helped that his name was Jay Glenn and mine was Glenn Jay," says Keller. "It was one of those nice little coincidences."

By the end of his car ride with Miner and Mitchy, Keller was won over. "I am like, 'I have got to work for this guy,'" he says.

One doubt Keller had was his lack of experience in the computer industry, or with personal computers of any sort. This was 1983, after all, and millions of personal computers had already permeated homes across North America. "I had done programming but I didn't understand the world of personal computers or indeed the world of Silicon Valley," he explains. "I hadn't been there."

Once at Koll Oakmead Park, Miner brought him into the shared office space with the whiteboards and block diagrams. Although Miner hoped the proposed system would have a great impact on Keller, he failed to get it. "I didn't really understand why the architecture was so great in a general sense, because I didn't know that much about where computers were at that point," says Keller.

Instead, he hoped his diverse electronics background would give him enough skills for the job. "I had done a lot of electronics but no chips," he says. "But I liked Jay and I always liked pretty colored wires. I had done a lot of different kinds of electronics. Being in ocean engineering, you do everything: digital, analog, interfaces, all that stuff. Even software. You do the whole thing. So I had a pretty broad base even though I hadn't done chip design."

Decades later, Keller sounds mystified as to why Miner would hire an oceanographic engineer into a computer company. "He hired me for some reason," he says, musing the reason might be because, "I guessed correctly the difference between a flip flop and a latch."

Most likely, Miner knew all he needed was an engineer with a good understanding of both analog and digital electronics for Portia. He could bridge the gap of chip design by mentoring a junior engineer. And the coincidence with their names probably made it seem like destiny.

Dave Dean

After Glenn Keller started work on Portia, Miner sought out a second hire in order to work on the graphics chip. Once again, Nicholson went to his contacts in the industry and found an engineer named Dave Dean from BTI Systems. "He was another person that I dragged along with me when Amiga started hiring," says Nicholson.

"We realized that we would need to do some lab prototyping," explains Nicholson. "So Dave Dean was hired around the time."

Most importantly, Dean had prior experience designing video at BTI Systems. "Dave Dean had done video chips before or had been in the chip world," recalls Keller.

With Dean working on Daphne and Keller on Portia, this left Miner to work on Agnus. "Jay took a little bit more ownership on the Agnus chip since a lot of the circuit design inside that was stuff that he knew how to do really well," says Nicholson.

Portia

Portia was, among the three chips of the Amiga chipset, the simplest to design. This also makes it appealing to study how it was designed by Glenn Keller, the mellow engineer who was brand new to the field of chip design.

By the time Keller arrived for his first day of work at Amiga in mid-April, the path before him had already been laid out by Nicholson and Decuir. "Joe Decuir and I did the block diagram, size estimates, timing estimates and stuff like that. The feature set and the specification," says Nicholson. "We had most of the block diagram of the four channel waveform audio before he got there as well as the registers."

Jay Miner gave him everything they had accomplished up to that point, some of it detailed, but most parts were undefined blocks in a diagram that needed to be implemented. Portia would be his baby. "It was the obvious thing because I was the junior chip guy and that was the one chip with the least complicated stuff on it," says Keller.

Miner also gave him a few more things to help him on his way. "He gave me books to read, *Principles of VLSI Design* and stuff like that," says Keller. "Later on I understood that stuff but in the beginning I didn't really. Like I said I was the junior guy."

The most powerful resource for learning chip design was of course Miner himself. "I talked to Jay and he was the best because he had a very deep understanding of this stuff," says Keller. "He knew exactly when to point you in the right direction, but also let you wander off and learn things on your own. He was very good at that."

Audio Chip Logic Gates

The designers used a Data General Eclipse MV/8000 minicomputer to run the chip design software. Ultimately, Amiga would need to produce a huge schematic that detailed all the resistors, transistors, and capacitors, as well as the snaking traces that connected them together. However, the first stage was another diagram that showed all the underlying logic gates that would perform the digital functions of the chip.

The logic diagram, which described the digital portion of the Portia chip, was composed of symbols that were a mix of rectangular, rounded, pointed, and triangular shapes. Each of these symbols represented a binary gate; one of AND, OR, NOT, NAND, NOR, XOR, XNOR that Keller learned in engineering. "I had to convert everything to standard logic too, so that was quite a big job," he says.

Helping Keller the entire time was Miner. "He taught me how to make adder chains, and carry chains for adders, and all that stuff. He taught me about the silicon itself, how fast it was, how big the wires were. Some of the things you needed to understand in order to design it."

Disk Controller Logic Design

Although audio was a big part of Portia, the disk controller was perhaps the most complicated system. The drive would spin a magnetic disk while the disk head sent a signal consisting of edges going up and down at intervals, representing binary data. An edge up means a 1 and an edge down means a 0. "The way a disk works is you have edges in your data, and then you have a bunch of zeros between them where there's no edges," explains Glenn Keller.

Keller had to program a phased locked loop—that is, a system that read data from the disk, looping over and over again. At the heart of this system was a voltage control oscillator (VCO) that could time the length of a 0 or 1 on disk. But to ensure the timing did not go out of sync, the phase locked loop adjusts the VCO slightly every time it encounters an edge between a 0 and a 1. This way it keeps the timing accurate as the disk spins around. "Your task as a phase locked loop, or a VCO, is to figure out how many zeroes you've got, and how many ones," explains Keller. "Usually an edge is a one and the spaces between them are zero."

A problem can occur when there are a lot of zeroes in a row, meaning the VCO can't calibrate its timing for a long period of time. "The farther apart you put the ones, the more stable your phase lock loop has to be, so it can tell how many zeros are between them," says Keller.

In the ensuing months, Keller would continue designing and refining his chip, both in the audio output and disk drive controller. When complete, the chip would have the power to revolutionize digital music.

Dave Needle

After Glenn Keller was a few months into his design of Portia, Dave Morse decided to bring in an experienced engineer to help with the simulation, testing, and design of the chipset. He found a 36 year-old electrical engineer named Dave Needle. "Dave Needle was brought aboard as a consultant to help Glenn," says Ron Nicholson.

Born in 1947, Needle was often stricken with illness growing up, which resulted in him staying in bed and reading. He became infatuated with science fiction stories, including a few dealing with aliens from Jupiter, known as Jovians (similar to Martians). These included Isaac Asimov's short story *Victory Unintentional* (1942), Edgar Rice Burroughs' *Skeleton Men of Jupiter* (1943), and Poul William Anderson's *Three Worlds to Conquer* (1964). This also led Needle to invent a language, but not one of this earth. Rather, he claimed it was the Jovian language, the language of the people of Jupiter and its moons.

Needle earned a BS in Electrical Engineering from City University of New York City College in 1969. He then worked for the Naval Air Station in Alameda, California starting in 1973. There, huge nuclear powered aircraft carriers docked regularly for maintenance and supplies.

At the time, David Bowie was touring under the persona of Ziggy Stardust, a messenger for extraterrestrial beings. This inspired Needle to take his Jovian schtick one step farther.

In the ultimate flight of fantasy, the eccentric Needle told others the real Dave Needle had passed away from illness as a child and was substituted with a Jovian. According to his childhood friend, Stan Shepard, "Long story short, the sickly child died and was replaced by a Jovian ambassador, whose mission was to be raised as a human and to inform humans that aliens were not what was being pictured in sci-fi."

In 1978 Needle (or perhaps his alien replacement) joined Tandem Computer, a recently formed company founded by ex-Hewlett-Packard employees. Tandem made a line of fault-tolerant servers dubbed "Non-Stop". These servers were sold to industries where uninterrupted service was critical.

While working at Tandem, a headhunter informed Needle of an opportunity for LSI design at Amiga. Bored with his work at Tandem, Needle agreed to an interview. What happened next shows the difficulty Needle had attempting to navigate social situations. "I go down to take a look," recalled Needle some years later. "I walk into the place. I'm arrogant as hell. I am, of course, the best designer there ever was in the whole wide world and I knew it."[1]

Needle was immediately impressed with the project under development at Amiga and the unique workplace culture compared to Tandem. "And I walked into this Amiga place and I saw the machine they were working on and it was stupendous," said Needle. "Just from the block diagrams and the paperwork, I drooled. It was awful. I wanted to be in on it. But I still hadn't calmed down from my standard arrogance."

The diminutive engineer, who had over a decade of experience, knew he wanted in. "So I saw Dave Morse, who was president there, and told him how great I was and what I was gonna do for him and he brushed me aside 'Little boy, don't bother me. We'll call you. Don't call us.' He shoved me out of his office. I felt like a real jerk."

Needle realized working at Amiga alongside industry luminary Jay Miner could be his dream job. So he tried again, this time with some genuine humility. "The next day I called him and I said, 'I'm real sorry. I know I came across bad. Please oh please I'll sweep the floors. I'll clean up. I really want to work there oh please oh please.'"

Morse had been trying to find competent engineers, a task made more difficult due to his tight budget constraints. The now desperate Needle sud-

---

1   *Wired* magazine. January, 1994. "Third Time's a Charm (They Hope)"

denly looked like a bargain, especially given his extensive experience with computers. He was in—but not as a chip designer. He would start on as a lowly technician, wiring prototypes together and cleaning up the lab.

From the start, Needle's coworkers knew he was unique when he revealed to them he was from Jupiter. "I don't know whether it was actually true or not," muses Glenn Keller. "In either case, it provided a philosophical base for Dave to expound on life, have a Jovian language, talk about a different form of culture (Jovian, of course) and its better and worse comparisons to our own."

Little by little, his new Amiga coworkers learned of his culture, such as having lunch at the "snaught pit" (pronounced "snot pit"). "Snaught is not expressed so simply in English," explains Keller. "It means something like, 'Can I do something for you or give something to you, but just because I want to and it is my pleasure, with no obligation or need on your part for a return favor.'"

As an alien ambassador from a highly technical society, Needle was able to contribute much more to the Amiga project than Dave Morse first antici-pated. "We didn't really split up the chips until it came time to pass them off to Dave Dean, Glenn Keller, Dave Needle, and two other engineers [Edwin Chu and Mark Shieu]," says Ron Nicholson. "At that time those guys split it off and did detailed logic design, one or two engineers per chip, Jay helping mostly on the Agnus."

Needle frequently strolled through engineering, took a glance at a trou-bled design, and was able to offer immediate fixes. He soon took on the task of wiring up Ron Nicholson's motherboard. More often than not, he was able to correct or improve upon Nicholson's design, often accompanied by a few biting criticisms. Within a short time be became the senior architect on the Amiga system, usurping Nicholson.

Jay Miner's list of tasks had grown, leaving him with less time to focus on chip design than he anticipated. Now he was not only mentoring Keller but also Needle, along with guiding Dean with the video chip design. Along with other duties such as hiring, it put him at a disadvantage to the young-er engineers who could focus carefree on their own chips. As a result, it was Needle who became almost as important on the Agnus chip as Miner. "Dave Needle proved to be extremely competent. He took over the lead of most of the logic design," says Nicholson. "Dave Dean, Dave Needle, and Glenn Keller did the lion's share of the logic design of the actual chips."

When Joe Decuir stopped coming around to Amiga, Needle inherited his desk in the large hardware engineer office. "There were the three desks in that room and eventually we moved a whole bunch of other people in there," recalls Nicholson.

In time, Needle had as much to do with the Agnus as Miner. "[Miner] never really was the detailed designer for the whole chip," says Nicholson. "That was being done by the other hires and consultants."

By the end of the summer of 1983, several of the chips were ready for prototyping. The simplest chip, Portia, was completed first, followed by the video chip Daphne. Agnus, the most complex chip, would be ready later in the year.

Prototype Chip Boards

Once the three chip engineers completed the logic, they had no immediate way to fabricate the chips. Unlike Commodore, with its built-in semiconductor plant, Amiga Corporation had no access to chip manufacturing. For the time being, the engineers would have to find another way to test their chips.

Instead of miniaturizing the circuits into microchips, they built them full sized using regular components on breadboards. It was as though the engineers used an enlarging ray on their silicon chips. As can be expected, these mega-sized chips would take up a lot of space.

To create the prototype boards, Jay Miner hired an outside company in Silicon Valley. "We contracted those out," says Nicholson. " Dave Needle would drop schematics and send them to a contract prototyping facility."

Prototyping a custom chip meant implementing the logic of the chips using discrete gates, available in off-the-shelf parts such as DIP (Dual-Inline Pin) packages, and hooking the gates together with wire. If the design called for an AND gate, a 74HC08 could be used which gave 4 AND gates in a 20 pin package. Of course, as well as being connected to other gates for input and output, it also needed its own power and ground signals, adding further wiring.

By following the schematics, relatively unskilled technicians could insert the correct IC chips and wire together the corresponding logic gates. Because each prototype required up to eight separate prototype circuit boards (all wired together), the employer would assign one worker for each board in order to get the prototype assembled quicker. "This is all being managed by someone who had connections with all these hand laborers all over the Valley who could actually do a lot of hand labor and contract that cheaper than companies could hire full-time employees to do it themselves," explains Nicholson.

Although the work was low-skilled, workers nevertheless had to be meticulous, systematic and organized, remembering to check off each gate on the master schematic as it was connected to another chip. "It was basically Japanese, Chinese, or Vietnamese women who, as their business, were sent a board with instructions how to wire wrap it," says Nicholson. "They'd wire wrap it and send it back to a technician who looked it over."

If the board passed the tests, a senior technician connected the different boards together with ribbon cables. These connected along one side of each board, resulting in a stack of boards that opened up like a book.

Each breadboard had up to 150 IC chips on it, with potentially eight breadboards in total, all bundled together with multicolored spaghetti wire. Each of the breadboards was spaced apart with metal spacers, and when in use, they simply stacked all the breadboards together into a large box shape. All this to implement a circuit that ultimately would end up as a single chip smaller than a fingernail.

For the next few months, the company produced each of the three major chips that would make up the chipset as massive prototype versions of the chips.

During this time, the engineers picked up on some problems within the Amiga company. Morse kept the business side of the company isolated from the engineers so they could concentrate on engineering, but soon it became obvious to the engineers that things were beginning to fall apart. "I was vaguely aware that we were getting behind on our payables," says Ron Nicholson. "The first hint that I got that there were money problems was when some of the contractors that we'd contracted out doing some of the wire wrapping and other things in the chips started giving me calls asking, 'How come you're not paying us? The accounts payable guy keeps giving us BS stories about the check is in the mail.'"

Amiga was able to defer payment long enough to receive all three prototypes by late 1983. As expected, the chip boards required some additional work. "Dave Needle and his team did the bulk of the debugging," recalls Nicholson.

Glenn Keller recalls the patience required to test or "buzz out" the prototypes. "You go back and check every single connection with an ohmmeter," he says. "Once you sit down and start doing that, you'd be surprised how much you can get done in one day."

Needle meticulously planned the testing process to slowly inch the chip boards closer to full operation. "If the thing doesn't work, it wasn't like you started out with running software on the thing," says Keller. "You started out with a switch and light box. If the thing doesn't work at all, maybe you can write a register. Maybe you can toggle the thing and have the signal get partway through the board. In doing that you can debug it."

The work demanded a patient personality, common among Jovians. "You have to be slow and steady for that," says Keller. "I think that part of being the hardware guy is boring."

Ron Nicholson had been designing and building a prototype motherboard, which he named Peace. Once the prototype chips were debugged, Needle connected it to the Peace motherboard. "I did a little bit of the debugging since they plugged into a motherboard which I had designed and knew how it worked," says Nicholson.

The prototype chip boards had one other important feature. If the chip designers decided to change or improve on the original schematics, they could make a change to the chip boards and see exactly how the change behaved. This was possible because all the IC chips in the chip boards were socketed. This meant that the Amiga team could locate the appropriate part of the circuit, unwire any or all of a particular IC, pull out IC's, and replace them with different ones to make a new circuit. Thus as the schematics evolved, so would their prototype chip boards.

By August 1983, the team had a working Portia prototype and would soon have a prototype of the Daphne chip. The effect this had on the hardware designers' morale can not be overstated. Only Agnus remained. However, it was enough for them to begin testing the chips and writing code. In the meantime, Amiga Corporation began to prepare for an influx of new engineers to begin work on the actual software.

Dancing Fools
1983

Once Amiga Corporation had some of the chips prototyped, it became possible to begin programming those chips—testing them out, plumbing their depths to see what they were capable of, and developing system software. That system software would allow programmers to create powerful games more easily than they could on the current generation of video game consoles. How sophisticated that software became surprised even those who worked for Amiga.

The Software Developers

Dave Morse had originally planned for Ron Nicholson to handle the programming efforts on the video game system. After all, how hard could it be to program code for a simple game console? The Atari 2600 had almost no system code, other than that in the cartridges, but had very limited potential. The Amiga was a completely different proposition.

Thanks to the relative complexity of the Amiga chipset, the engineers wanted to make things easy for programmers to create games. "The guys at Activision and Imagic, all these other people doing VCS games, had had to struggle to figure out how to build the screen," recalls Joe Decuir. "For this machine, they wouldn't have to struggle, and they could build world-beater stuff."

Instead of fighting off third-party developers, as Atari had, Amiga would embrace them by creating programmer libraries that would make it easy to create sounds and graphics. Developers could use high-level languages such as C for software and games that ran within an operating system, but it would require a lot of effort on Amiga's part to create these libraries—more than one person could handle. "I sold myself to Dave Morse as someone who knew a little bit about software, but of course, when I got there I realized that I had bitten off a lot more than I could chew," recalls Nicholson. "We definitely needed to bring some real software people on board."

Bob Pariseau

Amiga Corp turned to Ron Nicholson's contacts at his old employer, BTI Systems. He told Miner and Morse, "Here's this guy with really good people skills. A good stand up guy if you ever need someone to be in meetings to talk to software vendors and stuff."

"And that was Bob Pariseau," says Nicholson. Pariseau had previously helped develop a Pascal compiler at BTI. "Bob Pariseau impressed me, not only as a sharp engineer but he had a good personality. He wasn't a manager then but he had impressed me that he had those people skills."

According to Jay Miner, his strategy for hiring employees was based on the enthusiasm they showed when he revealed the project to them during interviews. To show off what the machine could do, Nicholson ran his Apple II graphics program that simulated the blitter. "I wrote early demos to show what it could do that helped us figure out how to design hardware," says Nicholson. "When we were interviewing Bob Pariseau, we showed him some of the things that it can do."

Pariseau responded with the required level of enthusiasm, especially when he saw the overall architecture. "We bring in Bob Pariseau and interview him and he looks at the whiteboard and that convinced him," says Nicholson.

Nicholson was now free to design the system board, while Bob Pariseau would lead the software development. "He agreed to come on board as director of software engineering. I was there as director of hardware engineering," says Nicholson.

Pariseau had a definite goal and timeline in front of him. Amiga intended to demonstrate the video game system at the January 1984 Winter CES in Las Vegas. Although Pariseau had prior programming experience, his skills in that area were not immediately required. "There weren't really tools to do any coding on," says Nicholson. Pariseau would need to set up a software development system before he could hire a team of programmers, who would then set about creating the tools they needed to program the video game system. All in six months.

Ideally, the team wanted to display the video game system at the upcoming CES with working software. However, the hardware would not be ready until later in 1983. Instead, they would focus on demos and the software library used to access the chipset.

They also hoped one day to develop software on a possible Amiga home computer, but for now they would have to do cross development on a different system. Pariseau bought the cheapest multi-user system he could find, called the Sage IV system. It was a Motorola 68000 based machine with a 40 MB hard drive and 512 K of memory.

To overcome the absence of real chips, the software team would write small pieces of code to simulate some of the functions from the chip specification. "They wrote some code to do in software what the hardware would do, but not in terms of emulating what the final results would be," explains Ron Nicholson. "They may have written some software graphics routines that did what the hardware would later do–similar to how Apple II game programmers had to write it all in software. They wrote that on a Sage multi-user system that was less powerful than a Mac 128 K."

With the exception of Bob Pariseau, the first wave of Amiga employees were hardware engineers. With chips becoming available in mid-1983, at least in prototype form, it was time to start hiring the second wave of employees who would program the hardware.

Sam Dicker - Audio Programming

Because the Portia chip was the first prototype completed, Bob Pariseau would hire an audio programmer first to begin developing the all important sound libraries that other programmers would rely on, as well as audio demos to help promote the console.

Pariseau naturally turned to the video game industry for his audio programmer. After all, he wasn't likely to find the skills he needed anywhere else. "I had worked for three years for Williams Electronics in Chicago on their first and phenomenally successful coin-op video games before coin-op collapsed in late '82 and early '83," says Sam Dicker.

By 1983, the Williams Electronic Manufacturing Company had been responsible for a string of hit arcade games, most notably *Defender* in 1981. Sam Dicker was the audio programmer of Defender, who used a dedicated 6800 processor and a Digital to Analog Converter to produce the rich sounds in the game. Dicker did not confine himself to audio programming, however, and was the lead game programmer on *Sinistar*, in which he designed the multitasking kernel, game play, animation, and sound effects.

After Sinistar wrapped, he became tempted by other industry colleagues. "I was jealous of a few generously paid staff programmers at Atari who received royalties for their hit games," he says. "Two of my favorite co-workers had left Williams and started a small company selling the games they programmed to Williams. They didn't tell me before they left, since Williams had gotten me to sign a contract that restricted me to working for them if I stayed in Chicago."

Dicker decided it was time to leave Chicago. "I was young and didn't know the first thing about negotiating, so I hired a talent agent in L.A. who decided to move into representing video game developers," he says. "At the time, we were all starting to feel like rockstars exploited by record companies in our dealings with coin-op manufacturers."

Soon he was bound for California. "The agent sent me to a bunch of video game startup companies in California when I made a trip there in the Spring of '83," he says. "Somehow he had heard of Amiga and their amazing design for a home computer with graphics and sound that was light-years ahead of even the most advanced coin-op hardware on the drawing boards. Even though I knew I wouldn't be making games at Amiga, I couldn't resist the opportunity to help bring a product like that to the masses and change the world."

In June 1983, Dicker accepted Pariseau's offer and the two continued setting up terminals, installing development tools, and hiring other programmers. "In the beginning, the software group was just Pariseau and me. In the next few months that followed, we interviewed and hired the rest of the original Amiga software team."

Once the prototype chips became available, Dicker began his quest for improving computer audio. "Sam mainly wrote the audio library and then he also did a lot of testing of the audio, and also wrote a lot of cool little audio tricks and sounds and instruments," says co-worker Carl Sassenrath. "He also wrote a lot of the early demos and things."

Although one of the goals of Dicker's audio demos was to show off the power of the Portia chip, Dicker himself had trouble showing off what he made. "He was just an amazing, amazing guy from the audio side, but he was very shy about showing people stuff," says Sassenrath.

Portia had been designed around the concept of looping digitized audio sounds, so one of the first things Dicker experimented with was recording musical instruments and then playing them back with different pitches. "A lot of the magic of the music was from [Sam Dicker]," says Dale Luck.

In this way, realistic music could be played dynamically. "He was so funny because he was so modest," says Sassenrath. "He would record a bunch of musical instruments, load them into the memory, and then play stuff. This would be like one o'clock in the morning, late at night. He'd say, 'Listen to this Carl.' It was amazing audio. We were like Sam, you gotta show other people this stuff. This is great."

Dale Luck - Graphics

Hiring a team of programmers proved more difficult and time consuming than anyone anticipated. By August, Amiga had only Sam Dicker to show. Though they had interviewed many candidates, none had the qualities Dave Morse was looking for.

Then a contact from Tandem, the company Dave Needle formerly worked for, opened a door to a pool of quality applicants. "[Bob Pariseau] contacted the recruiter that he knew at Tandem," recalls Nicholson. "Her name was Marina Eisenzimmer and she had deep hooks into HP. Somehow she knew all the good people at HP."

At the time, Hewlett-Packard was well regarded for defining the Silicon Valley business culture. "They were all in her calling book. We convinced her to start calling up really cool people at HP and that included Dale Luck and Carl Sassenrath," says Nicholson. "We interviewed some others that didn't make the cut. She brought those names to Pariseau. Then the bunch of us, Bob and I, interviewed them and we hired the rest of the software team into the mid and latter half of '83."

Pariseau soon found a promising addition to the programming team: Dale Luck, who was 25 at the time he joined Amiga. The former Midwesterner sported typical eighties feathered hair and moustache. Members of the Amiga team called him Luck Trucking Dale. "My dad was a truck driver," he says. "He had a trucking company called Luck Trucking."

Luck was born in 1958 and grew up in Beaver Dam, Wisconsin. In his early teens, he began playing pen and paper role-playing games made by a company called SPI (Simulations Publications, Inc.). "As a kid I was into games, and at that time I was also into strategy and tactics games. There was a company that was making these games with hexagon shapes. You got little pieces and then you would create your strategy for moving them around and getting the supply lines and things like that, all on this piece of paper with a grid and you would play it on a table. We would play war games, basically."

Luck's love of role-playing games led him into programming in 1972 at the age of 14. "Math and science came pretty easy to me," he says. "I started writing programs when I was in ninth grade. We had a little teletype hooked up to a timeshare system at high school."

Luck attended Wayland Academy, a private boarding school with about 200 students. The high school had several teletype machines connected to a PDP-8 timesharing system, which was physically located 30 miles north at Ripon College. "I was trying to create games on the teletype," he recalls, laughing. "It didn't have a video screen or anything like that, and the teletype only ran at 110 baud, so it was 10 characters per second. It was like a typewriter, and it had a paper tape reader and a paper tape punch. That was how you could store your programs."

After high school, Luck enrolled at Michigan Technological University in 1976 and received a degree in computer science in 1979. After university, he joined Hewlett-Packard, specializing in computer graphics. "I worked on graphics terminals and graphics software. That was my forté," he says. "I worked on a product that came out. Some would say it was a good product, but it didn't really get the market share we thought it would."

After spending three years of his life on the HP-2700 graphics terminal, it disappointed Luck to see it fail. He blames the failure on the $20,000 price. "Typically at that time, Hewlett-Packard made over-designed, some would say overpriced, stuff but it did the job that needed to be done. I helped a little bit with the design at Hewlett-Packard. If they were to do all custom chips, it would have cost a lot less. But they weren't doing much of their own custom chip design at that time."

For the next year, Luck worked on a UNIX graphics package before Hewlett-Packard began moving away from multitasking UNIX development. "By that time, in 1983, I had started looking around to see if there was something else that would be interesting to do."

Luck hired a recruiter and interviewed at several Silicon Valley businesses. "I had actually interviewed at Mindset and a couple of other places. Some places didn't want to consider me because I didn't wear a tie," he says. "The recruiter told me I probably should have dressed up and worn a tie, but that's not really me."

Luck came very close to missing his opportunity with Amiga. "I forgot my first interview and blew them off because I was at an HP 'beer bust' with some friends," he recalls, referring to HP's Friday after-work gatherings. "I looked at my watch and said, 'Oh crap. I just missed an interview that I was supposed to be at.' So I called them up and they said, 'No problem, just come in the next day.'"

At his interview, Luck found out about Amiga's secret project. "What I worked on at Hewlett-Packard sold for $20,000. What I saw at Amiga was almost the exact same thing, and it was going to be $1000," he explains. "It was the same performance, but it was a magnitude decrease in price. So I thought, we're going to make millions of them! This was a company where I thought we were going to change the world."

Luck felt confident the product was possible. "I saw Jay's background and history in terms of what he did at Atari," he recalls. "So when they drew out the block diagrams, I could see that this would work. They showed me what they were going to do with the custom chips. I could add up the cost of the parts, and I could say, 'This is going to be great. This is some-thing that I've always wanted to have myself.' Because at that time, I hadn't bought a computer for myself yet."

Luck described his experience programming graphics hardware to Bob Pariseau. "We kind of clicked together," says Luck. "The PC was out, and the Lisa just came out. I kind of talked about all the things that I thought we could do with it."

"They apparently were impressed enough that they said, 'When can you start?' It was primarily because of my graphics experience and my enthusiasm."

In August, Luck sat down in front of one of the Sage IV terminals and began programming the Daphne prototype chip. "There weren't very many people at Amiga at that time," says Luck. "There was Bob Pariseau, Jay Miner, Dave Morse, and a couple of hardware guys. That was about it."

The software side was even emptier. "I was the second software person there," he says, "Sam Dicker was the first person."

In the early part of development, as he became familiar with the chipset, Luck worked closely with Jay Miner. "He was great," says Luck. "He was fun and easy to work with, a good manager and very intelligent. He had some stories about being on a Navy ship which were kind of funny."

Luck began planning the low-level code that would allow Daphne to dis-play graphics. "My contribution was the graphics library in the ROM," says Luck. "The blitter stuff in terms of software, and I invented the hardware line draw using the blitter. I programmed the screens how they moved up and down. You could have multiple screens that were at different resolutions."

Carl Sassenrath - System Kernel

After finding Dale Luck, Bob Pariseau continued harvesting engineers from Hewlett-Packard. He needed someone to program the kernel of the Amiga operating system, the central part that would execute code, manage memory, allow access to hardware, handle drivers, and integrate with a disk operating system. In August, he found a promising HP engineer named Carl Sassenrath.

Sassenrath was born in 1957 and grew up in the seaside town of Eureka, California. As a child his hobbies included electronics, amateur radio, photography, and filmmaking. In 1970, at the age of 13, he became a cameraman for the local PBS station. A year later he became a cameraman for an ABC affiliate broadcasting television station named KVIQ. He worked his way up to technical director, overseeing news broadcasts, commercials, and local programming.

In 1976, using the income he raised working at KVIQ, he entered University of California, Davis, graduating in 1980 with a degree in Electrical Engineering and Computer Science.

Sassenrath briefly considered a career in the military. "When I graduated from college I looked into joining the military to give a few years of service to the country," he says. "I looked at the Navy, specifically its nuclear Navy. I went down for the interviews and met this Admiral Rickover guy that was running the nuclear Navy at the time."

While he was considering the Navy he received an offer from the top company in Silicon Valley. "[The Navy] sounded interesting to me but I got an offer from Hewlett-Packard. And HP at the time was the company to work for in engineering. They were very engineering friendly and engineering innovative. So I went to work for Hewlett-Packard."

Sassenrath worked for Hewlett-Packard at the same time as Dale Luck but found it less appealing than he imagined it would be. "I worked for them for a few years and I got kind of discouraged because of the internal politics and all the things that are part of a big company," he explains. "I joined Hewlett-Packard because I wanted to learn from the best and I was kind of disappointed that HP had these various failings in terms of the way they built products and the way they managed people. Don't get me wrong, it was a great company but it wasn't as good as I thought it could be."

In 1981, he took a break and joined the Antarctic research team from Stanford University as a research scientist at the South Pole. "I was flipping through an electronics magazine, a professional career kind of magazine, and in the back there was an ad for Antarctica," he recalls. "They were looking for someone who was both a computer person and also had the scientific background to do this work in Antarctica. I went up and talked to them and it sounded kind of interesting so I ended up getting into that whole Antarctica thing."

The 24-year old expected Antarctica to be the ideal place for scientific exploration. "It was pretty exciting and adventurous but I was pretty young and idealistic when I went down there," he says. "I figured Antarctica, man you can't mess up down there or everyone dies. So I figured this has got to be as perfect as we get in terms of its organization and management."

Sassenrath arrived at the Amundsen–Scott South Pole Station in late September of 1982. The region has 6 months of daylight followed by 6 months of night—literally one solar day per year. With temperatures as low as -100° F (-73° C), the camp had a large geodesic dome to protect the wooden buildings from the elements. "There were 17 of us, the permanent people, and three of us were scientists and the other 14 were support personnel," he recalls. "They were the ones that ran generators and cooked the food and ran the radios and all that kind of stuff to keep the base going. And then there were three of us that were the scientists that ran the experiments and collected all the data."

Research at the station focused on the upper atmosphere. "It was actually an interesting year because one of my coworkers down there ran the air quality experiments, air sampling. One day he said, 'You gotta come out to my lab.' That was really far away from the main base because it had to have completely pure air."

Sassenrath trundled out to his colleague's outpost and became one of the first people to learn of thin spots in the ozone layer. "He's showing me these plots and stuff. He's saying you know it looks like there's a hole in the ozone layer. This is really interesting if you look at these. They look like there is a hole in the ozone and that's where the holes in the ozone first appear were over the poles because earth is rotating and the atmosphere tends to bow out around the equator."

The isolated conditions he experienced were similar to those in *The Thing* (1982). The movie so well depicted the living conditions at the South Pole that it became an annual tradition for the crew at the Amundsen–Scott South Pole Station to view the film on the first evening every winter. "The more interesting and eye-opening part of it for me was just the psychological side of it. People can get a little strange in places like this," observes Sassenrath.

When his six months were up in late March 1983, Sassenrath was looking forward to leaving. "When I was there, I actually found it was kind of the opposite. It was chaos. It was gross mismanagement and it was very political. So it was completely the opposite of what I was looking for."

Upon returning from the South Pole, HP extended an offer to Sassenrath that he couldn't refuse. "If you come back to Hewlett-Packard you can do whatever you want. You don't have to have a boss."

Sassenrath accepted. "I thought well that's a really interesting offer. I took them up on that and went back to Hewlett-Packard and I did a lot of fun stuff there." At the time, HP was an alpha-test site for SmallTalk, an object oriented programming language developed at Xerox PARC. "Xerox PARC had done a fabulous job creating it and making the whole Smalltalk environment. There was that going on and I got involved in that."

As Sassenrath learned more from Xerox PARC, and learned of GUI based operating systems, he tried to convince HP to develop a GUI OS. "HP didn't make anything like that but I was trying to convince them to build some bitmap graphic computers," he recalls. "But I was up against a whole bunch of people who said no, there is no future in that. Having character mapped graphics is the way to go, it really conserves a lot of memory, it's much more efficient, it can refresh faster. All these arguments."

Sassenrath endeavored to show HP what a true GUI system was capable of. "I found this kid working on a system up at Stanford and his name was Andy Bechtolsheim and he was building something he called the Sun Workstation," he recalls. "He really didn't have anyone doing any programming on it. He had gotten it running. Its operating system came up running UNIX. It barely came up and had this really minimal graphics library but I convinced him to give me one of the few prototypes that he had built."

Now Sassenrath had something on which he could demonstrate a GUI for HP. "I got one of them, brought it back to Hewlett-Packard and then over the next month or so I built a user interface that had a mouse and a pointer on the screen and fonts and windows and all that stuff. It was kind of cobbled together but it worked and it worked well enough to show the concept and started to get other people at HP interested in the idea." He called his demo the Probus (professional business) workstation.

When Sun released the SUN-1, HP was one of its first customers. "I got HP to buy some of these very first units of the SUN-1 from him. We bought 4 or 5 of them and started programming and really building this concept of windowing and graphic user interfaces." The features for Probus were impressive, including a bitmap display, icons, fonts, a mouse, hyperlinks, and remote procedure calls to a database server.

With demo in hand, Sassenrath showed it to as many people as he could at HP. "We actually proposed the project then at Hewlett-Packard to build the ultimate business machine. It's hard now in this era to even imagine what computing was like before a mouse or any kind of pointing device. It was all text based. It was all scrolling console style text windows. So it was really eye-opening for people to see this demo. We would go around Hewlett-Packard and we even showed it to the president of the company. And everyone's like wow this looks like it could be the future."

The demo paid off and HP agreed to start a project for a GUI based computer system. "The result of that was HP reorganized and they decided to start a division to work on that. But at the same time in that time frame, that's when the PC was coming out." Instead of a pure bitmapped graphics machine, HP decided to create a hybrid IBM PC machine. "We'll put those two together in the same division, form this new division in Sunnyvale and work on those projects. And I was like no, this is not an IBM PC. We're getting it totally wrong here guys."

The rift between the visions at HP caused Sassenrath and his team to begin looking for work elsewhere. A friend who had interviewed at Amiga and turned them down in favor of a job at Symantec ended up telling Sassenrath about Amiga. "The thing that really hyped me about the Amiga was I had this problem where there were no good inexpensive bitmap display systems around. The Sun was a fairly expensive computer. Back then it was $25,000 for a Sun computer. And when I went to interview, Bob Pariseau had on the wall this block diagram. The block diagram actually showed the basic architecture of the Amiga and its DMA channels, co-processor, that kind of thing. And it was all built in VLSI. Jay Miner was like, 'You know, we're going to build this all out of chips. We're not going to wire wrap the boards or make big boards, we're going to make this all on a chip. Even Sun wasn't doing that at the time. So I was like, 'Wow this is fantastic. All this capability and these chips will really do exactly what I need to do.'"

Amiga ended up giving Sassenrath the kind of open-ended offer he couldn't refuse. "I went in for the interview and they made me an offer by the time I finished the interview there. The promise was you can come here and write whatever operating system you want. We don't care what it is. It's your vision."

The scrappy, underfunded Amiga had just won out over Silicon Valley's stalwart HP. "At that point a bunch of us quit. The whole team. I quit as well."

Life at Amiga

The three programmers, Dale Luck, Carl Sassenrath, and Sam Dicker all worked out of the software office with Bob Pariseau. The office inspired a dreary name. "They were windowless rooms that were totally dark," recalls Sassenrath. "We called it the software cave. The desks were just jammed in there because we were a little startup company and couldn't afford nice cubicles. We left the lights off and we each had a little desk lamp."

Contrary to being detrimental, the close quarters fostered a spirit of cooperation. "It was kind of nice because we communicated really well that way," says Sassenrath. "You could easily hear what others were doing and make comments and suggestions. It really did unify the team early on. I think that's why the Amiga team was such a tight knit team because of those early days."

At the head of the software team was Bob Pariseau. "Bob was really interesting," says Sassenrath. "Managing engineers is not an easy thing to do. You can piss them off pretty quickly. But he had a style about him in the way that he managed the project and followed up with what you're doing, got your status that was totally non-hierarchical. I think he deserves a lot of credit for the creation of the Amiga because he had this fabulous management style that was very encouraging. It made us want to work together as engineers and really try to achieve this whole dream. Bob was pretty incredible."

The Amiga development team had a surprisingly clear focus on documentation early in the project. " Rob Peck came in to do documentation," says Dale Luck. "He started very early because he was helping to get the documentation ready so the software guys would have something more than just scribbled notes to work with. Then we started getting some QA people and some software people."

Amiga purchased a state-of-the-art Apple Lisa computer to produce the documentation. "We'd actually bought a Lisa and a Mac for the software group because we've got this great publications guy who was documenting and writing up the stuff we had done," recalls Ron Nicholson. "In fact he was keenly responsible for copying down some of the stuff that Joe had on a whiteboard and actually putting it in hard documentation before the cleaning people could wipe it off."

Amiga Exec

Both Dale Luck and Sam Dicker had developed code that displayed graphics and played sound. To integrate their code together with the operating system would require a different approach that was years ahead of competing operating systems.

The kernel of Sassenrath's operating system was called the Exec. This miracle of programming for 1983 allowed the operating system to run more than one program at a time. "He wrote the multitasking kernel of our machine," says RJ Mical. "Carl did the Exec, and that thing was a work of art."

Sassenrath was able to begin developing Exec without any of the Amiga chips because he only required the 68000 processor, which the Sage IV systems all contained.

The ubiquitous whiteboards often came in handy when things became complicated for the programmers. "Dave Morse liked to have one wall in each of the rooms that was a white board," says Sassenrath. "It was the very beginning of whiteboards. Whiteboards were really cool technology, right. He'd make sure that one of the walls was just a whiteboard from wall to wall and ceiling to floor."

Peace

Ron Nicholson had been working on a motherboard since April 1983. It was merely meant to prove the Motorola 68000. "The first one was just to demonstrate that we knew how to build-in the 68000 and get proper timing out of it," he says. "I knew we could do it with the Mac but I wanted to demonstrate to Jay and Dave that we were competent and knew something. The first one I actually wired up myself."

His next two motherboard designs would incorporate the Daphne, Portia and Agnus chips. "The second two had empty sockets for the three chips," he recalls.

Instead or wire wrapping his own board this time, he had a Santa Clara company called Twin Industries manufacture a proper PCB. "The other two I contracted out and finished off when they came back. Of those two that came back, I only got one working reliably." The first motherboard, which he stuffed with components in roughly October, he named Peace.

Carl Sassenrath was responsible for the "bring up"; creating the code to allow access to the computer, such as running executable files. "I had to get it running so that Dave Needle and everyone else could plug in their prototype chips," says Sassenrath.

The first attempt did not go well. Before Sassenrath could begin programming his operating system, he needed to work with Ron Nicholson, who was designing the Amiga system board. "I was writing the operating system and his main component of the system was really the motherboard," recalls Sassenrath. "But when he delivered the first motherboard to me it didn't work."

The software and hardware designers did not get along at first. "Those teams always have a little bit of friction," says Sassenrath. "Why doesn't your board boot? The first real Amiga board he gave me didn't work. We had some words about that."

After some study, and some help from Dave Needle, the problem was traced to the system board design. "I had to go through it with the scope and I found that he hadn't tied down all the interrupt lines," says Sassenrath. "There were a lot of floating pins on the 68000 so it was getting messed up, just from noise on the pins." It was now possible to run code directly on the hardware.

Nicholson finished the second revision of the motherboard in December 1983, which he called "War". Now the team had two motherboards, *War and Peace*, named after the novel by Leo Tolstoy.

However, War proved to be problematic. "I think Dave Needle was unhappy with me that I couldn't get the second one working because he had more experience breadboarding and stuff like that."

Disk Operating System

The team was able to load demos onto the Peace motherboard with the help of the Sage IV system, simply by loading memory from Sage into the Peace RAM using a simple stub of an OS written by Carl Sassenrath. "I'd written a little demo, what was called the demo file system that all of the hardware engineers and testing teams were using to verify the chips and load all the demos that we had when we went to CES," says Sassenrath. "It was a little file system I wrote that was 10K and it actually worked really well, it loaded really fast."

This worked for bootstrapping a prototype demo but they needed a more formidable Disk Operating System, or DOS. Pariseau contracted a small company to develop the Amiga DOS. "It was a small contracting company of three or four guys that were supposed to get it done," recalls Sassenrath.

The operating system would resemble Unix, the engineer's favorite operating system. "It was a file system but very Unix-like," says Sassenrath. "The implementation was also Unix-like because the design of Unix had been published in the *Bell System Technical Journal*. These guys were kind of following that design."

Bob Pariseau hoped to have the DOS ready by CES in January 1984. Unfortunately, the contractors were not up to the task. "I think they had other contracts going on and they neglected us a lot," recalls Sassenrath. "They would show up and they wouldn't have much progress and things were going very poorly on that project. We'd fly down there and visit and they would not have much to show us. I don't know if they were in over their head or what the deal was but it wasn't going really well."

As the date inched closer towards CES, it became more and more doubtful the company would have the DOS ready in time.

RJ

In early September 1983, Amiga hired another programmer, RJ Mical. Like sound designer Sam Dicker before him, Mical came from arcade manufacturer Williams Electronics and had worked on the arcade game Sinistar. "RJ was one of the junior programmers on my last game at Williams in Chicago," says Sam Dicker. There, Mical was responsible for game logic and visual effects.

The employees all received a stake in the company. "The best companies that I've been involved with are the ones where everyone owns a piece of the action," says Mical. "Amiga was one of them where, be ye big or little, you've got a stake in the company. Some of the more significant guys were up in the five to seven percent range."

As a new employee, Mical received his stake, but not as much as the founders. "My piece was small, but I'm not sneering at it," he says. "It was well worth it to get a chance to come out to California, join up with all these wacky people, and do that company together."

Mical's first task at Amiga was to create the software library that would allow programmers to animate and manipulate graphical elements. Mical would go on to name his system GELs, short for Graphical Elements.

Mical embraced his new mission with a hyperbolic sense of humor and fun. Dave Needle recalled, "The first time I saw RJ, I'm working at Amiga in the early '80s and I know I'm gonna like this guy because he's rushing down the hallway pushing people saying, 'Get out of my way, I'm a busy guy.' It was amazing. There was energy and vibrancy and power, and that was the kind of thing I was looking for. I knew that was the right kind of person to be working with."[1]

Dale Luck, who was working on the low-level graphics code, worked closely with Mical on the graphics library. When Luck first met Mical, he thought Amiga Corp. was hiring straight from high school. "He's so bubbly and full of energy. When he first started, I thought, 'Here's this young kid that's coming in from Chicago. This guy is a really young boy.' Then I found out he was actually older than I was, and I thought, 'This guy, he's got a really young heart.' And I really admired that in him."

The two programmers became fast friends. "He was the greatest guy," says Luck. "He has this Chicago accent. Of course, I had also come from the Midwest so my accent wasn't too far away."

"Dale is a brilliant engineer and a warm, loving, compassionate, decent, kind, excellent human being," gushes Mical. "He is one of the best humans I've had the pleasure to get to know well in my whole life."

Bob "Kodiak" Burns

In October, Pariseau hired a third programmer from Hewlett-Packard named Bob Burns. An experienced engineer, Burns had worked with HP for over four years.

Unfortunately, the Amiga programming group now faced a crisis as they had reached the upper limit of Bobs. "In the old days, before I moved to California, I used to be known mostly as Bob, but when I went to California to help build the Amiga I became one of four Bobs in the Amiga software team," recalls RJ Mical. "During the first week that we worked there together, so many people came in the room and said, 'Hey, Bob' that we all got whiplash."[2]

In programing, unique names are used to keep track of variables. When the Amiga programmers were faced with too many employees with the same name, they did what any good programmer would do and changed the variable names. "So the boss got to be Bob [Pariseau] while suddenly the rest of us became Rob [Peck], RJ [Mical] and Kodiak [Burns]. That's Kodiak as in the Kodiak bear. And for good reason."

---

1   *Wired* magazine. January, 1994. "Third Time's a Charm (They Hope)"

2   *Info Magazine* Issue 13, Jan/Feb 1987. p. 46. "How We Created the Amiga Computer" by Robert J. Mical.

Now that Amiga had five programmers, they had exceeded the four terminal limit of the Sage IV. This could be temporarily overcome by having one round of programmers come in at night, but with Pariseau wanting to log in to check on code, it made sense to obtain another Sage IV system. In keeping with 1860's Russian novels, they named one system "Crime" and the other " Punishment" after the Fyodor Dostoyevsky novel.

At Amiga, "Kodiak" was tasked with the multifaceted job of OS subsystems. This would eventually include drivers for the keyboard, mouse, joystick and printers. He would also program the text display, which included the font subsystem, and functions such as copying and pasting from a virtual clipboard in memory.

Burns' job was surprisingly complicated. Eventually he became the guy who handled the text. "Bob worked on some of the device drivers like the print device driver and fonts," explains Sassenrath. "He and I actually did a flow diagram from when you press the key on the keyboard through all of the different modules of the system that key had to travel to print the letter A out on the screen. It was a neat diagram but it took the whole wall to describe it. By today's standards it's simple but back then we were like, 'Wow, this is amazing how much has to happen just for the letter to come out on the screen.'"

Dancing Fools

Since he began at Amiga, Carl Sassenrath had planned out the features he wanted to include in the operating system. This being a video game console, the developers had no ambition to upgrade it once it was completed. "The original idea was to put the entire system; all the graphics, all sounds, kernel, file system, everything was to be put into ROM," explains Sassenrath.

Sassenrath had completed most of his Exec but he needed a way to load in the parts of the operating system his coworkers contributed. "As I was developing the Exec and getting all that running, there was RJ and Dale and Sam Dicker and folks that were also working on their parts of the system," explains Sassenrath. "To be able to build the system, you had to put them all together and link them and run the tools over them basically to get them loaded into ROM. And the synchronization on that was way too complicated and difficult to do."

This chaos led Sassenrath to rethink the operating system into something more manageable. "So I came up with this system of modularizing all of that code into libraries. That was the birth of dynamic libraries," he explains. "The first was the ROM library. And when the system booted it actually scanned the ROM and looked for what libraries were in it, built a list of libraries, and then initialized them all. It was a really cool modular system."

He called the first part of the operating system Kickstart, which shared similarities to a modern day BIOS (Basic Input/Output System). "It's a lot more powerful than a BIOS though," says Sassenrath. "Kickstart is the loader at the beginning of the Exec that gets things going. When you see the Kickstart want the floppy disk [the Workbench], we're talking about the old original design, it's already got most of the system running from the ROM, so it's just waiting for you to load in the disk and then from the disk there's some script files that actually initialize the rest of the system. You can bring in any additional libraries, device drivers, that kind of thing."

By September 1983, all three chips were simulated on breadboards. However, because of the many wire connections, they were error prone. Miner recalls, "Those were a nightmare to keep running with all the connections breaking down." The circuit boards had no cooling system, so they threw off enough heat to make the air shimmer when in use.

According to RJ Mical, the engineers constructed a special area for the massive chips using anti-static flooring and walls. The room was wide enough for one person to enter, much like a confessional booth. Mical claims they also placed signs saying, 'Ground Thyself', which gave him the impression he was entering an altar to a technology God.

In the same month, the software group had enough information to begin programming their software libraries, giving them only four months to program everything before CES. During this time, the key programmers sometimes turned in 100-hour weeks.

The software developers began to appreciate the economical Sage IV computer. "The Sage computer was a remarkable machine," says Mical. "It was a 68000 machine that was an extremely low-cost, wonderfully high-powered multi-user computer. It could support up to four users and it did a darned good job of it."

In the early stages of software development, the computer was ample for the programmers, but things soon changed. "It was a four user computer and we ended up with ten users," says Mical. "If you think four people compiling at the same time made it slow, try five or six or seven."

Soon the engineers began calling the Sage IV " Agony". The programmers adopted a routine of adding a few lines of code to their program, then waiting for it to compile. "If you changed one of the critical data structures that are at the heart of the system, you ended up having to recompile the whole system in order to make sure everything is fresh," says Mical. "When we did that, it could go five or even ten minutes, sometimes 15 minutes if you were doing a full load. We used to find interesting ways to fill the time when we had to do that."

The hardware engineers like Jay Miner worked for long uninterrupted periods and then took catnaps for a few hours. Dale Luck found it more efficient to work his sleep schedule around the compiler. "We had this program that we created for the Sage called 'beep', and if you typed 'beep' your computer made a loud obnoxious sound," explains Mical. "Our computers had a type-ahead buffer where you could type more instructions than what you could see on the screen. Dale would type the commands to do his builds, then type ahead the command 'beep', so that when the build was done it would execute the command 'beep' and make this loud obnoxious sound." The engineers made sure to add this feature into the Amiga's own command line interface.

"Dale had a pillow on his lap, and he would type in the build command, type in the 'beep' command, then put his head down on his pillow and fall asleep for five minutes," recalls Mical. "The computer would say, 'Beep!' and he would sit up and get back to work. It was the most astonishing thing. He would sneak in five minutes of sleep here and there."

With September the hottest month in Los Gatos, heat became an issue. "Boy did we need fans in those days," says Mical. "All the equipment we had jammed in those rooms threw off a lot of heat. The people who worked there slowly cooked as the day went by, so we always had fans running to move the air around. This type of ventilation system is also called a convection oven." As a result, it became more practical to work evenings and into the night to avoid the heat.

The after hours work also meant there were fewer programmers on the Sage system at night. "We did long late night builds," recalls Mical. "Dale and I would work through the night and just grind non-stop."

The two programmers fought a constant battle against fatigue. "We would need to keep ourselves pepped up," says Mical. "When the going got long and the trade show was tomorrow, you've got to deliver. So we would play loud music to keep us awake. We played Led Zepplin and the two of us would dance and dance to keep awake. We would dance together sometimes or just dance with your computer."

The regular Amiga employees were oblivious to the late night insanity of their programmers until one morning. "One of the sales guys shows up

early for work and gets there at 7 AM," recalls Mical. "The music is booming out of the software lab and he comes around the corner, and there's the
two of us dancing together in the middle of the room. Thereafter, we were
known as the dancing fools."

As CES approached, enough of the GELs system was programmed by
RJ Mical and Dale Luck to demonstrate the graphics and animation ca-
pabilities of the machine. The blitter objects were designated "BOB's" by
Mical, an ode to the number of Bobs present on the software team.

The software development process was strenuous, so Mical developed a
method to sooth his nerves using the Joyboard. According to Mical, "There
was a Guru Meditation game that we used to play on the Joyboard. You
would put the Joyboard up on a chair and then you would sit on it. The
game was to attempt to remain motionless for as long as you could stand it."

The Guru Meditation game became popular among all walks in the
company. "Almost all of the Amiga people were there to play: art, sales,
marketing, accounting, manufacturing, hardware, and software," says Mical. "We sat motionless atop high chairs with eyes closed and hands and
fingers raised in enlightened poses. Our legs were crossed, and beneath
our bottoms were Amiga Joyboards. There was a faint hum in the air, the
thought song of machine and man."

The designers loved the Guru Meditation game and decided to incorporate it into the operating system. When a system crash occurred, impatient
users were shown a 'Guru Meditation Error' on the screen.

Begging for an MMU

With a multitasking operating system, users could create programs that ran
at the same time. However, this posed problems if not implemented correctly. If a programmer created code that crashed, it could bring down
the whole operating system. "In all modern operating systems, programs
can crash one at a time," explains Carl Sassenrath. "A bug in one program
doesn't affect another program. We don't even think about that anymore.
We run a computer and we have a hundred tasks going, a hundred separate
computer programs written by several people and occasionally a browser
tab crashes or the word processor crashes or something like that, but it
doesn't take down the whole operating system."

Sassenrath wanted his operating system to be protected from bad code by
using something called an MMU. "Prior to the memory management unit,
a bug in one piece of software could affect the operation of another piece
of software. The entire memory space was writable and so a bug in one

program could corrupt data in another program. And that really limited the utility of a multitasking operating system."

Sassenrath was aware of the concept of the MMU, typically contained in higher-end computers of the time. "It was common in the UNIX world at the time," he says.

The MMU allocated a segment of memory to each program, called Virtual Memory; essentially segregating programs from one another. "We needed memory management hardware, so we couldn't really do virtual memory," he explains. "Everything was just in the same memory space and if you had a bug it could easily just trash other parts of the system and other applications."

Sassenrath argued for including an MMU into the Amiga system design. "Folks like Dale and myself were from the professional computing market that were already using MMU's and virtual memory," says Sassenrath. "In fact Dale showed how you could take a fairly small inexpensive memory chip and turn it into a memory mapping so that the Amiga memory could be mapped into different segments and that kind of thing. Some segments could be protected and other segments could get read-write access."

Unfortunately, with the focus on a games machine, the idea did not gain much traction. "But it added like 25 cents or 50 cents to do that," says Sassenrath. "And we pushed it pretty hard because we knew this particular memory issue but Jay was like, 'No. It's a game machine, it's not a computer. We do not need this.' It was a trade-off we made in the design early on because the focus was on the consumer market and not the professional market."

Due to this decision, Amiga would have to rely on third-party programmers coding very carefully so their programs did not interfere with one another. If one programmer of a single application made a mistake, it could bring down the entire OS. "It was pretty tricky. You had to obey all the rules really carefully," says Sassenrath.

CHAPTER 9

Help!
1983

After the video game crash, of 1983, Dave Morse realized his company could no longer fund its own operations. As the existing funds began to run dry, Morse began looking for options to keep Amiga afloat. He would start with the original investor, InterMedics. But if they couldn't keep Amiga alive, he would have to find someone else, and that would not make Inter-Medics happy.

Losing InterMedics

Dave Morse felt comfortable running a retail company, but when financial decisions started to get complicated, he wanted outside help. He turned to an old college friend named Bill Hart. A native of New York, Hart was a former IBM salesman who went back to get his MBA from Tuck School of Business, where he was a classmate of Dave Morse. "That's where our relationship began," recalls Hart. "We actually shared two halves of a duplex student housing building. We were both married when we went back to graduate school. Our families were friendly and then I went from there into the management consulting business and didn't have a lot of contact with Dave except perhaps Christmas cards and stuff like that."

Hart decided to throw caution to the wind and founded an investment company in the early eighties called Technology Partners. "I just decided to leave the management consulting business and start a venture capital firm," he says. "I didn't have any investment track record, and really no entrepreneurial track record. I had successfully solved a lot of difficult business problems and had a pretty strong information technology background."

Rather than aggressively looking for seed money, Hart quietly helped new companies in the hopes that the relationships would become mutually beneficial. "I began just building a network in Silicon Valley and trying to find worthy startup companies that I might be able to help," he says. "Writing business plans, lining up initial seed capital and that sort of thing. There was a real need for that at the time because the venture capital community wasn't going to pay a lot of attention to a pretty raw situation that needed a little bit more structure added."

Hart had last met with Morse in 1982 at Tonka Toys in Minneapolis, when Morse was contemplating becoming an entrepreneur. "The next thing I knew, I got a call from Dave and he said, 'Guess what? I'm here in California! We've moved and I'm running a startup company in Silicon Valley. Why don't you come down?'"

Hart became a business advisor to Morse, someone who would look out for his interests and not necessarily those of InterMedics. "I was still working with individual projects trying to build my track record so that I could actually raise a blind pool type fund," explains Hart, referring to the type of investment where the investors are not aware of which companies the fund will invest in. "I went to see Dave. He was fully funded by their corporate sponsor InterMedics, a cardiac pacemaker company."

Hart immediately saw the precariousness of the situation. He told Morse, "It looks like an interesting project, Dave. It's going to be challenging because you're in a marketplace with the big boys. Your money is coming from a company whose main businesses is somewhere else and you've got to be careful that you don't someday find the rug pulled out from under you."

"And sure enough that's exactly what happened," recalls Hart.

Four times per year, Morse was obligated to report the status of Amiga to the board of directors, which included investor and chairman O. Wayne Rollins. Morse would often bring support people from Amiga with him, such as the VP of finance. For the mid-October board meeting, Morse presented an honest report that included good news and bad news. The good news included sales of Power Sticks and the progress of the Amiga game system, whose chipset was now demonstrable with the prototype chip boards. The bad news, of course, was the video game crash.

O. Wayne Rollins had originally funded the company based on projections for a cheap 8-bit video game console that would fund itself on sales of products to the booming video game industry. The company would also be a source for ROM chip production of sister-company Xymos. When Jay Miner came on board, it evolved into an even more expensive 16-bit console. Now, with the video game crash, there was talk of making it a home computer with a keyboard and mouse. Miner and Morse hoped InterMedics would go along for the ride, putting their faith in the old saying, "In for a penny, in for a pound."

However, with the bottom falling out of the video game market and the daunting prospect of fighting against established companies like Apple, Commodore and even IBM with its forthcoming PCjr, the board of directors started to get cold feet. InterMedics also had problems of its own. "Their general business tanked on them and so the cash flow that they could have directed our way pretty much dried up," says Don Reisinger. "When you're depending upon a company like that for your funding and their business goes south, it is definitely going to impact you too."

In the fall of 1983, Rollins made a decision. "InterMedics ran into some FDA issues and their profits declined," recalls Hart. "They decided that they would withdraw their support from Amiga." The board told Morse to continue operations of the company and to fund it internally with sales, just like they agreed to earlier.

It seemed like Amiga Corporation could be heading for disaster. "When InterMedics stopped the funding, we were basically hand to mouth," says Reisinger. "Dave and Jay did a bunch of things to make sure that we were going to be making payroll and stuff like that."

To meet office expenses, Morse and Miner began charging as many of the expenses as they could to their personal credit cards. To make payroll every two weeks, they had to take drastic action. "I found out later that Dave Morse had sold his Porsche and Jay Miner had taken out a second mortgage on his house to float the company," says Ron Nicholson.

The gestures meant both men had extraordinary faith in the Amiga concept. "The computer was still viable as a personal computer and the work continued, but with severe financial restrictions," recalls Jay Miner. "It seemed like we owed money to every supplier in town. I had to mortgage practically everything I owned personally to help meet the company payroll."[1]

Morse remained steady, calm, and upbeat through this troubling period. "It comes down to the leadership of Dave Morse," says Reisinger. "He said, 'We will take care of this. Don't you worry about it and we'll get funding somewhere.' And at that time he brought Bill Hart in. Bill had been involved to a degree but really got very involved after the InterMedics thing fell apart. At that point he was much more visible in our place."

---

1 *Amiga User International.* June 1988. "The AUI Interview" p. 20

Hart recalls, "Dave called me and said, 'Well it happened. Can you come down? Maybe you can help.' I had visited previously but that was really my first serious collaboration with Dave on this."

Morse no longer needed general business advice, he needed cold, hard cash. "He called me because he knew he was going to have to find some funding to continue the company," says Hart. "While I didn't have the money all ready, I had been able to help other companies assemble that kind of money. I was his main business advisor as well. I proposed to Dave that I form a partnership and line up the funding that would get him through."

As he had done with other Silicon Valley companies, Hart essentially worked for free. "I didn't get a stake in the company directly, although subsequently I did get some stock options for the consulting help that I gave Dave," recalls Hart. "I never got paid anything and I didn't want to be paid anything when the company was struggling to survive."

Since early 1983, Amiga had invested in the development of almost a dozen unique video games. When Morse cancelled the Amiga Power Module, only a few of those dozen games made it to production as cartridges for the Joyboard. Morse later determined it was worth trying to salvage those costs and proceed with alternate plans to release those games.

At the June 1983 CES retailers had been more receptive to budget video game titles. Morse the marketer would employ a slightly different tactic by offering multi-game cartridges containing 2, 3, 4 or 5 titles in one cartridge and selling them at $30 to $40 retail.

Morse also intended to licence the rights to pre-existing Atari 2600 games and bundle them together. He went to Imagic, US Games, and Telesys for those titles and hoped to have five cartridges ready for the January 1984 Winter CES.

Atari Enters the Picture

While Morse salvaged the line of Atari 2600 games, Bill Hart tried to line up an angel investor for Amiga. And failed. "The venture capital community at the time didn't really have much of a record of funding consumer products companies," explains Hart. "At least the West Coast faction here. They were much more into backing business-to-business kinds of companies."

Most VC's were dubious of the investment due to the video game crash and the possibility of fighting with established computer companies like Apple and IBM. According to Hart, "We went ahead and the project progressed but it became increasingly clear that it was going to be difficult to get major venture capital money because of the stir that had been caused in the market by Apple, the Mac and IBM with what they called at the time the Peanut, which became the PCjr.

One by one, Hart visited the big angel investors, hoping one of them would fund Amiga. But the investors were astute and realized it would cost a lot more money to launch a computer. "We had many of the very top venture capitalists of the day in and they were all impressed with what we had but they thought the risks were very high," recalls Hart. "Plus I think everyone in the venture capital business at that time suspected, probably correctly, that it was a lot of money. So that was one of the big unknowns. 'If we invest in this, how much additional funding would be required over the first couple of years to get this thing established? Especially when you're against companies that have huge marketing budgets.'"

In many ways, a pool of smaller investors, who were more willing to roll the dice, worked better precisely because they were ignorant of what they were stepping into. "We finally reached the conclusion that we should keep talking to venture capitalists but probably there was a good chance we weren't going to get the money from this source," says Hart. "So we began to look for other funding sources."

To save Amiga, Morse and Hart decided to pay a visit to Jay Miner's old company, Atari Incorporated. As Miner knew, Atari would be looking to build an updated game console because many analysts cited the aging Atari 2600 technology as one of the key reasons for the video game crash. And Atari had the necessary funds and resources to help finish the chipset and fabricate chips.

In November 1983, Morse, Miner, and Hart approached Atari with their proposal. "The idea was that Atari would be able to use technology for purely a game machine and we would introduce a computer based on the same technology," explains Hart. "Any of the game software would work on the computer as well as on the Atari device."

The trio from Amiga met with their contact at Atari, Michael Albaugh, who, as a programmer, had assisted Miner and Decuir when they were designing the Atari 2600. Albaugh was a coin-op video game programmer and now had a foot in both the consumer division and the coin-op division of Atari.

The meeting allowed Miner to introduce the chipset technology to Atari. He came to the table with a detailed 38 page report on the Amiga chipset features. The purpose was to tantalize Atari with the chipset. The business arrangement was still up in the air at this point. "We entered into an agreement to negotiate a license agreement with Atari," says Hart.

The letter of intent was signed by Albaugh on November 21, 1983. Albaugh would later present it to Atari management in the hopes that it would spur development of a new video game console, and the chipset could also be used in Atari's coin-op video games.

The positive reception by Atari was a ray of hope at last for Amiga, and the firmest interest expressed by any company so far. For the time being, Amiga would attempt to hide from Atari just how desperate they were for cash.

If Atari accepted the licensing deal, it would be a beautiful arrangement for Amiga. They would have the money to continue development for the near future. Atari could worry about navigating the video game crash and Amiga could focus its efforts into a home computer instead. Now all they had to do was refocus their own engineers towards a vision of a personal computer.

Pivot

When RJ Mical was interviewed by Amiga back in September 1983, he noticed there was some ambiguity about the game console. "It was originally a console but we weren't sure exactly what it was going to look like," he says. "They told me when I was interviewing there, 'We're working on a game console. It's going to be a next generation thing; big and powerful and just run circles around the other guys.'"

Mical spotted some odd features for a game console. "I talked to the hardware guys as part of my interview process," he recalls. "I'm looking at this whiteboard and there's this port that's marked 'kbdprt', which is like, 'Keyboard port?' And there's this other box, 'extdrv'. External drive on a game console?"

Mical and his fellow engineers realized the game crash threatened everything. "Suddenly we were about to release a game console that no one was going to want," says Mical.

With the disfavor shown to video games, it would be a disaster to launch a video game console into the market. Retailers believed it had been just another fad. "It definitely almost took out Amiga since we were designing a game machine," says Ron Nicholson.

Silicon Valley entrepreneurs have become renowned for "pivoting" by changing course midway to release a different product to capture a larger market. Now, it looked like Amiga was due for a pivot.

As the video game crash solidified, and as Bill Hart went out looking for investors, the goal began to change. "I have a lot of the original documents from way back then regarding industrial designs and drawings, and some of their presentations to venture capitalists way back in 1983," explains Dale Luck. "In those designs, there was an Amiga, a mouse, a keyboard, and a monitor. It was a personal computer."

Jay Miner was the first to come up with a concept for the computer. "I drew several sketches for the outside of the computer showing a large IBM style box with lots of card slots and a large IBM keyboard," says Miner. "Dave Morse had his own ideas about what a computer should look like and he felt that the card slots were too expensive for the machine he wanted to sell."

Miner created seven different concept sketches to illustrate the potential for a unique look for the computer. The computer system would be modular and stackable, like stereo equipment. Early sketches show a base unit, which slid open like a drawer for storing the keyboard. The next unit contained a cartridge port and connectors for other devices. The top unit shows two floppy disk-drives side by side. It was a radically different approach to system design.

Amiga would now attempt to appeal to the same market opened up by the C64. "The original philosophy behind the Amiga was to capitalize on the rising consciousness people were having on computers," says Mical. "Computers like the C64 had become pervasive. There were millions of those things sold. A lot of people were getting used to not just having it as a toy, like the Intellivision and the [Atari] 2600. Instead, it was a system that you actually worked with and it came with a language."

The engineers wanted a home computer targeted to casual users. "We saw that the usefulness of these things in the office was going to end up in the home," explains Mical. "There was a different mentality for what you would do for software in the office and what you would do for software in the home. It was like somehow we became a different human being when we were in the office than when we were in our homes."

The Amiga computer would be accessible to anyone. "We set out to do a computer for the home that was easily understandable and easily usable by anyone," says Mical. "You could grasp the concepts of it and interact with it no matter how old you were. It would be a good, powerful computer that anyone could afford."

The vision for the new computer was formed between Miner and Morse. "Jay and Dave had an amazing vision that was well before its time," recalls Hart. "They said eventually people are going to have a computer in their home that's going to be the center of their entertainment system. It's going to be able to play games. It's going to be able to control their stereo and their TV and maybe eventually HVAC and so on. We think we can build a computer that would have those capabilities."

Due to the features of the chipset, especially Portia, pivoting wouldn't be too difficult. "We, by luck, stuffed enough of that into the Amiga that when we had the pivot, because Atari destroyed the game market, the Amiga was an acceptable personal computer," explains Nicholson. "As a purist, since I was given the goal to design a great game machine and an acceptable personal computer, I just considered it an acceptable personal computer. I would have done things very differently if I was told to design a personal computer multimedia machine. Which, in retrospect, I know I wasn't competent to design back then."

The key feature that allowed to team to pivot was the disk controller on the Portia chip. "It was a little thing in the corner that just happened to be a great asset when we definitely had to pivot and put in a disk controller," says Nicholson.

On the software side, when the team decided to switch from a game console to a home computer, Sassenrath and the programmers had very little to change. "It was a multitasking OS all along, from the beginning," says Mical. "It really wanted to be a computer."

The software developers would now attempt to create a full featured operating system called AmigaOS. "I started as manager of the graphics software," says Dale Luck. "We knew it was going to have preemptive multitasking. It wasn't clear what kind of GUI it was going to have, but we knew it was going to have some kind of graphical thing. It was going to be user friendly, it was going to have fantastic audio built in, it was going to have a [voice] synthesizer built in, and it was going to be great. It was really supposed to change the world at that time."

To design a graphical user interface at the operating system level, Bob Pariseau and Dave Morse approached the people who started it all. "We actually tried to hire someone out of Xerox PARC first since that has a big name for the people doing the leading edge software having to do with GUIs and user interfaces and stuff like that," says Nicholson. "But he looked at us and said this is impossible for you to do."

In many ways, the crash was a blessing in disguise. Now the engineers could focus all their energies on a true home computer. "Fortunately for us, it really was a computer and it only took a little bit of extra work to convert it from being just a game system into a full-blown proper personal computer," says Mical.

Lorraine and the Rush for CES

When Jay Miner worked for Atari, it was tradition to name prototype systems after wives and girlfriends. Pong was codenamed Darlene, the Atari 2600 was codenamed Stella[2], the Atari 400 was Candy, and the Atari 800 was Colleen. The early business plan by Larry Kaplan listed three prototypes after his wife and kids. At Amiga, CEO and President Dave Morse continued the tradition by naming the prototype Lorraine in honor of his wife.

After the hiring spree of software programmers, Morse spent time in September and October 1983 travelling to all the major computer magazines, industry pundits and even other industry players. His mission was to tantalize them by describing the incredible capabilities of the Lorraine computer. And most importantly, he invited them to come and visit Amiga's booth at the upcoming CES show, where he promised the in-person demonstrations would definitely show that this computer was like no other. By establishing these relationship early with the press, when the release came, it was likely they would cover Amiga.

As CES neared, hope began to fade for a working disk drive with the system. There were still too many bugs in the Portia chip and too many technical issues to figure out. Not to mention the company they had contracted to develop a disk operating system had utterly failed to perform any development. For now, to load demos into the system, the engineers used the Sage IV system and a terminal. Luckily the Sage IV was portable enough to travel to CES.

Lorraine could demonstrate most of its hardware features at the show. The 4-voice stereo sound was working, and the engineers were able to connect a standard speaker system to produce booming audio that would capture the attention of CES attendees. The keyboard was also working, thanks to the efforts of Bob "Kodiak" Burns. And Morse would bring along the concept sketches of the Lorraine to communicate the stylish vision they had for the computer.

Near the end of the year, as CES loomed on the immediate horizon, the software developers and engineers began practically living at the Amiga offices in order to finish the demos. "I remember there was a huge push around the end of '83 into '84," recalls Glenn Keller. "One of the things I

---

2   Stella was actually named after Joe Decuir's bike.

did which I regret is, I missed one of my sisters' weddings because of that. I was so involved in the thing, but I was sad."

In fact, most engineers and management were making personal sacrifices to their family lives in order to make the Amiga happen. At this point, there was no option. They had all invested so much in the product and to skip CES would be to miss out on potential investors to keep the project going.

The Divorce

By December, Bill Hart had succeeded in gathering together a number of small investors for Amiga under his investment fund Technology Partners. "I lined up the funding," says Hart. Together, the pool of investments amounted to a million dollars.

There was one big obstacle that prevented Hart from investing the money: InterMedics, which had ceased funding Amiga earlier in the year, still owned the company. "The problem was that the residual interest of Inter-Medics hadn't been resolved," explains Hart. "They still owned a hundred percent of the company."

Delicately, Morse and Hart would have to approach InterMedics, fronted by multi-millionaire O. Wayne Rollins and his lawyers, and tell them, "By the way, we'd like our company back now, please."

Dave Morse, adept as he was at actually running a business, was not as adept at handling the financial side of business arrangements. As a result, he did not even own a small sliver of Amiga, an unusual situation for a company founder and CEO. "At the time of the negotiation with Inter-Medics, they owned 100% of Amiga and its technology," says Hart. "They had promised equity to Dave but I'm not sure how binding that promise would have been."

As the sole owner of Amiga, InterMedics' role was to fund operations. Now that they had cut off funding, they became an anchor around the company's neck. Bill Hart needed to bring additional investors on board, but that would require gaining ownership back from InterMedics. "The money that I lined up wasn't going to go into the company until we resolved the issue of how we buy them out," says Hart. "We made it clear that there would be no investment by Technology Partners in Amiga without satisfactory settlement of this issue."

As Morse's business advisor, Hart had attempted several times to clear up the situation with InterMedics. "We kept asking to get together with the InterMedics people and they kept deflecting us until we got a call in December," says Hart. "All of a sudden there is great urgency to get together with us to resolve the issue."

The meeting would take place on Rollins' home turf. "We were invited to come to a meeting in Lake Charles, Louisiana at the offices of the attorney for the owner of InterMedics," says Hart.

That owner, of course, was O.Wayne Rollins. Now that the relationship with Amiga was somewhat strained, Rollins let his lawyers handle the face-to-face meeting entirely. "So we met with them on the 31st of December 1983. The reason I remember that clearly is because we flew in the night before and we had hoped to get out of there and get home for New Year's Eve. We were thinking that perhaps we can get this thing resolved in a few hours."

The meeting did not get off to a good start. "It was sort of farcical because we walked in there and there was nobody there from the company," says Hart. "The lawyers had been charged with negotiating this and we didn't even have a lawyer with us. So we sat down with them and their idea of how to negotiate with us was fairly strong armed. They yelled and shouted and postured."

The two tried their best to present their side of the case to the lawyers from Rollins Inc. "The kind of deal we have to have is one that will allow me to induce the investors I have lined up to put their money in," explains Hart. "If I don't like the deal, I'm not going to do that. I'll just look for something else. We've got to come up with something worthwhile or we could go home without a deal."

The attorneys had clearly been given different instructions and did not respond well to the proposal at first. "These guys would yell at us. 'If you think you are going to steal this company out from under us, you are mistaken!'"

The two remained patient. "Dave and I are fairly low key guys and we just kept caucusing and coming back and telling them the same thing," says Hart. "Dave could be tough when he needed to be but generally came across as a pretty easy going guy."

The reason Morse and Hart were so calm was because they knew they just needed to wait as the clock ticked closer to midnight before the Inter-Medics people would have to strike a deal. Any deal. "The one thing that Dave and I knew, and we didn't bring it up because it wouldn't have been smart, was there was a reason we were sitting there on December 31st. And that was, if they didn't have a deal by the end of the day, InterMedics would have to write off its investment of about five million dollars in Amiga," explains Hart. "I believe their auditors were going to insist on recognizing this loss in 1983, if the matter had not been settled."

With the tax year ending, and InterMedics having to perform an audit up to the December 31 period, they had a deadline to the auditors. "Clearly Amiga was a distressed company at the time and any reasonable auditor would have required them to reserve the full amount of their investment as a likely loss," explains Hart. "And we understood that. We knew that they weren't about to walk away from that table without a deal."

Hart tried to offer a deal that was likely to equal the amount invested, or perhaps give InterMedics a small profit on its investment. "We calmly and steadily worked our way through it," says Hart. "We were telling them that the only way the company can survive was to raise more money and that the only way we were going to raise more money is if there was enough equity for the new investors and for management. The fact that they put a lot of money in was irrelevant. What mattered was we could give them a deal that might give them a reasonable chance of recovering their investment."

InterMedics essentially wanted Amiga to pay back the investment it had made in the company. "InterMedics claimed the venture owed them for support of its operations up to that time, something in the $5 to $7 million range as I recall," says Hart.

Throughout the day, the lawyers went back and forth to speak with Rollins and explain the offer that was on the table. "I'm sure that they were told to try to get 50% or something like that," says Hart. "They didn't want to have to go back and tell their client that they couldn't do it. So they were caucusing a lot as well talking to the client and the client was probably talking to his board. There was a lot of behind the scenes stuff going on."

As the day wore on, it was becoming clear to InterMedics that the way to recoup its investment was to give Amiga a fighting chance. "Their alternative was to record a substantial loss on the investment they had made," says Hart. "InterMedics was already dealing with some operating setbacks in their pacemaker business, so further losses might have had a substantial adverse impact on their shareholder value."

Late in the day, with both parties mentally exhausted, a deal was struck. InterMedics would not have to add another $7 million loss to its annual report. "We finally reached a tentative agreement and signed a Letter of Intent," says Hart. "In return for forgiveness of the debt, we agreed to give them 25% of the then existing equity. We called our wives and said we're not making it home for New Year's and came home the next day."

So much had gone wrong for Amiga, but for once something went right. The timing of the InterMedics compromise was in Amiga's favor. Amiga had been low-key about their computer up to this point. There was no buzz about the company or its computer. Now, with the January 1984 CES a few days away, that was all about to change. Amiga would soon seem like a very valuable company indeed.

Boing!
1984

After formally obtaining 75% ownership of Amiga Corporation from InterMedics, Dave Morse and Bill Hart were now in a race to find investments in the company to continue operations. Their big push would come at CES where they hoped to lure investors. Meanwhile, Atari had already lined up to do business with Amiga for the chipset. If things went well, Amiga Corporation would soon have the money to fabricate its chipset.

The Boing Demo

The Amiga engineers had worked almost non-stop through Christmas 1983 preparing the Lorraine prototype for the CES show. Now they had to disassemble the prototype and prepare it for a short flight to Las Vegas. Transporting the prototype was a nightmare. "There was a core of us engineers who went to every show because the system was so fragile," says RJ Mical. Rather than shipping the chipboards separately, they packaged them carefully in boxes and brought them aboard the flight.

Once at the show, Jay Miner had a chance to survey the competition along with the 90,000 other attendees. Atari was there, still showing off the Atari 800XL, which was a small update to the Atari 800 that Miner himself helped design years earlier.

Commodore was also there, triumphantly announcing revenues of a billion dollars. However, its latest computer, the Plus/4, was greeted with a resounding 'So what?' Apple was not at the show but it would debut its comparatively primitive black and white Macintosh in the same month. Looking at the rival machines, Miner must have felt a degree of satisfaction; his computer was ahead of the competition by at least half a decade.

Despite the video game crash in 1983, Dave Morse decided to bring Atari 2600 Power-Sticks, Joyboards and games to CES. "It was something to occupy everybody's time when they were waiting to get in to see the demos more than anything else," says Don Reisinger. "Once the market fell, there was really no reason. We didn't even need to bother to bring this stuff but we figured what the hell, we've got the space."

It was one last attempt to turn their efforts into cash and to carefully control who got to see the Lorraine. "At the first CES, we were concealing what we were really doing, or at least attempting to," says Mical. "There was the external portion of the booth where any casual visitor could see a display of joysticks, Joyboards, peripheral products, and some software that we had created that used these devices."

Only select industry people would be allowed to view the Lorraine, provided they signed the appropriate non-disclosure agreement. "Keeping it quiet was just because we believed we had an excellent idea," says Mical. The joysticks and Joyboards were merely a distraction. "It was what we told people we were doing, while meanwhile, what we were really doing was kept under wraps."

According to Mical, the ruse worked. "I believe until the end it was a well kept secret," he says.

Amiga rented a simple gray booth in the West Hall at CES with an enclosed space behind the public display to show off the Lorraine. Unfortunately, the enclosure had no ceiling, so crafty attendees snuck glimpses of the Lorraine by riding up the escalators and craning their necks as they reached the top.

" There was a guarded door that let you into the inner sanctum," recalls Mical. "You had to be with one of us to be able to get through the door. On the inside was the computer. It was still in its prototype stage and we had the three chips in their prototype form on a table with a skirt around the table."

Morse made sure the software engineers presented the demos that they had put so much work into. "He was the kind of guy who wasn't interested in taking credit for things," says Bill Hart. "He wanted to see his people get credit for their creative genius."

Bob Pariseau, VP of software, led the choreographed demonstrations of the Lorraine to a succession of groups. "There was a whole presentation that we made," says Mical. "We talked about the machine and [Bob Pariseau] stood up in front and gave the spiel."

Pariseau had a light heart that made his presentations appealing. "He was one of the guys there with a good sense of humor," says Ron Nicholson.

The Lorraine looked rough and unfinished to most potential investors, lacking even a case for the system board, so the engineers had to reassure them the final product would look better. "That was part of the spiel," says Mical. "We had to explain, 'This is the state of it right now but we're going to take all of these big stacks of silicon and chips and wires that you see here and turn it into three chips. It's going to be a nice little computer that is going to look like these drawings someday.'"

The Lorraine hardware was incredible for 1984, especially compared to companies like Apple, Atari, IBM, and Commodore. "We had various interesting whiz-bang demos that we put together to exercise the various capabilities of the system," says Mical. "One engineer would sit at the computer console and launch one demo after another to show off all the capabilities."

Through the first day of the show and well into the evening, Mical and Luck programmed. "We never stopped working," says Mical. "We were constantly refining and polishing the demos, making them more impressive and exciting."

The experience was amazing for the two programmers, who finally had a chance to explore the machine in a creative way. Mical was no stranger to flashy graphics and sound, having come from the arcade company Williams Electronics. The two programmers planned to create an ambitious demo showing a large, rotating, checkered polygon ball bouncing up and down on the screen.

They called it the Boing Demo and it would become one of the most iconic demonstrations of a new computer. Mical and Luck developed the demo in C language. "We had stayed up all night working on the Boing demo," says Mical. "The sales and marketing would just love us because every day they would come in during the trade show itself and there would be the two of us exhausted in one of the back conference rooms sleeping with our heads resting on the table."

The demonstration stunned those who saw it. Not only was there a smoothly animating 3D sphere spinning and bouncing on screen, but it was big! Behind the ball was a shadow, flawlessly cast onto a purple grid. The illusion was perfect. Where the shadow fell, the grid darkened appropriately. No one had ever seen anything like it. It was an incredible vindication of the machine.

Sam Dicker also had an audio demo ready for CES which amused former Amiga contractor Joe Decuir. "We recorded a dog barking and then in the demo we hooked it up to some software and an [electronic synthesizer] keyboard," recalls Decuir. "If you pushed it with your left hand the dog is woofing [deep tone] and if you push it far on your right hand it's a Yip-yip-yip. So you can play four dogs barking at different frequencies at the same time. I saw this demo and it was hilarious."

Mical loved the demonstrations. "We had just a whole wonderful collection of demos," he says. "There was probably a dozen of them that we showed."

Dave Morse hoped that someone attending the demonstration would be interested in investing in the project. "I know Commodore visited," says Mical, referring to Commodore's VP of technology, Lloyd "Red" Taylor.

After CES, Amiga sent press releases to the major magazines announcing the features of the Lorraine. *Byte* magazine commented, "Joystick maker Amiga Corp. is developing a 68000-based home computer with a custom graphics coprocessor. With 128K bytes of RAM and a floppy-disk drive, the computer will reportedly sell for less than $1000 late this year."[1]

Creative Computing took a firmer stand on the Lorraine, with writer John J. Anderson proclaiming, "If there was a hit of the show for me, it had to be my first glimpse of the supermicro code-named Lorraine by Amiga." He went on to say, "As far as I'm concerned, the Lorraine demo was reason enough to have made the trip to Las Vegas."[2]

Anderson also urged Amiga to make the Lorraine compatible with the IBM PC software library, and also the IBM PCjr saying, "Okay, fellas. Let's put the Joyboard behind us and get credible."

The enthusiastic response lifted the spirits of the Amiga team; however, they received no additional investment offers. Amiga also failed to make any serious sales of their joysticks or games, confirming the Atari 2600 market was as good as dead. Money would soon become their most pressing issue.

There was one bright spot, however. Since meeting with Atari in November and presenting a description of the system, Atari had been able to present the chipset documentation to management and there was keen interest. Now that Atari executives and engineers had viewed the Lorraine graphics and sound in the metal, so to speak, they wanted to move forward

---

1 *Byte* magazine (April 1984), p.10.

2 *Creative Computing* magazine (April 1984), p. 150.

with negotiations to acquire the technology for a system of their own. Bill Hart even offered the possibility of Atari investing in the Amiga company, a deal that could potentially be beneficial to both parties.

Back to the Lab Again

Now that the back-room reveal at CES was over, it was time for the engineers and programmers to go home and turn their rough prototype into a working personal computer. But before they could do that, there was one other thing to deal with. "We went to the January 1984 [CES] show and the thing worked and it did its thing," recalls Glenn Keller. "We got back and a couple days later the breadboards stopped working. So Dave [Needle] debugs it."

After an anxious, prolonged search, Needle was able to narrow the problem down to a single mysterious cause. "He finds a missing wire. It's not there. Not like it was broken but a completely missing wire," recalls Keller. To the engineers, it appeared as though the wire was absent the whole time, even during CES. "The thing could have never worked. He put in the wire and the thing works. So how did that ever work at the show?"

To this day, the engineers continue to muse about the mysterious missing wire. "Nobody knows what happened but it's a nice story," says Keller.

With the problem rooted out, the programmers could continue development on the OS while the hardware engineers worked on the chip layout and motherboard.

At the January CES, Morse had been telling potential investors that Amiga planned to have working chips fabricated by April or May of 1984. This meant Amiga would have multiple working Lorraine computers available for demonstration at the next CES in June and possibly even developer systems for software houses.

All personal computers in 1984 came with the BASIC programming language, and that included Amiga. Company documents at the time curiously don't call it MS BASIC, but rather "Apple compatible" BASIC, perhaps wanting to ride on the coattails of Apple's success. They planned to include BASIC in a 64KB ROM, along with other system code.

RJ Mical credits Jay Miner with the vision for the system. "Jay was the whole hardware side of the system," says Mical.

It was a tall order for the Amiga team. After all, they were trying to create a computer superior to the Macintosh with far fewer resources than Ron Nicholson's former group. "The Mac group had massive resources, whereas the Amiga was done on a shoestring budget," says Nicholson. "We had everything we wanted in the Mac group. In the Amiga group, we struggled to buy the stuff for chips and boards or anything like that."

The lack of resources was most noticeable on the chip design. "With the Macintosh, we had two teams to do each chip," says Nicholson. "On Amiga we barely had one team on three chips." However, with Jay Miner there, seasoned veteran that he was, chip development progressed at a rapid rate.

The software spec was another tall order. Morse wanted to be able to show off the integrated text to speech package. Mical, Luck, and Sassenrath all had lots to do on the operating system and graphics libraries. Sassenrath, who had dabbled in GUI designs while at Hewlett-Packard, wanted a GUI for his OS.

Although at the time there was no concerted effort at developing a GUI for the Lorraine operating system, they knew they would have one eventually. Sassenrath wanted the GUI to include Windows, Icons, Menus, and a Pointer (WIMP). And if you have a WIMP GUI, you also need a mouse.

Owing to the well-received designs for the Amiga Powerstick, Morse returned to his contractor and hired him to design an Amiga mouse. "Not only did he do the joystick and the Joyboard based on some switching technology but we also chartered him to design the first prototype mice for the Amiga," recalls Nicholson.

Bill Hart and the Quest for Funding

In January, Morse and Hart dealt with the aftermath of Amiga's separation from InterMedics. Soon, Amiga would be primarily owned by Amiga employees. All that remained was to determine who owned what. Dave Morse, Jay Miner, and Bill Hart worked together to formalize an ownership plan.

Informal arrangements and agreements had been made with employees as they were hired by Amiga. Now it was time to give them their shares, along with InterMedics, and determine how much Bill Hart's investors would be entitled to.

Prior to the meeting, it had been agreed that InterMedics would have 25% ownership of Amiga, or two million shares. Now the three had to deal with the remaining 75%. The trio agreed on 50% ownership by employees, or 4 million shares. Of those, 500,000 shares were reserved for employee stock options. Morse and Miner, as cofounders of the company, would own the majority of the employee shares.

And finally, the remaining 25%, or two million shares, would be available for Bill Hart's investors at Technology Partners. Hart himself would receive a cut of the shares that he sold to his investors. The more he sold, the larger his cut.

Now that they had an idea of how the company ownership was divided, Morse and Hart had to agree on approximately how much the company was worth, in dollars. This was vital if Hart were to offer a fair sale price to his investors. "I discussed with him a valuation of the company that, of course, would define what my partnership stake would be," explains Hart, referring to his Technology Partners investors.

It was natural for Dave Morse to want to value the company higher, in order to make each share cost more. It was also natural for Bill Hart to want it valued lower, in order to maximize the ownership his investors received. This natural tension worked well for the pair to arrive at a reasonable and honest valuation of what Amiga was worth. After all, if Morse overvalued the company, Hart would be unable to sell shares.

In December, InterMedics had insisted that its cut of the company was worth $5.8 million dollars, or $2.90 per share. However, this was what InterMedics hoped one day to get back from Amiga. For now, the two arrived at a minimum share price of $2 per share. Hart could, by agreement, not sell shares for less than that price. "We had a tentative agreement on the valuation of the company," says Hart. With 8 million total shares valued at a minimum of $2, it meant they valued Amiga at somewhere north of $16 million dollars at the start of 1984. Confirmation of this valuation would arrive later if investors indeed purchased shares for $2 each. If no one wanted to buy in, it meant they had overvalued the company.

Since late 1983, Hart had been hard at work, knocking on doors of anyone who might want to invest in Amiga. For every potential investor who showed interest, multiple prospects rejected his offer outright. But, after a lot of footwork, Hart had managed to line up almost one million dollars in investments. "That took a while," says Hart. "Without a track record, I couldn't exactly go out there and induce people to give me a lot of money, especially institutions, which was where the larger money comes from."

It was a bit of a chicken and egg problem, in that no one wanted to be the first investor in a start-up company with a totally green fund manager. Hart soon targeted those who would invest in him based on personal trust. He ended up approaching friends and former classmates from the East Coast. "There were a couple from Boston," says Hart. "The ones from Boston and other places in the country were classmates of Dave's and mine. When we put this thing together we approached them."

Once he had some investors, it became easier for others to invest in Amiga. Soon, Hart began concentrating purely on investors in California. "Most of the money came from a network of interested investors that I had established, which was made up of Silicon Valley company CEOs and other prominent San Francisco executives," he explains. "There were a bunch of Goldman Sachs partners. There were some Transamerica Corporation people. These are just people that I had gotten to know or had been introduced to. In fact, there was one investment advisor who liked it and put his money and his clients in as well. It was kind of an eclectic group of people."

Prior to 1984, Hart merely had his investors lined up. No one had written any checks. Now it was time to collect those investments, or as Hart puts it, "close". "Subsequently, I was able to close on the money that I had lined up," he says.

That eclectic group added up to a significant investment in Amiga. "I eventually put about a million in from various sources," says Hart. "But a million wasn't going to last more than about 7 or 8 months. We knew we had to get subsequent funding."

Hart never gave up trying to obtain major investors in Amiga. "In the meantime, we did have venture capitalists visiting just to begin to see what kind of interest there might be, because the kind of funding I was going to put in wasn't going to take it very far."

Two other things happened as Hart travelled the Valley talking with CEO's and investors. Many investors said no to investing in Amiga, due to their fear of competing with Apple and IBM. However, they were open to other investments. And Hart also learned about other investment opportunities. For example, a startup called Trimble was entering the emerging civilian GPS business. Hart dutifully filled up his Rolodex with names and phone numbers, which he called his investment network.

Eventually he raised a further one million dollars in a non-Amiga related investment fund. "In March, I closed on my first venture capital fund, which I had been working on raising," he explains. "I was able to put another $250,000 from that into Amiga."

Although Hart had yet to generate a penny of actual income for himself, things started moving for him. Each investor gave him more credibility, and soon making investments became easier.

Dealing with Atari

Bill Hart's investment gave Amiga some much needed relief and would carry them through for most of the year, but as he knew, it was not going to get them to the finish line. However, the first few days of 1984 had been unusually kind to Amiga. Not only had they regained control from Inter-Medics which allowed Hart to close on his investments from his company Technology Partners, and not only had the private unveiling of Lorraine at CES gone spectacularly well, but Atari had a chance to see the Lorraine's graphics and sound for the first time. And they were impressed. Discussions with Atari were now getting serious.

Atari's first priority was to license Amiga's three custom chips for a proposed 16-bit game console. Atari would pay Amiga $2 for each machine they built that included the chipset. Atari, of course, would pay to manufacture its own chips. The deal could prove lucrative for Amiga. Atari had sold tens of millions of Atari 2600 machines. If Atari ended up producing 10 million of the new consoles, it could be worth worth $20 million to Amiga, paid quarterly over several years.

As part of the agreement, the two companies would make their respective systems software compatible. This would be an incredible benefit for the Lorraine system, due in no small part to the fact that Amiga would probably struggle to win over game developers. Atari not only had some of the best games and games developers in the industry, but it had the attention of third party game developers.

And lastly, Atari would pay Amiga $15 per chipset for each coin-op arcade game it produced. This was an exclusive license to Atari, provided they paid Amiga at least $100,000 per year in royalties for the chipset. Over the space of a decade, provided Atari's games exceeded the minimum, it could amount to a regular source of revenue.

The licensing deal was a mutually beneficial business arrangement. However, it was far into the future before Amiga would receive any royalties on the chips. Amiga needed development funds now, otherwise the chips would never be completed. This is where Bill Hart stepped in.

Hart offered Atari 1,000,000 shares of Amiga outright. Atari was interested, but they were more interested in the chipset than an investment in Amiga. Therefore Atari tailored its investment around Amiga chipset milestones. Specifically, Atari would loan Amiga $500,000 for signing a letter of intent, $1 million for signing the final licensing agreement, and $500,000 for each chip ($1.5 million for all three chips). In total, Amiga stood to receive $3 million in cash by the time Miner and crew delivered the chipset.

Once the chips were ready, Amiga would pay back the $3 million to Atari by selling 1,000,000 shares at $3 per share to Atari. At this time, Amiga's debt to Atari would effectively be cancelled by paying back the loan with shares. The $3 per share might sound audacious, considering Hart was selling shares for around $2 each, but by the time the chipset was done, the value of Amiga would have naturally increased due to the chipset being complete. After all, a hardware company with a complete chipset is worth more than a hardware company with a partially working chipset.

As a side benefit of this deal, Hart could tell his investors that a major company was buying shares at $3. Anything less was a deal.

Amiga currently had 8 million shares. Hart would allocate another 1 million shares for Atari to purchase, for a total of 9 million shares. This gave Atari greater than 10% ownership, while slightly diluting the ownership of the other shareholders in Amiga. "InterMedics had no anti-dilution protection, so if the venture had gone ahead with further equity financing, the 25% would have been diminished substantially," says Bill Hart. In exchange, it gave Amiga enough reserves for development of the final chipset. Even better, at $3 per share, it would theoretically cast Amiga as a $27 million dollar company, on paper.

There was also a huge potential upside in the investment for Atari. Morse and Hart hoped to launch Amiga with an Initial Public Offering (IPO) at some point. If that happened, Atari could benefit handsomely. In fact, should a public offering of Amiga occur, the agreement lists the minimum sale price per share of Atari's stock at $7.50 per share, ensuring Atari more than doubled its investment.

Amiga had been initially ecstatic about its dealings with Atari. After all, for a small sacrifice of the game console rights, Amiga stood to benefit to the tune of several million dollars. However, soon Atari began asking for non-exclusive home computer rights to the chips. In other words, Atari wanted to make a home computer that would compete against the Lorraine. "As we got deeper into the negotiations, it seemed to us that they kept wanting to move it more in the direction of allowing them to introduce a product that would compete with us," recalls Hart. "We kept telling them that that would not work for us."

The additional requests clearly rankled Amiga's employees and set off warning bells for Morse. Morse tried his best to talk Atari out of its plan for a home computer. "As the negotiations got closer to that deadline, we became increasingly concerned that they were trying to leverage their position to get more out of us," says Hart.

In the end, the best Morse could do was put restrictions on Atari's home computer in the contract. Specifically Atari would at first only be able to sell a keyboard and disk drive upgrade module that expanded its console into a personal computer. Furthermore, it could not sell this product until June 1, 1985, at which point Amiga hoped to have its own computer launched.

Atari felt it could push Amiga into whatever agreement it needed. "They sensed that we were really up against it," says Hart. Atari persisted with its demands and wanted the option to sell its own standalone personal computer. In the end, Morse was only able to stall the release date in the contract of a full-blown personal computer to March 1986, at which point Atari could release a personal computer.

Curiously, the agreement stipulates Amiga can only market its computer in "value added distribution channels" and Atari can only market in mass market channels until April 1, 1986. After that date, either party could market its product freely.

It's worth mentioning that, as desperate as Amiga was for development funds, Atari was also a little desperate and running out of time. The marketplace was clearly done with the Atari 2600. The Atari line of home computers, launched in 1979, were also fading. It needed something spectacular to replace them. Atari even clearly stated in the Letter of Intent, "Our objective is to enter into, *as soon as feasible*, a formal stock purchase agreement and a license agreement between Atari and Amiga."

As much as they disliked the terms of the loan agreement, Morse had no choice but to sign, otherwise Amiga would run out of development funds. Morse signed an interim loan agreement, which delivered a $500,000 loan on March 7, 1984 to Amiga.

However, the final licensing agreement would not have to be signed until the summer, should both parties choose to move forward with the agreement. Escape for Amiga was clearly stated in the letter of intent: "For value received, the undersigned Amiga Corporation, a California corporation (the "Borrower"), hereby promises to pay to the order of Atari, Inc. (the "Lender") the principal sum of Five Hundred Thousand Dollars ($500,000) on June 30, 1984 at the office of the Lender at 1265 Borregas Avenue, Sunnyvale, California…"

If Morse wanted to continue the deal with Atari, he would sign the licensing agreement by June 30. If he wanted to get out of the deal, he would be required to pay back the $500,000 loan in full by that date.

The third option, Morse not signing the agreement and not paying back the loan, would result in Atari receiving all of the Amiga technology. This was a safeguard for Atari that Amiga would not leave it high and dry with nothing to show for the loan.

To guarantee Atari would get the technology, the agreement stipulated that Amiga must, within a week of signing, send documentation and instructions for all the technology and code to the Bank of America, to be held in escrow. The escrowed materials included the logic diagrams for the three chips, source listings for the software library, a complete functional description of the three chips, the full specification for the emulator (the prototype chips). And the final guarantee for Atari was an irrevocable letter of instructions to the eventual chip manufacturer, signed by Amiga, that the manufacturer was to sell chips to Atari at the request of Atari.

Still, it was anything but guaranteed that Amiga would sign the final agreement with Atari in June. "Because they had loaned $500,000 at the beginning of this process and if we couldn't repay it when it was due or hadn't entered into an agreement with them, it was secured by the technology," says Hart. "So they could foreclose on the technology."

Atari was so confident in the deal, its engineers began to design a personal computer system around the Amiga chipset. Owing to Dave Morse's pitch of the chips producing Saturday morning cartoon quality graphics, Atari even codenamed the machine " Mickey". It was also internally called the Atari 1850XLD.

Joe Pillow

The legend of Joe Pillow, the most mysterious developer of the Amiga Lorraine, was born during a March 1984 flight from New Orleans. "RJ and I were voted to go to New Orleans to try to entice developers to write programs for the Amiga," recalls Dale Luck.

The two Amiga developers were attending the annual Softcon to promote the Amiga. "We were at one of these computer conventions," says Luck. "There's a whole bunch of companies there and they all have literature, so RJ and I were grabbing literature from these companies that we may want to get in contact with later to do software or hardware development for the Amiga."

After a long week, Luck and Mical arrived at the airport on Friday afternoon to return home to California. "We were coming back from Softcon in New Orleans," says Luck. "Both of us had backpacks full of stuff we picked up at the show. We sat down in our seats and there was an empty seat between us, and that's where we piled our backpacks. As the plane filled up, we saw no one use that seat, so I took my suit coat off and put it around the backpack and then we grabbed one of those paper airplane pillows, and drew a face on it and stuck it on there, and kind of propped him up and started playing with him."

Very few empty seats remained. "Everyone who had gone to the show was now leaving and going home," says Luck. "The plane was going to be packed, it was probably oversold like planes are. And there RJ and I are with Joe Pillow sitting between us."

The head stewardess began a headcount to determine how many stand-by passengers could board. "She's walking down and looks right at us and counts, then she continues to the end of the plane and then goes back up to the front."

After a few moments, the remaining passengers boarded. "The people who are walking down the aisle are kind of looking at us like we're nuts because we still have this here. And then I look back and there's an empty seat behind us. Where we thought she counted Joe Pillow as an empty seat, she actually counted the seat behind us as an empty seat." Luck began to get nervous.

"When everybody got on board and sat down, the plane looked like it was full. They locked the door and started backing the plane away. The stewardess who had previously just counted started walking back down the aisle and she noticed there's this pillow head there on a seat on the airplane," says Luck. "She was so pissed, she grabbed his head and ripped it off. She said, 'You guys, you ain't getting away with this,' and then stormed to the front of the plane. But the plane had already left the gates. By that time also there were about 20 people roaring in the plane saying, 'How did she not count this guy?'"

The incorrigible software developers took another pillow, replanted Joe Pillow's head, and continued amusing their fellow passengers. "We had already changed one of our driver's licenses, and put a little picture of a little pillow guy on the driver's license and wrote in the name Joe Pillow," recalls Luck. "Joe Pillow was starting to make friends by that time. He tried to buy a drink and they carded him."

Soon, even the other stewardesses were treating him like a passenger. "He got food. He read a book for awhile. He got tired and fell asleep, so we turned the pillow over and drew a sleepy face on the side so he could sleep on my shoulder."

Although the rowdy Softcon attendees made fast friends with Joe Pillow, he was not without his critics. "There was a little girl, I think she was about seven years old, sitting in the middle seat in front of us with her folks. In the middle of the flight she gets up, stands on the chair and leans over, looking right at us, and she says, 'Boy, you guys are weird!' Then we noticed her mom elbowing her, and she tells her, 'Shut up or you're going to end up growing up and being like those guys.'"

Luck still remembers the time fondly. "Joe got the phone number of one of the stewardesses too, which was kind of neat," he says.

HAM Version 1

Jay Miner was a creative man and believed in experimentation, even though it was already late in the development cycle. In early 1984, Miner added a very clever hack to the Daphne chip to produce a revolutionary graphics mode called Hold and Modify, or HAM.

Miner had previously designed the CTIA chip for the Atari computers to allow a palette of 16 colors, similar to the C64's VIC-II chip. However, CTIA could allow 8 luminance values per color (the brightness) for total of 128 colors. Now he would use the same idea for the Daphne chip, only improved for use with the 6 bitplanes the design supported, providing 32 base colors and 32 luminance levels.

At the time, the Daphne chip was tailor made for a video game system, and Miner used the Hue, Saturation, Luminosity (HSL) model of color production common for video game consoles attached to televisions. By playing with the luminance signal, Miner's chip could produce incredible images.

As Jay Miner recalled, "Hold and Modify came from a trip to see flight simulators in action and I had a kind of idea about a primitive type of virtual reality. NTSC on the chip meant you could hold the hue and change the luminance by only altering four bits."

Miner's work amazed Bil Herd, who was surprised to see so many colors displayed on a standard television set; something he thought previously impossible. "I started in the TV repair field, so I actually know why you can only make so much color in a certain amount of time," says Herd. "The color crystal frequency is 3.58 MHz, which means you can only have 40 transitions of that across your screen. If you change the information faster than that, you get that rainbow effect, where one side of a character is red and one side is green."

The rainbow effect had plagued earlier computers from other companies. "The Coleco Adam had those rainbows running through it," recalls Herd.

"On the Amiga, they said, 'Fine. We will change the color as fast as the TV will go, but we can change the black and white [luminance] part of the signal twice as fast.' They were right," explains Herd. "In TV sets, that's why you can see the little black line between people's teeth. That's the black and white modulation, which is going much faster."

Miner exploited the fact that the luminance signal on a television set is faster than the color signal. "That's what the Hold and Modify for the Amiga was," says Herd. "They would put a color out there, and then you could change the brightness of the color for the next pixel. You couldn't change the color, or else you would get these artifacts, but you could change the brightness of the existing color. It was the first time somebody had broken that barrier about what you could see on a TV set."

The addition of HAM completed Miner's goal of making the chipset capable of running sophisticated flight simulator software. The polygons rendered by the chip could now display in many colors and many shades, making for a more realistic flight sim experience. And it was plenty fast for a flight simulator. Unknown to Herd or Miner, HAM would undergo a dramatic change by the time the final chipset emerged, one that was not necessarily for the better.

Dale Luck's Line Draw

Although the hardware and software engineers were in opposite ends of the engineering area, they collaborated together. "In a lot of companies, the hardware team throws a spec over the fence and the software team is stuck implementing it. They throw the final product over the fence and no one's happy with the result," says Ron Nicholson. "We knew that the way to do things right was to put the software and hardware people together and let them collaborate and influence each other's designs."

The engineers were open to ideas and collaboration from the software team, but they were on a tight schedule to get the chip layouts done. The last thing they needed was another feature suggested by someone in the software group. But that's exactly what happened. "When Dale Luck came in, he said we need line drawing," recalls Nicholson. "I said no, the design is late, it's too big. And he said but we can do it with this minor addition."

Luck was not naive and knew it was a lot to ask at this late stage, but he also knew how important hardware line drawing would be to the speed of the Amiga GUI. As a result, he made sure his idea was solid and workable before approaching the hardware engineers. "He built a software model of it and realized that with a small tweak, it could draw a line," explains Glenn Keller. "That modeling is a very effective thing. I've used software models and you can see the overall picture easier than when you're thinking about the little gates."

When word reached Dave Morse that the chip schedule could be in danger due to the insistence of a persuasive software engineer, he asked Miner to throw Luck off the idea. According to Keller, "They were trying to convince Dale not to do it because the schedule was tight and we are trying to get the thing out the door. Then Jay and Dale went to lunch," says Keller. "Morse had told Jay to convince Dale not to do it, but it didn't work. It worked the other way around. They went out to lunch, and then Jay said, 'We're putting it in.'"

When Nicholson saw that Miner was taking the idea seriously, he took another look at the proposal. "[Dale] sat down first with Jay and he convinced Jay and then he sat down with me and he said we can do it by adding only this many gates to the design," says Nicholson. "Both Jay and I relented because we saw that, in spite of being a software guy, he knew enough about the hardware design."

The line logic turned out to be an important addition to the Amiga chipset, one that would be used to give the Amiga lightning fast GUI abilities, wireframe graphics and to some extent, faster polygons. "To my recollection we have no polygon engines in there but with the line draw engine, if your code was clever enough you can draw the lines in the right manner to make a closed polygon," explains Nicholson.

Chip Layout

In the original Amiga business plan, co-authored by Larry Kaplan, the scheduled release date of the 8-bit Pixel video game console had been June 1984. Although much had changed with the business plan and system, Dave Morse still planned to release the computer in 1984. In multiple interviews given by Morse throughout 1984, he claims the Lorraine will be released by Christmas. In order to meet that schedule, Amiga would need a working computer by June and then begin moving it into production.

For the chip designers, their next big goal was to have working chips produced in time for the June CES. Chip runs for all three custom chips would be expensive. With funds barely adequate to pay the engineers, there would be no second chance if errors cropped up in the first run of chips. It was imperative that the layouts for all three chips contained minimal or minor errors if Amiga hoped to show actual working prototypes at CES.

Jay Miner, Dave Dean, and Glenn Keller had handed off the schematics to the chip layout guys, Shieu and Chu, in the third quarter of 1983. Since then, they had been hard at work performing the mind-numbingly detailed work of manually laying out each transistor on each chip. "That was mostly done by Mark Shieu," says Keller. "He headed up that effort."

The engineers designed the Amiga chipset for a 5 micron NMOS process, the same process chip companies like MOS Technology had been using going back to 1975 with the 6502. "The chips were designed in NMOS," says Dale Luck. "I don't think there were any automated layout tools that were done. Agnus was 50,000 transistors all hand laid out."

Keller and some of the other hardware engineers helped out a little on the layouts, but for the most part, they left the work for Shieu and Chu. "I didn't do that much of the layout," says Keller. "I had to understand some of it later on, but for the most part, I handed off the schematics."

In the modern age of chip design, semiconductor designers relied on CAD tools, but Amiga was a little more primitive. "The CAD tools that we had were Edwin Chu and Mark Shieu," explains Nicholson. "Chu and Shieu had a remote terminal running SPICE printing out the results of how fast transistors would be."

The chip designers had access to a Data General Eclipse MV/8000 minicomputer with a digitizer puck attached to it. They moved the puck over the layout, pinpointing each corner of a polygon and each trace, inputting the chip design into the computer. A Design Rule Checker ensured the layout met all the rules required for high yield manufacturing, such as the appropriate space between polygons representing transistors.

Many parts of the surface of the chip repeated, which meant Shieu could hire out relatively unskilled workers to perform the more tedious, repetitious parts of the chip. "He hired people to do that," says Keller. "But he did the hard stuff."

Checking the Layouts

Miner, Needle, Dean, and Keller, the actual chip designers who created the schematics, became integral to the layout process when it came time to verify the layout work. "In order to check the layout, we did it by hand, with big pieces of paper," says Keller. "One person with the schematic and one person with the layout and both have yellow pens. You would do it one transistor at a time and check, 'Is that transistor there? Does it connect to this guy?'"

Typically the person who designed the schematic looked at their own schematic, while the person who did the layout looked at their own layout. "I was on the schematic side," says Keller. "There was somebody else on the layout side and we would set them out on the floor, get on our hands and knees and check them."

With approximately 20,000 transistors per chip, and multiple connections between each transistor, it was a considerable task. As Edwin Chu had done the layout for most of Portia, he partnered with Keller. "The way you did it was, I had this big picture of the schematic with every transistor showing," explains Keller. "He had a picture of the layout with every transistor showing. We would start at some wire, like a pin, and he'd say, 'Okay, this goes to X Y. This goes to a transistor at such and such a size.' Then I'll say, 'Okay, I see that on the layout.' Then he'd say, 'Well the gate of that goes to this. The source of that goes to ground.' 'Okay, yes, it does on the schematic.' 'The drain of that goes to this other transistor.' Okay, yeah, I see that in the layout.'"

With so much verbal communication required, each person talking all day, every minute of every day, for a long stretch, it was not uncommon for the engineers to start going hoarse by the end of the process. As time went on, and each diagram became more covered in yellow, they could see their progress. "We go through and then every time we check something, we mark it with the yellow marker to show it was checked," says Keller.

Each gate on the chip consisted of two or three transistors. The engineers were lucky to check 1,000 transistors, each with multiple connections, in a single day. "It took a week or two weeks to systematically check the entire thing," says Keller. "It's only like 5,000 gates or something. Compared to today's circuits it's not that complicated."

By the end of the process, with both engineers hunched down on their hands and knees the whole time, their bodies felt thoroughly fatigued and sore.

Surprisingly, even in 1984 the engineers would have to create the design on large sheets of Rubylith. "All three chips were done with tape on Rubylith," says Nicholson.

Rubylith was a red transparent material that could be cut with a scalpel. The engineers would crawl over the sheet of Rubylith, in socks so they didn't damage the surface, cutting out all the parts of the circuit that would become different layers. Each chip required several full layers of rubylith in order to make the final chip.

Once the Rubylith layers were complete, the design engineer and mask designers would spend days hand-checking the rubylith for problems. These were many, and included peeling errors, nicks, and unintended cuts. They also checked for design rule violations, such as too-thin wires or transistors.

"By today's standards, it's pretty much a miracle it all worked," says Nicholson. "I don't think today's engineers, with their training, would think it possible or even dare try. They would think we were nuts."

Finally, in March, the engineers were ready to send the patterns to the chip vendor for production. Jay Miner rented a Calma GDS II system to digitize the layout. "This involved using a puck on a large light table to mark the positions of each transistor and wire on the rubylith layout sheets, and convert all the rectangle coordinates into digital data," explains Nicholson. "This digital data was then sent to the chip vendor on a magnetic tape." Engineers referred to this as the "tape-out".

Now it would take around two months before silicon arrived back at Amiga, ready to plug into the Lorraine board. "Jay had done this before so he knew what he was doing," says Dale Luck. "We were just getting those chips in right around February-March."

Luck estimates it cost Amiga around $50,000 to fabricate a run. "I don't think it was that much because we had done all the design, we just needed a fab house."

Amiga Chips Fabbed

After receiving the $500,000 windfall from Atari, Miner sent the chips for immediate fabrication. Morse also used some of the money to alleviate the cramped engineering work-spaces in the two offices. Morse ended up purchasing Herman Miller office cubicles, which were seeing popular emergence in business in the 1980's. Cubicles and a few office tables were set up in the main workspace area between the two large offices in the engineering department.

In late March 1984, the chips went into production and in early April they arrived back from the chip fabricator. For Jay Miner and his chip designers, this was a special moment. "We had the block diagram in roughly by the end of the first quarter of '83 and we got working chips back in the second quarter of '84," says Nicholson. "Any reasonable opinion would be that this is a miracle!"

It was especially fulfilling for Nicholson to see his miniaturized bit blitter. "We had to take the logic that was in this delivery truck," says Nicholson.

"Here's how it was done before Amiga, this rack of cabinets the size of a delivery truck and here's how we actually did it."[3]

Unfortunately, the euphoria of receiving the chips was somewhat offset by a debilitating problem with Portia. "There were a couple bugs in the very first tape out," recalls Nicholson. "But that was a minor issue."

Despite the verification process done by Keller and Chu, bugs remained. When the developers attempted to use the disk controller, it could not read data properly. "You can make mistakes," says Keller. "That's in fact why the disk controller didn't work."

Keller debugged the chip and finally tracked it down to a single error in the layout with one transistor. "We missed one transistor. We had cross traced it incorrectly," he says.

Although it was a minor error that would be easy to correct on the next production run of chips, it meant the Lorrine would not have a working disk drive for the June CES.

Keller was also not completely satisfied by the audio output of the chip. "The audio was hard in an analogue way because when the first chips came back, we had to tweak the sizes of the transistors to get the DNL (Differential Non-Linearity) better on the DACs (Digital to Analog Converters). That took some doing," he says.

Amiga started stockpiling Motorola 68000 chips to insert into the systems as well. The timing of the Amiga's release after the Macintosh couldn't have been better. "Between Jay and the purchasing guys, they had a good idea of what they could negotiate Motorola into," says Nicholson. "Of course, as far as volumes were concerned, we knew it was pretty likely the Mac would get shipped before us, which would run Motorola's volumes up. The larger volumes would allow us to get volume pricing as well."

Amiga intended to hand out hundreds of development systems to software developers. However, it would take months of testing with the chips before they could release them, likely after the upcoming CES.

---

3   Although it seemed like a small miracle to take the blitter and put it on a chip, Nicholson notes that in 1984, the size of the transistors on each chip was massive compared to later technology. "We had transistors that were over a hundred thousand times bigger and a lot slower," he says. "I was talking with one of the designers of Commodore who went on to work at Intel. We estimated in current technology, we could take one of the chips in the Amiga and put it on top of one transistor of the original Amiga. In other words, in the area we designed four gates, we might be able to put the whole Amiga and the 68000 on top of it with today's technology, roughly."

As soon as the chips began arriving, Amiga handed out samples and documentation to Atari. Atari had been working on a Motorola 68000 based computer codenamed Gaza, which they soon cancelled in favor of the Mickey computer based on the Amiga chipset. Amiga engineers visited Atari to lend assistance during development. It seemed the Amiga-Atari relationship would soon bear fruit.

CHAPTER 11

Changing Sides 1984

Dave Morse had at one time seen Atari as his savior, especially when it handed over $500,000 to keep Amiga Corporation afloat and allow the company to fabricate the Amiga chipset. Unfortunately Atari wanted to use the chipset in a home computer, while Amiga wanted to restrict them to the video game console market. By the time the summer CES rolled around, Morse was looking for a way to get out of the deal.

June 1984 CES

Sunday, June 3, 1984 was the opening of the four-day Consumer Electronics Show in Chicago. The event attracted 98,271 attendees, a new record. Most of the attendees belonged to electronics retailers, along with over 2,000 members of the press. They all came to see over 1,400 exhibitors in the 811,000 square foot hall, so many it would be near impossible for a single person to visit them all.

IBM and Apple were not there this year, but Commodore, Atari, and Amiga were. It was an anxious time for all three companies who, in the next few months, would either be merging, selling, acquiring, or suing one another.

Commodore unveiled the SX-64 Executive portable computer, a repackaging of the C64. At 26 pounds, it was meant to compete with the luggable systems by Osborne and Kaypro. However, those two systems were business computers running CP/M, while the C64 was clearly a home computer for entertainment. Although the $995 price was competitive with systems from Osborne and Kaypro, it was not a great fit with the business world.

With Commodore already working on a truly portable computer, the SX-64 was almost obsolete by the time it debuted. "They had a CRT type of portable but that was already sort of going out the door so to speak, technology wise," says David Baraff.

Commodore also had a large display of its production Plus/4 and C16 computers, which failed to impress the original Commodore 64 design team. "We were disappointed that there were no exciting follow-on products in a [C64] family," says Charles Winterble. "Where is the 128K version?"

True backward compatibility was obvious to Commodore's competitors in the computer industry, such as IBM and Apple, who released successively improved versions of their computers. It was obvious to magazine writers. It was obvious to computer sellers. It was obvious to 13-year-old teenagers with computers in their bedrooms. At CES, it finally became obvious to Plus/4 designer Bil Herd.

Herd received his first taste of the importance of backward compatibility when he showed his Plus/4 computer at CES. "Everybody was like, 'Why the hell didn't you make this compatible!' They would show me their software they had invested all their time in, and I'm going, 'Yeah, why didn't we make it backward compatible?'"

Herd relayed his concerns to Irving Gould during the show. "That day, around the other side of that booth, I got into a conversation with Irving about the Plus/4's compatibility problems," he recalls. "I was loud, and I probably had alcohol on my breath." He presented Gould with a scathing critique of Commodore's failure to pursue backward compatibility. "I said, 'Our next computer should be compatible. I'm catching all kinds of shit over this compatibility problem and compatibility wouldn't have been that bad [to implement].' He tolerated me, but I don't know that he ever did anything from it."

Rumors spread during CES that Jack Tramiel was in talks to purchase Atari from Warner. They were, of course, true. The Tramiels wanted Atari for its large manufacturing facilities and distribution network. At the Atari booth, Jack Tramiel and his son Sam met with Warner executives.

At the same show, Japan attempted to enter the North American market with the MSX standard. Microsoft even organized a lavish launch party at the show, but ultimately MSX met with a lackluster reception. "The Commodore 64 just killed MSX," says Chuck Peddle. "MSX just never got anywhere."

For Amiga, the show would be much different from the previous CES in Las Vegas, where it demonstrated the Lorraine system to potential investors. This time, Amiga would be loud and bold, showing off the system to the media at large and hoping to get noticed by investors, albeit still behind closed doors, since the final system design was not complete and ready for public consumption. Dave Morse was particularly motivated because he needed to pay back Atari $500,000 by the end of the month, otherwise Atari would gain control of the chipset for a game console.

This time, Lorraine used actual silicon chips for Daphne, Agnus, and Paula rather than the bulky breadboards. "We did fly the breadboards out just in case as a backup plan," says Dale Luck.

The reason a backup plan was needed was due to the problems with the Portia chip. "There was a bug in the disk controller and I realized that if I could cut this wire on the chip, we could get it to work and bring it to the show," recalls Keller. "I pulled out a microscope and an X-Acto knife and tried to cut the wire."

The task seemed impossible, given that the wires on the chip were about a tenth of the diameter of a human hair. "The first three or four tries I wasn't able to cut it," he says. "The geometries weren't that small. Five microns is small but not like today."

Keller was ready to give up, but Stan Shepard, Amiga's director of quality assurance, convinced him to soldier on. "I was able to cut one or two wires and then I gave up, but Stan convinced me to keep trying," he says. "After destroying about 10 chips, I finally got one that worked and we took it to the show."

The Daphne chip in particular impressed visitors. One demo, called the rainbow demo, displayed all 4096 available colors at once. This was startling for people who were used to seeing very few colors displayed simultaneously.

Dale Luck and RJ Mical also improved on the original silent Boing Ball demo, creating a truly multimedia spectacle. Thanks to help from Sam Dicker, now people outside the booth heard the rhythmic banging of the ball coming through the thin walls, followed by the gasps of those who were lucky enough to see it firsthand.

Every time the ball hit the ground, the Lorraine produced a thunderous sound, in stereo. According to Miner, "The booming noise of the ball was Bob Pariseau hitting a foam baseball bat against our garage door."

The ball had previously moved only up and down, but the programmers added a side to side motion, as though the ball was bouncing inside the box bounded by the edges of the monitor.

Boing relied mainly on the three custom chips, using only 8% of the main CPU time. This allowed for an impressive show of multitasking. "You could have the Boing Ball running in the background and have your workbench running," says Luck. "You could have another graphic thing up, and you could just slide them up and down."

Many attendees were skeptical of the Lorraine, believing it was a fraud. "It was wonderfully gratifying because the more savvy people invariably walked up after the demo and gave a good look at the machine," says Mical. "They would get down on one knee to lift up the skirt and look under the table to see where the real computer was. They thought there must be some trick that we were pulling off under the skirt, but it was nothing but power cords."

The Mac and Amiga computer were fated to share some of the same code due to a partnership with a third party speech software developer. "Some developers had a product called Software Automatic Mouth," explains Ron Nicholson. "They first came out with an Atari product. They had a C64 version too. And then they came out with an Apple product that had a 6-bit DAC (Digital to Analog Converter) on it. That was one of the first chances I had to play with a waveform based audio on my Apple II."

The product, called S.A.M. (Software Automatic Mouth), was developed and marketed by a small company, Don't Ask Software. It was an ear-opening demo when released in 1982. "Since I was familiar with the product, I introduced the developers of that product to Dave Morse at Amiga," says Nicholson. "It turns out that Steve Jobs was also negotiating with them to do Macintalk for the Mac around the same time frame. They actually came in and they worked together integrating their software with our software."

Amiga licensed a 16-bit software package called SoftVoice from Don't Ask Software. SoftVoice was a simple text to speech utility, similar to the one used earlier on the Lorraine. "The technology was quite good, but taking it from good to really great was an art form that a lot of us were involved in," says Mical. Mical's experience with the Williams arcade game Sinistar, which also had speech capabilities, helped him on the project.

Mical particularly enjoyed an interactive demonstration Narrator, as the speech module was named. "One of the demos was the *Talking Heads* demo," he recalls. "It was a couple of robot heads and they were nicely done. The male was Mr. Amiga and the female was a reporter asking questions. The reporter would ask certain questions about Mr. Amiga and he would describe his capabilities and the technology."

The select visitors loved the final part of the demonstration. "We proved to the audience that it wasn't just good at doing canned speech, but that you could get it to say anything you wanted," says Mical. "We would ask the audience to throw sentences at us, and we would type them in and it would speak those sentences for you right there. It was impressive to people."

When the Amiga team spotted a Sears representative, they tailored the demonstration just for him. "We wanted Sears to carry the machine," says Mical. "When one of the bigwigs at Sears was in there seeing the demo, without warning, the guy who was riding the keyboard typed in, 'I buy all my tools at Sears,' and the place lit up in a great roar of laughter. It was a wonderful little touch."

The designers also handed out detailed spec sheets to software houses and peripheral makers in an attempt to encourage third-party development for the computer. "One of the things we were doing was looking for more programmers to join the Amiga," says Luck. "We also exposed some of the hardware specs because people wanted to develop hardware for the Amiga."

The Amiga spec sheet still claimed it would be a 128K system, the same amount of memory used by the Commodore 128, with a 5 ¼ inch floppy drive. Since the previous January CES, there were a few notable changes. The Amiga now boasted a coprocessor slot, which Amiga claimed would allow an Intel 8088 processor in order to run MS-DOS software. And a mouse was promised with the computer.

Morse had previously stated the computer would retail for less than $1000. Now, six months later, he would only say the cost would be less than $2000. Morse was clearly no longer attached to the idea of an affordable home computer for the masses. He also still claimed the computer would be ready for Christmas 1984, something *Compute!* magazine had doubts about.

Post-CES, the Lorraine received even more praise, with Compute! magazine saying it was "possibly the most advanced personal computer ever."[1]

One question that came up repeatedly at the show was whether the Amiga would be MS-DOS compatible, like the IBM PC computers that were dominating businesses. These questions affected Morse and Miner in particular, who started to rethink the Lorraine.

Amiga and Atari Clause

Even before CES, the industry was aware that Atari was in talks to distribute an Amiga system. When asked about it, CEO Dave Morse's reply should have sent alarm bells off for Atari executives. "There have been a lot

---

1   *Compute!* magazine, "Software Power!" (August 1984), p. 32.

of rumors about what's going on with Atari," Morse said. "Amiga is interested in licensing its technology in areas we don't intend to compete. We're intending to market and distribute this computer as an Amiga product. We won't do any licensing arrangements that would conflict with that."[2]

When rumors began to swirl at CES that Jack Tramiel was about to purchase Atari, Morse began feeling especially apprehensive about the company's pending licensing agreement. Remembering Tramiel's turbulent visit in May, he suspected the future looked dismal if Tramiel purchased Atari. "That was another thing we were concerned about because we knew that once we lost our protection here, Tramiel was a ruthless businessman and we would be dead in the water," says Bill Hart.

But the main concern was still that Atari wanted to release a personal computer with the Amiga chipset. "We told them that what they were trying to get was not what we had entered into these discussions thinking would be the outcome," explains Hart. "And that they had to be realistic. Yes, we were up against it but we were going to find another solution."

Morse had less than a month to find a way to divorce Amiga entirely from Atari before he would lose control of the technology his employees had worked so hard to develop. "Atari at this point had locked us into the terms of a deal and had given us an advance on money so that we could keep making payroll and keep the effort going," explains Mical. "We had a timeline; a month to either say yes to the deal and sign the deal, or say no to the deal and give them their money back."

Amiga would forfeit their technology to Atari if they failed to pay back the $500,000 loan by June 30th. "This was a dumb thing to agree to but there was no choice," said Miner. John Ferrand of Atari also believed he had a verbal agreement with Morse that Amiga would not sell to five prominent computer companies, including Apple, IBM, Commodore, General Electric, and Philips.

Unfortunately, Amiga did not have the cash to pay back Atari. In fact, all the two founders had was massive debt. "Dave had borrowed on his personal credit to keep the company afloat, as had Jay Miner," says Hart. "They both had a lot of skin in the game as they say."

Worried about the possibility of turning the Amiga chipset over to Atari, Morse worked tirelessly lining up potential suitors for Amiga. He gave presentations to Sony, Hewlett Packard, Philips, Apple, and Silicon Graphics. Unfortunately, most companies were concerned because the Lorraine was not IBM PC compatible. Steve Jobs of Apple even criticized the Lorraine architecture, saying there was too much hardware in the machine. It seemed like Amiga was destined to go to Atari

Post-CES Amiga Changes

After the huge push for CES, it was time for Amiga to sort a few things out. First, the Amiga systems engineers began producing 100 Lorraine developer systems to hand out to companies like Activision, Electronic Arts, Infocom, and Microsoft. At the time, Commodore programmer Andy Finkel was helping Infocom in Cambridge to port its games to the C64. "That was where I first got a hint of the Amiga," says Finkel. "There was this locked room where I couldn't go, even though I could go anywhere else in the building. The Infocom tech people would sneak in and work on the computer. They told me there was a secret computer that they couldn't talk about."

The Amiga PC

Since unveiling the Lorraine in January, a chorus of voices began asking about MS-DOS compatibility. *Creative Computing* in particular urged Amiga to adopt IBM PCjr compatibility. After the most recent CES, the volume only intensified. Potential investors, not always the most savvy about PC technology, were particularly concerned about PC compatibility. "During that timeframe, we were starting to run out of money, and so a lot of ideas were starting to come out to make the product more attractive," says Dale Luck.

Mainly, Amiga wanted to be able to claim the existence of business applications that could run under MS-DOS. "At the time, I don't believe we had that many third party developers that would write applications for us," says Luck. "There wasn't really any productivity software at the time. It was thought that with some form of PC compatibility we could get that for free."

The Amiga team had already incorporated a coprocessor slot and now they continued work on an Intel 8088 coprocessor card, which would allow the system to boot up MS-DOS. It was almost like an IBM PC with an exceptional video and sound card far in advance of anything the PC would receive for the next five years.

CAOS Begins

Bob Pariseau had attempted to hire a contractor to create a disk operating system for Lorraine. However, lacking direction, the company failed to produce anything. "There was a file system that we contracted out to a company down in Arizona," says Carl Sassenrath "The file system was really suffering at this point. They were not getting it done on time. They were just really slow on it."

The Amiga team regrouped and found another contractor to deliver a DOS. This time, Amiga would give a specification for the developers to work towards. "I wrote a spec for the file system and called it CAOS," says Sassenrath, referring to Carl's Amiga Operating System. "That's what they were sort of implementing but they had their own variation on it."

Sassenrath, a perfectionist, improved the specs as the months went by. "I continued to develop the CAOS idea," he recalls "For instance, one of the ideas of CAOS which is actually implemented in Linux these days, was the fact that part of the file system would also reference the different objects of the kernel. You could see a list of them and they would look like files to the file system. Show me all the tasks of the system, as a listing of files. Show me all of the interrupts of the system. Show me all the libraries of the system. You could reference that namespace through the file system."

Although Sassenrath was motivated, the contractors did not embrace his new specs. "That was part of the CAOS design but what they were implementing was really strictly a UNIX inode based file system," says Sassenrath. "They were pretty far from the whole CAOS specs. I really don't feel that we could call what they were implementing CAOS but I guess it was. I was disappointed that they really couldn't do much of what I was spelling out."

Other developers at Amiga were able to collaborate with the contractors to make the code work better with the chipset. "The disk driver was a really interesting thing to get running, for the floppy disk, because we used the blitter on the Amiga to actually form the bit patterns that would be written out to disk," explains Sassenrath. "Neil Katin, who was one of the engineers there, actually went ahead and implemented that design and made it work really quite well."

While CAOS lacked some of Sassenrath's more high-minded concepts, the DOS was still outstanding in the minds of the other Amiga developers. "The original file system that we had designed for the machine was just beautiful," recalls Mical. "It was exactly what you would want a modern multitasking operating system to have."

lationship established already, but the call was, 'We've heard things and we want to know whether or not there is an opportunity here for us.'"

Amiga's marketing side had sensed the dire problems within Amiga, but suddenly they noticed a change in Morse's attitude. "The first time we had an inkling something was going on was because Dave would tell us, 'Don't worry about the Atari thing.' Ok, Dave. We're not going to worry about it… much," says Don Reisinger.

On June 19, Dave Morse flew out to Pennsylvania to meet with Marshall Smith and other executives. He emphatically told the Commodore executives that the situation was urgent. In response, Commodore sent a team of engineers to inspect Amiga's technology. "I was told to lead this team of engineers out to do an evaluation of Amiga," says Bob Russell. "I went out there in this big rush because we have to do this before Atari takes possession by default. I took a bunch of chip designers, software guys, and hardware guys out there."

One of the team members was Andy Finkel, who soon realized the secret computer he heard about at Infocom and the Amiga were one and the same. "They were having Infocom work with them to port some of the adventures to the Amiga," says Finkel. "When Commodore bought the Amiga, I was talking to some of my Infocom friends and found out that was what they were doing at the time."

When Russell arrived in California, he noticed that Amiga was close to the old Commodore headquarters. "They were actually just across the street from our Scott Boulevard location," he says. "There was this little office park of single story buildings with a ton of little companies in it."

The Amiga executives were forthright with the engineers and described the predicament they were in with Atari. "They were concerned about trying to find sources other than Atari," says Russell. "Atari was just going to take it for the money they had already put into it and those guys weren't going to get anything out of it."

According to Russell, the Amiga engineers tried repositioning the Lorraine yet again in one last attempt to entice investors. "Those guys were desperate when I was out there trying to come up with a way not to sell it to Atari," he says. "They had worked real hard and were thinking real hard about PC compatibility at that point in time. We talked with them about the original design of the product and what it was becoming. We asked why they were changing it. Apparently they had run into [investor] problems with it not being PC compatible."

Russell learned as much as he could about the company, the situation, and the Lorraine technology and presented his findings to his executives. "I called back with the evaluation and said, 'Here's a tentative off the cuff impression. They're doing the wrong thing by trying to make it PC compatible, but they've got exactly what we need as far as a chipset core and features. It's definitely a step up.' The other engineers I was with chipped in on the phone." In Russell's mind, the Amiga technology would be perfect for a low cost Commodore 64 replacement computer.

On June 27, Commodore sent an engineering manager and a corporate lawyer Nicholas Lefevre to California with a draft agreement. "In the summer of '84 we went to talk with Amiga about taking a license for the Amiga computer," says Lefevre. "I went out with a fellow named Martin Schabelski and the two of us were negotiating with Amiga."

Sitting across from Commodore at the negotiating table were Amiga's three main representatives, "It was the three people that should have been involved," says Reisinger. "It was Dave Morse, Jay Miner, and Bill Hart. Bill was there because he had led a group that did some financing for us so he had a protected interest there. Dave was obviously to protect the interests of the corporation. And Jay was trying to make sure that the technology was actually going to get used and not just stuck on a shelf."

There was every possibility Commodore would also sense the desperate situation Amiga faced, but the Amiga camp felt that Commodore itself was in a situation of its own. "Commodore was a big dog at that time. They were a billion dollar corporation," says Reisinger. "They were flying high but boy they needed a new product because they had nothing and I mean nothing in the pipeline."

True to form, Morse laid his cards on the table and gave Commodore the full story about the loan from Atari and the impending deadline. According to Hart, "Dave basically said to them, 'Look, before we go any further, we need you to give us some good faith money.' Without a loan, there was nothing for us and nothing for them because Atari would own the whole thing."

Morse was well aware of the Atari/Tramiel-Commodore rivalry and knew it could only benefit the negotiations. "And of course that provided quite an incentive for Commodore to bail us out as you can imagine," laughs Hart.

According to Lefevre, "We started negotiating a deal that would get Amiga that money and get the technology for ourselves."

Commodore had taken the bait and now Dave Morse saw an escape from the Atari deal and Jack Tramiel. "On the phone call, it sounded like it was a done deal and we were going to go ahead," recalls Russell. "I even remember talking about how many million dollars we were going to pay to get chip rights, rather than buy the company. They were willing to sell the chip rights for a few million dollars, rather than making us buy the whole company."

Russell was in favor of purchasing computer rights for the chip technology, and leaving the rest for Atari. "The only thing Atari was going to end up with was the right to use that chip in a game machine," says Russell. "We were like, 'Hell, let them have the game machine. We'll buy the computer chip rights for $2.4 to $4 million.'"

Although negotiations would continue in the weeks ahead, in the short term, Commodore agreed to give Amiga a lump sum of $750,000 to pay back Atari and continue operations. "Commodore loaned us the money," says Hart. "They gave a loan that would convert into equity after we agreed on a deal. It was probably a little more than that because we were running short on operating funds."

Not so coincidentally, the meeting happened a day before Dave Morse was to have a scheduled meeting at Atari with Ken Nussbacher, the Intellectual Properties lawyer for Atari. At the last minute, Morse cancelled the 1:30 pm meeting because, on the same day, he and Commodore were signing a letter of intent.

An Unwelcome Check

On June 29, 1984, instead of signing a licensing agreement with Atari, Amiga planned to deliver a check to Atari's John Ferrand for $500,000 plus interest. They hoped this meant Atari could not claim ownership of the chipset technology held in escrow. "Dave and I knew that this was going to be sensitive, so we sat down and carefully crafted the words that we were going to communicate to Atari," recalls Hart. "They were true but we had to be very careful how we said this. So we wrote it all down and we called and asked for a meeting with the Atari guy. And we knew at that point that Jack Tramiel was in the process of taking over Atari."

Morse and Hart showed up at Atari headquarters to meet with John Ferrand, check and letter in hand. "We went to see the guy we had been negotiating with and Dave read him the statement," recalls Hart. "It basically said, 'Having negotiated in good faith and having seen that the direction Atari wanted to go in was not compatible with the spirit of what we had entered into, we have decided to terminate the negotiations and returned in full the money.' And we handed them a check for half a million bucks." According to a New York Times article, Morse also claimed the chipset did not work, an issue which would resurface later.

Atari, which was well into developing the Mickey system based on the Amiga technology, was not likely to be happy. "This guy was just totally surprised and he said, 'I'm not going to take this,'" says Hart.

Atari's John Ferrand had a slightly different recollection of the meeting: "Dave said that he had to do it because under the terms of the letter of intent, they had to deliver the chip sets by the end of June or Atari could go into escrow and obtain the schematics for the chips. I said, 'Well, Atari has no intention of doing that. If that's your reason, there's no need to give the money back. Why are we going through this process?' And so they persisted in wanting to give the money back. And I said, 'Well, I'm sorry, I don't even know whether I'm in a legal position to accept the money. I will go and speak to my attorney,' meaning Ken Nussbacher."[4]

Morse stood with the check hanging in mid-air for a moment before Hart said, "Well that's interesting. I don't know what we're supposed to do. Why don't you call your people and we will call our people and figure it out."

"So we called our lawyer and said, 'What should we do? He doesn't want to take the check.' The lawyer said, 'Put the statement you just made in writing and leave the check on the table and walk out,'" recalls Hart.

Amiga now had its plan of action and Morse began writing out a formal statement according to his lawyer's advice. Meanwhile, Atari was in another room trying to figure out what its plan of action should be.

Coincidentally, Jack Tramiel was in a meeting with Atari wrapping up negotiations. "This guy called up Jack, who was in an executive's committee meeting," says Hart.[5] "This call came in and Jack didn't really know much about Amiga. He had done his diligence on Atari and knew a lot about Atari and I don't think he was quite aware of the significance of the Amiga technology. So when the guy called him and said, 'What should I do?,' Jack said, 'When somebody hands you a check for $500,000 you take it. You get it into the bank quickly.' So when the guy came back he was still angry but he said, 'Okay, I'll take the check. I don't like this. We're going to have problems.' And we left."

---

4 John Ferrand's sworn testimony in the ensuing trial.

5 Hart subsequently heard what went on in the meeting from an Atari executive who was present.

CHAPTER 12

The Acquisition
1984

Dave Morse and Bill Hart had successfully escaped from the Atari deal, thanks to an alliance with Commodore. Now the two would see how far Commodore was willing to go to support Amiga Corporation. If negotiations went well, it could be the beginning of a mutually beneficial relationship—one that could end up revolutionizing the computer world.

Jack Buys Atari

Within days of Amiga handing the check to Atari, Jack Tramiel was on the brink of signing the acquisition of Atari's home computing and game console divisions from Warner. Both parties agreed on a deal and set up one final meeting to work out the details that began Sunday, July 1. Tramiel unleashed his tough negotiating style, and by the early morning hours of July 2, TTL owned Atari for no money down. Deftly, he had managed to work out an exchange with Warner whereby Warner would receive stock equivalent to 32% of the available shares in Tramiel's newly forming Atari Corporation, as well as a promise of $240 million in long-term notes.

When Warner announced it had sold Atari, Warner shareholders greeted the news enthusiastically and the stock price shot up. Tramiel was able to pocket several million dollars on the stock surge. It was the type of deal only he could negotiate. The deal was sweet success for Tramiel, who was largely responsible for bringing Atari to its knees while at the helm of Commodore.

Commodore engineer Dave Haynie believes Tramiel's next move proves he had previously wanted his sons to run Commodore. "What did he do? He went and bought Atari, started up a computer company, and put his sons in charge," he explains. "If he could have done that at Commodore, why wouldn't he? You can draw some conclusions there."

Kit Spencer, Commodore's former director of marketing who was responsible for the massive marketing success of the VIC-20 and C64, recalls his reaction to the purchase. "I was on a sailing trip through the Bahamian islands at that time and I picked up a newspaper and read Jack's little start-up bought Atari from Warner Communications, largely on an exchange of notes. I thought, 'I bet there's a phone message when I get back.' Sure enough, when I got back home there's a message from Jack, 'Please call, I'm back in business.'"

Spencer immediately returned the call. "I got a phone call when he got back and he said, 'Kit, I'm bored. I'm going back into business again. I've got a technical startup and I've got one or two people you might know from the past. I'd like you to come in as one of the founding partners. It will be a year or so before we have a product to market.'"

Spencer knew each department head would need to downsize their department in order to stop Atari from bleeding out. He told his former boss, "Thank you Jack, I appreciate the offer but I'm enjoying the life and I don't enjoy firing people."

Tramiel did not get where he was without being persistent, and he continued trying to woo his former marketing superstar. Spencer loved a good marketing challenge, but he was just starting his early retirement. "I was tempted because it sounded quite interesting, but I decided I was quite happy," he says. "And things have a habit of changing when you work with Jack. So I said, 'No, I've made my decision to spend a couple of years here and start doing some things other than business.'"

It was the last communication the two would ever have. "He didn't do the Atari gig, which always surprised me," says Robert Russell. "Jack and Kit fell out because Kit stayed with Commodore."

"Fortunately, I found I enjoyed life too much. When he asked me to come back a couple of times and rejoin him after he left Commodore, I decided I didn't want another change of lifestyle back to the high pressure environment I had been through in my time with Jack in Commodore and declined his offers," says Spencer. "I talked to some of my old colleagues that went there with him and it was certainly high pressure again."

Commodore soon experienced an exodus of employees to Atari. The sunny location at 1196 Borregas Avenue in Sunnyvale, California surely appealed to Commodore's employees stuck in chilly Pennsylvania. Approximately 35 managers, technicians, engineers, and executives put their faith in Tramiel and left Commodore. It was a vindication of his magnetism as a leader. They trusted him to come out on top, a large gamble considering the dominant position Commodore enjoyed.

Even Commodore's European employees were not off limits, including the GM of Commodore UK. "Bob [Gleadow] was a Jack Tramiel loyal man and when Jack left he was immediately appointed by Tramiel," says Commodore UK's David Pleasance. "He was a very capable guy." Fortunately, Gleadow was the only Commodore UK executive or employee to depart. Most wanted to stay with Commodore UK because it was flying high in 1984.

Not everyone departed Commodore for Atari. Tramiel did not ask Michael Tomczyk, the original VIC-20 marketing executive, to join Atari. He left Commodore anyway, feeling it was no longer the same company without Tramiel.

Russell became nervous that he would lose some of his key project engineers, so he made an agreement with Shiraz Shivji. "[Shiraz] called up and we discussed it after he had left the company," says Russell. "He said that he wasn't going to take those engineers." In particular, Russell wanted to retain a Z8000 engineer until they completed the project. "Shiraz promised me that he would let him wrap his stuff up."

In July 1984, Russell attended a meeting in the UK where anxious Commodore executives contemplated the threat posed by Jack Tramiel. "We were at a meeting in London. All the big general managers were there, maybe 20 people," says Russell. "I was there because I had the Z8000 project and I was doing reports to the board on engineering. The Amiga was part of it. I knew what was happening with Atari and Jack and their engineers."

While Russell was away, Shivji suddenly backed out of their agreement. "I was at a board meeting in London when this engineer just left," says Russell. "I got a phone call at the board meeting that he was gone, and that just pissed me off to no end. I thought I had an agreement with Shiraz."

Russell soon tipped off Commodore lawyers about possible theft of trade secrets. Russell thought it would be a good idea to inspect what the ex-employees were moving out of Commodore. "We put a lawsuit and we opened up their moving vans," recalls Russell. "They were taking people's personal goods. When the lawyers cracked open the moving truck, we found all kinds of Commodore documentation."

In a suit filed July 10 in Chester County Court, Commodore charged that Shivji and three other former employees had stolen information on new products Commodore was developing. A *Washington Post* article soon appeared with the headline, "Commodore Says Four Stole Trade Secrets".

Commodore obtained a preliminary injunction against releasing a new Atari computer.

Tramiel was furious. He was triumphant from negotiating the deal of the century to purchase Atari and now the injunction would stop him from marketing his new computer. To make matters worse, he had no means to fight back immediately.

News of Tramiel's departure, his purchase of Atari and the exodus of top talent from Commodore all had a devastating effect on Commodore's stock market price. If Irving Gould knew how poorly his shares would fare, he likely would have given a second thought to replacing him. Through 1984, the price fell from $60 to $20. It was clear investors thought Tramiel was the true reason for Commodore's success. They had little confidence in Irving Gould or Marshall Smith.

According to Russell, Irving Gould held his cool in the midst of all the bad news. "Shit was hitting the fan all over the place," he recalls. "My engineers were already leaving with Jack and they knew Jack was doing something. The C64 was starting to lose its momentum then. You could see that the company had turned the corner in some respects. It was pretty bad as far as how the regional people were doing. They were getting slammed."

While former Commodore employees flowed into Atari, Atari employees flowed out. Within the first week of starting Atari Corp., Tramiel closed all 8-bit computer projects and froze all other operations pending an evaluation. He also announced his intentions to reduce the size of Atari's staff to just 200 people.

Atari Inc. had already suffered massive layoffs, starting the previous summer when 600 employees lost their jobs, followed by a monstrous winter layoff of about 6,300 from its worldwide staff.

By Thursday, employees received notice that most of the departments outside of the main research and engineering groups would be closed or drastically reduced. On Friday, about 95% of the staff in each department received a notice of termination.

In the meantime, Jack's son Leonard and John Feagans began the process of interviewing engineers from Atari Consumer as well as Atari's old coin-op division (still owned by Warner and renamed Atari Games). Some engineers were asked to stay on at the new Atari while others were offered a severance package.

Departures

In July 1984, Commodore changed its flagship magazine from *Commodore the Microcomputer Magazine* to *Commodore Microcomputers*. As the popularity of the magazine increased, Commodore began publishing bi-monthly. By late 1984, the magazine also began giving more coverage to third party hits like *M.U.L.E.* and *Archon*. "We probably did three or four million dollars a year in revenue from the magazines by the time I had finished with it," says editor Neil Harris. "We got the circulation up over 100,000 copies per month and put it on newsstands all over the country. Aside from being a nice little profit center, it made the shareholders happy. They could say, 'Look on this newsstand, there's this magazine by this company that I invested in. Look how great it is.' It was seen as a good thing all along."

Despite the success of his magazine, Harris felt unfulfilled. "I thought the air went out of the balloon at Commodore when Jack left. I just watched bad decisions being made and felt like the company was going nowhere," he says. "I came to work for [Commodore's VP of software] Sig [Hartmann] for a few months but honestly at that point, I was more focused at finding my next job because I just didn't think the company was headed for a good place."

Harris decided to try his luck with Atari. "In the summer of 1984, I called Greg Pratt, who had been my boss for a while at Commodore. He was one of the VPs at Atari. I said, 'So what's going on?' He said, 'Glad to hear from you. We have a perfect position for you. Are you interested in coming out?' I said, 'Fly me out for an interview and let me see what's going on.' They made me an offer and I took the opportunity."

It was an amazing reversal. Former Atari engineers like Jay Miner would soon be designing Commodore computers, and former Commodore engineers like Shiraz Shivji, John Feagans, and Leonard Tramiel were now designing Atari computers. However, Commodore would soon have Amiga and arguably the most advanced personal computer technology at the time.

Dismissing Ron

Back at Amiga Corporation in Santa Clara, Morse began housecleaning the organisation to make it more attractive for an acquisition. There was one small issue among the employees that needed to be cleared up. Some of the employees were not all that happy with Ron Nicholson's work—specifically the War and Peace motherboards.

Nicholson had also become redundant, given the goals of the Lorraine and the skills the other engineers possessed. The other grating factor was that Nicholson had negotiated a high salary when Hi-Toro was flush with cash from O. Wayne Rollins. "Coming from Apple, as you could probably understand, I negotiated a very healthy compensation package," explains Nicholson. "I was highly paid, not necessary for the selling of the company, which I did realize was going on at the time."

And to make matters worse, Nicholson had been given founders shares. Though not at the same level as Morse and Miner, it was still a larger share than any other employee. On top of that, Nicholson had the most time to accumulate stock options, which he could choose to exercise and receive even more shares in Amiga. This did not sit well with other employees who were now making larger contributions to the project than Nicholson had. If an acquisition occurred, Nicholson would profit more than the other employees, which could cause a revolt.

Morse decided it was time to let Nicholson go, and Amiga running out of money was a good pretense to base it on. "I became an expendable expense right about the time that they ran out of money," recalls Nicholson. "They just said, 'Thanks for working here, Ron, but we don't want you here anymore.' Dave Morse said that specifically."

When Nicholson was asked to sign his termination agreement, he didn't like what he saw. "On my termination they actually shorted me two months of founder's stock. So that became a slight issue between Dave Morse and myself."

If Morse expected to see Nicholson walk away without a fight, he was disappointed. "We talked and before I pulled lawyers in, we resolved the issue," he says. "I made sure when I separated from Amiga that, as a good gamble, I exercised every possible option. I had this nice discussion with Dave Morse about the exact number that I would be able to exercise. When Commodore did their exchange, I got Commodore stock as part of the deal."

In the end, Morse achieved his goal of not upsetting the other employees by keeping Nicholson's final compensation a secret. "Part of the understanding was I would go off quietly and not rock the boat. And so I disappeared from Amiga history at just the time that they were cutting Amiga out from underneath Jack Tramiel."

Although his tenure with Amiga ended on a slightly bitter note, Nicholson has no regrets about his experience. "I'm very happy that I got my name on four patents with Jay Miner. He's one of the luminaries of the

Valley and I got to participate in that. How many people get to participate in all these interesting things?"[1]

Commodore Buys Amiga

After the Atari acquisition by Jack Tramiel, Irving Gould watched as his former partner garnered all the headlines. Gould desperately wanted something to trump the magnificent move that Tramiel had just played. An acquisition of Amiga began to look like just the thing to steal back the headlines and stop Commodore's plummeting stock price.

After Russell's recommendation on the Amiga chipset, Commodore entered negotiations with Dave Morse, Jay Miner, and Bill Hart on behalf of Amiga. Morse planted the idea in Commodore's legal council, Nicholas Lefevre, of a full acquisition of Amiga Corporation, rather than just the technology. "Over the weekend we got to talking with the founder and CEO of Amiga and he suggested, 'Why Nick are you guys not just buying us?' I said, 'Well that's something that really we should consider if you're interested.' And they were. So we started working on a potential acquisition of Amiga."[2]

Commodore was thorough in analyzing the deal before committing to it. The executives consulted with their key engineers, including Bil Herd. "By that time, I had a reputation for how to make shit work, and how well it works, and whether it's going to work well," says Herd. "I was asked some questions about it fitting the Commodore style of manufacturing, but nothing instrumental. I didn't really change the course of anything."

Herd had questions of his own regarding the new acquisition, which occurred right as he was starting to think about an 8-bit successor to the C64. He felt the spec for the computer was poorly defined. "Adam [Chowaniec] had shared with me the preliminary stuff," says Herd. "It was funny to have those original documents and see little pictures of Atari tanks all over them. When they asked my opinion of some things, I kept coming to, 'What is it supposed to do?' That was a natural question to be asking but we all knew the next machine had to be 16-bit."

---

1   Nicholson holds a special place in history as the only person to have his name inside the plastic molding of two iconic computers, the Macintosh and Amiga, despite leaving both projects before they were completed and released.

2   Antic: The Atari 8-bit Podcast. "ANTIC Interview 46 - Nicholas Lefevre, Attorney for Commodore & Atari"   .

Back in California, the Amiga team awaited their fate. "The last minute negotiations with Commodore were intense," says Mical. "Those were tense and scary tightrope walking days. At the time, it was so terrifying to have the company so close to the brink."

Adam Chowaniec's analysis of the pros and cons of acquiring Amiga revealed a lot of pros. In trying to keep pace with Atari, it would give Commodore the most advanced graphics and sound technology in the personal computer industry. It would also deny Atari and Jack Tramiel the Amiga chipset, shutting down the Mickey system.

With Morse on the brink of selling the company to Commodore, the possibility of employee revolt became a possibility. After all, Amiga enjoyed its own culture built on the dream of releasing its own computer. If key engineers departed, it would make the acquisition less valuable.

Most employees were proud that Amiga was a different company based on creating a very different computer. Now, if an acquisition occurred, they would not be a different computer company. They would be a cog within Commodore, an established company with its own unique culture. For many employees, an acquisition could signal the death of a dream. Morse and Miner now had to break the news to their employees.

In July, Morse invited his key marketing people for a talk. "He called Gary McCoy and myself and said I'd like you guys to come to my house because there's some business stuff we've got to talk about," recalls Reisinger. At the time it sounded a little ominous, given the circumstances. "We go over there with not a clue about what the conversation was to be about."

Given the possible scenarios swirling through Reisinger's head, he was happy to learn all was not lost. "We sat by his pool in the backyard and he said, 'We have an offer on the table from Commodore. Let me tell you about how we got here.'"

Morse explained what had happened and the offer currently on the table by Commodore. Morse assured the two that Amiga would also be able to pay back the many outstanding debts. "They're going to get us out of the Atari deal. All our vendors that we owe money to are going to get paid—right down the line. You're going to be able to come out of this and not feel guilty about anybody. They didn't get paid when they wanted to but they did get paid."

Finally, Morse urged the strengths of the deal. "He said, 'We've got to be practical here. We might be able to get financing, we might not. We might be able to get out from underneath the Atari deal, but if we don't get the financing, we're not. This is the bird in the hand versus two in the bush, guys, and it's not a small bird. Let's take it and run with it."

Reisinger and McCoy didn't require anything more. "We said, 'You know what Dave, we've followed you this far. We're going to follow you right to the end,'" says Reisinger.

Jay Miner had the equally delicate task of breaking the news to his band of fickle engineers. Reisinger recalls, "I said, 'I kind of thought Jay would be here.' He said, 'Jay's got his own hands full. Jay wants to do the deal and quite frankly Jay, Bill, and I are the only three that count because if we say yes then everybody else can say no and it doesn't make any difference.'"

Miner knew his team could have a problem with the deal, given how integral they were to finishing the project. According to Reisinger, Morse noted, "Jay is concerned that the engineers are probably not going to, in general, be in favor of a deal and he's got to try to hold it all together so we can finish this thing, otherwise nobody is going to make any money out of the deal."

The repercussions of an engineer revolt could be monumental. "There was some concern that some of the engineers would have said, 'Well if we're not gonna do it then I'm out of here,'" recalls Reisinger.

In the end, the engineers' dedication to the Lorraine project prevailed. "Much to Jay's credit, he did pull everything together," says Reisinger. "I don't recall anybody leaving. Not a single engineer left."

Marshall Smith handled Commodore's negotiations, along with his consultant Steven A. Greenberg and Commodore's attorney, Nicholas Lefevre. Contrary to Russell's suggestion, they decided to purchase Amiga outright, rather than acquiring a licensing agreement for just the chipset. Several machines, including the C900, were stuck in development hell with no guarantee the engineers were capable of finishing the projects. Gould and Smith wanted finishers; they wanted Jay Miner and his team.

Morse was a surprisingly firm negotiator, despite his tenuous financial position. "Dave Morse had already mortgaged his house and sunk a lot of his own money into Amiga to keep it going," says Dale Luck. "That would have scared the bejesus out of me. I think he sold his Porsche. He had faith in being able to pull this off."

In order for the deal to happen, both sides had to arrive at an agreed upon price for Amiga as a company. This was easy for Amiga, because Morse and Hart had already negotiated for a valuation of the company earlier in the year.

During the time of the proposed Atari deal, there could have been up to nine million total shares, including the million Atari would purchase. With Atari willing to pay $3 per share, this gave Amiga a maximum valuation of $27 million, on paper.

However, Bill Hart never did end up selling all two million shares that were reserved for him. In fact, only a limited number of investors were willing to purchase stock at the minimum $2 value. So even though Morse and Hart valued the company highly, many investors did not.

As of July 1984, Amiga had only 5,647,059 shares, with 2,352,941 reserved for future investors and employee stock options. If each of those 5,647,059 shares was valued at $3, it meant Amiga was worth $16,941,177 on paper.

At the low end of the company's valuation was the $1 per share offered by Jack Tramiel earlier in the year, which would have valued the company at $5,647,059 if his offer had been accepted.

Morse sensed that Commodore had already decided that it must acquire Amiga. He also perceived Gould himself wanted to deny Tramiel access to the Amiga chipset. Now that Bill Hart and Dave Morse had become aware of this rivalry, they would use it to leverage a higher price for company and pushed for the maximum $27 million valuation.

Amiga had a lot of talent by July of 1984. "By this time Amiga was probably 45 people," says Dale Luck. "They were going back and forth, with Commodore saying, 'This is our final offer.' Then, even though it was a very fair offer, Dave Morse came back and said, 'No that's not good enough.' He was very close to blowing the deal, but at the same time getting them to up the ante to make it work. After that whole negotiation, I would never want to play poker with Dave Morse. He was too good at bluffing."

Marshall Smith, for his part, emphasized that Commodore shares had recently fallen from $60 to $20 based on the news of Jack Tramiel departing and purchasing Atari. Given that the company faced no financial concerns and revenues had increased dramatically in the past few years, it seemed like a reasonable expectation that the value was depressed only for the short-term. There was every expectation that the good news of the Amiga acquisition could send Commodore's share price skywards, even doubling in value.

According to Michael Tomczyk, not all of the negotiations occurred around the boardroom table, as CEO Marshall Smith was well known for appreciating a good drink. "In the wee hours of the meeting with the Amiga designers, the CEO of the company, who also knew nothing about computers by the way, and our corporate attorney, decided to go have a drink somewhere with the group."

Unfortunately, closing call had already passed. "They couldn't find a bar because the bars were closed and they came back to the office. They had a bottle of booze in the desk, so they all proceeded to share that. Unfortunately, our team drank more than their team. The next thing we know, there was a $23 million deal on the table without any requirements for the Amiga designers to stay involved. That's my understanding as it was told by one of the meeting participants."

Commodore developer Andy Finkel had mixed feelings about the deal. "I believe Commodore probably overpaid," he says. "The story that went around was that Irving was willing to pay top dollar to get it instead of Jack, since Jack was preparing to take ownership of the Amiga chips because Atari had lent Amiga money. Irving also wanted to show Jack that he knew technology as well."

Although a deal was arrived at in July, it would take much longer to draw up a formal legal agreement to make the deal official. "It didn't take us too long to reach a deal with Commodore," says Hart. "In fact, there may already have been a tentative deal when Commodore gave us that money. It just takes a lot of time to execute these deals." In the meantime, word leaked that a deal was imminent.

Atari Lawsuit

Jack Tramiel was still seething from the lawsuit by Commodore but he soon found a way to counteract. In late July, Leonard Tramiel found a cashed check for $500,000 to Amiga, along with the loan agreement. He immediately showed it to his father. They soon learned of the original Amiga deal and realized Atari had a project codenamed Mickey to use the Amiga chipset.

After absorbing the new information, Tramiel regrouped and launched a legal assault. "As the Commodore transaction became public, Tramiel sued Commodore," says Hart. Tramiel contacted Warner and renegotiated with them, claiming the value of Atari Inc. was diminished by the loss of the Amiga deal. On August 9 Warner transferred the contract to Atari Corp.

On Monday, August 13 (two days before the Commodore-Amiga announcement), Tramiel filed a countersuit against both Commodore and Jay Miner personally, charging breach of contract.

Bill Hart believes the reason for Tramiel's lawsuit was to try to block the sale of Amiga to Commodore and delay Commodore's plans. "There's a long history of successful lawsuits when someone interferes with an ongoing negotiation," he says. "Texaco was the classic one that cost their shareholders a fortune because they interfered with an acquisition discussion that was ongoing. There had been a big judgment, and people are always afraid of that. So he sued Commodore."

Some felt Tramiel still wanted the Amiga chipset. "There was a drama taking place that I didn't know about at the time," explains Mical. "Commodore had let the Tramiels go in circumstances that were unhappy for people. The Tramiels went to Atari, and part of their intention was to take over the success of the C64; to take that away from Commodore and to have that success be Atari's success. They wanted the Amiga [chipset] to be the C64 killer and sink the ship of Commodore."

Atari charged that those chips were now being used in Amiga's new computer that Commodore intended to sell. Atari Corp. requested a permanent injunction to prevent Amiga from transferring the chips to Commodore and also asked for $100 million in punitive damages.

"Atari at that time was lawsuit happy," recalls Mical. "Their legal department was a profit center for the company. I don't know if this is true or not, but we used to joke that half of their business came from their lawsuits, and only half of it came from their actual products. They sued everybody. They just sued and sued and sued. It was laughable."[3]

On the surface, it looked like Amiga was free and clear of any wrongdoing. After all, it had paid back the $500,000 loan to Atari within the allowed time-frame and no licensing agreement was ever signed. The only documents signed had been the letter of intent and the $500,000 loan agreement.

Morse had undoubtedly strung along Atari, hoping for a better deal to come along, but kept the licensing deal alive in case he needed to fall back on it. He had also lied to Atari when John Ferrand had asked if Amiga was dealing with any other companies. And according to Ferrand, he had stated that the chipset did not work, a questionable assertion given it was demonstrated at the most recent CES. However, none of this was illegal per se.

There was, however, a line in the agreement which stated, "Amiga and Atari agree to negotiate in good faith regarding the licence Agreement." This was questionable. At the time, Amiga had happily negotiated for the sale of the video game console rights to the chipset. But as Atari insisted it wanted to design a home computer, Amiga soured on the deal.

---

3   Atari also tried suing Nintendo in 1989, alleging Nintendo prevented game developers from porting their games to other consoles.

When news of the lawsuit hit, Joe Decuir's worst fears were realized. He never did receive his indemnification from Morse, which he badly wanted when working for Amiga. However, Miner volunteered to help protect Decuir. "Because of the indemnification problem, and particularly when Jack Tramiel, who had acquired Atari Corp., decided to sue Jay Miner personally for patent infringement and theft of trade secrets, Jay Miner's instructions to me were, 'Become invisible. Make sure that Jack and his lawyers don't notice you.'"

As a result, Decuir kept his contribution to the Amiga a secret within the industry. "I did a really good job of being, as they say in Monty Python, not being seen. So I didn't have to spend all the money that I had to pay lawyers," he says. Although once the Amiga gained praise, it was also painful not to acknowledge his contribution. "On the other hand, I didn't get to hang out with these people," he says.

Commodore backed up its newly acquired company by paying for Amiga's defense fees and stepping in to take charge of the case. "We didn't do anything wrong," says Mical. "We followed the letter of the agreement with them and did everything right. They were just frustrated and lashing out."

It's Official

If Tramiel's plan was to stop the sale of Amiga to Commodore, it didn't work. After settling the details of the deal through the remainder of July and into August, the papers were finally signed. Commodore agreed to purchase Amiga Corporation for $4.25 per share. Commodore would make the official announcement on August 15, 1984. "I came back thinking it was going to be a four million dollar purchase and we would have the rights to use the chips in computers," says an exasperated Bob Russell. "Then the next day they were like, 'We're buying the whole company for $24 million.' I'm like, 'Say what? We could have got it for a tenth of that. Why did we buy the whole damn company?'"

It could be argued that Commodore paid a fair price, or at the very least didn't overpay by that much. After all, $4.25 is very close to $3 Atari was willing to pay earlier in the year, and Amiga had developed a lot more of the operating system and chipset since then, plus the public reveal at CES was met with unparalleled enthusiasm.

Regardless, Commodore now owned 100% of Amiga Corporation. Russell believes Irving Gould and Marshall Smith intended to thwart the Tramiels. "I'm sure part of that $24 million was spite," he says.

Michael Tomczyk believes Commodore could have negotiated a far better deal. "We got the Amiga machine for $23 million which was grossly overpaid and we never required the Amiga engineers and designers to stay involved," he explains. "They were just given the money and allowed to walk away. The whole thing was screwed up."

The Amiga employees were now worth significant sums after the deal. "If you were in the two to three percent range, you were considered one of the major shareholders in the company," says RJ Mical. "It would be good." In fact, three percent would be worth over $700,000 in Commodore stock. Not a bad haul for less than a year's worth of work for some employees.

The partners in Amiga, including Jay Miner and Dave Morse, were finally able to wipe out their debts and then some. "Their stake was pretty substantial," says Hart. "It's rare that the founders can get away with having 30 percent. I'm guessing they might each have taken 20%. It was more than the rest of the other employees." If it was 20%, Morse and Miner now each benefited by $4.8 million on paper.

Things also worked out for Intermedics, which originally invested $5.8 million in Hi-Toro. With 2 million in shares, Intermedics walked away with $8.5 million worth of Commodore stock. "I was told that every one of the investors who put any money in all did very well when Commodore bought the company," says Mical.

Mical himself was not a major shareholder, but his 2% share gave him a good return for his year at Amiga. "I was a lowly engineer," he says. "I rose to be director, but I didn't get a commensurate increase in my stock. I was young and naïve back then, and I didn't know to ask for it. I should have asked for it."

Although everyone involved seemed happy, Robert Yannes recalls the frustration of his friend Bob Russell. "When [Bob Russell] found out what they paid for the company, which was some outrageous sum of money, he called me and he said, 'Yeah, it was a good thing to buy but not for that much money! You could have taken that money and divided it up among the engineers and each would have gotten several million dollars. I guarantee you they would have designed something better than the Amiga.'"

The entire Amiga enterprise was renamed Commodore-Amiga and incorporated as a subsidiary of Commodore. Jay Miner insisted on one important clause in his contract. He wanted Commodore to allow his cockapoo Mitchy to become an official member of the Commodore-Amiga development team. "I wouldn't say they were okay with it," says Mical. "They tolerated it because it was Jay and who's going to argue with Jay?"

Bill Hart Exits

Once Amiga belonged to Commodore, investment expertise was no longer required and Bill Hart departed. Hart felt gratified that he had helped Amiga survive through a difficult period while benefiting his investors. "My funds in total walked away mostly with Commodore stock that was valued at the time of the transaction at $5-6 million," he says. "It was not a world-beating deal but the turnaround happened in less than a year. From the time they put their money in, until the time they got the stock back was less than a year. Even though the return might have been five times on their money, when you can make five times in less than a year that's a very large rate of return."

Throughout the period, Hart had suffered financially as much as Morse and Miner. "I had built up a fair amount of personal debt just trying to get my venture capital firm started. It took a lot longer than I thought, about five years. My daughter was starting to go to college and I was just really wondering how we were going to make it."

However, he had been given Amiga stock options, which he exercised before the Commodore deal. "I did have stock options personally but basically it all belonged to my funds," he says. "I ended up selling it and probably would have been better off selling it all as quickly as I could have because it went into decline shortly after that. But I still got enough out of it to certainly put me on my feet. All of a sudden I had several hundred thousand dollars and life turned around."

Hart also immediately transferred the Commodore shares to his investors. "When you have a success, you distribute it to the partners, you don't reinvest it," he explains. "We distributed the stock out to the partners. The investors can make their own decision."

Hart's involvement with Amiga also put him on the map among Silicon Valley investors. "That was the first liquidated investment that actually had a cash return that I had made," he explains. "I had other investments that were doing very well but they were more long-term in nature. As one very experienced venture capitalist said to me at the time, 'You just made it!' It only takes one really audacious deal to establish your credibility for going out and raising venture capital."[4]

---

4   Bill Hart grew his venture capital fund, Technology Partners, into a $450 million powerhouse by the end of the 1990's and remained friends with Dave Morse.

1-1

3-1

3-2

3-3

1-1   Marshall Smith, CEO and President of Commodore (AP Photo)

3-1   Gerard Bucas, director of business systems (photo courtesy of Gerard Bucas)

3-2   DEC VAX-11/785 minicomputer

3-3   Commodore PC-10, the company's first PC clone

4–1

4–2

4–3

4–4

4–1   Jay Miner, father of the Amiga (photo courtesy of Joe Decuir)

4–2   Dave Morse, founder of Amiga Corp. (photo courtesy of RJ Mical)

4–3   Joe Decuir, co-designer of the Amiga chipset (photo courtesy of Joe Decuir)

4–4   Mitchy, co-designer of the Amiga chipset (photo courtesy of Joe Decuir)

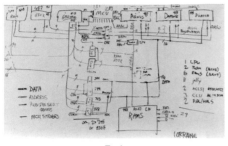

5–1

6–1

7–1

7–2

7–3

8–1

5–1   Lorraine block diagram on whiteboard (photo courtesy of RJ Mical)

6–1   The Joyboard and Power Sticks
(photo by Chris Collins from the Dale Luck collection)

7–1   Dave Needle, chip designer and Jovian (photo courtesy of RJ Mical)

7–2   The Agnus prototype chip board
(photo by Chris Collins from the Dale Luck collection)

7–3   Glenn Keller next to the Portia prototype (photo courtesy of RJ Mical)

8–1   Carl Sassenrath, exec developer (photo courtesy of RJ Mical)

8–2

8–3

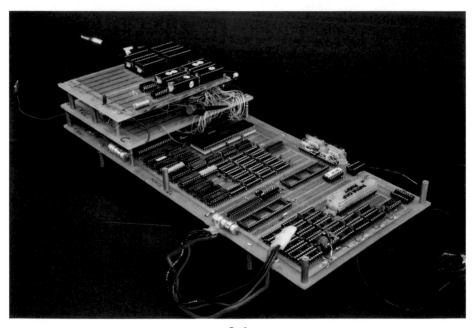

8–4

8–2 Dale Luck waking from a compiler catnap (photo courtesy of RJ Mical)

8–3 Amiga's Sage IV computer. The sticky note identifies it as "Agony".
(photo courtesy of Chris Collins from the Dale Luck collection)

8–4 Ron Nicholson's Peace motherboard
(photo by Chris Collins from the Dale Luck collection)

9–1

9–2

9–1   Lorraine concept sketches

9–2   Amiga developer system with wooden keyboard
      (photo by Chris Collins from the Dale Luck collection)

10–1   10–2

10–3

10–4

10–1 Displaying Joyboards at the CES Amiga booth (photo courtesy of RJ Mical)

10–2 RJ Mical and Dale Luck catching up on sleep at CES (photo courtesy of RJ Mical)

10–3 Bob Pariseau (r) and Glenn Keller presenting demos inside the Amiga booth (photo courtesy of RJ Mical)

10–4 RJ Mical, Joe Pillow, and Dale Luck (photos courtesy of RJ Mical)

11–1

13–1

13–2

11–1 June 1984 CES registration lines

13–1 Dave DiOrio (left) and Bil Herd (photo courtesy of Dave Haynie)

13–2 Commodore LCD Portable

13–3

14–1

15–1

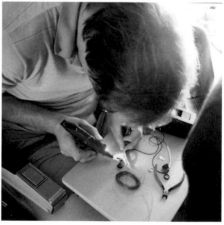

15–2

13–3 Dave Haynie wearing his C128 Animals sweater (photo courtesy of Dave Haynie)

14–1 Commodore-Amiga headquarters in Los Gatos

15–1 The ill-fated Plus/4 computer (photo courtesy of Phillipe Rouxete)

15–2 Greg Berlin soldering aboard an airliner on the way to CES
(photo courtesy of Dave Haynie)

A True Sequel 1984

Despite everything happening with the Amiga acquisition, Commodore still had a business to run, had its own projects underway and was set to release the Plus/4 to retail stores in late-summer 1984. Its executives had no reason to doubt its impending success and began thinking about their next home computer. The man who would take on that task was currently working on the LCD portable, though he would soon pass that system off to someone else.

Backward Compatibility

Up until 1984, Commodore had three hit products: the PET, VIC-20, and C64. Each successive computer was not software compatible with the previous one and the company saw no reason to change that direction. While customers saw a huge reason to have backward compatibility with the C64 library, within Commodore it didn't seem to matter much. This momentum would be hard to change within the large organization. But after some grumbling at the Plus/4's CES launch, some engineers began to realize they needed to build on the C64's success rather than attempt to compete with it.

With so much momentum behind the C64, there was still plenty of time for Commodore to decide on a true successor. Bob Yannes was sure Commodore would attempt to create a sequel. "I would have made something that would have led them to continue the Commodore 64 line; a Commodore 64 that had an 80-character screen that was improved in every area: more memory, better sound, better everything," he says.

An incompatible sequel called the D128 (not to be confused with the C128D) was already in the works by Dr. Kong Sui, but the project lingered in development hell. "He had some good ideas and just couldn't get them to work," says Dave Haynie.

Many in Commodore thought the D128 was not on target. A marketing consultant had previously convinced management that they did not have to do anything new to retain the low-end computer space. "Later on we had these marketing experts who would come in and say, 'Well you guys own this space, so you don't need to do anything about it,'" recalls Russell. "As much as people protested, corporate listened to them."

Russell listened to the experts in disbelief. "I plainly remember sitting in a meeting and the marketing people came in and started drawing. 'Here's the computer market in four quadrants. You own that space where the C64 is at in that quadrant. You don't need to do product in that.' All the management is saying, 'Okay. Yeah. That makes sense.' We're saying, 'No! No! We own that, but how do we maintain it?'"

Even though Russell patiently screamed that they needed to figure out how to continue the C64 success in retail, management felt they could retain a perpetual lock on the low-end market with the current C64 design. Russell knew users did not want to lose their software library when they bought a new computer and the best way to retain them was to release a backward compatible C64 with more memory, a faster processor, and better features.

Commodore's magazine division obviously knew the importance of backward compatibility. A March/April 1985 *Commodore Microcomputers* article starts, "Ask a Commodore 64 owner what kind of computer they would like to see Commodore produce next. They would probably chuckle and say, 'A compatible upgrade of the 64.'"

Bil Herd maintains the idea did not occur to the engineers or management of Commodore. "Nobody thought about doing a C64 sequel," says Herd. "There had been this weird-assed thing called the P128, and it was more like a PET than anything."

Most of Herd's engineers felt the task would be too difficult without the original C64 engineers. "Nobody thought about C64 compatibility. Nobody even thought we could do it again. Nobody even knew what it meant, because the guys who had done it were gone," explains Herd.

Herd made it his personal mission to convince Commodore to take backward compatibility seriously. "The idea of doing another C64 compatible machine started with me literally because I put up with all that crap at the CES show," he says. "Everybody else, it didn't faze. I swear to God. Nobody else was walking around talking about ever doing a C64 machine again. I'm not trying to grab credit, but I was the one who said, 'Whatever we do, why don't we make it C64 compatible?' They said, 'You can do that?'"

Herd wrote a lengthy memo to his coworkers and managers, including Joe Krasucki and Adam Chowaniec, titled, 'Yes Virginia There is Compatibility'. "It was written a couple of months after the Plus/4 show," says Herd. "I made some fairly brash statements regarding my opinion of product strategy."

The high-school dropout's memorandum was unrefined and strident in tone. "It would have been written in bad English that changed tense. I didn't write good English back then and we didn't have good spell checkers," recalls Herd. "It would have looked like it was written by a maniac to the wrong person. I think I went over the edge in a sentence or two and got derogatory at one point. I wrote like I talked, so I had curse words in there. It was passionate and pissed off. I didn't have a lot of patience for people who didn't see the obvious."

Looking back, Herd wonders how he got away with it. "I would hate to try to put up with me now like I was then," he says. "When I wrote it, I didn't know what would become of it." If Herd expected an immediate response from his letter, he did not receive one.

Conceiving the Next 8-Bit

The glacial pace of D128 development began to frustrate engineering manager Robert Russell. "Kong Sui was one of those guys who you wondered why he was around sometimes," laments Russell.

After many of the early Commodore engineers departed, the company had trouble finding engineers who could finish a product. "We really didn't have the same development people there anymore, apart from buying in the Amiga technology from outside," says Kit Spencer. "When they started to bring in new developer teams, I'm not sure they ever got a team that could drive a great new product."

Bil Herd also noticed the sharp contrast between Dr. Kong Sui's knowledge and lack of practical ability. "He was mathematically brilliant but couldn't really march a product downfield," he says. Commodore needed someone with real world experience.

Herd got involved with the D128 project while working on the LCD computer in the same lab as Dr. Kong Sui. According to Herd, "Freddy Bowen was sitting there with Kong Sui behind me in the lab, and I'm working on my LCD thing, and I keep hearing [Sui say], 'I don't understand how it can be doing that!'"

As Herd listened, he realized the problem was due to a short circuit. "Finally I lean over and say, 'It's because you've got contention,'" says Herd. Dr. Sui was reluctant to accept the explanation, telling Herd, "You must be wrong."

Herd delved into the problem. "I looked over and grabbed this photocopy of his PLA. He had photocopied it crooked and so close to the edge that he was missing the last column of terms," recalls Herd. "I showed him and said, 'Look, you're missing a column, you have two outputs turned on at the same time.'"

In minutes, Herd had solved a tenacious problem that had occupied the engineers for most of the day. Even more impressive, the project was unfamiliar to Herd. "Freddy Bowen looked at me and said, 'You know, I need Herd.' I said, 'That looks interesting, but can we make it compatible?'"

Herd received the plans for the D128. "By the time Herd got it, we had already sketched it up several times and gone through several iterations," says Russell.

According to Haynie, Herd discarded the plans. "We really didn't look at it much before getting into the C128," he says. "At that point there was very little left that described what they were trying to do."

Herd shared engineering tasks with Dr. Kong Sui and began pushing his concept of backward compatibility. With the brash young Herd around, Dr. Sui began to lose his position on the project. "He was who I shared the title of C128 designer for a week with, and then he was kind of on the outs," says Herd. "People who didn't belong there got scorched real fast and would get pushed to the side."

To incorporate backward compatibility, Herd started over from the beginning. "The D128 had that funny-assed processor and other things, and it used a color 6845 chip. It didn't use the VIC chip at all, and how can you not start with the VIC chip?" says Herd. "I looked at the existing schematics once and then started with a new design based on C64ness."

One part of the LCD machine Herd brought with him was the Memory management Unit. "I took the MMU spec with me to the 128, it was the first chip defined and got into the design process first," he says.

Herd directed planning sessions with the software and semiconductor engineers. "We commandeered the office all the way to the left of engineering row," says Herd. "It was Freddy Bowen, Terry Ryan, myself, and Dave DiOrio. It literally started with four of us in a room with a whiteboard, drawing big blocks." With the coup complete, the four rebels began planning a true C64 successor.

Early on, the discussions revolved around how to increase capabilities while allowing the computer to run the C64 software library. According to Herd, Fred Bowen believed the advanced 128K mode should not be compatible with the C64. "Freddy Bowen started this thought and I went with it. It made sense to me," says Herd. "He said, 'No, keep it different. Don't try and be a bigger C64, because then you will really fuck with the definition of C64 compatibility.'"

After much discussion, the engineers decided to have two separate modes: a mode with C64 compatibility, and a 128K mode with more memory and features. "We didn't want a hybrid definition of compatibility, and I applaud that thought that he started with," says Herd.

The decision for two modes was controversial. As hardware engineers it seemed to solve the problem of allowing users to continue running their old software library, but software developers were not as enthusiastic. "The only thing that really bothered me about the C128 was the mode switch," says Andy Finkel. "I would have tried to make it so you could use part or all of the capabilities in the same program, rather than having to switch modes."

After the meeting, Herd created the schematics. "I wrote the schematic from scratch, starting with a VIC chip and starting with a 6510 alias; the NMOS version [called the 8502]," he says.

Herd found himself competing with his old LCD project for resources, namely Jeff Porter. It was a holdover from the Tramiel years. "Jack was gone at this time, but he made it so the departments competed with each other for resources," says Herd.

Dave Haynie began working on the LCD project until Herd poached him for the C128 project. "I actually worked on [the LCD computer] for about a month before Bil asked me to come on the C128 project with him," recalls Haynie.

The engineers gave the computer the appropriate name of Commodore 128, or C128 for short. "When we started the Commodore 128, we always knew it was going to be called the Commodore 128," says Haynie. "It wasn't like it was a secret project or anything."

Marketing had a heavy hand in the Plus/4, but they were notably absent from the C128. "Nobody told us what to do, as far as the design. We drove the design, and it was a rare opportunity in history," explains Herd. "This would never happen at IBM or another company."

The unique freedom was due to a power vacuum left by Tramiel. "The reason I think there wasn't that process where marketing reviews everything is because under Jack, it wasn't necessary," says Herd. "Jack called the shots. With Jack gone, the engineers were free to say, 'Hey, look what we've got for you guys.'"

An aggressive engineer who passionately believed in backward compatibility now led the C128 project. Commodore would have a C64 successor. Although it was already August 1984, the C128 would have to be ready for the January 1985 CES show. With most computer companies focusing on 16-bit technology, industry analysts wondered if the market was still interested in 8-bit computers.

LCD Project Post-Herd

Once Bil Herd took over and effectively cancelled the D128 in favor of his C128, the LCD portable needed a new engineer to lead the project. The obvious replacement was Jeff Porter, who came to Commodore with an ambition to design computers. "I did the LCD design on graph paper, got interested in the D128, and he was obviously competent enough," recalls Herd.

Porter's promotion to project lead came from Herd himself. "I met with Joe [Krasucki] and said that Jeff could clearly handle the project, and I was moved to the D128 as a co-project lead with Kong Sui," recalls Herd. Joe's last words were 'time to cut the cord', a positive statement about his confidence in Jeff. At that point we actually handed off the LCD to Jeff Porter."

Porter, the engineer creating modems for Commodore and an internal version for the LCD, would continued working on his modems while leading the LCD portable. "It took three months to build this modem and then the LCD project came along," says Herd.

Jeff Porter was not involved in the genesis of the project but he would become its biggest cheerleader. "The LCD factory was well underway by the time I arrived, so I'm sort of the 'tail end of the dog' here," he says.

Although he had felt like he had been suckered into designing Commodore modems, when his ambitions to design systems came true, he committed fully to the project. "When Jeff Porter took over the LCD design, he put his heart into it," says Herd.

Meanwhile, David Baraff had samples of his LCD panels ready for Porter to use. "We made several hundred displays in a development facility," he says. "The displays were 80 character wide by 20 rows high. Across the display were 480 pixels and down the display were 240 pixels. The displays had horizontal and vertical viewing angles of plus or minus 45 degrees where the contrast was 10 to 1 or greater."

Porter was justifiably proud of the specs for the system. "We made an 80 character wide display that was 16 lines," he says. "So it had a lot more resolution in terms of LCD display."

At the time, Radio Shack was coming out with the Model 200 portable LCD computer, a successor to the Model 100 that inspired Commodore. "Our display was slightly larger and the contrast, viewing angle and speed were much faster," claims Baraff. "Our display was black and white television compatible; the TRS 200 display was not."

Many of the internal chips were similar to those used in the C64. "We came up with our own display controller and IO parts and CMOS 6502. So it was pretty traditional technology that built the C64," says Porter. "We didn't use any of the C64 chips like SID that were not CMOS. They were power hungry son of a bitches."

Battery technology for portable computers in 1984 was primitive. However, by using the efficient CMOS 65C02 processor developed by Bill Mensch, the LCD portable could operate for 15 hours. "It was a CMOS 6502 based system that ran off of 4 AA batteries," Porter says. "It was an 8-bit CPU that was in CMOS, so it got many days, depending on how many hours per day you used it. It was pretty good."

While it lacked a disk drive, the computer contained 32 kilobytes of battery-backed memory to save data. "It had static RAM," Porter explains. "Most laptops today still have DRAMs in them. Turn the power off and the data goes bye bye. Static RAMs were an easy way to keep data in memory back then, but they were more expensive and lower density."

To store documents in a more permanent form, data could either be uploaded to another computer with the modem or saved to an external 1541 disk drive. "It had a standard Commodore serial bus, so you could save it to a 1541 or 1581," Porter explains. "It had a modem in it. It had a Centronics printer port so you could hook up a normal printer and print out your document."

The LCD computer weighed only five pounds. "It would have been great," says Andy Finkel. "It had 80 columns and was fairly light weight. Its big competition at that point was the TRS-80 Model 100 from Radio Shack."

Commodore estimated the LCD computer would retail for only $500. Marshall Smith told Porter that if he could acquire enough orders at the upcoming January 1985 CES show, the product could go into production. According to Herd, "They told him, 'Go get 15,000 and we'll talk.'"

LCD Portable Software

The LCD required two types of software. The low-level system software would be programmed by a recent hire named Hedley Davis. The applications software would be handled by long-time Commodore game programmer Andy Finkel and his team.

Davis remembers working overtime on the LCD system software. "I worked feverishly on that," he says. "We worked day and night."

One problem with working on the system at night was the building shut down after everyone else went home. "I remember being in there in the development systems in a lab and they would shut off the air conditioning at like 6 p.m. and by like nine it would be like a hundred degrees in there," he recalls, laughing. "I would strip down to my underwear to write code because it was so hot. Sweat pouring off."

Somewhere in his feverish mind, Davis sensed a portable laptop computer could have a bright future in computing. "I was going to be a fucking billionaire because I wrote all the systems code for the LCD," he explains. "I did a whole bunch of development on that. It was kind of revolutionary and I knew somewhere in the back of my mind that if some system came out and you knew that system inside and out and you could develop software for that system better than anybody else, that somehow you could make a lot of money. And this was my ticket, this machine. It was going to be awesome."

As was usual, the hardware designers and software programmers sometimes clashed. "To this day, Porter and I disagree about a problem that machine had starting up," Davis recalls. "Something in memory would get changed and I had code in there to check that. So it was throwing errors. There's all these machines, the five or six that exist, you would turn them on and oh, something's wrong because the code says something even though Porter says there's no problem whatsoever. We're still fighting about it."

While Davis worked on the system software, Andy Finkel worked on the application software. Michael North's specification for the machine carried forward the Plus/4 idea of integrated software applications in ROM. "The most interesting thing about the LCD was that all the productivity software built-in was done in-house, and it was excellent," claims Haynie. "It was everything the Plus/4 hadn't been."

For the applications, instead of using an existing software suite as the Plus/4 had, Commodore used its internal programmers to develop the software. "Andy Finkel and some of his guys worked on the apps because it had a built in word processor and spreadsheet and terminal program and things like that. It was pretty awesome," says Porter.

Finkel was overjoyed to be a part of the project. "We called it an LCD machine but it was a laptop really," he says. "At Commodore we always wanted to do a portable. We had the Executive 64, which was a Commodore 64 in a case with a fairly heavy five-inch monitor, but it still weighed a ton."

The software included eight applications, including a word processor, file manager, address book, scheduler, calculator, memo pad, and a telecommunications package for the built in modem. "I did some stuff for the C128 but at that point I was more focused on the LCD machine," says Finkel.

Choosing a Processor

While the suit and tie wearing Jeff Porter, Hedley Davis and Andy Finkel put together the LCD computer, across the hall in another lab, the slightly more rowdy C128 team began piecing together the C128.

One of the most important decisions Bil Herd and his engineers had to make was choosing the processor for the C128. The engineers knew customers would expect an improvement between the C64 and C128, especially with processor speed. They had several choices, but they looked the hardest at two: the 8502, a depletion-load NMOS (called the HMOS-II process) version of the 6510 that ran at faster speeds, and a new 16-bit chip by original 6502 co-designer Bill Mensch. His chip, called the 65816, was fully backward compatible with the original 6502.

By March 1984, Bill Mensch had samples of his 16-bit 6502 processor in the hands of both Apple and Atari. Although Atari declined, Apple showed interest in the chip for a system it called the Apple IIx.

Mensch then approached MOS Technology, as it seemed logical to him that they would want to fabricate the processor. Bob Russell compared the 65816 to an earlier 16-bit spec called the SY6516. "I was sitting there looking at the 6516 saying, 'Damn, that was pretty good architecture.' But he did even a better job with the real one," he says.

Unfortunately, Mensch found very little interest from MOS. "When I negotiated with Michael Channing, the vice president of engineering at MOS Technology at the time, he said, 'No, we've got an 8086 based platform we're building, so we have no use for a 16-bit 6502 type of product.' I said, 'Oh, alright. Fine. Well if you change your mind, call me.' Which I thought they would for sure."

Mensch wanted to sell a license to MOS Technology to produce the chips. "I gave Commodore 50% off my standard license fees for the other chips but they would have had to pay full fees at that time or $250,000 to $500,000 for the '816." he says. "I was giving them a good deal. But they didn't come back for it because it really quite frankly didn't fit in with their way of thinking. Commodore was having a bad bout of NIH (Not Invented Here) so it really didn't surprise me they didn't use the '816."

When he approached Commodore directly, he ran into Bil Herd. "I had a conversation about using it one day," says Herd. "I was in my office and he called me. He said, 'Hey, you should look at building this in. I'm trying to get Apple to build it in and then there will be this common code.' I'm like, 'So you're trying to tell me Bill that because my competitor is using it, I have to use it.' He didn't like that comment."

Mensch's marketing skills failed to impress Herd. "I had tried to treat the call with the reverence of speaking to one of my elders but the logic got lost in the sales attempt," he says. "The Apple comment wasn't a compelling argument to a young engineer looking to do the things the best way, not what's best for the vendor."

Herd was also studying Motorola's 16-bit processor at the time. "We were looking at the 68000," he says. The 68000 design used many registers, compared to the minimal registers in the 65816. "I completely disagree with the attitude that having less registers by design is better than having more," explains Herd.

"His final attempt to get me to use the chip was, 'Well, the 68000 has got those 16 registers, and that's just so much stuff you have to store every time you get an interrupt. My chip has only got two registers, so it's easy.' I couldn't believe that. I'm like, 'So what you're saying is it's less powerful so therefore it's quicker, but if I wanted to I could use two registers on the new chip and it would be just like yours.' He goes, 'Uh, yeah, I guess.' That was the only conversation I had with Bill Mensch about using it."

Herd felt Mensch should have consulted with Commodore engineers during his 65816 design process. "If Mensch had talked with Freddy Bowen, he would have got good feedback earlier on in his design cycle," says Herd. "Fred would have read him the riot act on how to make a kernel for a C64 compatible user system."[1]

---

1   A company called *CMD* later released a C64 upgrade called the *SuperCPU.* The device uses a 65816 chip to upgrade a stock C64 to 20 MHz and 16 megabytes of memory. It was surprisingly backward compatible, drastically speeding up 3D games such as *Freescape, Mercenary*, and *Sentinel* while maintaining the correct timing.

Out of the engineers, Bowen was the primary antagonist against using the 65816 because it would be up to him to program the system software. Aside from his criticisms of the processor, Bowen felt it would be harder to work with the chip because of the lack of a mature assembler for the 65816 in 1984.

In the end, the lack of control over the 65816, the extra cost of buying the chip from an outside vendor, immature development tools, and the inevitable bugs in the new chip led the engineers to side with the 8502 instead. In retrospect, this was probably a wise move if they wanted to keep to their challenging schedule.

The C128 Animals

After the engineers handed off the Plus/4 to production, six of the seven Plus/4 engineers eventually moved on to develop the C128. Bil Herd, Dave Haynie, and Frank Palaia would design the hardware, while Fred Bowen, Terry Ryan, and Von Ertwine developed the system software.

Management realized the tight January 1985 deadline meant the engineers would have to work overtime, so they did everything possible to keep the engineers busy at Commodore until late hours. "We occasionally got bribed," recalls Haynie. "Occasionally, a manager would say, 'We're bringing in beer and pizza at 10:00 or 11:00 [at night]', but it wasn't like we were drinking beer on the job all the time."

Management set the precedent, and soon Herd began bringing his own alcohol to work. "I got the guards used to seeing me walk in with a case of beer on my shoulder," recalls Herd. "My record was 11 days without leaving, and given the fact that I drank a lot back then, I couldn't live at work without a refrigerator with beer in it. They were told to leave us alone on that."

Herd worked with a 6 foot 8 peripheral designer for the C128 named Greg Berlin. The two became best friends. "Bil was working on the motherboard primarily and I was doing the disk drive," recalls Berlin. "Bil and I were thick as thieves back in those days. We were best buddies, we partied together. He's wound so tight he's just gotta be go, go, go; a hundred miles an hour."

Beer became a constant companion to Herd while he developed the C128. "I had a refrigerator in [Greg] Berlin's office," says Herd. "Anybody was welcome to put their beer in there, but there was a beer tax, which meant we would take as much as we wanted. One time, a guy had shown up with this San Francisco brand beer, and when he came to get one, they were gone. We just said, 'This time the beer tax was 100%. Sorry.'"

Herd's ways spread among the other engineers. "Bil was a crazy man and he dragged me down," recalls Berlin. "But it was good."

When direct management was absent from the engineering rooms, things often got out of control. "They were like teenagers, just totally out of control," recalls Hedley Davis. "Him and Herd where best of buds. Herd used to physically fight 6 foot 8 Berlin because that's just the way he was wired."

When Davis came into work, he noticed some damage to the drywall and no sign of Herd or Berlin. "There was a man sized hole in the wall one day where they got into it just screwing around," laughs Davis. "And Berlin separated Herd's shoulder." The two were at the hospital and Herd returned with his arm in a sling. "It was funny. We were largely unsupervised, unmanaged kids in a toy store."

When not destroying Commodore's premises, Berlin designed the C128's custom disk drive. "I was doing the disk drive for that and that was the 1571," he recalls. He was determined to improve on the slow speed of the 1541. "It was kind of compatible with the 1541 but it had the serial interface done in hardware so it was faster."

The engineering culture changed radically under Herd compared to the days when Chuck Peddle and Charles Winterble ran their respective systems groups. "It was kind of wild," recalls Haynie. "It was the kind of place where you were encouraged by the fact that you could be wild. There was a lot of camaraderie there. We pulled lots of late-night hours and I kept a sleeping bag under my desk. It was a very, very creative environment."

The unruly behavior of the C128 team soon earned them a nickname. "We were collectively known as the C128 Animals," explains Herd. "The term Animals was used by the highest management levels I was aware of at the time and described the effort and spirit of the team."

Haynie laughs at the old moniker. "We kind of looked like animals," he recalls. "Me and Bil had the long hair and we sometimes smelled like animals after too many days without going home."

To management, the group barely appeared civilized. "I walked around without my shirt on a lot and without shoes occasionally," says Herd.

Computer engineers have a reputation for leading staid lives, but Herd feels the C128 Animals challenged the stereotype. "I went into the Plus/4 with wild-eyed enthusiasm and by the next year I was cocky like a Jet fighter pilot," he says. "There were no geeks on our team except Terry Ryan. He was the resident vegetarian who wrote BASIC 7.0."

Commodore had moved to West Chester in the summer of 1983, and soon employees became patrons of a local bar called Margaritas. "When we started going there, it was kind of this little biker bar place," recalls Haynie. Margaritas soon prospered due to the close proximity to Commodore headquarters.[2] "We called it the 'house that Commodore built' because they added an extension and it got real fancy."

Herd fit right in at Margarita's during its early biker-bar phase. "I could walk right into a biker bar and you would never know I knew anything about computers," he says. "If anything, I was probably more dangerous than a normal person and hopped up from all the testosterone we got at work."

Although Haynie restricted his Margaritas visits to Fridays, Bil Herd sometimes used it as a conference room. "To get out of the office (this was in the days before cell phones) we would go down to Margaritas," recalls Herd. "Dave DiOrio and I had the bartenders in the area trained if we showed up in the afternoon. We pushed a couple of tables together and spread our schematics out, and that was how we would work all afternoon. Some of our schematics actually had rings in the corners from the beer mugs holding them down."

While the C128 Animals enjoyed their freedom, management started building up. "In the C128 days, they had installed a needless layer of middle management that pretty much did nothing, at least that I could determine," says Haynie. "Rather than reporting directly to the director of engineering, we were reporting to this middle-guy."

Herd grew frustrated seeing resources wasted on unproductive projects. "To give you an idea of how middle managers dog-piled on the department, we got a manager in charge of components," says Herd. "He didn't know anything about the real life aspect of Asian markets or cost and availability overseas that I could detect."

The situation appalled Herd. "He officially had more salary and people to support our ability to use the microfiche than we had designing the C128 computer," says Herd. "He hired a couple of more people and set up a computer-indexed version of data books that used microfiche. The microfiche was sort of out of date and I had several hundred data books anyway that actually traveled well to the local bars."

When the C128 Animals found someone without a purpose, they attacked. "The manager's name was Elroy, and rarely did we ever just say

---

2 A Margaritas bartender amused patrons by stopping a fan blade with his tongue. He later became semi-famous after winning *Stupid Human Tricks* on *Late Night with David Letterman*.

his name," explains Herd. "We usually sang it in a sentence, as in, 'Our Boy Elroy' [from the *Jetsons* TV show]. Whether you were in an intense discussion with management or a meeting, or at the bar, you didn't say Elroy, you sang it."

The middle manager provided one side benefit: access to executive emails. "I never complained about the microfiche program as it was my favorite backdoor into the VAX system with manager privileges, since he had installed it incorrectly," reveals Herd. "If you hit Ctrl-C at the right time, it would break to the prompt and you would be logged on as Our Boy Elroy. [It was] great for finding out what managers were up to."

When marketing released promotional material for the C128, Herd's goal was set even higher. "We never said it was 100% compatible. We called it compatible-like," says Herd. "Then we found that Julie Bauer over in the marketing department had put out a brochure that said, '100% C64 compatibility.' So we said, 'Great, I like a challenge.'"

Achieving 100% compatibility became a mission. "The whole thing with the C128 became live or die whether it was compatible or not," explains Herd. "Anytime somebody thought they found a reason that it wasn't compatible, it was, 'Aha! We found why it will fail.' We created the culture that C64 compatibility was a must have, and compatibility meant 100% not 95%."

Herd tried fixing several problems in the C64 but those fixes inadvertently created new problems. "I started out as one of the only guys who knew where all the glitches were," says Herd. "I designed them out, and you know what? Cartridges stopped working."

The problems encountered while recreating C64 mode originated with the C64 team as the chips determined a lot about the hardware. "So in effect the guys who designed it weren't hardware engineers, they were chip designers," says Herd. "There is a different way of thinking. I have nothing against the guys who developed the C64. They were pioneers and they did it first, so this is not a swing at them or anything."

"The chip designers just didn't know some of the basic rules," he says. As a result, developers often discovered programming tricks which relied on glitches. "The guys who designed cartridges would use the glitches on the IO select lines to clock data. It was like, 'No, no! Use the clock, not the address lines changing.' But they had found something that happened repeatedly."

It was disheartening to recreate the problems. "I had to put them back in," laments Herd. "There was a wire on the C128 and next to it, it said, 'Puts glitches back in.'"

Herd's attitude carried the project through. "The whole thing with Commodore 64 compatibility was you couldn't sit there and argue about why something wasn't compatible and blame the guy that did it," says Herd. "You had to make it compatible."

Dave Haynie became the engineer most responsible for compatibility. "On the C128, I basically turned into the compatibility guy," he says. "I was getting all sorts of add-on hardware and when it didn't work I had to sit there and figure out why, and then figure out if they were doing something I considered legitimate."

Haynie used an old Bally-Midway game to test compatibility. "Our favorite cartridge was Wizard of Wor because that one did all kinds of crazy-assed things," he says.

Herd had very little time to make the 128 project happen. Five months remained until the computer's CES debut. "You'd think if we were smart we would have started in January for next year, but I think I started in August for next January," says Herd.

It was up to LSI engineer Dave DiOrio to continue the VIC and SID chip legacy. "He was instrumental in the design and capabilities of the C128," says Herd. While the C64 designers had nine months to complete their chips, the C128 team had only five. However, the design changes were not as ambitious.

For sound, the C128 used the new 8580 SID chip, which received no improved functionality over the 6580 SID. "The only difference was we got a 9 volt SID chip instead of a 12 volt SID chip," says Haynie. "We didn't have two chips for stereo, but it was something that had been talked about."

Yannes had plans for further development of the SID chip. "If I had stayed at Commodore, I think I would have had time to refine it and make it a much better sounding product," he says.

Commodore only slightly improved on the SID chip after Yannes departed with the new 8580. "They had a guy named Radovsky but he was the wrong guy to try it," says Herd. "He was supposed to be the analog guy, and he was a case. He tried an NMOS version of the SID chip, and the rev I saw was visibly worse. He broke a lot of rules."

The alterations by John Radovsky created a loud thump sound when the SID chip became active. "Capacitors are attached to the sound chip, because it's an analog device," explains Herd. "You have to respect that these things are out there holding charge. So Radovsky tried to improve the SID chip, and he really didn't. He moved it backwards for a while. He brought back the thump."

Building the Herdware

Software developers usually create software for the largest platform available. Since that was the C64, the 128K mode would have to be very similar to the existing C64 standard so that programmers could develop one program that would work on a normal C64 *and* the enhanced 128K mode. Even though the enhanced mode may not run all of the old software, it would run the new C64 software faster and better, encouraging existing C64 owners to upgrade. Call it forward compatibility. This was the path taken by IBM and Apple.

On paper, the C128 appeared to be exactly what users and software programmers wanted. "I would have wanted 80 columns, more colors, and more sprites," says Andy Finkel. "Basically, a C64 on steroids." Indeed, Herd set out to produce a machine with 128 kilobytes of memory, a 2 MHz processor, and 80 columns. The only thing it lacked was a true successor to the VIC-II chip, with more colors, better resolutions, and larger, more detailed sprites.

Adding an additional 64 kilobytes of memory required ingenuity from Herd, since 6502 processors only addressed 64 kilobytes. "The CPU can only put out 16 bits worth of address, or 64K of memory," explains Haynie. "So no matter how much memory you have, the CPU can only talk to 64K at a time, no matter what you do."

Al Charpentier and his LSI engineers had already included a simple method of allowing more memory on the C64 called bank switching. "We handled that in the 6510," says Charpentier. "There was a port register that allowed you to do extended addressing."

By 1984, Charpentier's method of bank switching was outdated. "We didn't use that other banking scheme that was there [in the 6510]," says Herd. "Time had passed, so it was no longer the ideal way."

Herd and his team devised a Memory Management Unit chip, or MMU. "As far as I knew, I was inventing it, although I'm sure I hadn't," says Herd.

The results were impressive. "The way we did it in the C128 was the right way to do it," says Haynie. "You put an MMU in there and let the programmer manage the memory that you are banking between."

The MMU made it more difficult to add features while retaining backward compatibility. "If you change the memory map around at all, you will lose some compatibility," says Haynie.

Herd initially attempted a faster, better C64. "We had uber C64s," reveals Herd. "We had it working at one time. It was a C64 with an MMU. There were all kinds of addressing modes and other things. You could actually go into dual speed mode." The description sounded like the mode most people expected.

The "uber C64" had less C64 compatibility but more features for programmers. "We could run a C64 program, stop it, and it was really a C128 with all the resources at its command," explains Herd.

Unfortunately, the VIC-II chip could not keep up with the 2 MHz processor. "He was trying to do something faster, but once again, there were problems with MOS getting chips to run faster," says Russell.

Herd wanted his "uber C64" to work with older software titles. "You would be hard pressed to find a game that didn't screw up somehow, because you needed room in the memory for the Memory Management Unit to sit there," explains Herd.

To the engineers, it seemed pointless to attempt backward compatibility with a more powerful system. "The [C64] programmer's reference guide told the users how to do every damn thing and how to get to every bit," says Russell. "People were doing weird stuff with peeking and poking, so to be 100% compatible was too difficult."

Instead, due to a suggestion from Herd's coworker Fred Bowen, he decided to concentrate on a radically different C128 mode that retained very little compatibility. "We not only added a better kernel, and a better version of BASIC, but we put a ROM monitor in there and some other things," says Herd. "That's why it's not compatible with the old. None of that crap fit in the bag."

Commodore 64 designer Bob Yannes claims he would have followed a similar path taken by Bil Herd for a C64 sequel. "I probably would have made the C64 a subset of a new machine," he says. "I wouldn't want to cripple the capabilities of the new machine in order to be compatible with the C64."

Programmer Terry Ryan improved almost every aspect of BASIC, including better graphics commands and disk commands that were more like Microsoft DOS. The C128's starting screen even displayed, 'Microsoft BASIC copyright 1977,' which was a first for a Commodore computer. According to Robert Russell, Microsoft was behind the change. "They came in and demanded that we put Microsoft back on the BASIC, even though they didn't contribute anything," he says.

While Herd drove the hardware design, Fred Bowen developed the system software. "Fred was really the hands-on software guy then," says Russell. "Herd and Bowen were much more into implementation and what was really getting done on the product."

The software engineers had a surplus of ROM memory available, so the design team decided to add their signatures to the computer in the form of Easter eggs. Users who typed SYS 32800,123,45,6 received a message:

```
Brought to you by...
Software: Fred Bowen, Terry Ryan, Von Ertwine.
Herdware: Bil Herd, Dave Haynie, Frank Palaia.
Link Arms don't make them.
```

Terry Ryan also added messages of his own. An early message said, 'Veni Vidi Vici' (I came I saw I conquered). Herd and Ryan attempted to verify the message in the ROM code. "One time we spent two hours looking for a message to come through the analyzer," recalls Herd. "Finally I said, 'Nope, just a bunch of Vs.' [Ryan] stopped, looked at me, his moustache twitched and he mouthed the word, 'Shit.'" As it turns out, Herd was not familiar with the saying. "I didn't recognize it as English and it had been working the whole time," he says.

Ryan changed this to another message that reflected his thoughts during the cold-war arms race. "He of course was the author of, 'Link arms don't make them,'" says Herd.

Games Are Dead. Long Live Games.

Commodore had always worked hard to make sure each of its home computer platforms, the VIC-20 and C64, launched with dozens of software titles to give users something to do with their new computer. Even the recently launched Plus/4 attracted hundreds of commercial games to the platform. The man responsible for this success was VP of software Sig Hartmann, who would be expected to bring the same quantity of game and productivity software to the C128 when it was time to launch the system—if Marshall Smith could hold onto him.

Commodore, like many other computer companies, established an educational software division going back to the early 1980s. In early 1984, sensing educational software was not significantly affecting the fortunes of Commodore, Hartmann closed the division. The last educational game was *Lemonade*, a copy of the popular educational game *Lemonade Stand*.

Commodore also released a few more popular games in 1984. Andrew Spencer of Commodore UK followed his *International Soccer* hit with *International Basketball*, which used much of the same code from his previous game. This time the game featured a random crowd, a scoreboard, and courtside advertisements for Kellogg's, Coca-Cola, and of course Commodore. He followed up the game with *International Tennis*.

Satan's Hollow was Commodore's final in-house Bally-Midway port. Commodore's relationship with Bally-Midway ended in 1984, after which Sega Corporation began converting Bally-Midway games for the C64. In late 1984, Sig Hartmann, the man who established the software division at Commodore, began to doubt the company's future under Marshall Smith. On October 24, 1984, Hartmann resigned and went to work for none other than his former boss, Jack Tramiel at Atari. Commodore's software output soon decreased to almost nothing.

Curiously, just prior to leaving, Hartmann decided Commodore should also release its games for the IBM PC, Apple II, and Atari 800. In an interview with *RUN* magazine, Hartmann said, "If we were to sell it for only one system, we'd be missing the boat. That's why we're pushing to get maximum exposure in the marketplace."[3]

In the aftermath of his departure, Marshal Smith and Irving Gould let the software division wither and die, feeling the video game crash meant Commodore should exit the games marketplace. "The game division kind of dissolved when we were in engineering and working on other things," explains Andy Finkel. "I think Commodore was getting out of the game publisher business. There were just so many other publishers. Commodore never really understood game publishing."

With no internal software division creating games and finding lucrative deals, the C128 now had no real hope of receiving any game development for C128-mode, even by third party game developers. And with games being the lifeblood of home computers, especially in the 8-bit world, it would have a profound impact on the legitimacy of the C128 as a true successor to the C64.

---

3   *RUN* magazine, "For Gamesters Only" (December 1984), p. 24.

Commodore-Amiga
1984

After the initial shock of Commodore acquiring their company wore off, the Amiga engineers realized they had more resources at their disposal than they could dream of. Commodore also had demands for the new system and wanted it to compete against the Macintosh and IBM PC in the business world. It was time to step back, reassess the goals of the project, and begin forging forward. On the software side, Bob Pariseau's team still needed a disk operating system, a GUI, the BASIC programming language, and some launch titles. It was a tall order, but with the schedule pushed back to the summer of 1985, the team felt they had plenty of time. First, they needed to set up their new office space.

Velvet

In late August 1984, Jay Miner took his seat as General Manager of Commodore-Amiga. The engineers were thrilled with the arrangement. "Commodore did the best thing they possibly could have done to make sure that the product they bought was successful: They left us alone," says RJ Mical.

Miner continued designing and improving his chips at the lowest levels. Although Mitchy was slowing down, she continued working with Miner developing the chips. "Mitchy was really kind of an old dog during the Amiga days," says Mical.

"I never met Jay Miner but I have a lot of respect for him," says Bil Herd. "The only thing I ever heard bad about him was that his dog stunk. One of the programmers was like, 'Oh, I hated that dog!'"

Commodore-Amiga moved ten miles from the small offices on Scott Boulevard to a spacious rented facility at 983 University Avenue in Los Gatos,

California, Building D. "It was a nice big facility with a huge kitchen and offices for everyone. It was great," says Mical.

The new location, a few minutes walk from Vasona Lake County Park, uniquely suited Mical's style. "There was a lovely green courtyard in a gorgeous, lush setting," he recalls. "It was close to good restaurants and close to a beautiful huge park, which was great for walking. I've always been a walker. My best meetings and my best design thinking sessions have taken place out of doors. It was a beautiful place for that."

The Los Gatos area also had all the cultural necessities for young engineers. "There was this wonderful pizza parlor that we always used to go to and play video games and drink beer and eat pizza," says Mical. "We would go there together quite often. We were real close friends with each other, as well as coworkers, so we would regularly hang around and socialize in the evenings."

Dave Haynie recalls the best part about Los Gatos. "I only went out there a couple of times and I really liked being out there in Los Gatos simply because there were no Commodore management types wandering around," he explains.

The Amiga engineers enjoyed their arrangement with Commodore. "They had this brilliant group of engineers who had put this machine together and they just left us to invent the thing ourselves without interference," Mical says. "In the beginning, we were all vastly in love with Commodore and their way of doing business because we were going to be able to finish the Amiga the way we intended."

Although Commodore's contract with Amiga had no retention agreements, most stayed. "There were a couple of hardware engineers who left, but by that time most of the hardware engineering was done," says Dale Luck, referring to Joe Decuir and Ron Nicholson. "Most people were dedicated and loyal to wanting to bring the product out. None of us were there just to make money."

Once the Amiga engineers were comfortable in their new workspace, Dave Needle began designing a new version of the motherboard, different from Lorraine. Revision 0 and 1 had been designed by Ron Nicholson and Lorraine had been revision 2. "On the Amiga prototypes, each motherboard had a code name," explains Dave Haynie. "The first codename was the Lorraine. That was the one in the black metal cases and they still had the 5.25-inch floppy."

Needle codenamed his new revision Velvet. Like Lorraine before it, Velvet was designed for 128 KB expandable to 256 KB. Now that the engineers wanted a serious business computer, several of the home computer elements were removed. First to go was the game cartridge slot, for obvious reasons. The internal 300 baud modem was also removed, since that speed was now considered obsolete. It was not replaced by a 1200 baud modem because modem speeds were clearly evolving.

After seeing the Atari ST at the most recent CES, it became clear the Amiga needed a disk drive upgrade. And for good reason. All those graphically intensive applications required more data storage. The prior year, Lorraine used 5.25 inch disks which stored about 320 K per disk. Now, the engineers swapped it out for a double sided, double density 3.5 inch drive, which stored up to 880 K of data.

Up until now, the Amiga computer had been showcased in a plain black metal box. Once at Commodore, the Amiga finally received a professional case design. The case had come a long way since the far-out concept sketches from 1983. But in a nod to the original modular designs, the keyboard slid underneath the computer in a small compartment, giving the Amiga a tidy appearance when not in use. Developer units of Velvet shipped in early 1985, looking very refined.

By mid-1984 there was still a lot of work left for the software engineers. "At that time there still wasn't a disk operating system," says Dale Luck. "We had a cross compiler that ran on a Sun computer. So the amount of other software to make the machine usable was still really very much limited to some games and demos we had going."

At this point it was obvious the late 1984 release date Dave Morse had been touting earlier in the year was no longer realistic. Even if the computer was completely done, they had missed taking pre-orders at the June CES that were vital for a launch. The new launch date for the computer was pushed back to June 1985, with shipments expected to go out in September.

Commodore gave the Amiga engineers the proper resources and tools they needed to develop the system. "They gave us a huge infusion of cash which allowed us to buy new computers for ourselves and hire some extra people that we needed," says Mical.

The Second Pivot

Amiga previously wanted to release a video game console. Then Amiga stated that they would release the "Amiga PC" in late 1984. After the acquisition by Commodore, the team pushed the release date back to 1985 because it was about to pivot to a business computer.

It would not be easy for the developers to meet the new date and the Amiga's transformation from a home computer into a business machine would cause delays. "It was entirely due to the fact that we wanted to turn it into a real computer," says Mical. "It wasn't just the user interface. Some of the other things were smaller but equally significant. We needed a word processor, we needed a good graphics program, and we needed the basic set of tools that could also do some businessey officey things."

Andy Finkel believes the delays were justified. "The Amiga was the most complex computer Commodore had gotten involved in. It was way more complex than the MS DOS machines, way more complex than the C128 or B256 or any of those others. The three custom chips, the huge operating system, all that just took a lot more development time and effort than we thought."

Internal turmoil between Dave Morse and Commodore began not long after the acquisition, when Commodore wanted to manage the company more closely. "I frankly think they wanted to get control of Amiga from a management standpoint," says Bill Hart. "A lot of companies will do that when they buy a company."

Adam Chowaniec in particular felt there would be a better chance of making deadlines with someone from Commodore to monitor the Amiga operation. "They were a loose bunch of engineers in some ways," says Gerard Bucas. "As they grew, they needed to be managed."

In September of 1984, barely a month after the acquisition, Commodore hired a former Apple Manager of Advanced Development named Rick Geiger. The idea was that Geiger, a West Coast native, would keep an eye on the Amiga group and report back to Commodore management on the East Coast. "This guy was brought in by Adam to manage them," says Bucas. "He was handed the VP of the Amiga division and of the engineering side of the Amiga division."

Over the next six months, Geiger watched over the Amiga project, reporting back to Commodore management in West Chester. This began to rub Dave Morse the wrong way because he was used to his freedom. "Geiger was never involved in the design architecture but more of a manager than anything else, which Dave [Morse] didn't like that much quite frankly," says Bucas. "Dave wanted to be free spirits and all that."

The Rocky and Bullwinkle Show

Commodore provided the Amiga team with powerful tools for development. "At Amiga, we used the Sage and it was miserable and slow," says

Mical. "We instantly went from ten people on one Sage to each guy having his own Sun workstation, with massive power and its own hard disk and its own CPU. Those were heavenly days."

Each Sun-2/120 workstation, decked out with two megabytes of memory, SCSI hard drive, Ethernet card, and tape unit cost Commodore $26,400. The workstations required names to differentiate them from one another on the local network. Neil Katin decided to name the file server Natasha. This caused Carl Sassenrath to name his system Boris, in reference to the 1960's cartoon *The Rocky and Bullwinkle Show*. And with that, other developers started naming their systems Rocky, Bullwinkle, Peabody, and Dudley.

Amiga also received its own VAX-11/785 minicomputer along with a number of PET terminals to connect to the system. Now engineers could send intercompany memos to each other, and soon to Commodore's West Chester headquarters and beyond.

With the tremendous resources now available to Commodore-Amiga, Jay Miner felt they should go after IBM. In his mind, IBM was vulnerable because of its relatively primitive chipset.

This was a huge shift from the low-cost video game system originally envisioned for the chipset. "It did start out as being less than $500 but it quickly ran up from there," says Sassenrath. "The target for that changed a lot when Commodore got involved."

Although Commodore left the engineers alone, there were still discussions at the management level between Commodore engineers like Robert Russell, Commodore marketing people, and Jay Miner. Arguments occurred over which market they should target. Russell was in favor of a low cost, high performance product to replace the Commodore 64. Jay Miner wanted a high cost, high performance machine for the business marketplace. According to Miner, "This battle of cost was never ending, being internal among us as well as with the investors and Commodore."[1]

Russell had a valid point, since Commodore had their biggest success in the low cost, high performance market dominated by the Commodore 64. "I wanted a cheap Commodore 64-space replacement," says Russell. "That's why I pushed them to buy the computer. It most certainly wasn't the PC compatible they were trying to turn it into and it most certainly wasn't a business machine."

---

1   *Amiga User International.* June 1988. "The AUI Interview" p. 20. (All subsequent quotes from Miner are from the same source.)

Russell's assessment of the product matched the original concept of the Lorraine as a personal computer that also played games. "As far as I was concerned, it was a personal computer," says Russell.

The first move Russell insisted on was to undo the PC-compatibility revisions made to the Lorraine. "They had to go back and take some stuff out and repurpose it, and make it once again 68000 based," he says.

One of the biggest disagreements occurred over memory. The original Lorraine prototype used only 128 kilobytes, the same as the C128 and Macintosh computers. Over time, the Amiga engineers realized they would need 512 kilobytes. "[Commodore] wanted a 256K machine as the 512 was too expensive," says Miner. "Back in those days RAM was very pricey, but I could see it had to come down. I told them it couldn't be done as we were too close to being finished, it would spoil the architecture."

Miner compromised on 256 kilobytes with an additional memory expansion slot on the front of the machine. "The 256K RAM was a real problem," says Miner. "The software people knew it was inadequate but nobody could stand up to Commodore about it. We had to really argue to put the expansion connector on the side and this was before the deal was finalized so we were close to sinking everything."

HAM6 and Denise

The Amiga engineers continued development of the Amiga chipset at Commodore. Dave Dean had finished the design of Daphne earlier in the year and had departed the company. His work on the chip was then taken over by an engineer named Akio Tanaka, in order to see the chip completed to production.

After Commodore decided to make the Amiga into a business machine, Jay Miner realized the Daphne chip, which had been designed as a video game console chip, would no longer be suitable in a business computer. Daphne used the HSL model of color production, the standard commonly used by video game consoles at the time. Instead, Miner would change the chip so it could use RGB (Red, Green, Blue), the standard for displaying color on a computer monitor.

To retain HAM mode, Jay Miner would have to modify the chip. The new HAM mode could either set the color of a pixel to one of 16-colors in a color palette, or it could change one of the RGB values—either red, green or blue—rather than changing the luminance value of the pixel.

As history shows, HAM would later be qualified as a lossy compression technique that allowed more color detail. Ron Nicholson claims he showed the technique to Miner, something he picked up from his previous job at Compression Labs. "One of the methods of compression is called differential encoding compression," explains Nicholson. "You can do two things: you can take data of a certain size and make it smaller or for a given size of data you can represent more detail. Hold and Modify essentially is differential encoding of color. Given the limited number of bits we have we could represent more colors."

Because of the changes, the engineers renamed the chip to Denise. There was one downside to the change: HAM6 was not as fast as it had been in HSL, and due to the lossy nature of the compression, colors tended to bleed on a television. Though the Denise graphics chip was impressive for 1985, Miner did not quite realize his dream of creating a computer capable of producing incredible flight simulator graphics. He was hoping programmers could use the delicious HAM mode to display 4096 colors using polygon graphics. While HAM was great at displaying color images, it was much slower than he had hoped.

According to Miner, "I said that wasn't needed any more as it wasn't useful and I asked the chip layout guy to take it off. He came back and said that this would either leave a big hole in the middle of the chip or take a three-month redesign and we couldn't do that. I didn't think anyone would use it. I was wrong again as that has really given the Amiga its edge in terms of the color palette."

The new version, called HAM6 due to the 6-bits of data per pixel, made it possible to show 4096 colors on screen at once, producing photo-realistic images. It was a first for personal computers, with the potential to revolutionize the industry.

Without HAM, only EHB mode would remain, which could display 64 colors at once—the last 32 of which were half as bright as the other colors in the pallette, hence the name. While 64 colors were impressive, it did not produce photorealism, a key feature that would become a major selling point. "There's two things that happened with the HAM mode," recalls RJ Mical. "One was video and the other was frame capture technology that took advantage of the HAM mode."

According to Jay Miner, Commodore's LSI engineers also helped improve the chip in other ways. "Commodore made a lot of improvements in the things that we wanted but we did not have the resources to accomplish."

Miner had previously created the prototype Amiga chipset using a process dating back to 1975 called NMOS, with internal wires of 5 micron thickness. In order to take advantage of the economics of vertical integration,

Commodore decided to manufacture the Amiga chipset using Commodore Semiconductor Group (CSG).

CSG would manufacture the chips using the slightly more efficient depletion-load NMOS (called the HMOS-II process) with a reduction to 3.5 microns. This was the same process CSG had been using for the 8563 VDC chip and 8564 VIC-II for the C128. As a result, Mark Shieu and his team at Los Gatos began a new HMOS-II layout in late 1984.

CSG also would require an equipment upgrade in order to produce HMOS-II chips. VIC chip designer Al Charpentier believes CSG (formerly known as MOS Technology) may have become a burden to Commodore as the years went by. "It is such an extraordinarily expensive proposition to be in the chip business that at the end of the day, it was more of a drag than an asset in my opinion," he says. "I think it created an environment where they didn't want to look outside the box because they had the fab. It created an environment where they kept saying, 'Well, we've got to buy it out of our own fab.'"

CSG no longer attempted to sell semiconductors to outside companies. "At that time they were only building Commodore chips," says Robert Russell. "It was probably 95% captive. We would sell random parts to people, but not as a sustainable business."

Managers and executives within Commodore began to have doubts about the long term viability of CSG, and whether Commodore should sell it off.

CAOS Chaos

Prior to the Amiga acquisition, Amiga had contracted a company to work on the disk operating system known as CAOS. After the acquisition, the acronym was modified to stand for Commodore Amiga Operating System.

CAOS was the part of the operating system responsible for managing files on disk, separate from EXEC and Intuition. "CAOS was the original file system for the Amiga," says RJ Mical.

Mical admired the work done by the third-party engineers, but despised their duplicity after Commodore bought Amiga. "It was being developed by these guys who I believe were extremely good engineers, but they were also cutthroat businessmen," says Mical. "When Commodore bought our company, these guys saw an opportunity to get a much better deal for the operating system out of Commodore than the deal that they made with us."

In many ways, it had been easier to make business deals without Commodore. "We were a tiny little startup of starving artists trying to do something big to change the world," explains Mical. "Now they are dealing with big fat Commodore with big fat checkbooks, big fat guys smoking big fat cigars, and they wanted some of that big fat money. So instead, they tried to extort a bunch of extra money out of Commodore."

Through the latter half of 1984, the engineers held out hope that the CAOS developers would honor their original commitment to Amiga. "What a drag that whole situation was," recalls Mical.

While the Commodore engineers familiarized themselves with their new programming tasks, it became more apparent the developers of the CAOS disk operating system would not honor their original contract. "Commodore tried to negotiate with them in good faith, but the whole thing fell apart in the end," says Mical.

"We didn't use any of what they had produced. It was hugely disappointing," says Sassenrath.

Decades later, the incident continued to upset Mical. "That was a damnable thing for us," he says. "To have it so tantalizingly close but never get a chance to use it was such a heartbreak. I feel very badly about the evil business thing that they did to try to make money rather than to live up to the commitment they made to us. It was a jerk-butt thing that they did there."

The engineers started to contemplate what to do about a true disk operating system. "As it was getting worse, and as we were becoming more doubtful as to whether they were going to do the right thing for us, we started working on Plan B," says Mical.

It was the second time an attempt to acquire a DOS for Amiga had failed. Carl Sassenrath and another engineer named Neil Katin felt it was time to do it themselves. "Neil and I agreed that we need to write the file system now because it was not getting done," recalls Sassenrath. "We went to the management of the company, Dave Morse and to Jay and Bob Pariseau and we said we want to write the file system. We think we could do it in a couple weeks but we need a file system real badly."

Sassenrath had written a utility to load in demos from disk, but felt he could take it farther. "It was just like, can we expand this and make it into a real file system? But they turned it down," he recalls. Commodore felt that the Amiga, now targeting the business market, needed something more substantial for the business market and continued searching for an alternative.

Microsoft BASIC

Commodore wanted BASIC in the Amiga. Unfortunately, it could not use the 8-bit 6502 BASIC it had long ago purchased from Microsoft. Sig Hartmann, prior to departing for Atari, had to go back to Microsoft and negotiate for a 68000-based BASIC. "Microsoft got their revenge when Commodore tried to negotiate a BASIC for the Amiga," explains Jim Butterfield. "Not only was that reportedly costly to Commodore, but Microsoft also insisted that the next 8-bit product, the Commodore 128, show the Microsoft name or the deal was off."

"Sig was an effective manager and was also effective at bringing things in and dealing with the Microsofts of the world," says Russell. "They were starting to get to be in a position of power."

As Microsoft ported BASIC to the Amiga, the engineers attempted to interest them in further development. Unfortunately, the $24 million lawsuit Jack Tramiel had started over Multiplan soured any interest. "We'd go out there and show them the Amiga and try and make them appreciate how wonderful it was," says Andy Finkel. "We got Microsoft BASIC ported but never got the deal done to Microsoft's satisfaction, so we never really got that relationship going the way we wanted."

The Search for a GUI

With Amiga now at Commodore, the engineers began to realize their computer was lacking one important component. "We did an inventory of what a computer needed to have and what ours had, and the user interface was the piece that it lacked," says RJ Mical. Commodore-Amiga needed a WIMP GUI.

In late 1984, the Amiga developers began looking around for a GUI to purchase for the Amiga. They arrived at the steps of a small company headed by visionary programmer and founder, Brian Dougherty. "We were talking to a company called Berkeley Softworks who did a graphical user interface for the C64 called GEOS," says Dale Luck. "There were about three guys we talked to. They had a GUI they thought they could port over."

Dougherty had previously approached Commodore in 1982 with an offer to develop the disk operating system for the C64. Now he would propose a similar offer for the Amiga, even though GEOS was little more than a glimmer in his eye at the time. "We were in discussion to help them on the Amiga operating system," he says. "I think we could have made something way better than the Mac. It had the same processor and better multimedia support."

Dougherty felt that having a team dedicated to the GUI part of the operating system would produce a superior result, instead of something that was an afterthought. "The Amiga hardware and some of the software was good, but there wasn't a concerted effort behind doing a great graphical

OS on the Amiga," he says. "We would have been prepared to step up and develop a much more flushed out operating system and productivity suite for the Amiga."

Berkeley Softworks would not create the entire operating system, however, as Microsoft did. "That was more of a user interface," says Luck. "There was no operating system there as I recall."

The Amiga designers wanted something more original than Dougherty's proposal. "This may have been unfair, but part of it was we thought GEOS looked too much like a Mac; a color Mac before there was a color Mac," says Luck. "It was felt that we could do something a lot better."

Dougherty had a hard time convincing most Commodore executives to take the user interface seriously. "Other than Clive Smith, the rest of the people internal to Commodore were really from a low cost manufacturing background," says Dougherty. "They never really got software. Clive was the only guy there who got software and it got frustrating for him to try to get the rest of the management team to realize that it was important."

With a whole team at Berkeley dedicated to the GUI and applications, it would potentially cost Commodore more than using its own software engineers. "We had those discussions going with them but they were never willing to get behind it," says Dougherty. "Commodore just wasn't willing to pay for that. As a result, they weren't able to turn the Amiga into what the Macintosh is today."

It would have been a tremendous boost to Berkeley to be an integral part of the Amiga OS. "I talked to one of those guys. As I recall they were really hoping to be able to do the thing for the Amiga, so they were fairly disappointed when it was decided not to go with them," says Luck.

Unknown to Commodore, Berkeley also had discussions with Jack Tramiel at Atari for an operating system. "We talked to Jack," says Dougherty. "Jack Tramiel was doing something similar with the Atari computers." In the end, however, neither Amiga nor Atari used GEOS.

Both Commodore and Atari were also investigating the GEM user interface developed by Digital Research, the same company that had developed CP/M. GEM stood for Graphics Environment Manager and was developed by Lee Lorenzen, a former programmer from Xerox PARC, which had invented the GUI. The GUI was remarkably similar to the Macintosh GUI. Commodore even went so far as to purchase a license to use GEM.[2]

2 *Byte* magazine. June 1985. p. 455. "A GEM Seminar"

However it did not use that license when it was revealed that Atari would be using GEM for its upcoming computer, a direct competitor to the Amiga.

As 1984 wound to a close, the Amiga engineers felt mixed emotions. They were elated with the new resources Commodore was able to provide them, and they had used much of the year setting up new systems, installing new tools, and becoming familiar with the new technology. Yet they were also disappointed with the slow progress of the Amiga operating system. It still lacked a GUI and even a basic disk operating system. Worst of all, it felt like they were running out of time.

CHAPTER 15

Animal House
1984-1985

Bil Herd and his team, the C128 Animals, would spend the remainder of 1984 designing Commodore's next 8-bit computer—this time with backward compatibility. Herd himself would have to quickly choose the features and components that would make the C128 into a business-friend-ly 80-column computer. The year 1984 was not only exciting because he was starting a new system design, but also because his previous creation the Plus/4 would finally go on sale. But in the aftermath, many employ-ees and executives within Commodore would lose faith in Commodore's leadership.

Video Display Controller

Kim Eckert originally designed the 8563 video chip for the C900 UNIX machine, but in 1984 it became a contender for Bil Herd's C64 sequel. As Herd recalls, "Bob Olah came to me, who was Dave DiOrio's boss and head of the chip designers at this point, and he said, 'I've got a chip for you.' I was going to use the industry standard 6845. It was my understand-ing that this part had the same operating parameters as the 6845, a very common graphics adapter. I said, 'Hey, this looks cool. This is a 6845 with these additional features,' and they said, 'Yes.'"

The 8563 chip had features not available in the VIC-II chip, such as 80-column text display and 640 by 200 resolution. However, it lacked other features of the VIC-II, such as sprites. Since the 8563 had no support for VIC-II graphics modes, the C128 required a separate VIC-II chip.

"The [8563] chip used in the C128 for high resolution was actually done for the Z8000," says Russell. Even though it was not developed for use with a 6502 family processor, it would still work.

By mid-1984, the 8563 was already on the second revision. Herd assumed that the technology would be stable. "The chip had actually already been around for a year and a half," he recalls.

After he added the 8563 chip to his C128 prototype, he began noticing problems. "Not scrutinizing the chip for timing differences the way I normally did any new chip was a mistake I made," he says. "I blame myself as this really is the type of mistake an amateur makes."

Prior to Herd discovering the chip, the 8563 project was plagued with problems, even though Eckert used more advanced design tools than Al Charpentier had on the VIC-II. By mid-1984, the 8563 was far from complete. "The 8563 took nine revs before it could just display some characters correctly," says Herd. "That was a troubled chip."

Dave Haynie felt frustrated by the lack of communication from Kim Eckert. "I always had problems because of lack of documentation because it wasn't like many of our chip designers wanted to write up specs," he says. "They said, 'Here, design something with this chip. Oh, by the way, we're not going to tell you how it works.' They would basically give you the notes they used to design it with, which were sometimes exactly what the chip did, and sometimes they weren't."[1]

Herd became more and more disappointed with the 8563's fundamental design. The video chip's main function is, of course, to draw pixels on a screen. Each time the video chip draws a line, it tells the processor it has finished so it can get the next line of data (when it isn't using DMA like the Amiga design). The video chip signals the processor that it needs attention by raising an interrupt, causing the processor to stop what it is doing and respond. Interrupts are a cornerstone of system design as they free a processor from waiting for something to happen in a subsystem, while allowing appropriate attention exactly when needed. The alternative is for the CPU to poll regularly, which is inefficient as it wastes CPU cycles if polling is frequent, and if polling isn't frequent enough then subsystems don't get notified in time. To Herd's astonishment, early 8563 revisions had no interrupt facility built in.

After complaining frequently about this, Herd sat down with Eckert to find out why the chip lacked an interrupt. According to Eckert, an interrupt was redundant because the processor can check the status any time by

---

1   After the release of the 8563, programmers discovered undocumented features, such as an 80-column bitmap mode. "Apparently [Kim Eckert] never mentioned it to anyone," says Dave Haynie.

checking on the video processor. In other words, instead of the video chip telling the processor when it is done, the processor keeps checking to see if the video chip is done.

The explanation amused Herd. In Eckert's mind, it seemed like the system would do nothing else besides talk to his 8563 chip. Herd used the analogy of a phone to describe the architecture. When a phone rings, it is effectively interrupting you to tell you someone is on the line. Eckert thought it was better to eliminate the interruption and rely on the user to keep checking the phone by picking it up and saying, "Hello?"

This became a sticking point between Eckert and the C128 Animals. During heated discussions, someone would stop, excuse himself, and pick up the nearest phone to see if anyone was on the line. According to Herd, "This utterly failed to get the point across but provided hours of amusement." Whenever a phone was nearby, one of the C128 Animals picked it up and said, "Hello?" This behavior puzzled the owners of Margaritas, who wondered what fixation the Commodore engineers had with their pay phone.

To make matters worse, Commodore Semiconductor Group was having problems producing 8563 chips that even powered up. Occasionally the video chip would literally self-destruct and spew bad odors when it attempted to load in the fonts. Herd turned to the black arts. "Sometimes, all I had to do was touch the board in a mystical way and then back out slowly, accompanied by ritual-like chanting and humming. This became known as the 'laying of hands.'"

CP/M

CP/M was released in 1974 and was one of the first mass market operating systems for personal computers. Gary Kildall, the programmer of CP/M, was familiar to many computer users in the eighties as the co-host of the PBS series *Computer Chronicles*. According to host Stewart Cheifet, "Kildall was the rare combination of genius and gentleman."

Commodore had promised CP/M compatibility with the C64 since 1982 and Bil Herd also wanted the C128 to be compatible with the CP/M cartridge. By 1984, the CP/M cartridge for the C64 remained under development by an engineer his coworkers called "Shooting Star" but technical problems plagued the project. "It took him a long time to even make it somewhat functional," says Bob Russell. "There were some serious timing problems with that card that kept it from coming out."

According to *Byte* magazine, the FTC took notice. "Commodore Business Machines signed a consent agreement in Aug-84, under which Commodore agreed not to advertise capabilities that don't yet exist. Commodore had advertised CP/M capabilities for its Commodore 64 computer long before the optional Z80 coprocessor was available."[2]

"This guy was supposed to design a Z80 cartridge for the Commodore 64," explains Herd. "One of the things I noticed when I did the C128 was that the Z80 cartridge didn't work in the C128, and it *really* didn't work in the Commodore 64; they just thought it did."

Then he discovered the problem. "I'm going through this pile of papers a year later and I find a schematic for a Z80 cartridge," he recalls. "I open it up and look at it, and lo and behold it's the Z80 coprocessor card for the Apple! Shooting Star ripped it off and that's why it didn't work."

Herd studied the schematic and realized the CP/M cartridge used more power than the C64 or C128 supplied, largely due to it having a full Z80 processor inside. "I got paid to be cheap and I couldn't afford to pay for half an amp that I would only use if somebody had the CP/M cartridge," he says. "I couldn't afford to add five dollars to the cost of [the C128]."

He then moved CP/M off to the side and tried another cartridge whilst considering alternative approaches. "Then we got the Magic Voice cartridge in from Texas and it wouldn't work," he says. "I looked at it to see why it was crashing my C128, because until then I had a good record. There were these lines called the game lines in the C64 that would cause the memory map to shift, and they were using it in a new and unpredictable way."

To fix the problem, Herd required the C128 to start at memory address zero, but the 8502 started elsewhere. "One night, everybody left and it was broken," says Herd. "During the night, I said, 'I have no way to fix this, unless we start-up by not starting at that address.' I said, 'Hey, Von [Ertwine]. The Z80 chip starts from zero, doesn't it?' He said, 'Yup.' I said, 'Cool. I need somebody wire wrapping tonight.'" Herd's audacious solution would be to hack the Z80 into the C128 itself.

The hour was too late to purchase a Z80 chip, so Herd looked elsewhere. "Everybody had doorstops that were actually Sinclairs," he recalls. "I went and tore open my doorstop because we didn't own a Z80 chip in the place."

The C128 Animals spent the night reconfiguring the C128. "By morning, we had written enough of the kernel and wired this other processor in," he explains. "When you turned on the thing, it would wake up at 0000, set up the MMU, and then [the Z80] would look to see if there was a cartridge before turning control over to the 8502." After the changes, Magic Voice worked.

Herd also used the Z80 to load disk programs automatically when the user turned on the C128. This made a disk-based operating system more viable. Users could also select which mode they wanted by holding down different key combinations when the C128 started.

In the end, Herd had three good reasons for including the Z80 processor in his C128. "One, I couldn't afford the CP/M cartridge. Two, I couldn't afford the black eye from not being compatible with Magic Voice. Three, I ended up using it to boot the thing. So the first dual processor home computer was born," he says.

To be clear, the C128 now had three modes: C64, C128 and CP/M, all built into the same computer. The new franken-computer approach was almost diametrically opposite to that of the Amiga. The C128 had two processors, only one of which was active at a time, and two graphics processors, only one of which was active at a time, and effectively two operating systems in ROM plus the disk-based CP/M.

Greg Berlin now changed his design of the 1571 disk drive to allow CP/M disks to be read by the C128 while in CP/M mode. Most CP/M computers used MFM encoding, so Berlin added MFM support, meaning users could buy off-the-shelf disks for Osborne or Kaypro CP/M computers and pop them right into the 1571.

Others were unenthusiastic about the additional processor. "Commodore Australia wrote us a telex that said, 'We will tear the Z80 out of every C128 before we sell it!' We thought that was funny. They could try it, but where are they going to get the code to run it, because it boots from the Z80," says Herd.

CP/M also served a tactical purpose in the C128. "We had CP/M in there because we wanted the C128 to hit the ground running with a bunch of software that would be somewhat useful for business," says Haynie. "We understood, especially after the Plus/4 and TED stuff, that it was going to be hard to get people to write new programs."

The engineers were well aware that CP/M was antiquated and losing market share to MS-DOS by 1984. "It definitely was," says Haynie. "But we walked into it with our eyes open. We knew that was a transitional thing."

Plus/4 Sales

While Bil Herd and his animals worked on the C128, it was becoming apparent their previous creation, the Plus/4, was not faring well. "The Plus/4 was doomed to be somewhat of a disaster because it had no compatibility with Commodore 64 software," says Commodore UK's National Accounts Manager of Consumer Products, David Pleasance. "When you launch something and it's called the 'Plus' whatever, then people immediately think it's a better version of an existing product when in fact it was a different product entirely."

When Commodore attempted to market the Plus/4 at full price, it failed in every market it launched in. "In the UK we tried to sell it and it didn't sell very well at all," says Pleasance. "The retailers didn't accept it."

Unlike in the US, which had a weak sales & marketing department, the UK tried valiantly to market the product. At the time, the short-lived GM of Commodore UK was Nick Bessey, who lasted all of three months before he left for New Zealand. "He was in charge at the time when we had all of the Plus/4 surplus stock," recalls Pleasance. "I remember him coming through to my office and saying, 'David, how can we get rid of all these Plus/4's? What can we do?' And I said to him, 'What you should do is put an extra incentive on it.' And he said, 'Well what sort of thing are you thinking?' I said, 'I don't know.' He said, 'What about some Champagne?' I said, 'Well that's a good incentive because all the salespeople and their partners will drink that as well.'"

Commodore UK would now hand out Champagne to company salesmen based on sales quotas. "He put forward a formula like a bottle of Champagne for every 24 Plus/4's sold," says Pleasance.

Although Commodore UK's salesforce was now more motivated, the prime obstacle remained the reluctance of retailers, who preferred stocking the bestselling C64 to the Plus/4. It looked like Commodore UK would be stuck with excess inventory like all the other regions. But then good fortune smiled on Pleasance. "A guy came into my office one day. He sat on the chair in front of my desk, leaned back, and he put one of his feet up on my desk," laughs Pleasance. "And he was picking his nose, I swear to you on my life. And he said, 'I've got twenty million quid to spend on you. I want all your Commodore 64's for this Christmas.'"

David Pleasance's heart sank, as he knew Commodore was already sold out of stock until at least early 1985; too late for the holiday season. "I said, 'Fine, excellent. But you've got no chance.' He says, 'What are you talking about?' I said, 'Because they are already sold. Everything is booked in, the orders are in place and I've got full distribution. I can't get any more.' He said, 'I can't believe you are turning down more than 20 million quid!' And ladidadida. He went on and on. He was a right *London wide boy*."

Pleasance was quick to spot an opportunity. "He said, 'Well I can't leave here without buying something.' So my brain clicked into gear and I said, 'Have you heard of the Plus/4?' He said, 'No, what's that?' And I said, 'That is a computer that I can probably do a deal with you on.' I didn't tell him that it wasn't C64 compatible. Mind you, if he had asked the question I would have said. But he didn't know anything about what he was doing anyway so why am I going to tell him a negative. So anyway, he cut a deal and we sold all of the Plus/4's that we had in stock, which is quite a lot."

As a bonus, Pleasance capitalized fully on the sales incentive program he had previously suggested himself. "Three weeks later I did that deal and I ended up with 144 bottles of Champagne," he laughs.

Although much of the excess inventory was cleared out, the product sat on retail shelves. By October, it was clear they were not moving and the prices were slashed, along with bonus software items thrown in. "We put a package together for them," says Pleasance. "We put in some pretty average software but it was a pack. We always bundled stuff. They were able to sell that for 99 quid because we just had to get rid of it."

Once the Plus/4 received a lower price, more in line to the price Jack Tramiel originally wanted, an incredible thing happened. "They put them on sale around the end of October and people started buying them for Christmas," recalls Pleasance. "They sold and sold and sold. Of course nobody opened them up until Christmas day. So they came back to us and said, 'We want some more! We're selling them like crazy! We've never known anything like it in our whole lives.'"

Suddenly the UK was selling them like no other region could. The problem was, the UK had already sold out of its inventory. "I then got in touch and I got all the stock from all around the world of Plus/4's," laughs Pleasance. "And we sold them all out as well. And we sold all the peripherals, because they had dedicated Plus/4 peripherals that were gray in color. There was the 1551 drive and monitors and all these sort of things that were all dedicated to the Plus/4. They took everything. And I can remember coming out of their offices and doing cartwheels in the car park! I just made such a massive sale."

Even though David Pleasance led a successful retreat from the marketplace, in the end Commodore lost money on every Plus/4 sold at £99.

But it was better to get something back rather than having them clog store shelves. "It was a dog of a product," recalls Pleasance.

Quality Assurance

Commodore had a quality assurance (QA) group that examined and verified products before they could be released to the public. Everything from joysticks to software to computers passed through their hands. Usually the QA process began early with computers, as soon as developer systems were ready. "Early in the design I thought that the QA department might indeed help us assure the quality of the design," recalls Bil Herd.

Within engineering organizations, certain groups often clash; none more so than engineers and QA, due to the core mission of finding flaws and criticisms of the engineers work.

At Commodore, the QA manager was Bob Shamus. Eventually relations deteriorated to the point where Herd openly mocked members of the QA team. "The culture became, see who can poke a hole in the C128," he says. "It became a pastime for a lot of different groups."

"We had product assurance people running every piece of software on the C128," recalls Haynie. "They came up with this Island Graphics paint program, which was a pretty popular program."

Herd continues, "Somebody downstairs had tried a Koala Paint cartridge and I'm glad they did. He sent a runner up to tell me it had failed, so I knew about a minute before everybody else that there was about to be a problem. [The runner] just said the Koala Paint crashed, and I was thinking, 'This could be real serious, but let's see what it is.'"

Herd prepared himself. "I was eating a sandwich at the time," he recalls. "I leaned back to get a little Zen-like trance going. Sure enough, they come down the hall looking like *The Witches of Eastwick*. The doors open and in comes one of the managers, and there's the QA guy, there to say, 'I told you so,' and probably three or four others in an entourage. They have one thing on their mind: to prove that the C128 has a problem."

Herd felt as though he was under attack but tried not to show it. "I'm still eating a sandwich being cool about it. I said, 'Alright, let's walk to the lab. Show me what you've got.'"

Haynie recalls the unusual bug. "With their startup screen, they would draw a pretty picture using all the Island Graphics painting functions," he explains. "One of the things they did was read the characters out of the ROM, blew them up real big, and then they would paint them."

"We plug in the cartridge and it says, 'Koala Paint,' and it spells 'koala' and then the word 'paint' under it," explains Herd. "The characters are a couple of inches high."

On the C128, programmer Terry Ryan had improved the original C64 font set. "The characters are what's called the Atari font," reveals Herd. "We called it the Atari font because we took it right from Atari. If you look at the early Atari computer, it's 100% the same. Well, guess who we made ROM's for? The rumor is we lifted their font right off their cartridge. If we didn't, we copied it bit for bit, byte for byte."

Ryan attempted to replace the old Atari fonts. "Terry Ryan had put in a real Times-New Roman font so in C64 mode it looked different. You would think the text looking different would not make it behave different," says Herd. The seemingly innocuous change came back to haunt the team.

Herd watched the screen and spotted the problem. "It works its way through all the characters, and when it gets to the 'i' in paint, it missed the dot," he says. "The dot in the 'i' had moved to where it looked better. So instead of painting the dot in the 'i', which would have been very quick, it had missed it and hit the background."

"It proceeded to paint the entire background," says Haynie. "As well as doing that, it erased a bunch of stuff. The next one would come along, and so on. When you ran it on the C128 in C64 mode, it took about half an hour to start up." Terry Ryan's seemingly benign change to the font set rendered the software unusable.

Herd came up with a temporary solution. "I said, 'Grab a C64 ROM and brick lay it on there.' I went back to eating my sandwich, and in less than ten minutes, they have a C64 ROM soldered to the top of a C128 ROM, and it's working," says Herd.

The glitch showed how close the engineers had to stay to the original design for 100% compatibility. "Anything that you could think of on the Commodore 64 was essentially part of the hardware description, even if it was software because somebody somewhere had figured out a way to use it in ways you would never think of," says Haynie.

Herd felt vindicated for solving the problem in front of his detractors. "All the people who were gunning for me again had to go off mumbling to themselves," he says.

Herd's relationships with management also deteriorated. "When I was working there, designing the computer wasn't the only obstacle," he says. "In fact, that seemed kind of easy compared to trying to navigate the middle management morass that was there."

Herd acknowledges his role in antagonizing the managers. "I would do things and I would piss them off, and if they did something wrong I let everybody know it," explains Herd. "They didn't actually have a lot of power, hence they were ragged at me because they couldn't do anything to me."

Jack Tramiel's absence contributed to the management problem. "They were rampant at this time. It was like too many deer and they needed to be thinned out because there were no Jack Attacks," says Herd.[3] "There really wasn't any accountability for bad management. They had completely broken the cycle of, 'Do a good job and you'll stay, don't do a good job and you'll leave.' Instead, it was open ended."

Herd got along well with the VP of technology, Adam Chowaniec and often relied on him for support. "Adam Chowaniec had done a real good job of managing the technology," says Herd. "I got along with him great."

However, Herd felt Chowaniec should have been tougher with his staff. "What Adam didn't do until later was fire a bunch of people who needed to be fired where it wasn't like you could redirect their efforts and get them going in a positive fashion," he explains.

Herd's nemesis at Commodore was a software manager named Julian Strauss, who was also Fred Bowen and Terry Ryan's manager, two engineers Herd worked closely with. "Julian was one of those managers who said, 'I can see the advantage of deciding not to decide this right now.' I said, 'So you are going way out on a limb in that you're not even going to decide to decide something? Good going, Julian.' I couldn't stand not making a decision. That's what I learned from people there; how to make decisions."

As usual, Herd openly courted confrontations. "One time I dragged in one of the plants and set it next to him, as a reference to which one you could get a better answer out of," says Herd. "I really hated this guy."

Herd's rivalry with the QA manager, Bob Shamus, also escalated. "At some point the head of the QA department declared that the C128 pretty much wouldn't work," says Herd. "I guess he meant it was a matter of time before we all achieved the same level of enlightenment that he had. He basically hovered about waiting for every opportunity to be vindicated." With so many enemies, it was doubtful Herd would survive at Commodore long enough to finish the C128.

---

3   A Jack Attack was the name for a savage lecture by Jack Tramiel, followed by job termination if employee behavior did not improve.

Braindead Company

In the latter half of 1984, as the Plus/4 flailed in the marketplace, many of Commodore's own began to lose faith in the company. Those watching closely noticed signs that could lead to insurmountable problems in the future.

Bob Welland continued his work on the C900, occasionally taking breaks to stroll through the manufacturing area and warehouse. In the second half of 1984 the manufacturing area became especially busy, churning out Commodore 64s and disk drives in anticipation of the approaching Christmas season. Likewise the warehouse overflowed with rows and rows of identical boxed machines. "It's hard for people to imagine," says Welland. "They sold a lot of Commodore 64's and peripherals and that warehouse was enormous. I don't know the dimensions but it was just incredibly huge."

When they ran out of space in the warehouse, the parking lot became a storage area. "They would stock it up with stuff getting ready for Christmas and then they would start parking enormous trucks in the parking lot," recalls Welland. "Just row after row of these trucks which they would fill up with Commodore 64 stuff to send off."

Welland thought it was amazing the company could continue to be that productive even though he had noticed management problems within his first few months. "The part of Commodore that was extraordinary was its ability to just make this incredible number of things, even when the top of the company was brain dead as far as I could tell," he says. "I remember this exact thought when I was there. It was like the Sorcerer's Apprentice, like there's no brain and the thing can still churn out millions and millions of things. It was kind of spectacular."

Although the company continued to operate based on the products introduced during the Tramiel years, there was a sense that success was slipping away. "It's unfortunate that Jack Tramiel left and I think the spirit of the higher end of the company had vanished and with it a lot of the passion," says Welland. "I had never met Jack Tramiel but my sense is that he was an extraordinary human being and really was the heart of what made Commodore."

Looking for a New CEO

In November 1984, Commodore's board of directors voted in a new board member, Alexander Haig.[4] The retired four-star general, who was once the

---

4 *Bloomberg Business.* June 16, 1991. "Al Haig: Embattled In The Boardroom"

NATO supreme commander in Europe, had recently retired from the Reagan administration and was now working in the private sector.

Haig must have noticed the same problems noted by Welland and he began pushing for better management. Commodore's fourth quarter would not be as profitable as it had been a year earlier under Jack Tramiel. Even though revenues had continued increasing, mainly due to the C64, expenses had crept too high. Haig urged Gould to take a hard look at his aging president and CEO, Marshall Smith.

It was clear to Haig that Commodore lacked marketing and he suggested finding a replacement for Smith. Earlier in the year, Steve Jobs hired John Sculley, the former CEO of Pepsi, to head Apple. The announcement received positive press. Gould wanted his own John Sculley. In late 1984, Gould hired a search firm and included Marshall Smith in the decision. After all, he wanted Smith to work closely with his replacement to ensure a smooth transition.

Among the candidates, the search firm found Thomas J. Rattigan, a former Pepsi vice president. "Sometime later in that year, I got a call from a search firm," recalls Rattigan. He talked with both Irving Gould and Marshall Smith. "We had some discussions in late 1984. Commodore was looking for somebody to run their North American operation, which was the United States and Canada, with the indication that once I came in and did that for a while, I would be taking over from Marshall Smith, who was then the CEO."

For the next few months, Gould and his board interviewed and discussed possible candidates, and hoped to have a replacement installed by early 1985.

The CES Panic

With five weeks before CES, stress levels peaked among employees. Suddenly making the deadline became more important than designing a functional computer. "It was a weird time because you didn't do the product as best you could," explains Bil Herd. "You had a relatively narrow window to shove the shit into the bag and you spent the rest of the time making the bag a good bag."

However, Herd never doubted they would make it. "I can honestly say that it didn't seriously occur to me that we wouldn't be ready for CES," he says.

The worst bugs, called showstoppers, prevented the computer from working. Sometimes the engineers encountered as many as three showstoppers in a single day. With CES nearing, all the C128 Animals cared about were killing showstoppers. If it was a minor problem, they did not address it. "Often we didn't get it right; we just got it done on time," says Herd. "You could not make that date otherwise."

The C128 Animals adopted a new attitude in the face of the imminent deadline. According to Herd, he frequently quoted Clint Eastwood from *The Outlaw Josey Wales* to his engineers, "Now remember, if things look bad and it looks like you're not gonna make it, then you gotta get mean. I mean plumb, mad-dog mean."

The hectic schedule played with the engineers' sleep patterns. "At most places, you're not allowed to sleep but I would sleep in the middle of the day if I was tired," he says.

Herd inspired the C128 Animals with his own diehard example. "I certainly stayed for multiple days," recalls Haynie. "I went home, got a good night's sleep, and then came right back and stayed for a few more days."

Herd was perpetually exhausted during the final month before CES. "One afternoon the phone is ringing. It continued ringing in spite of the fact that three people were gathered around a terminal only a couple of feet from it," recalls Herd, who had been fast asleep. "My door opens and I come out with a metal leg I had previously wretched off of a desk, walk to the phone, and do a hard Samurai bash on the phone. This had the effect that the phone stopped ringing immediately. The three people had turned to stare at the phone like it had just appeared there, and I, with the leg of a desk slung back over my shoulder, went back into my office to go back to sleep."

As Commodore became their life, the C128 Animals had little time for family, home-life, commuting to work, or even eating. Throughout November, a dedication to build the C128 overrode everything else, including Thanksgiving. The young engineers skipped visits home to family and concentrated on the computer. Herd's guardian angel, Adam Chowaniec, was kind enough to bring in some turkey and stuffing for Herd and his C128 Animals.

Employees grew out large beards because shaving cost an extra five minutes per day that could be used towards engineering. Bil Herd's personal record for consecutive days at the West Chester facility was 11 days. He kept an air mattress under a table for when fatigue overtook him. Herd did his best to maintain grooming habits, despite the lack of showers at work. "I may have lived there, but I had been in the service and I knew how to stay clean," he says. "I would take a birdbath, which is what we called it."

Most of the engineers kept toothbrushes, sponges, and washcloths at work. "It wasn't unusual for someone to walk into the men's bathroom about six in the morning and I'd be standing there in my red bikini underwear washing myself out of the sink with cold water," he recalls.

Birdbaths were especially unpleasant because hot water was not available on the late shift. "At night, the hot water would turn cold because of power saving," explains Herd. To make his birdbath more pleasant, he found an alternate solution. "I got this brown bin and I would go over to the vice president's coffee machine, and I would fill it with hot water. So now I at least had hot water in my birdbath."

As CES closed in, the lack of working chips became a running joke among the systems engineers. The 8563 was especially problematic, with a long list of glitches. The latest revision no longer displayed a solid screen. The first couple of characters on each line were either missing or partially formed. When the chip heated up, the characters disappeared altogether while other characters on the screen seemed possessed. According to Herd, "The 8563 also had a problem where the 256 byte transfer didn't always take place properly, leaving a character behind. This ended up having the effect of characters scrolling upwards randomly." Other problems mysteriously appeared. If a pixel was by itself, it became invisible. The problems gave the engineers nightmares.

Incredibly, the two 8563 chip designers went on vacation in December, leaving behind a non-functioning chip. "That was Kim and Anne Eckert," says Herd. "They may not have been married at the time, but they did get married. They were gone, off on an island or something."

Near the end of December, the only custom chip that worked flawlessly was the 8502 CPU. Herd waited patiently for MOS to deliver new batches of chips, which arrived in sealed cardboard tubes. When chips are fabricated, a percentage of them work and the non-working portion is discarded. It's not unusual for new chips to yield less than 50% working chips. In the case of the 8563 video chip, the yield was much lower. "The 8563 video chip had gone through a lot of revisions," says Welland.

When MOS Technology delivered another run of chips in late December it was up to Herd to sift through the chips to find those that worked. "Bill would take a chip from one of the tubes, put it in a zero-insertion force socket, and turn on the machine," explains Welland. "Mostly nothing happened and he would take out the chip, throw it into the trash, and try another one. He did this for a very long time."

It was up to the engineers to find working 8563 chips among thousands. "[We] were going through vast quantities of these to find a handful that would work. They barely yielded," recalls Haynie. "Naturally, we're doing all this last minute stuff between Christmas and New Years."

The results were not promising. "Going into December we had a chip with 0.001% yield," says Herd. "The yield of chips that even worked this good fell to where they only got three or four working chips the last run." A run produced upwards of ten thousand chips and cost between $40,000 and $120,000. "It was a pretty expensive couple of chips."

After testing the latest batch of 8563 chips, Herd concluded they were worthless. That night, delirious from testing the chips, he was inspired by the classic jelly bean jar contest. He placed a sign on a jar reading, 'Guess how many working 8563s there are in the jar and win a prize.' "If the number you guessed was a positive real number, you were wrong," says Herd. The C128 Animals were in real danger of missing CES.

After days of testing, a very determined Bil Herd managed to scrape together enough chips to use in a few prototype C128 machines. "I think he eventually got enough to demo the machine at CES," says Welland.

Unfortunately, even the "working" 8563 chips had problems. "If they worked at all, they didn't synchronize properly," says Haynie. Herd decided to make a timing circuit and bypass the chip circuit altogether. While Haynie sorted chips, the engineers produced a three by three inch printed circuit board.

Herd's fellow engineers were amazed by his ability to continue development even around problematic technology. "Bill Herd had very little formal training but he read like nobody's business. He had an excellent memory," says Hedley Davis. "He had some kind of killer instinct that really allowed him to excel as an engineer."

Survival at Commodore meant the engineers had to push themselves to extremes. "Engineers were like Jet fighter pilots," says Herd. "We were cocky because we needed to be. It didn't matter if they liked you. Either you were good or you were in the way. There was no middle ground."

Engineers began contemplating bizarre solutions to make the chips work during the CES demonstration. According to Herd, "On our side, there was talk of rigging cans of cold spray with foot switches for the CES show."

The relationship between management and engineering seemed dysfunctional at Commodore, especially when compared to Amiga, where management advocated for their staff. Herd clashed with his own manager, Joe Krasucki, over the MMU design. "The MMU was designed to go a full

512K," says Herd. Unfortunately, Krasucki wanted to limit the MMU to 128 kilobytes. "We had gotten an MMU done fast so we could keep developing and I had slated for one more [revision] that had more address lines on it. Joe Krasucki, my boss, pulled the plug on the next rev of the MMU."

Herd was used to going around managers to get things done, but in this case, it would be impossible. "He said, 'Nope. Not authorized.' He told MOS not to do another chip. If he would not authorize the whole transaction between the two companies, who am I to go over there and say, 'Hey, I need you to do another rev of the chip.' So we were stuck with a maximum of 128K."

The decision infuriated Herd. "Even though Joe Krasucki was his boss, Herd had to fight to do what was right," says Russell. "That's where I got respect for those guys. Krasucki would do something stupid and you would wonder sometimes what the hell they were smoking."

The passion of creating a new computer drove Herd and his team on. "I had a drill sergeant who one day said, 'You know, gentlemen, I know it hurts. I know it's pain. Just live with it.' And that's what it was."

Christmas was a minimal affair for Herd and his girlfriend. "We went to Greg [Berlin]'s house," recalls Herd. "Our Christmas Eve consisted of stopping at somebody's house on the way home." The intense work schedule had put a halt to the engineer's personal life but the Animals had succeeded and would get their machine to CES.

CHAPTER 16

Finishing
What You Started
1985

Commodore would decline to show the Amiga computer at CES in January 1985, but the company hoped to release it mid-year. There was still a lot of work to do to complete the system, especially when it came to the system software. After CES wrapped, it would take a concerted effort by the Amiga engineers to complete two of the most important aspects of the operating system: the graphical user interface (GUI) and the disk operating system (DOS).

January 1985 CES

The C128 Animals had mostly completed their demonstration hardware at 2:00 am, just in time for their 6:00 am departure for the January 1985 CES in Las Vegas. As they were packing, they heard the unofficial C128 theme song on the radio, Peter Gabriel's *Solsbury Hill*. Bil Herd took this as an omen that things would go smoothly at CES. "Several hapless programmers were spared the ritual sacrifice that night. Little do they know they owe their lives to some unknown disc jockey," says Herd.

One engineer, Greg Berlin, continued working on his hardware during the long flight from West Chester to Las Vegas. The engineers brought a record number of prototypes to the show. "I guess we had about 30 prototypes by early January," recalls Dave Haynie.

Haynie was in for a shock as soon as he landed. "Bil and I are sharing a cab on the way in from the airport," he recalls. "We see this big billboard about the C128, and guess what it says? It says it's expandable to 512K. We didn't know that! Naturally, when we got back to West Chester, we had to find a way to make the thing expandable to 512K."

The presence of Jack Tramiel was evident to everyone who drove in from the Las Vegas airport. Tramiel had rented land owned by the Howard Hughes estate along the highway and posted a series of signs reminiscent of the famous Burma-Shave signs from the 1920's. The series of signs ended with the proclamations, "Welcome to Atari Country" and "Regards, Jack".

Trouble began almost as soon as the C128 Animals stepped into the *MGM Grand Hotel* to claim their reserved rooms. "We showed up in the lobby and you know something is wrong when the line at the desk is only full of Commodore employees," says Herd. "We found out that our hotel reservations had been canceled by someone who fit the description of an Atari employee."

The Commodore employees tried their best to avenge themselves. "We assumed we knew who it was. I heard somebody on the phone saying, 'Hi, this is Sam Tramiel. Cancel my hotel rooms, we won't be needing them.'"

After the accommodations were settled, the engineers presented the C128 computer to Marshall Smith in the Commodore suite. "When we would go to show it to [Smith], I was the guy who was standing right behind them answering his questions," says Herd. "He said, 'Where does the 512K [memory expansion] go?' My boss Joe Krasucki puffed on a cigar and said, 'In the back.' Me and another guy looked at each other and started working our way out the back of the room because we knew we would have to go make the changes that Smith just asked about that my boss said existed, when they didn't exist."

Herd felt frustration with Krasucki, who had previously overruled 512K expansion. "It was supposed to be 512K expandable from day one and we were told not to do it," says Herd. "I told him, 'So you are telling us to do what we said we wanted to do all along?' By that time, me and Krasucki were starting to rub each other more and more the wrong way, and he just said, 'Shut up.'"

On Saturday, January 5, the doors to CES opened. The Commodore booth was one of the biggest ever. "Commodore had this battleship grey booth that was huge," recalls Haynie. The Commodore 64 occupied most of the space, even though they had launched it three years earlier. "When the C128 was announced, sales of the C64 started up again," says Haynie. "They had the normal stuff, like C64s all over the place, and then they had a special section with the C128 showing off the new things. They also had the Commodore LCD machine."

Commodore's employees demonstrated the C128's diverse functions. "There were stations set up that would do different things," says Herd.

"One would be showing CP/M, one would be running C64 games, and one would be showing 80-column mode and 40-column mode."

The different C128 stations kept the engineers busy. "Normally, it would be smooth sailing and you could have a good time, because you worked hard for it," says Haynie. "There was plenty of that, but it wasn't the whole story."

The fickle C128 prototypes required special attention from their creators. "When you turned the voltage up too high the 80-column chip didn't work, and when you turned it down too low the VIC chip didn't work right in multicolor character mode," explains Herd. "I had made the power supply adjustable, which saved my life, and I carried a little blue tweak tool with me. Some power supplies were adjusted for 5.25 volts and some were adjusted for 4.75 volts and I would match up what you were displaying to your power."

Herd gave the marketing people very strict instructions. "Somebody would come and get me and show me sparkles and I would get in the cabinet and the sparkles would go away, and then I would say, 'Now don't let anybody change what you're doing here without coming to me,'" says Herd. "We crafted what was seen by the public there."

Temperature also played a role in the demonstrations because of the faulty 8563 chip. "The way that the 80-column chips were made to work required this phase lock loop circuit," explains Haynie. "The problem with locking circuits like that is that their locking points change when they get warm. You would have to adjust it with this little tweaking tool."

Haynie spent the show running from demonstration to demonstration, adjusting the locking point and keeping the temperatures down. "One of my jobs became instantly clear. I was the guy who ran around with a can of freeze spray and a little tweaking tool," says Haynie. "Anytime a marketing guy shut one of these machines off and couldn't get it to turn back on, I had to spot it, go right over there very discretely, and get this thing back up and running. I had a whole week of that."

Herd disliked the cold-spray solution. "To call me, they would actually just start using their cold spray, because I hated them using the cold spray," recalls Herd. "I'm like, 'You're going to break it one of these days and I'm not going to help you!' So they used it as a hardware engineer call. I'd come running and they would be smiling because they were nowhere near the breadboard with it."

Not all the C128 machines could display every mode properly, but some marketing people were overzealous and attempted to show them off anyway. "You couldn't quite convince these people," says Haynie. "There were also some where the 80-column chip worked well enough to run, but not really well enough to let people look at. Yet you had a really hard time getting the marketing guys to not try to show off the 80-column chip on the machines that we had deemed unacceptable."

With crowds everywhere, the C128 Animals had to attend to the problems covertly; otherwise, the C128 might gain a poor reputation. "I would occasionally have to walk over and say, 'Oh, they need you over there,' and then I would switch it back before anyone saw that it looked like crap," says Haynie.

Commodore aimed their CES marketing campaign squarely at the competition. "They were running this campaign where they had arrows going through the Charlie Chaplin hat from IBM, and arrows going through apples," explains Haynie.

Jeff Porter demonstrated his laptop computer, although the term had not yet been coined. "They didn't have PC laptops then. They didn't exist," he says. So Commodore continued referring to it as the LCD portable.

The show would be used to gauge support for the LCD portable. "There's two CES shows, the winter CES in Las Vegas in January and then the summer CES," explains Porter. "You do all your trial balloons in the winter to see whether people are interested in the product or not. After the show you go visit them and see if you can get the orders."

Normally Commodore's marketing department would take on conversations with retailers, however, no one in marketing or management stepped forward to support the machine. As a result, Porter the engineer temporarily stepped into a marketing role for this particular CES show. "When the higher ups started hemming and hawing about whether to try marketing the machine, Jeff took it on himself to try and sell it," recalls a coworker, Jim Redfield.

For now, Porter would do his best to estimate how many of the computers retailers were prepared to order. If there appeared to be enough demand, it was likely he could convince management to manufacture the product.

Hedley Davis was intrigued by the attention the LCD display received by Japanese manufacturers, who were themselves soon to become the major LCD producers of the world. "It was a very cool system and it had a really good LCD display," he says. "A bunch of Japanese guys at CES came by and they stood on the left side and then right side because it had a great field of view. It could maintain contrast over a very large field of view. And there was a lot of conversation about it."

After viewing the product and getting a feel for the device, most retailers were interested in the wholesale price and the estimated retail price. "The cost of goods on that was on the order of a couple of hundred bucks, and we sold it for $400," says Porter. Retailers would then sell it for their own price, but were given a suggested retail price starting at $600. "That was normal markup for Commodore in the day."

One strategy by Commodore to attract retailers was to get a large retailer to sign orders. Then Commodore could tell other retailers, who often took their cues from the large retailers. At the show, Sears expressed serious interest in the product, but Porter would have to follow up with them after the show.

CES was the time to flaunt success and Commodore had a lot to say at the show. For fiscal 1984, Commodore reported its highest revenues ever of $1.3 billion, which landed Commodore on the Forbes International 500 at 380th position for the first time. Subtracting the costs of doing business, Commodore earned a profit of $144 million, largely attributable to Jack Tramiel's reign.

However, Smith and Gould were accentuating the positive aspects of their financial year. In truth, they already knew the Plus/4 had not performed well since its launch in mid-1984. The only thing left to do was tally up the results. For the quarter ending December 1984, profits were down 94% from the same quarter a year before. The rapid expansion of Commodore, increased hiring of employees, and failure to recoup its massive investment in the Plus/4 was bringing Commodore's bottom line dangerously close to a loss in what should have been its most profitable quarter for the year.

Commodore also announced the retirement of the VIC-20. According to *Compute!* magazine, Commodore sold 2.5 million VIC-20 computers before discontinuing it in January 1985. The same year, *Computer Chronicles* credited the VIC-20 with starting the home computer phenomenon. "It was a cool little computer and it was the first computer to sell over a million units so a lot of people must have liked it," says its creator, Bob Yannes.

Owing to the massive video game crash, which still lingered, the software section of CES was a ghost town. Despite the recent shakeout among home computers, competition was fierce at CES, mainly between the two surviving companies in the home computer space, Commodore and Atari.

In just a few months, Jack Tramiel had a line of computers ready to compete one on one with every offering from Commodore. All of Atari's new computers had cases designed by Ira Velinsky, formerly of Commodore. Atari proclaimed a new slogan, espousing Tramiel's lifelong philosophy, "Power Without the Price."

To compete with the powerhouse C64, Tramiel released a redesigned Atari 800XL computer with 64 kilobytes of memory, retailing for $99. Rather than calling it the Atari 64, he named it the Atari 65XE—one better than the C64. To compete with the C128, he would release the 128 kilobyte Atari 130XE for $150.

To everyone's surprise, the engineers were able to bring dozens of fully working next-generation 16-bit computers, called the Atari 520ST.

Although the Amiga was not shown at the Winter CES, the Amiga team attended the show. They were skeptical the 520ST could match the Amiga with such a short development cycle. "The Atari engineers didn't have time to keep working on it, to refine it, to make it into a machine that would be the equal of the Amiga," says RJ Mical. "They surely had the engineering talent but Atari couldn't wait for them to go through the whole cycle that we went through."

Now that they were at the show, the Amiga engineers were eager to review the Atari competitor. "That was the proposed Amiga killer that was in its own rights a good machine," recalls Mical. "It had a lot of good capabilities and there was some good engineering that was done to it, both hardware and software. But the Amiga was superior."

Although the Atari ST trailed the Amiga in technology prowess, the computer was an amazing feat nonetheless. The rapid production of the Atari 520ST garnered both fear and respect from the Amiga team. As Mical recalls, "In the end, it was a contender, and Atari was aggressively pricing it so it was more than a contender."

Unfortunately, the Amiga was not on public display at the Commodore booth. "They were showing everything behind the scenes," says Dave Haynie. Commodore rented a suite for the Amiga where they showed it to select individuals.

Since the Amiga was incomplete and lacking both a disk operating system and a Windowing GUI, the engineers loaded programs into the Amiga using one of their new Sun workstations.

CES was the first real meeting between the Commodore 8-bit engineers and the new Amiga team. "They called a bunch of us who were there into a room and showed us the early demos," recalls Haynie. "This was January 1985 and they hadn't finished the operating system but parts of it were working. We got to see the Boing demo and RoboCity and some of those famous demos."

Haynie immediately knew the Amiga was a groundbreaking piece of technology. "It was really impressive because nobody had ever seen anything like that on a computer," he says. "It was different enough from anything any-body had done that it was quite profound, especially for people who designed these things."

There was instant chemistry between the West Coast Amiga engineers and the East Coast Commodore engineers. "We got along because we were the same kind of people," says Haynie.

RJ Mical recalls meeting the Commodore engineers. "There were a lot of really brilliant people," he recalls. "Bil Herd was great. I hung around with Bil at CES and a lot of other shows as well."

That evening, Dave Haynie and Bil Herd had a chance to study the inside of the machine as the Amiga engineers took it apart. "We went up to the big suite they had rented for them and they showed us the inside of the Amiga 1000," recalls Haynie. "Herd and I ended up hanging out with some of the Amiga guys. I think it was Dale [Luck] and Dave Needle, the guy who did hardware and chips."

Herd remembers his first encounter with Dave Needle, who was still evi-dently very committed to his role as a Jovian ambassador to Earth. "When we first met the Amiga guys, the guy that had done the hardware design had claimed to be from Jupiter," says Herd. "We just looked at him and said, 'We're from Pluto, man. We've got you beat.' He was still in the inner planets as far as we were concerned."

The Commodore engineers received a thorough education on the Amiga when one of the display models broke down. "One of them was broken and we ended up taking the whole thing apart to get it to run at the show," explains Mical.

As usual with Bil Herd, the night was not complete unless it included alco-hol. "After that we went out and got drunk together," he says.

The Mad Scientist

Upon returning from CES in January, Robert Pariseau and his Amiga soft-ware developers realized how desperate their situation had become. The Amiga was supposed to launch in mid-1985 and yet they still did not have either a DOS or a GUI for the operating system. It was time for Pariseau to make some decisions.

The Amiga software developers decided to hand over development of the GUI to Robert "RJ" Mical. "I'm a Chicago boy," says Mical, who was born in 1956. "I got my love of science and math from my parents. Both of my parents were good at math or science and good logical people."

Mical was born with a distinct birthmark on his forehead, called a Port-wine stain, resembling the lightning bolt made famous by Harry Potter. Self-conscious of the mark as a child, he grew out his bangs and combed his hair over it.

Mical's early life was guided by an influential children's book by author Bertrand R. Brinley. "There was this book that was called *The Mad Scientists' Club* that I read when I was very young," he recalls. "It's a delightful tale of these five boys who have a club and they get into all these shenanigans."

Like many electronics engineers, Mical had his first hands-on experience with a kit. "When I was almost a teenager I started loving science," recalls Mical. "My parents got me a toy called a Heathkit. Heathkit was an electronics play toy with a simple circuit board and you got all sorts of electronic components: resistors, capacitors, tuners, and variable pots and things. The kits included great instructions for how to build your own radio, how to build your own telegraph set and all this stuff."

Mical branched out and began experimenting himself. "I built my own AM radios and I built my own telegraph systems," he recalls. "That was cool, but then I discovered that if you played around with it you could make other interesting electronic toys. My favorite one that I discovered was that if you plugged it all in just right and then grounded one of the capacitors with your finger, the speaker made this eerie squealing noise."

The Mad Scientists' Club inspired Mical to mischief with his new invention. "I took the speaker and mounted it inside a shoebox and ran the wires underneath the floorboards from the closet in my sister's bedroom into my bedroom, where I hid the Heathkit under my bed," explains Mical. "On a regular basis, I would go and make that speaker in her bedroom squeal. It wasn't quite like a mouse; it was more like a ghost mouse."

The prank confused his family, much to Mical's delight. "It had my parents in there for weeks trying to figure out where that noise was coming from and what was wrong," says Mical. "My sister was terrified. Then finally one day, there's my father standing in the doorway of my bedroom with the shoebox in one hand, holding the wires in the other."

With his hoax exposed, he turned to more benevolent pursuits. "Then came my first real big project," says Mical. "When I was 14 years old, I built my first computer, a tic-tac-toe playing computer. It was made out of D batteries, flashlight bulbs, and relays."

The young Mical learned how to represent logic in electronic switching relays. "I had just learned about relays and was fascinated by the things," he recalls. "A relay is this electromagnetic thing where you put electricity to it and it causes a contact to close. If you take the electricity off it, it opens. It's like a big clunky transistor."

Unschooled in logic, Mical's tic-tac-toe game was not a model of efficiency. "They were so big and clunky, and I used dozens of them to implement the tic-tac-toe logic," he recalls. "I was stupid and naïve. There were all these tricks I learned later, and I could have done it with ten transistors to play the whole game."

Despite his lack of understanding, Mical's game performed impressively. "It worked really well," he says. "It went through a set of D batteries in three games but it worked! You couldn't beat the thing."

Mical's idyllic childhood shattered when his father left the family. "My dad was trained as a chemical engineer," he says. "After my dad split on us, my mom had to get a new life together for herself. She got back into doing office work in a medical place."

Mical attended the University of Illinois intending to earn a degree in English, while harboring ambitions to enter journalism. Despite taking courses in English, Mical gravitated towards technology and computers. "Anyone at the university had access to an account, and if you were a student you could play on this one computer," he explains. "At this point, I had already taught myself how to program and by then I knew Fortran and BASIC."

Sometime in 1977, Mical's natural inclination to create games blossomed "I had an account and I had written a bunch of my own programs," he recalls. "I had created my own version of a Star Trek program. Star Trek was really popular then, and there was a Star Trek game on these simple teletype computers where you would give coordinates and your ships would move around. It was clunky and I wanted to do a better one, so I did a better one."

Like many students, Mical was unsure what he wanted to do with his life. "I was having a terrible afternoon sitting in the computer lab," he recalls. "I'm trying to figure out what I'm going to do with my life. I'm worrying and fretting over it, and then taking a break from worrying to play with my computer game. Then all of a sudden, it dawned on me. 'I could do this! I would love this!'"

Mical entered engineering. "I had this epiphany to go off and be a computer scientist," he says.

Four years later, in 1981, Mical began working for a Chicago industrial company, Sciaky Brothers. "Right after University I got a very nice job but not a game job," he says. "It was working with electron beam welding equipment."

The company soon began using Mical for all their computer needs. "I was writing utilities and writing database managers for them, having a grand old time," he says. "But the whole time I was doing it, I was feeling like it was just a job. I wasn't doing something significant. I was making money and living for the weekends."

After working for more than a year, Mical followed his feelings. "It nagged at me until I finally decided that I needed to go see the world and get my head straight," he says. The young engineer took nine months off to travel around the world, including Japan, the Soviet Union, and Europe. According to Mical, the experience changed his life.

When Mical returned, he sported long, unkempt hair and an even longer Doctor Who style scarf (of the Tom Baker era). The self-described artist, poet, and musician decided to pursue his dream. "When I got back it was time to change my life and go to the next big thing," he says. "I didn't want to just make a living. I wanted something meaningful and significant; something that was good for me that brought together all of my skills and my art and my music and my love of computer science. So I had the idea that I ought to go into video games."

Mical began looking for an appropriate company. "I went to two of the arcades and looked around for who was doing the best games," he says. "By far and away, Williams had the best games at the time. They did Joust and Robotron and Defender; all of those wonderful, classic games. I wanted to be part of that."

At Williams, Mical helped create the cult favorite *Sinistar* with Noah Falstein. "He was already involved in the Sinistar project so I jumped in. The project was largely done when I joined," says Mical. The Asteroids style game featured crisp, scrolling graphics. In the game, players try to thwart a group of robots from assembling a giant Juggernaut ship known as the Sinistar.

The speech was adored by arcade players, who delighted as the ship taunted with statements like, 'I live.' and 'Run, coward!' "I did special effects and worked on the voice stuff and some of the underlying code," says Mical.

After his stint with Williams, Mical interviewed with Jay Miner and became an Amiga employee in September 1983. Mical became fast friends with Amiga's most important employee. "I was Mitchy's second best friend at that company," says Mical. "I used to keep a bag of dog treats in my drawer. Mitchy would come trotting into my office without warning and jump up onto my lap. I had no family and I hardly knew anyone, and here was this dog that was friendly to me."

Intuition

At Amiga, RJ Mical began single-handedly coding a GUI for the Amiga while other computer companies were beginning to embrace the GUI paradigm originated at Xerox. "The Mac would have influenced the decision, but less so than some of the more sophisticated machines that we were using at the time," says Mical. "We were using Sun Workstations and they had very powerful user interfaces that were much more powerful than what the Mac had."

The Amiga still lacked key components when he began, making his task slightly more difficult. "Carl had primarily written the kernel, but we had not done a disk operating system," says Dale Luck. "RJ was doing the high-level software; the user interface stuff. He started programming his system on January 30, 1985."

Mical sought to create a WIMP (Windows, Icons, Menus, Pointer) user interface, which he affectionately named Intuition. "Intuition was the input mechanism for the whole system," explains Mical. "It gave users that experience that we are familiar with now: windows, menus, using a mouse to move a pointer around on the screen, and dialog boxes which we called requesters that would give you options."

With his new responsibility, Mical was given a new title for his business card. "That gave me the best title I have ever had in my entire professional career," he quips. "For a while there at Commodore, I was their Director of Intuition."

The software engineer had to forgo things others take for granted, such as having weekends off, going home, and sleeping. "I took on that job and spent seven months of my life working on average six and a half days a week to do that thing," recalls Mical. "Almost every week was a 100 hour week."

Mical was able to concentrate on the appearance and functionality of the GUI because of Dale Luck's graphical routines. "Intuition used my library to do overlapping windows, the screens moving up and down," says Luck. "I wrote all the software that controlled the sprites, all the line draw support, the polygonal area fill."

Using the Daphne graphical chip and Dale Luck's graphical library, Mical was able to deliver unheard of features, such as displaying different screen resolutions at the same time. "It could interleave those different screens on the same output display in the same way you can interleave windows now and overlap them, but with the different display resolutions," says Mical.

One big part of modern operating systems were the fonts; the character set that allowed different text styles in documents and applications. "Another fellow, Bob 'Kodiak' Burns, came along in 1984 and he wrote all the text code for the fonts and stuff," says Luck. "He and I had worked together at HP and he had done a lot of font stuff at HP. That was kind of his forte."

The Amiga employees were careful not to put themselves at risk of a lawsuit over their GUI. "We started out passing around design docs. The actual implementation was done completely behind the walls so that there was no knowledge of what anyone else had done," says Mical.

Because of this policy, Amiga did not receive any infringement lawsuits based on their GUI. "Not a one; not from anyone, ever," says Mical. "I attribute that mostly to the fact that once I decided that I needed to do a user interface, I slammed the door and drew the blinds and invented it completely and entirely on my own. I didn't look at any other computer system through that whole period. We wanted it to be as clean-room as possible."

Mical was even able to introduce several new innovations to the GUI concept. According to Mical, "Because of that, it turned out that I scored several patents for stuff that I created on the Amiga; one patent of which was violated by Microsoft up until just recently."[1]

Intuition easily outclassed the Macintosh operating system and had more in common with Windows 95, which was still ten years away. One powerful feature that distinguished the Amiga operating system from the Macintosh was the Command Line Interface (CLI). This allowed users access to powerful DOS commands using command line arguments.

Throughout most of 1984, Amiga lacked a true graphics artist. The demos, which often contained cartoon characters, were created by programmers with no visual training. This resulted in demos that showed off the hardware specs but didn't truly represent the possibilities of the new graphical chips.

Sam Dicker and RJ Mical knew who they wanted on the team to fill the void. At their former employer, Williams Electronics, the two had worked on the arcade game Sinistar with a third person. "Jack Haeger was an artist

---

1 As of 2004, according to Mical, "You go over an icon and press the right mouse button instead of the left, and a menu appears that has menu items. If you select one of those items, it can cause a secondary menu to appear and you have other choices you can make. I got a patent for that technique."

on it," says Sam Dicker. Haeger was the art director for most of Williams games, including Joust, Sinistar and an ambitious laserdisc arcade game called Star Rider.

With the new resources from Commodore, it now made sense to hire an art director full time, and Haeger joined the team. He was tasked with creating art assets not only for demos but also for Intuitions icons and other graphics.

TRIPOS

The Amiga developers intended to use CAOS for their disk operating system, but when that deal fell apart in late 1984, they had no choice but to find another option, preferably one developed in C language. "Plan B was TRIPOS, the operating system that came out of the UK," says RJ Mical.

A computer scientist named Dr. Martin Richards developed TRIPOS at the University of Cambridge Computer Laboratory starting in 1976. Richards was also the inventor of BCPL, the forerunner to the C programming language. Originally, he developed TRIPOS for the IBM 3081 mainframe computer using BCPL. Later, in the early 1980's, he adapted it to the PDP-11.

In 1984, a University of Cambridge alumni named Dr. Tim King had joined a company called MetaComCo to market TRIPOS. Commodore UK's director of software Gail Wellington found MetaComCo and brought the company to Pariseau's attention. Starting on January 6, 1985, with amazing speed, MetaComCo began porting TRIPOS to the Amiga using a prototype Lorraine computer.

Within a few months, an alpha version of TRIPOS was already running on the Amiga. Carl Sassenrath was both surprised and bitterly disappointed with the outdated mainframe operating system. "This one company TRIPOS from England came in and said, 'We've implemented our API on top of your exec.' I don't know how they got it, we must have sent them one of our prototypes and here it is! We're going to show you a file system running on the Amiga," says Sassenrath.

Sassenrath saw that TRIPOS, which was not developed to target a floppy disk system, would cause problems for the Amiga. "That was a disaster. It was a huge problem for the Amiga earlier on," he says. "TRIPOS was not very compatible with a floppy disk. It was very, very slow and there were a lot of operations that you wouldn't want to do on a floppy disk."

One particular problem was TRIPOS expected a hard disk that was never removed from the drive, whereas on the Amiga, a user could pull out a floppy disk at any moment. "If you pulled a floppy disk out before it has written back its caches, or in the process of writing back its caches, you could easily destroy the floppy," says Sassenrath. "Then you've lost your data. That was why those file system recovery programs become really popular really quick. It was a huge disappointment to me."

Mical was also disappointed with already antiquated TRIPOS. "No disrespect to the guys who invented it, but it was not meant to be on a class of machine like the Amiga," he says.

In the minds of the developers, TRIPOS was clearly inferior to what CAOS would have been. "That file system had a lot of problems, but its biggest problem was that it had been designed for an 8-bit world, and the Amiga was a 16-bit world," says Mical. "The whole thing was just a mess because of it. All the file system operations had to go through this translation mechanism to get into their code."

Mical also found the institutionally developed BCPL code less than efficient. "Their code was University quality code, where optimized performance is not important, but where theoretical purity was important," he explains. "We were getting University quality engineering where it was bad and it was slow and it turned out to be buggy too."

After working so hard to create the perfect system, it was a difficult compromise. "Everyone was upset from top to bottom," recalls Mical. "The only guys who weren't upset were the TRIPOS guys."

Atari Lawsuit Intensifies

After witnessing the Atari 520ST at the January 1985 CES, Commodore-Amiga knew it had a worthy rival. Some even claimed the Atari 520ST would be superior to the Amiga. Meanwhile, the lawsuit for breach of contract and counter-lawsuit for IP infringement, launched the previous year, hung over the heads of both companies.

To make matters worse, on April 10, 1985, Tramiel launched a second lawsuit against Commodore for patent violations. The lawsuit alleged the Amiga chipset resembled those used in the Atari 400 and 800 computers. It was clear Tramiel was out for revenge against the company that spurned him.

The new lawsuit was especially significant for Joe Decuir, who was laying low in order to avoid getting swept up in any lawsuits. "I'm glad that I was never forced to sit there on the stand in some random court somewhere and explain this under oath," he says. "Jay was careful to not suck me into it at all."

The Amiga engineers began to see Jack Tramiel as a ruthless enemy. "I had a picture of him on my door at Amiga," recalls Carl Sassenrath. "It was a picture of him and his mean looking face. It said underneath, 'Never forget.' Don't forget who we are dealing with here because business is war was his motto. We did not need an adversary like this, so let's not mess around."

Lack of Promotion

Ever since the acquisition of Amiga, Commodore did very little to promote the new computer. *Compute!* editor Richard Mansfield called Commodore 'aggressively silent' with respect to the Amiga. This was puzzling because usually companies attempt to pre-hype products.

As the avalanche of non-news continued, *Compute!* editor Tom Halfhill decided to force the issue. In early May, he showed up unannounced at the Los Gatos Amiga offices, along with fellow program editor Charles Brannon. Though it was a brash move, the two believed they had a chance at success. After all, Commodore would not turn down free publicity if it showed up on the doorstep. They were wrong.

Unknown to them, Commodore-Amiga president Dave Morse was in the midst of a conflict with Commodore. The two editors ran into him in the parking lot expecting to arrange a meeting, however he drove off hurriedly. The two then spoke to the receptionist and asked for someone, but when a marketing manager arrived, all she had to say was, "We aren't saying anything publicly at this point. We aren't saying anything at all." The two asked to speak with General Manager Jay Miner but the manager said he was not around.

Later, *Compute!* complained in an editorial that Commodore gave a hands on demonstration of the Amiga to a competing magazine, *Byte*, but denied the *Compute!* editors a similar preview. It seemed like Commodore was shunning free publicity for the Amiga.

The Founder Departs

For his part, Morse always favored the Amiga as a games machine and probably felt more comfortable in the toy business than the computer business. When the tension between Dave Morse and Commodore's Marshall Smith and Irving Gould increased due to the recent lawsuits, something had to give.

Although Amiga engineers were able to dissuade Commodore from suing Morse outright, they were not able to save Morse's job. In May, with Morse on the way out, Rick Geiger replaced his duties fully. "They replaced the company head," says RJ Mical. "They took Dave Morse, who is a brilliant guy, removed him from being president of the company, and put their own guy in, Rick Geiger."

For his part, Morse remained on as a consultant with Commodore, though it was on paper only. "They entered into a consulting contract with Dave Morse that allowed them to establish a noncompete for a certain period of time," says Bill Hart. "They kept him out of the business and he was available to consult with them."

As time went on, however, Morse did little actual consulting. "I doubt they ever used much of that consulting time because you know you're in a business where there's a lot of egos," laughs Hart. "I'm sure that they didn't need another ego in the mix."

It had been a sometimes stressful two years for Dave Morse as CEO of Amiga. "He was ready to move on," says Dale Luck. "He took a little bit of time off and then he went off to do some new stuff."[2]

Amiga Chipset Fabrication

By early 1985, Mark Shieu and his team at Los Gatos had completed the new NMOS layouts of the Amiga chipset: Agnus, Denise and Paula. Commodore Semiconductor Group (CSG) ramped up its staff in early 1985 in preparation for the Amiga chipset production. "They brought more people in, especially as we were getting into the Amiga stuff," says Haynie. "We had our share of resident wizard types who were just really, really smart guys. They were transitioning from a chip company where just making a chip made sense, to this company that was supposedly vertically integrated to deliver consumer products."

Commodore funded a new NMOS process, called HMOS II, at CSG, located in King of Prussia, Pennsylvania. "They were trying to get a better process when they were doing the Amiga line," says Russell. "They basically cleaned out the side of the building that had the cafeteria and put in a new production line. That was when [Commodore] ran into money problems."

Upgrading CSG from the old PMOS process to NMOS required a large capital expenditure. There were voices within Commodore that called for the company to purchase chips from third party vendors instead. "Everyone was arguing that we can buy it cheaper from other suppliers," says Russell.

---

2   Morse went on to instigate the Lynx portable game system at Epyx.

The chip engineers designated numerical designations for each chip. Agnus became the 8361, Denise the 8362 and Paula the 8364. Only a percentage of every batch of chips manufactured would work, called the *yield*. The chips would undergo multiple revisions before they would yield a high enough percentage to become cost effective. By February 4, 1985, Denise yielded 50%, while both Agnus and Paula yielded 0%.

The engineers continued the process of refining the layout, producing another small run of chips, and testing and debugging. By May 3, Agnus yielded 40%. Finally, by June 13, Agnus yielded 77%, Denise 83.7% and Paula hovered around 50%. The vast improvement meant they could now produce the Amiga in large numbers when the time came.

The chips themselves, nothing more than small flecks of silicon, cost between $1.63 for the simplest chip, Denise, and up to $2.89 for Agnus, the most complex. But the technicians placed the chips into plastic or ceramic packaging, which cost $0.48 and $3.12 respectively. Given the low yields at the time, which hovered around 60%, and the fact that they could not test the chips until they inserted them into packaging, it could end up making the chips quite costly.

Surprisingly, the meticulously designed Agnus by Jay Miner and Dave Needle was the only chip that ran cool enough for a plastic package this early. As a result, Agnus only cost $6.47 while Denise and Paula cost $8.21 and $10.43 respectively. But with time, those prices would drop below $5 per chip once the yields improved and they all moved to plastic packaging.

It was, at least for the time being, perhaps a vindication of the vertical integration strategy of using CSG to produce the chipset.

Zorro

Earlier in the year, Amiga "Velvet" prototypes arrived to developers with just 128K of RAM. By May of 1985 it became abundantly clear that the Amiga needed more memory. The recent additions of a GUI and DOS to the operating system left barely any memory for user programs. Dave Needle now needed to redesign the motherboard. "The next generation of that was called the Zorro," says Dave Haynie.

Zorro doubled the memory potential of the Amiga. Needle designed the new motherboard to handle 256K of onboard RAM with another 256K expansion. But this came with a price, because memory was one of the most expensive costs in a computer.

Luckily, the extra year of development gave an advantage to the Amiga compared to when the engineers began designing it. "By the time the Amiga came out, memory was orders of magnitude cheaper," says Joe Decuir, comparing memory costs with his initial days designing the Atari 2600.

Even in mid-1984, Dave Morse would only say the Amiga computer would cost less than $2000. But now, even with the recent addition of RAM memory, Commodore estimated the computer would cost between $1100 to $1500 for the basic 256K model. With a full 512K and an RGB monitor, the price increased to $2000.[3]

Transformer

While Commodore ramped up operations for the Amiga, marketing began talking about IBM compatibility. Those Amiga developer systems that had been handed out earlier, the Lorraine and Velvet, were now starting to bear fruit. A company called Simile Research had developed an IBM PC emulator called the Transformer.

Jay Miner felt it was a mistake to attempt IBM-PC compatibility. According to Miner, "It's funny but I never really saw MS-DOS compatibility as being that important for the Amiga. I said at the time to Commodore 'Hey, we're different. Try to take advantage of that, not imitate or simulate other people.'"

To keep costs down, the emulator was programmed entirely in software. The only piece of hardware required for the Amiga was a 5.25 inch floppy disk drive, which was the dominant format for the IBM PC at the time. Commodore hoped to offer the Transformer at the launch of the Amiga later in the year.

System Software and WCS

The Los Gatos engineers found themselves in a difficult situation as the Amiga release date neared. The problem was not in the usual area of manufacturing the custom chips. MOS Technology was producing a reliable quantity of Denise, Paula and Agnus by the time pilot production began, not to mention the controller and support chips.

The problem was with the software. Behind the scenes, the operating system was unstable and crashing frequently. Dale Luck blames the problems on the inexperienced team. "A lot of the software was written fairly quickly by some inexperienced engineers, like myself," he admits. "One of the issues was memory allocation."

---

3   *Compute!'s Gazette*, Sept. 1985. P. 28. "Amiga at a Glance"

The core part of the operating system, called the Kickstart, was originally going to go into ROM chips, similar to the C64 system software. However, the engineers did not trust the code would be stable enough to warrant fixing it permanently in ROM chips. "The A1000 was designed to have the operating system in ROM, which by the way is an entirely stupid idea," says engineer Bryce Nesbitt.

"The software was in enormous flux and they were probably just terrified," explains Bob Welland. "They couldn't make a ROM when they made the A1000 because it would have been too buggy or would have been too incomplete."

The daughter board, the Writable Control Store, allowed engineers to quickly upload system code onto the Amiga, rather than having to burn new ROM chips every time. "This was clearly not originally intended to be part of the chipset architecture and I suspect that it was really a debugging aid during OS development," says Welland.

However, this temporary daughter board became part of the final design when they realized the Kickstart would need further improvements. "The operating system wasn't ready, so they produced this memory board that went upside down," says Nesbitt. "It actually plugged into the ROM sockets. It was hideously expensive, and it was doubly expensive because it was a separate piece of hardware."

Not everyone at Commodore was a fan of the WCS. "It would be a much simpler machine if it wasn't there," says Welland. "It would have been much more in the spirit of what Jay Miner was doing. I mean if you look at that machine and you ask yourself, why is it mechanically so complicated? It's because there's a board in there that shouldn't be there. It's as simple as that."

The added cost of manufacturing a daughter board and including additional memory pushed up the cost to manufacture dramatically, which either pushed up the retail cost or decreased Commodore's profit margin. "They put the burden of not having [the OS ready] on the cost of the machine, unjustifiably," says Welland. "How they managed to convince themselves that that was okay is a mystery. I think they did it because they didn't have the software ready yet and they had to do it that way. But that means what they did is made a hundred thousand prototype machines."

Commodore Reinforcements

After the completion of the C128 and uncertainty for the LCD portable, many Commodore engineers were without a project. "I was on the LCD machine up until it was cancelled," says Andy Finkel. "So they needed to do something with the people who were working on the LCD machine, the software guys anyway."

The Amiga team ended up recruiting many of Commodore's best engineers. "The Amiga people said we need more engineers out here to finish this thing," says Finkel. "We were the natural sacrificial lambs to be sent out to help them on the project. We basically were grunt software engineers."

Four of the East Coast engineers relocated to the West Coast. "I didn't have to move though," says Finkel. "It was a temporary six months to a year kind of thing."

The Los Gatos offices impressed the East Coast engineers, who did not rate an office window at the West Chester facility. "That was a pretty nice building," says Finkel. "It was around a central square, sort of a courtyard. There were offices all around. It was a typical California office building."

The computer industry was going through a change from primarily assembly language programming to the C language. "Our first job was to learn C and that was a real shock," says Finkel. "We were all assembly programmers. Because of all our 6502 based stuff, you had to work in assembly. So we learned C, learned the Amiga, learned all the new operating system stuff."

After weeks of learning, the Commodore engineers were each given a specific part of the operating system to work on. "We were two in an office for the most part, except for the software lab where there were four people. I did printer drivers and the printer driver subsystem as well as some of the Workbench stuff," says Finkel. "We basically all filled in where people were needed."

While all this was going on, the UK developers from MetaComCo continued to improve TRIPOS out of the Los Gatos offices. "Tim King and his crew would camp out there when they were in town," says Finkel. Commodore renamed the Amiga version of TRIPOS to Amiga DOS.

The Amiga team appreciated the extra help on AmigaOS, particularly from Andy Finkel. "I thought he and the Commodore engineers were great guys to work with," says Dale Luck.

The software engineers found time to sneak Easter eggs into the system, which users were quick to discover. By holding down both Alt keys and both Shift keys, and pressing one of the function keys a message would appear. Finally, by pressing F10 while doing this, users were treated to a message saying, 'Moral Support: Joe Pillow & The Dancing Fools'.

The completed operating system would use two separate disks. The disk called Kickstart essentially contained the system ROM, the equivalent of the PC BIOS (Basic Input Output System). Once the system booted, the user inserted another disk called Workbench, which contained the graphical user interface and operating system.

The engineers, especially RJ Mical, who was busy finishing off Intuition, had a definite goal of mid-July to finish everything. The reason was because Commodore had decided to launch the Amiga in lavish style in New York on July 23—barely a month away. The engineers were now up against a difficult timeline.

CHAPTER 17

Pepsi Challenge 1985

After Marshall Smith's disastrous first year as CEO, Commodore had over-spent by purchasing the entire Amiga Corporation rather than just the chipset. They were working on too many products, which led to out of control hiring and spending on new technology. And many of Commodore's key employees, who felt Smith was a poor substitute for Jack Tramiel, had left the company. At the urging of board member Alexander Haig, Irving Gould was ready to bring in new leadership and get Commodore's finances under control.

Nosedive

After announcing at the January 1985 CES that Commodore had landed on the Forbes International 500, it became apparent that Commodore's finances were about to take a nosedive. *New York* magazine noticed Irving Gould's reticent attitude. "When an executive with whom you've had a friendly relationship for seven years suddenly ducks your phone calls, you know something's wrong."[1]

Post-holiday season, with sales tabulated, the scope of the Plus/4 failure became apparent. It was an unmitigated disaster, even in the UK where Commodore was able to liquidate its inventory at a loss. In other parts of the world, Commodore would have a hard time moving its remaining inventory of Plus/4 computers, software, and devices.

Although Commodore UK had found clever ways of liquidating its Plus/4 inventory, Commodore US was having much more difficulty even

---

after steep price reductions. Finally Marshall Smith decided to wash his hands completely of the debacle by selling off the inventory to an Orange County, California company named Pacific Tri-Micro. Under the agreement, Commodore would pass off sales and customer support of the Plus/4 exclusively to Pacific Tri-Micro.

Even in the UK, buyer's remorse seemed common among Plus/4 owners, who inexplicably believed their computer was software compatible with the C64. "On Christmas Day everybody opens up their product and they're fine for the first few days because they are playing with the games that we put in the pack, but as soon as they go out and try to buy some C64 software, it doesn't work," says David Pleasance. "The shit hit the fan as they say."

With Commodore UK being used as a dumping ground for liquidated Plus/4 computers, there was some possibility the fiasco would tarnish its reputation. However, David Pleasance doesn't think it did. "It was never said anywhere in any of our documentation that it was compatible with the C64," he says. "We weren't guilty of anything."

But what about disappointment with the Plus/4 product itself? "Perhaps there was some of that negativity," he says. "We never really witnessed it much ourselves. But what I can tell you is that loads of those people, once they got into computing, they then bought other things. They'd only paid 99 quid for a complete package that could do everything."

With the Plus/4 debacle now behind Commodore, there were new issues to deal with. Rapid growth of the company payroll and multiple projects began having a negative toll on finances. Not only was Commodore burdened by excessive costs from producing and marketing the Plus/4, it had also shelled out excessive amounts of cash acquiring Amiga. On top of that, Commodore had spent millions in 1984 upgrading its tools and technology; not just with myriad minicomputers, workstations and servers, but all the equipment to keep up with semiconductor manufacturing and move to new fabrication processes.

As an example, Commodore Semiconductor Group previously tested all its chips in a custom handmade chip tester, but by April 1984, it was no longer able to keep up with production quantities and Commodore began looking for better chip testing equipment. CSG department head Ted Lenthe ended up purchasing a $2.3 million system called the MegaOne. This also came with additional expenses for training employees, service contracts costing hundreds of thousands yearly, and installation costs.

Marshall Smith began looking for ways to save money. Soon after announcing the end of production of the VIC-20 at CES, Smith took action. Jack Tramiel's former Commodore headquarters at 3330 Scott Boulevard in California continued to manufacture PET and VIC-20 computers and to house components imported from Asia. In early 1985, Marshall Smith closed it down.

The layoffs included factory workers, VIC-20 and PET product managers and personnel. The portable C64 computer, the Commodore SX-64, would also fade into oblivion.

The Choice of a New Generation

For the quarter ending March 1985, Marshall Smith reported an embarrassing loss of $21 million. Commodore stock plummeted from a high of 60 $5/8$ in mid-1983 when Jack Tramiel controlled Commodore, to a low of around 10 in April 1985 when the announcement of losses was made. Gould suffered a paper loss of $300 million in less than a year.

Most analysts pinned Commodore's recent losses on the Plus/4, which they believed Jack Tramiel conceived. *Fortune* magazine concluded that under Tramiel, Commodore was "a one product company whose management gave little thought to planning for the future."[2] Tramiel had let research and technology slip while he was at the helm. CSG did not even have a 16-bit microprocessor to succeed the 6502 because Tramiel never pushed for one.

A May 5, 1985 *New York* magazine article titled "Commodore's Big Dive" explained that the C64 itself was a "dead duck" and would soon fade away.

Others in the industry felt it had been wrong for Irving Gould to hire Marshall Smith, a president and CEO with no prior experience in the computer industry. "In the mid eighties there were all these management gurus. At that time they were preaching you didn't have to know anything about the industry you were in. As long as you understood general management concepts, you could do the job—which is totally fallacious," says David Baraff. "So they brought in this guy who made a lot of bad decisions."

Ironically, many of Commodore's managers appreciated Marshall Smith exactly because he lacked knowledge of the computer business. "There weren't that many clashes with him," says Gerard Bucas. "Marshall was much older of course and was really more or less dependent on Adam

2 *Fortune* magazine, "How Commodore Hopes to Survive" (January 6, 1986), p. 30.

[Chowaniec], which was good from an engineering point of view. They were actually interesting because Marshall Smith really needed Adam Chowaniec to guide him and basically set the product strategy."

Under Smith, Commodore went from a small, lean company to a big company with lots of staff, similar to Apple. It didn't last long as the latest cutbacks attested to.

Gould had seen enough to know it could not go on under Smith's leadership and conducted interviews for a new president and CEO throughout early 1985. Out of the candidates, a former PepsiCo executive stood out to him.

Thomas J. Rattigan was born in Boston, Massachusetts on July 20, 1937. His father, Thomas F. Rattigan, was a World War II army veteran. "I was brought up during the Second World War and was from a working class family," says Rattigan. "My father, Thomas Francis Rattigan, served in the U.S. army. I grew up in Boston but when my father went into the service we were living in Springfield, Massachusetts."

At the age of 19, Rattigan married Jane Beaumier on September 1, 1956. Around the same time he enrolled at Boston College and received a degree in Business Administration in 1960. He then pursued a master's degree at the Harvard University Graduate School of Business Administration, graduating in 1962. Rattigan immediately took a job with General Foods, where he worked in marketing. "I spent eight years at General Foods from 1962 to 1970," he recalls.

He then joined PepsiCo Incorporated as a marketing executive in 1970. In 1982, he began investigating irregularities within the international regions of Pepsi. As it turned out, the president of PepsiCo International was inflating profits by colluding with executives in other countries.[3] As a result, PepsiCo dismissed the president and Rattigan assumed the vacant job.

Rattigan describes his strategy against Coca-Cola. "We tried to operate like the Viet Cong during the war, where you try to hit them where they weren't and hopefully outflank them. A head on assault would have been disastrous." Perhaps his knowledge of fighting against a larger competitor could help Commodore survive.

In the mid eighties, Pepsi was one of the most dynamic and respected American companies, largely due to effective marketing. The slogan, 'Pepsi, the Choice of a New Generation,' was having an impact, and Pepsi was

---

3   *Toledo Blade.* November 9, 1982. P. 23.

growing fast. Pepsi always seemed to have the latest pop sensation pitching its famous product. Gould hoped he could bring some of that success to Commodore. It was an inspired decision by Gould and could potentially straighten out the weakness in Commodore marketing.

Rattigan was no longer with Pepsi when Gould began his search. "[Commodore] didn't really lure me from Pepsi because I had left in the spring of 1984," he recalls. During several meetings with Gould and the board of directors, Rattigan pitched himself as a "fixer" who could analyse problems and get the company back on track. And he had proven this ability by clearing out corruption while at Pepsi. Rattigan stood out as the ideal fit for the troubled period Commodore was in.

Commodore's former VP of marketing and sales Kit Spencer wondered if Rattigan could adjust to the microcomputer industry. "If you'd come from a big company like Pepsi or Coke, you were fighting over a 1% market share change in a year, and you'd think you did a great job," he says. "If we weren't changing 50% in a year at Commodore, it probably meant nothing was happening."

At the time, Rattigan was spending time with his family. "We had four children," he says. Skiing was a major source of leisure for the family. "There were two places; either north of New England, largely Vermont, or in the west in Utah and Colorado."

When taking time for himself, Rattigan enjoyed reading. "Most of it was non-fiction and a lot of it was biographical and/or historical in nature," he says. "I'm not one of these guys who walks around quoting books that I've read. I read them for enjoyment."

Gould needed a big announcement to help revive Commodore's stock. He wanted Commodore to look more like rival Apple, who had a former Pepsi CEO at the helm. In the end, Gould chose the former PepsiCo president to lead the new Commodore.

He gave him one overriding task: make Commodore profitable. As Rattigan stepped in, Commodore planned to launch five products in 1985, including the C128, Amiga, C900, LCD Portable, and a line of PC compatibles in Europe.

Rattigan negotiated a five year contract. For his service, Commodore would pay Rattigan $600,000 for his first two years and $400,000 for his final three years. Starting in his third year as CEO, Gould would allow Rattigan to purchase $2 million per year worth of Commodore stock for $5,000.

Once Rattigan joined Commodore, it was inevitable Marshall Smith would be out. "We both understood that at some point in time he would be leaving and, assuming I was doing what they hoped I would be doing, I'd move up into that slot," says Rattigan. In the meantime, Smith would continue as CEO of Commodore International, retaining control of the technology and finance departments. He also retained his vice chairman status on the board of directors. "I went into Commodore on that basis; taking over responsibility for the North American operation, reporting to Marshall."

On April 10, 1985, the *LA Times* announced Thomas J. Rattigan as the new president and CEO of Commodore's new North American division (not to be confused with Commodore International). Rattigan seemed to hold promise for a new Commodore culture. At 44, he was relatively young, resembling actor Vince Vaughn with a dash of the TV Batman, Adam West.

Most Commodore engineers saw a bright future under the new boss. "Rattigan really was on the marketing side of things. I thought Thomas Rattigan was a sharp marketing guy," says Bob Russell. "He was definitely more on the ball than Marshall Smith was."

His transition from a soft drink company to the technology business required a quick education. "It was a new business to me," recalls Rattigan. "The company was in many ways living hand to mouth based on what the economic scenario was. All of a sudden, I've got a fair number of people reporting to me who I don't know. The early months really were just familiarizing yourself with the people and the business as best you could."

Commodore's most successful regions were in Europe at the time. David Pleasance, Commodore UK's marketing manager, felt Rattigan should have at least become familiar with the European operations, given their importance to the company. "Even in those early days the UK was doing better than anybody else but they hardly ever came to see us," he says. "The first thing I would do if I was in a position of that magnitude is I would go to my biggest earners and say, 'What is it you guys are doing right that the other people aren't doing?'"

Often, new corporate presidents begin their tenure by firing and hiring a new executive team. "I didn't want to be spending my time on that," says Rattigan. "I really wanted to spend time on how we were going to move the goods, how we were going to reduce our manufacturing costs, and how best to take advantage of the technology we had in hand."

Andy Finkel had mixed feelings about Rattigan. "He was a guy in the John Sculley [who moved from Pepsi to Apple] mold. We used to joke, 'Now we have our own soft drink executive.' He was very to the point; very direct," he recalls. "I was never sure if he really got the computer business. He definitely didn't really have a vision for computers."

Others pined for their former leader. "They brought in a guy from Pepsi-Cola who knew marketing but again didn't understand the industry he was in," says David Baraff. "They would have been so much better off if they had just kept Jack. It's a what might have been kind of story."

What Rattigan lacked in computer experience, he substituted with business savvy. "You have to learn the language and that was part of the equation," explains Rattigan. "You had to try and understand what the problems were and what opinions you might have on them. I was sitting down with Marshall and other people and discussing those kinds of things. It was a quick and short breaking in period, but that's where I spent a lot of my time."

The engineering division, which had enjoyed almost total autonomy under Marshall Smith, was about to come under more control. "There was always a clash between engineering and Tom Rattigan, that's for sure," says Bucas. "He was younger than Marshall and obviously a faster learner and a smart guy."

A new era was about to begin for Commodore. If Rattigan could convince consumers to take the "Pepsi Challenge" against the Macintosh and IBM-PC, the Commodore-Amiga could thrive.

The End for LCD

Jeff Porter was ready to supplant the luggable SX-64 with his portable LCD computer. In fact, he was driven. With no support from management or marketing, he took it upon himself to make his beloved LCD laptop happen. "Jeff Porter did an excellent job of selling that," says Bil Herd. "He had the LCD computer ready to launch."

Porter planned to secure LCD orders and prove to management that his product would generate profit for Commodore. After the solid leads he collected at CES, he gathered several willing allies from Commodore for a road trip. "At that time, Commodore sold a lot of product through mass merchants like Sears and Toys 'R' Us," says Porter. "I remember going out with some of the sales people to meet the key buyers for Sears in Chicago and some of the regional offices."

On one such trip, Porter struck gold. "There was one guy up in the Pacific Northwest who was kind of the computer geek for the buying group for them," he recalls. "He bought into it. Once he decided he wanted to do it, then all the other regional buyers said, 'Well if Bill from the Northwest is going to do it then I'll do twice as many as him.'"

With each visit to a Sears regional office, preorders started pouring in. Soon Porter believed the rationale for his project would be unassailable. "We had initial orders from Sears for 50,000 or 100,000 units," says Porter. With those kind of numbers, there was every chance Commodore could outsell RadioShack in the portable computer market.

As it turned out, Marshall Smith had been gathering his own intelligence about portable computing. "Marshall Smith, the CEO of Commodore, told me he had a conversation with the CEO of RadioShack," recalls Porter. The RadioShack CEO told Smith, "There's good news and bad news about the laptop market. The bad news is there is no market for this stuff. The good news is we own it."

This was enough to dissuade Smith from entering the market. "Marshall cancelled the program," says Herd. "Commodore didn't produce an LCD machine after a conversation with our competition telling us not to produce it."

Herd believes RadioShack misled Smith. "I had an article hanging on my wall that said, 'Tandy's number one selling product of all RadioShack products,' and it had a picture of their little stupid LCD machine," recalls Herd. "That was back when it was golden-blue displays and they had 30 columns by eight rows."

The engineers sensed Commodore was missing out on the future of computing. "I went to the shows and brought home all the literature and put them in individual files, so I knew what the competition was announcing or had out," says Robert Russell. "I knew that there was a glitch [with the Tandy LCD computer] but it was a temporary glitch because they had such an inferior LCD screen. They had a tablet with a tiny LCD display and it was nothing like an LCD computer."

But was RadioShack truly trying to deceive Commodore? The former released the Model 200 in 1984, which was more laptop-like than the previous model. Then in 1985 it released the final portable in the line, the Model 600. If the line of portables was such a success, why would RadioShack end it?

At the time, RadioShack was limited to selling its portable LCD computer in RadioShack stores, whereas Commodore could sell them in all of its many retail channels. And, as history shows, laptop computers proved to be a lasting market.

Porter had worked tirelessly for almost a year on the project. Now it seemed all his hard work was destined for the dust bin. "He freaked. He had a cow," recalls Hedley Davis. "He pushed and pushed and pushed but at the end of the day he just didn't have the management points or whatever it is that was necessary to override that decision in the project. It was very sad."

Ultimately, Marshall Smith had to do something if the Amiga was going to survive. "We ran out of money," says Andy Finkel, who created the software for the LCD portable. "The Amiga cost Commodore a lot more than we expected to finish development. It basically came down to one day we would have had to buy tooling for the case for the production version of the LCD machine and we just didn't have that several hundred thousand dollars to dedicate to that project at that point. We said no, the Amiga needs that money to finish."

Commodore could ill-afford a long-term product that would take many years to build a market. "Commodore had the Amiga, it had the PC line it was trying to start up, it had the C128, it had another machine called the C900, it had the LCD. At the end of the day they just could not afford to bring all these systems to market. So the LCD got the axe," says Davis.

Commodore's new president gave a more coherent explanation of the decision. "We had to set our priorities, and we feel that the 128 and the Amiga machine have more short-term potential for us right now than the LCD," explained Thomas Rattigan. "I don't know of many other companies coming out with two new computers this year, much less three. We had to allocate our people and finances."[4]

Porter grew to understand the decision was not based on the merits or shortcomings of his LCD machine, but rather the financial situation of the company. "Think about how much R&D money you need to develop five separate product lines," explains Porter. "Yes, the C64 was a good cash cow, but that's a lot of stuff."

Out of all the products, in the minds of marketing, the LCD had the smallest market in the short term. "Commodore was a billion dollar garage shop. Adding another whatever to the bottom line needs to be a significant number, otherwise it doesn't hold water," says Porter. "It never really was given chance because they didn't have the option."

---

4 *Chicago Tribune.* June 5, 1985. Written by Christine Winter.

Dave Haynie chuckles at the shortsighted decision. "It was one of those things. 'Who needs a portable computer?'"

With time, Porter became more sanguine about the decision. "Yes it was sad that they cancelled my baby, but I had a mentor at Kodak who gave me a good life lesson. He said, 'Jeff, don't expect you will hit a home run every time at bat. Occasionally things are going to go down, sometimes not even because of you. Shit happens. As long as you keep going up to bat you'll eventually hit a home run. Just keep plugging away and you'll do it.'"

Hanover Fair

Although the C900 was not ready for unveiling at the January CES, the team felt it could be ready for the April 1985 Hanover Fair. Rico Tudor had been especially hard at work programming a GUI for Coherent Unix, complete with mouse and windows.

Gerard Bucas, the standard bearer of Unix among Commodore's management, was thrilled by the result. "In today's terms, it was almost like Ubuntu desktop. It was literally a whole graphics screen, which was at an incredible resolution," he recalls. "It was a complete graphics workstation with a Unix operating system. It would have blown a lot of other things away."

In the eighties, professional developers prized screen real estate above color graphics. This meant high-resolution output. "We even had a special monitor developed for it," says Bucas. "Obviously we had a lot of clout with monitor suppliers because Commodore with one of the biggest customers of large monitor suppliers like Philips. We basically had them develop a special high resolution."

Although Commodore made appearances at CES and COMDEX in North America, the Hanover Fair dwarfed both shows. "With Commodore the big annual trade show was Hanover," says Bucas. "It was the biggest show that was the European equivalent of COMDEX in those days."

Bucas sent his engineers along with C900 prototypes to help set them up and ensure they remained functioning. "George Robbins and I were there but since we didn't speak German, we were just there to make sure the machine worked," says Welland. The team included Bob Russell, George Robbins, Bob Welland and Hedley Davis.

He also wanted his engineers to look professional in case they were asked to help demonstrate the C900 to prospective buyers. "It was suggested that we bring suits, as we might have to interact with the press or something," says Welland. "I had a nice suit and brought it."

The unkempt George Robbins, however, was the polar opposite of the business professional. "The idea of George owning a suit was rather absurd," recalls Welland. "However, when we got on the plane, George had a backpack and a paper bag. I asked him what was in the paper bag and George said, 'My suit.' I found this an odd way to carry a suit."

The mystery continued to build in Welland's mind and was revealed after the show began. "Later in the week I was going to get breakfast with George and dropped by his hotel room," recalls Welland. "In the hallway was the paper bag and in it, his suit. I asked him about it."

As it turned out, the suit was unwearable. "He conveyed that his since-deceased cat had been sleeping on his suit for years and he was having an allergic reaction to it. It was a corduroy thing and it was in a ball and covered in cat hair. To this day I cannot imagine why George bothered to bring the thing but that was George."

Welland's trip to Europe was memorable if not scary for a young man used to being cloistered in an engineering lab. "When we went there, it was when there had been some terrorist thing that had happened," recalls Welland. "George and I, we brought the hard disks for the C900 onto our carry-on luggage because we didn't want to leave them in the machines. I remember getting to Frankfurt. We had to transfer somewhere to fly from Hanover to Braunschweig. I had this hard disk and at the customs place are these 18-year old kids with submachine guns. I thought, I hope they know what a hard disk is because if they think it's something offensive, I'm in trouble."

This year, Commodore Germany showed off prototypes of the C128, the Commodore PC-10, and of course the aforementioned C900 prototypes. The Amiga computer was conspicuously absent, much to the disappointment of attendees. "All those exhibit spaces were permanent at the Hanover Fair in those days, so they sat there all year," explains Welland. "They were very elaborate. Commodore's was two stories. It had a bar and a restaurant and all the big ones were the same."

The Commodore PC-10, for better or for worse, was a near perfect clone of the IBM PC model 5150. "Some of the European companies wanted to deal with one vendor for everything," he explains. "They might like Amigas but if you didn't have PC clones you couldn't get their business, which is why Apple was just doing so well in Europe—they weren't of course. Nobody was buying Apple and they were wickedly overpriced there at the time."

Commodore had no problems selling the clones in Europe and announced it had sold over 5000 Commodore PC's in Germany and almost the same in the UK in the first year. "If you went to Europe, Commodore really had a very different perspective because they had maintained all their connections with the small computer stores in Europe," says Welland. "It had a distribution channel that they had kind of destroyed in the United States."

The C128, seen as a true successor to the C64, was also highly anticipated, although it was disappointing no games were on display for the machine.

But the most sophisticated computer on display was the C900. "What got demoed at Hanover was the Z8000 motherboard plus Ferenc [Vadovszky]'s video card," says Welland. "The Windows system we demoed in Hanover was something [Rico Tudor] wrote."

Unfortunately, Welland's bit blitter card was not yet working and he was unable to demonstrate it.

Although Robbins and Welland had been brought to the show to maintain the hardware, they were rarely needed. As a result, they spent most of their time in Commodore's restaurant. "You go sit up on the second floor and you could look over the show," says Welland. "We were next to the Xerox booth and they also had a restaurant and a bar. It was just this kind of strange thing, very different from what was at CES. We just sat upstairs drinking beer."

The whole scene was surreal for Welland, who usually worked with male engineers in windowless labs. "These waitresses were young women and they were quite good looking," he recalls. "One day I'm up there having a beer and this woman is making steak tartare. It was such a weird thing to see this beautiful waitress with raw hamburger. Like what am I doing here? This was a very strange place."

Surveying the crowds every day, Welland eventually spotted three familiar faces from a rival workstation company. "Unix being my background, I had spent a little bit of time at Sun. There were three people," explains Welland. "Bill Joy and Scott McNeely of Sun came by and looked at it for a long time. The third person might have been Andreas Bechtolsheim who was the guy who designed the original Sun machines."

Welland and Robbins came down from their perch to have a closer look at their competitors. "It was interesting. They came up to the booth and we had the Windows system running, we had the hi-res graphics card running and they stood there for a long time," laughs Welland. "It was very fun for us because we knew who they were and the idea that we were scaring them was actually quite appealing on some level."

Sun had every reason to fear Commodore's entry into the workstation market at the time. "The hope behind that machine was that you could get a low-cost Unix-centric workstation out in the world," explains Welland. "Sun charged an astonishing amount of money for those machines. It's hard to really comprehend how they got the premiums they got, particularly when you consider that the Mac was from a hardware perspective not terribly different. We saw them coming and they sat there and they looked concerned and that made us happy."

Robbins and Welland also watched from above as other competitors tried to show off their wares. "Next door to the Commodore booth was the East German technology booth," says Welland. "This would have been before the wall came down. In the East German technology booth, the two things I remember were: they had a printer and they had a Z-80 machine. The Z-80 machine looked kind of okay, kind of crude. But the printer was literally a typewriter where they had put solenoids on the keys. It was kind of like a thing out of a David Lynch movie. You walked up to it and you couldn't not laugh."

Over and over from their perch, they saw the same bemused reaction. "Everyone who walked into this booth would see this 'printer' and you'd just start laughing," says Welland. "You see this poor guy in the booth, who is like the representative of East German high technology, and you'd feel bad for him. And then you think, 'Oh but he's probably a good Communist and that's why he gets to go here.' It was a very strange thing. It was like, why are they even here? I guess they wanted to demonstrate something."

Hedley Davis attended with the C128 prototypes but wanted to find out more about the competition. "Hedley, because he was working on the C128 at the time, I think he was keenly curious about what was in the Apple IIe," says Welland.

Davis, who rarely sat down for very long, recruited Welland to help him with a mission. "At the Hanover Fair, you could hang out late at night if your company was there," says Welland. "So we went over to the Apple booth. The Apple IIe been announced and that was a competitor to the C128 and the C64. Hedley and I, not seeing anyone around, actually took the whole thing apart and then put it back together and went back to our booth."

With the 10-minute mission a success, they pushed their luck even further at the Atari booth. "We got our hands on an Atari 520ST and we took that apart," says Welland. "It was probably a bad thing to do but we couldn't resist. That was kind of the culture."

CHAPTER 18

Launching the C128 1985

While the Amiga engineers in Los Gatos raced to finish the Amiga in time for a mid-1985 launch, the C128 Animals of West Chester had a battle of their own. They had engineered the C128 prototype in less than six months to bring to the Winter CES. Now they needed to bring the C128 into production ahead of the Amiga launch. And to make things more difficult, Commodore was running low on resources. But a new executive at Commodore felt an online service could help to balance Commodore's books.

C128 Production

Commodore planned to launch the C128 in May or June 1985 to make room in the schedule for the Amiga launch. It would take an extraordinary effort to have the C128 ready for production in time.

Bil Herd had many enemies within Commodore management, but he could always rely on one executive. "Adam Chowaniec was my guardian angel at that point," he recalls. Unfortunately, Chowaniec was away at the Hanover Fair at the time and Herd's protection disappeared. "He was out for about ten days in Germany and the head of the drafting department had come to see me and said, 'Well, we're going to stop giving such priority to the C128. This has gone on just far too long.' Those were his exact words."

Herd was appalled. "I thought, 'Really? How can I tell you to just fucking do your job? You've decided that the C128 shouldn't be the top priority at this phase of the design.'"

For ten days during Chowaniec's absence, the C128 project fell behind schedule. "Adam got back and wanted to know what asshole stopped the C128," recalls Herd. "It was like, 'As long as you hurt him later, I'll be okay. I'll get this fixed for you, but I want to see him bleed later.'"

Getting the project back on schedule was Herd's main concern. Herd ran three eight-hour shifts of PCB engineers to catch up. The design area became Herd's temporary home. "I took an air mattress, and my army coat because it's very air-conditioned in that area," says Herd. "I just stayed in this room with these guys for the next three or four days in three shifts. They were doing one guy per shift, and there's three designers, but I was there for all three shifts."

The air-conditioned room was great for the computers, but to the humans working there it felt like a refrigerator. "There's something about working like that that makes you like junk food," says Herd. "On Friday I had bought Burger King breakfast biscuits. I bought four or five, and they were sitting on a bookshelf next to me on Friday. It was so cold in that goddamned room that by Sunday they were still good and I ate them for lunch."

The crunch-time paid off. "We would have had time to do it in the ten days, but we knocked it out in three. We killed ourselves to catch up for what a manager had done," recalls Herd. "That was an example of middle management just fucking something up." As a remembrance of their efforts, the designers included a small message on the board that only they could appreciate. It said, 'RIP HERD FISH RUBINO.'[1]

"It was the layout guys who put the RIP, rest in peace message," says Herd. "The syntax refers to an inside joke where we supposedly gave our lives in an effort to get the FCC production board done in time."

Made In Japan

With the PCB design complete, Bil Herd sent the layout to Japan for production. Commodore paid over $120,000 per year to RCA Global just to lease a communications link between the VAX systems in North America with the one in Tokyo. Despite this, the Japanese wanted Herd on site to help work out production issues. "Bil was there for a week, maybe two," recalls Dave Haynie. "He was basically just babysitting. They would make the boards there and ship them off to Europe or America for final assembly."

Communication with the Japanese was mostly in English. "They all knew some English, some more than others," say Herd. "Engineers speak a common language."

---

1 Inexplicably, the third PCB engineer's name did not appear on the board. "It should say Guay on there because he was the third one," says Herd.

But Herd had improved his Japanese comprehension since the Plus/4 days. "He was really trying to learn Japanese," says Haynie. "Every time he went out with the Japanese guys, he'd have them teach him a word or two."

While in America, Herd also had a chance to practice his Japanese with Yashi Terakura and another Japanese engineer. "We went over there and we got them coming over here," says Herd. "One of the guys I call a friend, [Sumio] Katayama, would come over [to America] and I would put him up at my place."

For Herd, learning Japanese was for the cause. "It was part of being a better engineer to break down that wall that existed between Japan and us," says Herd. "I took the time to learn Japanese because it was one more thing that increased our chance for success."

During meetings, Herd's colorful descriptions of the 8563 video chip amused the Japanese engineers. "I called it a 'dead piece of shit'," says Herd. "It was a phrase I said in a meeting that just had the Japanese roaring."

Normally, the Japanese engineers redesigned the PCB layout to fit their component insertion tools, but Herd gave them a head start. "Instead of designing it to be redone by Japan, I worked with it so the version I was done with could go straight to production, and that hadn't been done before," says Herd. "Every single chip could be inserted with a Panasert machine [made by Panasonic] for the Japanese runs, or a Universal, which is the American machine."

Herd's drinking habits helped him bond with the head of R & D, Yuichi Okubo, and his Japanese colleagues. "One night we were sitting around and everybody was relating what their last names meant. I thought about it and said that my last name meant 'many animals'. The happy drunk Japanese engineers all said, 'So!' in unison. They were quite pleased with the revelation and my Japanese nickname *doobutsu* was born that night, which means animal," says Herd.

"Doobutsu" got along well with the head engineer. "I liked Okubo, who ran the shop," says Herd. "Me and him got to be good friends. He gave me a very touching letter that was very Japanese in that it said, 'With this I wish you well with your life.' You could catch from the letter that he meant it. He gave me a little present that meant a lot to him, which was an ink pen of all things."

Although Herd embraced his Japanese counterparts, he soon became restless. "There was nothing to do," says Dave Haynie. "That's why Bil wanted to leave, because he said, 'There's no reason for me to be here.'"

Haynie soon found himself on a plane to Japan to fill in for Herd. "They were insistent upon somebody being there, so he said, 'Dave, come on over to Japan.' I said, 'Okay, great. No problem.'"

Commodore Japan consisted of two facilities: the offices and the production lines. "The place in Tokyo was just an office," says Haynie. "It was exactly what you would expect a Japanese office to be in the mid-eighties. There was a manager at the end of a row of desks. Of course, there were some Americans there who were there full time. They were off doing whatever they wanted to do."

The Japanese engineers excelled in finding cheaper ways to manufacture products. "They occasionally did some serious engineering, like cost reductions on the C128," says Haynie. "Sometimes after you make a couple of thousand of something, you find a problem or you find a better way to do it. After you make a hundred thousand, you find a cheaper way to do it. That's the kind of stuff they did there."

Haynie felt equally unneeded during his stay. "At that time, they were bringing up the C128 into production," says Haynie. "They basically wanted somebody who understood it better than they did to be on hand in case something went wrong. For about ten days, I was there and so was Greg Berlin, who was on the 1571 drive. They would have a few questions, but I think they were just being very polite. We were just waiting for an emergency to break out and it never did."

Haynie and Berlin developed a truncated workday schedule. "We would kind of come in around ten, hang out until lunch time because nothing happened, then we would go to Akihabara," recalls Haynie. "Akihabara is a section of Tokyo where all the electronics are. You could buy components off the shelf and you could buy stereo gear. Greg was outfitting his car, so we were loading up his credit card and then we were starting to load up my credit card with all his purchases."

Favorable dollar to yen exchange rates made shopping in Tokyo in the early eighties extremely appealing. "Back then the exchange rate when we first started in Japan was probably 300 to 1," says Berlin. "The first time I went to Japan, I went to Akihabara, the big electronics mecca. It was a huge area and you could buy any electronics. I bought about 1,500 bucks worth of car stereo equipment for me and more for my brother."

CD players were starting to pervade, something that would one day become important for computers. "They actually introduced the first car CD player that was available in the world," says Berlin. "It wasn't available in the US yet. I bought it, brought it back and put it in my car and my brother's car. Everything was so cheap back then in Japan it was totally insane."

Although Haynie felt unproductive in Japan, the trip was a needed diversion after working so hard on the C128. "It was just really neat being there and it was kind of like a vacation," he says.

Even though it was a business trip, the two young engineers took in the tourist sites. "There was some kind of big technology fair outside of Tokyo called the Tsukuba Science City," recalls Berlin. "He and I went to that. I was kind of a freak show for all the kids there. I'm 6 foot 8 inches and there's all these school kids and they're climbing me like a tree the whole day, freaking out. It was amazing."

A Costly Mistake

Back in America, it seemed like everyone was against the C128 Animals. "These were the middle managers that couldn't or didn't embrace what we were truly trying to do," says Bil Herd. "They either wanted to stake out their territory, were mortified that the rules were being broken, or they simply wanted to be noticed."

Herd continued battling with QA manager Bob Shamus after making a costly mistake. "We didn't have design-checking tools back then and we had hand-created the font for the gate array," says Herd. "If you held out the green and white computer paper, it would extend almost to the floor. There was a term on each line. Well, one of them was wrong."

As a result, one single letter in the font set displayed improperly. Herd released the set of terms before anyone had verified them. "We had released it aggressively to MOS because I knew that if you slowed them down, it would be us that were hurting when we didn't get the chips on time," explains Herd.

Without realizing the error, the MOS Technology technicians created a half-run of PLA chips, which came out to over ten thousand chips. "If you turn it over to production, it's five weeks before you see your chips," explains Herd. "We had gotten the first half and they were screwed up."

The error resulted in Ultimax mode not working properly while in C64 mode. "Who used Ultimax mode? Well, it turns out the English soccer game did, so when you plugged in the soccer game into the C128, it would actually come up with big black and white checker blocks," explains Herd.

Herd looked into the problem and traced it to the gate array. "I went to go and find out why, and sure enough, on this huge piece of paper where there should have been a one there was an X," says Herd.

The small error turned out to be very costly. "It cost a couple of hundred thousand dollars," says Herd. "Basically it was my fault. Somebody in my group missed it but I took all blame for anything."

The managers summoned Herd. "I go into this meeting and the two heads from QA are there. One was from the QA engineering group, who had never done anything useful in his whole time there," says Herd. "There was also the president of MOS Technology and the vice president of Commodore."

Herd instantly noticed the mood was heavy. "The one guy pushes this little stack of paper forward and says, 'We have proof that you approved the bad font.' I said, 'Yeah, I fucked up.' And those were the words I used in this big meeting. I said, 'Here's how we're going to fix it.'"

Herd sensed the QA manager had an ulterior motive. "There was a plan [to have me fired], but I didn't think for a second I was in jeopardy," he says.

Bob Shamus cut Herd off before he could continue. "The guy cleared his throat and he says, 'Ahem. No, we have proof that it was you that messed it up.' I said, 'Yes. I. Fucked. Up. And here's how we're going to fix it,' and I started to outline it."

Shamus was determined to make Herd squirm. "He starts to do it again!" recalls Herd. Luckily, Herd had an ally in the room, Ted Lenthe. "The president of MOS, who taught me how to make a decision, cleared his throat and the room goes quiet. He said, 'I think Bil is on it and he's trying to tell you how to fix it.'"

Herd had a plan to save the other half-run of the PLA chip by making a minor correction to one of the layers. "We made a mask that we would never use again for layer six, which was metal, and we were able to recover one of the split lots," says Herd. "We corrected it in less than a week and we got half a run out of it."

Herd continued to battle middle managers right to the end of the C128 production cycle. "The middle managers were all scrabbling to make a name for themselves or clear an area for themselves," says Herd. "[Julian Strauss] had said, 'From now on, you can't release anything to MOS without my approval.' I said, 'If you go fast, I don't have a problem with that. But you need to go at my speed when you do that.' He said, 'Okay, no problem.'"

Herd passed the corrected character ROM to Strauss, as instructed, and waited. "We gave him the font for the character set, and we asked, 'Is it done yet? Is it done yet?' He said, 'No, I'm looking at it.'" The inaction frustrated Herd and he decided to resolve the problem himself.

"There were all these cubicle offices with the managers," says Herd. "They had had some thefts, and there was actually a memo that said, 'Anybody caught breaking into an office will be terminated on the spot. This means engineers too.' They were trying to treat it very seriously."

Herd felt secure because of his critical position on the C128 project and he had no fear of reprisals. When an obstacle blocked his path, he went through it or around it. "We broke into his office by popping the ceiling out, climbing over his office walls, and dropping down," reveals Herd. "I cut my arm on the top metal thing, got the EPROM out of his desk drawer, put the tiles back in his ceiling, swept up the mess and left."

Strauss was unaware that anything had occurred until the engineers met for a meeting. "Three days later, we said, 'So how's that font coming?' He said, 'I'm almost done looking at it.' I looked at him in the meeting and said, 'I broke into your office, I stole it out of your desk drawer, and I released it to production almost three days ago.'"

The admission had Strauss cornered and revealed to everyone he was slowing down the process rather than helping. "Here I am admitting I had committed a thing that would get you fired," says Herd. "But the point was, this is already done and you're lying about it." Herd survived the confrontation but he was rapidly losing popularity with management.

Soon it seemed like managers were making decisions merely to thwart Herd. "Later they would try and tell us what to do as far as being destructive," says Herd. "I built a fuse into the C128 power supply, which I was told not to and I did anyway. They took it out later, and somebody rubbed my face in it."

Middle managers were increasingly frustrating Herd. "Near the end, because there hadn't been any Jack Attacks, we were starting to get up to our ears in bad middle managers," says Herd. "They had stopped culling the herd. These people would define their existence if they could mutilate something. That was as good as doing something good, as far as they were concerned, because they got their mark on it."

It was important for Herd to release an 80-column monitor with the C128 so users could take advantage of the advanced graphical modes. However, management significantly slowed down the release of the monitor. "The C128 was one of the first computers to try and sell a monitor to home users," explains Herd.

Commodore rarely adhered to standards. "On the monitor interface, there were no monitor standards because there were barely any monitors out there," says Herd. "On one standard, the syncs were both negative, and on the other standard the syncs were both positive. I was told [by Joe Krasucki] to make one negative and one positive so that only Commodore monitors work with it."

The manufacturer, Mitsumi, waited on a final design from Commodore. Herd decided to bypass his manager's instructions and design the monitor interface as he saw best. "We got conflicting information on how to do it, so I made up my mind one night and said, 'Well, we're going to do it this way,' and that's how Mitsumi made the monitors."

Rather than face his boss, Herd chose to deceive him. "A couple of days later, I looked [Joe Krasucki] square in the face and lied to him," reveals Herd. "I said, 'I did it.' Well, I didn't. I actually researched which was the most compatible and which had more monitors out there. So I lied to him and had actually done what I thought was the pure way. I didn't care if I got fired at that point. We were at the end of the [C128] cycle and I was expendable." Today Herd feels he made the right decision, rather than allowing a bad management decision to stand.

By June of 1985, Commodore started shipping the C128 to retail stores with full packaging and manuals. Unlike the Commodore 64, the engineers were still around to contribute to the manual. "The manual itself was done in-house by our technical writers," says Haynie. "I wrote part of the technical reference manual and Fred [Bowen] wrote part of it."

Even Herd contributed. "If you ever see a sentence that starts with the word 'additionally', I wrote it," says Herd. "Unfortunately, my English skills weren't quite as good as they are today."

The high-school dropout with no college education had succeeded in designing the computer he set out to design, with virtually 100% backward compatibility. "I never doubted," says Herd. "Not because I was egotistical but because I knew that I would do everything in my power to succeed. Looking back, I think that it was that drive that was responsible for the fact we did succeed." Despite management interference, Herd believes he achieved his vision of the C128. "I can't say I would have done too much different."

June 1985 CES

Commodore planned to stagger the launches of the C128 and the Amiga in order to focus company resources on each respective system. The C128, being the consumer model, went first so as to capitalize on Christmas sales. The Amiga, which was somewhere between a personal computer and a business computer, would launch later in the year.

The June 2, 1985 CES in Chicago starred the C128 exclusively. *Compute!'s Gazette* noted, "The long-awaited Amiga computer was not a popular topic with Commodore representatives at CES. Although the machine was said to have been ready, Commodore was putting full emphasis on the 128 at the show."[2]

Commodore's marketing department had hired an advertising firm to create a series of C128 advertisements narrated by actor Burgess Meredith. As was typical, the ads premiered at CES ahead of broadcast on television.

Thomas Rattigan announced that 100,000 pre-orders for the C128 had been received prior to the start of CES. He predicted 15 percent of C64 owners would upgrade to the C128 within a year, which proved to be quite accurate.

With previous 8-bit computers, Commodore created its own software library. Each computer launched with games and applications that showed the way for other software makers. Under Marshall Smith, Commodore did not produce any new software titles in C128 mode. Either due to oversight or intentional omission, it was an ominous sign that Commodore marketing was leaving the C128 to fend for itself.

The only titles Commodore brought to the machine were lacklustre CP/M applications Perfect Writer, Perfect Calc, and Perfect Filer. All that was required by Commodore was to copy the files to 1541 compatible disks. Unfortunately, Perfect Writer would go on to be named runner-up to "worst word processor of all time" by PC Magazine.

As for third-party games for the C128, there were almost none. Normally Commodore sent developer systems to game companies in order to spur development. However, the industry was still in the shadow of the video game crash. Executives and engineers alike believed it was a selling point that C128 mode did not have games. And besides, it ran all those games in C64 mode anyway so, in their minds, there was no reason to create new games in C128 mode.

Along with the C128, Commodore marketed the usual peripherals of disk drives, printers, and modems. Commodore demonstrated the 1571 disk drive, as well as a proposed dual-drive called the 1572. The concept of a dual-drive was deemed by management to be a throwback to the PET days and never made it into production.

---

2   *Compute!'s Gazette.* September 1985, p. 36.

It was also the public debut of Jeff Porter's 1200 baud modem, the 1670. Porter demonstrated the modems next to a VCR which played the C128 ads in a loop, driving him crazy from repetition.

One surprising new product was a mouse for $49.95. Commodore Hong Kong had sent a simple mouse that plugged into the port of a C64 or C128. "It just kind of showed up," says engineer Hedley Davis.

The mouse fit the joystick ports of most 8-bit computers. It was not a true proportional mouse, but rather a joystick disguised as a mouse. In other words, dragging the mouse left was like pushing left on a joystick. While not practical for most joystick games, it was useful for applications that used a pointer, such as paint programs, or even games that used a pointer arrow.

Commodore planned to launch the mouse later in 1985 as the 1350 mouse, once the engineers pushed it through FCC testing. Curiously, the promotional materials at CES and the manual only recognize C128 support. No support for the C64 is mentioned, despite working perfectly with the computer.

Commodore also liked to show off what they were up to without necessarily taking orders. Rattigan brought out the PC-10 and PC-20 models of MS-DOS compatible computers. These had recently launched in Europe to great success, as well as a moderately successful Canadian launch. Commodore also showed off the C900, although it acknowledged it would be launched in Europe in the fall, with perhaps a later U.S. launch date.

CEO Marshall Smith hosted the annual Commodore CES press reception. When asked about Commodore's declining stock price and press reports about Commodore's future, he became openly upset. However, he gamely tried to convince the press that they had optimism about the C128 launch, the continued success of the C64, and of course, the impending launch of the Amiga.

As Commodore continued pushing the C64 at the show, a new and unexpected rival popped up. Nintendo of Japan debuted a redesigned version of its Famicom system, called the Nintendo Entertainment System, or NES. It was the first time the machine would appear in North America but it would take many years before it found success.

After the introduction of the C128 at CES, attendees visited Commodore's booth in the following days. Most felt $300 was a remarkable value, considering the C64 debuted at $600 years earlier.

As *Byte* magazine later noted in its 7-page review of the C128, the basic performance of the C128 was actually superior to the Apple IIe and even the IBM PC. This was due to the efficiency of the 6502 processor versus the

Intel based IBM PC. "It was faster than the 8088s running at 4.7 MHz," explains Herd. "They came out with a 6 MHz 8088 but they would have needed an 8 MHz to take us on."

Commodore magazines warmly received the C128. *Run* magazine reviewer Margaret Morabito liked the price to feature comparison with the IBM PCjr and the Apple IIc. Though the base price of the C128 was $300, with a 1571 disk drive it cost $550. This favorably compared to the Apple IIc for $1100 and the IBM PCjr for $1000.

Compute!'s Gazette provided a seven page overview on the computer that was generally positive, though they noted C64 users had to wait three years for a true encore to their favorite computer.

The former C64 designers attended CES with their company, Ensoniq. This included engineers Bob Yannes, Al Charpentier, Bruce Crockett, and product manager Charles Winterble.

Bob Yannes had reservations about the lack of a strategy to continually improve the 8-bit line. "The C128 should have happened much sooner than it did," he says. "It didn't come out for three years. By then, it was like, 'Who cares?' I would have followed up the C64 with a 128K version within the year, as quickly as possible, just to keep people moving up in the line, and then gradually take it up higher than that."

Despite the release date, Yannes felt the C128 was in keeping with his vision for an expanded C64. "I think the C128 is probably close to what I would have done for a sequel to the C64," he says. He also appreciated the look of the C128, which resembled the case he hoped would enclose his C64. "It seemed like a pretty nice product. I never had one, and I never really played with it but I saw one and it looked nice."

On the other end of the spectrum, Charles Winterble, the project manager for the C64, was unimpressed. "What we wouldn't have done is what they did," he says. "They came out with this computer which was a C64, C128, and CP/M. What the heck? Are you out of your minds?"

Perhaps the biggest weakness was that C128 mode was not close enough to C64 mode to allow developers to write one piece of code for both computers. "It was only C64 compatible when it was only a C64. The C128 in C128 mode wasn't really C64 compatible," says Herd. "It just shared the same chassis."

The thing that would have motivated C64 owners to run out and upgrade their C64 computers to C128 would have been a C64 mode with more memory and a faster processor. That one change would have made the C128 very desirable by C64 owners looking to boost the speed of their existing software library.

Another change that would have motivated buyers is if the C128 mode had significantly better graphics and sound. Overall, there were few reasons for a C64 owner to make the upgrade.

While demonstrating his new computer at the CES show, Herd felt some disapproval. "I had a kid criticize me for this at a show one time," he says. "This little punk wiped his nose on his sleeve and in a whiney voice proclaimed that if he had designed the C128 he would have found a way to keep the MMU in the memory map in C64 mode. I explained to him that I actually took it out on purpose; I wasn't just so stupid that I couldn't figure out how to map a device in."

The "little punk" would one-day work for Commodore. "This guy's name was Bryce [Nesbitt], who later went on to become a Commodore engineer after I had left," says Herd. "I never did get a chance to backhand him."

Years later, Nesbitt understands the reaction to his criticisms. "I don't have that kind of inhibition so I would have done something as stupid as going up to a company and criticizing their products right on the floor," he says. "Given the age difference and the professionalism difference, I'm sure it wasn't an inappropriate thought. Like who are you?"

However, he still believes his analysis of the C128 was accurate, even though he was a teenager at the time. "I think that I picked up on that immediately when I heard about the C128 and just slapped my forehead even at age 17," he recalls. "It's like, how could you do something so dumb? You are asking people to develop two versions of all the software. Why would you take your developer software base and divide it in two? You're developing a new platform and putting it out there with essentially no software right next to something that's got great software and now you're damaging both. So now you look at buying a C64 and you go, 'Oh well that's the old model. I don't want that. Oh, that's the new version, I don't want that.'"

Robert Russell, who helped develop three of Commodore's previous hits, has mixed feelings on the C128. "I worked real hard to get a Z80 card in the original C64," begins Russell. "I liked the fact that the [Z80] chip got used, but why couldn't we have done our own piece of silicon that was both 40 columns and 80 columns? That's what I really wanted at that point in time, but we didn't have the design engineers to do that."

In Russell's opinion, MOS Technology lacked the capability to produce a VIC-III chip. "We didn't have the personnel when it was needed," he says. "We could do a simple 80-column display chip but we couldn't do an integrated one."

Although it had a somewhat controversial CES reception, the true test of the C128 would occur over the next six months, as the product found its way across the world on store shelves. And with Commodore quickly running out of money, the C128 could either make or break the company.

CHAPTER 19

The Debut
1985

Commodore had kept the Amiga under wraps from the public and press since acquiring the Amiga technology. The Amiga employees felt Commodore had done an excellent job bringing the Amiga farther along to production. But with a rival about to launch a competing machine, it was time to introduce the Amiga to the world, and Commodore would attempt to do that in a spectacular fashion.

Atari 520ST

Unknown to the public, both Commodore and Atari were in a desperate race to release their computers to store shelves first. Although the specs of the Atari 520ST were not as good as the Amiga, it was in the same class of machine and going after the same market. As *Compute!'s Gazette* reported, "It seems likely that the Amiga and the new ST from Atari are going to revitalize the personal computer industry. These machines represent a leap to a higher level of technology."

Prototypes of the Atari 520ST debuted at the January 1985 CES, but it was still not on store shelves when summer arrived. Atari believed Commodore would announce the retail release of the Amiga at the Summer CES show on June 2. Atari executives began pushing for a May release in order to claim they were the first to market. When engineers failed to meet the ambitious release schedule, Atari marketing did the next best thing and lied.

In late May, when it became clear production models would not arrive for at least another month, Atari's VP of marketing, James Copland, gave an interview to *InfoWorld* with the very misleading title, "Atari Ships New 520 ST". In truth, as the article revealed, hand-built demo units had shipped to dealers, user groups, and of course developers—something Amiga had also done since 1984.

But when the Summer CES show arrived, no one was more surprised than Atari when Commodore failed to show the Amiga, given that the Amiga engineers had a long head-start on the Atari engineers. Behind the scenes, Commodore's developers were still working out issues with the new user interface, Intuition, and Amiga DOS. With the Amiga launch scheduled for July 23, the team was in overdrive, with RJ Mical sometimes working all night until 8 in the morning before retiring for some sleep. This went on until July 15, when the code was finally locked for the upcoming show.

And then, just before the Amiga launch party, Atari began to trickle out the production model ST computers to store shelves. Despite the obvious financial trouble at Atari, and despite the shorter development period, Atari was able to get the Atari 520ST on store shelves in July 1985, ahead of the Amiga. "The Atari beat the Amiga 1000 to market by about a month. And, because of Tramiel's tenaciousness, it caused us a lot of anxiety," recalls Bob Welland.

It was a testament to the drive, determination, and business shrewdness of Jack Tramiel. He made executives of other computer companies look lazy by comparison. Commodore could now only hope to play catch up with Atari's head-start in the marketplace.

Amiga Launch Party

To launch the Amiga, Irving Gould and his board of directors approved a massive budget of $25 million, to be spent in the latter half of 1985.[1] This figure included both advertising and marketing costs.

One of the first major expenditures from the budget was a lavish debut for the Amiga, something Commodore had not done in the past for any of its computers. "The Launch Party came from the Amiga marketing people," says RJ Mical. "The Amiga marketing people were a brilliant bunch."

The new idea for a launch event came from the minds of the Los Gatos marketing team. "The marketing effort was headed up by two people: Jerry McCoy and a woman named Caryn Havis," says Mical.[2]

---

1 *Compute!'s Gazette.* September 1985 p. 26

2 "She sports a different last name these days," says Mical. "Her name is now Caryn Mical and she and I met during the Amiga days." RJ and Caryn married and had four children.

On July 23, 1985, the official Amiga launch took place in New York. Commodore rented the renowned Lincoln Center for the event. Its modern architecture and vast theater was an appropriate setting to unveil a revolutionary computer.

Hundreds of people attended the event, including technology writers, editors, reporters, market analysts, employees, software developers, and even some celebrities. "We had Debbie Harry there," says Mical, referring to the lead singer of Blondie. Irving Gould ensured much of the crowd consisted of Wall Street investors and journalists.

The scale and grandiosity of the event impressed the Amiga developers. Jay Miner and his entire Amiga team flew out from California for the launch. According to Mical, "We were intensely involved with setting the whole thing up, getting it all organized, getting the software to work, figuring out the plan for how it was all going to flow. It was a gigantic group effort that involved the whole company." Irving Gould spared no expense and flew in the engineer's wives and girlfriends as well.

The event started late in the day and continued into the night. "As I recall it was late afternoon but I think it was still light when we arrived," says Mical. "We were assembling and getting the whole cast together."

Attendees wore their best attire. "The engineers and the Amiga staff were all elegantly dressed in tuxedos," says Mical. Attendees packed into the reception area of Lincoln Center, chatting and periodically stepping up to the fully stocked bar for free drinks. A woodwind trio played soothing tunes while a small laser show kept the crowd entertained.

Marshall Smith indulged his thirst for martinis. "Marshall liked to drink a lot," recalls Bil Herd. "There's a film of him doing the Amiga intro and he had already been into the martinis, and it was just kind of sad."

Looking like James Bond himself in his black tuxedo, Thomas Rattigan garnered much of the interest from the press. "It was a hell of a party!" says Rattigan. "We had a good crowd there and we got pretty good press out of it." The press questioned Rattigan on his Amiga strategy. Still new and understandably shaky, Rattigan tried his best to give meaningful replies to some difficult questions.

At 6:30 PM, attendees entered the darkened Vivian Beaumont theater for the Amiga demonstration. After years of effort, it was time for the engineers to unveil their creation. "We were all just so nervous because we needed to exude confidence and professionalism," says Mical. "It was a thin veneer underneath where a bunch of sweating engineers were praying that the demos wouldn't crash and that this whole thing would come off flawlessly."

The natural person to present the show was of course Dave Morse, who had brought the company so far. Although he attended the launch event and still consulted with Commodore, he was no longer truly with the company. Instead, Commodore-Amiga chose one of its own as the master of ceremonies. "The overall presenter was my boss, Bob Pariseau," says Mical. "He was smooth and slick; an excellent presenter and an excellent spokesperson who did a fantastic job at the launch."

Cameras were positioned to capture close-up images on the user and computer, as well as a direct feed from the Amiga onto large screens above the stage. "It was a carefully crafted presentation," says Mical. "Pariseau did a brilliant job of getting the material together and figuring out all the dodges they might have to make if things crashed."

Pariseau showed off Intuition, which allowed switching between multitasking applications, including the iconic Boing Demo. The window smoothly scrolled to reveal multiple programs running simultaneously.

Commodore recruited musician Roger Powell of Cherry Lane Technologies and Mike Boom of Everyware Incorporated to compose music for the Paula sound chip. For many, it was the first time they had heard computer synthesized music as it echoed through the auditorium.

To demonstrate the graphics, Commodore relied on a software package called GraphiCraft developed by a startup named Island Graphics. Commodore had assigned a junior developer named Jeff Bruette to help with development. "I was assigned to monitor the development of the Images and Animator graphics programs being developed by Island Graphics in Sausalito, California," he says. "For about four months I had a fully furnished apartment right in Sausalito."

The company also created a signature demo for the Amiga. "Another thing that Island Graphics was doing for Commodore was creating the ballet sequence that appeared in the Amiga launch," says Bruette. "I oversaw that at Island Graphics facility, while Gail Wellington was in charge of it."

For the finale, Pariseau welcomed two artists on stage to show off the graphics capabilities and ease of use of the Amiga. "I remember Debbie Harry and Andy Warhol. I briefly met them while they were working with Jack Haeger, who was our graphics artist," says Dale Luck. "He was working with Andy Warhol teaching him how to use the paint program."

Warhol had been approached by Commodore's Clive Smith for the Amiga launch. Preparation for the demo was months in the planning, which included training (or attempting to train) Warhol to use GraphiCraft. Bruette was tasked with training him. "I had no clue who this character was. All

I knew was he had people such as band members from The Cars coming to his studio when I was there," says Bruette. Warhol's use of drugs hampered his short term memory. "He was very difficult to instruct. We would spend the morning going over basic drawing tools and understanding the difference between the right and left mouse buttons. We would break for lunch. Upon returning to the Amiga after lunch, he had forgotten everything we had gone over."

During a rehearsal for the show, the young engineer found himself seated next to Debbie Harry, who was something of a sex symbol in the eighties. "During rehearsal when Debbie Harry was there at the Lincoln Center, I was sitting next to her while we were all waiting for some other portion being rehearsed," recalls Bruette. "She had on a sequined top that was about mini-skirt length. She had a matching skin-tight pants/boots. This made her sequined from neck to toe."

Bruette made some small talk that led to one of the most memorable moments of his youth. "I mentioned to her that it looked like it would be uncomfortable and scratchy. She proceeded to pull up the shirt portion and pull down the pants portion." This revealed everything to the young engineer. "She accompanied this by saying 'Actually, it's really soft on the inside.' I am sure I turned all shades of red. I was speechless."

To some, Warhol appeared to be a curious choice to demonstrate the Amiga, since he did not represent mainstream sensibilities. His one connection to Commodore was that he was a native of nearby Pittsburgh, Pennsylvania. "He was considered really avant-garde in New York and in art circles," explains Guy Wright. "He did lots of films and installations. All he really did was take snapshots of the world at those periods in time— Marilyn Monroe or the Campbell soup can. He was also quite famous among celebrities because if Andy Warhol did a picture of you, then you knew you had made it. So celebrities were always trying to get him to paint their portraits."

As one attendee reported, "Warhol and Harry didn't seem to know why they were there, which probably matched the feeling of the audience."[3]

Warhol lacked knowledge of computers, which gave the engineers a chill as he approached the Amiga. "Andy Warhol was a lovely guy and a fascinating artist," says Mical. "He had a good grasp of the fact that technology

---

3 *PC Magazine* (January 14, 1986), p. 119.

was going to change everything but at that time he was not into sophisti-cated computing. No graphics artist was because it was a brand new tool."

To offset Warhol's inexperience, Commodore made sure one of their employees was on hand to supervise. "Our chief artist at the time, a guy named Jack Haeger, stood next to Andy and made jokes with Andy through the whole thing," says Mical. "He was the perfect counterpoint to Andy Warhol because Warhol is in an odd environment where things are queer and foreign."

For his presentation, Warhol used the mouse to paint an image of Debbie Harry. One screen showed Harry live, a second screen showed the Amiga screen output and a third screen showed Warhol working away at the com-puter. Before hundreds of attendees, Warhol created one of his signature celebrity prints.

"There were some incredibly dicey moments," recalls Mical. "He digi-tized her and then he was going to paint in her face. He was only supposed to use the paintbrush because the flood-fill was known to crash every sec-ond time you used it. He went to reach for the paintbrush and grabbed the flood fill. 'Click click clickedy click.' I was like, 'It's going down! It's going down!' And it *didn't*. The engineers in that audience willed that art program collectively. If there is such a thing as the Force, we used it that day to keep that flood fill from crashing."

Luckily, Jack Haeger was on hand to politely steer Warhol to the paint tool. "The only time we saw a real crack on [Jack's] face is when Andy starts clicking around with the flood fill," says Mical. "Jack was smooth right through that but you could see, behind the eyes, he was getting ready for the joke that he's got to make when the machine crashes and we've got to reboot the machine."

To the relief of the Commodore-Amiga engineers, the presentation came off flawlessly. "It was a great big party and it came off really well," says Mical.[4]

After the show, attendees were invited to the lobby area where stations were now set up to demonstrate the Amiga software. Attendees went from one Amiga demonstration to another, set up by developers like Electron-

---

4   The portrait was saved for posterity. "After the interview, I returned to the Amiga that had the Debbie portrait on it. Just for the heck of it, I saved the image," says Jeff Bruette. "After the event I asked Andy if he wanted a copy of the disk with the image. He told me no and said I could do whatever I wanted with it. I asked him to sign the disk for me, which he did."

ics Arts, subLOGIC and Infocom. "I remember there was a whole front lobby full of third party developers," says Dale Luck. "Arthur Abraham of A-Squared Development was there showing the *Live! Digitizer*, there was a Genlock, and there was a demonstration of a word processor program."

Commodore also debuted the Transformer, the software-based IBM PC emulator for the Amiga. The booth demonstrated an Amiga running the PC version of Lotus 1-2-3. However, it was noticeably slower when running on the Amiga than on an IBM PC. Attendees wanted to know if it was capable of running *Flight Simulator*, the most taxing piece of software for the IBM PC at the time. It was not.

The stage magicians Penn & Teller were also at the event. "They were there as guests, not so much as presenters," says Commodore software developer Eric Cotton. "Penn was a big Amiga advocate back in the day as I recall."

Although Commodore successfully promoted the Amiga at the launch party, the Amiga would not appear on store shelves for months after the event. Commodore still had to manufacture and distribute the computer and there were plenty of problems to overcome.

Amiga Production

After the July debut of the Amiga at the Lincoln Center in New York, Commodore began production of the Amiga hardware. Jay Miner thought it would be appropriate to give credit to the entire Amiga team right inside the case. All 53 team members, including the original Amiga team and the new Commodore engineers, had their signatures inscribed on the plastic mold. "There wasn't any real thumbprint of Commodore's on it except some of the Commodore guys got their thumbprints on the lid, and those were good guys," says Mical. Alongside the signatures was Mitchy's paw print, in tribute to her enduring loyalty. The tiny signature of the mysterious Joe Pillow was also included.

Jack Tramiel's earlier mandate that all products be manufactured internally still applied for most of the chips produced by Commodore Semiconductor Group, other than the 68000 processor. However, Adam Chowaniec decided to use an outside company for production of the motherboards and assembly rather than Commodore's Hong Kong factory.

Chowaniec found a VCR factory in Japan instead. "The A1000 was was manufactured by Sanyo and that was orchestrated by Adam, mainly because he didn't have any confidence in the quality of the Commodore factory in

Hong Kong, which manufactured C64s and a couple of other things," says Gerard Bucas. "He decided he wanted a quality manufacturer."

Chowaniec sent Dave Needle to Japan to supervise the manufacture of the Amiga because he was the motherboard designer. When the first Amiga rolled off the production line, Needle posed with his Japanese hosts for a picture of the momentous occasion.

Jeff Porter had a chance to examine the Amiga's construction in detail and was not impressed. "Why is it so expensive? Well, it's built in Japan. It's expensive to build shit in Japan. It has this internal power supply. Really? Wow, that's expensive. It has this internal floppy drive. Wow, that is really expensive. Everything was fricking gold plated in that. It was incredibly expensive."

The profitability of the Amiga was lower as a result. "In a certain sense that was a mistake because the cost was much higher and the pricing was much higher and probably one of the reasons why the A1000 didn't do too well," says Bucas. "Plus that meant Commodore really didn't make any money on the A1000."

There was plenty of blame to go around for the high cost of the computer. Ultimately the blame would fall to Adam Chowaniec, Commodore's VP of engineering. Although he was well liked by engineers and executives, he had come from the telephone industry at Nortel and had no experience in consumer electronics.

Jay Miner and his engineers were satisfied with the Amiga, other than the disk operating system AmigaDOS and some minor bugs on release. "The Amiga 1000 is almost exactly what we intended," says RJ Mical. Now it was up to Commodore to tell the world about it.

An Uphill Marketing Battle

Commodore would rely on marketing executive Frank Leonardi to launch the Amiga. Leonardi had been hired away from Apple in January 1985 when Commodore decided it wanted out of the games market. Both Marshall Smith and Irving Gould believed someone from Apple could help to conquer the business sector. "This was still in the time when if you worked for Apple you must be a golden boy," says Jeff Porter.

When Leonardi took his seat as Commodore's VP of marketing, he began to devise a marketing strategy for the impending launch of the Amiga. "Something happened when the Amiga stopped being ours and started being Commodore's," says RJ Mical. "Their marketing and sales teams started kicking into gear and they took over the whole thing from us. Somewhere in that organization, someone or some group of people or perhaps all of them were insane. They did unbelievable, shocking, amazing, frighteningly stupid things with the Amiga."

Although the Amiga was revolutionary, it was difficult in 1985 to describe to the public at large how it would benefit them, especially given the small amount of software that would accompany the launch. "Not just Amiga, but everyone was grasping at straws trying to understand where computing would fit into the world," explains Carl Sassenrath. "Now we all know and everyone takes it for granted, but we had a lot of people resist. My father was a chemical engineer and understood technology but he said to me, 'Why would anyone want a personal computer? What would you do with it?'"

Leonardi was tasked with marketing the Amiga to the high-end business market. It was a risky move considering its strengths lay in the low-end home market dominated by the Commodore 64. "Such a change was needed, Gould said, because business was a bigger and faster-growing market than the home."[5]

"When Commodore launched the Amiga, in my opinion it was targeted very wrongly initially," says Kit Spencer. "Commodore targeted the business market and spent a lot of money on press adverts in things like *Business Week*. At that time the Amiga was not ready for that market. It didn't have the software, it didn't necessarily have the best distribution. It was going up against the PC."

Amiga marketing manager Don Reisinger knew he could not sell the computer to his existing Tonka base. "We did not see your traditional Toys "R" Us and Kay Bee Toys and Walmart and Target, who would be willing to carry that product was when it launched within the $1500 range. They were used to selling video game systems like a Commodore 64 for a couple hundred bucks. So they all said, 'We love you guys but we can't make this leap with you.'"

Since the early eighties, Commodore relied on mass-market retailers to sell their low-cost computers. Now, they were jettisoning that strategy in favor of attempting to copy Apple. "It all backfired when the Amiga came along and you actually needed a distributor," says Dave Haynie. "That wasn't a machine that would sell well in Kmart." The Amiga engineers now became spectators, watching as Commodore carried the fate of their computer.

5 *The Philadelphia Inquirer*, "A New Strategy" (May 4, 1987), p. E01.

Earlier in 1985, Commodore had publicly stated it had plans to sell the machine for less than $1000.[6] Most analysts believed it could sell for no lower than $700. These estimates were reasonable, considering Atari had prematurely announced its low-end 130ST machine would sell for $399. However, the cost of required RAM resulted in a more expensive machine.

Commodore gave the Amiga a business price of $1295, without a monitor. It appeared Commodore was going after the Macintosh market. The price put the Amiga out of reach of most Commodore 64 owners. However, it was also about $200 less than Amiga had been estimating the computer would sell for at the June 1984 CES show, prior to Commodore's involvement.

The Amiga engineers were split on the cost, with Jay Miner favoring a more expensive computer. "I think that a lot of us that were on the main team really felt that it was way too high priced, especially coming from a company like Commodore," says Carl Sassenrath.

Commodore's biggest obstacle to selling the Amiga originated in the Jack Tramiel days. Since the Amiga was too costly for the retail market, only computer distributors could sell the machine. Unfortunately, Commodore had little credibility with computer stores since Tramiel undercut their prices with the VIC-20 and C64. Even in late 1985, according to the Chicago Tribune, "It is not uncommon, however, to find a retailer who still holds a grudge from the days when Commodore, then under the leadership of Jack Tramiel (now owner of Atari), double-crossed the specialty stores by also marketing the Commodore 64 through mass merchandisers. The discount and toy stores quickly slashed prices and left the higher-priced dealers holding the box, so to speak."[7]

"The biggest problem we faced is Jack Tramiel had set up Commodore computer retailers and then pulled the rug out from underneath them and moved the thing over to mass market," explains Don Reisinger. "Business-wise it made Commodore a billion dollar company, so you can't argue with it, but we come back in with the Amiga computer and the first thing that we got from all these guys is, 'When are you going to pull the rug out from underneath us this time?' It's like, 'Well Jack's not here!' 'That's fine, it's still Commodore.'"

---

6   *Chicago Tribune*, "Some Wary, Some Can't Wait For Commodore's New Computer", February 22, 1985.

7   *Chicago Tribune*, "Commodore On Tour To 'Mend Fences'", (August 12, 1985). Christine Winter.

Even before the Amiga release, the computer industry questioned Commodore's ability to market business computers in North America. *Compute!'s Gazette* editor Richard Mansfield wrote, "Commodore has a phenomenal computer, the Amiga, but a decidedly obscure marketing strategy for it." He went on to ask, "Is the Amiga so far beyond previous machines that Commodore doesn't yet know its identity and, thus, cannot yet position it or give it the right image?"[8]

Thomas Rattigan was well aware that Commodore had severed ties with its computer distributors. "Prior to my time, Commodore shifted to mass retail," he says. "All of that was recognized at the time. There was the issue of how do you regain the confidence of computer retail distributors who Commodore had obviously ignored because of the focus on mass merchants."

To combat the negative image of Commodore to computer resellers, executives mounted a 45 city tour in the third quarter of 1985, visiting the major computer resellers in an attempt to sway them to carry the Amiga. "We are rebuilding a series of relationships in this channel, because we want to be in this channel a long time," said Clive Smith.

The damage done to computer sellers under Tramiel was still visible during the tour, with computer sellers not trusting Commodore. "It does come up occasionally in discussions with dealers," Marshall Smith said. "They want reassurances that we won't do what we did before."

Curiously, Commodore seemed to have little confidence in the Commodore name. *Compute!'s Gazette* reported, "It has been decided that the Commodore name and company logo will not appear anywhere on the Amiga or its peripherals. Commodore's official comment on this was that they wanted the new machine to stand on its own. This probably means that Commodore is concerned that its name—so long associated with home computing—would prevent the business community from taking the Amiga seriously."

If management did not have confidence in the Commodore name, how could their customers? "Because it was coming from Commodore it had a feeling of being more of a home computer as opposed to a business personal computer," says Dale Luck.

Commodore marketing replaced the Amiga Boing Ball with a logo similar to the classic rainbow C of the Commodore 64. The rainbow checkmark

---

8   *Compute!'s Gazette* magazine, "Editor's Notes" (November 1985), p. 6.

was supposed to convey the vibrant colors of the Amiga. However, the Amiga team felt the new symbol was not nearly as potent as the Boing Ball, which was already well recognized.

Developer Carl Sassenrath believed the attempt to enter the business market was the wrong path. "They were trying to make a product that people would use in business but that was probably wrong. It was definitely a creative machine for game playing and making videos and doing all those things. That's what it was about, multimedia. It had been pushed the wrong way."

The Amiga played video, it displayed true color photographs, and it played recorded audio clearly. In other words, it handled media from multiple sources—photographs, audio, and video. In a word, the Amiga was a true *multimedia* computer. Unfortunately, Commodore marketing could not think of a buzzword to describe the computer.

"The Amiga was something of a shame," says Kit Spencer. "It had tremendous potential as a product and an opportunity to be a major new generation of computers but it never quite made it. The marketing, and some of the product development, got pretty screwed up."

Despite the marketing problems, Leonardi predicted they would sell 100,000 to 200,000 Amiga computers in 1985 alone. With those kind of numbers, the Amiga would surpass the Macintosh very quickly. It would now be up to Commodore's engineers, technicians, and manufacturing workers to get the machine on store shelves. Only then would the result of Leonardi's prediction be known.

Running on Empty
1985

The definitive product keeping Commodore afloat while it sorted out its next line of products was the C64, known internally as Commodore's cash cow. Now Commodore hoped to grow the cash cow with new products such as modems, monitors, disk drives, and of course the C128 to extend the life of the 8-bit computer line. But as the company chewed through cash at an alarming rate, it had already begun to falter; Commodore's accountants and executives would have to become very resourceful to pull through an impending financial crisis.

Financial Problems Deepen

Although Irving Gould refused to use Commodore's stock to raise capital for the company, he was relatively unrestrained spending Commodore's cash. "I've seen many companies where they get successful and then start spending a fortune," says Kit Spencer. "While I was with Commodore, we always tried to stay lean and hungry even when we were making lots of money. When they stop being lean and hungry, in the bad times they don't survive."

As the holiday season approached, Commodore's financial problems continued. The loss of $21 million in the first quarter of 1985 under Marshall Smith was merely a prelude to the rest of the year. For the next two quarters, Commodore continued to report losses and mount debts. By the end of September, Commodore owed $192 million dollars of unpaid bank loans, mainly to British, German and U.S. banks.[1]

---

1   *Chicago Tribune*, February 23, 1986. Christine Winter. "Now Commodore's Dodging A Bullet"

It was well known within the company that Commodore was having financial problems, as evidenced by the demise of the LCD portable and the sale of several factories. But in June 1985, the problem reached a crisis.

Unknown to the public, the company was unable to make the regularly scheduled repayments on its loans. Commodore went into technical default and was now at the mercy of international banks.

It was in both the banks' interest and Commodore's to keep the financial problems as quiet as possible. After all, hurting Commodore's ability to sell computers would not increase its chances of paying back the loans. Despite this, it soon became common knowledge that the company was in default and the share price plummeted to as low as $4.75 per share.

The banks now had two options: foreclose and liquidate Commodore's assets to get back as much money as possible or work with the company's executives to keep it operating, while slowly paying down its debts.

Thomas Rattigan, the vice president of Commodore US, inherited more responsibilities during the crisis. "It was kind of funny because there was an interim step in there where I became Chief Operating Officer but technology and finance continued to report to Marshall," he says.

Rattigan, Gould, and Marshall Smith visited the banks and negotiated for an extension on the next repayment. They wanted to be allowed to operate until end of January 1986. This, they said, would give Commodore enough time to recoup profits on holiday sales of the Amiga, C64, C128, and PC-compatible products.

Commodore would also have to stem the bleeding by cutting the workforce and closing some operations. However, no mass layoffs within manufacturing, sales & marketing or engineering would occur until after the Christmas season to make sure Commodore had a workforce capable of delivering those sales.

Commodore would meet again in February with the bankers, after it had restructured the company finances, at which time the banks would decide whether to foreclose on the loans or allow Commodore to continue operations with new loans. But first, Commodore had to make some visible cuts.

One of the most famous signs of Commodore's prosperity was Irving Gould's beloved Pet Jet. Although Gould owned less than 20% of Commodore's stock, the company provided him with use of the jet, all expenses paid. But in July 1985 Gould had to unload the burden from Commodore.

He sold the 8-person British Aerospace 125-700 to a company called Scientific Packaging for $2.75 million.[2]

Gould was not put out by the deal because he also owned Scientific Packaging. The deal allowed him to essentially transfer the money from one of his companies to another, while allowing him to retain the use of the jet. This deal would later come back to haunt him.

Because factory production was somewhat cyclical, and Commodore could always lease out factory space or contract out production, factories were always a tempting asset to sell off to raise funds and decrease costs. As a result, Commodore painlessly sold its partial ownership of two Japanese factories almost immediately.[3] But other cuts would become more painful as the year progressed.

Relinquishing the LCD Business

The LCD laptop was not the only product Commodore abandoned which turned out to have a bright future. The LCD screen itself was destined to go into not only laptops but replace desktop computer monitors, televisions, and appear in cameras, tablets and of course mobile phones—the cornerstone of several multi-billion dollar industries.

Although David Baraff was successful at designing his active matrix LCD display panels, none were ever mass produced or sold outside Commodore. "We provided prototypes but because we never set up for large scale production, we could not take any orders," he says.

Gould and Rattigan needed funds to continue development on the Amiga, and they saw Commodore Optoelectronics as a prime division to sell for quick cash. With no need for LCD technology, and no calculator or watch production, Gould and his board of directors authorized Rattigan to dispose of the LCD division. "They were looking for ways to sell off whatever they could, to have cash for their primary business which at that time was the Amiga," recalls Baraff.

Commodore Optoelectronics was much more valuable now that it had active matrix technology compared to when it could only produce simple segmented LCD panels. "Commodore sold off the LCD developer because who's going to need LCD's?" laughs Dave Haynie. "It's funny when you look back on some of that stuff."

---

2   *Philadelphia Inquirer*, "Commodore Questioned On Jet Deal", Nov. 23, 1988.

3   *Philadelphia Inquirer*, "Commodore Reaches Accord With Its Banks", Feb. 26, 1986.

Commodore had now definitively lost the opportunity to have vertical integration of LCD displays, something that would have given them a decisive edge over the competition when it came to building laptops. "That always pissed off every engineering person in the company," says Bob Russell. "I'm still pissed to this day. 'Oh, there's no future in LCD. None at all.' Argh!"

Thomas Rattigan sold Commodore Optoelectronics to a corporation infamous for its record of pollution where it manufactured batteries. "They sold the entire liquid crystal group to Eagle-Picher," recalls Baraff. Negotiations for the sale occurred in the latter half of 1985 and ended with a sale price of just under $10 million. This would go far in offsetting the cost of acquiring Amiga.

Baraff believes Commodore would have survived for decades if it had invested in LCD's instead. "That was one thing, in retrospect, that they were so well situated they could have done portable computers, they could have done laptop computers, they could have gone into the IBM compatible computers, but if they made any of those decisions they probably would have survived. Instead, they took the proprietary route to develop the Amiga and it just was not the right route."

Eagle-Picher

During this time, construction began on a new facility in nearby Chester County. "Eagle-Picher was forced to spend maybe five million dollars to set up another manufacturing facility," says Baraff. "So that took about a year and a half to two years because it was all clean rooms and you need all these water permissions. If you ever try building a manufacturing facility, you know the permit process can take years."

Although Eagle-Picher now owned the former Commodore Optoelectronics, it remained in the West Chester facility. "It was there for at least a year because we had to get another facility set up and that was part of the deal," says Baraff. "Eagle-Picher wasn't going to take it and do nothing for a year and lose all the people and all the rest. They were basically buying technology and equipment. So part of the deal was Commodore would let us use the facility." Commodore would receive rent while it leased out the building space to Eagle-Picher.

Eagle-Picher promoted David Baraff to vice president of research and brought in a new general manager to run the company. Things looked promising for the sole North American LCD manufacturer. "We finally got the facility up to start making the displays again. Our plan was to sell them to Apple or back to Commodore or whoever wanted to buy them."

And in fact, even though Commodore's executives had officially cancelled the LCD portable project, Porter and several engineers, including software and mechanical engineering, continued developing an LCD portable. Even Gerard Bucas, head of business products, knew the project had secretly continued. The engineers had gone rogue, hoping management would reconsider the project once Commodore emerged from its financial problems.

By early 1986, Gerard Bucas finally decided to pull the plug on the portable LCD project once and for all.

C128D is All Business

Following the release of the C128 in 1985, Bil Herd and his engineers took a much-deserved break. "After the C128 hit in June/July, I actually made all my guys go off fishing with me and got out of the building. New employees would wonder why we wouldn't be there for three days in a row."

Neither Herd nor Commodore had any plans to follow up the C128 with another C64 sequel. "The C128 was kind of meant to glue in the last of the 8-bit stuff while we moved to 16-bit, but it was as far as I wanted to push the C64 compatibility stuff," he says. "Besides, wasn't the Amiga a C64 on steroids?"

Instead, Herd and his team had spent a man-month designing an alternate model, called the C128D, in parallel with the C128. The new design was largely cosmetic, departing from Commodore's usual computer-in-a-keyboard design. The C128D looked almost identical to an Amiga 1000, with an internal power supply, cooling fan, and disk drive in a case, and a separate keyboard and mouse.

"We designed the PCB to fit both the regular C128 and the D version simultaneously," says Herd. "It slowed us down and caused lots of grief, but I was intent on having the built in floppy.

The C128D had been shown in 1985 behind closed doors. "We showed the D version at the June CES," says Herd.

However, after the C128 went into production, Herd moved onto other things. After months of intense pressure, he felt no desire to jump into a new project. "He basically did a little bit more than everybody else and eventually burnt out," says his friend, Dave Haynie, recalling the troubled period.

"He was burnt out, he was tired, and I think he was kind of frustrated. There were a lot of things that we would have liked to have done differently on the C128 that the management said, 'These are the resources you are getting.' He was tired of that and I guess some of it was the politicking that they had back then. He was just sick of the whole thing."

Haynie stepped in and led the effort to finish the alternate version of the C128. He targeted the machine to small businesses and made it somewhat portable by including a large carrying handle and the ability to lock the keyboard to the bottom of the case. "The C128D was actually something that Europe wanted," he says. "Bil was around for the beginning of that and I kind of finished it up."

It would be up to Commodore Europe's marketing to launch the C128D. However, given the growing presence of IBM in Europe by 1985, it was doubtful the computer would gain traction in the business community.

C64 Cost Reduced

Commodore had been cost reducing the C64 since the beginning, taking the retail price down from $600 to around $200. But there were further cost reductions possible by designing newer chips using the more efficient HMOS process, and also putting more functions of the C64 motherboard onto the chips (the "glue logic" as engineers called it).

Joe Krasucki and Robert Russell had instigated the C64CR project and Commodore Semiconductor had been at work designing the new versions of the HMOS chips since at least October 1984. This included HMOS versions of the 6510 processor, the 6567 VIC-II chip, and even the 6581 SID chip. Coincidentally, most of those chips would also go into the C128.

Although Commodore was struggling for cash at the time, the new project was not costly, requiring only a few engineers. Robert Russell, one of the original C64 engineers, had maintained the effort. "He kind of wore many hats because him and Fred Bowen were the standard bearers of the Commodore 64," says Bob Welland. "He would disappear and go do things related to that."

In August 1985, Bil Herd also lost his manager Joe Krasucki, whose head had been on the chopping block since the completion of the C128. Herd's new manager became Ed Parks. Unlike the tumultuous relationship Herd had with Krasuki, he got along with his new manager. "Ed and I never had a bad word between us," recalls Herd. A new manager named Ed Martello took over the business engineering group from Parks.

Ed Parks encouraged him to sleep while at work—provided he put in the hours. "If I really wanted to get some sleep, I had this sign that both Adam [Chowaniec] and Ed Parks had signed that said, 'Do not disturb under the authority of Adam Chowaniec and Ed Parks.' I put that on my door and you had to be at their level or higher to knock and wake me up," says Herd.

It was now Ed Parks, director of consumer products, and Clive Smith who primarily supported the C64CR. Rightly or wrongly, analysts inside and outside the company felt the C64's days were numbered. This affected managers and executives like Bucas immensely. "At that stage the C64 was declining, obviously," says Bucas. "The whole move was towards the Amiga and the C128, so the C64 was on its last legs."

When work on a redesigned C64 motherboard began, Parks put Bil Herd on the job, along with an engineer in Japan. Through the second half of 1985, Herd did liaison work for the Japanese engineer to cost reduce the C64, which the engineers dubbed the C64CR (Cost Reduced). "There was a cost reduced C64 that got made about the same time as the C128," says Herd. "I helped a little with that, but it was mostly done by an engineer from Japan named [Sumio] Katayama."

Herd's experience on the C128 project made him an invaluable resource to troubleshoot the details of the project. As before, Herd made sure to reintroduce all the bugs back into the C64CR, otherwise some software would not work properly.

Although the performance of the C64CR was identical to standard C64 computers, there were many improvements to reduce the cost of assembly. "In the Commodore environment, cheap was considered a type of performance," says Herd. The motherboard was smaller, with fewer components and it now used the 8500 processor. The old C64 used several different types of screws to assemble, but the new design used only two different types of screws.

Commodore Japan created a new case that looked more professional, with a standard off-white color. "He actually used the case styling that we used for the C128," says Herd. The new case was similar to the wedge-shaped case design envisioned by Robert Yannes and Al Charpentier, which they had planned to introduce sometime in 1983.

After Commodore released the C128, several executives believed it no longer made sense to concentrate company resources on the C64. "There was still, obviously, within engineering people that loved the C64 because this was their baby and all that," Gerard Bucas recalls. "Basically, my philosophy on the C64 was it's on its last legs."

Ever the comedian, Bucas had a favorite quote when referring to the wedge-shape of the new C64 case. "I said to the industrial designer who designs the case shape and form, 'Listen, make sure it's got good rubber feet.' Everybody's always asking me, 'Gerard, why do you always insist on good rubber feet?' I said, 'Well, the only useful feature of the C64, it makes a great door stop, so let's not take away the most important feature.'"

The comment said a lot about how upper management felt about the C64. There was very little confidence or respect for the computer that paid for most of the bills. With Rattigan looking to make cuts anywhere just to keep Commodore afloat, the C64CR project was given second tier status and manufacturing plans put on hold, in favor of the C128 project.

This view went all the way up to Irving Gould, who believed the analyst's stories in newspapers continually predicting the demise of the C64. As a result, Commodore was very conservative when producing C64's for the upcoming Christmas season. The results of the decision would later have a profound impact on the company.

Marketing Success

As sales of the C128 started in the summer of 1985, many within Commodore were luke-warm about the potential of the product. "My feeling on the C128 was it sounded like a follow-up [to the C64] but it had a niche with the C64 crowd," explains Gerard Bucas.

Throughout the holiday season, Commodore ran advertising campaigns for both the C64 and C128. One humorous C64 ad shows a poor college freshman whisked away on a train. Seconds later, he returns to the same train station. The announcer, Henry Morgan, suggests things could have worked out if only he had a Commodore 64. "They were guilting the parents into buying a C64 because their fat kid came home from college and didn't know what he was doing," says Dave Haynie. "They were extremely well done commercials."

Commodore also produced a campaign for the C128. As Herd recalls, "There was a TV commercial and it had Burgess Meredith for the voice.[4] In one commercial, there was a big drill that was drilling a hole in the side of an Apple IIe, and Burgess is saying, 'You would have to put more voices and better graphics in your Apple to do what the C128 does.'"

The commercials, dubbed the "Higher Intelligence" ad campaign by Frank Leonardi, visually demonstrated the benefits of the C128 over its ri-

---

4   Burgess Meredith played the trainer Mickey in *Rocky* and the Penguin on the sixties *Batman* TV series.

vals. "I think they were pretty ballsy coming after Apple and IBM directly," says Dave Haynie. .

As Rattigan had noted in June, Commodore already had 100,000 pre-orders. By October, Commodore was selling as many C128 computers as the factory workers could produce. It felt like vindication to the West Chester engineers who were starting to feel like second-class employees ever since the Amiga acquisition.

Herd was pleased with Frank Leonardi's marketing effort for the C128. "I think it was fair," he says. "I think it filled the hole waiting for the 16-bit [computers] to come."

UK Marketing of C128

Commodore UK's advertising campaign was similar to that of the US, comparing the C128 directly with the competition. One magazine ad stated, "When you look at the facts they do seem to weigh rather heavily in our favour."

Although the UK region dutifully advertised the machine, behind the scenes they were not enthusiastic about the new product. "It didn't really float our boats if you like but to be fair, we were still doing very well with the C64," says David Pleasance of Commodore UK. "The C128 was a better machine supposedly, and I guess it was really in most regards, but on the other hand I suppose they are very different animals. But it just means that we were confusing the consumer even more. And we were very good at confusing the consumers."

The UK's industry reporters held the same attitude. *Zzap! 64* reported, "Its successor, the 128, launched at last year's PCW show is not what anybody expected, or what many observers wanted."

"I think it hurt the machine to have the mode switching because it would never develop its own software base," says software engineer Andy Finkel. "If the developer could have taken the same C64 program and somehow added C128 capabilities and sold the same program for the C128, I think they would have had a better C128 software base early on."

Michael Tomczyk, who helped launch the VIC-20, felt Commodore's marketing team failed to attract software development for the machine. "In my personal opinion, the Commodore 128 was allowed to die by the legacy management team. The people who were left in charge of Commodore after May 1984 knew basically nothing about computers. They had no understanding of the marketplace. They were hostile to the home market and I know that for a fact. So they allowed the C128 to be under marketed and that lack of support resulted in killing the machine. Not only that, there was no design continuity."

Kit Spencer believes Commodore became unfocused with its product strategy. "I got the impression they were playing around with all sorts of things, but the bottom line is, what did they actually produce that sold or was successful? That's the one thing where Jack could be ruthless. If he thought an idea was good, he would push it through like crazy."

"We lost our ability to invent new computers, and so no new computers were basically designed in-house that were of any consequence," says Tomczyk. "Commodore's long string of engineering marvels came to an abrupt end."

PC Clone Results

Commodore also had success with its new line of PC clones. Since introducing the PC-10 in 1984, the company had created a successor called the PC-20. IBM was still perceived as weak in the German business sector and Commodore was able to use its brand name to leverage sales to businesses in the European market. "Within two years, maybe even less, Commodore became the largest MS-DOS PC reseller in Europe," recalls Gerard Bucas.

According to Winfried Hoffmann, for the final six months of 1985, Commodore had sold 55,000 PC-10 and PC-20 computers in Germany and another 20,000 in the rest of Europe. This gave Commodore a 35% market share of PC's in Germany.

Chuck Peddle, who was battling Commodore for the European market with the Victor Sirius computer, credits Commodore Germany with helping Commodore survive. "[Harald] Speyer ultimately wound up saving the company a couple of times," he says. "It kept Commodore in business while they were selling [IBM PC] clones."

Despite the success, others saw a pattern emerging that could have negative consequences for the company. "There was no impetus for innovation. In fact, the only strategy Commodore was pursuing was mimicry," says Tomczyk.

Before Commodore North America began to notice the success, however, they refused to sell the PC clones. In fact, it would be several years before a single PC clone was sold in North America by Commodore.

The success of the PC clones, and the video game crash had altered Irving Gould's thinking about Commodore's focus. For one thing, most of the industry started buying into the idea that videogames were a passing fad. Retailers certainly believed video games were done, and they refused to stock video game products. This led Irving Gould and Thomas Rattigan to consider abandoning game development at Commodore.

There was also one other negative consequence of the PC clone success. Commodore was making a business machine to compete with the IBM-PC, the aforementioned C900. Except the clone strategy by Commodore Europe signaled to the business community that MS-DOS PC's were the next business standard. Now as PET computers began being replaced by PC clones, which became more entrenched, no subsequent Commodore business machine would likely be accepted other than IBM PC computers.

As a result, the PC clones became a poison pill for Commodore, causing executives to question the C900 Unix strategy.

C900 Pilot Production

In the last half of 1985, Commodore was going forward with its plan to launch the C900 in Europe. "A thing that's interesting about Commodore is that in Europe, the way Commodore is perceived is completely different than the United States," says Bob Welland. "Around the time I was there, they actually owned a significant portion of the PC market in Europe. They were considered a viable business machine making company. In Europe [the C900] could have been a successful thing."

Commodore even promoted the C900 in the September-October issue of *Commodore MicroComputer* magazine, including photographs of a complete system. As of June 26, 1985 the Coherent OS was at version 0.7.3, and development would continue up until the disks were required for duplication during the product run.

The product had been in development for years and had been one of Commodore's more expensive engineering projects. "There were maybe ten people working on that project," says Bucas. "I don't remember the exact amount spent on it but certainly it would be in the millions, that's for sure."

For the pilot production, Commodore would require a parts supplier for every single part in the computer that was not manufactured by Commodore. As general manager of Commodore's business computer division, Bucas negotiated with other companies for the major parts of the computer. "For the C900 we needed a keyboard that was sort of similar to PC keyboards," he recalls. "It was because it was really going to be more or less a business graphics work station."

The Commodore version of a Unix workstation would stand apart from those made by other companies. Bucas, who came from Olivetti, remained in awe at how inexpensively Commodore could purchase keyboards compared to other computer manufacturers by using parts suppliers for the low-cost C64. "What is interesting, when you eventually go to your C64 keyboard supplier and say, 'Listen, I just need a few more keys and its shape to be a bit different.' What we negotiated was roughly a quarter of what companies like Olivetti were paying for keyboards."

Around August, the C900 entered pilot production, the process whereby the engineers set up the assembly lines. During this phase, the engineers created and refined the steps to assemble the machines, the testing, and bought the machinery needed to assemble them. "We built a number of them and certainly there were people testing them and that type of thing," says Bucas.

During this phase, the engineers would end up manufacturing dozens of computers themselves as they honed and refined the process. Once tested, those computers often ended up in the hands of salespeople, magazine editors, and software developers for early access. According to Bucas, "We went all the way to pre-production. I think we produced 50 of them or whatever."

Once the assembly line was set up, the workers and technicians would be brought in and trained by the engineers. After that, it would be up to them to run the assembly line for weeks or months at a time, churning out hundreds or thousands of computers per day. "It was exciting actually, I must admit," says Bucas.

C900 Demise

As the C900 was heading for full production, Thomas Rattigan was forced to put the project on hold. When Commodore had to choose priorities between spending the little money it had on parts for the much anticipated Amiga or the low-volume C900 business machine, well, there really was no decision.

On December 3, 1985 Gerard Bucas informed his engineers that the C900 was officially cancelled. "It was clear that they were making survival cuts at that point," says Dave Haynie. "They didn't believe they had the resources to launch two separate machines that were incompatible with each other."

If there was one major fault with the C900, it was the Z8000 chip. "There were a lot of issues with that machine, not the least of which was the choice of the Z8000, which is kind of a perverse processor," says Bob Welland. Practically no one else in the industry used the chip, meaning software development for the platform would have a hard time gaining a foothold. "So the

C900 had a lot of issues. It was a fairly ambitious thing for Commodore to try to do and it was in a domain that they were not really that familiar with."

When money problems hit Commodore, the C900 production was put on hold. "[The C900 was] basically a victim of the Amiga," says Dave Haynie. "It took some settling time, but once Commodore knew that the Amiga was their future, the C900 was no longer in the books. After they had finally gotten it working, it was cancelled."

Marshall Smith had let Commodore go wild with too many simultaneous projects. Even though it was true that Unix had a bright future in the world of computing, Commodore had almost no ability to market computers to businesses that used Unix. "It was difficult even positioning it marketing wise," says Gerard Bucas. "It was not going to be three or four hundred dollars. It was tough to hit a typical Commodore price point. I think it would have been difficult to position."

Rattigan also prioritized C128 production over the C900. "There were like five major product development things happening at Commodore at the time and there just wasn't enough money to go around for that," says Jeff Porter. "In the end they cancelled the LCD. They cancelled the Unix workstations. They managed to keep around the 128 project. And they kept the Amiga."

During the pilot production run in West Chester, the engineers had produced at least 50 C900 machines. "We actually had releases out because we were nearing completion on it," says Bob Russell.

Commodore sold the machines in Europe in late 1985 and throughout 1986 for approximately $2500 to $4000 each as development systems, gaining back some valuable cash which could be used to buy more Amiga components.

Although the C900 was not part of Commodore's plans for 1985, Gerard Bucas felt strongly that Unix itself would continue to gain popularity and Commodore should become a player in the workstation market.

Even in the midst of a successful launch of the C128, it was a demoralizing time to be an engineer in West Chester, with management and executives cancelling two of their three major projects. "We had three serious projects going on in engineering: the LCD machine, C900, and the Amiga," says Andy Finkel. "They ended up competing but they weren't supposed to. Commodore ran out of money to carry forward development on all three projects at the same time so Amiga won, and the C900 and LCD machines lost." Although things looked bleak for them at the end of 1985, a surprise was in store for them that would give them new hope.

Releasing the Amiga 1985

In spite of the lavish product launch earlier in the year, the Amiga would not be released until months later. Soon it would be time to communicate to the masses just what this revolutionary computer was all about. But first, Thomas Rattigan had to do more downsizing.

First Round Layoffs

Earlier in the year, Commodore closed several factories and laid off 700 workers. Now, in September 1985, the company was forced to hire back 350 factory workers to keep up with production of C128, Amiga, C64, and PC computers. But in order to pay those workers, a number of engineers were culled from the company. Every manager was asked to cut 33% of their employees to reduce the payroll expenses and provide Commodore enough cashflow to continue operations.

The first round of layoffs included employees who were not contributing significantly to the company, such as Benny Pruden, who had been working on a Commodore cash register product using Amiga technology. "They had a purging in the 1985 to 1986 years, and if you hadn't proved your worth, you were not going to stick around," says Dave Haynie.

In total, Commodore laid off 32 engineers in September alone. Bil Herd had built up his fair share of enemies within Commodore, but he had his chance for revenge when Commodore underwent the layoffs. "I had hired a new guy and he would bitch about me not being there," he says. Herd also still had to contend with Bob Shamus, the QA manager and Herd's sworn enemy.

Managers often rely on trusted personnel when it comes time for layoffs. "One day Adam [Chowaniec] called me in and said, 'I need to reduce people.' I said, 'I've got a guy for you,'" says Herd, referring to the new hire who complained about his absences. "I pointed at Shamus and I pointed at this other guy and said they should go, and they fired them."

The cuts continued in every department. In the meantime, Commodore did not have the money to attend trade shows or buy parts to manufacture more computers. It would be up to Commodore's VP of finance to skillfully use whatever cash flow he could generate to pay the parts suppliers just enough to keep the parts flowing. Thankfully the company had been pumping out product in the factories since July in order to prepare for the upcoming season, and they were able to get products on store shelves. Now all Commodore had to do was cut back expenses, promote its machines properly, and it could return to profitability.

Executives took a break from layoffs throughout the holiday season, not out of the goodness of their hearts, but because Commodore required employees to finish critical tasks such as manufacturing marketing, sales and distribution for the Amiga and C128 launch.

But knowing Commodore would have to face the bankers in February 1986 with an improved financial outlook, more cuts came in December. "As our company headcount was being reduced 33 percent in December 1985, operating expenses were reduced 37 percent. Our people started doing things the old fashioned way—they worked even harder," commented Rattigan.

Un-Advertising the Amiga

On the advertising front, the Amiga should have had a distinct advantage over the IBM PC and Macintosh. Both of those computers lacked color and did not translate well to a visual and audio medium like television. The Amiga, on the other hand, was made for television.

Commodore was prepared to spend $40 million throughout the year launching the Amiga, of which approximately $20 million was for advertising and $20 million for marketing. Some of it had already been expended for the lavish Lincoln Center debut in New York—including a significant sum to entice Andy Warhol to become an Amiga spokesman—albeit one who didn't really speak that much.

Commodore had a track record of creating successful ad campaigns that won awards, specifically for the launch of the VIC-20 and C64. The director of marketing communications at Commodore, Julie Bauer, had been with Commodore since early 1982 and had taken part in those campaigns, working under Kit Spencer to launch both products. After Spencer left, however, Commodore's marketing and advertising success had fallen noticeably flat.

When Thomas Rattigan was named president, Commodore hired a marketing executive from the food industry, Robert Trukenbrod, to oversee the advertising campaign for the upcoming Amiga release. Rattigan believed that, when spending millions of dollars on an ad campaign, a professional of equal stature was required.[1]

Rattigan intentionally looked for stronger marketing executives in the industry he previously worked within. "When you look at the Procter & Gambles of the world and General Foods or Kraft or Philip Morris, I think you would have to say that the marketing sophistication was much higher in those firms than it was in a host of other industries," he says. "I don't think you were going to walk into any of those [computer] companies and find five star marketing people by and large."

Trukenbrod had a history with Nabisco, the company that produced memorable, successful ads for Ritz crackers, Shredded Wheat, and Oreo cookies among others. While most of the ads were catchy and hip, one of its ads from the period for Milk-Bone was particularly nostalgia driven.

The *LA Times* reported, "According to Commodore's Trukenbrod, the new ads will depict the Amiga as 'a positive tool to help you.' The television campaign will include homey 1950s and 1960s childhood scenes in black-and-white film with splashes of color generated by the Amiga's graphic capabilities. He said it will speak to viewers who already have 'got their piece of the pie.'"[2] Whatever that meant.

The ad agency responsible for the commercials would be the Ted Bates advertising firm, established in 1940 (and the inspiration behind many of the characters in television's *Mad Men*). Michael Becker, agency chief creative officer at Ted Bates, would oversee production of the commercials. Ultimately Becker would come back with a proposed ad campaign to be approved by Marshall Smith, Irving Gould and Rattigan.

Television Ads

The Amiga engineers were ecstatic with Commodore and their treatment of the Amiga, and were suitably impressed with the advertising plans. And then the ads debuted the evening of September 23, 1985. They appeared

---

1   *InfoWorld,* July 15, 1985. Page 37. "Commodore President on Amiga and Competition"

2   *Los Angeles Times,* September 27, 1985. "Commodore Pins Hopes on Amiga Ad Campaign"

in prime time slots during *Dynasty*, *Miami Vice*, and *The Tonight Show Starring Johnny Carson* among others. It was obvious the ad agency did not understand the Amiga. "They had the most ridiculous ad campaign for launching it into the public's eye," recalls RJ Mical. "It was just nuts. It would have been laughable if it weren't for the fact that the machine that we had worked so hard on was being shat upon by these guys that didn't have a clue how to make it a popular device."

The first commercial did little to impress the engineers. "The launch television commercial of the Amiga had people almost zombie like, presumably in some sort of state of ecstasy but maybe it was more a state of mental disturbance, walking up towards this pedestal from which emanates a light," recalls Mical. "You finally see that there's some sort of computer monitor glowing with light."

The point of the ad baffled Mical. "Whatever it was, it did not advertise the machine," he says.

Mical was most disappointed the advertisement failed to highlight the groundbreaking Amiga features. "It did not show you the cool graphics, the cool audio, or the multitasking operating system," he explains. "This is a computer for the next generation!"

Bil Herd remembers the ambiguity of a second commercial in the campaign. "There was this fetus crying and then an old man walking up these white steps. It was kind of like *2001: A Space Odyssey*," he recalls. "We were like, 'What the hell are they talking about?' Well, they were trying to get across the dawn of a new generation."

Back in the engineering labs, the fetus became a daily joke. "We saw pictures of how they made the commercial and the fetus literally had a stick in it that they held up in front of the camera," explains Herd. "We got a hold of that picture and stuck it up. It looked like a tasty treat for dinosaurs or something. It was morbid actually. I mean, a fetus on a stick, oh my God. What were they thinking over there in marketing?"

For the second phase of the ad campaign, the Ted Bates advertising firm also produced a commercial with a nostalgic motif featuring black and white stock footage, with a tone similar to the aforementioned Nabisco Milk-Bones commercial. It showed images of children diving into a swimming pool, graduation, and teenagers doing the twist. The narrator says, "When you were growing up, you learned you were facing a world full of competition."

Print Ads

In order to attempt to expand the market for the Amiga, Robert Truken-brod ran ads in not only computer magazines, but also broader special interest magazines such as *Scientific American, Time, Life, National Geographic*, and *Psychology Today*. They even targeted Apple directly by advertising in *MacWorld*.

The print advertising also relied on nostalgic black and white stock photographs. Each print ad promoted the slogan, "Amiga gives you a creative edge." It was an ironic motto. One of the earliest ads ran in *National Geographic* in November 1985 and targeted the education market. It showed a black and white image of schoolchildren with the caption, "You've always had a lot of competition. Now you can have an unfair advantage."

The second magazine ad (and the first to grace the pages of *Byte*) came in January 1986. It featured a black and white photograph of boys running to their soapbox cars. The title was, "Today if you come in second, you've lost the race."

In Mical's mind, the old-fashioned advertising was misguided. "It was in sepia tones," he recalls. "Again, this is the message that you want to give people? 'Come get this new computer. It's got true colors!' They were just insane. The mind boggles that somebody out there thought this is a good idea. Let's sell this new, powerful, *color* graphics computer with an ad that shows sepia tones."

Jay Miner was equally unhappy. "I can't tell you how angry it makes me feel to see how the Amiga was handled. The advertisements they did have were absolutely awful. Old men changing into babies and kids competing in race cars. It was ghastly."[3]

The advertising did little to appeal to the target group of young computer users. Instead, it looked like Commodore was trying to market the Amiga to the retirement crowd.

Dave Haynie wonders how the commercials could have swayed anyone over to the Amiga. "I remember some of the early ads," he says. "I vaguely remember the first ones that were shown here and you didn't know what it was that they were advertising."

Herd agrees. "You could watch an Amiga commercial and not even known you had seen one," he says. "I remember seeing one or two and going, 'What was that a commercial for?'"

3 *Amiga User International,* June 1988. "The AUI Interview" p. 20

The new commercials fell far short of the standard set by earlier VIC-20 commercials featuring William Shatner. In the past, Commodore's most successful commercials were direct comparisons to its competitors' products. With the Macintosh so vulnerable, a direct comparison could change a lot of minds. The Amiga could even use a color printer, which would have made the black and white desktop publishing, the one niche market of the Macintosh, appear limited. If Commodore could get the message out to customers, it could make inroads into the desktop publishing market. Instead, the Macintosh outsold Amiga two to one, even with a higher price.[4]

When asked about the commercials, Thomas Rattigan distances himself from the effort, claiming he does not recall any specific ads. "I was not directly involved in terms of sitting down on the creative side and reviewing storyboards," he says. "I suspect whatever it is that we did, it was fairly modest dollar wise."

Dale Luck believed Trukenbrod could have produced better ads with the money he had. "I didn't sense that they were running out of money to do advertising. I sensed they weren't sure how to advertise it," he says. "For people who liked 2001 that was pretty cool usage, but we don't know how many sales that would have generated. A lot of their initial commercials were pretty out there. They weren't targeted very well."

Even with a more limited budget, Commodore could have produced smarter, more effective commercials by showing off the capabilities of the Amiga.

In contrast, people remembered the IBM PCjr ads with Charlie Chaplin. They were fun, distinctive, and caught viewers' attention. IBM had a marketing and advertising budget of $32.5 million for the IBM PCjr. Others remember the Orwellian Macintosh commercial, which ran during the Super Bowl. Despite the ultimate ineffectiveness of Apple's commercial and the subsequent slow Macintosh sales, people remembered the ad. Nobody, not even the president of Commodore, remembered the Amiga ads.

Looking back, Mical's frustration with the advertising campaign is apparent. "I don't know who it was inside the Commodore organization. Unfortunately, I don't have someone to point the finger at on that one," he says. "There must have been someone inside the organization who approved these ads, but out there somewhere is some ad agency that thought this was a good idea. All across the board, it was massive stupidity. I don't

---

4   According to the *Philadelphia Inquirer*, the Amiga sold 100,000 systems in its first full
    year, compared to 200,000 for the first year of the Macintosh.

know if Commodore guys told the ad agency, 'Give us sepia tone,' or the ad agency said, 'Oh my God! You've got to have sepia tones.' I don't know where that came from. Someone just go out and dump a bucket of ice water on their heads and then I will be happy."

Amiga Wide Release

By mid-September, Sanyo of Japan had produced approximately 35,000 Amiga computers. Because the Amiga chipset only supported the NTSC television standard, Sanyo shipped them all to the United States for distribution to retail stores. It would now be a test of Commodore's marketing department to see if its efforts would succeed.

Bil Herd believes Commodore did not put forward a strong marketing effort. "When the Amiga hit, they were sitting around with their feet on the table going, 'At last, a real computer that will sell itself. We're on the gravy train.' Well, of course it didn't sell itself. You've got to go out and sell it."

When the Amiga marketing and sales personnel merged with Commodore, Don Reisinger was transferred out of marketing and given his own region to manage. "I moved over to sales," he says. "I was running the West Coast—everything from the Colorado Rockies west was mine, including Hawaii."

Commodore tried hard to push the Amiga into established computer store chains, such as ComputerLand, CompUSA, Computer City, and Sears. "The bottom line is you need to be in computer stores," explains Gerard Bucas. "But getting into computer stores with the product line they had was not easy."

ComputerLand alone had over 800 stores worldwide by 1985 but Commodore was only able to get the Amiga into about 12% of ComputerLand retail outlets.[5] Although Commodore was unable to strike a deal with ComputerLand's headquarters, Reisinger was able to convince some individual ComputerLand stores to sell the Amiga, including 35 in California.

Unfortunately, by 1985 the big computer store chains were already doing very well selling IBM PC computers and were committed to IBM. Commodore and other manufacturers like Apple were largely cut out. "They were not selling it really through mainstream computer stores, and partly because mainstream computer stores were only starting to appear and they

5   *Los Angeles Times*, September 27, 1985. "Commodore Pins Hopes on Amiga Ad Campaign"

were all doing mostly PC compatible stuff," says Bucas. "The Amiga did not fit into the typical CompUSA."

Instead, Commodore was only able to attract specialty stores, which Bucas calls "mom and pop stores." This left Commodore in the position of having to ship to a multitude of diverse organizations, which required more paperwork for smaller volumes.

Despite this setback, when the Amiga finally started shipping to specialty stores in late October 1985, the demand for the computer easily outpaced supply. "All I can tell you is that the first thirty five or fifty thousand went through computer specialty stores like shit through a tin goose," says Reisinger. A second wave of product was slated to arrive in stores in mid-November. It seemed like the Amiga could be a tremendous success in the US.

Launch Titles

While the Amiga had been in development, Dave Morse had courted software developers to produce launch titles for the machine. "One of the things we wanted to do which was different, since we were going to be the different computer company, was to launch with a fairly robust library of software," recalls Don Reisinger. "We had gotten a number of people started on programs and when we had money we were funding it, but much to those guy's credit when they knew we had financial problems a lot of guys didn't abandon the project. They may have scaled it back slightly but they didn't quit."

Amiga initially lured several important software developers to create business applications for the Amiga. Autodesk began work on its popular 2D and 3D design tool, AutoCAD. Lotus Development Corporation began porting over the popular Lotus 1-2-3.

RJ Mical knew the machine was capable of hosting far better applications than either the IBM PC or Macintosh. "We had the IBM beat hands down," he says. "The only thing the IBM had on us was great business applications, so we went after that. We thought we had a roaring chance of taking over the industry with that machine."

However, Reisinger thinks things changed when Commodore took over the Amiga. "Commodore comes in and says this thing is so great you should pay us to be able to work on this computer. And they pulled all of the arrangements. When the product launched, there was hardly anything that you could do with it."

Most injurious was the lack of a killer-app. "The Mac came out in the summer of 1984 and it did very well in terms of desktop publishing with its little hi-res black and white display," explains Dale Luck. "But the Amiga didn't have a sophisticated word processor at the time."

The buggy AmigaOS 1.0 also prevented the release of many titles, since most developers held back releasing software until a stable platform appeared. With the computer industry agreeing that the Amiga was a revolutionary machine, it was yet to be seen if it would generate commensurate revolutionary software. "The trick was, it had all these capabilities, but could they be used, and by whom?" asks Glenn Keller. "That's why I think a lot of this stuff ended up being games, because those were the things that could use those capabilities effectively, with the hardware acceleration of graphics, and all that stuff."

One of the biggest supporters of the Amiga was Electronic Arts. EA had built itself on the Commodore 64 and it was not about to ignore Commodore's next computer, which was an obvious technological leap.

EA launched its first batch of Amiga software in September 1985. The same month, founder Trip Hawkins took out an ad in several computer magazines that would appear two months later. The two page spread announced, "Why Electronic Arts is Committed to the Amiga." Hawkins stated, "The Amiga will revolutionize the home computer industry. It's the first home machine that has everything you want and need for all the major uses of a home computer, including entertainment, education and productivity."

When the Amiga launched, EA released ports of its most popular titles for the C64. In fact, all of EA's games were ports from the C64, including *Archon*, *One on One*, and *Seven Cities of Gold*. In 1986 they followed with *Sky Fox*, *Arctic Fox*, *Bard's Tale*, *Marble Madness* and an intriguing creativity program called *Instant Music*.

EA also had a line of Construction Set software going back to *Pinball Construction Set* on the C64. It released several applications exploring the Amiga's creative capabilities, including *Music Construction Set* and *Adventure Construction Set*.

Electronic Arts had expertise in games, but it also wanted to exploit the productivity market. One of the first Amiga products EA announced was *Deluxe Video Construction Set*. The package aimed to create a new market by using the Amiga with a VCR for animations and video credits. It was brave new territory for both the Amiga and Electronic Arts.

The company followed up with a graphics program. It had previously written a graphics editor for the IBM PC called *Prism*. Though it was predictably lackluster on the IBM PC hardware, programmer Dan Silva rewrote it for the Amiga, taking advantage of the superior color palette.

Retitled *Deluxe Paint*, it launched in September 1985 and quickly became famous for an image of Tutankhamen's mask on the box cover. The startling image showed off the incredible graphics capability of the Amiga. Colors blended into one another seamlessly, giving a lifelike image no one had ever thought possible on a personal computer. The handicapped *MacPaint* could not even come close to competing with Deluxe Paint. "DPaint was the main product that came out from Electronic Arts that was the main seller for the Amiga when it came out," says Dale Luck.

Mical recalls the impact the program had with graphics artists. "We had the premier paint package at the time and for ten years," says Mical. "The best paint program that you could get was DPaint on the Amiga; hands down, on all machines, across all platforms."

Infocom released two adventure games, *Wishbringer* and *A Mind Forever Voyaging*, the latter of which took full advantage of the extra memory available to the Amiga. Activision released two adventure games as well, *Mindshadow* and *Hacker*.

Despite aiming for the business market, Mical was glad the Amiga received quality games. "Having good games became a secondary thing for us, although to tell you the truth that was never true," he reveals. "In our heart of hearts, we always wanted to have good games. And happily, the Amiga always did have really good games."

At the Amiga launch in New York, president of Microsoft Corporation John Shirley spoke of his company's "commitment to the Amiga". And by commitment, he meant releasing absolutely no software for the computer.[6]

Finkel thought they could at least tempt Microsoft into releasing its hit flight simulator. "I think we all wanted *MS Flight Simulator* on the Amiga really badly," he says. "It was a great demonstration of a computer's graphics. We thought, 'Of course they would want to support it.' But surprisingly, no."

In the end, BASIC was the only software Microsoft created for the Amiga. "The world would be a different place if Microsoft had gotten behind the Amiga," says Finkel.

---

6 *Amiga World*, November-December 1985. p. 7.

Critical Reception

In the last half of 1985, industry magazines released hands-on previews of the Amiga. In August, *Byte* magazine featured the Amiga on the front cover. It was rare for a specific computer to make the cover, signifying the Amiga was perceived at the time as a revolutionary new machine. Inside was a generous 13-page preview. It was a firm endorsement from the industry's top magazine.

Much of the article focused on Carl Sassenrath's OS. The article gave Sassenrath a feeling of accomplishment. "I've got that one framed on the wall," he says. "I'm of the age where I was graduating from college right at the very beginning of personal computing. I read Byte from the beginning and to have an article in Byte in 1985 was thrilling for me."

The article acknowledged the innovations Sassenrath brought to the operating system, and he was justifiably proud. "It was just years ahead of anything else in terms of being able to have a device driver or library load dynamically and also unload to be removed from memory if it needed to be," he says. "It was many, many years later that that actually became available on other types of personal computers and Windows."

There was one glaring flaw with the Amiga OS: the garish blue and orange colors of the desktop GUI. These colors were chosen because they offered the best contrast for televisions, but the colors did not help improve the Amiga's perception as a professional machine.

The same month, *Run* magazine launched the September-October issue of *Amiga World*, before the release of the actual computer. The aggressive launch schedule established Amiga World as the premier Amiga magazine. "We sold out the first three issues and we had a print run of 120,000," says editor in chief Guy Wright. "Commodore bought 30,000 and we sold 90,000 copies of the magazine. And nobody had the computer yet!"

The numbers indicated there was a clear interest in the computer, though not necessarily as high as the magazine sales. "I think people were just more curious about the machine and this was the only way they could get any information about it," says Wright. "Nobody else had one. Nobody else knew anything about it."

Wright also established a unique tone for the magazine. "It was also a different kind of magazine. I like to think of it as the *Wired* of 1985," he says. "We were doing weird stuff in a magazine; jokes and graphics, interviews with Andy Warhol and Timothy Leary. We had also an art director, Glenn Suokko, who was really good. He was pulling in all sorts of famous illustrators to do stuff."

When the January 1986 issue featuring Andy Warhol was released in December, reactions were extreme. "We got buried in mail on that one," he says. "Half the people thought it was great and the other half of the people wanted to come and kill us. 'Why do you have a pop artist on the cover? This is supposed to be a computer magazine, right?' But it's not supposed to be dry, boring and dead. People loved the magazine."

When the Amiga finally launched, engineers were still contending with bugs in the operating system. "In the very beginning, the technology wasn't as bug free and robust as it should have been," says Mical. "It started to get a bad rap for the flaky technology and it didn't get the boost in the public's awareness that it needed because of that."

The crux of the problem was the unstable operating system. "The 1.0 release of the operating system had a lot of bugs in it and it crashed a lot," says Mical. "People would use the machine and start getting something together, an art project or something, and then it would crash and they would lose all their work. The guru meditation error."

As head of the Amiga software group, Bob Pariseau took most of the blame from management for the AmigaOS problems. Thankfully, due to the writable control store, Commodore could issue upgrades on the Kickstart disk. "The Kickstart was a kludge but it turns out to be an important element of the Amiga success, because we were able to issue a new version of the operating system that people could just load," explains Bryce Nesbitt. "That's huge! The Amiga developers did not anticipate that. They were from the console world. They were thinking this is like a better video game console and you didn't issue an operating system update three years after you produced the computer, but we did. And we could only do that because of the kickstart boot board."

November 1985 COMDEX

COMDEX, the Computer Dealers' Exhibition, was established in 1979 and rapidly became the leading computer show. As the name suggested, dealers abounded, and it would be unthinkable for a serious computer manufacturer to miss the show. Apple, Atari, IBM, and Microsoft focused their promotional efforts at the show.

At the fall COMDEX, held November 20 to 24th, Amiga's main competitor, Atari, showed up with dozens of software vendors and displays. This gave a strong impression that the Atari ST had more software support than the Amiga. Meanwhile, as Computer Chronicles pointed out, the Commodore Amiga was conspicuously absent.

Commodore had attempted promotion of the Amiga earlier with ads and shows, but that promotion didn't last throughout the holiday season. The company claimed it was silent to heighten the effect of the launch. Let the Amiga speak for itself. "They went into this stealth silence mode so they could have some big splash knobby thing or other," says Mical. "Instead it was a splash in a puddle."

In reality, Commodore had planned to attend, and even reserved space at the COMDEX show, but ran out of cash when the banks refused to extend any more loans to the company. The space went unused and Commodore was left out in the cold. It was a miserable situation in the midst of launching the Amiga.

In response to a question about Commodore's no-show, an amused Jack Tramiel told journalists, "We sell more Atari 520STs than Commodore sells Amigas, and we sure want to sign up more dealers."

Atari also set up a "Pepsi Challenge" of its own. According to the Chicago Tribune, "To demonstrate the stunning capability of its new Amiga computer, Commodore often displays on its screen a surprisingly realistic picture of a colorful bouncing ball. So it was a deliberate challenge when, at a recent trade show, rival Atari placed its new 520ST computer beside the Amiga and displayed on its screen a virtually identical bouncing ball."

In contrast, Commodore presented a single press conference at COMDEX, truthfully claiming the company was selling all the Amigas it could make. It was an attempt to put up a strong front in the midst of financial disaster. If the company could make it through the next few months, it would have a shot at recovery and eventual success.

The Next Amigas 1985

The Amiga was now shipping in the USA, but over 50% of Commodore's business came from overseas, and the Amiga would not work anywhere except the USA, greatly limiting the market. Commodore's executives wanted something done quickly.

And those same executives realized that the much touted MS-DOS capability of the Amiga had disappointed everyone. The Transformer software seemed to run in slow motion compared to an actual IBM PC. To solve the problem, Commodore approached the people within the company who knew best: its engineers in Germany who designed and manufactured PC clones.

By late 1985, the West Chester engineers were starting to notice a pattern. First executives cancelled the LCD computer and next the C900 Unix workstation. Even the C128 amassed so much executive opposition it barely made it through to production. Though the engineers occupied Commodore's headquarters, they began to feel like they were playing second fiddle to the West German and West Coast Amiga teams. It was time to take back control.

Ranger

When Commodore acquired the Amiga, it reignited a tradition that had momentarily halted with the release of the Plus/4 and C128. The VIC-20 was a graphical and aural jump up from the PET, as was the leap to the the C64. And now the Amiga would indeed put the C64 to shame in every category. Perhaps it too would be the hit Commodore needed, although the price was certainly higher than any of its previous multi-million-sellers.

The Los Gatos Amiga hardware engineers began discussing concepts for an improved Amiga named Ranger with West Chester management as early as May 1985, even as they supported the manufacturing efforts of the Amiga. But once the production line was rolling, they passed everything off to Commodore and began working in earnest on the next generation of the Amiga.

Jay Miner wanted a more powerful machine. "There was a big market for designers and other people who would really like a computer with strong graphics capability that they can only get in workstations that cost $20,000 or more," says Bill Hart. "That was their vision."

Bill Kolb, Amiga's West Coast director of engineering called together an after-lunch meeting on Thursday, August 8, 1985 to discuss Ranger. Kolb proposed that Ranger, based on the original Amiga chipset, should be quickly designed and ready by the end of October so that the engineers could move on to a more advanced machine dubbed "Mitchie, The Ultimate Computer".

Kolb's vision for a new Amiga consisted mainly of features missing from the Amiga. For example, the expansion slot on the side of the Amiga was a bus to be used by modules, where the modules plug in side by side using the Amiga Zorro bus. This was very much a design decision by the former president and CEO of Amiga. "Dave Morse had his own ideas about what a computer should look like and he felt that the card slots were too expensive for the machine he wanted to sell," said Jay Miner. "Dave Morse was insisting however, probably because of the investors, that we make as low cost a game type machine as possible; even though the only computers that had done well at that time were ones with card slots, such as the Apple and IBM."[1]

The Ranger would be the first Commodore computer with true expansion slots, something Jack Tramiel had not allowed. "Part of that was Jack's big blind spot. He hated slots," says Andy Finkel. "It went back to the days when he sold these first PETs and he had one board design and you could populate it for 4K or 16K and people would buy the 4K version and add their own RAM chips and not buy the 16K version. So he felt he lost money on those and from then on, for all the rest of the computers, expandability was not really in the picture."

---

1   *Amiga User International.* June 1988. "The AUI Interview" p. 20.

Dale Luck explains the design goals of the Ranger computer. "The Amiga 1000 did not have slots, it had an expansion connector in the side. Ranger was an Amiga that had a place for plug-in cards. That was going to be the next generation of the Amiga that had expandability and built in slots called Zorro slots."

According to Haynie, the origin of the Zorro name came from the original Amiga. "In the back of [the reference manual] was a schematic called Zorro," says Haynie, referring to the name of the prototype mother-board produced after Lorraine. "That's actually how the [expansion bus] was named."

Kolb's proposed features included an internal SCSI hard drive, option-al LAN, battery backed-up clock, seven expansion slots, and Dale Luck's MMU, built around a Motorola 68010 processor. The new design, aimed squarely against the Macintosh computer, would not get any cheaper. In fact, it was liable to be much more expensive.

Somewhat controversially, the Ranger would retain the writable control store so it could boot different versions of Kickstart from disk. But it would not be a kludge this time; the extra circuit board that sat on top of the main motherboard would instead be integrated into the main motherboard.

By September 21, the team had a Plexiglas and Styrofoam mockup of Ranger designed by Rob Gemmell, formerly of the Apple Industrial Design Group. They narrowed down the design to two 3.5" floppy disk bays, one 5.25" floppy drive bay, and five Zorro slots. Later, an additional two ISA slots would be added to the design. Internally, the team wanted 1 megabyte of memory, or perhaps 1.5 megs if the costs allowed for it. LAN support was now put off until after the scheduled June 1986 release date (with PAL coming six months later). Total cost of goods was under $800, meaning approximately $2400 at retail.

The Amiga engineers were also beginning to tire of all the input from Commodore's marketing, whose ideas were espoused by Rick Geiger. They finally put their collective foot down, giving marketing until the end of Sep-tember for product input, at which point the specs would be frozen.

Ranger was not just a new computer. Jay Miner was also busy designing a whole new chipset. This time he would use Video RAM (VRAM) rather than dynamic RAM (DRAM). VRAM at the time was brand new on the market. Though it was faster than DRAM, it was also much more expen-sive. According to Miner, "This new type of ram—video ram—is a giant step in computer improvement because it frees up the bottleneck into memory caused by competition between the computer itself and the memory fetchers required for the high resolution display. Imagine having an additional gigantic parallel output port thousands of bits wide, just for video."[2]

Graphically, the new chipset needed to compete with the Amiga's two main rivals, the Macintosh and Atari ST. The latter had a 640 by 400 flicker-free hires mode that improved on the Macintosh monochrome display. Miner would include a 640 by 400 hires mode, which he called super-hires. He would also go one step farther and include a 1024 by 1024 mode, which he called ultra-hires. Both modes would be monochrome only, and would not implement Amiga concepts such as playfields and sprites.

Miner later explained, "These chips use video ram and can produce a very high resolution 1024 display along with the present Amiga display simultaneously. They increase the display address range to two megabytes."[3]

On the software side, Amiga engineers continued improving the operating system. "Part of it was due to the reputation based on the technology of the first few months," says Mical. "The 1.0 operating system was absolutely miserable and it had that slow disk operating system as well. It had a lot of shortcomings from an engineering perspective." The software developers began working on an improved 1.1 version, mainly bug fixes, for existing Amiga owners.

The Amiga engineers clearly felt that, what with their name being Amiga after all, and having just released the Amiga, they were still in control of the destiny of the machine they had brought to the world. They would soon learn otherwise.

The Euro Amiga

The launch of the Amiga in the United States was underway when Commodore turned its attention to the equally important European version of the computer. The company needed money fast and the European Amiga became a priority. In October 1985, Ed Parks, VP of business computing, assigned Bil Herd as the product manager for the European Amiga. "He was there for a little while, while the Amiga stuff was just starting up," recalls Dave Haynie. "He got one of the first books that described the Amiga."

Unknown to Herd, it was a sign of respect for his abilities that Parks give him the job. Almost every engineer at West Chester felt Herd was the best among them at troubleshooting difficult problems. Executives at the time

---

2 *Amiga User International,* June 1988. "The AUI Interview"

3 Ibid.

also saw Amiga computers as the future of the company and Parks was letting Herd into the club, grooming him for future Amiga work.

Although Herd was impressed with the Amiga, he felt the project offered him little of interest. "That was just paper. I would have changed some timings and told them how to cut a new chip but that wasn't really challenging," he says.

In the fog surrounding Herd after the C128 project wrapped, he didn't realize the experience could be a precursor to designing a new version of the Amiga. "My alcoholism was really giving me a fit, things had slowed down, and I was convinced that we were not going to do another [computer]," he says.

Within a week of starting his research, Herd quit the project and began looking for work outside Commodore. Disappointed, Parks began looking for another engineer to groom for leading Amiga development in West Chester.

After the cancellation of the LCD portable, the engineers were searching for projects to remain relevant at the company. "This left us rather unhinged, not knowing what we were going to do," says Bob Welland.

The obvious choice was Jeff Porter, the engineer who had previously inherited the LCD project when Herd handed off that project. "By the time they cancelled the LCD project, the LCD factory kind of went along with it. They put all of their eggs in the Amiga basket," says Porter. "That's where I got suckered into the Amiga."

Our PAL Jeff Porter

Jeff Porter was not only a capable, hard working engineer, but a professional from the Bell Labs mold who wore a suit to work. Better still, he was already experienced with Amiga technology. "There were very few people in West Chester doing Amiga stuff," says Dave Haynie. "Jeff Porter and Andy Finkel were doing an [Amiga] answering machine/modem that never got released."

Their creation would transform an Amiga into a personal secretary of sorts. "I had dreams of doing it from my Bell Labs days," says Porter. "We called it the AnswerMate."

Porter had developed two ideas he tentatively called OfficeBoy and MagicPhone. Coming from Bell Labs, where telecommunications was the center of activity, his product ideas were both telephone based. The cost of his products shows how consumer oriented he was already.

The OfficeBoy was a bargain basement FAX machine for the home. It relied on a normal Commodore printer and attached a simple scanner to the
print-head to convert the printer into an all-in-one scanner. The scanning
head connected to the C64 joystick port, and once scanned in, the modem
would send the image to another FAX machine. Total cost of parts, including cartridge based software, came to a mere $10.

Porter also proposed the MagicPhone, a touch-tone telephone with a
speakerphone, and an integrated LCD touch screen, useful for bringing up
an address book. He projected the device could retail for $99.

Neither of those two telecommunications ideas ever made it off paper.
Instead, Joe Krasuki mentioned that Joe Decuir had been working on a
similar idea at his startup company Teledesign while he helped design the
Amiga chipset. "When I was working as a consultant on the Amiga hardware, I was also writing a business plan for a startup to do an AnswerMate
type device for IBM PCs," explains Decuir.

In early 1985, Decuir had a chance to resurrect the idea, this time for the
Amiga. "I still had those ideas in my head," he says. "My consulting company Teledesign started some of that work in 1985 with Amiga."

By August 1985, Decuir and Porter had two functioning prototypes of
the product and they began building more for software development and
testing. Andy Finkel and Judy Braddock would work through November developing the alpha software, which ran on the Amiga. This would
go into beta testing in December. Assuming FCC testing went smoothly,
they expected to manufacture and ship the first 5,000 AnswerMates in
January 1986.

Then it was time for Jeff Porter to move onto the PAL Amiga project.
Unlike Bil Herd, Porter was eager to get the Amiga into Europe. The word
that best describes Porter's essence is *purpose*. "When the A1000 was introduced, it was a USA NTSC only computer," he says. "Commodore had a
lot of international business at that time. More than 50% of its business was
outside of the US."

Gerard Bucas officially assigned Porter to the PAL project in early October. "Gerard was assistant VP of engineering at that time. Since my LCD
project got cancelled, he said, 'Jeff how would you like to take over the PAL
A1000? Make it 220 volts, make it PAL instead of NTSC, get all the trans-
lations done, the keyboard drivers, get it certified in all the countries, and all
the other stuff that has to be done to sell it in all the other markets.'"

The project was not trivial because the Amiga chipset was designed so
tightly around NTSC. On Wednesday October 9, Porter travelled to Los

16–1   16–2

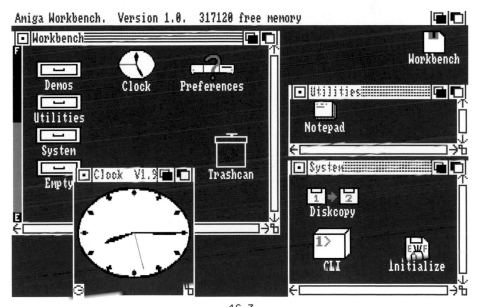

16–3

16–1 Commodore's January 1985 CES booth
(photo courtesy of Eric Cotton)

16–2 Jeff Porter (left) showing his LCD Portable at CES
(photo courtesy of Jeff Porter)

16–3 RJ Mical's Amiga Workbench 1.0

17–1

18–1

18–2

17–1 Thomas Rattigan, CEO of Commodore Inc.
(Commodore Magazine photo, Copyright 2017 Cloanto Corporation)

18–1 Dave Haynie (right) and Greg Berlin in Japan. T-shirt reads,
"Beer, It's not just for breakfast anymore." (photo courtesy of Dave Haynie)

18–2 Commodore 128, Bil Herd's sequel to the C64

18-3

19-1

19-2

18-3 Greg Berlin teeing his 1581 drive for a kick (photo courtesy of Eric Cotton)

19-1 Lincoln Center Amiga launch reception area (photo courtesy of RJ Mical)

19-2 RJ Mical with his white gloves at the Amiga launch event
(photo courtesy of RJ Mical)

19–3

20–1

20–2

21–1

19–3 Andy Warhol and Debbie Harry at the Amiga launch (Amiga World photo)

20–1 Commodore 128D

20–2 C900 Unix computer

21–1 Amiga 1000

21–2

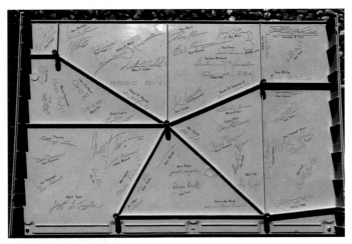

21–3

22–1   22–2

21–2 Deluxe Paint

21–3 Signatures engraved inside the A1000 case (photo courtesy of RJ Mical)

22–1 Ranger bezel and keyboard mockups
    (photo by Chris Collins from the Dale Luck collection)

22–2 Ranger Plexiglas prototype for airflow testing
    (photo by Chris Collins from the Dale Luck collection)

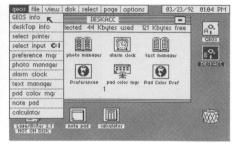

23-1

23-2

23-3

24-1

26-1

26-2

23-1 Habitat, the first MMO (C64 screenshot)

23-2 Geos desktop on a C64

23-3 Bil Herd on the night he hit CEO Marshall Smith (photo courtesy of Dave Haynie)

24-1 Adam Chowaniec, Commodore's VP of engineering

26-1 Participants entering CeBIT

26-2 Winfried Hoffmann, general manager of Commodore Braunschweig

28–1

28–2

30–1

31–1

28–1 Commodore 1351 mouse (and another example of marketing not quite getting it right)

28–2 Hedley Davis, designer of the 1351 mouse (photo courtesy of Bob Welland)

30–1 Bob Welland, A500 co-designer (photo courtesy of Bob Welland)

31–1 C256 prototypes (photos courtesy of Bo Zimmerman and Doug Cotton)

32-1

34-1

34-2

34-3

35-1

32-1 Dave Haynie (left) and George Robbins (photo courtesy of Bob Welland)

34-1 (l-r) Hedley Davis, Claude Guay, Jeff Porter and Dave Haynie at CES
(photo courtesy of Jeff Porter)

34-2 Commodore 64c, the cost reduced version

34-3 Amiga Juggler demo (Eric Graham)

35-1 Amiga 500, West Chester's version of the Amiga

Gatos to meet with the Amiga engineers and learn more about the issues he might encounter with converting the NTSC signal into PAL.

NTSC operated at 60 Hz and produced 480 scan lines. PAL, on the other hand, refreshed at 50 Hz but with 576 scan lines, requiring slightly higher resolution. To get the timing just right, the Motorola 68000 chip would run at 7.09 MHz in the PAL system (compared to 7.16 MHz in NTSC), meaning games were just a fraction slower on European systems. Anything using refresh rate timing, notably sound, would appear slower on PAL systems.

With Commodore low on money, it was vital to introduce the PAL Amiga into Europe on schedule. Porter would have until the March 1986 CeBIT Fair to have the PAL version ready. In the meantime, he would have to quickly get up to speed on the inner workings of the Amiga computer.

MS-DOS Compatibility

Commodore's executives (and most of the press at the time) considered MS-DOS compatibility to be of paramount importance to the success of the Amiga as a business computer. "There were a lot of issues to do with Amiga and the lack of PC compatibility of the Amiga," says Gerard Bucas. "The engineering side of Commodore didn't worry about PC compatibility but eventually that was forced on us by marketing and everybody had to be PC compatible. There was sort of that feeling in the company, 'What are we going to do with a non PC compatible computer? We can't sell it.'"

"They were like, 'We need to be able to run spreadsheets and word processors and all that kind of stuff so we can justify this $1300 price,'" recalls Carl Sassenrath.

The strategy for backward compatibility was similar to a move Commodore made previously with the C64. Commodore had attempted to produce a CP/M cartridge which allowed the C64 to run the existing library of CP/M software titles—the dominant operating system prior to MS-DOS. Thus, marketing could claim a large software base at launch.

The Amiga engineers themselves had attempted to create an MS-DOS compatible Amiga in mid-1984 around the time of the acquisition. They had called it the Amiga PC, but after the acquisition they rolled back those changes.

Commodore's first attempt at IBM PC emulation, the Transformer, was too slow. Thomas Rattigan openly acknowledged previous miscalculations. "I think we banked too much on the software emulator for IBM compatibility, which we saw as a bridge during the time Amiga's software was being developed," he said. "That obviously, in retrospect, did not pan out to the degree we had hoped."[4]

To achieve PC performance, engineers would have to include an Intel 8088 processor and dedicated memory. Neither of the US engineering groups were very supportive of an emulator, starting with Jay Miner on down. "The problem is the Amiga was based on a multitasking windowing OS," explains Bucas. "Application-wise, it was all based on multimedia. That's the key to Amiga: multimedia, audio, video compatibility with NTSC and PAL video. MS-DOS was single-tasking and no graphics in those days. The main thing people did in MS-DOS at that stage was Lotus 1-2-3 and WordPerfect."

Due to the lack of enthusiasm for emulation, Rick Geiger, the general manager of Amiga, hired an outside contractor to design the emulation hardware. He promised he would have hardware emulation ready by the end of 1985. Unfortunately, the expansion card never worked and Amiga grudgingly dismissed the contractor.

Despite the failures, Irving Gould believed IBM PC compatibility was the key to the Amiga's success, and he would attempt to personally make it happen. He had witnessed years of Jack Tramiel pitting divisions within Commodore against one another. Now he would attempt something similar. "I have met him many times and he was certainly an interesting character, that's for sure," says Bucas. "A little out of his depth in the technology industry but obviously he was a good investor and a smart guy."

Sidecar Engineering

The natural group to design a PC-compatible expansion, dubbed the Sidecar, was the German engineering group. "Commodore had a factory in Braunschweig, Germany," says Bucas. "The reason why they did the so-called Sidecar is really related to the fact that one of their jobs was to develop and introduce PC's for the European market. At that stage they were the only engineering group doing PC clones."

Although the German group fell under Gerard Bucas' purview, Gould went to the GM of the Braunschweig factory, Winfried Hoffmann, without Bucas' knowledge. "Basically his attitude was that, in his mind, the Amiga had to be PC compatible and we in US engineering weren't willing or able

---

4   *Commodore Magazine,* "What Next for Commodore?" (May 1987) p. 76

to do that," says Bucas. "So they convinced him they could do it and he started a secret project in Germany."

A German engineer named Wilfried Rusniok oversaw development of the Sidecar. He and his team of engineers produced the earliest prototypes by November 1985. But the Germans required programmers to make it run in the Amiga OS. "The sidecar product that was done over in Germany was to make something you plug into the side of your Amiga and it could read IBM PC disks and execute the IBM PC in a window," says Carl Sassenrath.

By December, Rusniok and his crew delivered 36 prototypes to the United States for dealer demos. It was an incredible turnaround time. The device connected to an external IBM PC disk drive and contained PC compatible ISA expansion slots and a 5.25 inch floppy disk drive, the dominant format for IBM PC computers at the time. The German engineers also promised more refined prototypes to demonstrate at the Hanover Fair and spring COMDEX, both to be held in April 1986.

Braunschweig's Amiga

While the Amiga engineers believed they were designing the next iteration of the Amiga in Los Gatos, other parts of the company also saw opportunities. In 1985, the Commodore engineers in Braunschweig, Germany, under lead engineer Wilfried Rusniok, were on a roll with the IBM PC clones and Sidecar.

Theoretically, the Braunschweig group reported to Gerard Bucas in West Chester, on paper at least. "Commodore had quite a big facility there, including an engineering team which reported to me," recalls Gerard Bucas. "From the beginning, even when I was the business system guy, they only did the business systems. They never did C64 and C128 and the Amiga stuff."

In reality, the German engineers reported more frequently to Winfried Hoffmann, the founder and GM of the Braunschweig factory. For the most part, Hoffmann and Rusniok operated quite independently of Bucas.

The Sidecar was essentially an IBM PC computer connected to the expansion port of an Amiga. This led Rusniok and Hoffmann to begin thinking of fusing those together into one integrated system with expansion slots. Shortly after they completed the Sidecar design, the Braunschweig engineers began designing an expandable Amiga computer. "They were trying to make an expandable machine—more expandable than the A1000 which just had the side connector," says Bob Welland.

This also solved Hoffmann's marketing dilemma in Europe. He had been pushing the IBM PC clones due to Commodore not having a viable business computer since the PET. Now Hoffmann needed to steer businesses away from IBM PC computers and back to Commodore's answer to the business computer, the Amiga. It was the perfect fit.

Within months, the Braunschweig team had built their expandable Amiga. It had IBM compatible ISA slots and was able to output video to a standard Amiga RGB monitor. In many ways it was a Frankenstein creation much like the C128, with several computers inside vying for the user's attention.

According to Bob Russell, the German engineers stuck their motherboard into a C900 Unix case. "It used my Z8000 keyboard and [case] because it was more of a business machine," he reveals.

The engineers also added the aforementioned Zorro expansion slots for proprietary Amiga expansion cards. "Germany took the A1000 reference design from a thin white book called the A1000 technical reference manual," explains Dave Haynie. "It had the autoconfig and everything, but it was fairly simply based on the 68000 bus with buffer.[5] It wasn't super creative, which is why it worked so well."

At the heart of the system was a special card with an Intel processor that plugged into both an ISA slot and a Zorro slot at the same time, bridging the IBM and Amiga worlds, and allowing the computer to emulate an IBM PC. Thus, the card became known as the Bridgeboard. The Bridgeboard was both fast and reliable. It could even run Microsoft *Flight Simulator*, a processor-intensive IBM PC game.

Hoffmann ordered his engineers to keep the project under wraps, notifying only Irving Gould. "Basically without a central engineering management knowing, which was me, Irving Gould went behind my back and convinced a guy in Germany, or the guys in Germany rather convinced him, that we really need to make this thing PC compatible, so we're going to design this bridge card," says Bucas.

Gould encouraged them to continue work on it and would unveil it to the West Chester executives in early 1986. The German team named the new computer the A2500, based around the projected retail cost of the machine in US dollars.

---

5 At the time, it was difficult to configure adapter cards in IBM PC computers. The Zorro slots were similar to *Plug and Play*, introduced later in Windows 95. The Amiga automatically configured the adapter cards.

There were now three engineering groups vying for Irving Gould's favor. Commodore West Chester was trying to succeed with the C128D business computer, with Dave Haynie as the lead engineer. The Amiga engineers in Los Gatos were working on the Ranger chipset, a new case, a new motherboard, and a new version of Amiga OS. They also had plans for a cost-reduced Amiga to be released in 1986. And now there was Germany, which appeared to already have Gould's favour. "It ended up being a kind of a race," says Bob Welland.

It would be up to Irving Gould, Thomas Rattigan, and Marshall Smith to choose which of these contenders would build the next product. They would choose the winner in 1986.

Resurrecting 8-Bit 1985

After the Amiga acquisition, support swung towards the new 16-bit computer as the best hope for Commodore. Suddenly very few people, especially in management, had any faith in low-end 8-bit computers. Acknowledging that it would take a few years for the Amiga to catch on, Irving Gould wanted someone to find ways to extend the lifetime sales of the C64 for a few more years. He hired Clive Smith, the Yankee Group consultant who had helped put together the Amiga acquisition, to work with him out of his Park Avenue offices in New York.

Throughout 1985, Clive Smith came up with several creative solutions to extend the life of the C64 and bring in more revenue. If all went well, revenue from the C64 would help pull the Amiga through its early days financially.

Showtime for GEOS

Clive Smith believed the C64 would require a GUI in order to remain competitive with other computers on the market in 1985. Commodore had risen to prominence as a hardware company, and it was never much of a software company. It had attempted a GUI suite of applications in 1983 called *Magic Desk*, which met with a mixed reception. In order to bring a credible GUI to the C64, Commodore would have to partner with an outside developer.

In late 1985, a company named Berkeley Software had a beta version of their GUI operating system ready for the C64. "We spent about a year in development. When we started it, I wasn't sure how good a job we'd be able to do because even the Commodore 64, as good as it was for the day, was limited compared to even the first Macs," explains company founder Brian

Dougherty. "We have an 8-bit processor and 64K of RAM versus a Mac, which has a 68000 and 128K of RAM. It doesn't sound like a big difference now, but then that was a world of difference."

There were other less obvious shortcomings too. Dougherty was disappointed that the C64 lacked the ability to load a program from disk as soon as the user turned on the computer. "All the routines that need to be there are there, but there should also be a facility for automatically reading the first track of the disk and booting a more sophisticated operating system into memory," says Dougherty.[1]

The Berkeley team used the same UNIX development tools they used for programming Data East games for the C64. "Back in that timeframe we used Emacs or vi, which were the popular UNIX editors," says Dougherty. "A bunch of our programmers switched about halfway through the Commodore GEOS project. You wrote in assembly language and we had a cross assembler that would then assemble that code down into the binary files that would get downloaded through the in-circuit emulator into the Commodore 64."

The final result looked and acted like the Macintosh operating system, right down to the location of icons on the desktop. Dougherty attributes their success to an obsession with code efficiency. "Once we got into it, one of the lessons, that I think unfortunately has been lost in the software world today, is that if you are willing to put a little more effort in, you can almost infinitely improve the efficiency of your code. That was really the secret to doing a graphical environment on an 8-bit 1 MHz processor. We had to get really clever about making the code efficient. At the end of the day, I was really pleased with how much we were able to deliver on the platform."

Despite being the CEO of Berkeley Softworks, Dougherty himself was the lead programmer on what he called the GEOS Kernal, which was the heart of the operating system. Since GEOS ran on the C64, Dougherty intentionally misspelled the word kernel as *kernal*, as the C64 developers had with their kernel.

In order to prevent GEOS from running out of memory while in use, the GEOS Kernal could use disk memory as though it was RAM. "What was amazing was that, as we got into it, we essentially built a little virtual memory system for the C64 where you had to have a floppy disk drive, even though it only gave you another 150K of storage on the disk drive," says

---

1   IEEE Spectrum journal, "Design case history: the Commodore 64", (March 1985), p. 48.

Dougherty. "We developed what we called the VLIR file system, which stood for Variable Length Index Records, which let us take and put arbitrary sized chunks of data on the disk and dynamically load them in and out of memory as you needed to work on them. That little dynamic memory management that we did expanded the memory space from 64K to 64K plus 150K of very slow memory, so you had to be very clever about preloading stuff and things like that."

In 1985 a mouse was an unusual sight for a home computer, so GEOS accepted input from a variety of sources: joystick, Commodore's 1350 mouse, Inkwell light pen, and Koala Pad, a touch tablet.

In late 1985, Berkeley Softworks released a beta version of GEOS for developers, which they referred to as 1.0, although it was not offered for sale. Dougherty hoped to see larger companies such as Microsoft, Lotus Software, WordPerfect and Electronic Arts develop software just for GEOS. "We had envisioned other companies writing for the Commodore 64 GEOS," he says.

In November 1985, Dougherty demonstrated GEOS to Commodore executive Clive Smith. "He was the senior VP of strategy who reported directly to Irving Gould," says Dougherty. "Clive Smith had come from the outside. He was a consultant from the Yankee Group."

Dougherty showed him the impossible: a Macintosh-like operating system running on a C64. "We came and showed Clive a demo of an early Commodore GEOS implementation and he was really impressed with what we were able to do," says Dougherty. "He was a really smart guy and saw the potential of Commodore GEOS in the early days."

The demonstration impressed Smith. People who couldn't afford thousands of dollars for an Amiga or Macintosh could still gain entrance into the world of GUI OS's, WYSIWYG fonts and mice, which seemed quite futuristic in 1985. Smith and Dougherty promised to meet again at the upcoming CES show in Las Vegas to discuss a partnership. The C64 was about to receive a significant upgrade.

Quantum Link Goes Online

Earlier in 1985, Clive Smith had decided to end Commodore's agreement with CompuServe and codevelop a new online service called Quantum Link. In order to satisfy its end of the contract, Commodore had to market and advertise the service.

In mid-August, Jeff Porter noticed no one was preparing for the Quantum Link software release. He complained to executives Adam Chowaniec,

Joe Krasucki, and Ed Parks about the situation. They immediately recognized a good opportunity and assigned him to coordinate the Quantum Link release. Porter went down to Virginia and met with the Quantum Link team to discuss details.

The plan hinged on selling hundreds of thousands of 300 baud modems, along with free Quantum Link software. But there was a problem. Porter now predicted the 300 baud modem would not be ready until October due to the FCC delay. This would have a severe impact on Commodore meeting the contractual target of 25,000 subscribers.

To compensate for the late launch of the 1660, Porter asked Thomas Rattigan to sign off on an additional 45,000 units of the 1200 baud modem, the 1670. It was a risky proposition. Quantum Link could only connect at 300 baud. Although the 1670 could also connect at 300 baud, it would be much easier to move large volumes of $50 300 baud modems than $200 1200-baud modems. But the good news was that 45,000 of those 1200-baud modems would be ready to ship September 23.

For the next two months, Commodore began aggressively shipping out the Quantum Link software and placing ads in magazines and newspapers. "It cost them several million dollars," says Kit Spencer. "It also allowed CompuServe to get out of the agreement that we had which would have continued churning out money for Commodore for years."

The deal meant that Commodore would not only promote Quantum Link but also pay royalties. "They put a disk in every C64 box and Steve Case made $1 for every C64 that was shipped," recalls Porter. "He made a lot of money on that deal because Commodore sold a lot of C64's."2

Quantum Link went live on November 5, 1985. Operating only during evenings and weekends, it cost $3.60 per hour for premium content, unlike CompuServe, which charged $20 per hour. "I saw demos of Quantum Link and thought it was interesting and fun," says Andy Finkel.

Unfortunately, as the launch date passed, Commodore had yet to ship any 300 baud modems. While other engineers might have grumbled to themselves and buried their heads in work, Porter dealt with the situation. But he also took his complaints right to the top, castigating Commodore for the pathetic release of his modems, pointing out that if they had gone

---

2   Thirty years later, Jeff Porter is amused by the disparity of wealth between he and
    Steve Case. "He used all that money to make AOL. He's a lot richer and bought half
    of a Hawaiian Island. I live in metropolitan Philadelphia and have been to Hawaii a
    couple of times."

to an outside testing house for FCC approval it would have happened 9 months ago.

Finally, the modem passed FCC certification and Commodore received 60,000 300 baud modems during Thanksgiving. All they had to do was package them up with disks and manuals and ship them out.

In retrospect, the deal Clive Smith had made no longer looked appealing. "So instead of receiving revenue every month, there was some possibility of some large payoff in the future that was never achieved," says Neil Harris. "In the meantime Commodore did all the promotion and had all the expense of operating the service, which was much higher than what it had been on CompuServe."

Although the ordeal meant Commodore had little chance of meeting the 25,000 subscriber quota, there was one positive effect. Management took notice that Jeff Porter was clearly an effective, hard-working employee. As a result, Gerard Bucas began mentoring Porter for a promotion.

Habitat

Although most executives felt little confidence for gaming in 1985, Clive Smith was a notable holdout. He wanted a killer app to make the Quantum Link service irresistable to C64 owners. And in 1985, the hot newcomer to the industry was Lucasfilm Games.

Smith was fresh off making the deal with Quantum Computer Services and looking for ways to ensure Commodore would meet its quota of new users. He explained to LucasFilm Games head Steve Arnold that he wanted killer apps for two new products: the Amiga and Quantum Link (using the new 300 baud modem for the C64). "Consequently, when Clive Smith came to Lucasfilm, he was shopping for two kinds of projects: things that would leverage modems and an online service, and things that would leverage the Amiga," recalls Chip Morningstar.

In December 1985, Morningstar started writing the code for his game, even though the LucasFilm-Quantum Link contract would not be signed until February 1986. He called the game *Habitat*. "Being based on the Commodore 64 was also advantageous since it meant that all of Lucasfilm Games' heavy duty development tools and our big bag of C64 and 6502 tricks could be brought to bear," says Morningstar. "It wasn't the slick, oomphy Amiga that we had originally been thinking in terms of, but it was a platform that we knew how to squeeze for every drop of performance it had."

UUCP, Usenet and JAUG

Commercial services like Quantum Link and CompuServe were not the only online services available to the public in 1985. There were also other services which were not owned and operated by one singular company. The person who would ultimately connect Commodore to this network was the unusual engineer known to his coworkers as GRR.

After the C900 was put on hold, George R. Robbins was between projects and began spending more time with the VAX machine. "We had a Unix system at Commodore and he basically administered it," says Hedley Davis.

As Robbins' love affair with the VAX machine continued, it became hard for him to leave every night. He often stayed late, hovering over a terminal, occasionally departing for a catnap in the back of his van. "He had a green van behind Commodore and he kind of lived there for a while," says Bil Herd. "He just never left."

According to Herd, this routine progressed until he rarely returned home. "He actually lived there, even when there were no projects going on," he says. "He didn't have a driver's license and I think his car was broken."

Commodore, like most other businesses at the time, did not have a dedicated Internet connection in 1985, despite the fact that the TCP/IP protocol had been formalized in 1982. Instead, the company used the VAXen to send inter-company emails.

However, now that the Amiga team was established in Los Gatos, the company wanted a way to exchange emails with them. It was up to Robbins to make that happen at West Chester's end.

The VAX system had a modem connected to a phone line, allowing it to establish communication intermittently with other regional Commodore offices. AT&T Bell Labs was always on the cutting edge of communications, and it had started developing a protocol in 1978 for exchanging files. This protocol, called UUCP, was rewritten in 1983 and became immensely popular after that. "There was this network, sort of a parallel network to the Internet, which was computers that were all connected with UUCP, which is Unix to Unix Copy Program," explains Commodore engineer Joe Augenbraun. "The VAX would have a dial-up modem hooked up to it and every day it would send a pile of files down the chain."

Some of those files were email messages. In a sense, UUCP allowed parallel services to those available on the Internet, even though it was not real time. "Commodore was not on the Internet, as far as I remember," says Augenbraun. "Commodore was a UUCP node. There is no IP address. You were on the Internet in the sense that you could email anyone, but there was no such thing as a website. There were all kinds of Internet services you couldn't do. You couldn't chat because there was no live connection; it was all batch files."

Robbins set up batch files to run periodically throughout the day, causing the VAX to dial into the Los Gatos server. Once connected, the servers could exchange email files, as well as making backups of important data.

He also established the node address for Commodore, which he called cbmvax. In turn, other servers on the UUCP network could dial into the Commodore UUCP node. This meant the engineers who used Commodore's VAX machine would have an email address. George Robbins' email address became grr@cbmvax.UUCP.

Because the ARPANET (the early name for the Internet) was connected to UUCP, Commodore employees were now able to email anyone on the Internet, even though they lacked a dedicated Internet connection. "This is when the Internet was brand new," says Hedley Davis. "He was the one responsible to get the CBMVAX domain name." This early peek at the Internet was a revelation to the engineers, even though Commodore itself would not receive Internet access for many more years.

Robbins soon learned of a burgeoning service called Usenet that allowed users to exchange messages publicly in an open forum. Usenet was pioneered at AT&T Bell Labs in 1979 and spread worldwide in 1983 at the same time that UUCP was rewritten. Here, hundreds of specialized forums, called newsgroups, allowed group conversations to take place.

A few years earlier, on April 23, 1983, a well known C64 software developer from the University of Waterloo math department named Brad Templeton established the net.micro.cbm newsgroup. At that time he had announced, "This group is for discussion of the computers made by Commodore Business Machines, whose numbers are growing in great numbers these days. This includes the PET, the CBM series, the VIC-20, the Commodore-64 and the new B and P series computers."

Although working for AT&T at the time, future Commodore employee Jeff Porter began posting to this group on October 4, 1983, discussing his favorite computer, the Commodore 64.

Robbins discovered Usenet in December 1985 and announced Commodore's UUCP node in order to have other servers on the UUCP network call the Commodore node. Even though the UUCP network relied on intermittent connections, it spanned the globe like a web, connecting machines together. Robbins also began posting to newsgroups, attempting to help Commodore users with their technical problems. A few months later, other users such as Dave Haynie and Jeff Porter began posting to Usenet groups. It was addictive.

Robbins' love of computers ran deep, and he enjoyed meeting new people through Usenet newsgroups. He soon encountered another UUCP administrator, Eric Lavitsky, and the two hit it off. "I loved George Robbins," says Lavitsky. "George and I were great friends because George ran all the VAXen, the mini computers at Commodore, and I was a bit of a VAX head because that's one of the many things that I did in my career early on."

Eric Lavitsky was a young programmer of the Kermit protocol for the C64 who had snuck into the Amiga launch party and struck up an acquaintance with Jeff Porter. "I ended up starting the first electronic public discussion group called Info Amiga, which was on the ARPANET, in early August of '85 after I came back from the launch at Lincoln Center," recalls Lavitsky. "That ended up becoming net.micro.amiga, which was the first Usenet group for discussing Amiga topics as well."

In October 1985, ahead of the West Chester group, the Amiga team connected to Usenet and announced themselves online. Neil Katin, Dale Luck, and Robert Pariseau began posting messages to Lavitsky's new group, answering questions and helping to promote the upcoming Amiga. The new Amiga group quickly became one of the top four most trafficked Usenet newsgroups, a source of some chagrin from administrators who didn't want to overload their server hard drives with so many postings.

Commodore's engineers found the newsgroups intoxicating. "It was just like everyone got hooked," explains Augenbraun. "There's sort of this weird curation that was happening then. Whatever topic you were interested in, you got the best and brightest in the world sitting there having a conversation on it, just because there is nothing else. It was really compelling in a way that nothing that exists now is."

This new technology came with a price, however. Commodore shelled out $1205 per month to RCA American for a land link to the West Coast, plus another $9373 per month to RCA Global for a connection to the Tokyo Pacific link. By contrast, Commodore Germany settled for an intermittent connection averaging 90 seconds a few times per day to the VAX machine. This was a bargain at DM 180 per month for the phone line, plus DM 0.20 per minute.

The VAX system and UUCP allowed Commodore's engineers to communicate better with software developers in a way upper management could scarcely imagine. "Rattigan had little if any contact with developers.

I mean, these people did not understand what developers were and how they were important to the lifeblood of a product like the Amiga," says Lavitsky, a developer himself.

Usenet allowed people with similar interests to connect and meet together in person as well. In August, two new Amiga user groups formed within days of each other. One was called FAUG, the First Amiga User Group, based in Silicon Valley. The second was JAUG, the Jersey Amiga User Group. "I ended up meeting a guy named Perry Kivolowitz and we formed what became the second Amiga user group in the country because FAUG had been founded only a few days before us," says Lavitsky. "We had a couple of small meetings and then we pushed the publicity, and in December that year we had the first big public meeting."

JAUG held its first meeting on Friday, December 20 at 7:30 pm in room 114 of Hill Center, Rutgers University. The inaugural guest was Jeff Porter, who demonstrated prototypes of the Amiga 1300 genlock along with his Amiga AnswerMate. "In the middle of a blizzard we had over 300 people come to our meeting," recalls Lavitsky. "And Jeff Porter came up from West Chester with Dave Berezowski, who was working at Commodore at the time. That was a great experience."

Through UUCP, Commodore was able to reach a large audience of enthusiasts and they in turn were able to reach Commodore. These connections in turn spawned user groups in support of the Amiga and other Commodore products, allowing groups like JAUG to lure other Amiga veterans such as Dale Luck to attend meetings and promote new products. Computer-to-computer communications was bearing fruit.

The Big Party

Before Christmas of 1985, Commodore's employees crammed into the historic Sunnybrook Ballroom in Pottstown, Pennsylvania. "There was a Christmas party where everybody was pretty damn looped by the end of it," recalls Robert Russell. "It was probably the biggest, best Commodore Christmas party ever. They were giving away all types of neat stuff and everybody was loaded up on tons of free booze."

Nobody enjoyed the free beverages more than CEO Marshall Smith. Surprisingly, the former steel industry CEO took part in some impromptu dancing more fitting of a punk rock concert. "Marshall Smith is a pretty big guy," says Russell. "All I can say is he was a good drinker and he could body slam with the best of them, as Herd can attest to. Herd and him were slam dancing, and Greg Berlin too. Drinking and body slamming; that's about the only thing I think he was qualified to do."

Bil Herd recalls fraternizing with his CEO. "I punched Marshall one night," he says. "I drank a lot and he got drunker through the night. At this time I had my hand in a cast."

Herd was edgy at the best of times but even worse when alcohol impaired his judgment. "He did that slap on face thing when you're talking to somebody," recalls Herd. "I whacked him back. I did it with my cast hand, so what would have been a whack came across harder. It knocked him back a little bit."

Most employees would worry if they punched their CEO in the jaw, but Herd was indifferent. "I figured he probably wasn't going to remember it but that wasn't the important thing at the time," says Herd. "I said, 'Don't do that again.' He looked at me and kind of staggered. We got along after that, sort of."

CHAPTER 24

Turning it Around
1986

Commodore had squeaked through 1985 by culling 33% of the employee workforce, skipping the fall COMDEX and liquidating some investments and assets. After the cuts, it appeared to be business as usual as those who remained launched the Amiga and the C128. All that was about to change as the new year rolled around, and executives would have to find a way out of Commodore's tenuous financial situation.

Winter CES

In January 1986, the seriousness of Commodore's financial predicament was apparent to all. For the first time since it entered the computer industry, Commodore was absent from the Winter Consumer Electronics Show in Las Vegas. Industry analysts were stunned, especially considering rival Atari was there showing off the 520ST. *Ahoy!* magazine reported:

> Understand that the last four CES shows in a row, dating back to January 1984, Commodore's exhibit had been the focal point of the home computer segment of CES, the most visited computer booth at the show - as befitted the industry's leading hardware manufacturer. Their pulling out of CES seemed like Russia resigning from the Soviet Bloc.[1]

"At that time they were having money problems," says Dale Luck. "They released the Plus/4 and a lot of these other products that they were trying to come out with. I don't know that any one of them was actually making a lot of money. The C64 might have been the only thing making money because they cost-reduced it so much."

---

1   *Ahoy!* magazine, "Scuttlebutt" (April 1986), p. 8.

Instead of hosting a booth, Irving Gould rented a hotel suite to demonstrate Amiga products. This was the first unveiling of the upcoming Sidecar project for the Amiga. In an interview with *Infoworld*, Commodore's Gail Wellington said the Sidecar would retail for under $1000, though Amiga developers believed the actual price would be $300 to $400 when released.[2]

Despite not having a booth, the engineers and executives attended the show as regular guests. Due to Commodore publishing two computer magazines, *Power/Play* and *Commodore Microcomputers*, the company requested and received official CES press passes. "Eric [Cotton] and I would go to CES in Vegas and would not work the booth," recalls software developer Jeff Bruette. "Instead, he and I would get press passes for *Power/Play* magazine and use the press status to get into competitor's press suites."

Commodore's Clive Smith visited the Berkeley Softworks booth where Brian Dougherty debuted GEOS 1.1 for the Commodore 64 at a price of $59.95. The demonstration impressed Smith, who had been in contact with Berkeley since seeing an early demo of the system. Smith put forth a serious proposal to include GEOS with the Commodore 64.

Second Round Cuts

Following the first round of cuts in 1985, Commodore had hoped to escape from its financial difficulties relatively unscathed. But when cash-flow became scarce, the banks wanted to see more efficiency. Thomas Rattigan knew he would have to close down some of Commodore's factories, which were the lifeblood of the company.

Rattigan tried to delay the closures right up to the last possible minute so they could pump out as much product as possible for the holiday season. But at the end of the year, with the upcoming banker meetings scheduled for February 1986, it was time to do the ugly deed. At the time he considered the main factory in the West Chester facility as the crown jewel, so Rattigan cast his eye to other parts of the world.

Commodore UK owned a state-of-the-art factory located in Corby, Northamptonshire, a small town that had recently been hit with the closure of a large steel factory. In keeping with Jack Tramiel's efficiency-oriented leadership, the purpose of the factory was to save on the high cost of shipping computers from around the world to the UK. Back in May 1983,

---

2   Infoworld, May 5, 1986. Page 5. "Amiga, Atari Ready PC Emulators"

Commodore had announced the plans for the factory, which would go on-line in September 1984.

All the UK employees located at 675 Ajax Avenue in Slough relocated to the modern premises. "When I joined them in 1983 they were in Slough Business Park," recalls UK marketing manager David Pleasance.

Pleasance recalls the factory as a core part of Commodore UK. "We bought a 10 acre site and had a purpose-built factory erected on it," he says. "It was very, very impressive. I think we had something like 530 employees and we were assembling C64s and VICs."

The factory was in a prime location and would fill Commodore UK's supply needs for the foreseeable future. "Northamptonshire is where it resided, pretty much in central UK," he says. "It was a good location to have a factory from a delivery point of view because it is quite central in the UK. They got a five million pound grant to build a factory, which was the subject of a lot of potential legal issues when they closed the factory down but I think they got away without paying it back."

The factory had opened in September 1984 and had taken over production of 8-bit computers from West Germany's Braunschweig factory, which began producing PC clones exclusively. The factory would go on to produce 200,000 VIC-20 and C64 computers per month, with a capacity of producing almost double that if required.[3] Approximately one third of the machines would go to the UK market, with the remainder going to Europe, the Middle-East, and Australia.

Just over a year later, it was time to shut it down. On January 9, 1986, Commodore made the announcement. "It was Rattigan who came in and was told to cut, out, cut," says Pleasance, "We went from 535 employees down to 13 overnight. They closed the factory and shut it down."

Pleasance thinks the cut had the potential to undermine one of the most profitable regions of Commodore International. "I certainly wouldn't have axed the most modern purpose-built facility that the company had anywhere," he says. "I wouldn't have done that. I would have gotten rid of some of the lesser ones if that was going to be the way forward."

The loss was especially painful for Commodore UK, which became little more than a marketing office. Ironically, it was because Commodore UK was doing so well that it was chosen for the factory. Now, because the factory was so valuable, it was worth more to sell it.

---

3 *Popular Computing Weekly*, March 29th to April 4th, 1984. "CBM comes to Corby"

The UK's loss was Germany's gain. Commodore moved production of the C64 and C128 computers back to the Braunschweig factory. "It was complete nonsense," says Pleasance. "They had another factory in Braunschweig which was a terribly old thing. They sold most of the equipment, the flow solder machine and all that kind of stuff. They sold most of that in the UK and then just relied on the German operation."

Commodore UK was not the only part of Commodore that was hit. Commodore also owned a chip-making plant in Costa Mesa, California. This was now closed, resulting in another 200 layoffs.[4] It would now be up to Commodore Semiconductor Group (formerly MOS Technology) in Pennsylvania to take up the extra chip production duties.

The Results Are In

By January 1986, Thomas Rattigan had been with Commodore for half a year, learning about the industry and the company as president. He was forced to largely follow the strategy set by Marshal Smith and release products that were well underway by the time he arrived. Now it would be his turn to steer the ship and set a new strategy for 1986. But first, he took a hard look at the sales figures from the recent holiday season.

Commodore had sold a respectable 250,000 C128 computers since that machine's release in mid-1985. The company estimated 20 to 25 percent of C128 purchases came from customers upgrading from a C64.[5]

At the top levels, the new computer was believed to be following in the path of the C64's success. "The C128, from some of the marketing people, was probably perceived as a much more natural success after the C64," says Gerard Bucas. "On the other hand, the C128 wasn't that cheap to produce. It was a lot more expensive to produce it than the C64."

If the C128 could attract developers for the C128 mode, it could prove to have some staying power. In any event, the launch had been a success, with Commodore hitting its sales targets.

The Amiga was a different story. Earlier in 1985, Commodore had publicly stated it hoped to sell 150,000 Amigas by Christmas. However, Sanyo was not able to build them fast enough and Commodore received only

---

4   InfoWorld, January 20, 1986. p. 12. "Commodore to Post a Loss For Last Quarter of 1985"

5   Compute!'s Gazette magazine, "An Interview With Nigel Shepherd" (October 1986), p. 28.

two shipments of 35,000 computers each.[6] When the financial default occurred, Sanyo began to worry about being paid by Commodore and wanted reassurances. "There were problems getting the next batch made so we had a fairly long period where there was no product to sell," recalls Don Reisinger. "And then the word got out: 'Well, Christ, there's no software for the thing.' So those two things caused the next batch to not quite sell as fast as the first batch."

Instead, Commodore announced that it had shipped between 40,000 and 50,000 Amigas in 1985. And it had spent $40,000,000 on marketing and advertising to do it—$800 per machine. Coupled with the low profit margin on the Amiga due to the extremely expensive manufacturing, there is no way that Commodore could have broken even with the release.

Sales continued into 1986, but it would be impossible to recoup the huge expenses. "They basically said we poured $55 million into the Amiga, and sold 75,000 units," recalls Porter. "That's a little bit less than $750 per unit on the Amiga 1000. It's a lot of money. They didn't make it back on the Amiga. They were basically wondering, 'Aw crap, what do we do? How are we going to fix it?'"

In contrast, Porter's cancelled LCD Portable had gained 50,000 to 100,000 preorders with little to no fanfare and no marketing effort. He could only wonder how the computer might have helped Commodore's bottom line over the season.

Meanwhile, Jack Tramiel's Atari had handily beaten the Amiga. The Atari 520ST sold for $999, which included a color monitor and a 3.5" disk drive. At the most recent CES, Atari announced the 1040ST with 1 megabyte of memory and a built-in disk drive for under $1000. It was reminiscent of Tramiel at Commodore, where he constantly destroyed price barriers. As before, his strategy was working. Reports at the time estimate the Atari ST was outselling the Amiga by ten to one. Rattigan needed to reverse this trend.

Marketing director Nigel Shepherd, who had replaced the previous director in January 1986, revealed the Amiga ongoing sales. "On Amigas, we're looking roughly at a run rate of 10,000 to 15,000 a month on a worldwide basis," he told *Compute!'s Gazette*.

---

6   *Los Angeles Times*, September 27, 1985. "Commodore Pins Hopes on Amiga Ad Campaign"

"It was tragic to have the machine do as poorly as it did," says RJ Mical. "In my opinion, it was mostly, but not all, due to the lack of marketing on the machine."

Herd blames the marketing failure on the lack of clear leadership. "When Commodore lost Jack Tramiel, we seemed to lose our ability to make decisions. We got technology like the Amiga and it lay there like a beached whale. That could have been something."

In response to the poor sales, Shepherd began planning Amiga price cuts. It was a painful decision to make for a computer with a low profit margin already.

There was more fallout as well. Jeff Porter and Joe Decuir's AnswerMate relied on the Amiga, as it was not a standalone product. "Commodore was resource bound in many ways," says Decuir. "In my opinion, they didn't have the vision to handle it. It was cancelled."

The engineers hoped to manufacture 100,000 units of the AnswerMate. It was a foregone conclusion that they would only be able to sell a fraction of the total Amiga sales. "It was a US-only product. The market in the US for Amiga stuff was pretty modest compared to the rest of the world," says Porter. "And there were not enough Amigas out there. Let me get back to the root problem: we haven't sold enough Amigas yet. So that project didn't go anywhere either. But that's fine. I kept going to bat."

One spinoff product from the AnswerMate was the A1680 modem for the Amiga. Porter springboarded off his knowledge of the RS232-based AnswerMate and its internal modem. He began designing a standalone 1200-baud modem in October 1985 and released it in August 1986. "I took the modem I built for the C64 and made it a standard RS232 one," he says. "That was a no brainer. I got one check in the box for that, meaning I got a single base run." The A1680 modem would become the last modem marketed by Commodore, due to the fact that the Amiga's RS232 port allowed competing modems from Rockwell and other companies to connect.

As for the financial results, Thomas Rattigan received the preliminary numbers by January 7. Commodore had just had a record quarter, bringing in $339.2 million in revenue, and it looked like it had generated a modest $1.05 million profit. Rattigan, eager for a turnaround, made the mistake of announcing to the world that Commodore had finally returned to profitability.

The preliminary report also detailed where the revenues had come from. Wall Street analysts had labeled Amiga the "save the company machine", but another computer kept Commodore alive. By early 1986, the company had sold between five and six million C64 computers. "The C64, in percentage margin terms, was the most profitable piece of equipment we had in the entire product line," says Rattigan.

Not only was it a highly profitable machine, it also accounted for 65% of Commodore's recent holiday sales. The other 35% was made up of sales of three products: the C128, PC compatibles in Europe, and the Amiga.[7]

The results were a definite slap in the face to Commodore's marketing department and executive teams. They had focused their efforts almost solely on the C128, PC compatibles and especially the Amiga. Almost no thought had been given to the C64, yet it dominated all others by almost double. The results were the inverse of where Commodore had spent its time and resources.

And Commodore could have sold even more if executives had been a bit less conservative with its production. "In retrospect, I wish we had built a lot more going into the season," Rattigan told the *Chicago Tribune*, indicating that backorders were in the six-figure range.

This must have been quite a shock to Rattigan, who had listened to those around him assuring him that the C64 was dead and Amiga would save the company. Rattigan found a new religion in 1986, and his object of worship was the 8-bit computer.

Someone to Blame

With the disappointing Amiga results fully tabulated, someone at Commodore had to take the fall. After VP of engineering Lloyd Taylor departed Commodore with Jack Tramiel, Marshall Smith promoted Adam Chowaniec to fill the position. Chowaniec hired Gerard Bucas to run the business division, while Ed Parks (and for a while, Joe Krasucki) ran the consumer products division. And it had not gone well.

Former marketing manager Kit Spencer blames the background of the executives for the failure. "You had people like Marshal Smith," says Spencer. "Quite frankly, he did not know the business. He was not technical. He was not in consumer electronics."

Spencer believes Gould and Smith also hired the wrong executives. "From the top of the organization, they brought in people who did not appreciate and understand the consumer electronics business," he says. "They just did not know the business they were in. I think they started to imagine

---

7   *Chicago Tribune.* January 07, 1986. " Boss 'Not Unhappy' With Amiga"

the computer business as it had been, whereas actually we had been terribly successful breaking most of the rules of the traditional computer business and establishing a new market."

On the consumer products side, the decision to release the Plus/4 had resulted in an unmitigated disaster. The C128 received a mixed reception; it wasn't exactly what legions of C64 owners wanted for a follow-up.

On the business side, things were a little better. The IBM PC clones released in Europe were doing well. And after many failed attempts, Commodore had finally succeeded at engineering a working Unix machine. Unfortunately, they just didn't have the money to go through with manufacturing it. But overall, Bucas had a good track record to show.

The Amiga, which didn't seem to fit into either the business or consumer product division, was another story. The West Coast Amiga engineers loved Adam Chowaniec. He was the "sweetheart" from Canada who got along with everyone and never said no to the Amiga engineers when they wanted the "gold plated" Amiga computer.

Rattigan, however, saw a different story. Chowaniec was responsible for the decision to manufacture the computer with Sanyo instead of Commodore's Hong Kong plant because he didn't have confidence the quality would be good enough. This cut the profit margin of the machine and made it expensive for consumers.

The low profit margin had resulted in difficulties marketing the Amiga into computer stores, who preferred the higher margins available with PC clones and Macintosh computers. "He had a major fallout with Tom Rattigan, who was the new CEO," says Bucas. "It was, I would say, more of a personality clash and vision differences. They had a major disagreement on the direction and a few other issues."

In late February 1986, Rattigan went to the board of directors and requested the dismissal of Chowaniec. It was approved and Chowaniec was out, forced to return to Canada. Gerard Bucas replaced him as VP of engineering. "When Adam left, I took over control of the whole engineering group, which included obviously the C64 and C128 family and then the Amiga family."

Other executives found themselves in the crossfire too. In March, Rick Geiger, Commodore-Amiga's replacement for Dave Morse, was relieved of his duties after barely a year and a half of employment. Under his watch, there had been delays with the operating system which had resulted in a buggy first version of the Amiga and the expensive Writable Control Store, which limited Amiga profitability.

Selling Out

Thomas Rattigan knew he had a technological advantage over his rival Apple, headed by former Pepsi executive John Scully. "I think it was pretty interesting technology [in the Amiga]," says Rattigan. "You had the same chip that the Mac had in it but you had the capacity for multitasking, which the Mac did not have at that time."

According to former Apple engineer Jean-Louis Gassee, Apple feared the Amiga. "When the Amiga came out, everyone was scared as hell," he says. "No one could figure out how they packed so much power into its off-the-shelf parts." Prior to the financial woes of 1985, it had seemed probable that the Amiga would usurp the Macintosh. Sales of the Macintosh were slow, and like Commodore, Apple was going through massive layoffs.

In the midst of Commodore's financial problems and the failure of the Amiga launch, a desperate Rattigan began to explore other options. "The best thing that could have happened really, in many respects, was if [Commodore] could have put themselves in the hands of a stronger financial entity in the business," he says.

Rattigan wanted to salvage the technology. "There was a real question at that time as to whether or not Commodore could pull itself out of this nosedive," he says. "You had the feeling you were on a Kamikaze plane dodging towards American battleships. So my attitude was, let's explore all of the alternatives."

Rattigan turned to Apple, where his former Pepsi co-worker John Scully was now in charge. He initially approached Commodore's board of directors. "I had told the board very early in my tenure, 'The ideal candidate [to acquire] this company is really Apple. Here's what you've got: number one, they have the school market locked. Like it or not, we've got the mass market locked. We've got the same 68000 chip in the Amiga as the Mac. We've got multitasking and they don't. They're buying a lot of their custom chips on the open market and we're producing our chips, so there's significant cost reductions for them on that side.' At that time, we were doing more international business than Apple was. So I told the board, 'I think we ought to explore doing something with Apple.'"

If Apple acquired Commodore, several of the board members, perhaps including Irving Gould, would simply have to take the money and go away. The idea was not relished. "Prior to my time, RCA had approached Commodore [to acquire the latter]," reveals Rattigan. "I gather there was some difference of opinion as to what the board composition should be and some other personal things like that. If true, I suspect that even if Apple had been amenable, that particular variable might have resurfaced in that equation."

Rattigan knew he would have to convince Irving Gould that his investment in Commodore would not be lost. He told Gould, "You've got six million shares and this may be a way to recoup your position and more importantly ensure the viability of the company, granted in the hands of a competitor." The board of directors allowed Rattigan to proceed with preliminary talks with Apple.

Years before, Jobs and Wozniak had tried to sell their company to Commodore. Now, Gould was trying to sell his company to Apple. "I flew out and met with Scully," says Rattigan.

Rattigan was hoping to discuss the proposal in person with John Scully, but the meeting did not go the way he had expected. "We sat down and John brought all of his staff in for some strange reason," he recalls. It was obvious Scully wanted his team to see the enemy on its knees. Despite this surprise, Rattigan maintained his composure and held back much of his proposal. "We had a general discussion," he says.

After the meeting, Rattigan had a chance to discuss the proposal in depth. "Then [Scully] and I met privately and I said, 'John, here's the things I didn't say in the meeting. We have some trade implications and some competitive implications that would work tremendously to your advantage. Internationally, here's some more.'" Unfortunately, Apple was not interested in an acquisition. "They were just so full of themselves at that point in time," says Rattigan.

Although the proposal failed, it showed a lot about Rattigan. First, he felt no loyalty to the Commodore name. Second, if his plan succeeded, he would be out of a job. "What I cared about was what's in the best interests of the company, what's in the best interests of the people, and what's in the best interests of shareholders," he says. "If that meant I was going to disappear in the equation, I didn't give a rat's ass."

Bankers and Lobster

Thomas Rattigan considered himself a company fixer when he interviewed with Commodore, promising he would fix the financial ailments much as he had fixed PepsiCo's international operations.

In December 1985 he had been promoted to president and chief operating officer of Commodore International, taking over from Marshall Smith. It was now time for Rattigan to live up to his reputation as a company "fixer". Commodore had been in technical default on its bank loans since the 4th quarter of 1985. On January 31, 1986, after cutting back on expenses and stopping the bleeding, Irving Gould renegotiated the terms of the loans. The banks were satisfied that Commodore's spending spree was at an end.

In early February 1986, Rattigan travelled to Europe to renegotiate the terms of Commodore's loan agreements with a consortium of German and UK banks. "The largest lender was Manufacturers Hanover Trust Company," says Rattigan. "Manufacturers Hanover, affectionately known as Manny Hanny in the old days, they were Commodore's lead bank. We had some banks in Australia, we had some banks in Hong Kong. We had some German banks in there."

Rattigan didn't relish coming to the high-pressure meetings. "When we were in trouble, you'd go to a meeting and you'd walk into a room full of bankers who have all flown in on your nickel, all of whom were going to Smith & Wollensky to eat three pound lobsters," he says. "The problem is, once the company gets into financial difficulties, there's a group, usually your lenders basically, who exacerbate the problem in terms of the kind of expense they bring to bear on you. And quite frankly, the management got the company into trouble, you live with the consequences."

Although Commodore was able to pay down its debt, which gave the banks confidence, they still thought the company's spending was out of control. As part of the negotiations, Rattigan and Gould agreed to allow an investment bank to help cut costs even more.

Investment banks help facilitate transactions between investors and companies, and often help out with financial restructuring—another term for layoffs and cutbacks. Gould hired Dillon Read & Co and a senior vice president, Mehdi Ali, to help with the cuts.

Ali devised a restructuring plan with Thomas Rattigan and presented it to the bankers. The plan convinced the bankers that they could safely continue loaning money to Commodore. As *Byte* magazine commented, "Commodore, in the meantime, seems to keep dodging the bullet that everyone thought would have been fatal by now. The bankers are apparently convinced that a live but ailing Commodore stands a better chance of paying off its debts than a dead one and that sales of the C64, C128, and Amiga are sufficient to keep Commodore alive for now. Smart folks, those bankers."[8]

---

8 *Byte* magazine. June, 1986. p. 348. "According to Webster"

As a result of the talks, Commodore was granted an additional $135 million line of credit. This came at a cost, however. The hatchet man, Mehdi Ali, would be there at Commodore, sitting in on meetings and working with executives to chop away the excess fat from the company for the rest of the year.

Following the successful renegotiations, Commodore's stock rose to 8 $\frac{1}{8}$, from a low of 4 $\frac{1}{2}$ months earlier. Gould promoted Rattigan to president and CEO of Commodore International. "There was a board meeting in February 1986 in the Bahamas," recalls Rattigan. "It was decided that I move up and take all of it, and Marshall would be leaving."

The board gave Rattigan a five-year contract, which would commence on April 1, 1986 and expire on July 1, 1991. It was clear Rattigan represented the future of Commodore—provided his promotion wasn't an elaborate April Fool's Day joke.

During the Marshall Smith era, despite the best efforts of everyone, Commodore stubbornly refused to become profitable. "You had to get the right people around you and you had to get them on board," says Rattigan. "Then you had to get people enthusiastic about how we can turn this company around."

One of the first decisions Rattigan made to focus the company on profitability and raise morale was to share the profits with the employees. "After we started getting on the road, one of the things we came up with was the idea that, rather than giving people raises, which they hadn't had for quite a while, I said, 'Let's reward them on the basis of what the stock price does,'" he explains. "The stock was trading at about five bucks per share at the time. We put a big board up in the cafeteria and said for every point the stock goes up, we're going to give a one percent bonus up to a 10% level. It will be a cash bonus payout."

The profit sharing even extended up to the executives. "Eventually, I have to give him credit, the company was recovering and was doing a bit better, and Tom Rattigan came up with a senior management bonus," recalls Bucas.

In the Tramiel days, Commodore lost engineers like Robert Yannes because they felt excluded from the success they helped create. Rattigan hoped another side effect of the profit sharing plan would be to retain the employees who had been bailing out on the company. Now, employees were full partners in the company's success.

Although Jack Tramiel had left Commodore in a powerful position, it had taken Marshall Smith scarcely a year to bring Commodore to near ruin, and another year to pull out of a nose-dive. "Marshall was gone shortly thereafter, and breathing a heavy sigh of relief in my opinion," says Rattigan. "Marshall was working his butt off, working very, very hard with what he had in terms of the people. In certain respects, I think that may have tempered the contribution he could have made."

The man who should have said no to Irving Gould when he was offered the job and who instead said yes, and nearly brought the company to its knees, was surprisingly well liked by Commodore employees. But then again, it's hard to dislike Santa Claus, and Smith was a very giving man when it came to Commodore's money.

When Rattigan became CEO, he stepped down as General Manager of Commodore North America. "I had moved out of the North American operation and had, over time, met most of the other senior people in the organization," says Rattigan. "I asked Nigel [Shepherd] to come in from Australia to take over the North American operation."

Shepherd impressed Rattigan with his aggressive style. "Nigel made it happen," says Rattigan. "He was the type of guy that, when you asked him to go through a wall, he would just ask you how thick it was so he could decide how fast he was going to run."

While Rattigan received praise for his cost cutting measures, others had doubts, such as David Pleasance of Commodore UK. "Rattigan had been told you've got to get profitable, so the only way you can do that is to cut costs," explains Pleasance. "He just slashed, slashed, slashed everywhere and then he got congratulated because within a year we showed a $25 million profit because he just slashed all the costs. But the long-term conse-quences weren't even considered."

For the time being, Commodore was stable again. When *Commodore Magazine* asked Rattigan how close the company came to bankruptcy, he replied, "I guess that depends on your perspective. Close is a funny word. If you're running along the edge of a cliff and it's a thousand feet down, I guess you could find that close. I don't consider it close until you start falling off the edge. We didn't fall off the edge. We may have gotten close, but we didn't fall."[9]

On a sour note, the same month Gould promoted Rattigan, Commodore released the official quarterly report. Embarrassingly, Rattigan was forced to retract the previous good news and announce a loss of $53.2 million for

---

9   *Commodore Magazine*, "What Next for Commodore?" (May 1987), p. 126.

the previous quarter, owing to a $22 million writedown on the sale of a factory and another $29 million inventory writedown for the Plus/4 hardware and software that went to Pacific Tri-Micro in 1985. On the upside, he had been able to pay down some of Commodore's debt to the banks, from $192 million to $140.2 million.[10]

Needless to say, Irving Gould was not amused by the revelation. Not only was it humiliating to have to backtrack previous comments, but Gould had awarded Rattigan a five year contract on the basis that he had helped return Commodore to profitability. It was a poor start to the CEO's relationship with Gould, one in which trust could become an issue.

10 *Chicago Tribune*. "Now Commodore's Dodging A Bullet" February 23, 1986.

CHAPTER 25

Saving the Amiga 1986

After the Amiga launch in 1985, there was a panic over the resulting lack-luster sales. The Amiga may not have been Gerard Bucas' first love (that was Unix) but as the new VP of engineering he knew something had to be done to rescue Amiga sales. "Commodore spent a tremendous amount of money on acquiring Amiga, developing the Amiga technology, getting the A1000 into production and then it didn't sell too well," he says. "It was probably marketed okay, but bottom line, price-wise, it was a little too expensive."

Most analysts identified the lack of business software, and on a related note, the lack of IBM PC compatibility, as the root cause of the problem. Engineers and executives alike recognized they would need sequels to the Amiga, using the same technology in a different package. While the West Coast Amiga veterans felt the computer should go upmarket, adding features and cost, the rest of Commodore was not so sure.

Bucas needed to find a way to get the Amiga into mass-market retail stores and those stores would not carry a computer selling for over $1000. It would require a different way of thinking to come up with the next generation of Amiga computers.

Carl and RJ Depart

The Amiga software engineers completed the bug fixes for AmigaOS version 1.1 by the end of December 1985. Several programmers who had been working since 1983 felt their work was done. "I was one of the first of the group to leave because I had finished exec and I was ready to do the next thing," says Carl Sassenrath. He was prepared to advance AmigaOS further but felt his ideas met with too much resistance. "They weren't really too open to what to do next. I said, 'Well I've got some other designs in my head that I want to pursue and I'm going to go leave and go do those." Sassenrath resigned in January 1986.

Intuition developer RJ Mical also felt it was time to leave. "I wanted to be free," he sings. "I had worked on the Amiga for about four years and there was an opportunity for me to go off and be a contractor, working not only on Amiga stuff but go on with my career and start working on the next thing. It was just the right time in my career to mosey on."

Amidst Commodore's cutbacks, Mical voluntarily departed. "I left as an employee in January 1986," he says. Although he would leave Commodore, he was not abandoning the Amiga. In order to address the lack of software for the new machine, Mical would make a heroic effort to develop Amiga software and even hardware over the next few years.

The Janus Project

As the Sidecar project progressed, Irving Gould realized he needed a software expert and he began asking key Amiga personnel for help. Unfortunately, even the US software engineers were unenthusiastic towards the PC emulator. Sassenrath recalls, "Irving called me and said, 'Hey, I really, really want you to do the Sidecar thing. Can you go over to Germany for six months and head up the project?' I said no, so RJ ended up going over and he was one of the main people on that project."

Mical soon became a consultant for Commodore Germany, where the secretive A2500 was taking shape. There was still one final but necessary software component. Sidecar (and Bridgeboard) required a special application to surface MS-DOS programs within AmigaOS. The engineers dubbed the software Janus, named after the two-faced Roman god who looked both forwards and backwards.

By February 13, 1986, Mical travelled to Braunschweig to help the Germans complete the Janus software. There, he got his first look at the A2500. "The A2000 was a good idea in all respects except it turned our sweet little delicate hi-tech box into this big industrial strength metal clad tank of a computer," he says. "It was contrary to what we wanted in terms of the cool sex appeal of the original Amiga."

The Germans expected Mical's portion of Janus would integrate with Intuition, allowing MS-DOS applications to run within an Amiga window. Mical was a fan of *Hitchhiker's Guide to the Galaxy* and he named his effort the Zaphod Project, after the galactic president with two heads.

He held meetings with the German engineers for the first week to determine the architecture for the Zaphod Project. "Shortly after I stopped working there I became a contractor," Mical says. "We dealt with the engineering people from the company; Henri Rubin and guys like that on downward."

He began coding in earnest on February 20, an endeavor that would take over two months to complete. Mical got along well with the bowtie wearing Rubin. "I liked him," he says. "He was very interesting to work with."

Rubin was a passionate supporter of the Amiga but he had a theory that it must support PC compatibility. A former Commodore dealer himself, he had heard from his own customers in South Africa that businesses wanted to purchase Amiga computers, but the companies would not allow them to purchase any computer that could not run the popular applications of the day, such as WordPerfect or Lotus Notes. Rubin believed if they could add PC compatibility, it would break through this barrier to entry because employees could claim it actually did run IBM PC software. This would allow the Amiga to enter the workplace like a Trojan Horse.

During this time, Mical began to enjoy significant influence over the Amiga through Rubin and even Irving Gould himself. "[Irving] had put a lot of trust and a lot of faith in Henri Rubin and Henri and I struck up a good relationship," explains Mical. "That led to me spending a lot of time with Irving through Henri. For a while there, I became one of the guys he was asking a lot of advice about. Those were some fun days."

Irving Gould never particularly hit it off with any of the East Coast engineers, whose remaining ranks were largely part of the C128 Animals. However, some of his employees, including RJ Mical, were a little more worldly and cultured. Mical had an artist's sensibility with the logic of a programmer. Gould, a collector of antique netsuke (small ornate sculptures from Japan) enjoyed talking with the passionate, engaging engineer.

Mical found his influence increase with time. "Very early on, after a lot of the original guys' relationships were falling apart with Commodore, there were a magical couple of months where I had the ear of the powers that be at Commodore," says Mical. "I had them convinced that it would be a good thing to spend the money to go back and hire Carl Sassenrath, the OS guy, to come in and redo the file system."

It was a lofty proposition but Irving Gould listened. "Commodore saw the wisdom in it and they were willing to at least fund the research into it," recalls Mical.

Sassenrath found Commodore wasn't done with him yet. "About a month after I left, I got a call from the chairman of the board of Commodore, Irving Gould," recalls Sassenrath. "He woke me up at 7:30 or 8:00 in the morning and he was like, 'This is Irving Gould.' I was like, 'What?' He was like, 'Carl, we want you to come back and fix this file system that we got from Tripos.' And I was like, 'Well it's already out there.'"

Sassenrath, who had once campaigned to develop the file system inhouse, felt it was too late. "I had to explain to him all these floppy disks that are out there have that format already on them," he says. "It's going to be very difficult to change it now because everyone's floppy is going to be that way. I ended up refusing him and told him no."

Gould persisted, perhaps believing Sassenrath could find a way. "He really tried to twist my arm, lots of different ways financially," says Sassenrath. "He did interesting things. He was like, 'You tell me your bank account and I'll deposit any reasonable amount of money in it.' I was like, 'Oh really. Who am I dealing with here?'"

Sassenrath held steady. "I just told him no. But I was stupid," he says. "I was idealistic and stupid because it was still the early days of the Amiga. At that point, maybe only a hundred thousand units or maybe even less had shipped. These days now, I realize I could have done a lot to fix it to make it work better—to find ways to maybe even have some kind of compatibility mode where it would detect certain files were written one way or other files written a newer and better way. But that's history. I feel bad that I didn't take him up on it."

RJ Mical felt disappointment when he heard back from Gould and tried his best to influence his friend. "I couldn't talk Carl into it," he says. "Carl was so disheartened with the entire Commodore experience and the way the whole thing had gone. He declined that opportunity. It was really a shame because it might have made a big difference in the final success of the Amiga."

TripOS remained an integral part of the Amiga operating system. "That was one of the things that sorely crippled the Amiga until the very end because they kept using that old file format," says Mical.

Sassenrath eventually joined Apple's Advanced Technology Group, working under Jean-Louis Gassée. There he would work on a next generation operating system for the Aquarius project, an early Quad-core RISC processor.

Mical completed the Zaphod Project on April 25, 1986. He immediately returned home to his sorely missed family in California, where he would continue to seek out contracting jobs with other Amiga software developers. "It turned out that I ended up spending a year and a half working on Amiga stuff as an independent contractor rather than an employee of Commodore," he says. "I did a bunch of different stuff that all kind of blurs together."

Bil Herd Moves On

The Amiga programmers were not the only employees within Commodore who were becoming restless. In the space of a few years, Bil Herd had worked his way up to becoming the engineer at the center of two out of three of Commodore's latest major product releases. But it had also taken a personal toll on him. "All this activity that was going on at Commodore and all the craziness you hear about, what you are hearing about is a young alcoholic in his prime when things are still working out," he explains. "It was obviously getting worse for those around me. What had been, 'Oh, he's a crazy man,' went to, 'He doesn't stop. He still isn't stopping.'"

Herd also wondered about his place at Commodore now that the company had released the Amiga. To make matters worse, Herd's protector was gone. "Adam [Chowaniec] had left, who was kind of my guardian angel at that point," he says. "I'm really pissing some people off about this time in my career."

To pass the time, the young engineer indulged his need for play. "My favorite game was *Kennedy Approach*, an air traffic controller game," he says. "It was good enough that I would come out of my office with sweaty palms and a slight shake. Later I would have dreams in which I could hear the screams of the people going down in the mountains outside of Denver due to my not being able to get them vectored for approach fast enough."

However, biding his time waiting for a new project did not last for long. "My ego wouldn't let me stay doing nothing and they didn't have a project for me to do."

By February 1986, Herd was already looking for a new job. "I was so damn hungry to keep doing what I was doing that I actually quit and took a job as the director of engineering for a startup doing image recognition," he says, referring to a short-lived local company called CBit. "There were a lot of Commodore people interviewed there. We all felt like the ship was rocking a little bit. They did a great job of appealing to a young man's ego."

Within months, Herd began to feel remorse for leaving Commodore. "I was hopped up on being a Commodore engineer. Why else would you sleep 11 days in your office?" he says. "It really was a great place to work."

Despite his lack of formal education, Herd made an indelible contribution to the company. "He did an exceptional job," says Dave Haynie. "To this day, if you are trying to fix something in hardware, Bil is the guy you want there in the lab with you. I've never seen anybody as good at diagnosing little weird problems as Bil and he learned it on the streets."

Like most former Commodore employees, Herd cherishes his memories with the company. "As my memory fades, I remember the good and forget the bad. Did I mention that Commodore was a fun place to work?"

Amiga-CR Study

With Bil Herd departed, a changing of the guard was occurring at West Chester. By early 1986, Jeff Porter had proven himself on several projects, including three modems that made it to production, the LCD portable, and the upcoming PAL Amiga. He was the type of engineer management liked; someone who ferociously attacked a project and finished it, while remaining professional.

Now he would have a chance to brainstorm a new 16-bit computer. "That was the thrill for me," he says. "As a kid, to be able to make these decisions without having a central marketing department or focus group or all the crap you have going on today. You could just do what you think best. In those days, I would build the computer I would want for myself."

His opportunity arrived when his newly installed boss, Gerard Bucas, began looking at ways to cost reduce the Amiga. Originally he spoke with the Los Gatos Amiga engineers. The Amiga they had just released had a very slim profit margin for both Commodore and retailers, and did little to help Commodore's bottom line. Glenn Keller, designer of the Portia and Paula chips, began working on an Amiga-CR shortly after the release of the Amiga in late 1985.

Keller stuck very close to the original Amiga design and was not able to significantly reduce the cost. At this point, Bucas went to his own team in West Chester. As the only West Chester engineer working on Amiga technology, Porter alone had a unique insight into the Amiga that others did not. "Since I got a full tour of duty making a PAL A1000, I kind of realized how much everything cost," he explains. "Damn, all this is really expensive."

Meanwhile, the Atari ST was dominating the Amiga in sales. "The Atari ST was out there and it was more like what the Amiga 500 was going to look like. It was just kicking some serious Amiga butt because it was so much less expensive," says Porter.

Bucas had his team study the competition first to see what Commodore could do better. "Gerard Bucas told Bob Russell, Jeff Porter, George Robbins and me to look at the Atari ST, which we were also worried about because it beat the Amiga out briefly," says Bob Welland. "The problem for the Amiga 1000[1] was it was very expensive to build. It was complicated and so it didn't fit into the Commodore manufacturing mechanism at all, which is: you have a single motherboard and a really simple case and maybe an integrated keyboard and things like that. What Gerard wanted was as inexpensive an Amiga as could be made."

The idea for a cost reduced Amiga, or Amiga CR, happened over the first few months of 1986 while Adam Chowaniec's career was hanging by a thread. "Adam Chowaniec and Gerard Bucas were the VP and assistant VP of engineering at the time I was pitching the A500 concept," says Porter.

Bob Russell, who had initially scoped out the Amiga technology for Irving Gould, felt Commodore should have gone after the cost-reduced market from the start. "The Amiga 1000 came out rather than the Amiga 500, which is what I was fighting for," he says.

When Russell first visited the Amiga team and returned to Commodore, he wanted Commodore to use its new acquisition for the low-cost market. "I was thinking Amiga 500 level immediately could come out of it," he recalls. "It took them a while to move from the A1000 to the A500 but technically there was no reason to take that much time."

Even several members at Commodore-Amiga on the West Coast felt a low-end Amiga was required. "The C64 is primarily a game machine; you hook it up to your TV. The Amiga could be made such that it was getting close to the price but having much better capabilities," says Dale Luck "They needed to do cost reductions to get it down into that area."

After the C900's cancellation, both George Robbins and Bob Welland were scrambling to remain relevant to Commodore. "Bob and George had a problem in that they didn't have a reason to continue existing, so they decided to jump into the Amiga," says Dave Haynie.

The engineers had access to an Amiga 1000, an IBM PCjr, and an Atari ST for close inspection. "Bob Russell, George Robbins, Jeff Porter, and I took apart an Atari 520ST to see how it was made and how much it was likely to cost Atari to manufacture," says Welland. "There was a lot to like

---

1 In January 1986, Commodore renamed the original Amiga computer the Amiga 1000 to differentiate it from other models that followed.

about the design and we drew on that machine for inspiration later when we proposed the design of the A500."

The simplicity of the Atari ST was familiar to the Commodore engineers. "We took the A1000 apart and we counted the number of screws it had. I think it had like forty two screws or something," recalls Welland. "And we took the 520ST apart and, because it's a Jack Tramiel machine, it was very Commodore-esque. It was very simple. It probably had nine screws in it and so we kind of viewed that as our goal: can we take the Amiga and make it like the 520ST."

There was little to learn from the IBM PCjr. "We got a PCjr and took it apart," recalls Welland. "What you're trying to do is see what decisions people are making and what are the good ideas and what are the bad ideas."

Unfortunately Porter would be tied up with the PAL Amiga until the end of April and unable to dedicate a full time effort to the Amiga-CR. In the meantime, Adam Chowaniec departed and Gerard Bucas took over, causing the momentum of the Amiga-CR project to slow down while the transition took place.

On February 26, Porter discovered that a popular coworker, Yash Terakura, was also trying to launch an Amiga-CR project. Terakura had been integral to the development of the VIC-20, Max Machine, and PET 8032. He was also one of a handful of Commodore employees who enjoyed the favor of Irving Gould (along with Bob Russell, Clive Smith, and Don Gilbreath) allowing him the freedom to pick and choose his own projects.

Porter became concerned that "Uncle Irv" was not aware of his current Amiga efforts and that the official West Chester engineering team could be overlooked on the Amiga-CR project. Not having the time himself, he immediately proposed to George Robbins that they should get ahead of Terakura by assembling a prototype and an in-depth cost analysis for an "Amiga in a C128 case".

Although the engineers respected the technology in the Amiga, they quickly found areas for improvement. "When we looked at that machine we thought why is this so complicated?" says Welland. "We spent almost zero time thinking about whether getting rid of the writable control store was a good idea or not. It was that simple. Like this shouldn't be here."

The writable control store was the last minute kludge added to the Amiga when it became clear the operating system software was not going to be ready. But in order to replace it with ROM chips, the engineers would need something from the Los Gatos engineers to proceed. "So what taking it out required of the software team was that they give us a version of the operating system that was going to be burned into ROM," explains Welland. "It meant that it had to be sufficiently stable because you couldn't upgrade it. And that's risky but that saves so much money and it simplified the machine so much that it it was the right thing to do."

More importantly, it would save money on the final cost of production, not only because they didn't have to produce an extra PCB, but because it would not need expensive DRAM. "The DRAM was a significant part of the cost of the machine and the writable control store was just more DRAM," says Welland. "When you're trying to cost reduce something, it's hard not to look at an $8 ROM versus something that was probably at least $60 or $70—I don't know what the number was, but it was a big number— and think all I have to do is make the software guys do the right thing."

The team identified other areas for cost reduction by using a combined keyboard-case, using cheaper parts—such as a low-cost disk drive and keyboard, using an external power supply and removing the television output circuitry via the composite connector.

With the study done, Robbins and Welland would now begin to look at how a new, cheaper Amiga could be assembled.

German Amiga Revealed

While the Amiga-CR project gained momentum, Commodore Germany continued developing the Amiga 2500 in secret. Their main goal was to create an expandable Amiga computer with IBM PC compatibility, including PC ISA expansion slots.

The secret was not well guarded, however. Commodore's QA group in West Chester helped the German engineering team with the Sidecar project for the Amiga 1000. In December 1985, a member of the German design team had let slip that they were also working on an IBM PC emulator card for the Amiga. Because the A1000 did not have slots for expansion cards, it was clear they must be talking about a different kind of Amiga. The QA team, in turn, informed Gerard Bucas of the project. For his part, Bucas played along and dutifully ignored it, hoping it would die on the vine.

The top executive authorizing the project was of course Irving Gould, who did not have the time nor the expertise to directly monitor the project. Instead, to keep the project secret from the rest of Commodore, he sent a personal friend named Henri Rubin to Germany to oversee the project on his behalf.

In April 1986, as soon as RJ Mical had the Janus software functioning, it was time to let the rest of Commodore know about the A2500 project.

Irving Gould gathered together the top people from Commodore International at his offices in the Seagram Building. "I was summoned to Irving Gould's office in New York," recalls Bucas. "There were people from Commodore Germany engineering, Commodore Germany in general and myself and Tom Rattigan and one or two other people."

Bucas immediately recognized a power-play when he saw one. Winfried Hoffmann was clearly hoping to gain a more prominent role for his Braunschweig team. "They literally just showed a prototype of a hacked up A2000 with this hacked up bridge card and all that," recalls Bucas. "This is where they unveiled the supposedly secret project. I was supposed to be surprised. Of course, I had heard all the rumors and they tried to keep me uninvolved in that. It was sort of interesting."

Gould made it clear that West Chester was now responsible for helping the Germans finish the Amiga 2500, the Bridgeboard, and the Sidecar. Bucas recalls, "He basically said, 'Guys, here is the result. If you don't like it, lump it.' We were still responsible for putting it into production so bottom line is, we had to back it up more or less."

To Bucas, it seemed like Gould was rebuking he and Rattigan for not coming up with the new system on their own. As for the A2500 itself, Bucas grudgingly admired the design. "It wasn't a bad idea. It was okay," he says.

Gould wanted the A2500 shown privately at the upcoming Spring COMDEX and ordered his generals to make sure they supported the project fully. He wanted the new system, along with a hard disk controller card, ready for production by May 16, 1986 (one month away). Bucas had no choice but to obey Gould's directives and quickly bring his own team on board the A2500 project.

For his part, Rattigan reminded Gould that the Los Gatos Amiga engineers were already working on an Amiga successor of their own called Ranger. Gould then told Rattigan to proceed as directed, with all resources going towards releasing the A2500.

COMDEX

The Amiga had only been available since before Christmas, but within months, the news media criticized the new computer for its small software library. One user publicly complained, "I laid out a lot of money for my Amiga and all I wound up with was an expensive doorstop."[2]

---

2 *Amiga World*. Sept/Oct 1986. p. 70 "The Amiga Shows Up"

Thomas Rattigan acutely felt the criticisms. "While there was a lot of enthusiasm, I think there was also a realization that we didn't have much software on the machine, and that was going to be a tough sell," he says. "[Programmers] don't like to write until you've got an installed base. They're interested in making money."

In response, Rattigan planned to turn the next COMDEX show into a software extravaganza for the Amiga. Commodore had missed the show in November 1985 due to financial difficulties and now the company wanted to make a big splash upon its return.

A month prior to the show, Nigel Shepherd, Commodore's GM of North America, authorized a $500 discount on the $1295 Amiga when purchased with a $495 Amiga 1080 monitor, essentially throwing in a free monitor.[3] This would spur on sales and give Commodore something to brag about when COMDEX rolled around.

The Spring COMDEX, April 28 to May 1, 1986, was held at the Georgia World Congress Center in Atlanta, Georgia. According to *Byte* magazine, "The Atari and Amiga booths were the center of most of the excitement. The Amiga Sidecar was particularly interesting. Scheduled for release this fall, this IBM PC hardware emulator allows you to run MS-DOS as an Intuition task."[4]

This was also the first time Commodore marketed the video capabilities of the machine with a unique device developed by the engineers in California. Bob Ryan of *Amiga World* said, "I had my first glimpse of the Amiga Genlock—the device that lets you overlay graphics images on pictures from a video source. You can display the result on your monitor and even save it to videotape." Other companies also displayed "frame grabbers", devices that captured digital images.

The Sidecar also generated interest from the press. Amiga World predicted, "The Amiga Sidecar is expected to hit your dealer's shelves in December. Although this is over a year since Commodore promised a viable MS-DOS option for the Amiga, the Sidecar may be worth the wait. If it satisfies both the needs of people who want to run MS-DOS and those who want to expand their Amiga, it will quickly become the most popular peripheral for the Amiga." However, it was noted that Commodore would

---

3   Chicago Tribune, March 26, 1986. "Commodore Amiga Price Cut"

4   Byte magazine. July, 1986. p. 271.

have to price the Sidecar significantly less than the rumored price of $600 in order to compete with $600 IBM PC clones.

Amiga Software Developers

Commodore made a special effort to promote numerous software titles now available for the Amiga by allowing other companies, such as EA and Activision, to display Amiga products right in its COMDEX booth, as Atari had done the prior year. *Amiga World* reported, "Looking like an off-shore drilling platform, the Commodore booth was 2,400 square feet of excitement and innovation. Dozens of developers were displaying their wares for the Amiga, putting to rest the notion that the Amiga is a machine without software and hardware support. The enthusiasm developers displayed for the machine was infectious, and the Commodore booth quickly became 'THE place to be' at COMDEX."[5]

Although EA had made a good first attempt at creativity applications with Deluxe Paint, it would take time to see what users really wanted. "The Amiga had so many capabilities and so much potential to do audio, graphics control, visual arts and all these different things that it was hard to decide what really needs to be concentrated on and where did the programs need to be written to really make it come out," says Dale Luck.

Multitasking was equally baffling to users. "It was even harder to explain to people why you would want it to do multiple things at the same time," recalls Carl Sassenrath. "Multitasking was a really difficult sell to people back in the eighties. And then for me it was so fun to watch it become a word within everyone's vocabulary, that they were multitasking. Now people say, 'I'm multitasking', and know what that means but you didn't know in 1985 when I was talking about it and trying to convince the world."

Sadly, Microsoft continued ignoring the Amiga, contrary to earlier statements that it was committed to the platform. "Microsoft was pretty busy with the PC at the time," says Luck. "They saw the PC having millions and millions out there and the Amiga was the new kid on the block. They had already started investing in Mac development. This would have been a third platform that they would have had to devote even more resources to. I think they just decided to do the top two in the market, which was the PC and the Mac."

When Amiga released a bug-fixed version of AmigaOS 1.1 in early 1986, software vendors who had been holding back waiting for a stable platform finally released several titles. The new software, along with the earlier $500 discount, led to sales of the Amiga 1000 doubling compared to previous months.[6] The Amiga was finally starting to catch on.

---

6 *InfoWorld*. May 26, 1986. p. 5. "Amid Losses, Commodore Plans Amiga 2000"

Amiga Invades Europe 1986

Throughout the recovery of Commodore International, the European region continued to be a stronghold for the company. The Amiga would soon be launched there by the business divisions, now facing off against MS-DOS based computers, which Commodore itself even sold. These business divisions would face a similarly difficult road encountered by the US Amiga launch.

Jeff Porter recalls, "In the process of making the A1000 in PAL, people asked, 'How will we sell more Amigas? This is going down in flames. This is not going well.' OK, we'll manage to sell more because we have a PAL version, but at $1200 it's too expensive for a home computer compared to a Commodore 64 at $200." Could Europe make the Amiga 1000 a success?

Pre-Launch Politics

Due to the differences in television standards, the Amiga launch came later in Europe than in North America. It was an excruciating wait for the business divisions who had been starved of a legitimate PET replacement for years.

Jeff Porter had largely completed the PAL Amiga by the end of December 1985. Unlike the 256K NTSC version, the PAL resolutions required over 25% more memory than their NTSC cousins, requiring Commodore to include 512K by default.

The PAL version also included a new video mode called Extra Half-Brite (EHB). This new mode could display 64 colors simultaneously without the restrictions of HAM mode.

Porter had created a universal motherboard for the A1000 that could be used in both NTSC and PAL regions. Only the Agnus chip differed, along with the included AmigaOS software on disk (the ROM was the same). Before he could release the computer, his system had to pass testing for both FCC and VDE (Verband der Elektrotechnik, or Association of Electrical Engineering).

According to his original schedule, Porter hoped to begin building the first 5,000 units on February 3, ship them on February 17, and then launch the product on March 3, 1986. Harald Speyer took this schedule literally and devised a launch schedule with perfect timing. He decided to hold a special launch event on March 5, one week before CeBIT began. This would generate press coverage, putting the Amiga on everyone's lips, and then when CeBIT began, the Amiga would be the focus of the show. It was a brilliant strategy.

When Jeff Porter found out about the firm launch date, he began to feel the pressure. After all, an American schedule is at best a guess, not a guarantee. In the field of engineering especially, production schedules have been known to slip. But he plowed ahead and hoped for the best.

Unfortunately, FCC testing revealed serious problems with Commodore Japan's layout of the motherboard and it had to go back for a revised layout, which added another month to the schedule, plus another month for retesting. In the meantime, Porter travelled to Europe on January 12 for VDE testing.

Gerard Bucas considered it too risky to rush forward to meet the launch date. Speyer, however, felt it important to sell Amigas in the Q3 financial period ending March 31 and insisted on the March launch date. With no choice, Bucas opted to manufacture and send NTSC Amiga units to Europe, equipping them with 50Hz 220/240V power supplies and optional NTSC monitors.

The decision did not sit well with the engineers in West Chester for several reasons. First, the PAL version of Agnus supported 320 x 256 lines, meaning all PAL software would likely support that resolution. By releasing NTSC units into Europe with only 320 x 200 resolutions, the software would probably not display properly.

The other problem was that the Genlock and Framegrabber devices would not work properly with the PAL market, which would expect PAL output, not NTSC.

Andy Finkel in particular felt dissatisfied with the plan but could make no headway reversing the executive decision. In response, Jeff Porter proposed including the new Agnus 256-line chip in the NTSC units, which would at least make the software compatible with the PAL units that would follow.

Finkel and his team would then create a special version of AmigaOS dubbed 1.1P (for PAL). The initial units would only display 320 by 200, but then in April when the actual European software was available, users could upgrade their existing Amiga to allow Intuition and other software to display the full 256 lines.

By February 20, it was clear the NTSC units would include the new Agnus chips. Jeff Porter attempted to convince Harald Speyer to offer an upgrade kit with new German keyboard and software in April, but Speyer would not agree. Porter had better luck convincing Commodore UK to delay the launch.

European Launch

In early March, Commodore International held a launch event in Basel, Switzerland. Over 350 people attended the posh dinner and dance—mostly dealers, software developers, and journalists. This was accompanied by a one hour presentation in which the Amiga rose up out of a cloud of smoke, accompanied by Amiga multitrack music, surrounded by five dancing girls in shiny white skin tight leotards.

After the dazzling opening, the technical presentation began, featuring a graphic artist and a musician using the Amiga. By all accounts, audience reaction was excellent.

On a rainy day on March 5, 1986, Jeff Porter travelled to the big launch in Frankfurt, Germany in order to provide technical assistance for the show. "I was a young kid making a trip around the world, and I thought, this is great! It was introduced in Frankfurt in the Alte Oper concert hall."

The lavish black tie party was so similar to the original launch in New York that it was almost plagiarized. "We tried to copy the marvelous show at Lincoln Center, NYC, of July 1985, in our Old Opera in Frankfurt," says Dr. Peter Kittel, a Commodore Germany employee who worked at the show. "But we did not really do it as nicely."[1]

The man responsible for Commodore Braunschweig's recent success with PC's led the introduction. "Winfried Hoffmann, head of Commodore Germany, got up there to do his little speech in German about how wonderful it is," says Porter. For around 15 minutes, Hoffmann gave a surprisingly candid talk in which he addressed Commodore's recent financial problems, before segueing to the Amiga. Most of the Amiga introduction was based

---

1 *Amiga Report Magazine*, Volume 3, Issue 10. May 17, 1995.

on the talk given by Bob Pariseau at the US Amiga launch, although Hoffman delved deeper into Commodore's marketing strategy.

The host for the evening was German radio and television personality Frank Elstner, who hosted the popular television show *Wetten, dass..?* ("Wanna bet..?"). Elstner worked with Commodore Germany's team of Dr. Peter Kittel, Walter Schmitz, and Peter Schneider to show off the graphics, sounds, and multitasking capabilities of the Amiga. The demos were, for the most part, the same as those used at the Lincoln Center launch in New York. In place of Andy Warhol, a graphics artist used a "frame grabber" to capture an image of a Campbell's soup can and duplicate it, similar to the classic Warhol painting.

For a change of pace, the "human computer" Erich Zenker, 57 at the time, showed off his incredible memory by learning the names of 30 random audience members and reciting them one by one.

The Amiga's MIDI capabilities were also demonstrated via a live one-woman concert with a musical keyboard connected to the Amiga.

The show concluded with Dr. Kittel demonstrating the Amiga's speech by having a humorous conversation with the host. Along with classical midi music, a ballerina animation was displayed along with an actual professional ballerina on-stage. Afterwards, the assembled crowd viewed personal demonstrations in the foyer of the historic Alte Oper.

CeBIT 1986

A week after the German Amiga launch event, Irving Gould's favorite trade show—the one he attended every year—began. "It's called CeBIT and that's the biggest computer show in Europe. Commodore was a major exhibitor there," says Gerard Bucas. "It had one of the bigger booths there in all the years."

Since 1970, the computer portion of the Hanover Fair was held in a subdivision of the show called CeBIT. Every computer maker from IBM to Apple attended the show. However, in 1986, CeBIT became so large that organizers decided to branch it off from the main show.

The head of Commodore Germany organized Commodore's entry at the show. "Hanover CeBIT ... was all organized by Harold Speyer obviously," says Bucas. "He was the boss of Germany, the MD—Managing Director. There was a pretty strong and close relationship between him and myself in organizing and orchestrating that show every year."

It was apparent to the engineers that Commodore Germany was the crown jewel of Commodore's empire. "They had very good advertising in Germany because Germany was always one of the best regarded places for Commodore," says Dave Haynie. "You could walk through an airport and see Commodore ads. The first time I went over there I was like, 'This is unbelievable.'"

Once at CeBIT, the Commodore booth itself especially impressed Haynie. "That was a big show for Commodore," he recalls. "They had a huge two-story booth with a bar upstairs. It was a bigger scale than anything ever done in the United States."

Commodore Germany used the reimagined CeBIT to take orders for the Amiga from its European customers. From March 12 to 19, Commodore gave demonstrations of the NTSC Amiga and the Sidecar running MS-DOS software. In the following weeks, Commodore would deliver shipments of NTSC units to sell to the German market.

Commodore UK Amiga Launch

After Thomas Rattigan closed down the Corby facility, Commodore UK moved to a new address in a small but affluent town a half-hour east of London's Heathrow Airport. "When they closed Corby down they moved to Maidenhead, which is a little bit more upmarket and a good address within commuting distance of London but not London prices," says David Pleasance. "It was a respectable place to be."

The move was still demoralizing for the UK staff, who now moved into the second floor of a three-story downtown building called Babbage House. From the new premises, Commodore UK would plan the launch of the Amiga. Unlike Germany, UK GM Nick Bessey decided to wait for the PAL version of the Amiga before launching. This pushed back the UK launch to May 1986.

As in the United States, Commodore was facing off against the Atari ST. In the UK, Atari was headed by former Commodore GM Bob Gleadow. Paul Wells, his replacement, was subsequently terminated by Commodore. "He was friends with Bob Gleadow and Jack Tramiel, so he joined them at Atari," says Pleasance. "We loved it because Atari was our enemy and we set about destroying them!"

The business division of Commodore UK, previously responsible for the PET and CBM computers, would launch the Amiga. Commodore initially estimated a price of £1700 for the Amiga before settling on £1475 (which came to over £1700 with taxes). At the time £1 was worth around $1.50 USD, making the base price equivalent to $2200 USD. "I think they forecast fairly modest numbers mainly because of its price point," says Pleasance. "It was very expensive at the time but it was probably well worth it."

Compared to the lavish US launch, the UK calculated a budget based on its forecasted sales. "We got five percent of our gross turnover," says Pleasance. "We were a hundred million pound company, so we got five million pounds to spend. Generally speaking, we were quite frugal with how we spent the money. We spent it very, very wisely."

Commodore UK officially launched the Amiga in London at its own 7th Annual Commodore Show. "We had our own Commodore show we did every year," says Pleasance. Normally the show attracted the 8-bit C64 community, so it was questionable whether it was the ideal venue to launch a business computer.

The show was hosted at a hotel complex called the Novotel at Hammersmith, London during the weekend of May 9 to 11. Over 150 booths were hosted in the hotel auditorium, with Commodore renting out a smaller theater to demonstrate the Amiga, which they called "Amiga village". This year was somewhat of a disappointment for the show, with a scant number of software publishers attending, meaning there was little to see and do for those who attended.

The launch of the Amiga was not well received. *Zzap!64* reported, "CBM themselves would have you believe that the most important event was the launch of the Amiga in the UK. This took place at a special champagne breakfast on the first day of the show... One representative from a dealer chain said afterwards, 'Everybody's worst fears were realised—the idiots put a £1475 ex VAT price on it.'"

Most thought it was overpriced. "Argue if you will that the computer is worth that much (bearing in mind that the main components of that machine were originally to form the basis of a £150 games machine), but I reckon it's still mismarketing a good product. The Amiga falls into too much of a void between the home and business user market."[2]

The ICPUG (Independent Computer Products Users Group) Newsletter reported, "...my only comment here is that the launch was really very feeble indeed. There was a distinct feeling that Commodore had only realised that there was a show in the couple of weeks leading up to it. Indeed, Commodore themselves did not have a stand and were only represented by their presentations in the Commodore Theatre."[3]

ICPUG concluded, "My own personal view is that the Amiga has been overpriced—so much so that it could easily kill the machine before it even hits the market."

As in the US, Commodore UK attempted to introduce the Amiga into the education market. "We had a dedicated education division, only one guy by the name of Peter Talbot," says Pleasance. "He was very good and so we got the product into education. We also did well in the audio-visual market. Where we didn't do well is in general business, word processing and stuff like that, because it was a lot of money for something that other machines for a lot less money could do."

The German introduction of the Amiga was far more substantial than the low-key UK introduction. The hype, such as it was, had been created. Commodore UK would await shipments of PAL Amigas to arrive on its shores. It would be months before the world learned if the Amiga would conquer Europe as the C64 had.

Amigas Arrive in Europe

One persistent question through the years is whether Commodore's US marketing had bungled the release of the Amiga, or whether the marketplace had rejected the Amiga. The Amiga PAL release might be able to answer that question. After all, both Commodore UK and Commodore Germany both had strong marketing, with their dealer networks intact, and they were well respected in the business community in 1986. So if the Amiga failed to sell impressive numbers in those countries too, it had likely not been a failure on Commodore's part.

Commodore US had hoped to sell 150,000 Amigas on launch, but instead sold in the neighborhood of 40 to 50 thousand. In West Germany, with around one fourth of the US population in 1986, and a slightly more computer-literate population, optimistically Commodore could expect 40,000 sales at launch. Furthermore, the software was more bug-free for the European launch and there were more software titles available, giving yet another advantage.

3   Independent Commodore Products User Group Newsletter, VOLUME 8 NUMBER 3. May/June 1986.

In the end, Commodore Germany was able to sell 27,500 Amiga 1000 computers—total, up to December 31, 1993.[4] How many were sold in 1986 remains unknown, but the dismal launch numbers were certainly on par with those in the US.

As for the UK, Kelly Sumner, a salesman at Commodore UK at the time who would later rise to GM, says, "It was tough, very tough. I can't say it was the most successful product ever." He estimates they sold around 14,000 units in a year.

The Amiga's price tempered any chance of a success. In light of this, the release was deemed a success. "I think they did quite well actually," says David Pleasance. "I think they did better than they anticipated."

It is also worth noting that, overall, the Amiga sold in similar numbers to the Macintosh in its first year. With Apple's strength in marketing and a less crowded field, even it had a hard time.

Although this evidence is not definitive, it indicates that the disappointing Amiga launch was probably not due to marketing problems, but rather, the configuration of the machine did not fit what the market wanted—not even in Europe, where Commodore distribution and advertising was strong. This, coupled with the universal comments offered by the UK press on the launch price of the Amiga, point to one thing: Commodore was not to blame. It was the expensive design along with a lack of expandable slots that sealed the Amiga 1000's fate.

Overall, however, Commodore Europe would remain the company's stronghold. "Germany was a very good market," says Thomas Rattigan. According to Forbes magazine, Commodore would remain a close number two to IBM in the business market and number one in the consumer market until the end of the decade. But to do that, Thomas Rattigan would have to set the company on the right path again.

---

4   These figures were provided by Dr. Peter Kittel of the Marketing department of Commodore Frankfurt. Source: www.amigahistory.plus.com

Plotting
a New Course
1986

During his tenure, Marshall Smith had let Commodore engineering run wild with little direction or strategy. Now that Thomas Rattigan was installed as the new CEO, along with a new VP of engineering, Gerard Bucas, it was time to get everyone on board Rattigan's vision for the company. He would attempt to focus his engineers' talents on projects with specific goals set by marketing.

Amiga Ranger at a Standstill

Jay Miner had always had a vision of using his chipset in ever more powerful machines. He considered the original Amiga computer the low-end entry into a line of Amigas that were yet to come. In fact, it was always Dave Morse pushing for a lower-cost version. Morse didn't want expansion card slots in the Amiga when Jay Miner did, and Morse originally wanted a video game system he could sell through retail channels.

"If you looked at it from the Los Gatos point of view, the A1000 was their cheap product and they weren't going to make it any cheaper because how could you," says Dave Haynie. "They wanted to move onto something bigger and better, which was codenamed Ranger."

Now, even in the face of a commercially disastrous Amiga launch, Miner didn't waver from his vision. Trying to launch the Amiga as an upscale business machine had failed. Whether it was Commodore's fault or Amiga's would become a bone of contention between the two groups.

Miner and his group wanted a high-end business computer with expansion slots, a hard drive, and expensive VRAM. It was the polar opposite of Rattigan's new religion of low-cost consumer models.

Everyone agreed Commodore needed to have something new to launch in 1986, and the Ranger would not be ready until 1987. Miner favored another project from his group: the cost reduced Amiga, designed by Glen Keller, identical in form to the original but with a cheaper design. It could be profitable to Commodore for around an $800 retail price. And like Ranger, it would retain the writable control store integrated on a single new motherboard that removed the kludginess of the original. "Those guys were working on a cost-reduced machine," recalls Bob Welland. "I don't know if anyone has ever described the details of that but I do think it had the writable control store in it."

Thomas Rattigan supported the proposed $800 cost-reduced Amiga. "I think the price also confused a lot of people," he says. "People seem to think that home systems are under $1,000 and business systems are over $1,000. There tends to be a lot of biases and preconceived notions as to exactly what differentiates home and business computers."

However, Rattigan had previously given the engineers a six-month window to create an Amiga to compete with the A2500. Not something expensive for the business market, but something more affordable yet powerful. "I don't think the higher end Amiga is going to go into accounting departments, but I do think it is going to go into areas where there is a degree of creativity, if you will," he says.

As Rattigan found out, the Amiga engineers had not followed his previous directive. They knew the German team was far ahead of them, and it would be pointless to waste engineering effort. So they had disregarded his plan in favor of concentrating on the next generation Ranger. Rattigan began to believe he needed more control over his Los Gatos engineers.

Rattigan also had a soft spot for the PC market. "That type of marketer is inclined to always want to go with whatever the latest trend is," says Gerard Bucas. "And the trend at that time was obviously more of a PC compatible. But PC compatible was more for the business side, whereas what he never really fully understood is that Commodore and Apple in some sense were the same. We were not really attacking the business side. Of course he felt that sales were not strong enough and therefore the only way to get into the mainstream of sales is to really be PC compatible. So you've just got to build another PC."

Although the German engineering team supported this idea, West Chester engineering was not as supportive. "Engineering resisted that typically because you just become another commodity builder," says Bucas. "There was always a tug of war. A number of people, obviously even in the sales and marketing, would agree with engineering because not everyone thought that way."

Come to Jesus

On April 24, 1986, Rattigan called together a meeting with top executives, including Clive Smith, Ed Parks, Jay Miner, Gerard Bucas, and the outgoing Marshall Smith, along with key engineers. There were heavy cuts coming and he needed to figure out which projects to begin, which to continue, and which to liquidate. "Commodore was this strange billion dollar garage shop. I remember being in a meeting with Rattigan, Marshall Smith, and a bunch of key guys from Los Gatos and myself and a couple of my second lieutenants," recalls Jeff Porter. "I remember Rattigan put up his feet and saying, 'Okay, this is a come to Jesus meeting. We're going to decide what's important for R&D to do in the coming year. We gotta do marching orders here. This is what we're going to do.'"

As a marketing person, Rattigan was bound to think differently from the engineering teams. "He came from Pepsi," says Gerard Bucas. "There is a quote from him, 'If I can be successful marketing bottled water, I should be able to sell computers.' That was the way he felt about it. The bottom line is, he was a good marketer. The problem is that he wasn't really a technology person."

Commodore's main product line included the C64, C128, C128D, and Amiga. The C64CR, a cost reduced restyling of the C64, was being worked on in Japan the prior year and had been shelved when Commodore ran out of money. The Los Gatos Amiga engineers continued working on the Amiga Ranger. Finally, the recently revealed Amiga/IBM PC hybrid from Commodore Germany was already a priority for Irving Gould.

Retail Retail Retail

At the meeting, Rattigan turned to Gerard Bucas and his West Chester engineers. The biggest moneymaker for 1985 had been the C64, much to the surprise of everyone, except perhaps Clive Smith.

West Chester held traditional Commodore values of low-cost mass market products, which aligned very well with Rattigan's new religion. "The Commodore West Chester side of engineering, they were very into the C64, C128 mindset," says Bucas. "A lot of that mindset has to do with costs."

Rattigan knew there was a path to success with low cost computers like the C64, but he really had no way to clearly verbalize what that new product looked like. He had no knowledge of video and sound chips, or the advantage of 16-bit processors, or experience with the steady evolution of computing power. "The closest most of us in those days got to computers was our secretaries buying Wang workstations," says Rattigan. "We were pretty much in the dark ages when it came to technology."

Rattigan asked his employees to begin thinking of new products for the C64 that would help extend its life and make it more popular, something Clive Smith had begun the previous year.

Gerard Bucas had the idea for a cosmetic makeover of the original C64, which had remained unchanged since its launch in 1982. "Eventually I was the one that came up with the idea, listen guys, what we need is a C64. Make it look like the new family look and effectively remarket it. In fact, I wanted it to be called a C64-II."

Thomas Rattigan also noted the success of the C128 compared with the Amiga and wanted something else to continue the line. But his VP of engineering couldn't have cared less. "There was always this thing about the C128: it's a very weak evolution of the C64 and that family," says Bucas. "I was not a supporter, quite frankly, of the C128. My attitude was cut it out completely. It's not worth it. Eventually they did but they spent far too much money on the C128. It was probably one of the biggest failures of Commodore."

Jeff Porter, who was working on the PAL version of the Amiga, had studied the computer and identified major cost reductions for the machine. He approached Bucas before the meeting and felt he could do an even more radical cost reduction than the Los Gatos engineers. Bucas recalls, "We decided to make a proposal to Tom Rattigan: 'Listen, we want to do something similar to the C128, but use the Amiga technology for that. And with MOS, we'll do a couple of custom chips in there to make it even lower cost to produce, etcetera. But it's going to be one unit: an integrated keyboard like a C128 or a C64, in a certain sense.'"

Sitting in front of many of the Amiga team, Porter took a breath and gave his presentation. "I proposed to management at the time, what if we take the core of the Amiga and make it more like a Commodore 64," he recalls. "I said there's no reason we can't do that with an Amiga. Watch me kick some serious Atari butt."

After his extensive travels in Asia to find cheap parts, he felt confident he was the one to do it. "We, as engineering, knew that we could dramatically cost-reduce it and get it down to maybe a $499 type product called an A500 if we totally changed the philosophy, totally threw out everything that the

A1000 was, which was separate keyboard, relatively expensive casework, and a few other things that were involved with the A1000."

The West Coast Amiga team, whom Porter hoped to impress, did not respond well. "Basically they were very negative on doing anything without a separate keyboard and doing a cost reduced version," says Gerard Bucas. "They just felt the Amiga needed to go up street, not down street. That was their feeling."

The Plan

At the end of the discussions, it was time for Rattigan to give his strategic battle plans to the engineers. He knew his company had $30 million in cash plus another $135 million line of credit with which to pursue a number of new projects.

Curiously, Rattigan chose to lean on Marshall Smith for his opinion. "So Rattigan puts his feet up on the boardroom table and says, 'Well I don't know. What do you think Marsh? What do you think is the most important thing these guys need to be working on?' And he said, 'I think the most important thing to be working on is the 128D cost-reduced.'"

Jeff Porter felt like he was in a mad house. "I just wanted to cringe," he recalls. "Really, you just said this to the key Amiga guys? Did they just tell the guys from Amiga that the most important thing they could be working on was the 128D-CR? They really did not have a clue."

The Amiga engineers looked visibly rattled. "The guys from California were not used to the shenanigans that went on in West Chester," explains Porter. "I was used to these cockamamie answers coming out of these guy's mouths that didn't know what the fuck they were doing. I had the attitude of, 'Okay, don't worry. I'll just do what is going to work.' So I kind of yes-manned him but went off to do what I knew we had to do. But the guys from California were like, 'Are you kidding me?'"

Although it might have appeared as a slap in the face to the Amiga engineers, it's possible Rattigan was using a page from Jack Tramiel's playbook of fostering competing teams. "I gather that with technology companies it's not unique to have different groups in the same company competing on the same project," says Rattigan. "To motivate them. And what the hell, it's better to have two in-house competing teams than one in-house and one out-of-house as one of your competitors."

Gerard Bucas gave a little support to the C128, but knew its future was limited. "I was a supporter only in the sense that you need to do something to follow up the C64," he explains. "It was an attempt by the C64 team to compete with the Amiga, which was in my opinion ridiculous and impossible."

In any event, Rattigan asked his engineers to develop more advanced versions of those computers in case the C128 did end up being the big successor to the Commodore 64 everyone hoped it would be.

In Rattigan's mind, it was also obvious the company needed a cheaper Amiga if the Amiga line was to survive. He wanted to bring the massive C64 user base over to the Amiga. "The C64 didn't have much life left to it because a lot of games on other machines were faster and better," says Dale Luck. "Commodore was in a mode where they needed to come out with a lower cost version to try and replace what the C64 had become."

"When I started leaning on them to go with the [Amiga] 500, that was recognition on my part that we better have an alternative," says Rattigan. "Maybe we better return closer to our roots than this pie-in-the-sky concept that we can be a true competitor to Apple."

Haynie believes there was no other choice. "Basically, whoever was at the helm at that time was going to push for that," he says. "It was inevitable that someone was going to come up with a lower cost Amiga."

Rattigan had to choose between the original Amiga engineers and his own engineers. "You had the West Coast group, and of course they were reluctant to fool around with their baby too much," explains Rattigan. "Then you had the West Chester technology group, who I gave the assignment to. I figured they would be more bloodthirsty."

Jeff Porter and his engineers in West Chester would begin researching the low-cost Amiga project.

The now somewhat perturbed Amiga engineers departed back for the West Coast where they would continue development of the Amiga Ranger, as well as a cost reduced Amiga 1000. Jeff Porter was not a fan of Rattigan after this meeting. He preferred non-interference from his CEO, as Marshall Smith had operated.

Everyone would meet at the June 1986 CES, where Rattigan would decide which products would make the cut. In the meantime, the bankers expected Rattigan to decide who was important for Commodore's current projects and cut the rest. If you were an engineer without a project, your days were numbered. It was time for engineers to jump onto projects. Anyone without one would perish. The mad scramble began.

The Next Mass Products

For the month of May 1986, Commodore became one big game of musical chairs. To join an active project meant you were safe and could sit down, but anyone left standing by the end of the month would find themselves out of a job. Luckily there were many potential projects for engineers to jump onto.

After the "Come to Jesus" meeting, it was crystal clear to management and engineer alike that mass market projects would be given priority by Rattigan. Employees began proposing mainly projects based around the C64 and C128.

Back in May 1985, prior to the launch of the Amiga and C128, Jeff Porter predicted the C128 would be a hit, due to its price and C64 compatibility. Conversely, he predicted the Amiga would flop because it was not a true business machine, it was overhyped, and it lacked expansion. "It was not expandable enough or business friendly enough to compete with the IBM PC back then," says Porter. "It didn't have any slots. It didn't have any plug-in cards. It fell in this cavern between game machine and business computer that was kind of no man's land."

By early 1986, those predictions had borne out and Porter began to receive respect for his marketing analysis. A week after the "Come to Jesus" meeting, Porter presented four projects to executives Gerard Bucas, Nigel Shepherd, Clive Smith, and Ed Parks: a sequel to the C128 he called the C256, a laptop C256, a C64 with a built-in modem and disk drive for the living room, and his Amiga in a C128 case. Of these proposals, only one would make it to production

The C256

For the C256, Porter turned to Dave Haynie, who worked on the original C128 project. "My group, which was me and Frank [Palaia], we were trying to figure out what we were going to do to try to stay valuable around here and not disappear," says Haynie. "So we had come up with a couple of different dog and pony shows around new variations on the C128."

Haynie thought of the C128 as a competitor to the Apple II line of computers. And much as the Apple II computers had evolved, he would attempt to take the C128 concept even farther by creating versions with faster processors and better memory options. To improve those options, he needed better chips than he had for the C128.

Commodore's LSI group began designing an MMU chip for the C256, named the 8725 chip, in early February, 1986. Bill Gardei, hard at work on a CMOS 6502 chip, the 4502, felt the MMU should be a real memory mapper and not use the budget "bank-switching" solution Commodore had used in the past.

As for the microprocessor, Haynie had been disappointed that in the 10 years since the 6502's introduction, MOS Technology had only succeeded in making a 2.05 MHz version for the C128, while other makers already had NMOS versions running at 3 MHz.

On May 13, Apple announced the Apple IIx, which would be released later in the year as the Apple IIGS. The machine used a 16-bit version of the 6502 processor, called the 65816, designed by the Western Design Center. This announcement immediately sparked interest among the Commodore engineers and they began looking at the possibility of using the chip in their next computers. An engineer named Dave DiOrio began trying to retrofit the 65816 into a standard C64.

Management even held meetings back in February with former Commodore chip designer Al Charpentier regarding the same Ensoniq sound chip used in the Apple IIx. Charpentier quoted them a price of $1.90 per chip in quantity, but ultimately nothing came of the discussions.

Dave Haynie wanted to design a whole new C128 using the 65C816 chip, which ran at 4 MHz and was capable of emulating the 8-bit 6502. Haynie planned to have the machine running in 8-bit mode at first, then allow software developers to take advantage of the 16-bit capability later.

The chip cost around $6 per unit, only $3 more than using the 8502 chip in the C128. The machine would come with 256KB of memory. Haynie also wanted to include a Writeable Control Store to load the operating system from disk into memory, much like the Amiga, using 64KB of that memory. Another 64KB memory would be dedicated to video, allowing a fully bitmapped screen with an advanced 8563 video controller chip. He called his new machine BMW after the car.

System programmer Fred Bowen, who would become part of the C256 team, had felt he wasn't getting any respect when it came to system design decisions. When he heard about Haynie's plans, he was as vehemently opposed to the idea of using the 65816 as he had been in 1984 when the chip had been proposed for the C128.

Despite the opposition, Haynie ploughed ahead, with the support of Jeff Porter. The latter asked for a system spec and prototype in time for the upcoming June CES.

The downside of Haynie's C256 was that it would not include a C64 mode, or CP/M mode for that matter, as the C128 had. This meant the millions of C64 owners would not be able to use their library of games on the C256. Haynie and Porter saw the C256 as a business machine, a sentiment felt throughout Commodore. Even two years after the video game crash, the company felt games were poison.

The team hurriedly began developing schematics and prototypes for the June CES show, where Rattigan would decide the fate of "BMW".

Portable LCD C256

Jeff Porter's greatest heartbreak at Commodore had been the rejection of his LCD portable. He had attempted several times in 1985 and early 1986 to revive the project, and now that Rattigan wanted a C128 successor, he thought he had an opportunity to revive an LCD project yet again and make use of the Eagle-Picher LCD plant that still resided in the West Chester building.

Porter proposed a portable C256 system, even more reminiscent of a laptop than the LCD Portable had been. However, Gerard Bucas had determined earlier in the year that Commodore simply did not have the manpower or budget to take on the new project while the company remained in survival mode. Porter's new proposal for the LCD machine went nowhere.

C64D and 1581 Drive

Porter also proposed a version of the C64 with a built in disk drive and modem, called the C64D (a name reminiscent of the C128D). He believed the modem was crucial, as it would allow a family to obtain news and information from outside sources, such as CompuServe or (especially) Quantum Link, essentially replacing the newspaper right on the living room TV.

Both Clive Smith and Commodore US president Nigel Shepherd supported the idea, but they felt something needed to be done about the slow, expensive 1541 drive. Around this time, many games began to overflow the storage limit on 5.25" disks, requiring multiple disks for each game. The two executives asked for a new drive based on the 3.5" disk, which was not only faster and cheaper, but also stored 800 KB versus 170 KB for the old 5.25" disks. Smith was especially interested in the 3.5" drive improving the performance of GEOS.

Jeff Porter determined Commodore could build the external drive, dubbed the 1581, for $98.26. He also proposed building the drive into the C64c, sharing the same motherboard, for an additional cost of $77.81 over the C64c base cost.

Both Clive Smith and Nigel Shepherd decided to go with the external 1581 drive for now. If that product caught on with customers and software publishers, they would then go ahead with a new C64 with a built in 3.5" disk drive.

Gerard Bucas did not want to lose his best engineers to the upcoming cuts and made sure to assign them projects to keep them safe. He assigned Greg Berlin to the 1581 drive on May 9, 1986 and by July 17, Berlin had his plan for the drive ready, and began building a prototype. For now, Berlin was safe from the upcoming cuts.

B52 Proposal

After helping launch the PAL Amiga, Jeff Porter decided to fly to Asia and hunt for low-cost parts for the Amiga-CR. He landed in Osaka, Japan, spending a few days visiting some factories, including Sanyo, Matsushita, and of course Commodore Japan Limited. He then travelled to Tokyo to meet with Mitsumi, Commodore's keyboard maker. While there, he consulted with a Commodore employee named Yoshi Narahara about cost reducing the Amiga. Porter estimated he could "128-ize" the Amiga for $175 plus $60 for a separate disk drive.

Prices were even cheaper outside Japan and Porter travelled to Hong Kong where he visited the Commodore factory. He also visited several subcontractors including Bremen, Universal Appliance Ltd. and Elec & Eltek. Then it was off to Taiwan where he visited Philips and Commodore Taiwan. Here he found the cheapest components, though there were some quality issues.

When Jeff Porter returned from his whirlwind tour on April 10, he was ready to begin planning the Amiga-CR—all while nursing a broken foot picked up during his globe trotting. Porter spoke mainly with Bob Welland and George Robbins, planning the Amiga-CR. He also pitched his ideas to Dave Haynie and others, who liked the ideas but were slightly concerned that the new Amiga could become regarded as a games machine.

On Friday, May 9 at noon, Gerard Bucas threw down the gauntlet to Porter, Robbins, Welland, and Bob Russell. He officially requested a detailed spec for a cost reduced Amiga, which he codenamed the B52 project. "We nicknamed the B52 after the bomber, not the rock group," says Jeff Porter.

"We either have to bomb the competition or we might as well bomb ourselves because we're going down in flames if we don't hit a home run here."

George Robbins would later write, "Long ago, when there were a number of proposals vying for the addition to the Amiga product line, ranging from something like an A1000 but a few dollars cheaper to something like an ST with zip for expansion, the proposal that eventually became the A500 was nicknamed the B52. This was no doubt supposed to indicate a Commodore strategic product with long range potential that would rattle the enemy's cage big time."[1]

Bucas wanted to, in his words, C128-ize the Amiga, with a total parts and labor cost of only $200. Using a small team, he wanted it done quickly, emphasizing a 6-month product schedule—pushing the original release date from late September to late October 1986. After all, nothing short of the survival of the company was at stake. In return, Bucas promised air conditioning at night and a budget for 1-day board turnarounds—an extremely expensive way to procure PCBs.

Controversially, he wanted a standard connector for RGB video so Commodore could avoid having to manufacture the costly 23-pin RGB cables used for the Amiga 1000. As an option, he suggested two dedicated MIDI ports to match the Atari ST computers. He gave the team until Monday morning to deliver a detailed proposal.

The team stayed until well past 10:00 pm that night before they had what they considered an accurate bill of materials (BoM). The total cost was $206.66. Jeff Porter wrote a response to Bucas, which he sent at 4:45 am the next morning.

Already the team had a name for the motherboard. As George Robbins later recalled, "After too many late nights working on the thing, it became obvious that B52 referred to the rock group of the same name, and that 'Rock Lobster' was an appropriate product designation."

Two hours later, early Saturday morning, Gerard Bucas had to inform the team that in their sleepless delirium they had missed around $20 in costs with the estimate, and in fact the BoM was $26 off. Bucas offered to chop $6 off by hammering his parts suppliers hard, but the engineers would have to find another $20 in savings.

On Monday, things began to move quickly. Bob Welland submitted a proposal for amalgamating the "glue logic" in the Amiga into one cheap

---

1   Newsgroup post to comp.sys.amiga, September 16, 1987.

chip, as well as the ability to address more memory. He immediately began designing the chips while Robbins began designing the motherboard schematics, which he would have almost finished by the end of the week.

By Friday, May 16, Jeff Porter had produced an accurate schedule for the B52. The schedule was aggressive and assumed everything went perfectly, including FCC approval and chips working on the first revision. Unfortunately, pilot production could only begin in December, with volume production beginning in January 1987. Bucas shared the bad news with Rattigan and other executives. It was a complete disappointment. The team had started just a few months too late to release the system in the current year. However, executives continued to hope for a miracle, while prodding and pushing for a 1986 release date.

On May 30, Porter presented a 12-page B52 Hardware Specification to Thomas Rattigan to sign off on. Specifically, the statement read, "I, Thomas J. Rattigan, have read, understood, and agreed to the information contained herewith." If the wording sounds impudent, that's because it was. On top of being condescending, it implies that Rattigan was legally bound to that spec and could have no further input once the project began. The mistrust between Jeff Porter and Thomas Rattigan was beginning to show itself.

Sitting among the executives was a new face, Irving Gould's man in Germany, Henri Rubin, who would become an important fixture at Commodore. "I made the pitch to Gerard and Henri for the B52," says Porter. "They bought off on that concept and I gave them a, 'Here's what I think it's going to cost, here's how much effort it will take, and here's how long it will take to design it.' And Henri accepted that, Irving accepted that and away we went."

With Rattigan signing off on the project, it now gained the necessary momentum. The rest of the company would fall in line to support the product. "That's when the West Chester engineering group proposed the A500, which is more of an evolution," says Bucas. "If you think of it from pricing/appearance and the type of target market, that was more or less an evolution of the home computer C64/C128 but with the Amiga technology. That's why they signed off on it. Of course that turned out to be the hottest Amiga ever."

If, in retrospect, it seems like the B52 project was slow to launch, it was because there was another major development happening at the same time that threatened to overshadow the B52.

Backing the A2500

The German A2500 project had been shown behind closed doors at COM-DEX, where the West Chester engineers had a chance to view it for the first time. The project did not sit well with them. At the recent "Come to Jesus" meeting, the project was mostly ignored and the West Chester engineers went off to work on a variety of mass market projects.

But then Irving Gould found out that his A2500 project was not being given the respect it deserved. "It eventually became a mainstream project and we had no choice but to do that," says Gerard Bucas. "As in all companies, if you have multinational engineering groups, there's always conflict between those types of groups because each group feels they are better than the next group, so the job of the boss is to resolve those issues."

On May 15, 1986, Bucas informed the LSI group that they were to immediately begin design of two chips for the German project. The first was a "glue logic" chip for the A2500 itself, while the second was a chip for the Bridgeboard. Ted Lenthe reacted poorly upon learning he now had to squeeze his employee's limited time into two unscheduled chips. But there was nothing to be done as "Uncle Irv" was backing the project.

On May 26, Commodore US president Nigel Shepherd revealed the project to *InfoWorld*. Commodore's US marketing felt Amiga 2000 had a better ring to it than 2500. He also publicly rebranded the original Amiga as the Amiga 1000. Shepherd even promised hard disk drive (HDD) support for the new computer upon release.

The German engineers had begun work on a hard drive controller board and handed it off to the Los Gatos engineers to complete, supervised by Bob Pariseau, earlier in the year. Confusingly, the engineers called the expansion board Ranger. Although the software to support the hard drive was in good shape, the hardware had major reliability problems.

Pariseau requested two engineers from West Chester, Lee Erickson and Jeff Boyer, to take over the project by mid-May. Now it would be up to the West Chester engineers to deliver the controller board.

On June 16, West Chester engineer Jeff Boyer flew to Braunschweig to begin working on the hard drive controller board for the A2500. Luckily he had already been working on a hard drive for the A1000, using the same Zorro bus.

The sudden emphasis on the German-designed Amiga did not sit well with the West Chester engineers, who believed the upcoming C256 and Amiga-CR would do far more to save Commodore. But now they had to divert their attention away from those projects and onto the German designed A2500. The sudden overabundance of new projects would threaten the timelines of them all.

Every Man's Macintosh 1986

In 1979, an engineer named Jef Raskin at Apple had begun an "appliance computer" called the Macintosh that was meant to be extremely cheap for the average consumer. After Steve Jobs took over the project in 1981, the cost of the Macintosh increased, ultimately missing the original low-cost goal.

Back at Commodore, Clive Smith saw several things coming together around the C64: a GEOS GUI, a mouse, and a cost reduction/redesign. He began to realize that Commodore held all the key ingredients to fulfill the original goal of the Macintosh project. If he could assemble a package containing a Macintosh-like OS at a cost effective price and enter it into retail space, Commodore could have another hit on its hands.

GEOS Comes to Commodore

In early 1986, a 29-year-old Brian Dougherty and his team were completing GEOS 1.2, the version they planned to release commercially. Now it was time to market the operating system. So far, Dougherty had been unable to convince any major software developers to create commercial applications for the operating system. It was a disappointment, but perhaps development would occur when the operating system was in wider release.

In the tech industry, the norm is engineers with poor communication skills. Dougherty was a rare exception: a programmer who was also articulate and understandable. This made it easy for him to move between the tech world to the business world. He had maintained a good relationship with Commodore's Clive Smith, and the latter had plans to partner with Berkeley Softworks.

Prior to 1986, articles in financial magazines all predicted the imminent demise of the C64 and Commodore considered ending its production in favor of the Amiga. "The C64 had been out for a while and Commodore was actually thinking about killing it at the time we developed Commodore GEOS for it," says Dougherty. "And then we sort of created a whole other life for the platform."

Clive Smith's plan to rebundle the C64 was cancelled in 1985 but quickly revived in early 1986 following strong sales of the original C64. The bundle was a brilliant plan, because many consumers at the time wanted to try a mouse controlled GUI for the first, but they didn't necessarily want to pay $2500 for a Macintosh, or $1200 for an Amiga, or even $600 for the upcoming B52. But many more could afford $200, even if the GUI experience did not quite measure up to the others.

Commodore's wunderkind executive, Clive Smith, approached Dougherty with an offer he could not refuse. "The guy who really made the deal happen at Commodore was Clive Smith," says Dougherty. "He spearheaded doing a deal with us with Commodore to bundle it with the Commodore 64."

Smith wanted to include an OEM version of GEOS with each new C64 sold by Commodore. The deal was similar to Microsoft's deal with IBM to include MS-DOS with its IBM PC computers. "There was a great business for us and it was a very profitable business," says Dougherty. The deal also ensured a large user base for GEOS.

Dougherty also made a deal with Quantum Link to include its software in every package of GEOS. "We ended up working with Commodore and AOL back when they were called Q-Link," says Dougherty. "We bundled GEOS and Q-Link together, which was how they got their real first user base which eventually became AOL." Although Berkeley Softworks helped promote Q-Link, the actual Q-Link software did not run from within the GEOS environment.

Commodore had released several RAM expansion units (REU's) around the same time the C128 debuted. First out was the 1700 and 1750 with 128K and 512K respectively, and then later the 1764 with 256K. Although the expansion had the potential to allow more complex programs to run on the C64, very little commercial software took advantage of the memory due to the low adoption rate.

GEOS was one of the few titles compatible with the 256K 1764 REU. "The real power users who were seriously using Commodore GEOS for desktop publishing and stuff like that, they got the RAM expansion unit," says Dougherty. "Once you had a RAM expansion unit, you couldn't imagine having worked without it because everything just happened instantly. You could go from application to application instantly because you could put several applications up in the RAM expansion unit and just click on it and it would instantly pop up. It was pretty snappy."

Berkeley also began developing a version of GEOS for the C128 to display at the June 1986 CES. Although the C128 had a superior processor, memory size, and graphics resolutions, Dougherty had mixed feelings. "The good points were you could run in a full 640 wide, so you got enough real estate to be a good productivity machine. From that respect it was pretty good," he says. "On the other hand, it was a pretty kludgy piece of hardware to work with."

Due to a tight development schedule for the C128, Bil Herd was unable to consult with outside developers such as Berkeley. "We wish we had been working with Commodore with the C128 because we could have helped them design a much better, easier-to-write-software machine than it was," says Dougherty. "By the time it came out, they already had the C128 almost done so we didn't get a chance to weigh in on what we wished the C128 had been."

1351 Mouse

One key ingredient of a GUI OS is the mouse. Commodore was about to ship the first 15,000 units of the 1350 mouse, developed by a Commodore engineer named Ian Kirschemann, but it was a joystick dressed up like a mouse and the performance wasn't the same as a true proportional mouse. The 1350 merely indicated directions to the computer. As a result, it could only move in 8 directions, allowing diagonal and straight lines, while curves were almost impossible to create within the GEOS drawing program. And if a user moved the mouse quickly, the mouse pointer moved at the same slow speed on screen.

Berkeley Softworks wanted a proportional mouse for GEOS that could not only comprehend true direction but also speed. "Initially we designed it to work with a joystick since most C64 users had one for playing games, but we really wanted a mouse," says Brian Dougherty. "We certainly pushed for the mouse since we were doing a graphical user interface."

Clive Smith heard Dougherty's concerns and in May he began a new project, this time headed by a Commodore engineer known for coming up with ingenious solutions to difficult engineering problems. "There was a British guy in management and he was all over a thing called GEOS, which was a windowing GUI system for the C64," recalls Hedley Davis. "Their big problem was that they didn't have a mouse."

Davis was enthusiastic about the project, mainly owing to the GEOS operating system that Smith had brought to Commodore. "He was trying to make something happen with this GEOS, which was actually insanely cool for what it did on a 6502," explains Davis. But it would also mean working with the 38 year-old Smith, one of Commodore's top executives. "He existed in a world I didn't. He was higher up in management. This guy wore a suit and dressed well, and he wielded power. I'm just some flunky down and in the engineering department."

At the time, Smith was out of favor with some managers due to the poorly negotiated Quantum Link deal. He was desperate to make the deal profitable and saw the rebundled C64-CR as the solution. "I remember that everybody said he was trouble and dangerous and you need to be careful around him," says Davis. "He would be fired at almost any time for all these different things he had done that hadn't worked out."

With Commodore in a tenuous position, if a project failed, it wasn't uncommon to fire the engineers on the project as well. Davis, a junior engineer at the time, had little experience with company politics but decided to do a little due diligence anyway. "I was totally impertinent. He was like four levels of management up from me and I was this punk kid," recalls Davis. "I remember asking how is it you're still here when you're doing all this stuff? And he said, 'Clean living.'"

Smith was also one of Irving Gould's favored employees, which gave him additional leverage—something engineering managers like Gerard Bucas didn't always like. Smith also saw the new mouse as another product he could package with Quantum Link disks, further helping Commodore to meet its targets.

Smith asked Davis to explore options for creating a truly proportional mouse. He also wanted the mouse to have a secondary mode that allowed it to imitate a joystick, just like the 1350 mouse. This would make the mouse useful for existing joystick controlled programs.

Clive Smith, like most managers, under-appreciated the time it takes to complete difficult engineering tasks. In his mind, he saw the new mouse, dubbed the 1351, as a minor tweak on the 1350 to make it behave like a true mouse. He hoped that, if Davis could complete the mouse on time and at a low cost, it would even be a candidate for including in the C64-CR bundle this year.

Designing a Better Mouse

Although the engineers who designed computers received most of the glory, there were other engineers who designed computer devices that were an important part of Commodore's revenues. These devices often presented unique engineering challenges. Hedley Davis' 1351 mouse was one such device.

The challenge was to create a cutting edge input device for a computer that was never designed to allow a mouse. Clive Smith gave him clear design goals based on current mice of the day. Davis was instructed to update the mouse pointer coordinates at 60 Hertz, the screen refresh rate of the C64, and to "make a mouse for the C64 that doesn't suck down the processor," he explains. "Mice in that day were 300 dpi. You would figure out how fast you want to move it—how many inches per second. You could figure out how many bits per 60 Hertz you needed to get in and it was just slightly less than seven, which left me a bit to deal with uncertainty."

Davis studied an Amiga 1000 mouse to learn how it worked. At the time, all computer mice used a mechanical design. It consisted of a heavy rubberized ball pressed against two rollers, each one translating movement along the X and Y axis respectively. Each roller was attached to an encoder wheel, which has slots in it through which light passes. An infrared LED shone light through the slots onto a photosensor in order to detect the rotation of the roller.

As for the circuitry, it would need to monitor the sensor and record movement along the X and Y axis at 60 times per second. And it would need to do so in hardware only, not software, so that it would be responsive to the user's hand movements.

Using the lessons he learned from a book he read called *Lateral Think-ing*, Davis examined the problem from every angle. He recalls, "I basically walked around the outer edge of the C64 and looked at every single port and said, 'How would I do it here? How would I do it here? How would I do it here?'"

The joystick port was of particular interest to Davis, due to its ability to read potentiometers; resistors that changed resistance when they rotated. "The joystick port had the ability to report the value of a potentiometer, because it supported paddles," explains Davis. "It had this specialized circuit in there for reporting the value of a potentiometer, which is multiple bits wide as opposed to being a single bit wide."

Curiously, the sound chip in the C64, called the SID chip, decoded the values of the potentiometers. SID had two pins that were analog-to-digital converters (A/D converters), called POT X and POT Y, in order to produce a digital value between 0 and 255. The C64 used a resistor-capacitor (RC) circuit to obtain a reading from the potentiometers. "It turns out that the register is 8 bits wide and it uses an RC charging network," explains Davis. "What happens is the SID chip discharges the capacitor for 256 clock cycles and then it releases the cap, and the cap charges up. When the voltage crosses a threshold, it captures that number and that number shows up in the register that you can read and it does so at 60 Hertz, which meant you could get 2 bytes per 60 Hertz into the system with a single register read."

Knowing this, Davis needed to get the C64 to accept the values from the mechanical mouse. "What Hedley wanted to do was convert mouse movement—you're basically counting the movement of a wheel—and be able to convey that to the joystick input," explains Bob Welland.

The joystick ports in the C64 allowed either analog joysticks or the rather obsolete paddles, but they both relied on reading values from potentiometers. "Joysticks are based on RC circuits," says Welland. "You basically charge up the capacitor and then the resistance is defined by the position of the joystick; one in the X-axis and one in the Y-axis. You charge the capacitor up and it dissipates through the resistor and when the voltage drops below a certain level, then you know where the joystick is."

Getting the timing of the mouse synchronized with the timing of the C64 was important. "What Hedley would do is he would see the voltage charge up and then he would start a countdown counter that was proportional to how far the mouse had traveled since the last time this sampling had happened," explains Welland. "And when it got to zero, he would just ground the circuit, which would effectively force the zero crossing and the joystick thing would happily think, 'Oh, the resistance is this value.'"

Welland was amazed at the insight required to come up with the solution. "It worked beautifully," he says. "It was such a pretty, elegant idea. I think that's actually one of the qualities that Hedley has. He'll come up with these real clean ideas and then he's very good at implementing them. He is a very clever man."

Davis sums up the concept. "That mouse interface circuit was just a really squirrely way to get in there and be able to get enough bits in, and get enough motion inside the vertical blanking interval without using a lot of computer time."

The final challenge was implementing two mouse buttons when a standard joystick only allowed one. This was accomplished by connecting the right mouse button directly to the POTX joystick port pin, which led to the

SID chip's POTX function. When the button is pressed, resistance is 0, and any other value means the right button is not pressed.

A few days after being asked to investigate a proportional mouse, Davis presented his findings to his manager, Gerard Bucas, for evaluation. "I spent a day or two investigating and came up with the idea of transmitting digital position data over the potentiometer ports," he recalls. "I wrote a single page piece of paper—because they asked for somebody to give them recommendations—and I outlined every single port, and why they were bad, and why this one was harder but it was good. I sent it off and then I got called into management's office and they said, 'Ok, go do this.'"

Now Davis would have to build a working prototype. Years earlier, in June 1983, AMD introduced the 22V10, a 24 pin IC chip, called a Programmable Array Logic (PAL). (The 22V10 name was derived from 22 inputs, V for versatile, and 10 for the number of outputs.) To construct his prototype, Davis would rely on the new IC chip to allow him to program the logic into the mouse.

He relied on several Amiga mice in order to test his prototype concepts. "The prototypes for the 1351 mouse used a regular Amiga mouse," he says. "The Amiga mouse plugged into the prototype box which then plugged into the C64. That box contained nine PALs which implemented the design."

Davis' mouse would not require batteries to power the PAL chips and optical encoder, since the C64 joystick port had a pin to provide 5 volts. He also added the joystick mode of the 1350 mouse, which was selectable by holding down the right mouse button when powering up the C64.

He then released a number of prototype mice to distribute to marketing people and developers, such as Berkeley Softworks. A company named Bremen was in the running to design the shell and internal mechanicals. "They did the entire mechanical thing," says Davis. "We built the PAL prototypes and we sent those around."

Davis could not help but be impressed with his own creation and considers himself lucky that the solution existed within the C64. "The planets were aligned and it was a good scheme," he says. Because it was a hardware solution utilizing very little CPU power, it produced fluid mouse motion on the screen with no lag or loss of data. Although the C64 did not match up to the Macintosh in memory or processor speed, the mouse movement in GEOS was every bit as competitive.

The mouse was more than Clive Smith could have expected. Smith asked Jeff Porter to assign the project a high priority, given how much the C64 could help Commodore survive through its financial turmoil. Davis would continue working on the mouse and getting it ready for production through-out the summer of 1986, with a schedule to coincide with the release of the C64-CR. It looked like Clive Smith would accomplish his dream of releasing a poor-man's Macintosh.

Cutting to the Bone
1986

In February 1986, Mehdi Ali, senior vice president of Dillon Read & Co. began his job of advising Commodore as it went through restructuring. This was, of course, a polite term for firing employees. In truth, Ali was hired to be the company hatchet man. "Mehdi was there as a consultant and mainly as a cost cutter," says Gerard Bucas. "That was his job."

Rattigan had already initiated two prior rounds of layoffs, one in September 1985 and one in January 1986. Since January, those layoffs had resulted in almost 1000 employees leaving Commodore, mostly from selling factories or cutting other divisions, but the cuts had mostly avoided the heart of Commodore in West Chester. Now it was time for a more serious round of cuts.

Commodore's engineering department rose to a peak of 253 employees in 1985 but would be whittled away through a series of layoffs. "It was just a paring down and actually the first layoff was a good thing," says Dave Haynie. "The second one was questionable. The third one was where they were actually hitting bone."

The urgency of this round of cuts was due to Commodore bleeding money for yet another quarter. For the three months ending March 1986, Commodore lost a further $36.7 million, although revenues rose from the previous year's quarter from $168.3 million to $182.3 million. Commodore maintained that some of this was attributed to a write-down for the cost of laying off employees and handing out severance packages.[1]

---

1   *InfoWorld*, May 26, 1986. p. 5. "Amid Losses, Commodore Plans Amiga 2000"

Executive Cuts

Mehdi Ali and Thomas Rattigan started cutting at the top, identifying weaknesses in Commodore's executive suite. There could be no arguing that in 1985, Commodore had spectacularly failed in many key areas, including sales, advertising, financing, investor relations, and the Amiga release. "I believe that the vast majority of the people at Commodore were highly qualified and they had their hearts in the right place," says Dale Luck. "But there were a few less capable high-level executives in advertising, marketing, and in helping to control the direction of engineering as well as sales."

On May 2, 1986 Commodore laid off three executives.[2] The first was Bob Trukenbrod, the advertising executive from Nabisco responsible for the failed Amiga launch campaign. Second was VP of investor relations Paul Lazovick.

And finally, Rattigan terminated John A. Widlicka, senior VP of sales. His most recent initiative had been to start an education division, mainly by giving a $500 discount to educational institutions. With Apple so entrenched in education already, it was a difficult road.

Although the executives lasted barely a year, they weren't suffering. "They all had ridiculous golden parachutes," explains engineer Greg Berlin. "They could totally screw the pooch and walk away with a shitload of money and it made us crazy. It was like a revolving door of morons who would come in and get paid lots of money to do stupid shit and walk away with a lot of money."

CFO

Thomas Rattigan's one misstep at Commodore so far had been to embarrassingly announce a profit of over $1 million, only to retract it and announce a $53 million loss. The mess Commodore had found itself in was due to poor financial forecasts by Marshall Smith's team, resulting in Commodore running out of money. Rattigan needed an accurate financial picture to "make sure the numbers we were looking at were the real numbers and that there wasn't a lot of pie in sky wishing."

Commodore was about to get executives as talented as those during the Tramiel years. "One of the first things I did when I was named CEO was hire a search firm to go out and find me a chief administrative officer,

---

who among other things, would have responsibility for the financial areas," says Rattigan.

Corporate decisions might seem simple on the surface, but there is a subtlety of how they get done properly. Under Marshall Smith and Irving Gould, these decisions lacked the attention to detail. Rattigan, on the other hand, put a lot of thought into hiring key players.

Not only did he hire a recruiting firm to find the perfect candidate, but he ensured he communicated clearly to the recruiter exactly what Commodore needed, otherwise the company could be stuck with yet another liability in the executive suite. But Rattigan had no financial experience, so he told the recruiter to talk to his former CFO at PepsiCo first. "I said, 'This guy is not a candidate for the job, but this guy will be able to give you the perfect template that I'm looking for. But then you have to overlay it with a guy who has some experience in electronics.' So I had them go up and interview the CFO who had worked for me on the bottling turnaround at Pepsi."

It seemed like a convoluted way to find a CFO, but it ensured a good fit. "So they interviewed the CFO at Pepsi. And then they went out and found at RCA a guy who they proposed was all of that plus has an electronics background. And that was Mike Evans."

Michael Evans had worked for RCA Consumer Electronics, once a leading corporation in the consumer electronics market until it was sold to GE in 1986 and broken up. "I interviewed Mike and brought him in," says Rattigan. "I gave him personnel, IS [Internal Security], and finance. He may have had a few other odds and sods basically, but largely the administrative side of the business." Now he would become a VP of Commodore International (essentially Rattigan's right hand man) and CFO.

With one of the biggest problems at Commodore now in the hands of someone more capable, Commodore's "fixer" could now get to work. "The first thing we had to do was get the fiscal house in order," says Rattigan.

Marketing and Sales Canned

Executives weren't the only heads that would roll. When Thomas Rattigan found his new religion about mass market computers, he decided to restructure Commodore's sales force. "Thomas Rattigan got antsy and decided we don't need this computer store stuff," recalls Don Reisinger. "We're not going to be able to do enough volume through them and he almost arbitrarily made the decision to yank the whole customer support; everything for the computer side of the business and go mass market."

Firing the sales and marketing department at Commodore was a tradition going back to the Tramiel years. "Marketing and sales went through a lot of turmoil," says Gerard Bucas. "It was all to do with this sort of tug of war between, 'We need to get more into the business market, like PCs,' but at the same time, 'We need to get more into the consumer and hobbyist market or maybe video production market.' Marketing obviously had to add some input and influence but they changed people too often. Because of this turmoil, there was never really a super strong driving force there."

Those on the Amiga side of marketing & sales, such as Reisinger, might have worked for Commodore, but that's not where their allegiances rested. Commodore executives like Rattigan often had to walk a tightrope when interacting with Amiga personnel. "I must have been an unmitigated pain in the ass because I was Mr. Amiga. All Amiga," says Reisinger. "I don't give a shit about Commodore and of course he was having to try to keep a lid on things there because he knew stuff going on that I was not privy to."

After the failure of Commodore's sales and marketing department with the Amiga, Rattigan shut it down. "I was part of the purge when Rattigan shut down the division," laments Reisinger.[3] "There was no need for regional managers when that happened. They were going to do everything out of West Chester. So the sales and marketing crew that was dedicated to the Amiga in the field and even back at West Chester was dismantled. Then a relatively short time after that they dismantled the development crew here in Silicon Valley."

Project Shutdowns

Commodore was a proud engineer-centered company. Even under Jack Tramiel, who was notorious for firing employees with gusto, the engineers were usually safe. Now things would be different. "The outside consultant [Mehdi Ali] was super negative on engineering," recalls Gerard Bucas. "They wanted to dramatically reduce costs. Effectively the engineering budget at one stage was probably 33 million dollars. They wanted to reduce that by more than 50 percent."

All managers were issued a hiring freeze until Commodore rebounded. Ali estimated Commodore would need to lay off 140 employees in the next

---

3   Reisinger went on to work for Sega as its VP of Marketing.

round of cuts.[4] This would mean cutting educated, well trained, valuable assets to the company.

Gerard Bucas had painstakingly recruited many of those engineers and was sad to lose even one of them. "So I resisted that," says Bucas. "I had a major conflict with Mehdi and this was a tough time at that stage. That was probably one of the most difficult times of my life."

Reluctantly, Bucas played along with the cuts in May. Since January, Commodore's engineers had either been assigned to projects or they hadn't. Those who hadn't were on the chopping block. "We had a number of lay-offs where people were getting chopped right and left," says Dave Haynie. "The whole 1985 to 1986 was not such a good year because they had spent all this money buying Amiga and all this money launching the product, and then they were waiting for money to come in. Meanwhile the 8-bit stuff was dying again."

Rattigan and Ali also cut back Commodore's diverse line of products. "He laid people off and shut projects down and sold off things that didn't make sense anymore," recalls Bob Russell. "We might have still had steel [furniture] manufacturing up in Canada and those types of things."

One of those projects was an attempt to enter the cash register market. Commodore had engineered a sophisticated 6502-based system called MUCTS, the Multi-User Cash Terminal System. It had been part of Jack Tramiel's previous efforts to capture market space owned by IBM. Now, Commodore would only focus on its core competency of personal computers.

The Axe Swings

When the cuts came in May, they came in waves. "The way that Mehdi Ali worked, he would never really give you a target," recalls Gerard Bucas. "He would just say, 'I want you to cut by, let's say 30 percent.' 'Is that the total?' 'Well, let's first do that.' And then once you've done that, 'I want another 30 percent.'"

The theory behind the gradual cuts is that by taking things slow, a little at a time, it was less of a shock to the whole organization. Bucas disagreed with the philosophy. "That eventually causes major morale issues. You can't expect to go through yet another cost reduction, which means layoffs, without affecting the whole morale. The whole place will eventually collapse."

---

4   *InfoWorld*. May 26, 1986. p. 5 "Amid Losses, Commodore Plans Amiga 2000"

Each time, every single group was forced to lay off one in three workers. These groups included Amiga, Braunschweig, Canada, CATS, Commodore International, Commodore Japan, Engineering Services, Executives, Hong Kong, the Layout group, Legal, LSI Design, Manuals, Marketing, Mechanical Design, CSG (internally referred to as MOS Technology), PCB group, Purchasing, Quality Assurance, Quality Control, Sales, Service, Site Management, Software Engineering, Special Projects, Human Resources, System Engineering, and the Unix Group.

When push came to shove and department heads were forced to cut, they usually went to their performance reviews. For example, Ted Lenthe, head of LSI Design, relieved Kim Eckert, the designer of the 8563 video controller in the C128 computer.

Bucas soon became a thorn in the side of Ali by ignoring his directive to cut more staff. "I refused a number of times. I absolutely refused to do it," says Bucas. "And he said, 'Well we're going to get rid of you.' And I said 'Great, do me a favor. I can do something useful with my life.' I had some serious fights with Mehdi."

Those fights eventually spilled into fights with Commodore's top executives. "I had major fights and arguments," says Bucas. "But strange enough, for whatever reason, they never actually fired me, which is amazing."

Part of Bucas' frustration was that he was being asked to support a myriad of projects without adequate staff: the C128D-CR, the C64-CR, the B52 and the Amiga 2500. Most people agreed the B52 showed great potential to expand the Amiga market. The C64 was a solid seller and a cost-reduced version could only improve profits. Plus the project barely counted as an expenditure, having only one Japanese engineer working on it.

Perhaps the odd-duck here was the C128 line of computers. Although Christmas sales had been positive, mostly due to the pent up excitement of Commodore finally releasing a C64 successor, it wasn't really the success Rattigan thought it had been. At the ground level of computer users and software developers, there was no real enthusiasm for it.

1986 was shaping up to be a repeat of the previous year with too many expensive projects in the works. At the very least, cancelling the C128D-CR would give Commodore a better chance of succeeding with its remaining products. Granted it was a difficult call in mid-1986 considering the C128 was one of the few successful products of the previous year. In any event, Bucas now had to chip away at the resources behind each project.

Special Projects

At Commodore it became something of a dark inside-joke that when you moved into special projects it was a prelude to termination. After Commodore cancelled the Z8000 project, Russell moved onto special projects. "It wasn't like I quit being an engineer," he says. "We all got special projects and ended up doing other tasks. Irving knew us and people respected us, but it wasn't necessarily what we had joined the company for or what we were real good at."

In April, he investigated the Nintendo Entertainment System, which had just been given a limited release in New York. Russell sent the chip to MOS Technology where they "decapsulated" the chip and took photographs, which were enlarged and printed to posters for detailed examination. "I remember we had the chip designer of the 6502," recalls Russell. "He scraped the [NES] chip down to the die and took pictures."

The excavation and subsequent report amazed Russell. "The Nintendo core processor was a 6502 designed with the patented technology scraped off," says Russell. "We actually skimmed off the top of the chip inside of it to see what it was, and it was exactly a 6502. We looked at where we had the patents and they had gone in and deleted the circuitry where our patents were."

The NES used a Ricoh 2A03 processor for NTSC regions and a Ricoh 2A07 for PAL regions. "The main reason Nintendo used 6502 for their NES was because Sharp and Ricoh were two companies licensed to manufacture 6502 in Japan at that time," explains Yash Terakura. "Sharp Corporation made the first Nintendo 8-bit machine."

Although there were changes, the NES microprocessor ran 99% of the 6502 instruction set. "Some things didn't work quite right or took extra cycles," says Russell. "I don't know if anybody else figured that out, but Rockwell also had the core at that time, and we thought maybe they got the core from Rockwell."

It seemed like the special projects only kept Russell busy, hovering in a holding pattern. He sensed he was becoming a non-entity within Commodore, passively accepting his assignments.

Robert Russell

One clear example of "hitting bone" occurred when Gerard Bucas was forced to pare down engineering. On the B52 project, Jeff Porter was the project lead, George Robbins was working on the printed circuit board, and Bob Welland was working on reducing circuitry and putting it into the chipset. "They were going to fire my engineers who I thought wanted to stay with the company; people like Bob Welland," says Russell.

Russell fought for Welland because a key part of cost reducing the Amiga involved miniaturizing some of the logic onto a chipset. He convinced Bucas that the project needed a dedicated chip engineer and Welland was the smartest one for the job—albeit not very experienced.

But someone still needed to be cut. When Adam Chowaniec departed and Gerard Bucas took over, Bucas wanted to install his own people in key positions. It was hard not to notice Jeff Porter, the suit-wearing engineer who also had excellent communications skills, keeping the higher-ups informed of major decisions while taking care of the little details. He also kept apprised of developments that could hurt or help Commodore, such as attempting to rescue the Quantum Link deal, even though it was not his project. Bucas decided he wanted Porter to lead the system design group.

Russell's final special project was heading an investigation into a house fire caused by a VIC-20. As it turned out, the power supply had overheated and come into contact with some light drapes, sparking the fire that destroyed the home.

Russell sensed the tenuousness of his position and soon Bucas made the hard decision. "I got let go later on too," says Russell. Bucas, Porter, and Robbins would attempt to take up the slack left by Russell when it came to manufacturing the B52. "I knew Irving and could have gone to him and saved my job, but you know, I said the hell with it. I'll move on. They're forcing me out because politically they didn't want me around."

"Maybe he got judged for the C900 as not having gotten done fast enough," offers Robert Welland.

The cut was a massive blow to the B52 project. "One of the major losses was Bob Russell, who, I think decided to leave," says Welland. "He was an excellent manager and I felt a bit lost when he left. I honestly was shocked because we had started working on the A500 and Bob, he's got a really good mind and he had a really good understanding of what Commodore can and can't do."

In the aftermath, Jeff Porter moved into the vacant office next to Gerard Bucas. As Bucas predicted, the cuts hurt morale for those who remained. Welland recalls, "It was pretty devastating for people in West Chester because all of a sudden you're wondering, 'Am I going to be the person who gets laid off because I don't have a project to work on?' At some point when they announced a big chunk of layoffs, it was probably half the engineering team."

Amiga Layoffs

The Amiga engineers in Los Gatos were not having an easy time either. After the bungled Amiga marketing campaign, the team lost faith in Commodore. "Everything was great, but there were a lot of choices they were making, both at the engineering and at the marketing and business level, that we disapproved of," says RJ Mical.

On top of that, the poor performance of Commodore's stock had made the Amiga acquisition look more and more unfavorable as the months went by. "Amiga was kind of a disappointment," says Carl Sassenrath. "We sold the company to Commodore and the company's stock was really pushed high at that point. But there was a restricted period of time in which we couldn't sell the stock and during that time the stock went from $25 a share down to like $5 a share. We lost the great majority of what we thought we'd won in terms of stock options."

Surprisingly, the engineers were not overly upset. "Anything is nice," says Sassenrath, who used his money to purchase a ranch he calls Sassenranch. "I'm not a greedy person and I'm not actually really that great of a businessman as a result but everything helps. I put a down payment on things."

Don Reisinger also did not dwell on the stock loss. "I got a really nice bonus for the two years worth of work," he says. "Way more than I would have gotten working for anybody else. It allowed me to do some things that I wanted to do. I bought an old car that I had my sights on for probably twenty years and I could finally afford to do that. I was breaking up with my wife at the time but I had money to put a down payment on another house with the new wife."

Brewing beneath the surface was another issue from the previous year when Commodore ran into financial difficulties. "There was a whole issue of the cost of keeping the Los Gatos Amiga group going versus merging them with the West Chester engineering," explains Gerard Bucas. "Can Commodore afford it? Those were already all top management discussions going on at the time. Before Adam [Chowaniec] left, he was the one involved in that. Obviously, when I took over, I was the main one that was involved."

Although Commodore itself once had headquarters in California, it had moved to the East Coast to save money. "Let's face reality, Los Gatos was a very expensive place to live," says Jay Miner.[5] "We had to pay 25 to 50% more to get good people. And our rent per square foot was twice what Commodore paid in West Chester. Commodore didn't like paying gobs of money to support Amiga when their German and West Chester design teams could design better boxes faster and cheaper."

Bucas understood two things: first, Commodore needed the Amiga engineers for their expertise. Second, the Amiga engineers were not willing to move. He had no choice but to resist the constant demands from Commodore's upper management. "Bottom line, I was a supporter of the Los Gatos side," he says. "My feeling was that West Chester wasn't quite ready for it and it would be difficult to replace some of the expertise in Los Gatos. Those people were certainly not prepared to move to Pennsylvania, so it was complicated."

Commodore also believed the Amiga engineers should be closer to CSG. "They weren't really set up out there to do chip design in modern terms," says Dave Haynie. "Commodore had sent a lot of equipment out there to help, but the fab and everything was out here. I think to a certain extent it was reasonable to at least have the chip people out here."

Although Bucas fought for the Amiga engineers, he could not protect them from the same reductions occurring to the rest of Commodore. On May 14, the cuts began at Los Gatos. "The Bank insisted that Commodore cut its expenses," says Miner. "So it cut heavily into the engineering facility in West Chester and also at the Amiga facility in Los Gatos. A 70% or so cut in engineering in West Chester still left 50 or so people in engineering but similar cuts at Amiga left only 10."

Among the engineers caught up in the layoffs were head of software development Bob Pariseau and Rob Peck, the documentation guy. Pariseau had previously taken the rap for the Transformer software failure, as well as the flaky AmigaOS performance and the lateness of delivering the finished product. His dismissal was seen as part of the housecleaning that included Adam Chowaniec.

The reduced complement of Amiga engineers continued developing the Hires chipset and the Ranger computer to bring to the upcoming CES. The few remaining software developers, including Dale Luck and Glen Keller, also continued working on Amiga OS 1.2.

---

5   *Amiga User International*, June 1988. "The AUI Interview"

Commodore's engineering ranks had grown to a high of 253 in 1985. Now it was left with just 74 engineers across the company in 1986. The massive cuts made Commodore self-sustaining once again. "[Rattigan] basically got it back under control, but he got it under control by cutting heads," says Bob Russell.

Rattigan planned to spend the rest of the year making sure Commodore came out with products its customers truly desired, rather than poring over financial reports looking for more ways to cut costs. Now it would be up to his engineers to make those products a reality.

Building a B52
1986

The drastic personnel cuts, which began in May 1986, were complete by the beginning of June. After the decimation, Commodore's offices in West Chester looked almost deserted. Those who survived the cuts would now move on, undistracted, working on the B52 and other projects that had kept them relevant. But there were morale problems brewing under the surface and a level of mistrust with the Los Gatos Amiga team, who wanted to kill the B52 project before it gathered steam.

Empty Cubicles

The recent cuts left a visible reminder to the remaining employees that things were not quite right with Commodore. "For about a month we would walk past cubicles that were essentially abandoned," recalls Bob Welland. "We ended up with a whole bunch of cubicles that were full of the detritus of people who had left. It was kind of depressing to walk by an office where literally, it's as though the person just disappeared and all their stuff is there and they just didn't bother to pick it up."

The solution to the dismal situation came from Commodore's resident outside-the-box thinker. "At some point, George Robbins decided that this was too depressing and so he decided to expand his cubicle to absorb the ones left empty," says Welland.

Commodore's engineering offices were built from the famous Herman-Miller cubicle system, with walls over six feet tall and doors that could shut if an engineer required uninterrupted concentration. "They were just standard cubicle walls and George got out the hex wrenches and started moving the walls around," says Welland.

With his experiment complete, Robbins decided to keep going and help out his co-workers. "George actually was the one who decided at one point that he would get out the Herman-Miller tools and just change the shape of all the offices," says Welland. "I did the same and soon we all had expansive offices."

With every employee now occupying double the space, the work area no longer looked half-empty. It was a brilliant solution! "That was a very wise thing on George's part because our spirits kind of rose a lot as soon as we did the work to clear out the old stuff and reclaim the space for ourselves."

One less-glamorous display of Commodore's deep financial troubles occurred when management briefly tried reducing the janitorial staff. "In fact they stopped the garbage removal for about three months and the place got incredibly stinky," says Welland. "They just stuck these big garbage bins at the end of the corridors and that was not a very effective money-saving mechanism. So they eventually returned the custodial services. It was an odd time."

Rattigan's Spies

After taking over the reins from Marshall Smith, Thomas Rattigan now had unprecedented power to do whatever actions he felt necessary to run Commodore. But of course, he was also accountable for the results, good or bad. If that was the case, he wanted to know everything that happened. Rattigan now took steps to monitor all levels of the company.

Rattigan found Commodore's organizational structure to be chaotic, a holdover from the Tramiel years. "That largely hearkens back to the way Jack ran the organization because Jack was the kind of guy who had absolutely no qualms about talking to absolutely anyone in the company on any day of the week on any subject," he says.

Rattigan was unfamiliar with computer technology but needed a way to keep track of what was going on. At this particular time, the West Chester engineers were viewed poorly by the upper ranks of the organization, likely due to the department's failure to produce a clear hit product since the C64 in 1982. The unruly reputation cultivated by Bil Herd and his C128 Animals also didn't help.

"It was an organization that, if you looked at it from a normal North American corporate structure point of view, was a nightmare," says Rattigan. "I didn't have enough time to change it, quite frankly, because you would have to fire a lot of people, and you'd probably end up firing a number of good people if you did that. So I had to ask, how do you constructively try to take advantage of this chaos?"

Rattigan, an avid reader, picked up the 1981 book *The Soul of a New Machine* to try and understand computer companies and formulate a strategy for Commodore. As a result, he ended up embracing Commodore's disorganized, non-hierarchical engineering department. "It's not all boxes and arrows and who reports to whom. My experience was—and some of the stuff I have read suggests—that there can be multiple lines and what appears on paper to be mass confusion but somehow or other it works. That sort of speaks to the very loose structure of Commodore and the various pockets of strength."

Rattigan also developed a corporate philosophy, similar to Jack Tramiel's, that competition within Commodore would improve product quality and hasten development time. "We'll create an in-house competitive situation and hope for the best," he recalls. To this end, he tried to have two competing cost reduced Amiga computers (the Los Gatos A1000-CR and a West Chester version). He would also attempt to pit the Los Gatos Ranger against the German A2500. Let the winner prevail. However, this strategy did not sit well with engineers or, more importantly, Irving Gould.

By now, Gerard Bucas was viewed as a thorn in the side of executives right up to Thomas Rattigan. Bucas' engineers, in turn, were not very supportive of Rattigan's attempts to gain control over the engineering projects. Rattigan had even done an end-run around the System Engineering group by asking Ted Lenthe of the LSI Design group to conceive of a new C128-CR. This led to some engineers, Jeff Porter included, giving their CEO the derisive monicker "Ratman".

Instead of dropping in personally to monitor Bucas' engineers, Rattigan would keep tabs on the engineering efforts by employing spies. He reveals, "Without telling anybody, I got to two of the lower level engineers and I said, 'I'm not telling your boss this but you guys are reporting to me directly now. You're going to be my conscience on cost because quite frankly, there aren't enough hours in the day to understand component costs. Every time the primary group working on it comes in, you're going to have a secret meeting with me afterwards and we're going to critique this thing.'"

Rattigan, being a responsible CEO, had a keen interest in the success of the C64 and was trying to figure out how best to continue that success. This obsession led him to consult with the very people who had been responsible for the C64's success.

One such consultant was Charles Winterble, the former project manager on the C64.[1] At the time, Winterble still had a Commodore lawsuit pending against him, initiated by Jack Tramiel, over the Atari 2600 keyboard computer. "I got a call from Commodore and they said, 'Would you come on down and do some work for us?'" recalls Winterble.

Rattigan wanted an experienced opinion on Commodore's current products. "I went in and I looked at their whole computer line," says Winterble. "They gave me samples of everything and I took everything apart and gave them some input on cost reduction. Mostly what Rattigan wanted me for was to re-examine the work their engineers were doing and to give them a second opinion on what they were being told by their engineers."

It was clear to Winterble that there were politics at work within Commodore. "It shows the distrust in the company when the management team doesn't even know if they can trust their own engineering team and they bring in somebody from the outside," he says. "Here I am being sued by Commodore, yet they trusted my opinion."

Winterble bluntly expressed his opinion about Marshall Smith and Thomas Rattigan's favored product, the C128. "When I saw their version of the C128, I think I didn't make people happy," he recalls. "When they asked about it, I said, 'Are you people out of your mind? What is this piece of crap, the Commodore 128? It's got CP/M and all this crap in there.'"

Rattigan felt the color drain from his face. He had previously been led to believe by Marshall Smith that the C128 could become the most valuable product in Commodore's arsenal, continuing the C64 success and hopefully building up to those amazing numbers one day. The meeting quickly disabused him of his love for the C128, and he started to realize the sales numbers did not necessarily mean the C128 would become the savior he thought it was.

Rattigan also brought in former 6502 co-designers Will Mathys and Bill Mensch, who had their own ideas on Commodore's direction. This rubbed many engineers, Jeff Porter among them, the wrong way as they felt he should be relying on them more than outside consultants.

Rattigan's apparent mistrust of his engineers, unruly bunch that he viewed them as, along with his attempts to rely on opinions from outside consultants did not sit well with Gerard Bucas. This began to have a corrosive effect on the relationship that would only get worse.

---

1   Winterble had joined Coleco to attempt to save the beleaguered Adam computer.

B52 Project Begins

Despite the differences between them, once Thomas Rattigan signed off on the B52 project, Jeff Porter and his engineers were off and running. As project manager, Porter was responsible for all the jobs that his two main engineers did not cover. "He didn't do any of the hardware but there were a lot of details," says Bob Welland. "He was responsible for the overall product management. He sourced the power supply. I'm sure he worked with Commodore Japan with the case. It's the kind of thing where he would say, 'Fifty thousand ROMs are showing up this week.' I know how to specify them but I don't know how you get them. He was more savvy about that kind of stuff."

The B52 team continued developing the cost-reduced concept in detail throughout early 1986, slowly creating block diagrams and detailed schematics of the motherboard. "There were a lot of people talking about what an A500 should be," says Porter. On top of removing the writable control store (WCS) and using an external power supply, more ideas came to the design. Porter wanted to incorporate his PAL modifications into the B52 so that it could be released in North America and Europe simultaneously.

Even before George Robbins defined the dimensions of the PCB board, Porter began working on the plastic case for the B52. He started early because the tooling required to make the moulds required one of the biggest lead times for the project.

Porter's first step was to find an industrial designer to create a concept sketch. After that, Commodore's in-house engineers would take care of creating the detailed schematics and create the moulds that would mass produce the cases.

Porter found Rob Gemmell, formerly of the Apple Industrial Design Group, for the concept sketches. Gemmell had designed the cases for the Apple IIe and IIc and in the process he helped define the renowned Snow White design language. When Steve Jobs left Apple in 1985, the group followed suit and founded a company called One Group. The Los Gatos engineers had hired Gemmell to create a Styrofoam mockup of the Amiga Ranger the previous year and referred him to Porter.

Porter gave Gemmell the basic design specs, including the number and type of physical ports. On the Amiga 1000, the expansion port was on the right side. However, Porter wanted the disk drive on the right side of the B52 because most people are right handed and would use that hand for inserting disks. Instead he placed the expansion port on the left side, which would make most A1000 expansion modules sit backwards. This design choice would later prove controversial with the original Amiga developers.

By late May 1986, Gemmell had produced a number of drawings for the B52 case. Porter passed them to Herb Mosteller of Commodore's mechanical engineering group to work out the details. After some discussion, Porter and the engineers were left unsatisfied with Gemmell's concept sketches.

Porter went outside Commodore once again and sought out a concept from the industrial design department at the Philadelphia College of Art. "Jeff went to see if there were any design students who wanted to design a case for what became the Amiga 500," recalls Welland. "We got this kid who was really creative. We showed him the Atari ST case, which is strange in some ways. He prototyped probably a dozen cases and they were all kind of rad. We were telling him which ones we'd liked."

Welland compares their favored design with the angular look of the Batmobile in the *Dark Knight* trilogy of films. "We finally settled on a case that he had designed and then it must have gone to Irving Gould or some management arm," he recalls. "They're like, 'No, we're not going to do that. Commodore Japan will design the case.'"

Only then did the engineers realise the major design decisions were out of their hands. "That is just one funny example of where you think you own something and then you go and you do a bunch of work and get excited and you get a kid really excited," recalls Welland. "He was pretty disappointed when they just scrapped it."

Although Porter's first attempt was jettisoned, he was thrilled by the industrial design by Commodore Japan engineer Yukiya Itoh. "He was absolutely an amazing industrial designer," says Porter. "He had designed a lot of high-end stereo receivers in his heyday before discovering his talent for computers. He made a few variations of the A500, but I absolutely fell in love with the final one."

Welland wasn't so sure. "The case we have is the case that was handed to us," he says. "The Commodore Japan case was boring. It is just very utilitarian. It's better than the 520ST case, which has these really bizarre angular function keys, but there's nothing interesting about it."

Once the concept art was agreed upon, it was up to Herb Mosteller to make it fit together, with all the interior parts. "We had to have a soft mould made and a hard mould and so there's a big interaction with manufacturing," says Welland.

The mould consisted of two pieces: a top and bottom. The rubber soft mould was less expensive and would produce cases for the pilot production run of about 500 computers. However, the soft mould deteriorates with usage, so when it came time to mass produce the B52, Commodore would create expensive moulds made from hardened steel.

Visiting Jay Miner

Once Welland had a detailed plan for the Fat Agnus and Gary chips, he shared them with the Amiga engineers in California. Jay Miner, the man who designed Agnus, would be critical to helping implement the changes. Unfortunately, since hearing about the plan for a low-cost Amiga at Thomas Rattigan's "Come to Jesus" meeting, he was not a fan of the concept. "The A500 was certainly not supported by California, that's for sure," says Gerard Bucas. "Because that was against their basic principles. They were very negative on that type of thing. And the A1000, which was their baby, unfortunately didn't sell well."

Jeff Porter, on top of his many duties, would have to pull the Californian team over to his cause. "Jeff Porter was the key project manager on the A500," says Bucas. "He almost, I won't say single handedly, because that's not true, but he certainly was the motivator of the A500."

One of the main obstacles to the B52 project was a competing A1000 cost reduction by Glenn Keller. The West Chester engineers had little confidence in the rival project. "In terms of the engineering group, Commodore was all about cost reduction and such," says Eric Lavitsky. "I think that there was definitely a sentiment inside West Chester that the Amiga technology was great but they didn't know how to build a consumer box and they don't know how to do cost reduction properly."

On June 3, a fax arrived from Keller in response to Welland's plans for the new chipset. The fax contained 14 points describing why the B52 chipset would not work and why West Chester should no longer pursue the project. "There was some 'high-speed' stuff we folded into Fat Agnus and there was some controversy as to if it was possible with the technology we had at the time," says Welland.

Both Jeff Porter and George Robbins individually replied to the fax with a point-by-point refutation. This was, in turn, replied to with another fax on June 9 explaining why the B52 project should include a detachable keyboard and should not compete with the A1000-CR. "California was very negative on that, because of course they were like totally anti-having a, for example, integrated keyboard," says Bucas. "That was against their philosophy and against their baby. That wasn't what their baby was born to do."

At the heart of the matter, the Los Gatos engineers doubted Fat Agnus would be fast enough to also take on the additional logic. "It's funny because, to do Fat Agnus, we got some pushback from some people," says Welland. "There's a 28 MHz clock that goes into it. We pulled in some stuff that had been discrete and there was some question as to whether the process could handle that speed."

Finally the team decided it would be best to hash out the disagreements in person. The engineers created a proposal for the West Coast engineering team, laying out the path to a low-cost Amiga computer. "We cobbled up a schematic and Jeff Porter and I went to California to talk with Jay Miner about our ideas," says Welland.

On June 24, Welland and Porter left for California. At the time, Miner and Mitchy were hard at work on his Hi-Res Ranger chipset, while enjoying his now un-mortgaged home and yacht. Ron Nicholson recalls, "His house is only four miles away from me so we'd go out and meet. He owned a 50 foot motor yacht which he kept out in the Sacramento Delta. I went out on a couple of weekend cruises with him a couple of years after all these events occurred. I still saw Mitchy and two smaller Pomeranians running around at that time. He didn't bring the Pomeranians into work but he did Mitchy."

Miner would have been impressed by Jeff Porter after he engineered the PAL version of his machine with improvements. "Jay was a really nice person and, in spite of the obvious tension of us proposing to do a design that the original Amiga team might also want a part in, he was cordial and helpful," says Welland. "I think what was really going on was that they were scared that if we ran with what we were doing, we would end up controlling the hardware. And I can understand that fear. They've done this startup, they've done all this work and there they are in California and there's some weird guys in West Chester, Pennsylvania presenting to Jay Miner a machine that they have no involvement in. We didn't consult them on the decisions that we made. We just looked at the machine and thought, 'Hmm, let's fix it this way.' So I can understand the frustration about that."

Out of the proposed cost reductions, there was particular pushback against four items: the external power supply, the attached keyboard, the removal of the WCS, and changes to Agnus. "There was a lot of hand wringing and consternation because who are these guys in West Chester to tell the Amiga guys in Los Gatos how to design a cost reduced Amiga," recalls Porter. "You're not putting the diapers on the baby correctly! 'Oh my God, you're not going to have a brick power supply, are you?' 'Yes.' 'Oh you're not going to have a detachable keyboard? That's sacrilege.'"

Perhaps because of the passion the Dancing Fools had towards the Amiga, it was the programmers who objected the most to any hardware changes. "I don't think it was Jay Miner. I think it was the software guys," says Welland.

Dale Luck had mixed feelings about a low-cost Amiga. "Commodore has always been a low-cost manufacturer and producer, so that kind of was in a different direction than most engineers would want," he says. "They wanted to see more performance and more capability."

Porter knew he could sway the engineers with hard numbers. "I said trust me, I know how to build cheap consumer products. Let me show you the costs. I know how to build an Amiga for $200. We'll sell it for $400 and the retailer will sell it for $500."

In the electronics industry, there are several price points that marketing people consider "magic" price points, at which a tipping point occurs with sales. "$500 is a magic price," explains Porter. "If we hit $499 we will sell a shitload. You want an internal power supply and a detachable keyboard? Now your computer is going to be $799. You are going to sell a fraction of the computers you will sell at $499. There is something magic about the $499 price point."

Despite his protests, Glenn Keller, who was leading the Amiga 1000 cost reduction at the time, respected the work done by Porter and his team. "The typical case for most stuff is two or three times smaller for the bill of materials. That was the typical industry thing," he says. "I remember I was working on cost reductions for a while. The Commodore guys were so much better at that. It was like, 'Hey, these guys are a hundred times better at this than I am.'"

Having hard numbers did little to soften Porter's opponents in the software division at the time. "This is kind of where most of the engineers really got pissed off at me because I could tell them how much something would cost before they had designed it," says Porter.

The engineers objected to the possibility of Fat Agnus working. "So various arguments came back as to why what we were doing was wrong," recalls Welland. "There were two that I remember. One was we don't want the writeable control store to go away. The second was we don't think that Fat Agnus will work."

According to Mical, they also believed the engineers should have pushed the chips farther. "There were a lot of people that didn't really like the decisions that were made with Fat Agnus because it wasn't enough," says Mical. "They didn't have enough of the extra graphics display capabilities that we were looking for. It was a good step in the right direction but it violated the idea of the bus architecture and actually slowed the machine down."

Mical was aware that some of their feelings could be misplaced. "We were concerned there was some 'not invented here' going on," he says. "We were always watchful that we were not just being emotional little jerks but that our protests were legitimate, and I think they were."

Porter appealed to the engineer who mattered most, and who also happened to be the most cordial. "Jay Miner is a sweetheart of a guy and a great IC designer," says Porter, who pleaded, "I promise not to screw up your baby. I promise to make it a hit. We absolutely can do this. I know how to do it, I've done it before. Let me do it."

Perhaps it was Miner's background in the army that enabled him to put his personal opinions aside, but he did end up helping Porter's cause. "And then Jay Miner squashed that. He seemed fine with it," recalls Welland. "In particular, he saw no reason that the 'high-speed' additions would not work. This gave us a lot of confidence."

B52 Chip Design

Throughout the spring and summer of 1986, George Robbins and Bob Welland continued work on the B52. Welland worked on Fat Agnus and Gary, the glue logic chip, while Robbins owned the motherboard, a complex job with many issues to sort out.

Welland is humble about his own contribution to the project. "This was not really a significant change to the Amiga chipset, it was a modest evolution of the system-level design," he says. "In fact, the A500 was designed to be identical to the A1000 in terms of the cycle-level operation."

Because of the recent doubts expressed about whether or not the new Fat Agnus chip would work, Welland devised a backup plan. "They did two things: they built the Fat Agnus and they built what they were calling the Fat chip," says Dave Haynie. "They built a chip that did all the Fat stuff outside of Agnus just in case the Fat Agnus didn't work."

Rather than using the 48 pin chips of the original Amiga chipset, Welland would begin using an 84 pin chip for Fat Agnus, almost doubling the inputs and outputs. "We got to use an 84 pin package rather than sticking with 48 pins. I had been working on chip architectures a fair amount so I understood as soon as we got that bigger package that we could pull some of the logic into the Agnus," says Welland. "The bulk of the design was looking at the A1000 schematic and trying to figure out if we have a gate array and a bigger package, what can we put where."

Welland worked with Robbins to determine where the chips connected and to determine what signal each pin on each chip produced. "Once the chip pinouts were fixed and the overall system architecture was complete, I focused on the implementation of the Gary gate array," says Welland. Meanwhile, the Fat Agnus alterations would be completed by LSI engineer Victor Andrade.

In the early 80's, the gate array was a new design and process for quickly creating new integrated circuits without requiring a completely new chip layout. It was first pioneered in the UK with the Sinclair ZX81 before being adopted by other semiconductor companies. A gate array consists of hundreds or thousands of logic gates (NOR and NAND gates) that are not connected in any way. In other words, the gate array is simply an array of gates. To make the chip functional, a layer of metal connections is printed on top of the existing gates to connect them together.[2]

In fact, Welland's chip took its name from Gate Array, which they shortened to Gary. Welland relished in the task. "I am a designer who most enjoys architectural challenges and then enjoys focusing on the details of something concrete, like Gary," he says.

Welland spent days at a time at Commodore during this design phase. "A tradition at Commodore was for engineers to work late into the night, often all night," he recalls. "In the summer when it got hot, I would often take a nap underneath my Apollo Domain CAD station because they were in an air conditioned room and the room was dark (in those days, high resolution color displays were not particularly bright so the room was kept dark). A lot of people ended up falling asleep there. Part of what made that a fun place to work is that people worked with an enormous amount of passion."

The passion was noticed somewhat belatedly even by the West Coast Amiga engineers. "The enthusiasm with which those people took that project, made it their own, and made it better, astounded," says Glenn Keller. "I noticed that everybody was nice, but I didn't really put it in context until much later how extraordinary that group of people was."

The pair of Robbins and Welland complemented each other's skills. "If I have an architectural-level thing, I can go and push that forward but when it comes to the minutiae of actually manufacturing something, I kinda get lost to be honest," says Welland. "You don't want someone like me doing it because it won't have all the ground covered that needs to be covered."

---

2   This type of gate array was a precursor to the field-programmable gate array (FPGA) that did not require a chip fabrication plant to connect the gates.

"Bob was a very good theoretical guy but he was one of those guys like [D128 designer] Kong Sui," says Dave Haynie. "You don't want to let him too near a soldering iron."

In contrast, George Robbins was comfortable with the complex, multi-faceted challenges of designing the rest of the computer. "George was the opposite. He handled every loose-end, every detail that might get by, and labored over, with passion and intensity, the details that have no boundaries," says Welland. "He stands in my mind as the rock for the A500 and deserves to be considered its standard bearer."

GRR

George Robbins, known as GRR to his coworkers, had been a consultant at Commodore since he started on the Unix C900 project, successfully redesigning the board. But he had been such an eccentric character, management had put off hiring him for as long as they could. Perhaps they wanted time to reassure themselves that he was a consistently valuable, stable employee.

At night, the engineer liked to liven the empty offices with music to keep his energy up. "George Robbins at some point set up a stereo in his office with a record player and some big speakers," says Welland. "Unfortunately, the offices were far from the lab. George's solution was to point a speaker up towards the ceiling and remove an acoustic panel from the false ceiling and crank the music up. The space between the false ceiling and the real ceiling acted like a sound guide and all you needed to do to get music was to remove an acoustic panel and the music would come pouring in."

A particular confluence of tastes came together due to the project's code-name, B52, and *The B-52's*, a popular American band. "Usually, that music was the B-52's and the theme song for the Amiga 500 was Rock Lobster, which I think had enough energy in it to keep us awake," says Welland. "Often we would stay overnight and whoever was left would head off to the cafeteria, which opened at perhaps 7 am. The best part of this time would be heading for the cafeteria for pancakes, looking disheveled, with the loud sounds of the B-52's suffusing the building, and watching as confused marketing type folks would arrive to this surreal atmosphere."

Working with Terry Fisher, Commodore's resident PCB expert, Robbins would spend months perfecting the B52 motherboard. "No one was more passionate, or contributed more energy and devotion to the A500 than George Robbins," says Welland. "He loves making sure all the details are covered."

The fact that Commodore was seemingly falling apart at the time only spurred on the engineers. "The collapse around us gave us a sense of urgency that the Amiga would either make or break Commodore. This gave us a lot of motivation," says Welland.

Rebound
1986

With the most painful cuts now behind him, Thomas Rattigan set out to build up Commodore once again into a revenue powerhouse. And he was determined not to fall into the same trap his predecessor, Marshall Smith, had fallen into of allowing too many projects to take root within the company. Instead, he would try to focus on a few core products and cut the rest. But first, he would bring Commodore to the Chicago CES to debut the resurrected C64.

Ranger Shut Down

Thomas Rattigan had attempted to cultivate two competing engineering groups with their respective Amiga successors. As was the tradition at Commodore, his plan was to view the systems at the June CES show and, along with Irving Gould and Nigel Shepherd, choose the winner.

The Amiga team had designed as much of the Ranger system as possible given that the chipset would not be complete until the next year. The prototype was little more than a clear acrylic glass case with cardboard internals representing a motherboard and polystyrene boxes representing disk drives. It looked like a thicker A1000.

Unfortunately, when Rattigan requested a demonstration of the prototype Ranger for the upcoming CES, the Los Gatos engineers had nothing to bring. Most of the Ranger was in the conceptual stage; a collection of good ideas and some lab investigation to prove certain hardware concepts.

It was now obviously too late for Ranger, especially with the A2500 almost ready for production. Rattigan had no choice but to cancel the project on May 30, 1986. "There was a lot of resentment about that," says Rattigan. "Obviously the Amiga group on the West Coast was disappointed because the old Commodores transitioned to being the new Amiga."

In truth, after the May 14 cuts that left Los Gatos with only 10 employees, there would be little chance of the engineers completing the Ranger design. "They chose the one that was designed by the Germans, the A2000," says Dale Luck. "That design was probably the lower cost design than we were doing out here, but our design looked a lot better."

Prior to Thomas Rattigan, Commodore seemed incapable of pruning dead-end projects, much to the detriment of the company. "They had gone crazy," says Robert Russell. "They were this billion-dollar company and they said, 'Let's hire everybody and let's start all these projects.' It was just that we were out of control; it wasn't like we couldn't be profitable."

Now, with Rattigan in charge, the company was capable of making hard decisions. "There are a lot of mixed stories on just how far they got on that," says Dave Haynie. "I never saw schematics or anything that claimed to be the Ranger, but of course that's kind of how legends are built. I could never really refute it either."

However, the cancellation did not mean the closure of the Los Gatos offices due to two main areas of development. First, the Amiga software developers continued working on AmigaOS version 1.2. Second, Jay Miner and his team of chip designers continued working on the Ranger chipset, which Commodore believed might be used in future Amiga computers.

After the Ranger cancellation, a few more key Amiga employees departed, including Bob "Kodiak" Burns and Sam Dicker. "People started giving notice and quitting but Commodore stuck to its policy of no raises and no replacements," says Jay Miner.[1] The departures left Los Gatos with around five employees in total. As a result, Amiga was chronically short on manpower.

With so few remaining employees, Gerard Bucas began selling off equipment to raise funds to continue Commodore's operations. As Bob Russell noted, in the previous year, Commodore had gone wild purchasing expensive equipment, including several new VAX computers. In fact, Commodore had so many they used a piece of DEC software called VMScluster, released in 1983, to connect them together (an early form of networking), which they called a VAX cluster.

---

1   Amiga User International. June 1988. "The AUI Interview"

Now, Bucas sold all but two of the VAX machines, getting rid of the one in Los Gatos and other groups. He sold the newer VAX 8600, two VAX-11/750's, the VAX-11/785 from Los Gatos, and a microVAX. He also sold off three Mentor 660 workstations from Los Gatos and two slower Mentor 600 workstations from West Chester. Commodore's excessive expenditures under Marshall Smith were now being reversed.

Choosing Products

Before CES began, Commodore's executives and engineers gathered together in a hotel suite to decide which products to display at the show. "Through most of Commodore, until the money got really bad, Irving Gould would of course have a suite at every one of these big shows," recalls Dave Haynie.

Clive Smith brought the C64c, along with a demonstration of GEOS 1.2, and the new 1351 prototype mouse. However, it was a fait accompli that the C64c would display publicly at CES, as the decision to go ahead with the C64c was made at the start of the year.

Although Dave Haynie had only recently completed the schematics for his C256 motherboard, codenamed BMW, he had a few prototypes to display to demonstrate the additional memory. "During many parts of this company's existence, engineering was bottom up as far as what the product would be," recalls Haynie. "I would build something and show it off to the bosses and they would say, 'Okay, that's very nice, maybe you could try something else,' or, 'We'll think about it.'"

Because he could not demonstrate a prototype with a 4 MHz 65816 chip yet, Haynie's co-worker, Frank Palaia, hacked together the next best thing. "Frank and I each took half the problem," says Haynie. "He made a version of the C128 that ran a 4 MHz Z80. I made a version of the C128 with a slightly different MMU that gave 256K of built in memory."

Haynie delivered his presentation of the machine, noting the final product would use the same 16-bit processor as the upcoming Apple IIx. He also told the executives BMW stood for "Big Mean Worm", something Apple should fear. The German executives loved the idea, since the C128 gained the most traction there. However, Nigel Shepherd of Commodore North America was not as enthusiastic, especially considering it lacked C64 compatibility.

The B52 Amiga was already eagerly anticipated by executives, in fact too much so for Porter's liking. Earlier in the year, Bucas had pushed Porter against his will for a 1986 release date. By now, Porter was already having misgivings about that date and attempted to dissuade management from the schedule. He told them tooling for the B52 case would not be ready before Christmas. Furthermore, dealers would be unhappy if the B52 launched alongside the A2500, undercutting their sales and hurting its chances of becoming established.

Instead, Porter urged management to focus on launching BMW in 1986, with an ambitious ship date of November 3. He estimated the Amiga B52 would only ship 100,000 units in the first six months, grossing $18 million, while the BMW would ship 200,000 units and generate $36 million. With tensions running high between engineering and Rattigan, Porter's suggestion was seen as something of a rebellion.

The Germans, along with Henri Rubin, brought their Amiga 2500. The Los Gatos Amiga engineers were not won over by the A2500 design, feeling their own Ranger would have been a true Amiga successor.

The Germans also brought over a reworked C128D-CR. Dave Haynie had originally designed the C128D, which did not pass FCC regulations due to noisy radio emissions. The Europeans reengineered the C128D to pass those tests and make it more profitable. "They cost reduced it in Europe and put it in a slightly more PC-ish metal case," says Haynie.

The new metal case shielded the stray radio emissions, allowing for a release in the US. However, it no longer had the stylish handle or keyboard dock of the previous plastic-case C128D. A cheaper floppy drive also reduced manufacturing costs significantly.

The decision around the C128 prototypes was more difficult because the C128 line had enjoyed a strange kind of success. Early sales were high and at the time Commodore could be forgiven for thinking it was merely the tip of a sales curve that would continue to grow higher and higher, replacing the C64. By June 1986, Commodore had sold an impressive 600,000 units. "[The C128] was supposed to be sort of a stopgap measure," explains Bil Herd. "It was supposed to have a year of climbing and then die off over the second year and give our 16-bit guys a chance. When they didn't market the Amiga very well, they kept the C128 alive longer."

However, the sales curve of the C128 was slowing down, likely due to the lack of software development for the platform. It was starting to look like further C128 product development could be a wasted effort, though Commodore would continue to manufacture the C128 for as long as it was profitable.

Rattigan, who earlier in the year had favored the C128 over the Amiga computers, now had a more stoic view of the system following the comments he received from C64 project manager Charles Winterble. Instead he emphasised making cost-reduced versions of the current models, rather than new models in the series.

June 1986 CES

With the pre-CES meeting over, it was time to focus on CES itself. The previous year, Atari had attended in a small meeting room on the upper floor. Now Compute! observed, "This year the tables were turned. While Atari occupied a large, crowded booth full of third-party software developers supporting the ST, Commodore occupied the mezzanine rooms showing its newly packaged 64."[2]

Commodore did not display the Amiga or related products at the show, instead choosing to save Amiga related announcements for COMDEX, where IBM and Apple showcased their products. Instead, it focused on the 8-bit line of computers at CES.

Commodore's showing at CES was not well received. As Robert Lock wrote in *Compute!'s Gazette*, "The seeming lethargy in market positioning that has stricken Commodore since the introduction of the Amiga is one of the most shocking turnabouts we've witnessed in the modern history of this industry. One wonders whether the bankers have begun to call the strategic shots at Commodore."[3]

Industry observers were curious if Commodore would attempt another computer in the C64 line, and were mildly receptive of the new C64c. Rattigan, who was from the soft drink industry, saw parallels to Coke Classic versus the New Coke. *Commodore Magazine* wrote, "Unlike Coca-Cola, Commodore kept the classic alive without the necessity of outcry."[4]

The most notable change was the refined case. As CBM General Manager Nigel Shepherd described it, "We decided that there should be, in appearance, more synergy between the 64 and the 128."

Gerard Bucas admits it was a small step. "For whatever reason, I think they eventually called it a C64c," he says. "I don't even think we added many features, quite honestly. It was really more repackaging, remarketing, rebranding."

---

2   *Compute!*, "Editor's Notes" (August, 1986), p. 6.

3   *Compute!'s Gazette*, "Editor's Notes" (September 1986), p. 6.

4   *Commodore Magazine*, "The Year in Computers" (January 1987), p. 71.

Commodore was also attempting to market the addition of the Quantum Link trial disk as a selling feature of the C64c. As per the agreement with Quantum, Commodore created several promotional videos, one for QLink and one for Habitat, made by same advertising company Commodore had used to create the Amiga sepia tone ads. The new ads both featured old newsreel footage as though done in the 1940's, complete with an old-time announcer touting the products.

Unfortunately, the QLink deal was not panning out as hoped. Commodore had increased the production of the 1200-baud 1670 modems for the C64 in an effort to include more QLink trial disks. The modem had sold 2000 per month since its release. As a result, the company now had 25,000 of the $199 modems sitting in the warehouse. Just prior to the show, Jeff Porter found out that another company would announce at CES a rival C64 Hayes-compatible 1200-baud modem for only $99.

The situation produced a nightmare for Nigel Shepherd, who would now have a difficult time unloading them. Porter recommended offering $100 rebates on the modems to clear them out, while moving manufacturing from US Robotics to Hong Kong, which could produce them for half the $60 manufacturing price. He estimated half of C128 owners would purchase a $99 modem from Commodore, for a total of 250,000 modems sold, and urged manufacturing to begin in Hong Kong.

Nigel Shepherd also found out from speaking with CES attendees that the C128 was not well respected in the US. Furthermore, most insiders he spoke to were not enthusiastic about a C128-mode only machine; there was far more enthusiasm for the C64. This confirmed Rattigan's suspicions since his conversation with Charles Winterble prior to CES.

NES Debut

One other important competitor to Commodore emerged at the June 1986 CES show. Japanese businessmen are known for their patience, but the story of the Nintendo Entertainment System is extreme, even by their standards. The first prototypes of the NES were created in 1982 (the year the C64 launched) and almost distributed by Dave Morse while he was at Tonka. However, due to the video game crash, Nintendo was unable to launch the console in North America.

So they waited.

Jack Tramiel had been famous for beating back Japanese competition in the computer industry and was fearful they would take over the home computer market. They never did, but they came in through an alternate route to compete against the C64.

In late 1985, Nintendo attempted to release the NES console to the New York market only. The launch was an abysmal failure, since retailers were still antagonistic towards video game consoles.

To distance themselves from the video game industry, they began including a very toy-looking device with the NES called the Robotic Operating Buddy. This gave the console a novel appearance and allowed it to become distributed by the established toy market.

With R.O.B. in tow, Nintendo launched again in February 1986, and met with success. With the marketing strategy perfected, Nintendo planned for a massive nationwide release in September 1986 for Christmas. The original set from 1985 sold for $249, which included a Zapper light gun and the Robotic Operating Buddy. This year the price dropped to only $199.99. The C64 was about to gain a formidable competitor.

Near the end of CES it was time for the engineers to celebrate. Irving Gould never stayed in the United States for long, even during CES. "He always left a day or two early, so his suite was always empty by the end of the week," recalls Haynie. This gave Commodore employees the opportunity to cut loose after the stress of preparing for CES. "Everybody would go there. We would have a party in Irving's suite every year. It was a standard company thing."

A2500 Product Review

Earlier in the year, Irving Gould believed the A2500 would be ready in time for a holiday release in both Europe and North America. However, an engineering meeting would determine the fate of the machine. "At Commodore, if you did a design, you would do a thing called a design review," explains Hedley Davis. "Basically everybody would cram into this conference room and they would just pick you apart. They would throw stones and rocks and needles and bombs. If you came out of that meeting unscathed, your design was probably pretty solid because nobody could find a fucking problem with it."

The A2500 did not fare well at its mid-1986 design review. "The Germans basically took the A1000 and put an expansion bus on it and put it in a PC case, and there's the A2000," explains Dave Haynie. "So [West Chester management] looked at that and said, 'This isn't going to work.'"

Nigel Shepherd and Thomas Rattigan decided they could not release it to the North American market. Since the A2500 was based on the expensive

A1000 motherboard, it was exceedingly costly to manufacture, especially with the additional hardware required for the expansion bus. Commodore could get away with selling it for a higher price in Germany, but it would not fly in North America.

The design of the German A2500 was also buggy, understandable because the German engineers lacked access to the type of development equipment used in the US, not to mention CSG. "The one that Germany built was not electronically reliable enough," says Commodore engineer Michael Sinz. Suddenly Commodore lacked a new Amiga for 1986.

Now Commodore was left with a $135 million line of credit to spend on manufacturing and advertising, but with nothing new introduce. It was an appalling situation.

Debate to Sell off CSG

Even after the layoffs and liquidation of expensive equipment, Thomas Rattigan and his executive team continued looking for ways to cut costs. After all, it would be months if not years until the new Amiga computers emerged and began adding to the bottom line. Even whole divisions within the company were no longer off limits.

Commodore had two divisions which, working together, produced semiconductor chips. The chipset design started with the LSI engineering group (Large Scale Integration) working out of West Chester. The director of LSI development had been Robert Olah, who was replaced by one of his chip designers, Ted Lenthe, in April 1986. Lenthe, a true Commodore man, would run the LSI division until the very end.

Sometimes engineers from outside the LSI group—such as system engineers Dave Haynie, Bob Welland, and Greg Berlin—designed "glue" chips to help them dramatically cost reduce the systems they designed.

The chip designers then handed off the final results, called the "tape out" or Pattern Generation, to Commodore Semiconductor Group (formerly MOS Technology). "The design of the chips was all done by engineering, which was my group," says Gerard Bucas. "MOS Technology just did manufacturing, they didn't do any design."

This artwork went to the CSG chip foundry at 950 Rittenhouse Road in nearby Valley Forge. Thomas Biggs, another Commodore loyalist who would stay with the company to the end, ran the whole operation. "The fab was not what I expected," says Commodore engineer Joe Augenbraun. "I expected people in bunny suits, everything painted bright white, and breathing apparatus. Really clean rooms."

In actuality, the operation was surprisingly low-budget, with inner walls of concrete cinder blocks. "It looked like classrooms in my old elementary school," says Augenbraun. "The process steps weren't done in order. They were running boats of wafers from room to room on AV carts and sticking them in the machines. And 98% of the machines looked like washing machines."

Despite the unimpressive appearance of CSG, engineers such as Hedley Davis and Bob Welland believed the chip foundry was key to Commodore's unique success in the computer industry.

Other managers had a different opinion. "The biggest problem with Commodore—to a certain extent was their strengths and their weakness—was MOS," says Gerard Bucas. "Building a new fab, obviously, cost more and more. Nowadays, to build a fab is a multi-billion dollar operation. That's why Intel is always one step ahead of everybody else, because they're the only ones that can afford it. But even in those days it was very expensive."

With Commodore yet to fully emerge from its financial crisis, CSG became a burden. The fab began with the PMOS process in 1975, which it used to produce the 6502 chips. In 1985 CSG adopted the NMOS process in order to fabricate the Amiga chipset. Now, scarcely a year later, a new process called CMOS, with its low energy requirements and cooler running temperatures, became a priority.

Gerard Bucas and Jeff Porter wanted CMOS gate array chips for the B52 and A2500, and they both felt it made more sense to have them fabricated by a chip foundry with the CMOS process. In June 1986, Ted Lenthe and Tom Biggs began researching the costs to upgrade to CMOS gate array technology.

CSG would only be a bargain for Commodore if it could manufacture it at 3 microns or less. "As technology changes and process technology changes, you are shrinking chips and the whole geometry of semiconductors," explains Bucas. "Commodore just couldn't afford to build a brand new fab and continuously shrink the actual geometry of the Amiga chipset, for example. They would need a new fab."

Commodore had already saved money by going from 5 microns for the Amiga chipset down to 3.5 microns. This small change resulted in a 30% size reduction, allowing CSG to produce more chips on each 5 inch silicon wafer. With three chips in the Amiga, and the massive volumes they produced, the reduction saved millions of dollars.

But CSG needed to keep up with the industry, otherwise if an outside foundry could produce smaller chips than CSG could, it made more sense to purchase from the outside vendor. Intel, for example, had already achieved 1.5 microns with the 80286 processor in 1982, but luckily for CSG it did not offer production to outside companies. "MOS was in-house and required a lot of ongoing investment all the time, whereas it would have been better to outsource that to a more up-to-date modern fab," concludes Bucas.

But to make the investment required a large capital expenditure, one Commodore would have a hard time managing in 1986. "This is really where the investment was not made," says Bucas. "So eventually the Amiga chipset became difficult to produce, because MOS was captive. They really didn't have the money to expand their operation and to grow as the whole chip technology improved. They couldn't make that investment."

In the executive suite, many felt it made sense to liquidate CSG, which would help refill Commodore's coffers and allow the company to fight another day. "From Commodore's management point of view, they wanted to get rid of MOS," says Bucas. "In fact, that was the right thing to do. But at the same time, you get rid of MOS then you can't produce your own chipsets anymore. So how do you do that?"

However, Tom Beggs, head of CSG, and Ted Lenthe, head of LSI, were more sympathetic to keeping CSG, despite Bucas' arguments to the contrary. "There was a major disagreement internally, and that was part of the tug of war between engineering and even management," says Bucas. "It was mostly between the three way side, which was Tom Rattigan, myself and the head of MOS at that time [Tom Beggs]. Of course, he was fighting for his side to stay alive and he needed more investment. I tried to stay out the argument but having said that, it was becoming obvious that MOS had a lot of limitations."

CSG eventually decided to develop a CMOS process but Bucas was reluctant to rely on the CMOS process for the Amiga. "The cost of production was not where it should be," explains Bucas. "And the yield of the chips was not where it was supposed to be. The bottom line is, my feeling always was, it's time to get out of that. But having said that, it's not so simple because the three main Amiga chips were not easy to move to somewhere else. It was very difficult."

Bucas favored transitioning to a manufacturing model similar to the PC industry, buying more off-the-shelf parts and using third-party foundries. "That was a transition—a mindset transition," says Bucas.

Bucas temporarily won the fight to have the chipset manufactured outside of Commodore and in November 1986, he contracted Toshiba to manufacture the 3 micron CMOS chips for the B52. "This obviously had lots of internal arguments even within engineering," says Bucas. "The reason is because people grew up with a concept of what makes us special, what makes us different is the fact that we have our own in-house chip and semiconductor manufacturing plant. And that's true, but eventually if you can't afford to invest in it and keep that up to the latest technology, that eventually becomes a drag on your performance. That was one of the key problems at Commodore."

However, in the long run, Tom Beggs was able to convince Commodore executives that it made financial sense to keep making their own chips. Commodore would give minimal funding to upgrade CSG to the CMOS process, initially for the smaller CMOS gate array chip in the 1351 mouse. Bucas was stuck with CSG for the future.

Atari ST Competition

By the middle of 1986, it was apparent that the restructuring of Commodore under Rattigan was making a difference. For the April to June quarter, sales were up 58% from the same quarter the year before and Commodore made its first profit after six consecutive losses. It was only $1.2 million dollars, but at least it was not a loss.[5]

Rattigan credits his new Chief Financial Officer (CFO), Mike Evans, for helping repair Commodore's financial house. "Mike made that happen in relatively short order and was a tremendous asset," he says.

As good as the recovery was, it did not match up to the rosy financial situation at Atari, where Thomas Rattigan was facing off against Jack Tramiel in the business arena. It was a challenge that could break almost anyone, but Rattigan was unfazed by his opponent. "He smokes cigars, so he can't be all bad," he says.

Although Commodore had started with a substantial lead, Atari Corporation was steadily closing the gap—some would say winning the war. Atari under Tramiel had increased revenues from $111 million in 1984 to $315 million in 1985. Meanwhile, Commodore's revenues had been dropping over the same period. And while Commodore had lost a whopping $237 million in 1985, that compared to a small loss of $14 million for Atari. By 1986 Atari had already turned a profit of $12 million by the middle of the year, the same point in which Commodore turned a $1.2 million profit.

---

5   InfoWorld, September 1, 1986. p. 11. "Commodore Turns Profit For Quarter"

The results sent chills through Commodore's empty halls. "Jack Tramiel was really the God of Commodore while he was running the company, so inside Commodore West Chester there was a great deal of fear about what Tramiel might do," recalls Bob Welland.

But there was some good news. Rattigan found out that the Atari ST was not as successful as analysts had first believed. Atari filed a prospectus with the Security Exchange Commission, which revealed the company had only sold 150,000 units of the ST as of June 30, 1986. This was only about double the number of Amiga units sold through the same period. The Atari ST had not outsold the Amiga 1000 by ten to one, as first reported.

Genlock Video

It took some time but the Amiga was beginning to find a position in the marketplace. The IBM PC had established itself with spreadsheets, databases, and accounting software. The Macintosh found a niche in creative desktop publishing. The Atari ST found a niche with music producers, luring in new wave bands such as Erasure. Now, the Amiga started to establish a reputation with music, visual art, animations, and incredible games. It was an exciting computer compared to the leading competitors.

It also had the potential to fill a niche that no other computer could, based on the curiously named genlock device, whose name comes from its ability to lock video synchronisation with an externally generated signal. A genlock allowed the Amiga to add special effects or text over a regular video image by synchronising timings, replacing the background color with live video from an external source. It was an important feature unique to the Amiga that could give it an advantage over other computers.

Work on the genlock adapter began in 1985, but after the original engineer resigned in late November there was no one to work on the product. It sat in limbo while Commodore concentrated on releasing the A1000 until the original Amiga team, supervised by Jay Miner, picked up the project again in early 1986. An engineer named Akio Tanaka redesigned the board and soon had working prototypes.

Commodore began showing the A1300 genlock expansion at the Spring 1986 Comdex. The flat white box neatly tucked underneath the rear of the Amiga 1000. A small square adapter on top plugged into the 23-pin RGB connector at the back of the A1000. The back of the box contained a row of composite connectors for video in/out and audio in/out, plus three knobs for adjusting the picture.

Progress on the genlock ground to a halt once again amid the West Coast Amiga layoffs. On June 27, 1986, the project was handed off to West Chester where engineer Ian Kirschemann took control of the product. In the September/October issue of *Amiga World*, the magazine mentioned its first glimpse of the mysterious device, which Commodore said would not appear on the market before 1987.

Jeff Bruette, a Commodore software developer, had early access to the device. Though only 25 years old in 1986, he was a seasoned veteran who was hired on the cheap. "This will show my naivety: they offered me $14,000 per year. I told them that wasn't enough. I wouldn't take less than $14,400," he says, laughing. One of the few remaining members of the VIC Commandos, he worked on the earliest VIC-20 and C64 games, including *Omega Race*, *Gorf*, and *Wizard of Wor*.

When the Amiga came along, Bruette was one of the Commodore engineers working to develop software for the Amiga launch. "The software that was developed by Island Graphics that I oversaw was eventually marketed as Aegis Images and Aegis Animator," he recalls. "I was intimately familiar with everything the programs could technically do. This led to Aegis Development offering me a job in Santa Monica, California." Given his low pay scale at Commodore, and the chance to relocate to a warmer climate, it was an easy decision. "I took that offer."

At the time, one of Hollywood's leading directors was developing a television show for NBC. "Soon after I had relocated, there was a request from Steven Spielberg's Amblin Entertainment asking if we could help with an episode of *Amazing Stories*. While there were a number of companies that were submitting proposals, I had an ace up my sleeve that got us the gig."

Bruette had kept in contact with his old company, and would continue consulting with them until at least the end of the decade. As a result, he was given access to new prototype hardware. "Commodore had let me have a prototype genlock. This was a device that would synchronize the Amiga screen refresh with an external sync source," he recalls. "Because I could offer that and nobody else could, we got the job."

If Bruette had any regrets leaving Commodore, they were soon dispelled when he began negotiations with Amblin. Because Bruette was the only video company in possession of an Amiga genlock, Amblin was eager to seal the deal. "They asked how much we would charge for 14 days of production. Keep in mind that the genlock had made us their only option," he says. "I told them that I had no clue on what would be fair. They responded with, 'Would $1000 per day for equipment and $1000 per day for labor be acceptable?'"

After Bruette finished pushing his eyes back into their sockets, he signed the papers. "They quickly got my answer that it was fine. Aegis and I had an understanding that, as I was employed with them at the time, we would split the income 50/50. At that moment, I instantly realized that in 14 days, I would be earning the same figure as my original salary offer from Commodore."

Bruette soon found himself on the filming set, working with actor Jeffrey Jones, who in the summer of 1986 became known as Mr. Rooney, the principal antagonist of the hit film *Ferris Bueller's Day Off*. "The studio built a room on-set for us to operate all of the Amigas," recalls Bruette. In the script, Jones plays a scientist who uploads his consciousness to a computer, requiring him to appear as a digitized ghost on the monitors.

To generate the actual visual effects, Bruette pointed a video digitizer at Jones and overlaid the effects using an Amiga 1000. "In addition to the genlock, we used prototype video digitizers by A-Squared called Amiga Live," says Bruette. "There were no prepared effects on tape. The technobabble on the screens and the processed video of Jeffrey Jones that appeared on the projection screen was all done live and in real-time through the Amiga computer."

Bruette used the genlock to properly record the video monitors in the scene. "You may have seen black lines running through computer screens that appear in TV shows," he explains. "This is caused by the computer refresh rate being different from the recording/filming rate. By using a genlock, the film camera could control the Amiga's refresh rate and thereby eliminate the black bar rolling through the computer screen."

Amblin was more than happy with the results. The show aired on December 29, 1986 under the title *The Eternal Mind*. Sadly, Bruette was denied a credit for the production. "They would not give us credits. If you noticed, the credits were very minimal. There were dozens of folks, many with specialty key responsibilities, whose names do not appear either."

Bruette had done well with his first foray into the entertainment industry, and soon the Amiga would become a major player in the new wave of digital special effects sweeping Hollywood. But he also realized he could have done much better if he had not had to split the contractual fee with his employer, Aegis. "The Amazing Stories opportunity gave me the inspiration to go on my own," he recalls. "As a result of experiencing working with movie studios, I left Aegis soon thereafter to provide computer graphics to the TV and movie industry."

As a result of Bruette's pioneering work, Commodore had a growing awareness of the potential for the Amiga to dominate the video production marketspace, something that could set the Amiga apart from the Macintosh in the creativity field.

CHAPTER 32

Two Amigas 1986

At the beginning of 1986, Gerard Bucas and Jeff Porter believed the West Chester engineers could focus mainly on B52, the low cost successor to the Amiga 1000. These plans were interrupted when Irving Gould revealed the A2500 to them, which would begin to steal the available resources within the engineering department. Soon morale became a problem as the two sisters competed with one another for the affection of the engineers.

B52 Schedule Issues

The elephant in the room dividing executives and engineers was the scheduled release date of the B52. Jeff Porter had never agreed to release it in 1986 because, well, that would be impossible. Normally a prototype would be shown at the January CES, followed by a production version at the June CES in which orders were taken for the upcoming holiday season. But at the June 1986 CES, Commodore did not even have a rudimentary proto type to display. In fact George Robbins would not begin working with the motherboard until the middle of July. Even in the most far-fetched dreams of executives, there was no way Commodore could release the B52 in 1986.

Yet every time Porter told executives it was impossible, they insisted Commodore needed the B52 released in 1986 otherwise the company would no longer exist, therefore he just had to make it happen. On June 17, Porter produced a compromised schedule that technically released pilot production models on December 15, followed by volume production on January 5, 1987. The schedule hinged on everything happening on time, including FCC certification. In other words, the schedule was pure fantasy meant to appease executives while they came to terms with the fact that it was a 1987 product.

Aside from beginning the B52 too late in the year, Commodore had other problems preventing the quick completion of projects. For starters, the recent layoffs had reduced manpower significantly within the engineering department. And the side effect of low morale took a further toll. Employees had not had raises in over a year and a half, and several employees left the company. In early July, three more engineers who were being trained up on the Amiga resigned. Porter would need to find other engineers to handle the upcoming Amiga products.

Things only got worse. During this time Henri Rubin became more and more visible at Commodore's headquarters in West Chester. Eventually it became clear that Rubin and Gould believed the A2500 was Commodore's savior project, even taking priority over the B52. This, despite Porter believing the A2500 had been struck down at its earlier product review.

On July 28, against Jeff Porter's wishes, George Robbins was sent to Germany to aid the A2500 project. Porter felt that the German engineers should be travelling to West Chester, considering that's where the prime engineering equipment resided. Instead, he was losing his key engineer, making it that much more difficult to complete the B52 on schedule.

Porter on B52

Although George Robbins owned the Rock Lobster motherboard, it was really Jeff Porter who achieved the low cost. "George Robbins was a good engineer and he definitely was the driver behind the actual hardware of the A500," says Robbins' friend Eric Lavitsky. "But Jeff was the management guy who drove that from the engineering management end."

In trying to cost reduce the Amiga down to something comparable to a C64, there were some notable problems. For starters, the C64 did not include a disk drive, which allowed it to retail for $200. Add the cost of a 1541 disk drive and the price nearly doubled. With the Amiga, there was no option but to include a disk drive. "That was non-negotiable," says Porter. "You had to have a floppy drive to boot the computer."[1]

Porter had to find other ways to save money. One cost reduction came to him from a competitor on a trip to Japan. "I used the ROM from the Nintendo game cartridges, believe it or not," says Porter. "In my tours of duty I discovered these incredibly high density mask ROMs that were used for

[1] The Atari 520ST does not have a built in drive, but it was included in the standard bundle. The GEM OS is in ROM and will load if there is no diskette.

cartridge computer games from Japan—the original Nintendo for instance. I said, 'Ooh, ooh, ooh! High density masked ROM, cheap, I need. 16-bit wide, I need!'"

As a result of the find, Porter could use a single 256K ROM chip to hold the Kickstart code. "Most of the EPROMs and ROMs that you'd have were 8-bit ROMs, and you would have to have 4, 6, or 8 of those suckers to hold the Kickstart; in essence the kernel for the computer," he explains. "Those were 16-bit wide ROMs."

Another saving, typically used by Commodore in its other computers, was the chip packaging. "I made a deal with MOS semiconductor to put all the chips in plastic instead of ceramic, so that was another key piece of cost reduction," he says.

Further cost reduction was found on the PCB. Instead of using a typical 4-layer PCB board, which had metal sandwiched in the middle of the board, he used the more primitive 2-layer boards. "I put the entire A500 on a 2-layer PCB, which was unheard of," says Porter. "That was a major cost reduction. A 4-layer board was way costlier."

The engineers could also save significantly by reducing the power supply unit (PSU). "The Atari 520ST had the power supply built into the case. That just seemed like a bad idea to us," says Bob Welland of the overheating concerns and servicing the machines. "So Jeff went off and tried to figure out, 'Can I get a power supply brick that'll provide that amount of current.'"

Porter ended up finding a low-power PSU. The Amiga 1000 came with a 90 watt PSU, allowing it to power the expansion module devices. Porter found he could get away with a much cheaper 35 watt PSU for the B52. It would not be able to power external devices, which would require their own power adapters.

Without an adequate PSU, Gerard Bucas knew the B52 would not be able to use many A1000 devices, such as a genlock. Privately he told Porter that if the other executives found out the B52 did not support genlock they would have heart attacks.

The B52 would also lack certain video capabilities. A selling point of the C64 had been its ability to connect to a standard television, something the B52 would lack. "That was another cost reduction," he says. "On top of that, it made the [A1000] board not international friendly because the RF modulator and television standards for the rest of the world were different. You had to have PAL and NTSC modulators for different parts of the world, so I took that out of the board."

B52 owners who wanted to connect to a color TV now had to buy a special adapter, called the A520. "If you really wanted to buy the RF modulator, it wasn't going to be a big deal, but I had to make that price point," says Porter. (As it turned out, Commodore UK included the A520 as part of a bundle. However, owing to the poor display on televisions, many owners opted to purchase a monitor from Commodore.)

Despite the intense drive to cut costs, Porter surprisingly did not compromise on the keyboard quality. "I insisted on a really good keyboard on the A500," he recalls. "Mechanical switches from NMB. It was awesome. I'm a pretty good touch typer, and I could absolutely fly on that baby compared with most other keyboards in their day."

Porter would attempt to find a cheaper 3 ½" disk drive. Adding to the cost reduction would be the falling memory and component prices. And this time, Commodore planned to manufacture the motherboards cheaply at its Hong Kong factory instead of outsourcing production to Samsung.

BMW C256 Axed

Despite a lukewarm reception at CES, Dave Haynie and his teammate Frank Palaia continued working on the upscaled C128 computer, BMW. "It wasn't really a replacement, it was more of an upgrade," he says. "I don't think anybody tried to position it as replacing the C64."

Throughout June and early July, Haynie continued researching the 65816 chip for BMW. With the 65816 costing around $5 each, Haynie calculated his BMW with internal disk drive would cost $158, meaning the retail cost would land in the $400 to $500 range, dangerously close to the B52's projected price.

In this post-CES time period, with Rattigan losing faith in the C128, the project began to lose steam with others. Finally Jeff Porter asked Gail Wellington, formerly of Commodore UK, if Commodore should proceed with the development of the machine. The tepid response told him everything he needed to know.

In early July 1986, with the BMW looking like it had no future, Porter began looking at other ideas for 8-bit machines for Dave Haynie to work on. At this time, Ed Parks, Nigel Shepherd, and Clive Smith were the three main executives who favored the C64 above even the Amiga. They also felt the C128 was a product with no future and began conceiving C64 alternatives.

Curiously, Ed Parks felt the C64 did not need enhanced processor specs, such as faster speeds or 16-bit processors like the 65816. He felt users were happy with the current speed of the C64 so there was no need to improve upon it. Instead, the slow disk drive was the main problem and he began investigating ways to speed up the 1541 drive, or to replace it with the 3½ inch 1581 drive Greg Berlin was working on.

Porter revisited his idea for the living room C64D he now called the LX64, which would be packaged in a VCR-like box and include a built in disk drive and modem. With an estimated bill of materials cost of $149.16, it would retail around $400 to $500—again too close to the B52's projected price.

For his part, Nigel Shepherd supported a new style of C64 with a built in modem and optional disk drives that would clip onto the side of the computer. This, he proposed, would allow Commodore to attach either a 1541 or 1581 disk drive to the case, allowing greater inventory flexibility.

With the C64c having just appeared on the market, there was no immediate urgency to pick a successor. For now, the next model in the C64 line was in flux and would remain so while management debated and discussed alternatives.

Switching Projects

After Dave Haynie had his C256 computer rejected by Thomas Rattigan, his role at Commodore became nebulous. "We were looking at maybe using a 65816 or something like that, but it was pretty much flogging a dead horse at that point," he says. "Once the Amiga was there, nobody was interested in more C128's."

The Amiga even began capturing Haynie's heart. "I played with [the C128] a lot when it first came out, but I have to admit having switched to an Amiga about six months after the C128 started shipping," he says.

Haynie was acquainted with the Amiga technology by August 1986. "I had already been programming it for nearly a year," he says. "I went out and got one as quickly as I could and then I was writing programs on it before I was actually doing any work for Commodore on it."

As other engineers fought to remain relevant during the cutbacks, something happened that saved Haynie's career. "I got into Amiga simply because George Robbins and Bob Welland needed some help on the A500," he says. "Everybody thought, 'Well, you're not getting very far with anyone wanting to do any more C128 stuff so maybe it would be a good idea to learn the Amiga. And I said, 'Yes, it would!'"

Jeff Porter decided to switch up the Amiga teams in order to get both the B52 and A2500 completed on time. On August 4, 1986, when Haynie returned from vacation, Porter officially tapped him to complete the B52 project. George Robbins, who was away in Germany at the time working on the A2500, would bring Haynie up to speed before moving over to a new A2500 cost reduction project.

At the same time, Bob Welland was in the process of delivering the complete Fat Agnus and Gary gate array designs. To help get Haynie up to speed, Welland directed him to run tests on his chip designs, which he did not expect in chip form until September. "We had gotten the A500 motherboard; the Fat Agnus chip was done and so we wanted to test the whole thing," recalls Welland. "So Dave Haynie did an emulator for the Gary chip. He came in on the project for a couple of months."

George Robbins Hired

At the beginning of August, two more engineers resigned, leaving Commodore even more short staffed. George Robbins remained a contract worker as he designed arguably the most important system for Commodore. "He came out of nowhere and has this really interesting history, but he was a find," says Bob Welland. "He was definitely a really important person."

The hiring freeze had prevented Robbins from gaining employee status. In time, management grew accustomed to his eccentricities. They also realized it was too big a risk to leave him on as a contractor who could leave at any moment for a better job. On August 25, 1986, Jeff Porter hired him on as a permanent employee.

Although Robbins was supposed to transition to the A2500 project, he continued working on the B52, debugging the motherboard and bringing up the computer. Both George Robbins and German lead engineer Wilfried Rusniok had to work together out of necessity because the two computers, the B52 and A2500, would share the same software and, to some extent, hardware. Thus it was important to have parity with the different connectors and ports.

Robbins also continued biking to and from work several times per week. "The more he rode, the better he got at it," says Welland. "There were days when he would ride to work and home in a single, long day."

Robbins' coworkers expected to see an accompanying change in his physique, but that curiously never occurred. "One of the mysteries of this whole saga was, one would assume, that George would get smaller. But this did not seem to happen," recalls Welland, who would solve the puzzle after a fashion.

To Welland, it didn't look like he ate more than his other engineers, despite having a high intake of cafeteria and restaurant food. "There was a cafeteria in Commodore so you could go get your breakfast and lunch," says Welland. "Most people went out afterwards to the pub, Margaritas, because we were all single. A handful of folks were married in the engineering group but most people weren't and so we all just worked ridiculous hours and hung out together."

The mystery of George Robbins' non-athletic physique in the face of his legendary exercise regimen was finally solved when Welland watched Robbins getting ready to depart. "The reason was perhaps revealed when one watched George prepare for his ride," says Welland. "He would duct-tape a couple of liters of Pepsi to the bicycle frame." The extra 850 calories per day presumably negated any health benefits.

One ominous factor that did not help with the B52 schedule was Robbins' creeping addiction to the Usenet newsgroups. "It was completely addictive," says Joe Augenbraun, a Commodore engineer. "No one who was introduced to newsgroups wasn't addicted. I mean it was just impossible not to be."

Some engineers, including Hedley Davis, wanted the Usenet system shut down. "People like George Robbins, he spent probably 80% of his life, I'm talking about including spare time, just on newsgroups and nurturing his VAX computer, which eventually can become a problem," says Gerard Bucas. "Eventually it became sort of an issue. People like Jeff Porter and Dave Haynie, they were certainly not addicted to VAX or spending too much time on newsgroups, but there was an element within engineering that actually got carried away with it, that's for sure."

Wanted: Experienced Engineers

In September 1986, for the third month in a row, several more engineers resigned. This time, both engineers were seasoned veterans of Commodore. The first was Frank Palaia, Dave Haynie's codesigner of the C128 computers. He decided to leave due to the cancellation of those projects, feeling Commodore was not going in the right direction.

The second was Frank Hughes, formerly the project leader on the C900 Unix project. With Commodore moving towards Amiga computers and low-end C64 derivatives, Hughes felt he had no future with the company.

Jeff Porter was beginning to feel the shortage of engineers acutely and projects began to suffer, including the A2500 and B52, along with the genlock and frame grabber Amiga devices. As far back as May, the axe had swung too far.

Despite the official hiring freeze, Gerard Bucas began to look for engineers to replenish his ranks. He considered hiring back Robert Russell, whose experience could help navigate difficult production issues. Ultimately Bucas and Porter decided he might be too expensive.

Another possible hire was none other than Bil Herd, who had since departed the local startup CBit. "At the time, I was actually between jobs, and at one point I said, 'Hey, can I come back?' By that time the regime had said, 'That wouldn't be a good idea.'"

Herd approached Jeff Porter on September 24, 1986. There were good and bad points for Porter and Bucas to consider. Herd was able to troubleshoot problems extremely quickly. Many of Commodore's engineers, such as Bob Welland, were excellent theoreticians but struggled when it came to hands-on electronics. Teaming up Welland and Herd would have improved the speed with which Commodore could achieve working and stable technology. And as far as the engineers were concerned, Herd was a lot of fun to work with.

On the downside, his presence tended to disrupt. Having him in the engineering group was like throwing a Tasmanian devil into a baseball game. He tended to add a lot of drama to what managers hoped would be a professional atmosphere. In the end, Bucas decided Herd would add too much negativity to the organization.

Herd believes Commodore management refused his reentry due to his past treatment of managers. "I'm basically a threat to anybody that has any authority," he says. Despite his pugnacious attitude, Herd was the best engineer Commodore had for fixing stubborn problems and getting projects out the door. "I heard one time somebody came out and said, 'Yeah, they admitted today that they wished you were here to fix this problem.' I was like, 'Yeah, but that's not going to get over my shortcomings, is it?' He said, 'No.'"

Fat Agnus Results

During this time the Los Gatos group aided Bob Welland as he developed the Fat Agnus and Gary chips. It was an uneasy relationship. "There was a lot of bad blood between West Chester and the Amiga group in California," says Welland. "It spilled over beyond just the bad management of Commodore and it spilled into the engineering group to a certain extent. I think that's unfortunate. I wish that they could have seen how hard everyone was working trying to make the A500 and then the A2000, and the work that was done after that. Everyone wanted the Amiga to succeed and the fact that the company had lousy businessmen is a completely separate issue from the passion of engineering."

Throughout these months, Welland remained cautious about whether his Fat Agnus would work. "That was the only thing that we were like, this might be a little bit iffy," he recalls. "I just had to trust the analog chip designer guys to be able to say yeah, that'll work."

A few months after Dave Haynie began testing and simulating the chip design, the results were in. It worked! The confirmation of the Fat Agnus chip design gave Welland a huge sigh of relief. "When the chip simulations were done, it didn't look iffy at all," says Welland.

Not everyone was happy about the results of the simulations. "Los Gatos was bent out of shape about that," says Haynie. "They didn't think it was going to work at all, and clearly it did."

However, Mical reveals that he finally accepted the decisions on the new chips. "In the end, I think it was largely the right choices that were made for Fat Agnus because it was more powerful and it was the next generation," he explains. "It was a careful step rather than a gigantic leap forward. A lot of the old software would still work."

The engineers now waited on the first run of Gary and Fat Agnus chips. This time, all the chips would be fabricated by the Commodore Semiconductor Group in Valley Forge. The engineers spent the remainder of the year racing to have sufficient numbers of A500 computers completed in time to demonstrate at the upcoming January 1987 CES in Las Vegas.

GRR Rebels

After realizing the German A2500 was not ready for a North American release, Gerard Bucas and Henri Rubin started a new project for a revision B of the Amiga 2000; one that would include a significant cost reduction. "That was largely in-house on the East Coast, with a lot of it being spurred on by this outside consultant that was working for the company at the time," says Thomas Rattigan, referring to Henri Rubin.

Back in early August, Jeff Porter had attempted to move George Robbins from the B52 project over to the A2500 Cost Reduction, as it was named. After all, Robbins had previously designed the high-end Unix machine, so in theory he was more suited to the project than the B52. Porter would hand off the B52 project to Dave Haynie to finish.

Haynie was, at the time, known as an engineer of low-end computers, having come from the C128 Animals. "They thought I was the senior ranking low-end guy after two years at Commodore because there had only been three of us and I was the top guy left," he recalls. "Of course, George and Bob had been the high-end guys because they did this little Unix workstation."

He also worked for several months on the B52 project and thus seemed like the ideal candidate to take over the project from Robbins. "The idea was I was going to learn the A500 and take it over," says Haynie. "The thing was, this was George's baby."

By August 7, most of Bob Welland's work on Gary and Fat Agnus was complete. Soon he would begin concentrating on bringing Unix to the Amiga. "I think George probably felt like if Bob is going to go off and do this other stuff, there's got to be somebody who's going to stick around and make sure the A500 evolves correctly," says Welland.

Robbins played along, helping Wilfried Rusniok troubleshoot and redesign the A2500 board. However his heart belonged with the B52 project, where he spent most of his time. On October 3, he regretfully informed Rusniok that the B52 required a second revision board and he would no longer be able to help with the A2500 project.

Robbins at this time was un-fireable, being one of a handful of Commodore engineers who truly understood the Amiga architecture. His refusal to leave the B52 project frustrated his managers, but there was nothing they could do. After months of trying to interest Robbins in the A2500-CR, Porter turned to his next best option, Dave Haynie.

Haynie was suddenly in charge of Commodore's high-end product. "It basically turned out that somebody was going to take over this A2000 project and you couldn't very well kick George off the A500 if he didn't want to because he started the whole thing," he explains. "So they put me on the A2000, which suited me just fine."

The Amiga Strategy

On October 3, 1986, Jeff Porter officially assigned the A2000-CR project to Dave Haynie. For the next two months he familiarized himself with the Amiga architecture and planned the specs out. "I *was* the design team for the A2000," says Haynie. "That's kind of the way things were there because we had had a lot of layoffs. I was working day and night and there still wasn't enough time to do everything."

For almost two months, Haynie plotted out the specs for his A2000-CR computer. Although his managers simply requested a cost reduced version of the A2000, he took his design much farther. Haynie added a special CPU slot to his A2000, along with the required bus logic in a gate array chip he cheekily named Buster. "It also enabled this CPU slot idea that I came up with that would allow you to plug in a card that had a different CPU on it without pulling chips out," he says.

A dedicated video card slot, something common decades later in PC architecture, was also added to the computer. "The Germans had the idea for a Genlock slot," says Haynie, referring to a method of outputting computer images over video. "They basically took the signals that went to the external video connector and ran it through an internal connector."

Haynie liked the genlock concept, but concluded that the Germans had done it wrong. Instead, he refined the concept by adding a dedicated video card slot. "George Robbins and I talked about that a little bit and said, 'This is not right,'" he recalls. "We should run every signal to that connector. That's what the video slot was for."

The A2000 revision B also added a composite video port on the back of the computer, allowing an RCA cable to connect to a monitor to display video output. This would be the only exterior change from the German A2500 case.

By the time Haynie started his design, Henri Rubin had become a permanent fixture in West Chester with his own office. He often strolled through engineering, brainstorming with the engineers and telling stories. He liked what he saw in Haynie's design and retroactively added it to an analysis of Commodore's long term strategy. Rubin had concluded that Commodore would not be able to keep up with the product release cycle of IBM PC clones. To combat this shortcoming, he proposed a strategy of making the A2000 expandable in every way, so that technological improvements in video chips and CPUs could be accommodated through expansion slots. When Rubin presented this plan to executives, Irving Gould was impressed.

Haynie poured his time into the A2000-CR. His only respite was the local bar. "That was on Fridays depending on the week," he says. "I got into a habit of working all Thursday night, pretty much every Thursday night, and going to Margarita's on Friday and then going home."

It was now up to Haynie to have his version of the A2000 ready in time for the summer CES in 1987. Meanwhile, George Robbins would need to have his B52 ready for display at the January CES show.

B2000 Begins

Although Haynie worked in Pennsylvania, he lived in Gibbstown, New Jersey, 30 miles southeast of the West Chester headquarters across the Delaware River. The long commute, which could take up to an hour in heavy traffic, often motivated him to stay nights at Commodore, much as George Robbins and other engineers did.

Having the mass market engineer in charge of cost reducing the A2000 computer provided certain benefits to the end product. "The motherboard for the A2000 was the A1000 chipset originally, and so they didn't have Fat Agnus or Gary. They did that completely independent of the A500," says Bob Welland. "And then the subsequent A2000 adopted the Amiga 500 chipset." This meant Commodore could realize the same dream Apple enjoyed: a large profit margin on a high-end machine.

Haynie would base his cost reduced A2000 motherboard on the B52 motherboard designed by George Robbins. Much like Rock Lobster, the motherboard was a 2-layer board to reduce costs. "It was a little scary because, other than conferring with George on various things, that was pretty much my show," he says.

Even though the project was officially designated the A2500 Cost Reduction, it was now called the A2000 even in Germany, leading to a naming crisis. The engineers soon began calling it the B2000. George Robbins later explained, "The B2000 internal designation for the West Chester design A2000 came about because things were just getting too confusing when you couldn't say A2000 without the respondent saying which A2000. While the customer in the US gets to deal with but one A2000, the purchasing and manufacturing people have to deal with two, at least on the international scene."

According to Dave Haynie, "The B comes from B52, which was the codename for the A500. That's because the B2000 uses the more highly integrated A500 chip set instead of the older A1000 chip set."

By December 9, 1986, Haynie knew enough about the Amiga architecture and began the actual design of the B2000 motherboard. He realized a further cost reduction could occur by taking the expansion bus circuitry and reducing it to a chip. "When I took over the Amiga 2000 project, in the fall of 1986 (well, after the shock wore off), I set out to implement the first Buster (Bus controller) chip," says Haynie. "This did with the expansion logic much of what Gary and the Fat Agnus did to the original Amiga 1000 logic: shrunk it in price and in size."

Haynie had an advantage over Bob Welland when it came time to design the gate array because the Germans had already designed the logic using PALs. "Since I was, in essence, copying the German design, I took the PAL equations from the Amiga 2000 on the left as my basis for the Buster chip," he says.

The programmer and system architect now added chip design to his list of skills. "I was probably the only one who had hardware, software, and chips all in one of the computers because I did a little bit of software and a tiny bit of gate array chip design," he says. "The Buster chip was my first gate array."

Working with the A2000 board gave Haynie a feeling of euphoria. "The designs, as done by the Los Gatos group, were just so radical for the time," he says. "They made me think about things better." With management eager to release the A2000 in the US, Haynie had a short development time measured in months before the machine would have to be ready for production in mid-1987.

From Hero to Zero
1986

Commodore was known in the industry as a hostile work environment for management, and most people assumed it was because of Jack Tramiel. But in truth, the company was littered with landmines that executives and managers alike were likely to step on as they navigated their way through the halls. In the latter half of 1986, Thomas Rattigan would step on several landmines. It was beginning to look as though the strife and turnover was because of chairman Irving Gould.

Engineering vs Marketing

In the middle of 1986, Commodore was in a battle of philosophies over whether the corporation should become marketing driven or remain engineering driven. Thomas Rattigan's "Come to Jesus" meeting had caused a lot of unhappiness within the engineering ranks. Although Commodore had a history of products being chosen with input from the very top, there was little marketing influence. Jack Tramiel had communicated directly with the engineers and they had come to enjoy almost complete freedom under Marshall Smith. Once Rattigan attempted to inject his marketing expertise into the process, the engineering group began to rebel.

To the engineers, it looked like Rattigan was hot on C128 products one second, then cold the next. One example was the cancellation of the BMW C256 (which Jeff Porter supported). The Amiga team, who had watched Rattigan put his feet on the table and tell them that the C128 was the future of the company, were aghast. Gerard Bucas started to receive reports that the lack of product direction was causing morale problems. All of this information eventually made its way back to Irving Gould.

Thomas Rattigan and Nigel Shepherd also committed an unintentional slight against Irving Gould that surely did not impress the chairman. Gould considered the A2500 his baby. After all, he and his buddy Henri Rubin had given the project life. Yet after a June review with West Chester engineers, Rattigan and Shepherd deemed the computer not ready for release in North America. Rattigan had made the decision in the best interests of the company, but to Gould it looked like Rattigan was calling his baby ugly.

Henri Rubin

It was no wonder then that when it came time for Gould to back his new CEO against the engineering department, Gould instead sided with the engineers. To keep Rattigan in check, Gould turned to a personal friend named Henri Rubin. He would attempt to get Commodore's products back under control. "When Commodore was faltering, Irving brought Henri in to help try to figure out what should be done from an engineering perspective," says RJ Mical.

As with most of Gould's recruits, he was an older man with gray hair. "They brought in a guy named Henri Rubin, who was one of Irving Gould's buddies," explains Jeff Porter. This was not by accident. Gould held a tenuous grip on Commodore, with only 20% of Commodore's shares. Instead of attempting to gain control by purchasing 50% ownership, he relied on bringing in people he could trust in order to maintain his grip. And those trusted friends could tell him exactly what was going on within the company.

Rubin had also proved himself to Gould with the A2000 and Bridge-board, the latter of which earned Rubin US patent # 4,954,949. The hopes pinned around this innovation were enough to earn Rubin a special place in Gould's mind—and in Commodore's engineering ranks.

Commodore's most successful products had, in the past, always originated with the engineers. This was about to change slightly. "Over the years, Commodore was unusually engineering driven," says Dave Haynie. "The people who were around us were not doing all that much marketing. Those who had the most direct contact with the market didn't have a whole lot of input."

Thomas Rattigan might be forgiven for believing he ran Commodore but he was about to find out where the actual power resided. Gould sent in Henri Rubin to West Chester in early July 1986 to choose Commodore's future products. Rattigan would now have little to do with product direction. It was as though Gould were chipping away at Rattigan's responsibilities.

Both Gerard Bucas and Jeff Porter felt Rubin was good to brainstorm with and, as a bonus, his friendship with Irving Gould meant he could keep Thomas Rattigan's marketing driven instincts at bay, though they did worry he could be another loose cannon like Clive Smith.

Rubin put those fears to rest by making it clear that from now on, Rattigan and Shepherd would no longer be dictating product direction. He told Porter, "We'll tell them what we got when it's done." Soon it became clear to every engineer that Henri Rubin was extremely pro-engineering. If engineers wanted to start a new product, Rubin was the only one they had to convince.

When Gould brought in Henri Rubin, this began to sour the chairman's relationship with his CEO. One of Rattigan's objections was the resulting design-by-committee. "That got to be fairly convoluted," Rattigan remembers, referring to Rubin. "We had one outside guy working on that technology with us. Some of that led to there being a lot of cooks in the kitchen as to what those machines should be."

Without a strong leader like Jack Tramiel, everyone attempted to exert their own influence on decisions. "Everyone was willing to give advice at that point," says RJ Mical.

Rattigan suddenly had a hard time steering Commodore. "It's very, very hard to have a meeting and get uniformity on technological decisions when you have a crowd of more than one," he explains. "Everybody is an instant expert and everybody has their own axe to grind, and that really slows the process down."

The CEO tried to force a different management style in opposition to Irving Gould, one that he knew might prove fatal to his job. "You just say, 'The hell with it! This is not going to be the normal corporate thing where we all sit around a table Japanese style to affect consensus.'"

In September 1986, Nigel Shepherd and LSI manager Ted Lenthe continued developing the C64 line of computers. This went counter to what Gould intended, and in October, Gould named Rubin as the official executive vice president and Chief Operating Officer of Commodore. Rubin did not come cheap. His yearly salary and compensation came to over $300,000 to start, and stock options would allow him to accumulate just under $1 million for every year he worked for Commodore.

Now, with his official COO title, he was in charge of all product decisions, and he could effectively neuter Rattigan and Shepherd's plans.

Raising Morale

Thomas Rattigan was facing increasing pressure from managers and Irving Gould to do something about the low morale within Commodore's ranks. Engineers had been quitting by the month, disrupting continuity and making product development all but impossible. A lot of this had to do with the lack of product direction and it seemed like Commodore had nothing new to sell when the holiday season rolled around in 1986.

During the holiday season, Commodore would have to rely on existing sales of the Amiga 1000 because not even the Sidecar was ready. The marketing department put the planned advertising for the Amiga 2000 on hold. Instead, in late September, the company hastily threw together another $500 discount on the Amiga 1000 system, a repeat of what they had done out of desperation earlier in the year. Miner complained, "An entire year was lost while there was no advertising and no PR for the Amiga, no push to sell 1000s. But IBM and Apple used that year to good advantage."

The company focused in particular on manufacturing the C64c and C128 computers and accessories. Rattigan was impressed with the work ethic of ordinary Commodore employees. "We had people coming in on Saturdays who would work at no pay," says an astonished Rattigan. "I'm talking about the people on the [factory] lines. They would come in and we would be loading trucks to get stuff out so we could build a shipment for that particular quarter."

Rattigan did what he could to reward the employees. "You would buy 20 or 30 pizzas and 20 cases of beer. What you were really trying to do was get them committed to survival and making it happen. Fortunately, we had that."

By October 1986, there could be no doubt that there was a financial turnaround under Thomas Rattigan. Whether or not this was attributable to others more than to him, the fact remains that it happened under his stewardship. And he hadn't even yet unleashed the two most significant products developed under his tenure, the A500 and A2000.

For the July to September quarter, Commodore took in $176 million in revenue and made $3.7 million profit, compared to revenues of $159.2 million and a loss of $39.2 million from the same quarter in the previous year.[1] It looked like Rattigan's employee bonus plan would soon pay off.

---

1   InfoWorld, November 17, 1986. p. 39. "Commodore Repeats Profit"

Rattigan started receiving good press in the latter part of 1986 for bringing Commodore under control—his control, that is. But a CEO taking control of the company made Irving Gould uneasy, as it always had going back to the Tramiel years.

Bucas and Rattigan

The consultants Rattigan had brought in were convinced that, for Commodore to succeed, it had to sell IBM PC-compatible computers. And Rattigan was inclined to believe them. "That was my goal," recalls Gerard Bucas. "I was being pressured from all side to cut costs, cut people, do more PC oriented versus Amiga. And even though I believed in both PC and Amiga, I certainly was a major supporter of Amiga."

Despite being stuck in the middle of the Amiga and PC camps, Bucas did his best to develop the PC clone business. "ATI had just done their first graphics chip and they had this little graphics board for the PC called the ATI Wonder board, which had both color graphics and text, which believe it or not in the PC market, that was unique in those days," he explains. "I was in Germany when I read an article somewhere on this about-to-be released board from ATI."

ATI was a new company from Canada pioneering IBM PC graphics cards. Its new product was capable of displaying multiple modes, including the IBM standard Hercules graphics mode, to different types of monitors. "The first couple of years on the PC there were all these green color monitors and Hercules was known to work best with a green monitor," says Bucas. "ATI had the first combined Hercules text and color board available for the PC and it wasn't on the market yet."

Bucas acted as soon as he read about the card. "I changed my flight from Germany through to Toronto and met with K. Y. Ho," he recalls. "The reason why it wasn't on the market yet was because they had just developed their own custom graphics chip, which is of course what Commodore used to do for the Amiga market. Their chip was not a hundred percent ready yet, so it took probably three to six months after I visited there. We were literally the first company to OEM it from ATI. And eventually ATI of course became super famous and become a major player in the PC graphics market and was eventually acquired by AMD."

In early October 1986, Bucas hired a dedicated PC designer named Jeff Frank, an employee recommended by former C128 designer Bil Herd. Frank worked at CBit (not to be confused with the computer expo CeBIT), a failing startup that Herd had also joined. Both Frank and Herd lost their jobs with the company in October but only Frank was welcomed into Commodore.

Upon starting, Jeff Porter gave Frank the task of designing an ultra-low cost PC compatible whose price would undercut that of the competition. Porter described the project as a C128-ized PC clone, which would have no hard drive or expansion slots. Because the new computer would be less powerful than the PC-10, the engineers dubbed it the PC-1, or (because it was targeted for Germany) the PC-Eins.

Commodore's belief that they could become a player in the ultra-competitive PC clone market was an attempt to hedge its bets, one that would take resources and attention away from the core Amiga and C64 products. These decisions had a big effect on the Los Gatos engineers. "Eventually the morale was very low and there were major problems with the people," recalls Bucas. "And I don't blame them."

In the second half of 1986, Bucas started to fall out of favor with upper management, including Thomas Rattigan and Henri Rubin. Part of it was the failure of the A2500 to materialize, but Rattigan was also disappointed that Bucas had not transferred the Los Gatos Amiga group over to the East Coast in a timely manner.

Meanwhile, the Amiga engineers remained unwilling to move. Rattigan became frustrated by the situation. "I was always the one that was in the middle of those two arguments, trying to protect the Los Gatos group against the senior management position, which said we're going to save money," explains Bucas. "They said, 'We're going to cut your budget. The only way to cut your budget is close down that facility.'"

The disagreements between Rattigan and Bucas came to a head in October of 1986. "I was almost independent and uncontrollable in some ways," laughs Bucas, recalling his clashes with the CEO. "He and I had a major falling out. His secretary had to come into the office because she heard us shouting at each other. So he decided to demote me for about three or four months."

Bucas and Rubin

After Rubin was officially installed as COO, Gerard Bucas no longer had direct control of his engineering budget. Instead, he had to seek out Rubin's approval for any expenditures within his department. "For about two or three months, he made me report to the executive vice president and chief operating officer," says Bucas. "And that's really where it became impossible. Part of that was Rubin would not sign anything."

Bucas put the delays with the B52 squarely on Henri Rubin's shoulders. "Another interesting story that was never told about Henri Rubin was the damage and other things that he caused," claims Bucas. "The best thing we can say about him is that he was tremendously good at never putting his signature on anything, never making a decision and just generally delaying things."

As COO, Rubin had a directive from Irving Gould to make sure costs did not spiral out of control as they had under Marshall Smith. "He was brought in to start major cost savings. His job was to cut costs and cut engineering and reduce wherever he can," says Bucas. "He was one of these people who never wanted to put his signature to any large expenditure. When you say, 'Listen, we've got to spend $100,000 on putting this custom IC into production,' he would never sign something like that."

Although the A2500 project received full support from Rubin, Gerard Bucas' B52 project was given a low priority. "Before that went into production, Henri Rubin arrived on the scene and he almost killed it," says Bucas. "He wouldn't sign off on final tooling and all that. Eventually I had to go over his head and just sign off on a couple of custom ICs, as well as production and tooling."

In order to have any hope of completing the B52 project, Bucas had no choice but to violate company policy. "Bottom line is, we had to go around him and just force the issue and approve it ourselves, putting ourselves at major risk," says Bucas. "We had to literally bypass Rubin and a few other people. The good news is it worked out and it paid off."

Return of the Dancing Fools

After completing the Janus software for the Bridgeboard, RJ Mical plunged headfirst into Amiga software development. It would be one of the craziest years of his life, allowing him to rub shoulders with some of the most creative game developers in the industry at the time.

Mical programmed the game engine for *Defender of Crown*, working with legendary computer artist Jim Sachs in the process. After that, he moved onto Electronic Arts where he began developing his own game, named *Baal*.[2]

But then an irresistible offer came from none other than Commodore, where Mical's friend Dale Luck was returning from a sabbatical. The company needed the AmigaOS developers back in order to get AmigaOS 1.2

---

2   Not to be confised with the 1988 game Baal by Psyclapse.

out the door. The two programmers returned to the company in early November 1986.

Things were much different for RJ Mical during his second stint at Commodore. Prior to 1986 he had been a lowly programmer, but since working with Henri Rubin and Irving Gould in Germany on the Janus project, he now enjoyed much more influence on decision making. And one thing that bothered both of the Dancing Fools was the lack of advertising for the Amiga. Mical would attempt to influence those at the top to take advertising more seriously.

But it was a tough sell in 1986 as the company was attempting to rebuild its reserves. "Basically the company was living hand to mouth," explains Thomas Rattigan. "When I was there, they weren't doing very much advertising because they couldn't afford it."

Even the $20 million dollar advertising budget for the Amiga launch had been scaled back and the company could not afford to pay television stations to run the ads regularly. "You had the company going into pretty serious financial straits," says Rattigan. "They had lost maybe a couple of hundred million dollars in the preceding six or seven quarters. Advertising, other than around Christmas time, really wasn't a priority. That was a luxury the company couldn't afford."

However, relatively inexpensive print ads continued, where Commodore finally began finding success. One of the most famous and strikingly effective print ads appeared later in 1986, showing a full-page screenshot of Tutankhamen displayed as an impressive color bitmap on an Amiga. For the first time, Commodore succeeded in showing off the graphics capability of the system. It said, "Amiga under $2,000. Anyone else up to $20,000." The approach was bold and it showed off exactly why the Amiga was different from other computers.

Print ads aside, the Dancing Fools were disappointed by the lack of televised ads—so much so that they felt inspired to prototype their own. "RJ and I, we made our own commercials," laughs Dale Luck. "There were a bunch of engineers sitting in the backyard trying to come up with crazy ideas to do a commercial, then running a video camera to capture our stupid ideas."

Luck and Mical filmed themselves doing a parody of the famous Bartles & Jaymes commercials of the eighties. The two even took a slight jab at the Amiga 500, joking, "The Amiga 999! Totally incompatible with any previous product!" Another engineer, Terry Ishida, did a spot-on impersonation of Apple evangelist Guy Kawasaki as "the resident Pathological Liar."

Though the ads did little to influence management, they made an appearance at the second Amiga Developers Conference banquet on November 7, 1986. *Byte* magazine later wrote, "However, these videos weren't slick, weren't professional, and weren't aimed at making you run out and be baptized by John Sculley. They were done by the crazies at the Amiga development group in Los Gatos, had no rock songs or heart-warming images, and were aimed mostly at having a good time."

Over the next five months, RJ Mical continued his friendly relationship with Henri Rubin and Irving Gould, which began to undermine Thomas Rattigan even more. After all, in the latter half of 1986, the Los Gatos Amiga group felt they had a lot to complain about, and now they could take those complaints directly to Commodore's boss. The constant barrage began to cast Rattigan's decisions in a bad light, even though Amiga products were actually about to enter a golden age of success.

Amiga Delays

Under Thomas Rattigan, Commodore's fortunes had turned around with profits and revenue up even prior to the launch of two major Amiga products, the highly anticipated A2000 and B52. It seemed like Irving Gould should have been happy with his new CEO, but he was not. Gould expected his baby, the A2500, to launch in 1986, especially after he saw how quickly the Bridgeboard and Janus software had come together.

After dumping the project onto the reluctant West Chester engineers at the end of April, things began to slow down. The A2500 required two custom chips designed and fabricated from scratch, which caused understandable delays.

As a result of the lateness of the two new Amiga products, Commodore skipped the November 1986 COMDEX show altogether. Officially, Commodore (along with Apple) were boycotting the show because the COMDEX organizers would not allow the companies to host third-party software makers in their booths.

No one felt the frustration of the delay more than Jay Miner, the father of the Amiga. "Those teams promised to have the 500 and the 2000 ready by September—that's September 1986," he recalled. "Both of those machines used the chips and software that Amiga designed but they were still more than a year late."[3]

---

3 Amiga User International. June 1988. "The AUI Interview" p. 20

According to newspaper articles, Gould was becoming impatient. "By November, Gould was telling a securities analyst that he was unhappy at the slowness with which the company was getting off the ground with two new models of the Amiga."[4] After the disastrous Amiga 1000 strategy, it seemed like Gould wanted instant success.

Rattigan dismisses the comments. "That was a manifestation of a whole host of things rather than the singular comment about the timing," he says. "The one thing I walked away from that industry knowing was that optimism in terms of due dates was often misplaced."

Although it is easy to excuse Rattigan, a former Pepsi executive, for not knowing how to push his engineers to complete a project on time, it's also apparent that his predecessor, Jack Tramiel, knew how. He exerted constant pressure, offering bribes or threats, until the product was done.

As a result of the delays, the A2000 had no hope of a 1986 release. In December 1986, Irving Gould requested a production model and brought it to his New York offices to display to the press, including *Byte, Compute!* magazine, *Compute!'s Gazette, Ahoy!*, and *Amiga World*. Security was tight during these inspections, and the press was sworn to secrecy until after February. Gould (along with Clive Smith and several Commodore engineers) proudly watched the proceedings and gauged the reaction towards his cherished machine. Clearly he felt a certain parentage towards the A2000, having had it developed in Germany without the knowledge of either Rattigan or Bucas.

The subsequent reviews for the Amiga 2000 were favorable, even though the press did not realize that the US model would be a complete redesign. At the time, Gould estimated the product would cost under $1500 without a monitor. *Compute!* magazine wrote, "Commodore answers those critics who have said that the original Amiga was too expensive to be a home computer and not powerful enough for a business machine."[5]

---

4   *The Philadelphia Inquirer*, "A New Strategy May be needed for Commodore" (May 4, 1987), p. E01.

5   *Compute!* magazine, "Commodore's New, Expandable Amiga 2000" (March 1987), p. 8.

C64 Lives!
1986

Throughout 1985, Commodore executives believed the low-end C64 was on its last legs and the company would soon exit the retail computer business, which would be replaced by business sales of the Amiga. Like everyone else, they were surprised by the C64's Christmas 1985 sales. But after the June 1986 Chicago CES, the company realized a new competitor, Nintendo, would pose a serious threat to the C64's dominance.

C64c release

The C64-CR project, which had been put on hold the previous year to focus on the Amiga and C128, was given priority early in 1986. Commodore's LSI division continued refining and testing the new HMOS chipset: the 8562 VIC-II, 8580 SID, and 8500 processor. The system itself would be a product of mainly Commodore Japan, begun by Sumio Katayama and completed by Yoshi Narahara

In June 1986, production ended on the original C64 and began on the new C64c. Nigel Shepherd raised the retail price of the new computer to $199, up from $159. The justification for the price increase was GEOS, the graphical operating system that imitated the Macintosh within a 64-kilobyte memory space.

Cost reducing the C64 while raising the price was a shocking move, given Commodore's history of price reductions on the C64. "The C64 only cost $35 to make, so if people wanted to buy them they were more than willing to make them," reveals Dave Haynie. It was akin to the pricing Apple used with its products. Times were tough and the increased price and lower manufacturing cost would make the C64 more profitable than ever for Commodore but as Nigel Shepherd let slip in an interview, "We needed the extra margin."

Although Commodore North America had moderate sales of the new C64, Commodore Europe was even stronger. "The C64c was born and it still had some legs at that point because everybody's all, 'Oh great, it's sort of a new look and feel and all that.' And it still lasted for a probably a year longer than it would have without that," says Gerard Bucas.

So how was the C64c received? When customers first heard rumors about the C64c (first known as the C64-II in Germany) there was enthusiasm. Questions began swirling. How much faster is the processor? How much more memory will it have? Which new video modes does the VIC chip have? How does the SID improve the sound?

Of course, it did none of those things. Along with the lackluster improvement to the machine, Commodore's marketing effort was predictably off-target. As *Commodore User* magazine reported, "The Commodore 64 currently sells for about $130 in the United States. The Commodore 128 sells for $219. The list price for the new 64C is $200. It doesn't make sense."

There were differing responses based on two different groups: those who already owned a C64 and those who were buying a computer for the first time.

For existing C64 owners—a huge number by 1986—there was no reason to upgrade to the new C64c. Their original C64 could do everything the new one could, minus the GEOS software suite, which could be purchased separately.

For those looking for a new computer, the C64c was a potentially attractive purchase. It had a large and mature software base, a graphical operating system, and a low price compared to other computers.

In the UK, the C64c debuted at the Commodore Show in Manchester in September 1986. Due to cassette tapes dominating over disks in the UK, the new computer did not come bundled with GEOS but instead would be sold separately. Prior to this, Commodore UK sold a C64 bundle including a datasette and games for £199.99.

Much like in North America, each European country had magazines devoted to the C64—Germany had a magazine called *64'er* and the UK had *Zzap!64*, both focusing on video games.

Perhaps because of the language barriers in each country, European marketing was not a joint effort. According to Dave Haynie, "One of the weird things that people never quite understood about Commodore was that every region was responsible for their own advertising and the way they wanted to sell computers to their country."

Some people felt Commodore should have coordinated marketing efforts to save money, with each region sharing the same ads. "My belief is that we were appealing to a particular target market and our target market in those days was teenagers," says UK marketing director David Pleasance. "I believe that teenaged children are pretty much the same all over the world. They have the same aspirations, the same desires. You might have to tailor things very slightly for each individual country, but essentially they all want the same thing. I mean, it's all peer pressure."

The initial C64c debut had a rocky reception from the UK press. Both *Zzap!64* and *Commodore User* were highly negative, with the latter writing, "Its slick new look may be right but the price is definitely wrong. The 64C will cost £199.99 and you won't get GEOS thrown in, or anything else for that matter. This sounds like nutty thinking on Commodore's part..." However, the magazine looked forward to seeing the expected Christmas bundle later in the year.

The Commodore 64 continued to have success through 1986. Despite the price increase of the C64c, sales soared with the added interest of GEOS. It was one of the last low-cost computers in the marketplace and superficially, it seemed to do everything a Macintosh did at a fraction of the cost.

Nigel Shepherd, who came from Commodore Australia where the C64 dominated sales, was a firm believer in the new system. He also had little faith in the Amiga, something excusable given the lacklustre sales of the Amiga 1000. This C64-centric view of Commodore marketing also spread to Thomas Rattigan.

Soon most Commodore executives realized the C64 had some life left, even though it was almost five years old. In a magazine interview, Shepherd predicted the future of the C64. "You're looking at a solid two to three years out of that machine," he predicted.[1]

However, the exclusion of a mouse in the new C64c-GEOS bundle and the lack of the C64c's ability to autoboot from disk somewhat hindered the cohesiveness of the package. And new users would soon realize they would need to shell out for a 1541 disk drive in order to use the GEOS disk, another savvy part of Shepherd's marketing. One can't help but wonder if the

---

1 *Compute!'s Gazette* magazine, "An Interview With Nigel Shepherd" (October 1986), p. 31.

C64c would have had a better reception bundled with a 1351 mouse along with the price increase.

1351 Manufacturing Delay

While Nintendo was planning to release a new console bundle, Clive Smith was putting together his own Commodore 64 bundle. The most important element of the bundle, aside from GEOS itself, was arguably the mouse, that revolutionary device that made GEOS feel like a proper GUI OS. However, his plan was about to run head-on into a brick wall.

Smith had anticipated including the 1350 mouse but after its disappointing performance he decided to hold off on establishing it as the standard while Hedley Davis developed the 1351 mouse. His C64c bundle was released without a mouse. He planned to include the mouse and 1764 memory expansion in a new bundle in early 1987.

In the meantime, Hedley Davis had completed his prototype mouse and began designing the production model. At the heart of the final mouse was a single chip. The engineer decided to use a gate array, the same technology Bob Welland was using for the B52's Gary chip. "We figured out what we needed to have in the gate array. Then I handed the PAL equations and everything over to the chip guys and they did all the translation to actually turn it into chips," recalls Davis.

Like the Gary chip, the 5717 chip would be manufactured by an outside vendor, GTE, until CSG developed its own CMOS process. "That was implemented in a Commodore gate array and it was one of the first gate arrays Commodore ever made," recalls Davis. "It was in an 18-pin package and it had two hundred and fifty two gates."

Davis found two potential companies to manufacture the mouse chassis. The first was Mitsumi, the company that manufactured the 1350 mouse. The second was Bremen, a California-based company that manufactured in Hong Kong. "It had the mouse mechanics, which we had built for us by a company that also built keyboards in Hong Kong," recalls Davis. "This company was supposed to have this mouse thing ready. They had never done a mouse before, so they were very interested in doing this."

Mitsumi, an experienced manufacturer, bid $11.30 per unit to manufacture the mouse chassis. Eager to enter mouse manufacturing, Bremen bid $8 per unit. With the additional costs of the chip, packaging, manual, disk, and shipping, the total cost was $11.80 per unit. Hedley Davis knew there could be more problems with Bremen due to its inexperience, but it was hard to overlook the $3.30 savings, which would translate to a more profitable product when it went to retail at $50.

Nigel Shepherd wanted to phase out the 1350 mouse and begin selling the 1351 to the North American market in September 1986, meaning Davis had a tight schedule with the first shipment expected August 10. However, by mid-July Davis began to have concerns over Bremen's ability to keep the tooling schedule.

When Bremen took longer than expected, Bucas pushed the release date back to August 20, but this too came and went with no samples from Bremen. Finally in early September samples arrived, but they had problems which required Davis' full attention.

On September 29, Davis experienced an engineer's fantasy of bringing his product to production. "I got to go to Hong Kong to help bring up the production line," he recalls. "They had a huge, huge facility over there with all these machines for stuffing resistors inside C64s and stuff like that, and a purchasing group. That project was just a boatload of fun!"

Predictably, being the first time Bremen attempted a mouse, the project had a few bugs to work out. "I'm supposed to be there for a week to do the bring-up on this mouse and they are just not ready," says Davis. "Their mouse doesn't work because the wheels get stuck and we're arguing about the mechanical clearances."

The young engineer felt Bremen did not hold up its end of the bargain and wanted vengeance. "I'm furious and I go back and talk to the sales guy at Commodore Hong Kong. I'm like, 'Kill em, kill em! Burn them to the ground! These guys have screwed us over. I'm not going to meet my schedule.' A totally immature engineer."

Davis did not get the backing he expected. "Being young and naive, I wanted them killed as a supplier because they didn't deliver on their promises. They messed up my nice pretty schedule! The purchasing agent over there would have none of it because in the bigger picture, Bremen also made boatloads of C64 keyboards. He's like, 'I'm not going to hurt these guys. Number one, I need these guys to buy keyboards from. They give me keyboards for a very cheap price. Your project is screwed up and yeah, you're kind of screwed, but in the big picture I still need these guys. You're sort of a negotiating token and I'll get something for it, but you've just got to ride it out.'"

Davis, who was originally scheduled to stay for less than two weeks, now had to settle in. "I knew it was going to be there longer than 10 days so I went out and found an apartment," he recalls. "They're like, 'What are you doing?' I'm like, 'Well, I'm going to be here for longer than 10 days and this apartment is cheaper than the hotel. And by the way, can you pay me some money because I ran out of cash?'"

Davis watched his production schedule slip all the way to November. "I was supposed to go over for 10 days and ended staying for something like two months while they got their act together," he recalls. "Bremen eventually backed off the tightness of how tight the wheels were."

To weed out faulty mice, Davis found a way to spot defects. "I wrote some test software for them that was designed to catch when you move the mouse in a diagonal direction. Does one wheel stop turning or the other one stop turning so that the line starts going vertical or horizontal? I made a pretty slick test and once I figured it out, then I came back and we were done. They were producing them and that was that. But I got to stay in Hong Kong for a few months and that was sweet."

There were also problems with the 5717 chips from GTE, who were only able to finally create samples of a completely functioning CMOS chip by October 22. On November 14 the first shipments from the pilot production began arriving in West Chester for testing, which continued into December. Finally in late December, Commodore authorized the production of 25,000 5717 chips from GTE. The mouse began shipping in volume on January 20, 1987, around five months behind schedule.

Davis was able to quickly get the cost down from $11.80 to $10.17 per unit. The easiest change was shipping units from Hong Kong via sea-shipping rather than air. "And then there was the 18-pin gate array from MOS Technology and lord knows what that cost," says Davis. When production of the 5717 chip moved from GTE to in-house production at CSG, the cost went from $2.12 per chip down to $0.75. "The whole MOS thing was like funny money."

Nintendo Moves In

ver since the video game crash of 1983 and 1984, most executives and anagement (including Irving Gould) thought videogames had been a assing fad. As the success of the NES started building, they began to real-e video games were here to stay.

Unfortunately, the entry of Nintendo into the US market had an unex-cted effect on Commodore's retail distribution. Commodore principally ld the C64 in the US through Kmart, where the latter engaged in radical ice cutting that undermined other retailers. "The sad, true story is that mmodore Incorporated (the US Sales company) had allowed Kmart to steal all the market share of C64 sales by not protesting about Kmart's policy to sell the C64 for $99 when they paid $98 for them," says UK marketing manager David Pleasance. "Kmart used this as a loss leader, which because the C64 was a hot seller, it got consumers into their stores in big numbers. They then sold C2N Cassette decks, joysticks, and software in big numbers at full price."

The strategy ensured the C64 sold in massive numbers in the US but Pleasance feels the low price was a strategic mistake. "By Commodore complacently allowing this to happen, because they were selling everything Commodore could get hold of, naturally all the other retailers stopped selling it. They could not justify stocking it."

The trap had been set. For the most part, Commodore's retailers abandoned the C64, all except for Kmart. And then disaster struck. "Nintendo knocked on Kmart's door and said, 'You know that product you're selling for 99 bucks? How about you sell one for 89 bucks and you can make twenty five percent margin on it.' So immediately Kmart dropped the C64 and and went with Nintendo."

Suddenly Nigel Shepherd found he had no retail customers with which to sell the C64. "They took all the distribution and took all the product that came in from Commodore US and then they dropped it like a hot potato," says Pleasance. "That left Commodore with no outlets to sell through."

Upon hearing that Commodore had lost its main retail distribution in the US to Nintendo, Irving Gould was understandably dismayed, even though it was not exactly something Thomas Rattigan or Nigel Shepherd could have anticipated or countered. After all, the relationship with Kmart had been established long before either man had joined Commodore. But as far as Gould was concerned, Kmart distribution fell apart under Rattigan's watch.

January 1987 CES

On Saturday, January 3, 1987, Commodore returned to CES Las Vegas in full force. For the first time in years, the company had a large two-story booth that was widely attended.

Commodore's focus this year was overwhelmingly on the 8-bit line of mass market computers, primarily the C64. North American General Manager Nigel Shepherd remarked, "I think if somebody had said to me, maybe in '85, what future do you see for the 64, I would have been very aggressive and said, 'At least through to '87' But I think today you're talking certainly past 1990. So it's not going to die."

His statements indicated a definite turnaround in the thinking within Commodore's management. No longer would the company attempt to phase out the computer in favor of the Amiga. "We finally said, 'Why should we try to supercede this product where there's still demand out there?' You're probably going to see some enhancements along the way with the 64. We're going to see how we can make it more attractive and more competitive."[2]

True to that statement, Commodore came to the show with plenty of products for the C64. First up was the final version of the 1764 RAM expansion, with 256K for $129. The new device was largely a reaction to GEOS and included software to allow it to function as a GEOS RAM disk.

The 1351 mouse also made its debut at CES, albeit belatedly, retailing for $49. It included a demo disk and an upgrade from GEOS 1.2 to 1.3, allowing for mouse support.

However, the mouse retail box reflected Commodore's poor marketing skills at the time, awkwardly proclaiming the mouse as, "The Perfect Solution for Alternate Keyboard Entry".

Despite the occasional misstep, Hedley Davis was jubilant to see his product on store shelves. "I saw one of my boxes in Walmart and that was my project," he says. "I pushed that from start to finish. As a design engineer, you want to build things that people like and that people buy and use. To see your product in Walmart was gratifying to say the least."

The success of the project also helped with Davis' visibility and prominence as an engineer within Commodore. Both Clive Smith and Brian Dougherty were overjoyed with the resulting product. "I distinctly remember that everybody was happy with the mouse," says Davis.

Another 8-bit announcement was a new 1581 drive at $399. It was compatible with the C64, C128 and even the Plus/4 line. At three times faster than the 1541, it stored a whopping 808K on each 3½ inch disk.

Commodore missed an opportunity to market the drive to GEOS users by partnering with Berkeley Softworks to release a single 3½ inch disk version of the GEOS operating system (the official GEOS came on four 5¼ inch floppy disks). This would have at least given GEOS users reason to purchase the drive. GEOS could have been a foothold to establish a new disk standard for the C64, but with no commercial software available on

3½ inch disks, there was little incentive for C64 owners to purchase the expensive drive.

Commodore also unveiled the new C128D-CR to the US business market, which featured a PC-style case and separate keyboard. "That's where it had the built-in drive," says Bil Herd. "The D version was originally supposed to come out at the same time [as the C128] but it just lagged by a couple of years."

Unfortunately, with a suggested retail price of $550, the computer was stuck in an awkward marketing position, being an 8-bit computer hoping to compete with IBM PC clones that sold for almost the same price.

Commodore also debuted two German IBM PC clones at CES. The PC10-1 with 512K retailed for $999, while the PC10-2 with 640K contained two floppy drives and retailed for $1,199. It was a premium price, even in 1987 when other clone makers charged as low as $600. Unfortunately, Commodore's announcement was undercut by Atari. Jack Tramiel announced two new Atari PC's at a price of $499 and $699. They both lacked expansion slots, but Atari planned to release an add-on later.

When Jeff Porter created his schedule for his B52, he planned to announce big at the January CES in 1987 and then release later in the month. It didn't happen, mainly because the Fat Agnus chip was proving difficult to manufacture. LSI head Ted Lenthe was only able to deliver 35 buggy chips to Porter for his prototypes by December 22, 1986.

Without a firm release date or production schedule, Nigel Shepherd decided instead to focus on the C64 at the show. Meanwhile, the B52 was finally given an official name, the Amiga 500.

The Amiga 500 was demonstrated to the press and selected dealers in a small room on the second floor of the Commodore booth. The A500 was well received, with a planned $650 price and 512K of onboard RAM— double what the original Amiga 1000 came with.

The new A500 impressed Rattigan. "They did an absolutely fantastic job and we got to the price point we wanted," he says.

For many of the Los Gatos Amiga engineers, it was the first time they set eyes on the new Commodore designed Amigas. Carl Sassenrath was one of the few original Amiga engineers who believed they should have released a cheaper machine right from the start. "What would have been the right step was to make the Amiga 500," he says. "And the Amiga 500 was ... much more in the concept of Commodore products they made before except just a really nice one, with multitasking and all that. I think that w the right direction to take."

As a result, Sassenrath had nothing but praise for the father of the machine, Jeff Porter. "Some of the team wasn't supportive but I loved it," he says. "I thought the Amiga 500 was just incredible. But Porter and I mostly always saw eye to eye. I have the highest respect for him. He's just one of the most brilliant engineers I've ever met."

Not everyone agreed. "They started making choices about the Amiga that we didn't like," says RJ Mical. "It was like they took our Amiga and made a C64 out of it. It was a toy version of the Amiga. The A500 came out as sort of a flimsy thing and it wasn't expandable in many ways."

Commodore also revealed the Amiga 2000 to the US public, although it was in fact the German A2500 they displayed, the one that would not make it to the US market.

Mical hoped for more from the Amiga 2000. "We thought it was going to be more powerful, a better bus, faster RAM, a faster CPU, and with more features in the graphics chip," he says. "That probably was a good choice in the end, all things considered, because it was less ambitious and therefore it had better performance and better compatibility."

Commodore had another killer demo to rival the original Boing Ball. With the advent of ray traced 3D images, Commodore introduced a new iconic demo at CES. The Juggler demo featured an abstract juggler with three glass balls, each perfectly refracting the light within the spheres. Most people had not seen pre-rendered graphics in 1987 and the effect was astounding.[3]

The demo was created by programmer Eric Graham. "In the fall of 1986, I was thinking of adding a room onto my house, and rather than start the work I decided to write a modeling and rendering program," he recalls. "It took about a week to get running, and then another week or two to make a few models and put the compression scheme together. That was November and the Juggler was born. The room never was added to the house."

In December 1986, Graham had sent his demo to Commodore. "Their legal department thought it was a hoax and that I'd done the image generation on a mainframe," he recalls. "So I sent Commodore the small program so they could run it themselves and generate the big Juggler file. Then they sent me $2,000 for the rights to use it for promotional purposes." Graham went on to develop and release *Sculpt 3D*, a modeling and rendering program for the Amiga.

The Juggler demo is seen in Tom Petty's 1987 video, "Jammin' Me"

Commodore then sent the code to Guy Wright at *Amiga World*. The image made the cover of the May 1987 issue instead of photographs of the A500, which was revealed in the same issue. The Amiga was finally coming into its own within the industry, appreciated for its superior graphics compared to other computers.

Although Commodore had a strong showing at CES, the belle of the ball this year was Nintendo, which had recently launched the NES across North America. The console had sold millions over the holiday season, reviving interest in 8-bit console gaming. Now, Nintendo was poised to expand on those sales by announcing a basic set with Super Mario Bros for $99.99, or without the game for $89.99. It was a magic price point that would tip sales into overdrive.

Incredibly, because most kids began receiving the NES on December 25, 1986, it meant the NES phenomenon really only began to take hold in 1987—five years after Dave Morse first talked with Nintendo while he was still at Tonka.

Commodore management began to consider options to make the C64 more competitive against Nintendo. "There was talk of making [the C64] a game machine, and less computer-like if you will," reveals Thomas Rattigan. "Obviously software compatible but also extending the life of the machine. That was going on as I was in the midst of Gould and I having our differences of opinion."

Results of 1986

Thomas Rattigan had achieved Irving Gould's goal of making Commodore profitable and he continued to increase profits. For the quarter ending December 1986, Commodore posted a net income of $22 million. (However, due to the first quarter losses under Marshall Smith, Commodore lost $127 million for the year.) Commodore had even reduced its bank debt by $110 million in the last 10 months. Soon, it would be a profit machine capable of full-scale advertising.

Rattigan also turned Commodore into a strategic success. When he took over, the company was still suffering from the short term strategies of Jack Tramiel, who delivered diverse, incompatible computers as though they were calculators. Now Commodore could concentrate on evolving its core platforms, the Amiga and C64. Its upcoming products targeted both segments of the market, with the low-end Amiga 500 and the high-end Amiga 2000. The Amiga 1000 would soon be phased out.

Rattigan was even garnering support from some of the biggest software makers of the day. *WordPerfect* was indisputably the most popular word processing package in the eighties and into the nineties. By early 1987, Commodore had lured the Word Perfect Corporation into developing its flagship product, WordPerfect 4.1, for the Amiga.

And as Nigel Shepherd vowed, Commodore would continue to look for ways to keep the 8-bit line relevant. Although the C64 was still the top selling computer in Commodore's arsenal, the C128 managed to impressively sell over a million units in calendar 1986.[4]

Unfortunately, the loss of C64 sales in Kmart had an immediate effect on revenues. During the Christmas season, Commodore pulled in $270.1 million. This was down from $339.2 million for the same period a year earlier.[5] Irving Gould did not like what he was seeing and would soon bring in an outside consultant to monitor Rattigan.

4   *Compute's! Gazette*, April 1987. page 6.

5   *Infoworld*, February 23, 1987. p. 30. "Tech Street"

Adios Amigos 1987

The original Amiga engineers had been together for five years, in various permutations, since 1982. Most of that time had been under the ownership of a faltering Commodore. Nevertheless, they had launched the Amiga 1000 and had hoped to continue designing improved iterations of the computer.

But then Irving Gould and his friend Henri Rubin began backing the A2500 from Germany, while back in West Chester, CEO Thomas Rattigan backed the low-cost Amiga 500. By early 1987, the designs of the two computers were complete. This gave management the confidence that it no longer needed to rely on the original Amiga team and they began transitioning for the final closure of the Amiga Los Gatos offices.

Amiga 500 vs. FCC

Jeff Porter had planned to begin mass producing the Amiga 500 in February 1987, but first it needed to pass FCC inspection. The FCC's goal was to ensure household devices did not interfere with radio frequencies that would degrade radio or television reception. Porter delivered a sample A500 to the FCC and filed the paperwork months before, in October 1986. However the computer had a "noisy board" as engineers called it, emitting too much electromagnetic interference. It failed to pass the FCC inspection.

The reason was obvious to Porter. Most engineers relied on 4-layer PCB boards to reduce electromagnetic emissions. The 2-layer board in the A500 posed more challenges. "It was even harder to get it to pass FCC," explains Porter. "When you have a 4-layer board, you have a power plane and a ground plane sitting in the middle, so by definition you've got a built-in shield. You don't have that with a 2-layer board." The engineers would need to find creative ways to reduce emissions enough to pass the FCC certification.

Commodore West Chester had a small wooden building, generally referred to by local Pennsylvanians as an Amish Shed, specifically for testing equipment. "I used to live out in the FCC hut before we figured out how to make that work," recalls Porter. "It was an Amish Shed in the parking lot of Commodore that had a big antenna and a big spectrum analyzer. You put the computer on a pedestal and you twirled it around and you wiggled wires, and had to make sure it didn't interfere within the emission limits."

Over time, Porter and Robbins learned the techniques required to pass FCC regulations. "The first generation board just sucked beyond belief," says Porter. "Eventually we figured out how to make that work."

The main weapon in the engineer's arsenal to fight against emissions were small, ceramic cylinders called ferrite beads. By placing ferrite beads in certain circuits, the iron in the beads choked off electromagnetic interference. Robbins placed 26 beads mainly within the video, audio, and joystick circuits, just before the circuits emerged at the actual ports. At two cents each, it was a cheap solution to the problem.

However, the beads alone did not provide a complete solution and the board still exceeded the emissions limits. Things came to a head on the weekend of February 21 as a record snowstorm hit Pennsylvania, laying down two feet of snow in some areas. Huddled in the Amish Shed on Saturday morning, Jeff Porter, George Robbins, and a representative from the FCC began the final push to pass certification.

The engineers measured the radio emissions with the sensitive equipment, then put their heads together to think of modifications to the circuitry to fix the noise. Once they agreed, Robbins ran back into the engineering lab, made the modifications on the fly, and then returned to test again. Occasionally Henri Rubin popped his head into the shed, told a few incorrigible stories, and then departed, leaving the engineers to their work.

Eventually the engineers settled on a two-piece metal shield that enclosed the entire PCB like a clam shell. The shield added to the overall cost, but it gave them a timely solution. "We worked with the PC board layout guys," says Porter. "We conquered that big-time and had it pass FCC."

With the FCC battle won, Porter would push through the modifications to the layout of the Rock Lobster motherboard. He was given an aggressive timeline for the A500 production and spared no expense in making sure he met that timeline. After the FCC delay, he was in a rush to get the final production layout for the motherboard done.

For a one-week turn-around, printed circuit boards cost tens of thousands of dollars for a small pilot productions run in the hundreds. However, by paying a premium, the PCB manufacturer would shift workers from other projects and work all night for a one day turnaround. However, the cost was often three or four times as high. Porter had no hesitation in spending the premium to make his deadline. "He obviously wasn't worried about where the money was coming from and he didn't have to deal with the politics," observes Gerard Bucas.

This made Bucas' job more challenging because of his ongoing battle with Henri Rubin's cost cutting measures. "Getting the Amiga 500 and customized IC's into production was incredible," he recalls. "Basically the system was going to prevent anyone from doing that because Rubin refused to sign anything."

To get the product out the door, Bucas ended up going around Rubin. "We've literally got to get the A500 into production, we've agreed on the production schedule but we've got to spend $80,000 in LSI (Large Scale Integration chips) and no one will sign the purchase order," recalls Bucas. "Eventually I personally signed it. Just screw everybody and you spend the money."

When the problem became apparent to Thomas Rattigan, Henri Rubin agreed to give Bucas back control over his budget. "After three or four months, he decided that well, maybe that wasn't such a good idea," recalls Bucas. "Then it went back to normal."

Rubin did not fight losing responsibility for the engineering department budget, which Bucas believes was because now he would not shoulder the responsibility should the A500 project fail. "If it wasn't a success, then Rubin could've said, 'I never signed off on that.'"

Although Rubin had more confidence in the success of his A2500, Gerard Bucas had little doubt about the importance of the A500 to Commodore. With the last of the motherboard problems solved, he had no hesitation to clear the A500 for mass production. After all, he and his right hand man, Jeff Porter, both believed their B52 would soon save the company.

Boston Computer Society

Commodore opted to introduce the A500 and A2000 at a low-key event, the Boston Computer Society general meeting on Monday, March 2, a date that roughly coincided with the European introduction a few days later. Thomas Rattigan delivered the keynote speech, with additional speeches b

Commodore's Henri Rubin, RJ Mical, and Gail Wellington. Several other engineers also attended, including Dale Luck, Steve Beats, and Jeff Boyer.

Rattigan used the opportunity to tout Commodore's newfound financial stability. "Not only did we return to profitability in the June quarter of last year, but we've been profitable every quarter since that time," he remarked. "Our bank debt is now down substantially, our cash position is at its highest level since March 1983 and our inventory level is at the lowest level since December 1982. All of this was accomplished by a substantial reduction in infrastructure, personnel, and expenses."

Rattigan was doing the right thing, promoting the recovery, shouting to the hills that Commodore was back and better than ever. He was taking a victory lap for having survived. According to a report in the Philadelphia Inquirer, the chairman did not approve. "Despite his success, Rattigan's high-profile manner was said to have annoyed Irving Gould…"[1]

Perhaps there was jealousy from Gould. "Other people have said that," says Rattigan. "There was an article in *Businessweek* or the *Wall Street Journal* where Irving was quoted as saying something that led you to believe he was spending a lot of time getting involved with me."

RJ Mical, who was less than a month away from losing his position at Commodore-Amiga due to its closure, gave a three hour talk on the history of Amiga, followed by a frank assessment of Commodore's marketing failures and a question and answer session. He even went so far as to recommend Amiga users hold onto their Amiga 1000's instead of upgrading to the Amiga 2000, an opinion that surely irked Commodore employees and management.

CeBIT '87

While the uncomfortable power struggle between Irving Gould and Thomas Rattigan continued, the UK and Germany, the stronghold of Commodore sales, launched the two new Amigas. However, the UK had suffered in recent years, where systems like the Plus/4 bombed, while the PC clones, C128, and Amiga 1000 were only marginally successful.

Commodore UK placed ads for the Amiga 500 in the *Sunday Times* in February. The ads gave a convincing pitch, proclaiming, "Now other home computers are just toys." It confidently explained how the Amiga was dif-

---

[1]   *The Philadelphia Inquirer* newspaper, "In the Executive Suites, the Pink Slip is Showing" (May 3, 1987), p. A01.

ferent from other computers in graphics, sound, video, windowing, and multitasking, and revealed the £499.99 retail price. And unlike US ads that left it up to the customer to seek out one of the few places selling the computer, it listed the three largest retail chains where it would become available.

Commodore Germany went all-out for the Amiga 2000 launch. A month before CeBIT began, the company invited 35 journalists to Fuerteventura, one of the Canary Islands off the coast of Africa. According to *c't* magazine (translated), "The ambience Commodore chose to present the new Amiga 2000 to specialised press almost a month before CeBIT '87 tells a lot about the pride about the new product. ... The multi-day event offered ample opportunity through talks and workshops to get to know every desired detail about the computer which was developed in Braunschweig." The magazine also noted the monitor flickered, and suggested, "...if Commodore now also introduces a crisp, non-flickering high-resolution monitor, the competition would have something to think about. Because then the Amiga would also be fit for demanding CAD-applications."

The big European launch of the A500 and A2000 occurred at CeBIT, held in Hanover March 4 to 11, 1987. "We did a lot of business there," says UK marketing director David Pleasance. "We would charter a private plane and we would take our major customers, the buyers from Dixons, Comet, and Currys. And we'd lay it on for them! We always wrote lots of orders there."

Commodore Germany continued its successful streak, pre-announcing the A500 in February in *Datawelt* magazine. At the show, the company pushed PC clones, the C128 machines, and especially the upcoming Amiga 500 and 2000. Jeff Porter sent 35 A500's for display at the show. "At CeBIT, we had a very big presence," says Pleasance. "It was much more focused on computer exhibition because there weren't all of the other consumer electronics products. It was pretty much computers and business products."

Winfried Hoffmann revealed the A2000 would be priced at 3995 DM, including a color 1081 monitor, mouse, 1MB of RAM, and two 3.5" disk drives. A more basic package without monitor would be announced later.

Although the C128 line did not match IBM PC sales, it managed to eke out a niche among small business owners in parts of Europe. The big announcement at the show for C128 users was Berkeley Softworks' GEOS 128. The company also displayed GEOS 1.5, a multilingual version of GEOS for the Commodore 64 developed by a German publisher named

Markt & Technik (publisher of the popular *64'er* magazine). The same company also ported GEOS to the Plus/4 computer.

International Amiga 2000 Release

On January 17, 1987, Commodore Braunschweig began assembling the first 500 units of the A2500, which would ship to distributors in February. Bridgeboard production did not begin until well into February 1987 because Commodore was still waiting on the fabrication of the custom Bridgeboard chips. All of this activity was in preparation for the March worldwide release of the system, which would be redubbed the A2000.

Back in December, at the same time Irving Gould debuted the A2000 to the press, Commodore Germany's Winfried Hoffmann had done the same with Germany's press. Around the same time as CeBIT, magazine previews of the A2000 began appearing in the leading German computer trade publications, such as *Amiga Magazin*, *Happy Computer*, *Data Welt*, *Chip*, and *c't* magazine.

Amiga Magazin, known for uncritical praise of all things Amiga, called it, "The absolute dream machine for freaks and commercial users." The magazine praised the internal floppy and hard disk drive expansion capabilities, memory expansion, the XT bridgeboard, CPU accelerators, slots, and genlock. It also criticized Kickstart 1.2 due to compatibility issues with some software titles, and the slightly slower PC graphics output when using the XT bridgeboard without a CGA card.

Happy Computer and c't magazine had similar praise for the A2000 but also criticized the bulky case design, sluggish hard disk speeds, and especially the flickery 512 line display in interlaced mode compared to the Atari ST. The magazine also reported on a rumor of a next generation Amiga running UNIX, using an 68020 CPU and mentioned the planned motherboard revision in the works back at West Chester, based on the A500 architecture.

Happy Computer saw the Amiga 2000 as a classic office computer, an ideal solution for everybody who wants to be able to use the vast MS-DOS software library but also wants to have the graphics and sound capabilities of an Amiga. The magazine predicted, "With the Amiga 500 and the Amiga 2000, Commodore presents two computers that might become the sensation of the year 1987."

Both the US and Commodore Europe had now primed the market for the release of both the A500 and the A2000. However, between December and March, Commodore US, headed by Nigel Shepherd, decided it made more sense to release one product at a time, starting with the A500. He would wait until Dave Haynie completed the B2000 for a US release. Commodore would sell the German designed A2000 everywhere except in the US, a decision that annoyed Irving Gould to no end.

The A2000 appeared in German stores such as Vobis, a large computer store chain, for for 2995 DM. This for the base configuration of one floppy drive, 1 MB RAM, and no monitor, which compared to the A1000 at 1695 DM.

The A2000 had brisk sales that allowed Commodore to retain a market share of 54 per-cent in Germany. Later in the year Winfried Hoffmann reported his subsidiary had sold 720,000 computers in the previous fiscal year (including C64 and A1000), and that there were 2.5 million Commodore computers in use in Germany.

Commodore planned to discontinue the A1000 later in the year, once the A2000-CR debuted in the US. The German A2000 would go on to sell approximately 60,000 units before being replaced by Dave Haynie's upcoming A2000 revision B.[2] It seemed like the new design might hit a sweet spot in the marketplace.

Settling Old Lawsuits

As Commodore launched two new Amiga products, the old Amiga lawsuit between Atari and Commodore dragged on. Even long-departed allies like Dave Morse and financier Bill Hart were obligated to give testimony before a court. "Dave and I were of course going to be the star witnesses," recalls Hart. "We spent hours and hours with Commodore's attorneys in Palo Alto, and those attorneys were very impressed with our case and our credibility. They said, 'We're going to trial. You guys will win because you can show that Atari overreached.'"

In March 1987, on the day of the trial, things suddenly changed. "I was literally dressed in my suit to go and testify when the phone rang," recalls Hart. "Dave said, 'Commodore settled last night with Atari.'"

Many within the company were relieved to have it over before it could enter a courtroom. "Nothing ever came of it," says RJ Mical. "There was a little bit of buzz, but it went away because there were no grounds." As part of the settlement, Commodore dropped all charges against Shiraz Shivji and the engineers who left with company documents.

---

2   Estimate by Dave Haynie in interview for this book.

As usual, Jack Tramiel came out on top from the settlement. "Some money exchanged hands and then people went away," says Dale Luck. "I think they just settled out of court for less than a million dollars to make it all go away."

Bill Hart suggests a different value. "They settled with Atari for quite a big piece of change, like $8 million."

Upon hearing this, neither Morse nor Hart felt relief. In fact, they began to worry Commodore would go after them. "I said, 'I hope they don't try to take recourse to us,'" recalls Hart. Amiga had given Commodore guarantees that there were no hidden liabilities at the time of purchase. "When you sell a company, the buyer has some recourse to the seller if it can be proved that we didn't act properly or whatever."

Now that Commodore had paid millions to Atari, it looked like there had been unstated liabilities. "But since they didn't consult us on the settlement, how can they take money from us? Dave said, 'Well, we just have to see what happens.'"

Commodore's legal counsel, Joseph C. Benedetti, began mulling over ways to reclaim the settlement from the shareholders. "They did subsequently attempt to get about two million from us," says Hart. "Us being all of the people who had benefited from the sale of Amiga, which of course included all the stockholders, many of whom were employees."

Benedetti's planned legal action against Morse, Miner, and Hart was quickly halted when the Amiga engineers, including Jay Miner and RJ Mical, took a stand. "Several of the key Amiga employees just went ahead and made it known to Commodore that if they continued to pursue this, they were out of there," says Hart. "The last thing Commodore wanted was to get into litigation with a group of people that included some of their key Amiga employees." As a result, Benedetti backed down from pursuing reparations from the shareholders.

Ranger Chipset Done

Jay Miner had started his Ranger chipset in 1985 and by January 1987 it was largely complete. The chipset now added 1024 x 800 NTSC or 1024 x 1024 PAL resolutions in monochrome. Due to its use of Video RAM, the chipset was blazingly fast. "These chips are completed and tested and only require a computer and memory to hold them together," Miner revealed at the time. "So keep your eye on video RAM and on the next generation of Amiga computers that will probably use it."[3]

Though the resolutions were amazing, video RAM had only become available in the mid-eighties and was still too costly to even consider incorporating into Commodore's low-end line of Amiga computers. Some video cards were using 256K and 512K of VRAM, but the Ranger chipset used a full 2 MB.

Jay Miner was frustrated that the price of VRAM had not fallen sufficiently by the time he completed the Ranger chipset design. He tried to rationalize the chipset to Commodore's executives on the basis that they could throw in the memory at cost. "There is a rule of thumb that your selling price must be three to four times your costs. And this is generally a good rule," said Miner. "However if I should add another 512K of ram to a product why should I charge the customer three times what I have to pay for it? It didn't increase my development costs. It didn't increase my marketing costs. This is just another way to gouge the customer instead of giving value."

As noble as this sentiment sounded, it was also unrealistic. All goods that go into a product must be acquired and paid for, and by taking a particular part and throwing it in at cost, the profit margin is further diminished. Companies that try to operate with slim profit margins usually find themselves going out of business.

At the very least, Commodore planned to use the new chipset in the high end Amiga line. In March, Miner handed off his chipset to the West Chester engineers to complete and fabricate. But as history shows, the Ranger chipset was never put into production by Commodore.[4]

Closing Down Los Gatos

It had been a tumultuous period for the Amiga engineers on the West Coast. With only six people remaining at Los Gatos, morale was at an all time low. Gerard Bucas did not have the authority to renew the lease on the Los Gatos building himself and therefore could not prevent its closure. The permanent closure of the offices would occur when the lease ran out at the end of March.

---

3   Amiga User International. June 1988. "The AUI Interview" p. 20

4   The fate of Jay Miner's chipset is covered in the followup to this book, "Commodore: The Final Years".

"That's really where the whole thing started having major problems," says Bucas. "One of those actions to save that money was to shut down the Los Gatos facility, pulling all of the design resources back into West Chester. Then, even after we did that, they wanted more cuts and more cuts and more cuts, which was pretty tough."

Financial problems at Commodore made the closure look appealing. "One of the reasons they wanted people to move back to Pennsylvania is because they were paying them two-thirds of what they're making out here," says Dale Luck.

Several promised products from the West Coast, including a digitizer and a genlock that Commodore wanted to market, were also repeatedly falling behind. The environment at Los Gatos was also viewed by West Chester as a little too casual. One employee sometimes came to work in a T-shirt with one arrow pointing up and another down, reading, "Sit here, suck here." Rattigan wanted a more professional work environment. According to Dave Haynie, "Regardless of what their reasons were, Commodore management ultimately really wanted to have more direct supervision over what was happening there."

It was an especially difficult time for Jay Miner. "He had to lay off all these people and it was clear that Commodore wanted to move the base of operations to West Chester," says Glenn Keller. "Pretty much nobody there wanted to move to West Chester. It was pretty clear that the place was going to close down."

Bucas once more dutifully asked the design team to move East. "I liked working for Amiga and working for Commodore was okay, but I hadn't signed on to work for an East Coast company," says RJ Mical. "I had signed on to do wild and exotic things in California; doing startups and inventing all kinds of new stuff."

Commodore ended up losing most of the Amiga team. "Anybody who wanted to move from California to Pennsylvania had a job there," says Luck. "There wasn't more than a handful of people who would even consider that. So everyone pretty much said, 'You know what, we like it out here in California.' I think they shut down the Los Gatos office too quickly. There was a lot of good guys they let go. I think that was probably one of their first mistakes."

In March, with a heavy heart, Bucas closed the offices. "I was eventually forced to be the messenger. But I did it in such a way that the Los Gatos group felt that I was the innocent party and it was all because of Commodore top management. I was never considered to be the bad guy. I was the person that had to go there and close the place down. We moved out the furniture and various other things. "

Unfortunately, due to Bucas's comments, the Amiga team now felt Thomas Rattigan was to blame for the predicament. Bucas had inadvertently put Rattigan in the ex-Amiga employees' crosshairs and many of them had a direct line to Irving Gould.

On March 31, the remaining engineers closed the doors on the Amiga offices. "I remember turning out the lights in the building in Los Gatos," says chip engineer Glen Keller.

The engineers hosted a solemn party in Los Gatos on the weekend after the closing. In the center was an open casket filled with old Amiga hardware. Jay Miner read aloud a reimagining of Mark Antony's famous speech, saying, "We come to bury Commodore, not to praise them."

At a subsequent talk a few days later at the San Diego Amiga User Group, Mical spoke openly about his disappointment with Commodore and bemoaned the fact that the German A2000 had won out over the Ranger. However, he was optimistic about A500 sales and toyed with the idea of finishing his *Baal* video game for Electronic Arts.

Ultimately he opted for a different project he had worked on during his final months at Commodore. Mical had helped develop the frame grabber software, an early attempt at image scanner technology. Initially, a company called A-Squared owned the technology and Commodore made an agreement to distribute the product.

After months of delays, the agreement with Commodore fell apart. Mical stepped in with a plan to finish the product. "There were some interesting scanning devices that were out there that automatically rotated colored filters in front of the lens of a black and white camera," he recalls. "There was all this really cool, interesting, mad scientist whizmo-gizmo stuff that people put together."

Along with some partners, he reformed a company called Grab, Inc. in June 1987 and began taking orders for the product. Days after demonstrating the frame grabber at Siggraph at the end of July, Mical left the company, reportedly over artistic differences.[5]

---

5   Mical and Needle next worked for Dave Morse at game publisher Epyx, where Morse employed a familiar business plan. Morse created a small red and black joystick reminiscent of the Power Stick called the Epyx 500XJ to fund development of a handheld game system called the Handy Game.

Out of all the highlights in Mical's long career, his days working with the Amiga stand out for him. "It was just an amazing thing to see," he says. "Those were such cool days; you just couldn't believe it. It was one of the most magical periods of my entire life working at Amiga. God, what an incredible thing we did."

The departure of the Amiga team created a frightening prospect for the remaining Commodore engineers. "It wasn't as bad a parting as it could have been under the circumstances," says Dave Haynie "I was actually a little worried about it because here we were taking over their baby."

The closure of Los Gatos, along with further attrition, left Commodore with only 49 engineers in the entire company, down from 74 the year before. Even longtime employees like Dave DiOrio began leaving the company. Commodore needed to reverse the situation fast.

Dark Echo 1986-1987

Often in business when a new CEO steps in, he replaces the team with his own people who are more likely to support him. When Thomas Rattigan came to Commodore, he left most of the existing management team in place, especially in engineering. Others he simply would not have been able to replace, such as Irving Gould or Henri Rubin. Over time, he had become a victim of attacks from well placed managers and executives. The cracks in his leadership were beginning to show.

The Last Straw

By early 1987, Commodore stock was on a rapid climb, having risen from 4 ⅞ a year earlier to 11 ¼. Thomas Rattigan's stock plan paid off for every employee at Commodore. The price continued rising to over 15 by April.[1] "We got it to 15 bucks and everybody got 10% of their pay," he says. This boosted morale within the company and helped to solidify his position with employees.

Many West Chester engineers held a positive view of Rattigan for pulling Commodore out of a nose dive. "I met him a couple of times and he seemed like a good guy to me," says Dave Haynie. Commodore's in-house magazine even presented a comprehensive interview with Rattigan, celebrating the recent successes.

However, many of the original Amiga 1000 engineers blamed Rattigan for the closure of the Los Gatos office. "He was always the solid business guy when our business guys dealt with him," says RJ Mical. "I know that

---

1   Amazing Computer Magazine. June 1987. p. 37

some people thought he was pretty strong while others thought he was pretty weak and had to go."

Many of the Amiga team continued voicing their criticisms to Henri Rubin and Irving Gould at the direction in which Commodore was going with the new Amiga computers. Rattigan began to sense people were undermining him. "[Gould] used to spend a lot of time on the phone talking to people," says Rattigan. "If he happened to talk to you, and you said something he found particularly insightful, then my phone would ring and I never knew where this was coming from."

Gould had in the past remained a hands-off chairman. "He had a small suite of offices in the Seagram Building in New York," says Rattigan. "In my tenure at Commodore, he was only down to West Chester once and I literally had to insist that he come down."

However, his recent foray into spearheading the German Amiga 2000 was something new for Gould. "He surprised me because in the beginning he struck me as someone who was just the money guy, who was out of touch with what was actually going on with his company," says Mical. "But that turned out to be wrong. He was a lot more in touch with what was actually happening with the company, where the engineering was going, and what sort of steps the company needed to take to become profitable."

Since receiving a five-year contract in the middle of 1986, Rattigan's reputation had faltered due to a few (perhaps unavoidable) missteps. Gould had dropped the A2000 project on West Chester in early 1986 and expected them to have it launched by September in Europe and the US.

When West Chester rejected the German A2000 design and decided to reengineer it for a US release, it did not sit well with the German team. "The dynamics were very complicated, very political," says Gerard Bucas. "Tom Rattigan is correct in that sense that he was probably as taken by surprise as much as I was on some things. The people that really influenced Irving Gould were really on the German side."

One of those surprises was the strong reaction from Gould himself. Gould had proudly given previews of the A2000 from his offices in December 1986. But in the same month, Dave Haynie began work on the A2000-CR (known internally as B2000) and Commodore opted to release it instead. This made Gould personally look stupid, as though he was announcing vaporware.

Instead, the US release was pushed back to the second half of 1987. This resulted in a less than stellar fourth quarter, with revenues down $69 million compared to the previous year. It was the last straw that broke the camel's back.

Henri Rubin also represented the German side and he enjoyed favoritism from Irving Gould that oftentimes seemed to overrule Rattigan's authority. When Rubin moved into West Chester, be became a more serious threat to Rattigan, able to undermine him from within.

The Amiga 500 was supposed to have launched in January 1987, but that had been pushed back to June instead, a situation at least partially caused by Henri Rubin refusing to sign off on development expenses. "There definitely was a lot of friction," says Andy Finkel. "I'm sure there were a lot of reasons why Irving and Thomas were unhappy with each other. Commodore was undergoing problems, things weren't ready and sales were down."

Jeff Porter thinks the drop in revenues was the source of Gould's displeasure. "It was the financial state in the year-end shareholder report for 1986," he says. "It was a public company and they had to issue a shareholder report. If your numbers are bad because you didn't sell a lot of Amigas, that's probably a bad thing."

When Rattigan celebrated Commodore's return to profitability with an interview in *Commodore Magazine*, it annoyed Gould. Steve Hull of *Amazing Computing* wrote, "Sources report that Gould had been dissatisfied with the performance of operations in the US and felt Rattigan may have been more involved in self-promotion than in the needs of the company. Among the examples cited; Commodore Magazine's May 1987 cover story, an interview with Mr. Rattigan headlined, 'What's next for Commodore?'"[2]

"He was a great guy but I'm sure at the end of the day it came down to his numbers weren't there," says Don Gilbreath, a Commodore manager who had an office close to Gould in the Seagram Building. "He was a guy who was overly confident and cocky and I'm sure that didn't sit well when the numbers were off."

Dave Haynie believes Rattigan also attempted to increase his control of Commodore. This bothered Gould. "From what I recall, [Rattigan] was definitely trying to increase his power base," says Haynie. "It wasn't like you could actually get rid of Gould, but you could certainly make sure that the people who reported to you were loyal to you and put your own people in place and take over from a functional point of view."

---

2 Amazing Computing. June 1987. p. 37.

Rattigan had built a team around himself of about 50 loyal employees, including his right hand man in North America, Nigel Shepherd, and chief financial officer Mike Evans. According to Haynie, Rattigan even tried to bring his own son into Commodore, a move echoing Jack Tramiel. "I originally thought his son was going to be some sort of rich daddy's boy thrust upon us, but the guy was actually a good guy," says Haynie. "He was just one of the guys, but you did kind of have to behave."

Haynie believes Rattigan wanted his son in a marketing role. "He seemed like he was in there and really wanted to learn this stuff," he recalls. "He was just kind of in there walking around learning. I guess he was going to be a marketing guy. He was really trying to learn every detail and that's what a marketing person should do."

In reality, Rattigan needed to take control of Commodore in order to reform and manage the company effectively. But Gould would never allow it. "In all fairness to Rattigan, I think that was absolutely something that was necessary in order to change the way things had worked," says Haynie. "I think [Rattigan] was doing the right thing."

Rattigan claims he did not intend to usurp control from Gould. "In the final analysis, he was still chairman of the board and he controlled the board, so there was no way I would be answerable other than to the board," says Rattigan. "If you didn't recognize that, you had an IQ less than 60. That's not a fight you pick unless you have a death wish."

Those words were ironic because Rattigan would be forced to pick that fight a few months into 1987.

Coup d'état!

Irving Gould hired Thomas Rattigan in early 1985, hoping to emulate Apple's success, with the latter becoming one of two former Pepsi executives to lead a major computer company. "Rattigan was a Pepsi guy, hired not too long after Apple hired [John] Sculley," recalls Jeff Porter. "It was in vogue to hire a Pepsi guy, but he didn't know much about consumer electronics or manufacturing. He certainly knew sales and marketing for sugar water. If you could sell that you could sell anything."

The conflict at Commodore echoed a similar conflict at Apple. Steve Jobs tried to oust John Sculley while the latter was away on a business trip to Japan. This coup was cut short when engineer Jean-Louis Gassée tipped Sculley off about the coup. In the end, Apple's board of directors sided with Sculley. Jobs was humiliatingly thrown out of his own company.

Now Gould believed Rattigan was slowly gaining control of Commodore and worried that before long he would not hold enough cards in his own favor.

Rumors began to spread through the company about tensions escalating among the top executives. "Everyone talked about it but I never saw it," says RJ Mical. "People knew that there was a lot of heavy hitting going on up in politics land at Commodore but we weren't privy to the actual details."

The first blow came in early April 1987 when Irving Gould once again brought in Mehdi Ali from Dillon, Read & Co. to examine management practices. "Mehdi was an investment banker who was responsible for funding Commodore during the time when the Amiga was not profitable," recalls Porter. "Believe it or not, he was pretty influential to keep the doors open while we were making the A500."

"Tom Rattigan was a powerful force but he was being undermined at that stage by Irving Gould and Mehdi, so he was in a difficult situation," recalls Gerard Bucas. "Irving decided to bring in an outside consultant because he felt that Commodore should grow faster but especially be more profitable. Obviously, he'd only bring in that type of person when you are not happy with the CEO."

The next seven days defied belief.

Within days of Mehdi Ali's analysis, Thomas Rattigan heard the results. "It was discussed internally," says Rattigan. "What Dillon, Read may have said in addition to what was discussed with operating management, God only knows. I suspect some of those discussions might have been somewhat richer than what people like myself were hearing at the time."

Rattigan was understandably suspicious of the consultant. "The job of any consultant is, 'How do I get my next consulting assignment?' It's self preservation. That's just the history of the industry."

Rattigan now felt his position was being directly challenged by Gould. Rather than allow his position to be further undermined, he took a page from John Sculley's playbook and attempted to win over board members to his cause. According to one magazine, "Some reports have it that Rattigan was marshaling board members against Gould in an attempt to gain control of the company, which truly would have recreated the Sculley-Steve Jobs scenario at Apple."[3]

---

3 *Computerworld.* May 18, 1987. p. 95. "Doin' the CEO Shuffle"

Commodore had only a few board members, including Rattigan and Gould. "It was a relatively small board," says Rattigan. "There were five or six. Besides Irving, you had at least two other Canadians; one was from the Royal Bank and one was from the Bank of Montreal."

The most high profile Commodore board member was Alexander Haig, a former Chief of Staff for the Nixon White House during the Watergate scandal and former Secretary of State under Ronald Reagan.

Rattigan had attended board meetings in New York, Toronto, the Bahamas, and Germany in the past and felt comfortable with the members: comfortable enough to try to turn them against Gould. "He tried to do a coup d'état on the board. He tried to push out Irving Gould and a few others," says Gerard Bucas. "He tried to change the board structure by getting more of his supporters on the board versus Gould supporters, and this apparently before a board meeting."

Unfortunately for Rattigan, he misjudged the board's support for Gould. "Rattigan was just trying to take over, I guess," says Porter. "He must have made some kind of play and it backfired because Irving Gould held all the cards. There were a lot of high stakes in that corner of the building."

Rattigan was well aware of Gould's tight grip on Commodore. "He had about six million of the 30 million shares," explains Rattigan. "In the public company sense, that really put him in the control position."

When one of the board members tipped off Irving Gould about Rattigan's attempted coup, Gould called an emergency meeting, without extending an invitation to Rattigan. "Everybody that was asked to attend gets notification," says Rattigan. "I just heard through the grapevine that there was going to be a meeting."

Since Rattigan was a board member, he had a legal right to attend the meeting. "My lawyers at the time said, 'If there's a board meeting, let's just consider it an oversight. You should attend that meeting.' It was obviously said tongue-in-cheek on their part."

On the day of the meeting, he surprised the board members with his unexpected arrival in Toronto. But Gould was prepared. "They had an outside lawyer there as well. It was all orchestrated," says Rattigan, referring to Commodore's corporate lawyer, Joseph C. Benedetti. "As soon as I saw the lawyer, I knew what was happening at the board level and how they had been instructed to handle themselves."

Rattigan was not given a chance to address the board. "When you know there's a meeting that you haven't been invited to, what are you going to say?" he recalls. "The meeting that I sat in on lasted 30 nanoseconds.

"They immediately called an executive session. I was not a member of the executive committee. That was just people going through set motions on a game board that had been pretty well determined in advance. The board members' loyalty at that stage was to [Gould]."

The meeting would reconvene the next day, without Thomas Rattigan. "Shortly after that I was on a plane back to the US of A," he says. "I talked to my lawyers."

When the executive committee met again to deliberate, they had some thorny issues to work through. They had given Rattigan a five year contract in order to make Commodore's leadership seem more stable to outside investors. They had also spent significant time bringing Rattigan up to speed, a process that would need to be painfully repeated with any new CEO they replaced him with. However, Gould convinced the board members that Rattigan had to go. "They literally fired him on the spot," says Bucas.

On Thursday, April 16, Commodore's lawyer, Joseph C. Benedetti, sent a letter to Rattigan informing him Commodore had suspended his duties. Furthermore, the letter stated, "the board of directors will make a determination as to the termination of your employment for cause at a special board meeting."

"He got crushed by Gould because Gould was always going to be the guy who was pulling the strings when he wanted to be able to pull the strings," says Haynie.

On the same day, Nigel Shepherd learned via a phone call from Gould that he was terminating four top executives, all of whom reported directly to Shepherd. These included the Chief Financial Officer, the Company Controller, the Treasurer, and the Computer Systems Director for Commodore North America. Shepherd objected and asked if he could talk with Rattigan before the firings went through. Gould told him that Rattigan was no longer involved with Commodore.

Once off the phone, Shepherd reached out to Rattigan. "I had lunch with Nigel Shepherd," recalls Rattigan. "He and I had a long conversation and drank a few beers."

When Gould learned of Shepherd and Rattigan's meeting, Shepherd ended up in the crosshairs. "He got questioned on that and I think Nigel told him to stuff it," says Rattigan. Gould immediately terminated Shepherd. The situation had all the hallmarks of a third-world coup.

"Nigel was very loyal to the company and he was loyal to me, and I think he could have been equally loyal to Irving," says Rattigan. "But I think [Nigel] saw this as an injustice, and he was the kind of guy who wore it on his sleeve and told it like it was."

The dismissal of Shepherd had an unfortunate effect on Commodore. Shepherd was one of the last remaining C64 supporters in upper management, along with Clive Smith. With him gone, there was one less voice keeping the C64 legacy alive.

One Last Try

Rattigan refused to give up without a fight and decided to test Gould's control of Commodore. On Monday, April 20, 1987, he drove to work in the morning as usual; after all, he had a contract that said he was the president and CEO until 1991.

But he noticed something different when he arrived. "He came back to work Monday morning and there were security guards in front of the building," recalls Gerard Bucas.

"We had a security team of probably 30 security guards in the company," explains Gilbreath. "They were watching a lot of inventory in the giant thirteen acre building."

Rattigan had cultivated friendly relationships with people at all levels of the company "The guards had been told not to let me on the premises," says Rattigan. "However, they did not stop me from entering." One of them commented, "What the hell am I going to do? The guy is running the company and turned it around, and I'm going to stop the guy from entering? Are you crazy?"

He walked past the guards and continued up to executive row. "When I went to my office, they had changed the locks on the doors so I couldn't get in," he says. The lawyers soon noticed him. "They asked me to leave, and I said, 'On what basis?'" The lawyers proceeded to give robotic legal statements.

Things turned for the worse when Rattigan took a stand. "I said, 'Well, I'm not leaving,'" he recalls. "So they called security and asked a couple of the guys to come up."

"They don't wear guns," says Gilbreath. "They could be your neighbor friend or whatever, yet their task was manually taking this guy out of the building. It was just a funny contrast of seeing these homegrown security guards acting like cops for a day."

It was a troubling moment for the guards. "They said, 'Would you mind accompanying me?'" recalls Rattigan. Realizing there was no way to win this fight, he relieved the tension with humor. "I said, 'Of course I don't mind accompanying you. Just don't throw me down the stairs.'"

Although Gould and his lawyers had rejected Rattigan, he still received support from these employees at the lowest levels of Commodore. "We were walking down the stairs and both of them said to me, 'This is insane.'" Rattigan assured them there were no hard feelings. "I said, 'Well, that's okay guys, you've got a job to do. Do your job.'"

According to an unnamed Commodore employee, "It was unreal. He couldn't even get the photos of his wife and kids off his desk." Rattigan stood in the parking lot to take one last look at the company he had helped save, wondering where it had all gone wrong. "I just got in my car and drove away," he says.

Contract Dispute

There was one problem for Irving Gould and his board: Rattigan's legally binding five-year contract with Commodore would run until July 1, 1991. According to the contract, Rattigan was to be paid $600,000 per annum in the first two years of his service and $400,000 per annum in the final three years. In the third year as CEO Gould would allow Rattigan to purchase $6 million worth of Commodore stock for the low-low price of $5,000. In the characteristic madness that is Commodore, Gould fired Rattigan only eight months into the contract.

On Wednesday, April 22, Rattigan filed a lawsuit against Commodore for breach of contract. He was seeking lost wages and stock options totaling $9 million. In the lawsuit, Rattigan noted that since January 1987, Gould had steadily diminished his authority and responsibilities. Among the charges, Rattigan accused the board of hiring and firing senior management without telling him.

The outside world found out about the dismissal on Thursday, April 23 when the *New York Times*, the *Wall Street Journal*, and the *Philadelphia Inquirer* reported the story. According to the Inquirer, it was "...a move that has astonished and confused both employees and investors."

In the interim, Gould named himself CEO and president of Commodore International until he could clear out Rattigan loyalists and ensure his position was no longer vulnerable.

The intrigue impacted Commodore's stock price. The day Rattigan filed suit, the stock started a slow dive that would last for years. At first, the stock dropped $0.50 from $12.37. Then when the news broke publicly, it dropped a further $1.50 to $10.37.

Gould went to the press to state his case. He claimed he had dismissed his top executives because of his disappointment in Commodore North America's sales figures. According to Gould, European sales accounted for 70% of Commodore International revenue at the time.

Days after his former CEO's departure, Gould began cleaning out the Rattigan faithful. As Rattigan recalls, "Anybody that I brought in or was high on was in some state of imminent danger." On Friday, April 24, Gould laid off 50 white-collar Commodore workers in administrative positions. The purging of Rattigan supporters continued for the next month.

On May 29, Gould eliminated Michael Evans, vice president and chief financial officer of Commodore North America. "Two gigantic mistakes they made were getting rid of Nigel [Shepherd] and the second one was when they got rid of Mike Evans," says Rattigan. "I heard subsequently that Irving said one of the biggest mistakes he made was letting Mike go. It was absolutely foolish. The guy was indispensable on the administrative side and on the financial side."

Rattigan believes many of the dismissals were due to the Dillon-Read consultants. "You have to ask: did Irving make the decision, or did somebody else influence him to make the decision? I think that was probably the outside consultants figuring they had to hit a double or a triple to show that they knew what they were talking about and get the extension on whatever contractual deal they had."

Ironically, an upbeat interview with Rattigan appeared in the May issue of *Commodore Magazine*, just as the turmoil began. The company magazine operated on a three-month lead-time for articles and was already in print by the time Rattigan departed. The article gave him credit for the turn-around, something Gould could not abide.

Commodore Magazine publisher Diane LeBold, who had previously run afoul of Irving Gould when she mentioned Jack Tramiel's legacy in her editorial column, was now in trouble again. With the three month publishing delay, LeBold's last issue was August 1987. The longtime publisher of Commodore Magazine departed the company.

On June 12, 1987, Commodore filed a $24 million countersuit against Rattigan. In the lawsuit, Commodore claimed that 'willful disobedience' by Rattigan cost the company millions in needless expenses. This was in reference to Rattigan having instructed his Los Gatos engineers to develop a competing system to the German A2000. Gould also claimed that Rattigan had behaved antagonistically and was therefore not entitled to the benefits in his contract.

Decades later, Rattigan remained amused by the countersuit. "I still have that on the top of my bills here. One of these days I'll write them a check," he laughs.

Rattigan feels Gould wanted to intimidate him into a lower settlement. "That's all posturing and nonsense," he says. "I guess the average person who got notification of something like that would reach for their chest and be in the throes of a heart attack."

As with most corporate lawsuits, Rattigan vs. Commodore would continue to plague the company for years, finally coming to a conclusion around the same time Rattigan's contract would have ended. In the meantime, the path set by Rattigan would continue to benefit the company for many more years.

End of an Era

Prior to Thomas Rattigan, Commodore was run by an elderly CEO and president, Marshall Smith. The decline of the company under Smith's tenure could not have been more stark. When he couldn't make a decision about which products to pursue, he pursued them all. This had devastating results on Commodore's financial bottom line. And the bungled, lacklustre launch of the Amiga 1000 had not lived up to Commodore's previous marketing success. Smith had lost an opportunity to capture a significant portion of the North American computer market.

Rattigan, by contrast, had opted to focus on Commodore's two strongest products; the Amiga and the C64 line. The results spoke for themselves.

Although his lawsuit hurt Commodore, Rattigan's stewardship left the company on a solid financial footing. "When I left, which is just a kind way of saying I was thrown out the door, we had built a very substantial eight-figure number on reserves and accruals that we had on the balance sheet," he claims. When pressed for the figure, he replies, "You wouldn't be wrong in saying it was greater than $50 million."

Commodore had money in the bank and could afford to advertise its upcoming computers, the Amiga 500 and Amiga 2000. "When bringing the company out of near bankruptcy, and then earning profits behind all of that, we had created an impeccably conservative balance sheet," says Rattigan. "It set them up for a long while."

The computers backed by Rattigan would prove to be just the products consumers were looking for. The success of the C64c and the A500 would keep Commodore profitable for years to come. Rattigan also backed the Los Gatos competitor named Ranger over the German A2000. Due to

Irving Gould opposing that system, we will never learn how it would have fared technologically or in the marketplace.

Rattigan, a former marketing executive himself, also had a strong marketing team in North America, headed by the highly competent Nigel Shepherd. They had planned the launch campaign of the A500 and A2000 prior to Gould dismissing them. Again, we will never know how marketing under Rattigan and his team would have turned out.

Instead, these two products would be launched by Irving Gould as CEO. Commodore was in a healthy position and was set up for success in the coming years, with the momentum of Rattigan's leadership carrying on into Gould's tenure. The success that had eluded Commodore throughout these years was just over the horizon.

Gould was not done with the incredible Amiga technology yet and would use it as the basis of many more products in the years to come. With emerging technology like networking, hard drives, CD-ROM, and the Internet, Commodore would have to answer with appropriate products or fall by the wayside.

Super Backers

Portia Level - The Group of 64

Alex Tucker
Andrew Chilton
Anthony M. Olver
Bryan Pope
Byron Jenssen
Chain-Q
Chand Svare Ghei
Christian Liendo
Darren Coles
Darren Webber
Dave Kelly
Dave Plonka
David Iwanicki
Dick van Ginkel
Dirk Vael
Ed Finkler
Edison Fernando Buitrago
Eero Rantanen
Filippo Santellocco
Francisco Cano
Gianluca Clos
Graham Crump

Helmut Fuchs
Hugo van der Aa
Ingo Devooght
Jarkko Kytölä
Jarkko Lehti
Jean Francois
Jeroen Knoester
Johan Bentzen
Johan Van Mensel
John Delisle
Joost Leisink
Kevin Anthony
Kevin Bagnall
Kevin Rutten
Lars Klaeboe
Lee Huggett
Luca Castiglioni and
Luca "skyluke" Spada
Marcel Franquinet
Marcin Kozinski
Mark Paul Corcoran
Markus Borgelin

Marvin Droogsma
Mary Feng
Matt Forrest
Michael Tedder
Mikko Riikonen
Nick Lines
Radikus
Robert Crossfield
Salvador Araya
Seppo Seppälä
Severin Stefan Kittl
Simo Koivukoski
Stephan Ricken
Steven Solie
Terry Moore
Tommy Spaberg
Torbjørn G. Dahle
Troy Davis
Ville Laustela
Wei ju Wu
Yves Grethen

Agnus Level

Balázs Szaszák
Ceri Stagg
Chris Collins
Chris Luke
Chris Van Graas
Christopher Masto
Dave Ross
Gareth Darby
Gene Johannsen
George Pantazis

Graham McAllister
Greg Soravilla
James Redfield
Laurence Gonsalves
Mark Burton
Nicolas Alejandro Spirdal-Jacobsen Mendo
Rob Clarke
Sebastian Bergmann
Steven Innell

Fat Agnus Level

Gary Wolfe
Herb Bagnall

Jason Robertson
Randy Epstein

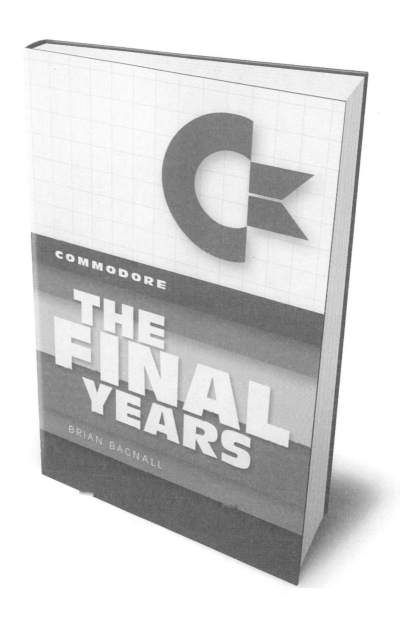

Concludes in 2018

ISBN: 978-0-9940310-3-7

Index